PRACTICAL APPLICATIONS AND SOLUTIONS USING LABVIEW™ SOFTWARE

Edited by **Silviu Folea**

Practical Applications and Solutions Using LabVIEW™ Software
Edited by Silviu Folea

Published by InTech
Janeza Trdine 9, 51000 Rijeka, Croatia

Publishing Process Manager Iva Lipovic

Technical Editor Teodora Smiljanic

Edition 2014

Additional hard copies can be obtained from orders@intechopen.com

Practical Applications and Solutions Using LabVIEW™ Software, Edited by Silviu Folea
p. cm.
ISBN 978-953-307-650-8

Meet the editor

Folea, C., Silviu, PhD, is associated professor at the Technical University of Cluj-Napoca, Automation Department, Romania. His research interests include embedded systems – hardware and software, reconfigurable systems, data acquisition, wireless networks and low power sensors. His software interests include LabVIEW graphical programming for Real Time, FPGA or PDA modules with courses taught at bachelor and master degree. Professor Folea has fifteen years of design experience in the embedded systems domain and in university teaching. He is the author of 6 books and book chapters and of more than 60 conference and journal publications, some indexed in international databases. He is promoting his research activity as a member in professional associations such as IEEE, SRAIT, etc. Professor Folea took part in more than 25 research contracts, international, national or with external industry partners such as Cores Electronic LLC from Austin, USA. Some of the most important and interesting research contracts were carried out in collaboration with National Instruments Corporate USA, between the years 2000 and 2007. Two patents resulted from these research contracts in the USA. He worked for National Instruments Romania between the years 2005 and 2007.

Contents

Preface

The book consists of 21 chapters which present applications implemented using the LabVIEW environment, belonging to several distinct fields such as engineering, chemistry, physics, fault diagnosis and medicine. In the context of the applications presented in this book, LabVIEW offers major advantages especially due to some characteristic features. It is a graphical programming language which utilizes interconnected icons (functions, structures connected by wires), resembling a flowchart and being more intuitive. Taking into account different objectives, LabVIEW can be considered an equivalent of an alternative to the classic programming languages. It is important to mention that the implementation time for a software application is reduced as compared to the time needed for implementing it by using other environments.

The built-in libraries and the virtual instruments examples (based on VIs), as well as the software drivers for almost all the existing data acquisition systems make the support and the use of devices produced by more than fifty companies, including industrial instruments, oscilloscopes, multimeters and signal generators possible in LabVIEW.

The LabVIEW platform is portable, being able to run on multiple devices and operating systems. Programming in LabVIEW involves the creation of the graphical code (G) on a PC, where it is afterwards compiled. Tools specific to different targets such as industrial computers with real time operating systems (PXI), programmable automation controllers (Compact RIO), PDAs, microcontrollers or field-programmable gate arrays (FPGAs) are used and after that the compiled code is downloaded to the target.

Chapter 1 presents a virtual instrument for image capture and display associated with the electrical capacitance tomography (ECT), a noninvasive measurement method for visualizing temporal and spatial distributions of materials within an enclosed vessel. According to the hardware circuitry configuration and the combination of electrodes for the ECT, the VI is implemented using seven major functional modules: switching control, data sampling, data normalization, permittivity calculation, mesh generation, image generation, and image display.

Chapter 2 describes a LabVIEW based NMR spectrometer (Nuclear Magnetic Resonance) working at low field. This spectrometer allows the detection of the NMR signals of both 1H and ^{129}Xe at 4.5 mT. The aim of this chapter is to present the advances accomplished by the author in the development of low-field NMR systems. The flexibility of the system allows its use for a palette of NMR applications without (or with minor) hardware and software modification.

Chapter 3 introduces a new version of drip irrigation design software (DH V 2.0) for usage with mobile devices like Smartphones or pocket PCs. It uses LabVIEW PDA as the programming language. The software allows the users of drip irrigation systems to evaluate their sensibility to changing conditions (water needs, emitters, spacing, slope, etc.) for all the diameters of commercial polythene drip lines.

Chapter 4 presents a new method for the design of computer-based measurement systems that can be seen in the use of up-to-date measurement, control and testing systems based on reliable devices. The measurement systems built with the help of the LabVIEW modular instrumentation offer a popular approach to nuclear spectrometers construction. By replacing the former single-purpose system, units with universal data acquisition modules, a lower-cost solution that is reliable, fast, and takes high-quality measurements, is achieved.

Chapter 5 describes a real-time rapid embedded control prototyping simulation and a simple power system case study implementation. The detailed implementation of an overcurrent relay for controller-in-the-loop simulation is described, including the setting and programming of a real-time digital simulator and the programming in CompactRIO, which includes the FPGA and the real-time processor by using LabVIEW. A synchronization technique which allows the readers to make the correction decision on the method to be used based on the application and its requirements is proposed and also discussed.

Chapter 6 presents a continuing research on the design and verification of an autopilot system for an unmanned aerial vehicle (UAV) through hardware-in-the-loop (HIL) simulations. The software development environment used for HIL simulations is LabVIEW. Different control methods for developing the UAV autopilot system design are applied and the comparison between the results obtained from HIL simulations is presented in this chapter.

Chapter 7 proposes a HIL-based system, where a Foundation Fieldbus control system manages the simulation of a generic plant in an industrial process. The simulation software is executed on a PC, and it has a didactic purpose for engineering students learning to control a process similar to the real one. The plant is simulated on a computer, implemented in LabVIEW and represents a part of the fieldbus network simulator FBSIMU.

Chapter 8 presents a solution for measuring object beating frequency from a video sequence using tools of image analysis and spectral analysis. It simplifies the methods used in present times and reduces the usage of the hardware devices. Using the LabVIEW environment, the authors created a fully automated application with interactive inputting of some parameters. Several algorithms were tested on phantoms with defined frequency. The designed hardware data acquisition system can be used with or without microscope in applications where the placement of kinematic parameters sensors is not possible. Intelligent regulation of condenser illumination through image feature extraction and histogram analysis enables the fully automated approach to video sequence acquisition.

Chapter 9 describes the design of a product developed by the authors using LabVIEW. It is named YF/XGYD atherosclerosis detection system. The hardware and software designs of the arterial elasticity measurement system are detailed. The system can diagnose the condition of arterial elasticity and the degree of arteriosclerosis.

Chapter 10 proposes a prototype of an ECG telemetry system that fulfills the requirements of real-time transmission of long term records, low power consumption and low cost. The software for implementing the acquisition, display and storage of the 4 signals (3 for ECG leads and one for battery voltage), the detection of the ECG R wave peak and for processing the R-R intervals based on LabVIEW was developed for the study of heart rate dynamics.

Chapter 11 presents an intelligent fault diagnosis system, where the noise produced by a fan is considered to be the diagnosis signal, a non-connect measurement method is adopted and a non-linear mapping from feature space to defective space using the wavelet neural network is performed. Modular programming was adopted for the development of this system, so it is easier to extend and change the characteristics of the network fault and structure parameters.

Chapter 12 describes a new shifted current method technique for determining ZnO ageing that was successfully implemented in LabVIEW software and was proven useful for on-site measurement purposes. The developed program provides convenience in the system management and a user-friendly interface.

Chapter 13 presents a remote measurement laboratory based on LabVIEW that has been designed and implemented. It provides the users with access to remote measurement instrumentation and a DSP embedded board, delivering different activities related to digital signal processing and measurement experiments. End-user Quality of Service has been measured and expressed in terms of satisfaction or technical terms.

Chapter 14 describes different digital image processing algorithms using LabVIEW. The chapter presents the image acquisition task and some of the most common operations that can be locally or globally applied. The statistical information generated by the image in a histogram is also discussed. A pattern recognition section shows how to use an image into a computer vision application through an example of object detection. All these, along with the use of other functionalities of LabVIEW lead to the conclusion that this software is an excellent platform for developing robotic projects as well as vision and image processing applications.

Chapter 15 presents the feasibility of a flexible and low cost monitoring and control solution using SMS, which can be easily applied and adapted to various applications. The developed system was applied to a RF signal procedure measurement for saving time and staff in this process. The tool development and its use in a specific application outline the LabVIEW versatility.

Chapter 16 introduces a new method for determining the coordinates of any cloud-to-ground lightning strike within a certain localized region. The system is suitable for determining distributions of lightning strikes for a small area by measuring the induced voltages due to lightning strikes in the vicinity of an existing telephone air line.

Chapter 17 presents a solution using two software development platforms, MATLAB and LabVIEW, for the proper control of a microreactor-based miniaturized intensified system. The use of the SIMULINK Interface Toolkit is presented. It enables the user to transfer measurement data from LabVIEW to the embedded control module in SIMULINK and also to apply the controller output to the system via LabVIEW.

Chapter 18 proposes a software and hardware platform based on a FPGA board to which a Wi-Fi communication device has been added in order to make remote wireless reconfiguration possible. This feature introduces a high level of flexibility allowing the development of applications which can quickly adapt to changes in environmental conditions and which can react to unexpected events with high speed. The capabilities introduced by wireless technology and reconfigurable systems are important in road traffic control systems, which are characterized by continuous parameter variation and unexpected event and incident occurrence.

Chapter 19 presents the development of a communication framework for distributed control and data acquisition systems, optimized for its application to LabVIEW distributed control, but also open and compatible with other programming languages, being based on standard communication protocols and standard data serialization methods.

Chapter 20 describes some general rules illustrated by examples taken from real life applications for beginner and advanced developers. The content of this chapter represents graphical programming techniques for better Virtual Instruments (VI) performance and rules for a better organization of the LabVIEW code.

Chapter 21 presents a collection of considerations and suggestions, some personal and others from LabVIEW manuals, in the direction of improving the awareness concerning what minimum knowledge is necessary for a developer in order to be able to develop rational, well organized and effective applications.

I wish to acknowledge the efforts of all the scientists who contributed to editing this book and to express my appreciation to the InTech team.

I'd like to dedicate this book to Dr. James Truchard, National Instruments president and CEO, who invented NI LabVIEW graphical development software together with Jeff Kodosky.

Silviu FOLEA
Technical University of Cluj-Napoca
Department of Automation
Romania

Part 1

Virtual Instruments

1

Virtual Instrument for Online Electrical Capacitance Tomography

Zhaoyan Fan, Robert X. Gao* and Jinjiang Wang
Department of Mechanical Engineering, University of Connecticut, USA

1. Introduction

Electrical capacitance tomography (ECT) is a technique invented in the 1980's to determine material distribution in the interior of an enclosed environment by means of external capacitance measurements (Huang et al., 1989a, 1992b). In a typical ECT system, 8 to 16 electrodes (Yang, 2010) are symmetrically mounted inside or outside a cylindrical container, as illustrated in Figure 1. During the period of a scanning *frame*, an excitation signal is applied to one of the electrodes and the remaining electrodes are acting as detector electrodes. Subsequently, the voltage potential at each of the detector electrodes is measured, one at a time, by the measurement electronics to determine the inter-electrode capacitance. Changes in these measured capacitance values indicate the variation of material distribution within the container, e.g. air bubbles translating within an oil flow. An image of permittivity distribution directly representing the materials distribution can be retrieved from the capacitance data through a back-projection algorithm (Isaksen, 1996).While image resolution associated with the ECT technique is lower than other tomographic techniques such as CT or optical imaging, it is advantageous in terms of its non-intrusive nature, portability, robustness, and no exposure to radiation hazard.

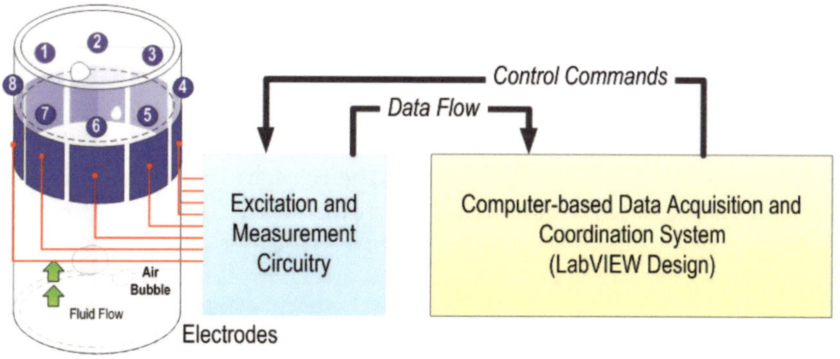

Fig. 1. Illustration of major components in an ECT system

As shown in Fig.1, an ECT system generally consists of three major components: 1) An excitation and measurement circuitry that drives the sensors and conditions the received signals; 2) A computer-based data acquisition (DAQ) and coordination system, to provide control logic for the sequential excitations of the electrodes and reconstruct tomographic

images of the materials; as well as 3) electrodes mounted on the outer (for non-metallic containers) or inner surface of the container.
According to the type of excitation signals being used, ECT can be divided into two categories: AC-based (sine-wave excitation) and charge-discharge-based (square-wave excitation). The former is advantageous in terms of measurement stability and accuracy, whereas the latter has lower circuit complexity (Huang et al., 1992). In recent years, studies have been conducted on sensing principle and circuit optimization to enhance the performances of ECT. For AC-based method, a multiple excitation scheme (Fan & Gao, 2011) has been designed and tested to increase the frame rate for higher time resolution in monitoring fast changing dynamics inside the container. The grouping method (Olmos et al., 2008) is another technique investigated to increase the magnitude of the received signals by combining two or more electrodes into one segment. ECT has also been applied to generate 3-D material distribution by mounting electrodes in multiple layers along the axis of the cylindrical container and detecting the cross-layer capacitance values (Marashdeh & Teixeira, 2004; Warsito et al., 2007). These efforts have expanded the scope of application of ECT, into such fields as measurement of multi-phase flows (gas-liquid and gas-solids, etc.) in pipelines, detection of leakage from buried water pipes, flow pattern identification (Reinecke & Mewes, 1996; Xie et al, 2006), etc. This chapter aims to introduce the realization of a computer-based DAQ and coordination system for ECT through Virtual Instrumentation (VI). Discussion will focus on the AC-based method, using single excitation and single detection channel, in which most of the basic functions required for various ECT techniques are included. The presentation provides design guidelines and recommendations for researchers to build ECT systems for specific applications.

2. VI design

According to the functions required for data acquisition, data processing, and circuit control, the VI is divided into seven major subVI's:

1. Switching control
2. Data sampling
3. Data calibration
4. Permittivity calculation
5. Mesh generation
6. Image generation
7. Image display

During a scanning frame, as shown in Figure 2, the **Switching Control** subVI divides the process into individual measurement steps according to the total number of capacitance values formed by all the electrodes. Connections of each electrode as well as the 8-1 multiplexer (MUX) in the measurement circuitry are controlled by the digital I/O (DIO) ports, such that the capacitance formed by each pair of electrodes is measured in each measurement step. After being processed by a pre-amplifier and lock-in amplifier, the voltage signal proportional to the capacitance value is sampled by the **Data Sampling** subVI. When all the capacitance values for a complete frame are sampled, they are normalized in the **Data Normalization** subVI and re-sorted into the form of matrix. The data is combined with the sensitivity matrix by the **Permittivity Calculation** subVI, and finally converted into an image representing the material permittivity distribution via the **Mesh Generation**, **Image Generation**, and **Image Display** subVI's. By looping the whole process frame by frame, the VI controls the measurement circuit and samples the signal continuously to display the dynamics of the monitored process.

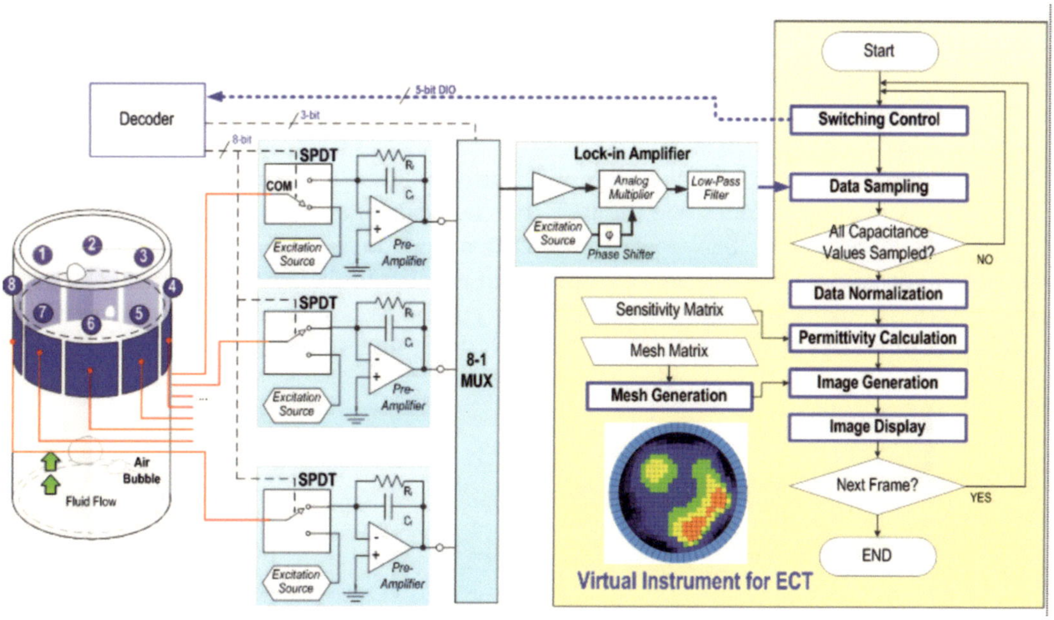

Fig. 2. A detailed view of an AC-based ECT system

2.1 Switching control

The basic procedure of AC-Based capacitance measurement is to apply a sinusoidal voltage signal to a pair of electrodes and measure the output current/voltage, from which the impedance or capacitance can be derived (Yang, 1996). Assuming there are N electrodes in the sensor being numbered from one to N, they are excited with the sinusoidal wave, one at a time. When one electrode is excited, other electrodes are kept at ground potential and act as detector electrodes. Physically, the function is realized by controlling the SPDT (Single-Pole-Double-Throw) switch and the analog MUX as shown in Figure 1. The common port of each SPDT switch is connected with one of the electrodes to enable switching between the non-inverting input of a pre-amplifier (detection mode) and the excitation source (excitation mode). In the detection mode, the output voltage amplitude of the pre-amplifier, V_{ij}, is a function of the measured inter-electrode capacitance (Huang et al., 1992), expressed as:

$$V_{ij} = -\frac{j2\pi f_e C_{ij} R_f}{j2\pi f_e C_f R_f + 1} V_e \tag{1}$$

where C_{ij} is the inter-electrode capacitance between electrodes i and j ($1 \le i, j \le N;\ i \ne j$). V_e and f_e are the voltage amplitude and frequency of the sine wave from the excitation source, R_f and C_f are the feedback resistance and capacitance of the pre-amplifier circuit. When the feedback resistance is chosen to satisfy the relationship $|j2\pi f_e C_f R_f| >> 1$, e.g. f_e= 700 kHz, C_f= 50 pF, and R_f=100 MΩ, the voltage amplitude V_{ij} is approximately proportional to C_{ij}. The simplified relationship can be expressed as:

$$V_{ij} = -\frac{C_{ij}}{C_f} V_e \tag{2}$$

Through the lock-in amplifier, the output sine wave from pre-amplifier is mixed with the original excitation signal and then processed by a low pass filter. Thus a measurable DC voltage equal to the value of V_{ij} is available from the output of the lock-in amplifier during each individual measurement step.

The measurement protocol in the sensing electronics first measures the inter-electrode capacitance between electrodes one and two, then between one and three, and up to one and N. Then, the capacitances between electrodes two and three, and up to two and N are measured. For each scanning frame, the measurements continue until all the inter-electrode capacitances are measured and the capacitances can be represented in a matrix, which is symmetric with respect to the diagonal. Due to $C_{ij} = C_{ji}$, the minimum required capacitance can be expressed as (Alme & Mylvaganam, 2007):

$$\bar{C} = \begin{bmatrix} C_{12} & & & & \\ C_{13} & C_{23} & & & \\ \vdots & \vdots & & & \\ C_{1,N-1} & C_{2,N-1} & \cdots & C_{N-2,N-1} & \\ C_{1,N} & C_{2,N} & \cdots & C_{N-2,N} & C_{N-1,N} \end{bmatrix} \tag{3}$$

With N electrodes, this gives a total number of M independent capacitance measurements, where M can be expressed as (Williams & Beck, 1995):

$$M = \frac{N(N-1)}{2} \tag{4}$$

For an 8-electrode arrangement, Equation (4) gives 28 capacitance values or a total of 28 measurement steps required for each frame. Given that the SPDT switch and the 8-1 MUX is controlled by one ($\log_2 2$) and three ($\log_2 8$) digital ports, respectively, a total of 8x1+3=11 digital ports are required to directly control the hardware. These digital ports can be either connected with the DIOs on the DAQ card directly, or through a decoder to reduce the control complexity as shown in Figure 2. The decoder translates the 5-bit digital number sent from the DIO into the 11-bit control codes to control the switches and MUX. Thus, the **Switching Control** subVI determines electrodes for excitation and detection in each step by sending a sequence number from 1 to 28 to the hardware decoder. Each of the sequence number corresponds to a specific inter-electrode configuration C_{ij}, as shown in Table 1.

Case #	0	1	2	3	...	5	6	...	9	10	...	14	15	...	20	21	...	27
C_{ij}	C_{12}	C_{13}	C_{23}	C_{14}	...	C_{34}	C_{15}	...	C_{45}	C_{16}	...	C_{56}	C_{17}	...	C_{67}	C_{18}		C_{78}
DT	1	1	2	1	...	3	1	...	4	1	...	5	1	...	6	1	...	7
EX	2	3	3	4	...	4	5	...	5	6	...	6	7	...	7	8	...	8

Table 1. Sequence of the inter-electrode capacitance measurement during a frame (EX: excitation electrode, DT: detection electrode)

Figure 3 shows the design of the **Switching Control** subVI. A *case structure* was created to generate the 28 sequence numbers in a binary form from 0x0001 (decimal 1, in case #0) to 1x1100 (decimal 28, in case #27). Within a **timed loop** structure, the loop counter [i] is used as a *measurement step indicator* to successively increase the control bit of the *case structure* till all the 28 capacitance values are measured. The time period of each measurement step is controlled by the loop timer, *dt*, with a unit of millisecond as shown in Figure 3. The value of *dt* finally determines the time resolution or the frame rate of ECT imaging. For example, when the value of *dt* is set to 4 [ms], the total time period for a frame is 28 x 4 = 112 ms, corresponding to a maximum frame rate of 8.9 frames per second. The minimum resolution of timer setting is constrained to one millisecond in the general LabVIEW system. Such a limitation is shortened to microsecond level by applying the LabVIEW Real-Time module, to further increase the frame rate of ECT at the cost of DAQ hardware upgrading (National Instruments, 2001).

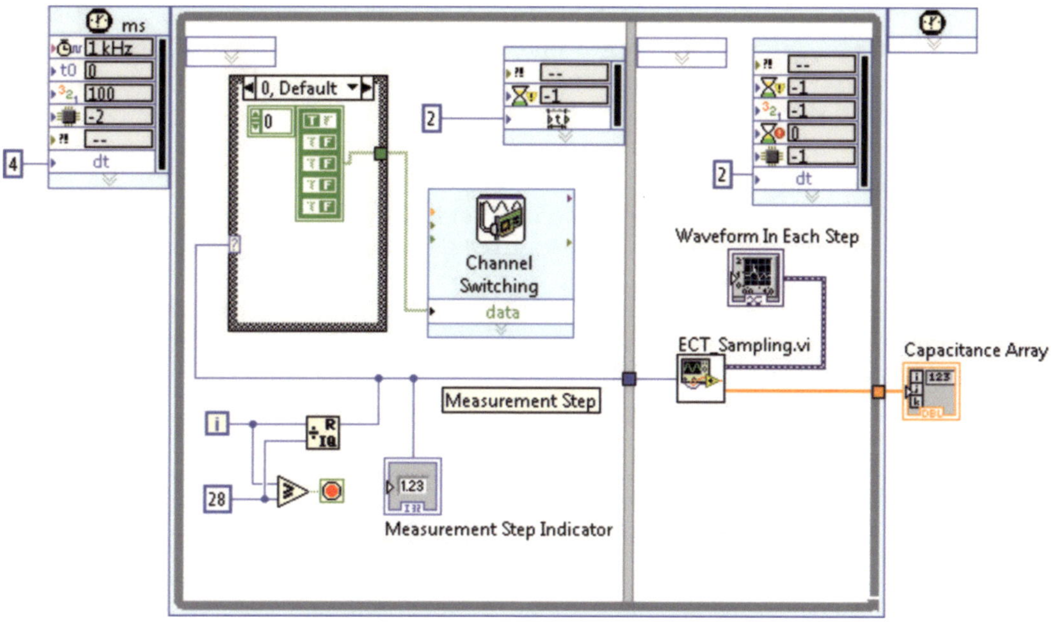

Fig. 3. Design of the Switching Control subVI within a timed loop

2.2 Data Sampling (ECT_Sampling.vi)

The **Data Sampling** subVI runs sequentially after the **Switching Control** subVI to read the voltage V_{ij} from lock-in amplifier in each measurement step. A detailed view of the subVI design is shown in Figure 4. To reduce the effect of noise from hardware components and DAQ card, the DC voltage V_{ij} in each measurement step is sampled 50 times at a sampling rate of 512 kSamples/sec. The results are averaged through a *MEAN* subVI. The capacitance value is calculated from V_{ij} with the known feedback capacitance, C_f, and excitation signal voltage amplitude, V_e. The relationship is expressed as:

$$C_{ij} = -\frac{V_{ij}}{V_e} C_f \tag{5}$$

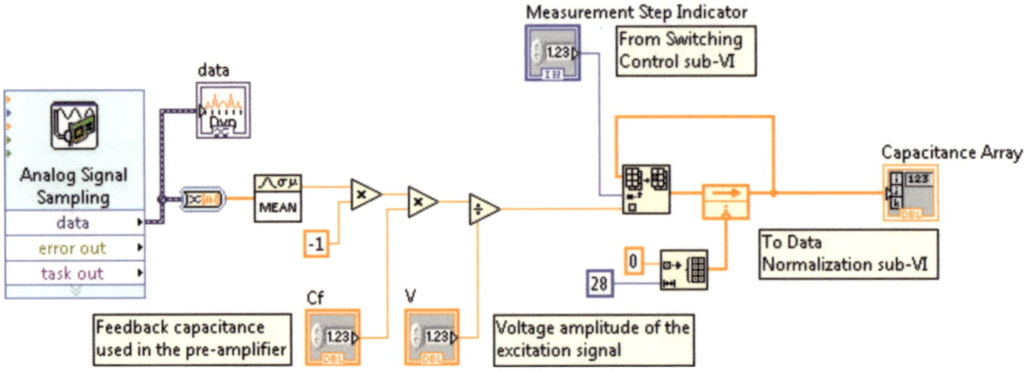

Fig. 4. Design of Data Sampling subVI

A 28x1 capacitance array is created as Table 1 to store all the calculated capacitance values for a scanning frame. As soon as one measurement step finished, the averaged value of V_{ij} is pushed into the array structure by referring to the *measurement step indicator* imported from **Switching Control** subVI.

2.3 Data Normalization

To retrieve the dynamic material distribution within the monitored space, the ECT systems (Isaksen, 1996) remove the effect of background material by normalizing the raw capacitance data with the data measured in two special cases where the ECT sensor is full-filled by the background material, and by the material being monitored. Suppose the corresponding capacitance values measured in these cases are $\{C_{ij}^b\}$ and $\{C_{ij}^a\}$, respectively, the normalized capacitance can be expressed as:

$$\lambda_{ij} = \frac{C_{ij} - C_{ij}^b}{C_{ij}^a - C_{ij}^b} \tag{6}$$

In the VI design, the normalization is realized by the **Data Normalization** subVI as shown in Figure 5. The values of $\{C_{ij}^b\}$ and $\{C_{ij}^a\}$ are measured from the preliminary test, e.g. for monitoring the air bubbles in the oil, the **Switching Control** and **Data Sampling** subVI's were run in cases when the pipe is full-filled with oil and air. Corresponding data from the *capacitance array* were copied and pasted into the array modules *C_a* and *C_b*, respectively, to calculate the normalized capacitance values as expressed in Equation (6).

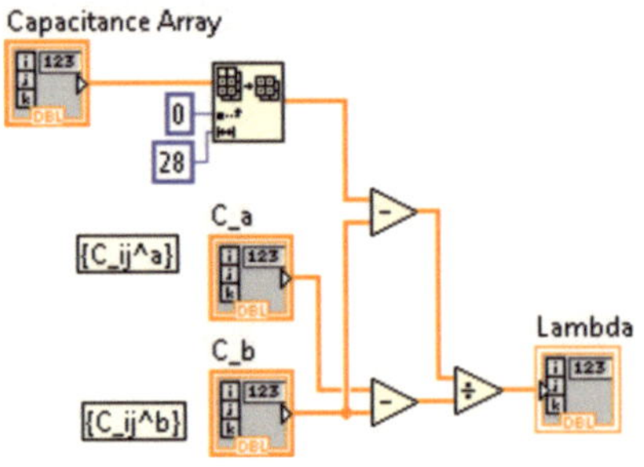

Fig. 5. Design of Data Normalization subVI

2.4 Permittivity calculation

Physically, the capacitance values are determined by the permittivity distribution $\varepsilon(x, y)$, by following a *forward problem*: $\lambda_{ij}= f(\varepsilon(x, y))$. The inverse relationship, called *backward problem*, i.e. estimating the permittivity distribution from the $N(N\text{-}1)/2$capacitance measurements (Huang et al., 1992), can be expressed as:

$$e(x,y) = f^{-1}(\lambda_{12}, \lambda_{13}, \cdots, \lambda_{ij}, \cdots, \lambda_{N-1,N}) \tag{7}$$

Unfortunately, it is not always possible to find a closed-form analytical and unique expression for this inverse function (Isaksen, 1996). Therefore, most of the ECT studies (Yang, 2010) apply numerical techniques, which divide the cross section area defined by the electrodes into K ($K \in$Integer) pixels, to simplify the boundary conditions and calculations. The permittivity in each of these pixels is assumed to be homogeneous. Thus, the forward problem can be expressed by using the linear matrices:

$$\underset{M\times 1}{\{\lambda_{ij}\}} = S \cdot \underset{K\times 1}{\{\varepsilon_k\}} \tag{8}$$

where S is an $M \times K$ Jacobian matrix, also known as the sensitivity matrix, and$\{ \varepsilon_k \}^T$ is a $K \times 1$ array in which the component ε_k is the permittivity of the kth ($1 \le k \le K$) pixel in the divided sensing area, calculated as:

$$\varepsilon_k = \frac{\varepsilon_k^A - \varepsilon^b}{\varepsilon^a - \varepsilon^b} \tag{9}$$

where ε_k^A, ε^a, ε^b are the absolute permittivity of pixel k, the permittivity of material being detected (e.g. air), and the permittivity of background material (e.g. oil), respectively. The sensitivity map Scontains M rows. Each row represents the sensitivity distribution within the sensing area when one pair of the electrodes is selected for capacitance measurement. For the 8-electrode ECT, M = 28, the rows are sorted along the sequence as listed in Table 1. Such a sensitivity matrix can be either experimentally measured (Williams & Beck, 1995) or calculated from a numerical model (Reinecke & Mewes, 1996) by simulating the inter-electrode capacitance values when there is a unit permittivity change in each of the pixels. Due to the limitation of signal-to-noise ratio in the practical capacitance measurement circuitry, the number of electrodes, N, is generally not greater than 16, to ensure a sufficient surface area for each electrode. Herein, the number of capacitance measurement M is usually far less than the number of pixels K. Thus, Equations (8) doesn't have a unique solution.

One of the generally used methods to provide an estimated solution for Equation (8) is Linear Back-Projection (LBP) by which the permittivity of pixel k is calculated as:

$$\{\hat{\varepsilon}_k\} = \frac{S^T \cdot \{\lambda_{ij}\}}{S^T \cdot u_\lambda} \tag{10}$$

Where u_λ= [1, 1, … 1] is a $M \times 1$ identity vector.

Practically, the LBP algorithm is realized in the VI design as shown in Figure 6. The vector of normalized capacitance values (*Norm Capacitance*) is imported from the **Data Normalization** subVI. The calculated sensitivity values from a numerical model are pre-loaded in the *constant Sensitivity Matrix (S)*. The operation of matrix transpose, matrix multiplication, and numerical division in Equation (9) are realized by using the *2D Array Transpose*, *Matrix Multiplication*, and *number division* modules as shown in Figure 6.

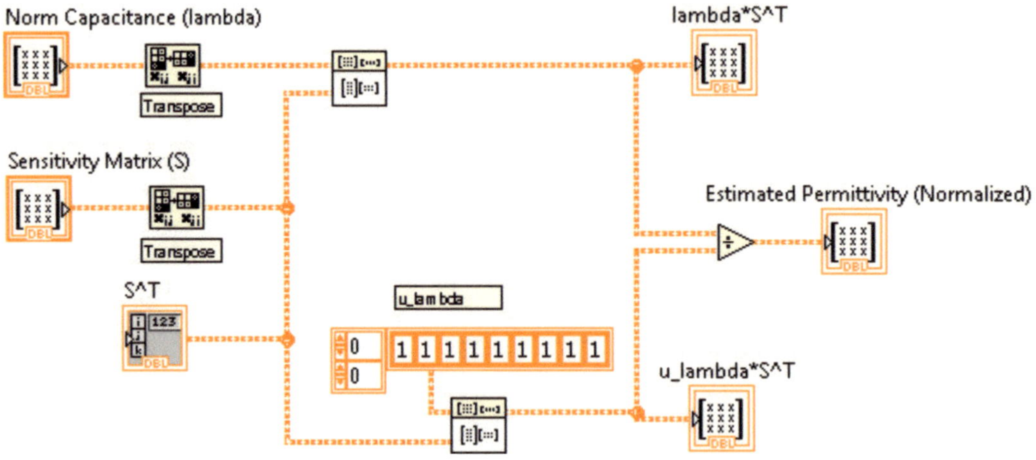

Fig. 6. Permittivity Calculation subVI designed with LBP algorithm

Mathematically, the LBP method uses the transposed sensitivity matrix S^T as an estimation of the inverse matrix S^{-1} in calculating the permittivity values. The LBP method can be further expanded by adding the additional subVI's to improve the accuracy in permittivity estimation. One of the optional methods is the Tikhonov Regularization (TR) developed by Tikhonov and Arsenin in 1977 (Tikhonov and Arsenin, 1977). The permittivity calculation using the general TR method can be expressed as:

$$\{\hat{\varepsilon}_k\} = \frac{S_{TR}^T \cdot \{\lambda_{ij}\}}{S_{TR}^T \cdot u_\lambda} \quad where \quad S_{TR}^T = (S^T \cdot S + \mu \cdot I)^{-1} \cdot S^T \cdot \{\lambda_{ij}\} \tag{11}$$

where μ is the regularization factor, I is an $M \times M$ identity matrix. As compared to Equation (8), the TR method replace the S^T with the matrix $(S^T \cdot S+\mu \cdot I)^{-1} \cdot S^T$. Thus, the *TR* method can be practically realized by applying a series of operations on the sensitivity matrix S as shown in Figure 7.

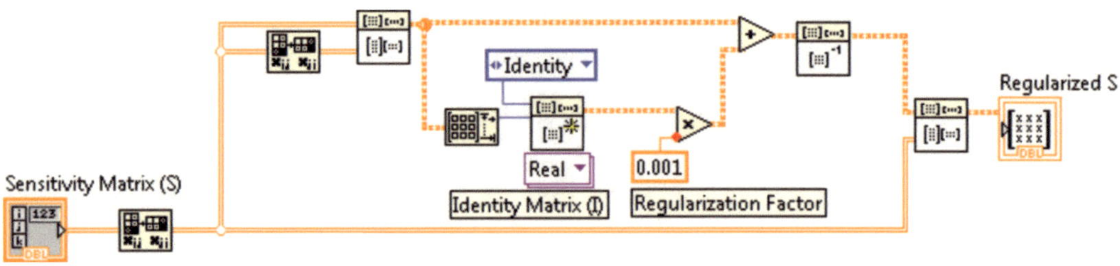

Fig. 7. SubVI design to realize TR for ECT

The accuracy of the TR method depends on the value of regularization factor μ. A small value of μ will result in a small approximation error but the result will be sensitive to the errors in measurement. In other words, the noise and fluctuation in measured signals produces large artifacts in the generated image when μ is small. Conversely, a large value of μ produces the image with small artifacts but increases the approximation error. Although some methods (Golub et al., 1979; Hansen, 1992) have been developed to estimate the optimal value of μ, they are not widely used due to the unavailability of prior noise information or the laborious calculation (Yang & Peng, 2003). In most of the applications, the value of μ in ECT is chosen empirically in the range from 0.01 to 0.0001. In the example shown in Figure 7, a value of 0.001 is adopted for detecting air bubbles in the oil.

2.5 Mesh Generation

When permittivity values are calculated for all the 512 pixels, a map of the meshed sensing area is created by the **Mesh Generation** subVI, as shown in Figure 8. The location and shape of these pixels are pre-written into a TEXT file in the format as shown in Figure 9.

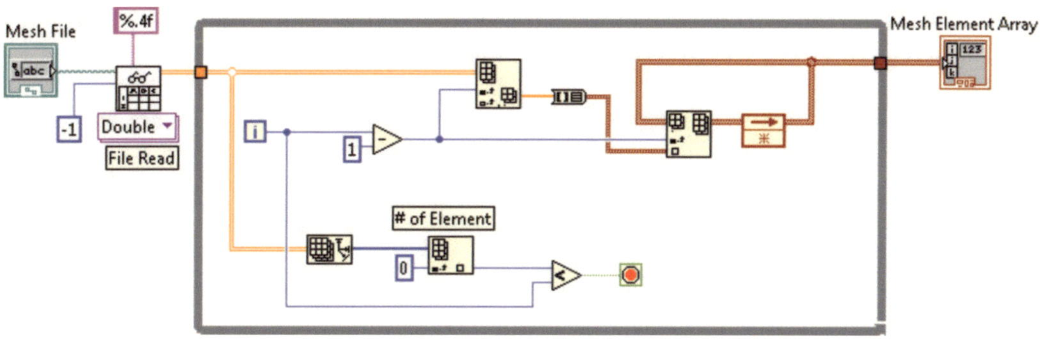

Fig. 8. Design of Mesh Generation subVI

The three columns of the file list x, y, and z (z=0 for 2-D display) coordinates of all the nodes. Since the sensing area is meshed with four-node pixels, the first four rows in the file represent the nodes included in pixel 1, sorted in counter-clock wise. Consequently the rows 5~8 represent the second pixel and so on. These coordinates are imported into the LabVIEW program by the *File Read* block, and then converted into a 2-dimentional array (2 x 2048), *Mesh Element Array,* which is readable by the **Image Generation** subVI.

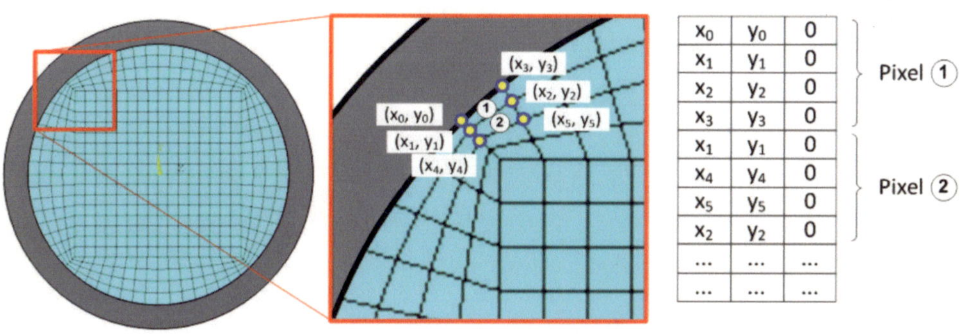

Fig. 9. Designed mesh for the 8-electrode ECT and the format of the Mesh File

2.6 Image Generation

Figure 10 shows the block diagram of the designed **Image Generation** subVI where operation functions are built within a loop structure. In each round of the looped operation functions, the **Image Generation** subVI organize the permittivity values measured through **Switching Control, Data Sampling, Data Normalization, and Permittivity Calculation** subVI's, together with the mesh information generated by **Mesh Generation** subVI to create a frame image showing the permittivity distribution within the sensing area.

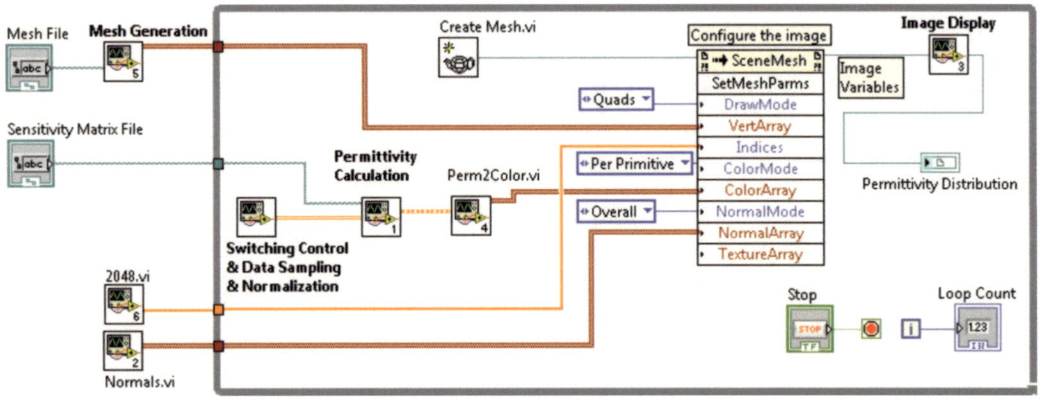

Fig. 10. Design of Image Generation subVI

Four functional subVI's, *Create Mesh.vi*, *2048.vi*, *Normals.vi*, and *Perm2Color.vi* are created in the **Image Generation** subVI to process the permittivity data as well as generate constant parameters for the image:

- The *Create Mesh.vi* generates a Cartesian coordinates array cluster of the node points of the permittivity mesh elements.
- The *2048.vi* produces an array of ordinal numbers, used to identify the order of the elements in the mesh.
- The *Normals.vi* produces the vectors to be normal to the elements in the mesh; this should be uniform to avoid shading discrepancies.
- The *Perm2Color.vi* converts the estimated permittivity values of each pixel, $\hat{\varepsilon}_k$, (in the range 0~1), to the RGB (Red, Green, Blue, 0~255) color series by following the relationship such that the material of being monitored is displayed in red, while the background material is displayed in blue. To highlight the interface between the two different materials, the permittivity close to mid-point $0.45 < \hat{\varepsilon}_k \le 0.55$ is displayed in yellow. The corresponding permittivity-to-color conversion can be expressed as:

$$\begin{cases} R_k = 255 \\ G_k = \dfrac{1-\hat{\varepsilon}_k}{1-0.55}\cdot 255 \quad \text{when } 0.55 < \hat{\varepsilon}_k \le 1 \\ B_k = 0 \end{cases} \tag{12}$$

$$\begin{cases} R_k = \dfrac{\hat{\varepsilon}_k - 0.45}{0.55-0.45}\cdot 255 \\ G_k = 255 \qquad\qquad \text{when } 0.45 < \hat{\varepsilon}_k \le 0.55 \\ B_k = \dfrac{0.55-\hat{\varepsilon}_k}{0.55-0.45}\cdot 255 \end{cases} \tag{13}$$

$$\begin{cases} R_k = 0 \\ G_k = \dfrac{\hat{\varepsilon}_k}{0.45}\cdot 255 \quad \text{when } 0 \le \hat{\varepsilon}_k \le 0.45 \\ B_k = 255 \end{cases} \tag{14}$$

2.7 Image Display

The image variables created by the **Image Generation** subVI, including coordinates of the nodes as well as the color set for each pixels, are finally processed by the **Image Display** subVI to show the permittivity distribution on the screen. As shown in Figure 11, a total of 6 *Invoke Nodes (IN)* are employed to combine the image variables into a data flow. The image variables are read via IN1 and IN2 as the drawable attributes in a 3D workspace. The IN3 and IN5 set up a ring in gray color to represent the dimension of the pipe container. The direction and diffuse color of the virtual light source are set by IN4 and IN6. The color map of the permittivity distribution is finally displayed by a Graphic Indicator in the front panel as shown in Figure 12.

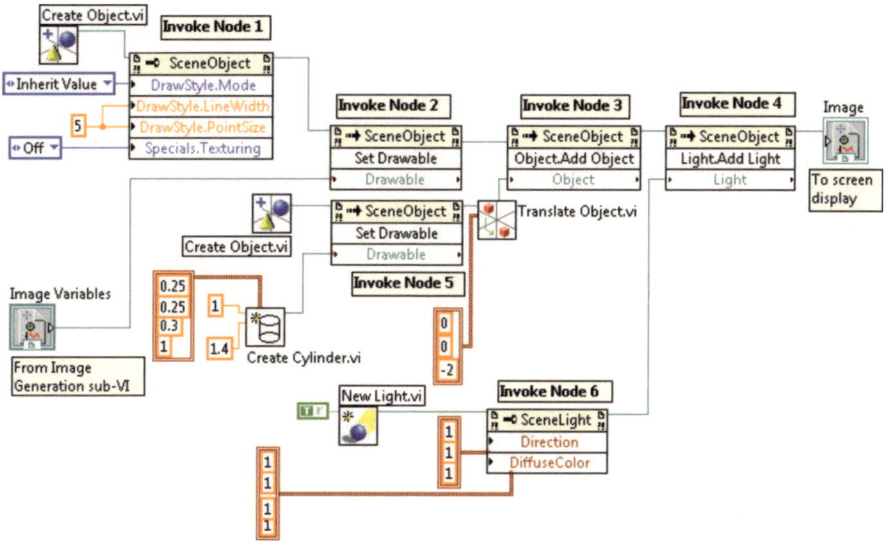

Fig. 11. Design of Image Display subVI

Fig. 12. Front panel of the Image Display subVI

Running on a desktop computer with 3.33GHz Core Duo CPU, the image generation and image display subVI's takes about 10 ms to process each frame of permittivity distribution.

The time delay is measured by looping the subVI's for 1,000 times. Such a time delay needs to be considered in the frame rate calculation as discussed in section 2.2, where the data sampling and circuit switching control take 112 ms per frame. Thus, the total frame rate for the online ECT VI can be calculated as $1/[(112+10)\cdot 10^{-3}]=8$ frames/s. It should be noticed that the frame rate is constrained by the timer settings in the general LabVIEW program. In case where higher frame rate is required, the improvement can be realized by employing the Real-time LabVIEW module or applying the multiple/receiving schemes (Fan & Gao, 2011).

3. Experiment

The designed VI together is tested with an 8-electrode ECT sensor as shown in Figure 13. The ECT sensor is built on a 40 mm diameter plastic pipe. The eight electrodes are installed on the outer surface of the pipe; each covers 42°along the circumference and 50 mm along the axial direction. At each end of the electrodes, a 10 mm wide circular copper foil is installed as guard-electrodes. During the measurement cycles, the guard-electrodes are electrically grounded to prevent the electric field from spreading axially out of the space determined by the electrodes. The measurement circuit includes the sine wave generation module, switching control logics, pre-amplifiers, and a built-in lock-in amplifier. The output voltage from the lock-in amplifier, V_{ij}, is sampled and recorded by the desktop computer via an NI PCI6259 DAQ card. Five digital I/O ports PORT0_Line0 to PORT0_Line4 are used to send switching control commands to the circuit. An ATMEGA 128L microcontroller is used in the measurement circuit as a decoder module to translate the control commands and initiate the frequency/phase setting of the waveform generators.

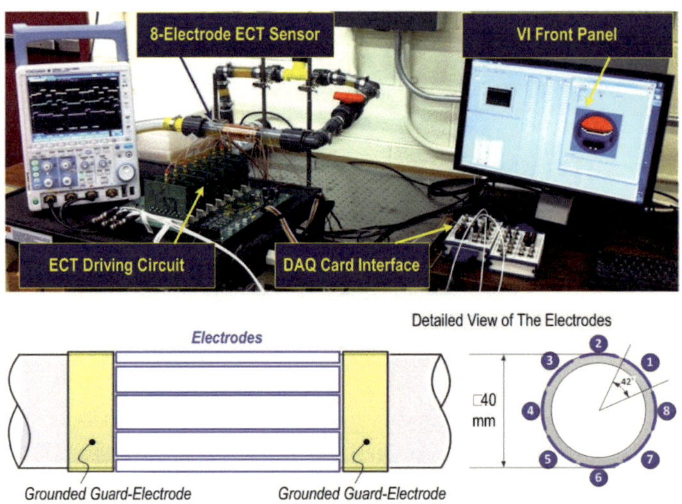

Fig. 13. Experimental setup for ECT

The flexible pipes and connectors in the experimental setup enable setting the ECT electrodes in either horizontal or vertical arrangement to monitor the fluid-gas interface of the oil-air dual phase flow. Figure14 shows the ECT sensor configured in horizontal arrangement to monitor the oil level. Controlled by an oil pump installed in the pipeline, the oil level is set between 35% and 60% of the pipe inner diameter. It is seen from the five frame images in Figure 14 that the actual oil levels are well represented in the retrieved images generated from the ECT VI.

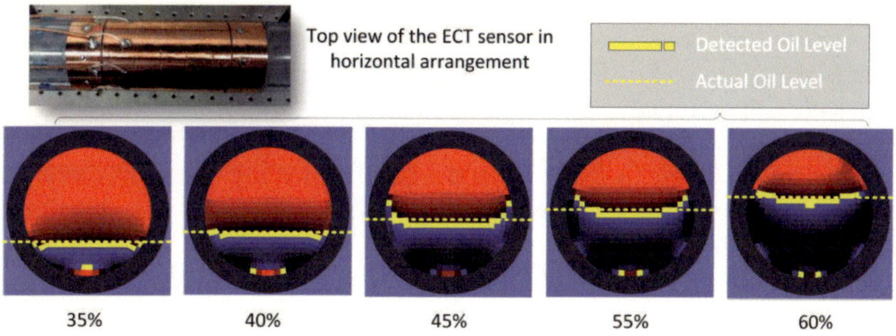

Fig. 14. Oil level monitoring in the horizontal arrangement

Another experiment is conducted to monitor the dynamics of air bubble in the oil in the vertical configuration, as shown in Figure 15. An additional air pump is added into the pipeline to inject air bubbles into the oil flow. Five consecutive frames generated by the ECT VI show the process when a single air bubble travels upward in the oil. Due to the fact that the sensitivity of the ECT sensor reduces at the top and bottom ends of the electrodes, weak signal strength is detected when the bubble enters or leaves the space determined by the electrodes along the axial axis. Variation of the bubble volume in the retrieved images validates such a phenomenon.

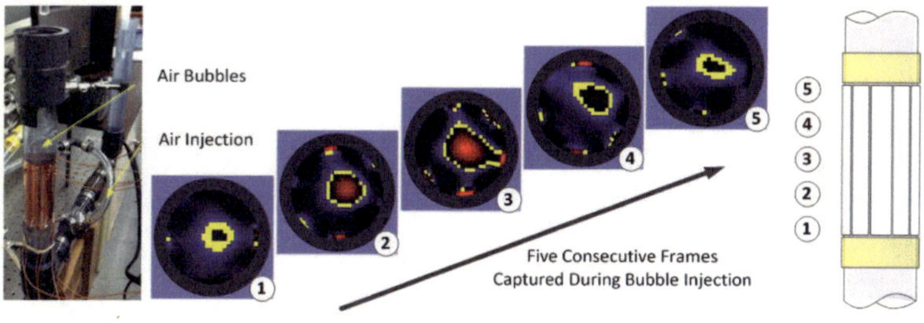

Fig. 15. Air bubble monitoring in the vertical arrangement

4. Conclusion

Electrical capacitance tomography is one of the widely used techniques for monitoring the material distribution within an enclosed container. This chapter introduces the design and realization of a virtual instrument for online ECT sensing. Based on the configuration of hardware circuitry and ECT electrodes, the VI is implemented using seven major functional modules: switching control, data sampling, data normalization, permittivity calculation, mesh generation, image generation, and image display. Each of the functional modules is designed as a subVI to control the measurement circuitry, sample the output signal, and retrieve the permittivity distribution image. Two image retrieving algorithms, Linear Back-Projection and Tikhonov Regularization are implemented in the permittivity calculation subVI. The VI is tested with an 8-electrode ECT sensor built on a 40mm plastic pipe for oil-air flow monitoring. Experimental results have shown that the VI is capable of detecting the oil-air interface as well as catching the dynamics such as the air bubble translation in the oil flow. The introduced VI design can be further expanded to include multiple-excitation (Fan & Gao, 2011), grouping schemes (Olmos, et al., 2008), and advanced image retrieving algorithms to improve the time and spatial resolution of ECT.

5. Reference

Alme, K. J. & Mylvaganam, S. (2007). Comparison of Different Measurement Protocols in Electrical Capacitance Tomography using Simulations", *IEEE Transactions on Instrumentation and Measurement*, Vol.56, No.6, pp.2119–2130.

Fan, Z. & Gao, R. X. (2011). A New Method for Improving Measurement Efficiency in Electrical Capacitance Tomography," *IEEE Transactions on Instrumentation and Measurement*, Vol.60, No.5, pp.

Golub, G.; Heath, M. & Wahba, G. (1979). Generalized Cross-Validation as a Method for Choosing a Good Ridge Parameter. *Technometrics,* Vol.21, No.2, pp.215–223.

Hansen, P. C. (1992). Analysis of Discrete Ill-posed Problems by Means of the L-curve, *SIAM Review,* Vol. 34, No. 3, pp.561–580.

Huang, S. M. ; Plaskowski, A. ; Xie, C. G. & Beck, M. S. (1989). Tomographic Imaging of Two-component Flow Using Capacitance Sensors. *Journal of Physics E: Scientific Instruments*, Vol.22, No.3, pp. 173-177.

Huang, S. M.; Xie, C. G.; Thorn, R.; Snowden, D. & Beck, M. S. (1992). Design of sensorelectronics for electrical capacitance tomography," IEE Proceedings G, Vol. 139, No.1, pp. 89-98.

Isaksen, O. (1996). A Review of Reconstruction Techniques for Capacitance Tomography. *Measurement Science and Technology*, Vol.7, No.3, pp. 325–337.

Marashdeh, Q. & Teixeira, F. L. (2004). Sensitivity Matrix Calculation for Fast 3-D Electrical Capacitance Tomography (ECT) of Flow Systems. *IEEE Transactions on Magnetics*, Vol. 40, No. 2, pp. 1204-1207.

National Instrumentation.(2001). LabVIEW Real-time User Manual. Available from http://www.ni.com.

Olmos, A. M.; Carvajal, M. A.; Morales, D. P.; García, A. & Palma, A. J. (2008). Development of an Electrical Capacitance Tomography System using Four Rotating Electrodes", *Sensors and Actuators A*, Vol. 128, No.2, pp.366-375.

Reinecke, N. & Mewes, D. (1996). Recent Developments and Industrial/Research Applications of Capacitance Tomography. *Measurement Science and Technology*, Vol. 7, No.3, pp. 233–246.

Tikhonov, A. N. & Arsenin, V. Y. (1977).*Solutions of Ill-Posed Problems*. Washington, DC: Winston.

Warsito, W.; Marashdeh, Q. & Fan, L. S. (2007).Electrical Capacitance Volume Tomography. *IEEE Sensors Journal*, Vol. 7, No. 3, pp. 525-535.

Williams, R. A. & Beck, M. S. (1995). *Process Tomography: Principles, Techniquesand Applications*. Oxford, U.K.: Butterworth-Heinemann.

Xie, D.; Huang, Z.; Ji, H. & Li, H. (2006). An Online Flow Pattern Identification System for Gas-Oil Two-Phase Flow Using Electrical Capacitance Tomography. *IEEE Transactions on Instrumentation and Measurement*, Vol.55, No.5, pp. 1833 - 1838.

Yang, W. Q. (1996).Hardware Design of Electrical Capacitance Tomography Systems. *Measurement Science and Technology*, Vol. 7, No.3, pp. 225–232.

Yang, W. Q & Peng, L. (2003). Image Reconstruction Algorithms for Electrical Capacitance Tomography. *Measurement Science and Technology*, Vol.14. No.1, pp. R1-13.

Yang, W. Q. (2010). Design of Electrical Capacitance Tomography Sensors," *Measurement Science and Technology*, Vol. 21, No. 4, pp. 1-13.

2

Low-Field NMR/MRI Systems Using LabVIEW and Advanced Data-Acquisition Techniques

Aktham Asfour
Grenoble University - Grenoble Electrical Engineering Lab (G2E-Lab), France

1. Introduction

Nuclear Magnetic Resonance (NMR) and Magnetic Resonance Imaging (MRI) have become powerful non-invasive analytical tools for a large palette of applications, ranging from solid state physics, to all the branches of chemistry, biology, medical research and medical diagnosis (Ernst et al., 1989). Nowadays, we are also witnessing new areas of applications for a variety of non-invasion measurements such as the quality control of food products (Asfour et al., 2004, Raoof et.al, 2002), etc.

To meet the needs for expanding research projects and applications, powerful and expensive spectrometers or imagers are commercially available. Although, these, usually high or medium field, NMR/MRI systems have many advantages, such as a high signal-to-noise ratio (SNR), resolution and high image quality, their use in some specific applications could be prohibitively expensive. Actually, in many cases, for particular purposes, one may only need NMR spectrometers or MR imagers having a subset of the features of a standard commercial one (Gengying et al., 2002). In addition, the use of low- and very-low fields (below 100 mT) could be sufficient in some cases. The cost of the system can then be dramatically reduced since these low- and very-low fields – with, sometimes, relatively poor performances requirements- could be easily produced. Moreover, the use of low fields simplifies the design and realization of compact and portable NMR systems which could be especially appreciated for the in situ applications.

Nevertheless, NMR spectrometers using low fields and so low frequencies (up to several 100 kHz) are not commercially available. A number of groups have worked to develop dedicated MRI/NMR systems by using compact low-field MR magnets. For example, we have proposed in a previous work a home-built and fully digital MRI system working at 0.1 T (resonance frequency of about 4.25 MHz) (Raoof et al., 2002). This system was based on the use of a high-performance Digital Signal Processor (DSP), a direct digital synthesizer (DDS) and a digital receiver. These very advanced hardware and signal processing techniques were typically employed in the base-stations of mobile phone. Based on this work, Shen (Shen et al., 2005) proposed another system working at 0.3 T and allowing larger imaging sizes than in (Raoof et al., 2002). Another work, carried out in (Michal et al., 2002) was focused on the realization of a wideband receiver for a home-built NMR spectrometer working at 55.84 MHz (high field).

Some groups have NMR systems working at low field for the specific application of measurement of the *polarization*[1] for the NMR of hyperpolarized gases (^{129}Xe, ^{3}He…). Most of these systems were actually developed by modifying high frequency and high cost commercial spectrometers. One research group has, however, developed its own NMR system (Saam & Conradi, 1998). This system was used for monitoring the *polarization* of hyperpolarized helium (^{3}He) at 3 mT. It was a fully analog system where authors performed a phase-sensitive detection of the NMR signal. They used then an oscilloscope for signal visualization. Despite the great merit of the original and elegant electronic solutions developed in (Saam & Conradi, 1998), the detection of hyperpolarized ^{3}He signals was relatively not a hard task since their levels were quite high (at least 10 mV). Actually, this spectrometer did not allow sufficient dynamic range to detect the NMR signal of the proton (^{1}H) at such field.

In any case, dedicated low-field NMR systems are still far from the experience of most NMR groups. Recently, we developed very low-field NMR spectrometers that allow detection of the ^{1}H NMR signals at 4.5 mT (Asfour, 2006, 2008, 2010). These developments were initially motivated by their application in the measurement of the *absolute polarization* of hyperpolarized xenon (^{129}Xe).

These systems were based on the use of data-acquisition boards (DAQ). These boards are adequate at low frequencies. Moreover, they have increased in performances and the related software (LabVIEW) made their use quite straightforward. In these new NMR spectrometers, we replaced as much analog electronics as possible with DAQ boards and software. We show that the use of advanced data-acquisition and signal processing techniques allow detection of the ^{1}H NMR signals at 4.5 mT.

The aim of this chapter is to present these advances in the development of low-field NMR systems. One of the underlying ideas of this chapter is to make these systems versatile and easy-to-replicate so as to help developers and research groups in realizing NMR spectrometers with flexibility, low cost and minimum development time. This is why we describe in some details the variety of the practical aspects of realization. This includes both hardware design and software developments.

For a reader who could be not familiarized with the NMR technique, we present, in a first section of this chapter, a brief and very simplified review of the NMR basic principles using classical physics. The second section is focused on the description of the hardware solutions and architecture of the NMR spectrometers. This architecture is mainly based on the use of signal generator and data-acquisition boards from National Instruments. The software developments (LabVIEW programs) and the advanced data-acquisition and signal processing techniques are presented in the third section. The last section will concentrate on applications and discussions. The use of the developed system for the measurement of the nuclear polarization of hyperpolarized gases will be particularly illustrated.

In addition to these new advances, general principles of the NMR instrumentation are sometimes illustrated. While these aspects could seem basic for confirmed NMR developers, we believe that they may be of great value for beginners, students and for education purposes. Actually, while many publications (academic courses, books, journals…) illustrate

[1] See section 5.1 and references (Asfour, 2010) and (Saam & Conradi, 1998) for the definition of the *absolute polarizations*.

the principles of the NMR, these publications usually concentrate on NMR physics rather than NMR instrumentation. We hope that this chapter could be of help for those who desire to learn about this exciting area. This is why schematics of the developed hardware, software as well as any detail about the design could be obtained by simply writing to the author.

2. NMR basic principles

As it is well known, when a sample, consisting of NMR-sensitive nuclei (^{1}H, ^{3}He, ^{129}Xe; ^{23}Na, etc.), is subjected to a uniform static magnetic field B_0, a net macroscopic magnetization M of the sample appears in the same direction of B_0. This magnetization is proportional, roughly speaking, to this polarizing field B_0, to the density of nuclei within the sample and to the characteristic gyro-magnetic ratio γ of the nucleus being studied.

In a typical one-pulse experiment, the sample is subjected to a short pulse (called excitation pulse) of a radiofrequency (RF) magnetic field B_1, applied perpendicularly to B_0 and at the characteristic Larmor frequency f_0. This frequency depends on the nucleus and of the static magnetic field according to the equation (1):

$$f_0 = \frac{\gamma}{2\pi} B_0 \tag{1}$$

For the proton (^{1}H nucleus), this frequency is about 42.25 MHz at B_0 = 1 T and about 190 kHz at 4.5 mT, while it is about 52 kHz for the xenon-129 (^{129}Xe) at this last field.

The effect of the excitation pulse is that the magnetization, M, is "tipped" or rotated from its initial direction (or from its thermal equilibrium state) by an angle α. This angle is called "*flip angle*". It is proportional to field B_1 and to its duration, τ, according to the equation (2):

$$\alpha = \gamma.\tau.B_1 \tag{2}$$

At the end of the excitation pulse, the NMR signal- called also the Free Induction Decay (FID) - is received at the same frequency f_0. This signal, which is proportional to the magnetization M (then to B_0) and to γ, is processed to be used for obtaining a "fingerprint" of the environment of the nucleus being studied.

The flip angle can be set through the adjustment of the amplitude, B_1, or/and the duration, τ, of the excitation pulse. For a one-pulse sequence, the maximum NMR signal level is obtained at a flip angle of 90°. However, the choice of the optimum value of this flip angle in more advanced NMR/MRI pulse sequences depends on many considerations which are out of the scope of this chapter.

One should also know that a variety of parameters contribute in the signal-to-noise ratio (SNR). Firstly, and roughly speaking, the SNR is proportional to the square of the static magnetic strength. The SNR, the image quality and spectral resolution are enhanced at high field. This is one of the main reasons for which NMR experiments are usually performed at high fields. Secondly, the SNR is proportional density of the nuclei within the sample being studied and its depends on the nucleus of interest (through the gyro magnetic ratio γ). Finally, for a given nucleus, a given B_0 and a given volume, the SNR depends strongly on the characteristics of the detection coil.

3. A hardware structure for low-field NMR systems

Based on these simplified principles, Fig. 1 illustrates the general hardware architecture of the developed low-field NMR systems.

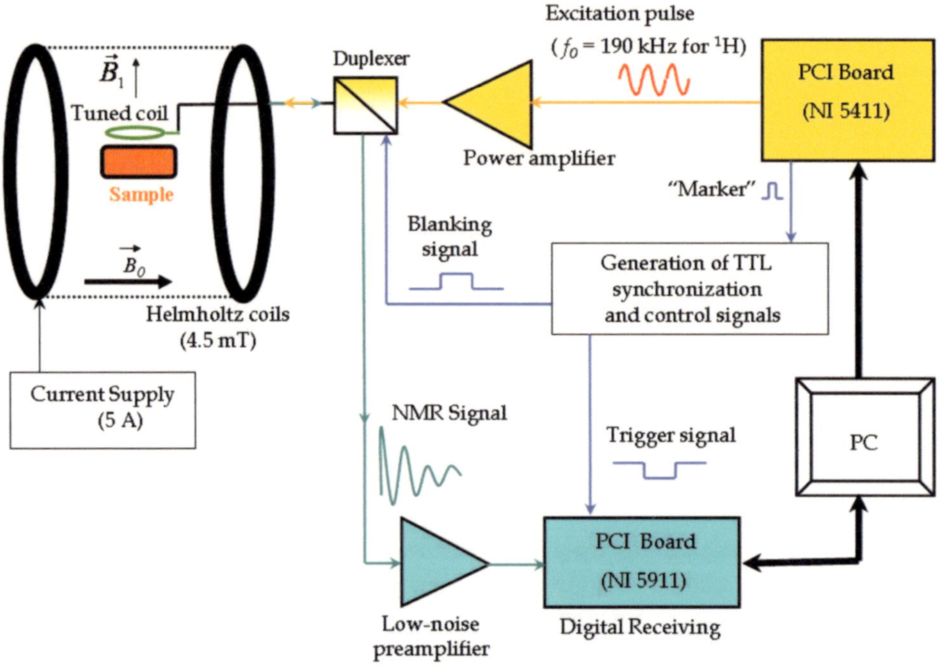

Fig. 1. The hardware architecture of the low -field NMR systems.

The static field B_0 of about 4.5 mT is produced by a pair of Helmholtz coils. The excitation pulse (at about 190 kHz for ^{1}H) is generated by the transmitter (arbitrary waveform generator board NI 5411 form National Instruments). This pulse is amplified by a power amplifier and sent, via the duplexer, to the well-tuned coil (at the working frequency of 190 kHz for the ^{1}H) which generates the excitation field B_1.

At the end of the excitation pulse, this same tuned coil detects the weak NMR signal. This signal is transmitted to a low-noise preamplifier via the same duplexer. The amplified signal is then received by the receiving board (A digitizer board NI 5911 from National Instruments) for digitalization and processing.

A monostable-based circuit generates TTL control and synchronization signals from a single and very short (about 10 ns) TTL pulse ("*Marker*") that could be generated from the NI 5411. At least, two signals are necessary. Since the same coil is used for both transmitting and receiving (i.e. a transmit-receive coil), a "blanking signal" is required to control the duplexer. This signal "blanks" the preamplifier input during the excitation pulse and it isolates the transmitting section from the receiving one during the NMR signal detection. Another control signal (trigger signal) is necessary for triggering the signal acquisition with the receiving board.

An example of the timing diagram of a one-pulse NMR experiment realized by the developed spectrometer is shown in Fig. 2.

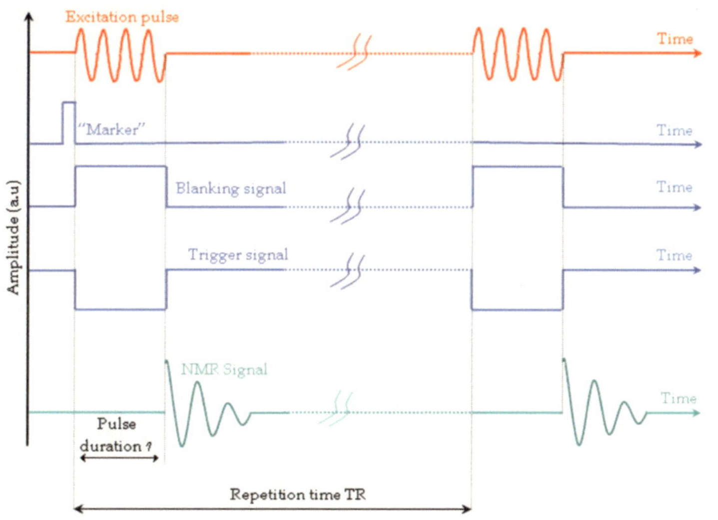

Fig. 2. The timing-diagram of a typical one-pulse NMR experiment.

The main elements of this hardware are developed in the next sections. Details about the hardware design are given to enable developer to easily replicate the system.

3.1 Magnetic field production: The Helmholtz coils for low and very-low fields

In low-field and very-low-field NMR systems, the static magnetic fields, B_0, could be produced using a variety of magnet categories and structures. The choice of a category and a structure is strongly related to the application, and its depends on many considerations such as the value of the magnet field, the desired performances (field stability, spatial homogeneity…), the cost and complexity of realization as well as the ease-of-use. These magnets can however be divided into two categories[2]: permanent magnets and electro-magnets. Permanent magnet of 0.08 T has been used in the development of an MR imager for education purposes (Wright et al., 2010). Permanent magnets with a typical field of 0.1 T have also potential industrial applications (quality control of food products) (Asfour et al. 2004). Some dedicated MR imagers using permanent magnets are commercially available for medical applications. Original and elegant structures of permanent magnets of 0.1 T have been proposed in a portable system for potential application for the high resolution NMR in inhomogeneous field (LeBec et al., 2006).
The main advantage of permanent magnets is that they do not use any power supply. However, these magnets could not offer a good stability of the field because of the temperature-dependence of their magnetization. Another disadvantage is the imperfections of the magnetic materials and may be the complexity of realization.
Electro- magnets can offer an alternative solution. Typically, the obtained field strength could be as high as 0.5 T. A water-cooled electro-magnet of 0.1 T was used in (Raoof et al., 2002) for a dedicated MRI system for both medical and industrial applications.

[2] High fields are generally created by superconducting magnets

In the systems developed in (Asfour, 2006, 2008, 2010), a pair of Helmholtz coils was used as illustrated by Fig. 3 (only one Helmholtz coil is shown). More homogeneous magnetic field could be obtained using four coils.

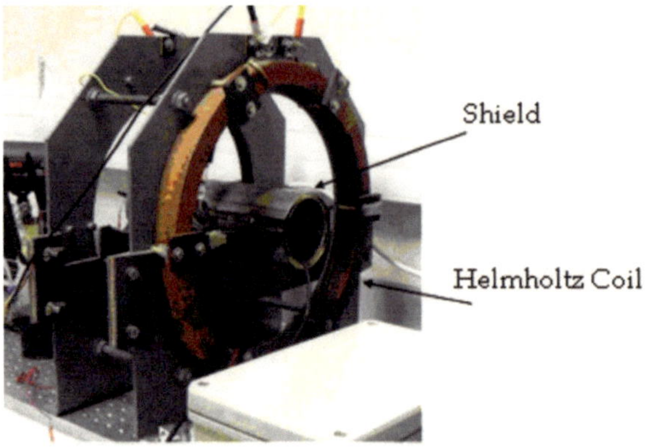

Fig. 3. Helmholtz coils producing a 4.5 mT magnetic field. A stabilized supply current of about 5A is used. A metallic shield serves for shielding the NMR coil when it is positioned inside the magnet

These coils produce a magnetic field of 4.5 mT when they are supplied by a DC current of about 5 A. The design of Helmholtz coils is well-know. It will not be developed here. It is however important to know that it is crucial to use a stabilized power suppler to maintain a constant value of the produced field and hence a constant resonance frequency. This is fundamental for the NMR, especially at low field where NMR signal averaging is still necessary.

3.2 The transmitter: Arbitrary waveform generator NI 5411

The excitation pulse at the working frequency is digitally synthesized using the PCI board NI 5411 from National Instruments. This device is an arbitrary-waveform generator (AWG) which has been chosen for its interesting features for the NMR, especially its high flexibility for pulse sequences programming and generation. The related NI-FGEN instrument driver is used to program and control it using LabVIEW.

The device can operate in two waveform-generation modes: Arbitrary mode and DDS (Direct Digital Synthesis) mode. This flexibility allows its use for a large palette of applications, and it is specially appreciated for the NMR. The paragraph 4.2 and the user-manual of the device give more description of these modes and their use.

In both modes, the digitally synthesized waveform is interpolated by a half-hand digital filter and then fed to a high-speed 12-bit DAC (Analog-to-Digital Converter). The DAC output is optionally applied to an output amplifier and/or an analog filter to generate the final analog output signal.

Digital outputs are also available. One digital output ("Marker") is a TTL compatible signal that can be set up at any point of the analog waveform being generated. This signal is used as a trigger pulse for the generation of TTL synchronization and control signals (see Fig. 1 and Fig. 2).

Full details and description of the board architecture and features could be found in the user manual of the NI 5411.

3.3 Power amplifier and generation of the TTL synchronization and control signals

The generated pulse from the AWG is amplified by a power amplifier stage. This stage was based on the use of the operational amplifier (op-amp) AD711. This op-amp was chosen for its high output slew rate (Saam & Conradi, 1998), (Asfour 2006, 2008, 2010). The amplifier was realized on the same board together with the circuit that generates the synchronization and control signals. Fig. 4 shows the schematic of the main parts of the board.

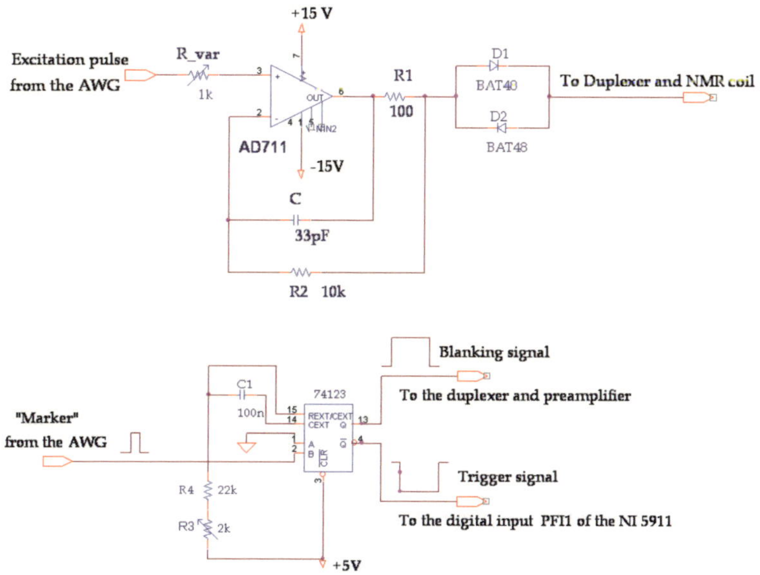

Fig. 4. Schematic of the power amplifier and the circuit for the generation of synchronization and control signals.

The stage allows more than 25 V peak-to-peak output measured on a high impedance oscilloscope. Since the amplifier is loaded by the duplexer and the NMR coil, the voltage across the coil should be lower and it depends on how well the coil is tuned during the transmitting period.

The design of op-amp-based power amplifiers for the NMR has to take into account the oscillations that could appear when the amplifier is loaded by the capacitive and inductive coil. The design in Fig. 4 employs a 100 □ resistor which enables the amplifier to drive large capacitive loads. The resistor effectively isolates the high frequency feedback from the load and stabilizes the circuit.

The synchronization and control TTL signals are generated using a monostable-based circuit (74123) triggered by the *"Marker"* from the AWG NI 5411. The circuit produces two complementary signals for blanking the preamplifier and for triggering the acquisition using the receiving board. The duration of these signals could be easily adjusted by external capacitors and resistors.

3.4 The NMR coil, duplexer and low-noise preamplifier

The well-tuned coil is one of the key elements for a successful detection of the weak NMR signals. Regardless the geometry of the coil, the equivalent electrical circuit of an NMR coil is an inductance which is tuned by one or more capacitors to form a parallel resonant circuit

at the working frequency. The geometry and the electrical structure of the coil are generally chosen to optimize the spatial homogeneity of the excitation field within the sample and/or the sensitivity of detection. For a given application, the coil structure depends strongly on these desired performances as well as on the working frequency.
A large number of geometries, electrical structures and coil configurations have been studied, published and use. The interested reader may refer to (Mispelter et al., 2006) for more information bout the NMR and MRI coils.
However, coils for low and very-low frequencies have actually not been widely investigated. A simple sensitive coil is proposed here. It is a transmit-receive surface coil of about 400 turns of a Litz wire with an average diameter of 2 cm and a height of 0.5 cm (Fig.5) The developed inductance is about 1.3 mH measured at 190 kHz. Fig. 5 shows the coil as well as its position, together with the sample, inside the magnet and the shield.

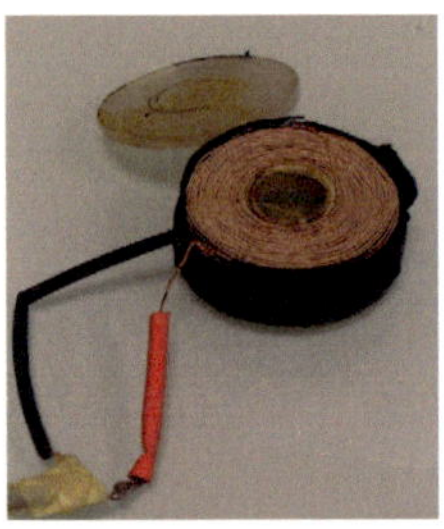

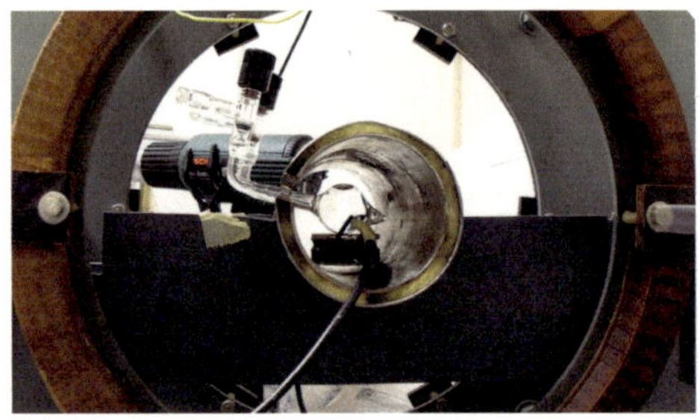

Fig. 5. The transmit-receive coil (left figure). On the right figure, the coil could be seen inside the Helmholtz coils and the shield. The coil is loaded by a sample consisting of Pyrex (a type of glass) cylinder filled with pure water.

Calculations have showed that a quality factor, Q, of the resonant circuit of at least 120 (at 190 kHz) is necessary for the detection of ^{1}H NMR signals. Even at this relatively low frequency, the use of a Litz wire was important to minimize the skin effect and to achieve a high quality factor Q. The measured quality factor of the final coil was 220 at 190 kHz and 130 at 52 kHz, about two times and a half greater than the one that could be achieved with solid wire of the same gauge and geometry.
Tuning the coil was achieved using fixed capacitors and variable ones. A software modulus allows displaying the resonance curve in real time for fine tuning (see paragraph 4.3). A same coil could be easily used for different frequencies. The only modifications are the tuning capacitors. To facilitate these modifications, tuning components could, if desired, plug-in on pin DIP component carriers. The coil is connected to the duplexer by ordinary coaxial cable; there are no tuning elements in close proximity of the coil.
A duplexer is necessary when the NMR coil is used for both transmitting and receiving. During the transmitting period, the duplexer must "blank" the preamplifier avoiding its overloading and its possible destruction by the high power excitation pulses. This same duplexer isolates the transmitter from the receiver during the receiving period. This avoids electrical noises from the transmit section.
Duplexers are usually built using quarter-wavelength lines. However, at low frequency, the length of such lines is very important and their use is not advised, at least from practical point-of-view. Moreover, for such line lengths, the signal attenuation could dramatically decrease the SNR and shielding requirements become more stringent to avoid external interferences.

Duplexers at low frequency have actually not been widely investigated. Here, a structure of duplexer is presented. This structure was inspired from the work in (Saam & Conradi, 1998). Fig. 6 shows the whole electrical circuit of the duplexer associated to the NMR coil and the first stage of the low-noise preamplifier.

The NMR coil inductance L is tuned to the working frequency using parallel fixed capacitor C_T and variable one C_T-var. The duplexer is based of the use of a Field-effect Transistor (FET) switch J108.

During the transmitting period, the blanking TTL signal is in high level. The "*Command of the switch* " (based on the bipolar transistor 2N3906) sets the gate voltage of the J108 to 0 V. The FET switch is then in its on-state, putting the preamplifier input to the ground and avoiding its overload. In the case of an eventual dysfunction of the FET switch, an additional protection of the preamplifier is achieved by the limiting crossed diodes D5-D6.

Notice that the capacitor C2 avoids the short circuit of the NMR coil when the switch is in its on-state. Also, during transmitting, crossed diodes D3-D4 conduct, putting C2 in parallel with C_T and C_T-var, and the NMR coil would not be well -tuned if an additional inductor L1 is not used. Indeed, this inductor offsets the increased capacitance. The value of L1 should be chosen according to the value of C2 so as the final resonance frequency of the parallel circuit- formed by L, L2, C_T and C_T-var and C2- to be closed to the working frequency.

During the receiving period, the "*Command of the switch*" sets the gate voltage of the FET switch to -15 V by charging the capacitor C3. The switch is now in its off-state. Diodes D3 and D4 are blocked. They isolate so the transmit section. On the other hand, they disconnect the additional inductor L2 from C2. This capacitor becomes now just a coupling capacitor to the preamplifier.

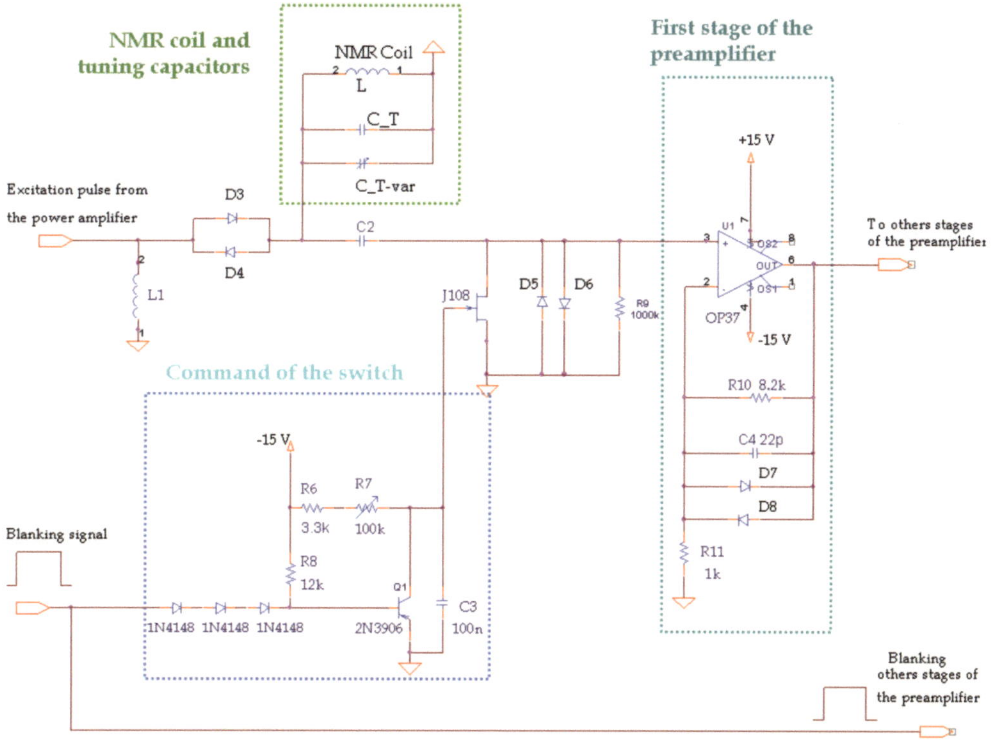

Fig. 6. Schematic of the NMR coil, duplexer and the first stage of the preamplifier.

The preamplifier is another key element for NMR signal receiving at very-low field. It is high gain, high dynamic range and low-noise. Several stages, based on the use of the OP37 (or OP27) low-noise op-amp, were associated. In Fig. 6, one can see the first stage which was realized, together with duplexer on the same printed circuit board. Crossed diodes D7-D8 in the feedback network prevent the overload of the following stage. In addition, the high frequency response is rolled off by a 22 pF capacitor (C4).
Optional analog filters could be used in adequate locations between the different stages of the preamplifier to optimize the SNR and/or the dynamic range. The total gain is programmable between 2 and 2000.
The design of low-noise and high gain preamplifiers is relatively complicated and requires some know-how. For developers who could not be familiarized with such development, the author could advise commercial low-noise preamplifiers. For example, the low-noise preamplifier SR560 from Stanford Research Systems is adequate for frequencies up to few 100 kHz.

3.5 The receiving board

The receiving board (NI 5911 from National Instruments) is the last receiving key element. This device is a high-speed digitizer with a flexible-resolution ADC (Analog-to-Digital Converter) and it ensures high sensitivity and high dynamic range. These features were the main crucial criteria in choosing the device for the NMR.
The analog input of the board -that could be AC or DC coupled- is equipped with a differential programmable gain input amplifier (PGIA). This PGIA accurately interfaces to and scales the input signal to match the full input range of the ADC so as to optimize accuracy and resolution. The ADC is 8-bits and is clocked at 100 MHz sampling frequency like a desktop oscilloscope. However, flexible resolution can dramatically enhance the final effective resolution of the ADC.
Full description of the board features could be found in the user manual of the NI 5911.

4. Software development: LabVIEW programs

4.1 Overall view of the developed NMR spectrometer program

The "*Low-field NMR Spectrometer*" program was developed using LabVIEW and associated instrument drivers (NI-FGEN and NI-SCOPE) of the NI 5411 and the NI 5911 devices. The architecture of the program is open which lets users build their own modulus if wanted. The main panel of the Graphical User Interface (GUI) is shown in Fig. 7.
User could choose the frequency, amplitude, and duration of the excitation pulse as well as the repetition time (TR) for a one-pulse NMR sequence. The gain of the low-noise preamplifier should be given when quantitative measurements on the NMR signal have to be performed. Other hardware configurations of the NI 5411 and the NI 5911 are not available in the main front panel, but they could be modified if required in the LabVIEW diagrams.
When the pulse sequence is defined, user can start the NMR experience using the "*NMR Signal Acquisition*" panel. The program allows NMR experiences at any excitation frequency up to 20 MHz. Currently, NMR signal acquisition and measurements are performed on two nuclei: proton (^{1}H) and xenon (^{129}Xe). The resonance frequencies are of about 190 kHz and 52 kHz, respectively.

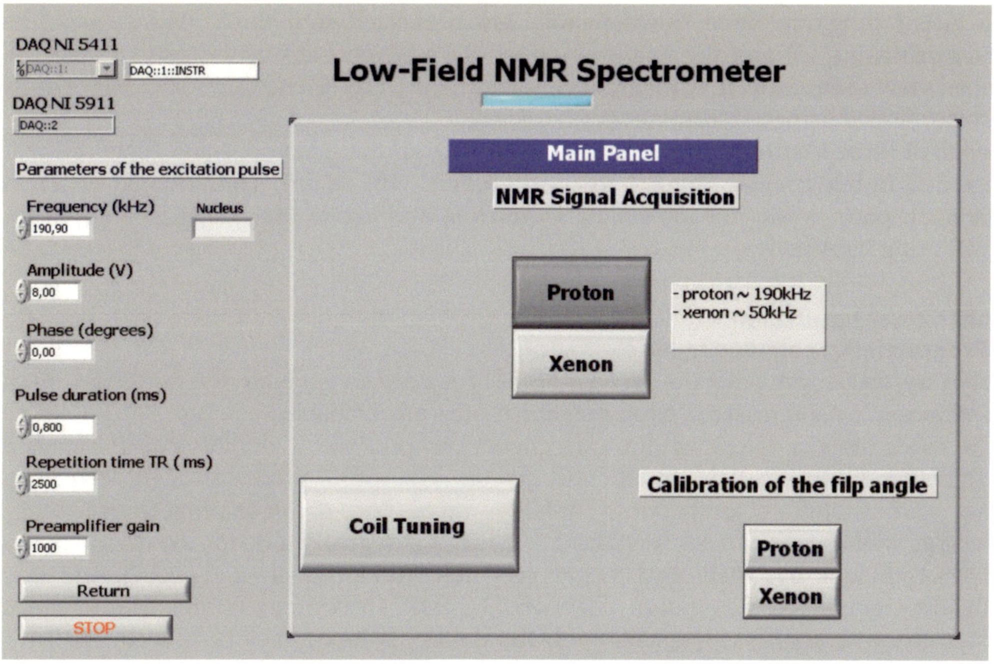

Fig. 7. The main front panel of the low-field NMR spectrometer

The developed program contains also two other main functionalities: the "*Coil Tuning*" and "*The Calibration of the Flip Angle*". These functionalities are required for an NMR spectrometer. In fact, each NMR or MRI experiment follows, at least, three fundamental steps in chronological order: coil tuning, calibration of the flip angle calibration of the excitation pulse and NMR signal acquisition and processing

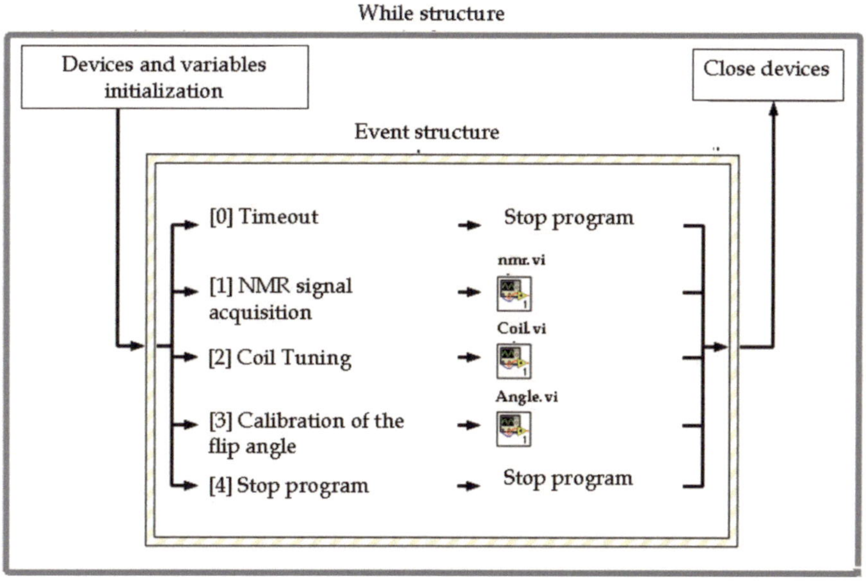

Fig. 8. The general structure of the LabVIEW diagram for NMR spectrometer

In the global program, these functionalities are organized into three *main sub-routines (Virtual Instruments VI)* and the whole program is based on LabVIEW *events structure*. A simplified view of the LabVIEW diagram is illustrated by Fig. 8. The three *main sub-routines* are also developed using sub-routines (VI).

Neither *all* of these VI, nor the general LabVIEW programming methods and functions will be presented in this chapter. Indeed, the next sections will be only concentrated on some specific main parts, ideas, advanced data-acquisition and signal processing techniques for the NMR using LabVIEW.

4.2 NMR signal acquisition

4.2.1 Programming sequences for excitation

The arbitrary waveform generator (AWG) NI 5411 is used to generate the excitation. As it was mentioned in paragraph 3.2, two operation modes are available.

A DDS mode uses a reference clock frequency to produce a digital waveform with programmable frequency, amplitude and phase. The DDS produces high frequency accuracy and resolution, temperature stability, rapid and phase-continuous frequency switching as well as low phase-noise. These features are of great value for the NMR. This is why DDS technique has been used in our previous works (Raoof et al., 2002), and it is actually now employed in modern commercial NMR spectrometers and MR imagers. However, the *arbitrary mode*, available with the device, is more flexible. Indeed, the DDS mode is well suited for applications that require continuous generation of standard waveforms that are repetitive in nature such as sine, square and triangular waveforms, etc.

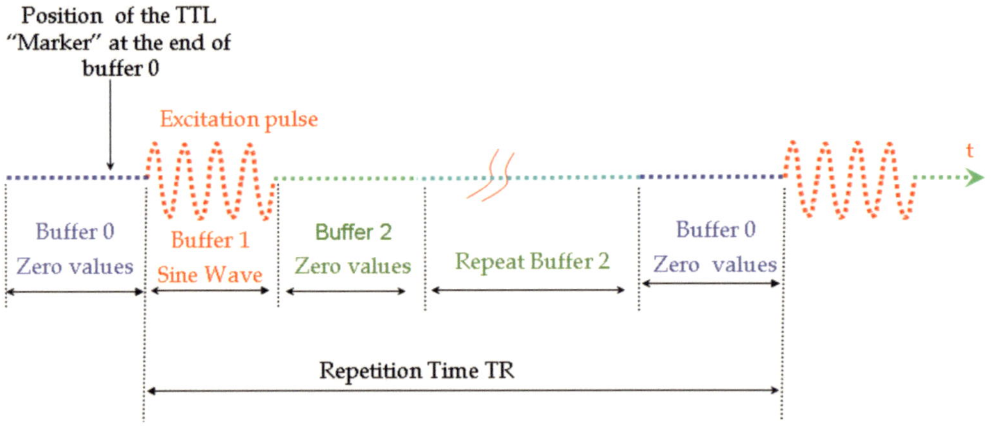

Fig. 9. The concept for creating a one-pulse NMR sequence using the *arbitrary mode*. The lengths of the buffers are programmable and they depend on the sampling frequency.

In a typical NMR/MRI sequence, the excitation pulse(s) must be generated during limited duration(s) within the repetition time TR. Unless the use of additional hardware (like a fast analog switch) in the excitation path, the DDS mode could not be suited since it generates continuous waveform. Arbitrary mode has more features and it is therefore preferred for the generation of the NMR pulse sequences. This mode allows defining waveforms as multiple buffers of samples. These buffers can then be downloaded to the memory of the AWG, linked and looped in any order to form a single sequence. In a one-pulse NMR sequence, at least two buffers are necessary: a sine waveform buffer of limited duration (τ) and a buffer of zero values. This zero- values buffer could then be repeated to obtain the final repetition time TR between two sine pulses. This feature is particularly useful for the implementation of more advanced NMR /MRI sequences (spin-echo or gradient-echo) where two or more pulses are required. Fig. 9 illustrates the concepts of waveform samples, buffers, linking and looping for a one-pulse sequence.

In addition to buffer 1 (sine waveform) and buffer 2 (zero values), and for the flexibility of implementation, the buffer 0 is used to position the TTL *"Marker"* signal which will be used to trigger the generation of the TTL synchronization and control signals. This *"Marker"* can be set at any position (time) of a waveform buffer. This position is specified by giving an offset count (in number of samples) from the start of a waveform buffer.

The creation of samples of each buffer is easily done and straightforward using general LabVIEW functions. These buffers (an array of samples) are then downloaded to the AWG's memory using the driver functions NI-FGEN of the device. Fig. 10 shows a part of the corresponding LabVIEW code.

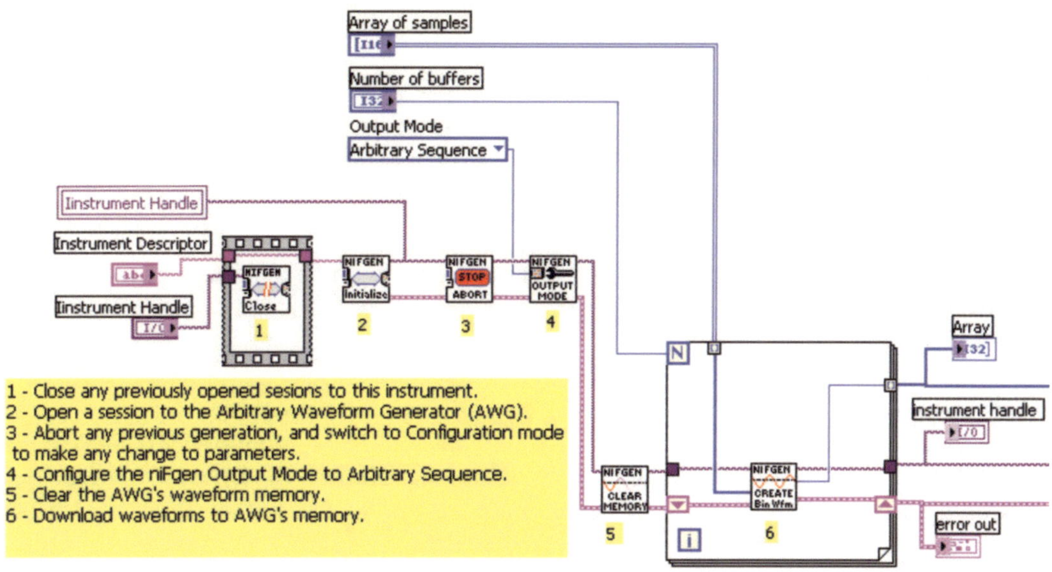

Fig. 10. The LabVIEW code for downloading the created buffers in the AWG's memory.

The waveform linking, looping and the sequence creation are then implemented according to the Fig. 11 of LabVIEW code. When creating the sequence, developer has to define the number of buffers (*sequence length*), the number of *repetitions (loops)* for each buffer. It is also important to enable the *"Marker"* signal and to route it to a digital output. The *position of the marker* in number of sample of buffer 0 must also be defined.

Other instrument configurations must be defined. These configurations include the *sampling rate* (up to 40 MHz) of the DAC, the use of the *digital filter* before the DAC, the *gain* of the output amplifier and the use of the output *analog filter*. The generation of the analog waveform could then be *enabled*.

Notice that other hardware configurations of the NI 5411 could also be defined (not shown in Fig. 11). The user-manual of the AWG NI 5411 gives you full description of the large number of functionalities offered by the device.

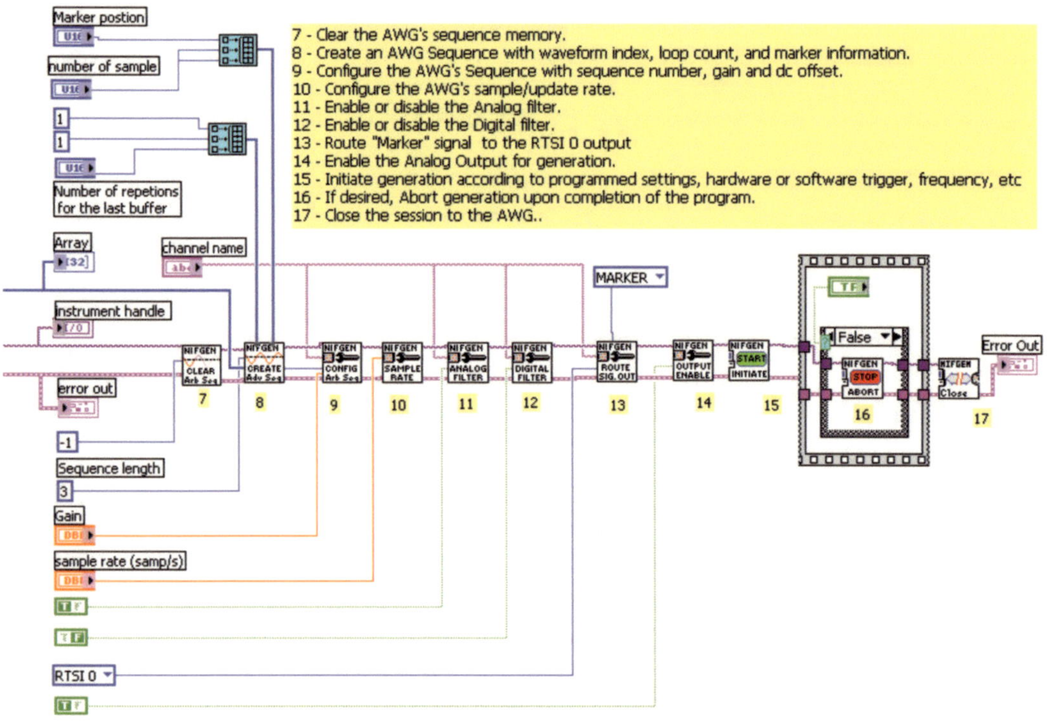

Fig. 11. A part of the LabVIEW code for waveform linking, looping and the sequence creation.

4.2.2 NMR signal detection and processing

After the end on the excitation pulse, the NMR signal from the preamplifier is applied to the analog input of the receiving board. The signal is scaled by the input amplifier (PGIA) of the NI 5911 and then sampled at 100 MHz with a resolution of 8-bits. Our previous development experience showed- and one could verify- that this resolution is far to be sufficient for NMR detection, especially at such low field.

The flexible-resolution of the ADC can dramatically enhance the ADC effective resolution.

In this flexible-resolution mode, the ADC is sourced through a noise shaping circuit that moves quantization noise on the output of the ADC from lower frequencies to higher frequencies. A digital lowpass filter applied to the data removes all but a fraction of original shaped quantization noise. The signal is then resampled at lower sampling frequency. In this way, the effective resolution is enhanced. A resolution of 11 bits is obtained at 12.5 MHz of sampling frequency. This same resolution can be as high as 21 bits for a sampling frequency of 10 kHz. In our experiments, a final ADC effective resolution of 14 bits at 5 MHz of sampling frequency was typically used.

The implementation of the NNR signal acquisition and of the flexible resolution is done using the advanced instrument driver functions (NI-SCOPE) of the NI 5911. Fig. 12 illustrates the main concept of the LabVIEW code for the configuration of the NMR signal acquisition with flexible resolution. Acquisition is hardware-triggered by the trigger signal applied to the PFI1 digital input of the device.

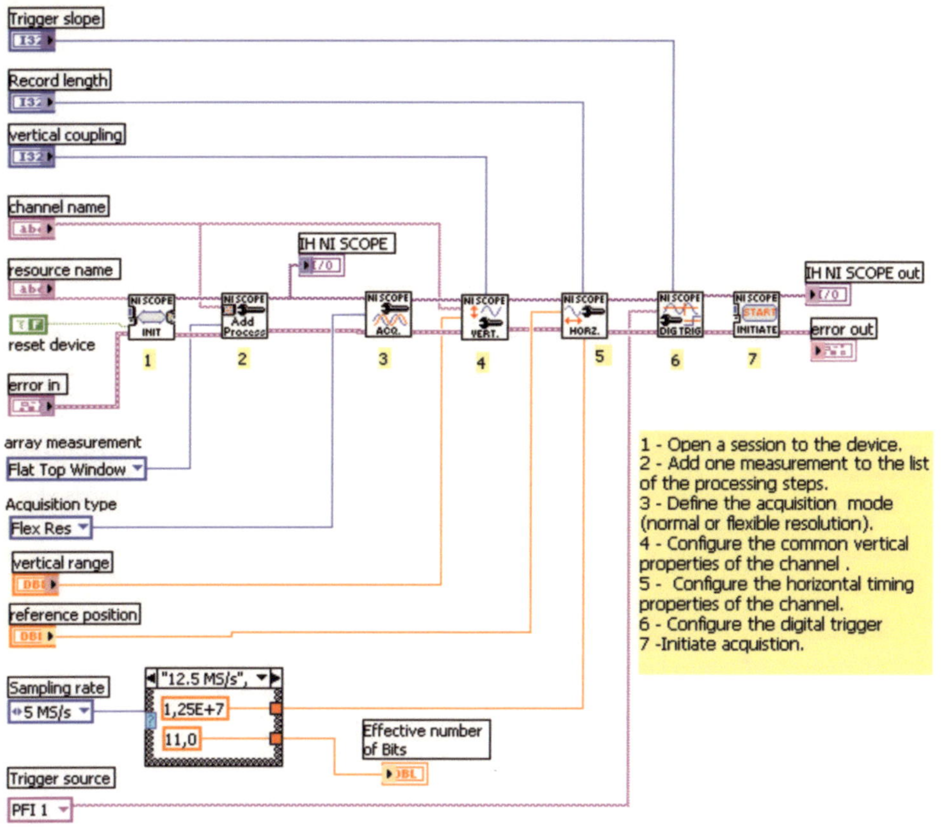

Fig. 12. A part of LabVIEW code for the configuration of the NI-5911 in flexible-resolution acquisition mode.

After acquisition with flexible resolution, data is read from the device memory and additional digital signal processing is performed by software. This processing is still necessary despite the flexible-resolution acquisition. This is why the digital data is fed to bandpass digital filter (Butterworth filter) with programmable bandwidth. The use of this filter is optional but it could be of great importance in noisy environments. In our experiments, the usefulness of this filter was still limited. After bandpass filtering, a quadratic demodulation or digital-down-conversion (DDC) is performed as it is shown in Fig. 13.

The DDC is achieved by multiplying the digital NMR signal (with N bits of effective resolution) by digital sine and cosine waveforms at the working frequency. Digital lowpass filters (Butterworth) -with programmable cutoff frequency and order- are applied. The quadratic base-band signals I/Q (In-phase and Quadratic signals) could then be obtained. However, since the useful bandwidth of these base-band signals should be no more than few hundreds Hz (depending mainly on the homogeneity of the static magnetic field), decimation technique with programmable decimating factors was implemented to improve the final effective resolution, dynamic range and the signal-to-noise ratio (SNR). In fact, the SNR is inversely proportional the total bandwidth. In digital systems, the useful bandwidth is limited by the final sampling frequency. Decimation decreases the sampling frequency and, when combined with *dedicated lowpass filtering*, improves the final SNR and dynamic range.

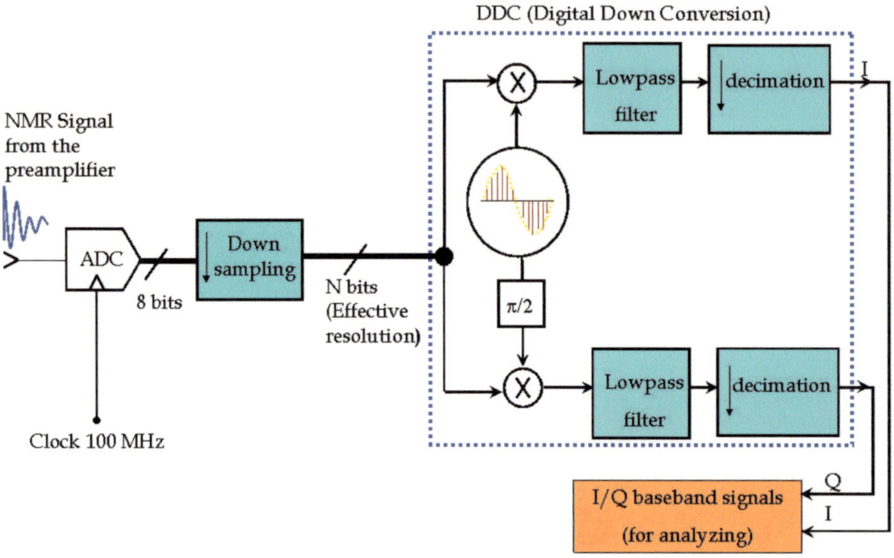

Fig. 13. Down-sampling and Digital Down-Conversion (DDC) of the NMR signals.

The simplified principle for implementing the DDC and decimation using LabVIEW is described in Fig. 14.

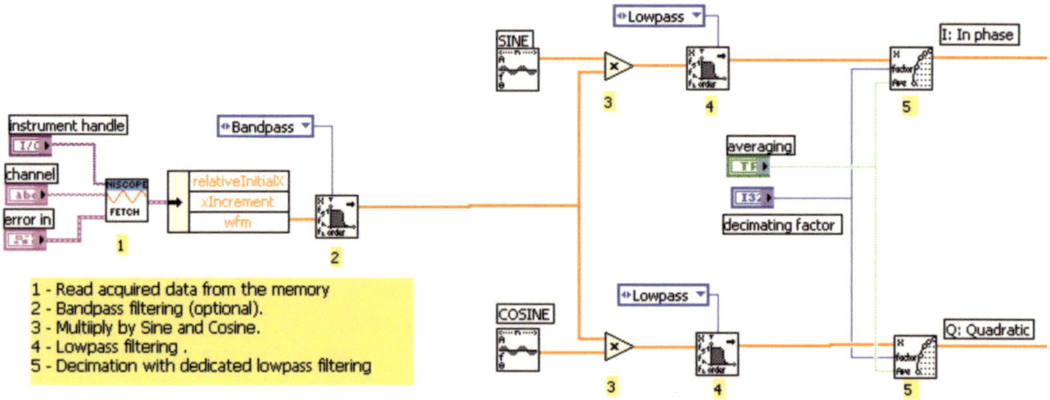

Fig. 14. Simplified Labwiew diagram for reading data from the NI 5911 memory and performing the digital down conversion (DDC) and decimation.

In Fig. 15, the "*NMR Signal acquisition*" Panel is shown. The user could choose the acquisition parameters such as the sampling rate for the flexible-resolution acquisition (The obtained effective ADC resolution is displayed for information), the cutoff frequencies and orders for the filters, the decimation factor, the trigger source, the scaling gain of the PIAG of the receiver, and the number of sample to be acquired, etc.

Starting the NMR pulse sequence is achieved by the event "*send pulse*" and data is acquired and displayed according to the defined parameters.

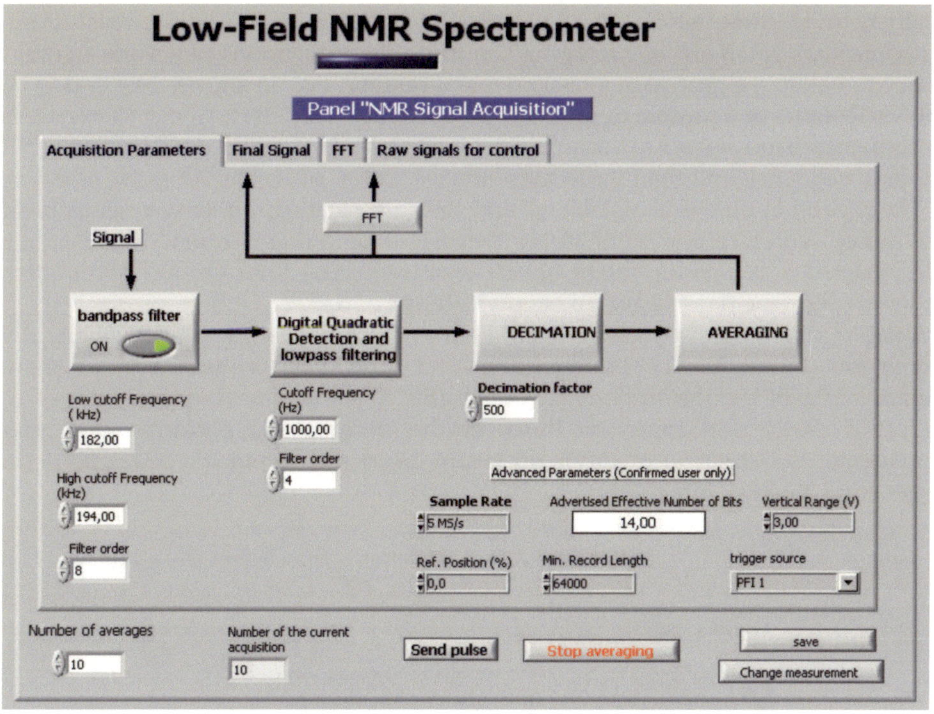

Fig. 15. The panel "NMR signal Acquisition".

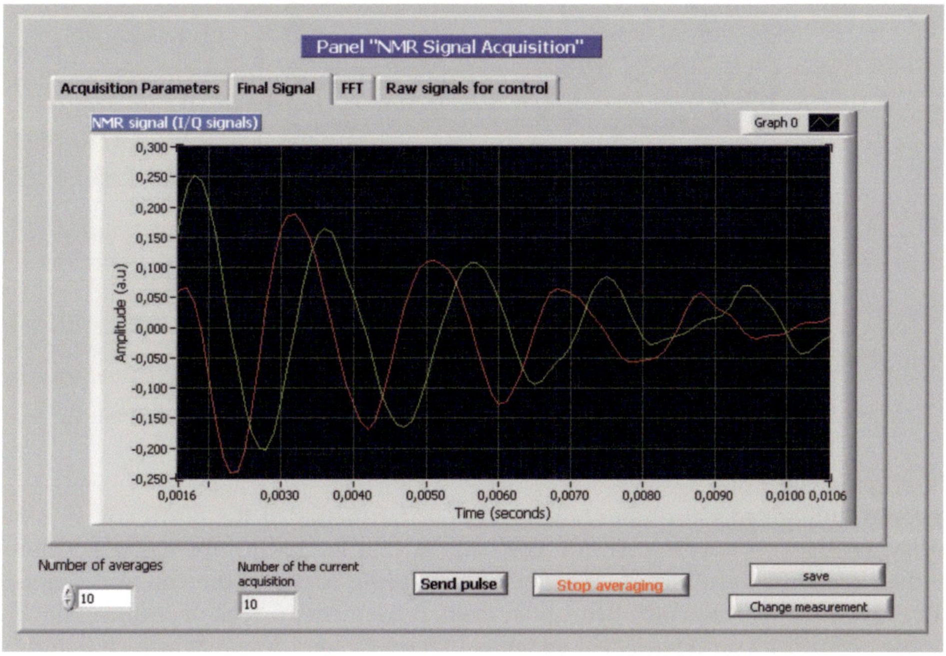

Fig. 16. The baseband I/Q parts of the ^{1}H NMR signal obtained at 4.5 mT with 10 signal averages.

In addition to all these advanced signal procession techniques (flexible-resolution, DDC with decimation), NMR signal averaging (i.e. multiple acquisitions of a same signal) is still necessary to obtain a signal with a measurement quality. Fig. 16 shows the I and Q parts of the ^{1}H NMR signal of a sample of pure water (about 100 milliliter). About 10 averages were used. These baseband signals are acquired with 500 Hz of off-resonance (difference between the Larmor frequency and the frequency of the excitation pulse). A 90° pulse of 0.8 ms was used. The repetition time was of 2500 ms and the gain of preamplifier was set to 1000. Data were acquired with a resolution of 14 bits (5 MHz of sampling frequency before the DDC). For decimation, a decimating factor of 500 was used. The final sampling frequency was about 10 kHz, and the positive useful bandwidth was of 5 kHz.

Additional signal analysis such as Fast Fourier Transform (FFT) as well as different measurements could then be performed in real time. For example, Fig. 17 shows the magnitude of the FFT of the NMR signal of Fig. 16.

Users could easily add more modulus in the program to perform other kinds of measurements on the signal or on its spectrum. Such measurements could be performed using general LabVIEW functions.

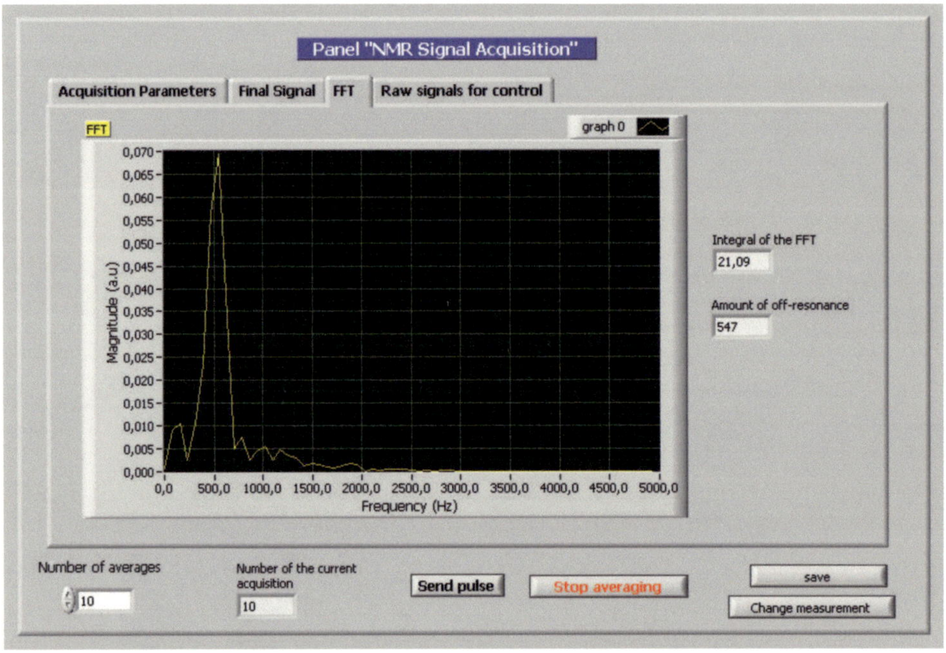

Fig. 17. Magnitude of the FFT of an-off resonance the NMR signal in the baseband.

4.3 Tuning the NMR coil

For a given tuning capacitor value, the resonance frequency of the NMR coil is generally shifted when the coil is placed inside the magnet and loaded by the sample. One might argue that this shift, resulting from capacitive coupling between the coil and the sample, could be small at low frequency. However, even at frequencies such as 190 kHz or 52 kHz, where the SNR of the detected NMR signal is inherently very low, we believe that it is still important to optimize the tune the coil for each sample and inside the magnet. The shift in the resonance frequency could dramatically cause losses in the SNR. Therefore, tuning the

coil must still the first fundamental step in each NMR/MRI experiment. The NMR spectrometer must then allow tuning the coil in real experimental conditions.
A simple method for tuning the coil is illustrated in Fig. 18. The NMR coil is excited by a continuous sine wave through the mutual coupling with coil 1. The response of the resonant circuit is measured by the pickup coil 2. It is important that excitation and pick-up coils be placed sufficiently far from the resonant circuit to avoid any modification of the resonance frequency which could be due to the mutual coupling between the coils.

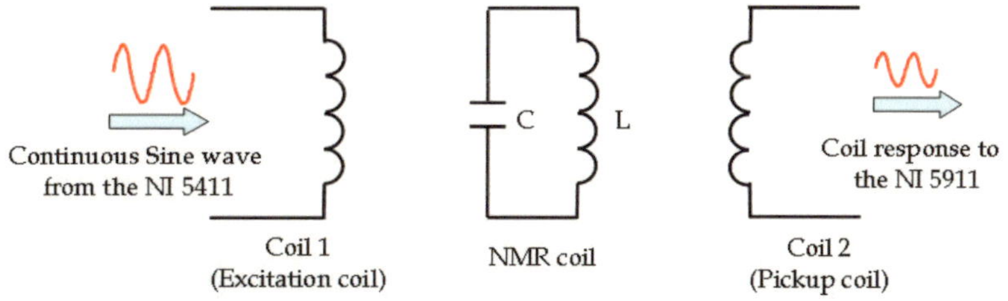

Fig. 18. A method for tuning the NMR coil inside the magnet.

The AWG NI 5411 was used in its DDS mode to generate sine waves of different frequencies. Each frequency is generated during a given duration. During this duration the receiver NI 59 11 was used to acquire the coil response.
Fig. 19 shows the "*Coil Tuning*" front panel where one can see an example of the resonance curve of a coil. User can choose and modify in real time some parameters like the frequency interval or resolution. The current resonance frequency, the bandwidth as well as and the quality factor of the coil are displayed in real time.

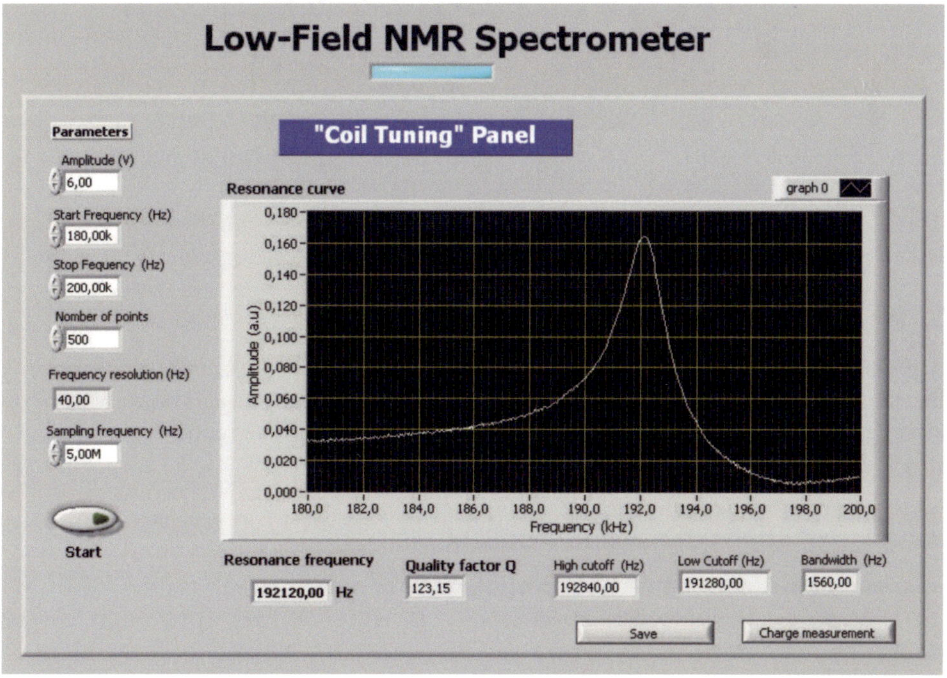

Fig. 19. "Coil Tuning" front Panel

The implementation of this procedure is accomplished using the instrument drivers of the NI 5411 and the NI 5911 and general LabVIEW functions. The use of the DDS mode was useful and quiet adequate for this purpose. The related driver functions could be easily used.

4.4 Calibration of the Flip angle

The third required functionality an NMR spectrometer is the "*Flip angle Calibration*". For a given sample, it is crucial to know, for a given pulse duration and amplitude, the resulting flip angle. In a one-pulse sequence, the maximum NMR signal is obtained at a flip-angle of 90°. More sophisticated NMR/MRI sequences require knowledge and adjustment of an optimum flip angle.

A LabVIEW modulus was developed to perform this calibration. Fig. 20 shows the front panel of this modulus.

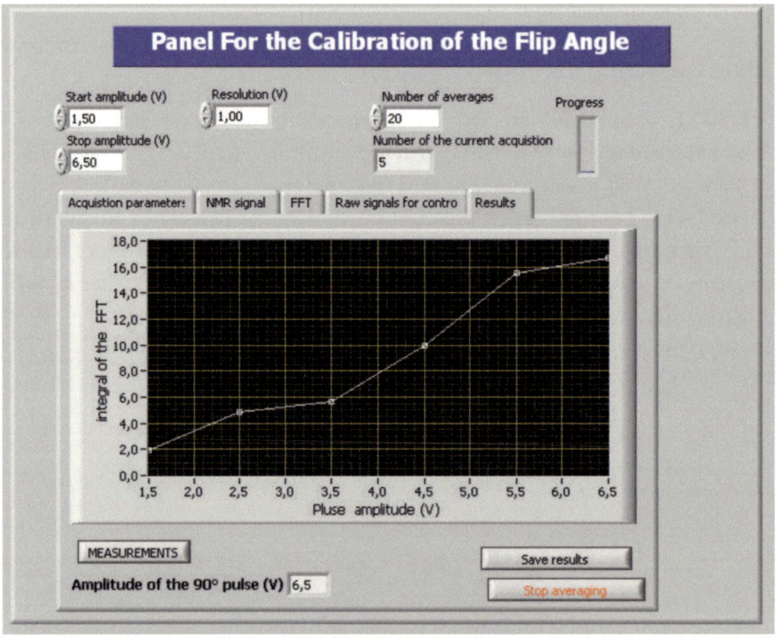

Fig. 20. The front panel for the "*Calibration of the Flip Angle*"

For a given pulse duration, a one-pulse NMR sequence is repeated for various pulse amplitudes. The NMR signal is measured for each excitation pulse. The maximum of the obtained curve corresponds to the 90° flip angle. For flip -angles greater than 90°, the NMR signal will decrease (not shown on the Fig. 20).

5. Examples of applications and discussions

5.1 Polarization measurements of hyperpolarized gases

The field of applications of this spectrometer is wide. A first application consists in measuring the *polarization, P,* of hyperpolarized gases. For a basic understanding of this parameter, one can say that the NMR signal, S, is related to the magnetization M and to the polarization by the equation (3), (Saam & Conradi, 1998, Asfour, 2010):

$$S \propto M \propto N.P \tag{3}$$

where N is the number of nuclei within the sample.

During the last decade, the MRI of hyperpolarized gases, such as ^{3}He and ^{129}Xe, had become widespread for a large palette of applications, especially medical research and clinical diagnosis. For example, the proprieties of xenon in biological environment make it a promising MRI probe for brain physiology and functional studies (Asfour, 2010).

Hyperpolarization is a technique which allows compensating the intrinsic low levels of NMR signal of such gases (when compared with the ^{1}H signal). Indeed, at equilibrium, and for a same magnetic field B_0, the NMR signal of a ^{129}Xe population is about 10000 lower than the one that could be obtained from the same volume of protons. This is because of the intrinsic lower gyro-magnetic ratio and lower density of the xenon.

The Hyperpolarization process can dramatically increase the polarization level of the gas before using it for the NMR or MRI in-vivo experiments. Consequently, the magnetization and the NMR signal levels are typically enhanced by a factor 100000. For a same volume, the NMR signal of the hyperpolarized gas becomes more important than the proton signal.

In our laboratory, the ^{129}Xe is hyperpolarized by spin-exchange with Rb optically pumped by laser at 795 nm. About 0.1 g of Rb is introduced in a 100-ml Pyrex container (cell), which has subsequently filled with a mixture of helium, nitrogen and ^{129}Xe at 5 bars at room temperature. The cell is heated to about 120°C, set in a 4.5 mT magnetic field produced by *Helmholtz coils,* and exposed to a circularly polarized laser. In few minutes, about 20 ml of hyperpolarized xenon can be obtained to be used for in vivo MRI experiments (generally at high field). Monitoring the available *polarization* of the gas during the optical pumping and at the end this process is critical. In fact, one must be able to quantify the effects of changing temperature, pressure, gas mixture, laser power, etc. The goal is to guarantee a maximum polarization or to diagnose eventual problems. The quantitative measurement of the polarization, during and at the end of the pumping process can actually be performed by NMR, since the gas being polarized is subjected to the 4.5 mT static magnetic field. The Larmor frequency f_0 for this field is about 52 kHz.

The measurement method of the *polarization* requires comparing the levels of hyperpolarized ^{129}Xe NMR signal to another reference signal such as a ^{1}H signal, (Saam & Conradi, 1998, Asfour, 2010).

The dynamic range of our systems allowed the detection of both the ^{1}H and hyperpolarized ^{129}Xe signals. Fig. 21 shows the quadratic base-band NMR signals of hyperpolarized acquired at 4.5 mT with the developed spectrometer the hyperbolizing process.

The sample (pyrex container or cell) has the same shape and the same volume that the one which was used to acquire the 1H signals of Fig. 16. These signals were collected by the same coil that was used for collecting the ^{1}H signals and which was retuned to 52 kHz by simply modifying the tuning capacitors. The gain of the preamplifier was set to 2 and no signal averaging was used. The excitation pulse duration was of the 800 µs with a repetition time of 2 seconds. The gain of the low-noise preamplifier was set to 2. The sampling frequency of the received signal before the DDC was of 5 MHz so as the effective ADC resolution was of 14 bits. The final sampling frequency in the base-band was of 10 kHz.

Comparing the NMR signals of ^{1}H and hyperplorized ^{129}Xe allow determination of the polarization P of the gas (Asfour, 2010). The system described here has been in use in our lab for some years and gives a reliable measurement of the polarization.

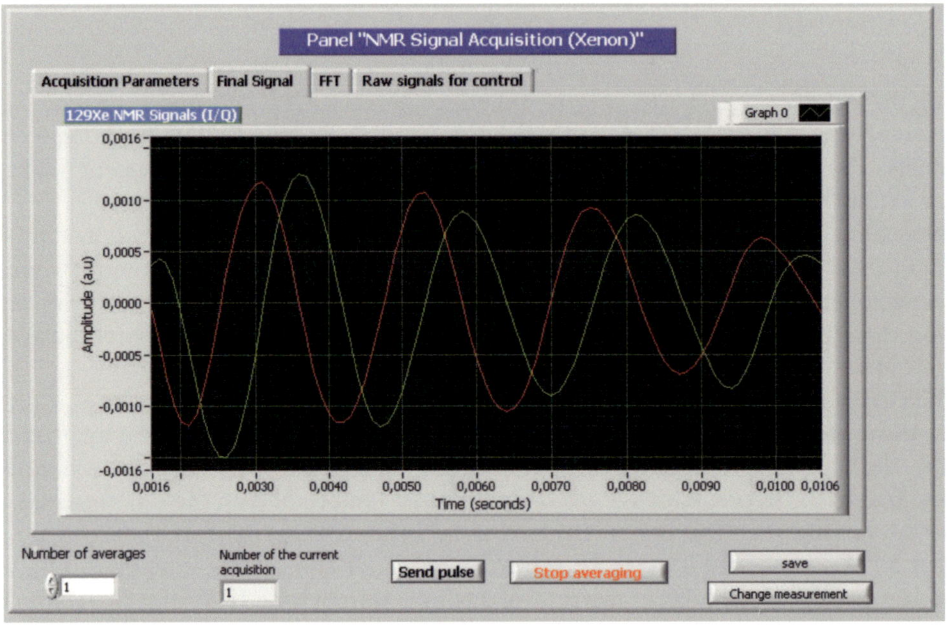

Fig. 21. The baseband I/Q parts of the hyperpolarized ^{129}Xe NMR signal obtained at 4.5 mT. No signal averaging was used.

5.2 Other applications

In addition to the measurement of the polarization, there are other potential applications of this spectrometer. Theses applications may especially concern NMR non-invasive measurements. A first application could be the measurement of the quantity of water contained in a given sample since the NMR signal is proportional to the density of water within the sample. One could then quantify the degree of humidity of the sample. This application could be generalized to concern the quality control of food product, etc.

A second application could concern the measurement of both transversal T_2 and longitudinal T_1 relaxation times of the sample. This could find application for temperature measurement of biological samples. Actually, NMR is a very important technique for measuring temperature of a sample in millikelvin and below through the temperature dependence of the spin-lattice relaxation time T_1 or through the measurement of magnetic susceptibility (Pobell, 1991). These measurements should be performed at frequencies below 1MHz to minimize power dissipation in the sample. Pulse sequences for such measurements could be easily implemented on our system without hardware modifications.

Another potential application of this non exhaustive palette of applications may concern educational purposes in the several areas: electronics, signal processing and biomedical engineering, etc. This is allowed thanks to the flexible and open structure of both hardware and software of the spectrometer. We are currently building another spectrometer in the Department of Physics Measurements at the Grenoble University. Practical courses and projects in electronics, signal processing, instrumentation and measurements, NMR physics could be take place during and after the development of the spectrometer. Students could simulate and build the Helmholtz coils, the power amplifier, the duplexer, the coil and the preamplifier. They could also develop their own applications for the control of the NMR sequence and the data acquisition using LabVIEW.

Notice finally that this low frequency NMR spectrometer could also be dedicated for other applications. It is low cost and easily transportable (for in situ experiments).

6. Conclusion

A DAQ- and LabVIEW-based NMR spectrometer working at low field was presented. This spectrometer allowed detection of the NMR signals of both ^{1}H and ^{129}Xe at 4.5 mT. The flexibility of the system allows its use for a palette of NMR applications without (or with minor) hardware and software modification. It is also easy-to-replicate.

7. Acknowledgment

The author would like to thank Christoph Segebarth, Jean-Louis Leviel, Emmanuel Barbier, Chantal Remy, Olivier Montigon, Lauriane Depoix and all the other members of Team 5 of the Grenoble Institute of Neurosciences (GIN) for supporting this work. The author is also very thankful to Jean-Noël Hyacinthe, from the Department of Radiology of Geneva University Hospital, for his help in preparing the illustrations in this chapter.

8. References

Asfour., A, Raoof., K & Fournier., J-M (2004). Promising new applications for permanent magnets: The low-field MRI, *HPMA'04 18th International Workshop on High Performance Magnets and their Applications,* Annecy, France, August 29-September 2, 2004.

Asfour., A, Hyacinthe., J.N & Leviel., J. L (2006). Development of a fully digital and low-frequency NMR system for polarization measurement of hyperpolarized gases, *Proceedings of the IMTC 2006 IEEE Instrumentation and Measurement Technology Conference,* pp. 1839-1843, ISBN 0-7803-9359, Sorrento, Italy, April 24-27, 2006.

Asfour., A (2008). A new DAQ-based and versatile low-cost NMR spectrometer working at very-low magnetic field (4.5 mT): A palette of potential applications, *Proceedings of the I²MTC 2008 IEEE International Instrumentation and Measurement Technology Conference,* pp. 697-701, ISBN 978-1-4244-1540-3, Vancouver, Canada, May 12-15, 2008.

Asfour., A (2010). A Novel NMR instrument for the in situ monitoring of the absolute polarization of laser-polarized 129Xe, *Journal of Biomedical Science and Engineering (JBIS),* Vol.3, No.11, (November 2010), pp. 1099-1107, ISSN 1937-6871.

Ernst., R. R, Bodenhausen.G & Wokaun., A (1989). *Principles of Nuclear Magnetic Resonance in One and Two Dimensions,* ISBN 0-19-855647-0, Clarendon Press, Oxford, New York, USA.

Gengying., L, J., Yu, Xiaolong., Y & Yun., J (2002). Digital nuclear magnetic resonance spectrometer , *Review of Scientific Instruments,* Vol. 72. No. 12 (December 2002), pp. 105101-105108, ISSN 0034-6748.

LeBec., G, Yonnet., J-P & Raoof., K (2006). Coil and magnet design for Nuclear Magnetic resonance in homogeneous field, *IEEE Transactions on Magnetics,* Vol 42, No. 12 (December 2006), pp. 3861-3867. ISSN 0018-9464.

Michal., C. A, Broughton., K & Hansen., E (2002). A high performance digital receiver for home-built nuclear magnetic resonance spectrometers. *Review of Scientific Instruments,* Vol.73, No. 2 (2002), pp. 453-458, ISSN 0034-6748.

Mispelter., J, Lupu., M & Briguet.A (2006). *NMR Probeheads for Biophysical and Biomedical Experiments: theoretical principles and practical guidelines*, Imperial College Press, ISBN 1-86094-637-2, London, United Kingdom.

NI 5911 User Manual (2001), High-speed Digitizer with FLEX ADC, National Instruments (2001).

NI 5411/5431 User Manual (2001), NI 5411 Pxi/PCI/ISA High-speed Arbitrary Waveform Generator, National Instruments (2001).

Pobell.,F (1991), *Matter and Methods at Low Temperatures*, Spring, ISBN 978-3-540-4635-6, Berlin, Gremany.

Raoof., K, Asfour., A & Fournier., J-M (2002). A complete digital magnetic resonance imaging (MRI) system at low magnetic field (0.1 T). *Proceedings of the IMTC 2002 19th IEEE Instrumentation and Measurement Technology Conference*, pp. 341-345 , ISBN 0-7803-7218-2, Anchorage, Alaska, USA, May 20-23, 2002.

Saam., B. T & Conradi., M.S (1998). low frequency NMR polarimeter for hyperpolarized gases, *Journal of Magnetic Resonance,* Vol. 134, No.1 (September 998), pp. 67-71. ISSN 1090-7807.

Shen., J, Xu., Q, Liu., Y & Gengying., L (2005). Home-built magnetic resonance imaging system (0.3 T) with a complete digital spectrometer , *Review of Scientific Instruments,* Vol. 76. No. 10 (October 2005), pp. 105101-105108, ISSN 0034-6748.

Wright, S. M, McDougall, M. P & Bosshard, J. C (2010). A desktop imaging system for teaching MR engineering, *Proceedings of EMBC 2010 32nd Annual International Conference of the IEEE Engineering in Medicine and Biology Society*, pp. 6653 – 6656, ISBN 978-1-4244-4123-5, Buenos Aires, Argentina, August 31- September 4, 2010

3

DH V 2.0, A Pocket PC Software to Evaluate Drip Irrigation Lateral Diameters Fed from the Extreme with on-line Emitters in Slope Surfaces

José Miguel Molina-Martínez[1],
Manuel Jiménez-Buendía[1] and Antonio Ruiz-Canales[2]
[1]*Technical University of Cartagena,*
[2]*Miguel Hernández University,*
Spain

1. Introduction

Modernisation in irrigation systems allows farmers to adapt easily to requirements in crop production to contribute to environmental protection and optimize water resources, among others. The majority of the processes in the modernisation of the irrigation systems imply the change of surface irrigation systems to pressure systems. One of the main pressure irrigation systems is drip irrigation (Valiantzas, 2003; Yitayew et al., 1999; López, 1996).

High water use efficiency is a feature on drip irrigation systems (Ko et al., 2009; Rodriguez-Diaz et al., 2004; Yitayew et al., 1999). Precision in water and fertilizers application under adequate design conditions is another advantage of this irrigation system (Bracy et al., 2003; Pedras and Pereira, 2001; Holzapfel et al., 2001).

The design of a drip irrigation system calculation implies two phases: agronomic design and hydraulic design. For the agronomic design some specific data are needed (crop water demand, type of soil and data of drip emitters, among others). The hydraulic design is based on several data (characterization of chosen emitter, field topography, etc.). In order to design an irrigation subunit (drip line and sub main pipes), it is necessary to combine the hydraulic calculation (flow, diameters and pressure of drip line and sub main pipes) with the irrigation net distribution plane. Drip line calculation is the first part in the hydraulic design of a drip irrigation system.

Drip line calculation is integrated in the hydraulic design of drip irrigation subunits (Yildirim, 2007; Provenzano and Pumo, 2004; Ravikumar et al., 2003; Anyoji and Wu, 1994; Wu, 1992; Wu and Gitlin, 1982). As in the design of drip irrigation system, in drip lines calculation the agronomic and the hydraulic design phases are included. Moreover, in the drip line design some specific agronomic features are used (plant frame, crop water demand…) (Cetin and Uygan, 2008; Narayanan et al., 2002). The number and the distribution of the emitters are the results of the design (Gyasi-Agyei, 2007; Medina, 1997).

For the future design of micro-irrigation systems several aspects must be considered. Some of these aspects were established in 2004 by Kang and Liu that presented the challenges to design micro-irrigation systems in the future. Firstly, to develop more perfect methods in order to minimize the total cost of a whole system (e.g. da Silva et al., 2005; Kuo et al., 2000 and Ortega et al., 2004); other aspect is the improvement of present-day methods by applying modern geographic information sciences such as GIS (geographic information system), RS (remote sensing) and GPS (global position system) for computerized input of field topographic information; and finally, to develop intelligent computer software with functions where this field topographic information can be input automatically, layout and parameters of a whole system can be optimized automatically, and ground plans and installation maps can be created automatically. This software achieves the last challenge partially. Nowadays this software is designed just for drip line calculations in specifics conditions but new tools are currently being implemented as part of this project.

The objective of this paper is to show a new version of software (DH V 2.0) capable of evaluating the adequate commercial diameters in the design of a pipeline for drip irrigation (micro-irrigation) systems with several changing conditions.

As the crop grows it is usual to add new emitters in order to supply the increasing crop water needs. In some cases, when the farmer wants to increase the plant density or decides to change the crop maintaining the existing irrigation system, the system has to be adapted to the new situation. This implies to change the number of emitters in the drip line to fulfill the new water requirements. In this case, if the flow and pressure required at the beginning of the drip line are known, it is very useful to provide software that allows the user to know if drip line is ready to these changes. It is necessary for this software to be quick and precise. This software would indicate immediately the farmer or the installer what decision he would make.

Some software for drip irrigation design is used under Windows operative systems (Pedras et al., 2008; Rodrigo and Cordero, 2003) but not in mobile devices for agronomic and hydraulic design in drip irrigation. One adequate solution is the installation of developed software for mobile devices as Smartphone or pocket PC. In the last years several programming languages have been used in mobile devices. One of this is LabVIEW®, which is a revolutionary system of graphical programming used for applications that includes acquisition, control analysis and data presentation (Berg et al., 2008; Lajara and Pelegrí, 2007). This software is being used in engineer applications because of its great versatility and simplicity of use.

This document shows a new version of the developed software (DH V 2.0) for this type of mobile device that uses LabVIEW PDA® as programming language (Molina-Martínez and Ruiz-Canales, 2009). This is an executable freeware and it is not necessary to install LabVIEW PDA®. This programming language has some advantages. During programming phase, this it allows to configure several algorithms that compute in parallel. Additionally, it allows implementing algorithms in a friendly and intuitive way. Another advantage is presented during the phase of use: its graphical interface elements to collect and show information are very attractive and easy to use. The use of this freeware is limited to the next conditions: a) drip lines fed from the extreme, b) with a varying slope terrain, c) on-line emitters at the same distance from the beginning of the pipe to the first emitter and between emitters and d) standard dimensions of the emitter connection. This software can be downloaded from the next links:

DH V 2.0 (with slope surfaces support): http://decibel.ni.com/content/docs/DOC-4771.

DH V1.0 (without slope surfaces support): http://decibel.ni.com/content/docs/DOC-3851

2. Theoretical considerations

The theoretical base of used equations in the hydraulic design of drip irrigation considers that flow distribution in a drip line is coming close to a continue distribution. A description of the calculation procedure is detailed in the next lines.

Head losses Dh (m) in a pipe of Length (m), have been calculated with the next equation:

$$Dh = F \cdot J^{*} \cdot Length \tag{1}$$

Where F is the Christiansen's reduction factor in a pipe with emitters located at the same distance from the beginning of the pipe to the first emitter and between emitters. J* (m. m^{-1}) is the unit head losses coefficient that includes major and minor head losses.
The equation used to estimate the Christiansen's reduction factor is:

$$F = \frac{1}{1+\beta} + \frac{1}{2n} + \frac{\sqrt{\beta - 1}}{6n^2} \tag{2}$$

Where the value of β is 1.75 in the Blasius formula for polythene pipes and n is the number of emitters in the drip line.
Unit head losses J*, have been determined using an empirical formula that includes the minor head losses of the emitters by means of the next expression:

$$J^{*} = J \frac{Ee + fe}{Ee} \tag{3}$$

Where Ee (m) is the distance between emitters and fe (m) is the equivalent length of the emitter that depends on the inner Diameter (mm) of the drip line (Table 1) to estimate the minor head losses. This software version is only for on line emitters and standard dimensions of the emitter connection.
Unit major head losses, J (m m^{-1}), have been determined using the Blasius's formula (with a standard temperature of 20° C) in polythene pipes:

$$J = 0.473 \frac{(Qdripline)^{1.75}}{Diameter^{4.75}} \tag{4}$$

Where Diameter (mm) is the inner diameter of the drip line and Qdrip line (l·h^{-1}) is the flow in the beginning of the drip line. Qdrip line value is obtained multiplying the number of emitters Ne in the drip line by the nominal flow of the emitter qe (l·h^{-1}).

Diameter (mm)	**fe (m)**
10.3	0.24
13.2	0.15
16.0	0.11
18.0	0.08
20.4	0.07
28.0	0.04

Table 1. Equivalent length of pipe fe (m) as a function of the inner pipe diameter (mm).

Pressure distribution in a drip line is shown in Fig. 1 and Fig. 2. Fig. 1 is the pressure distribution in an upward slope terrain. In Fig. 2, the pressure distribution in a downward slope terrain is presented.

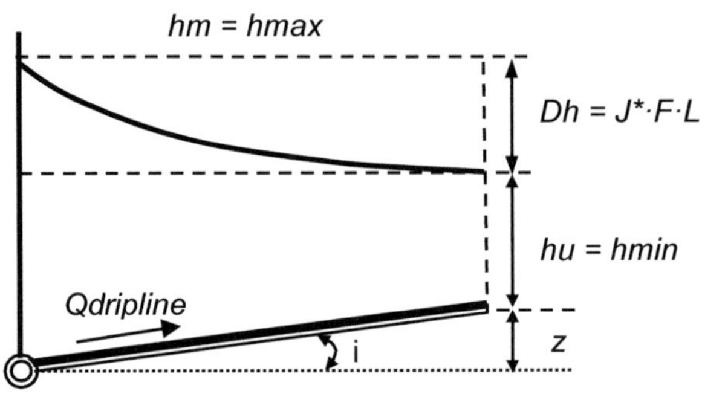

Fig. 1. Pressure distribution in a drip line fed by the extreme in an upward slope terrain.

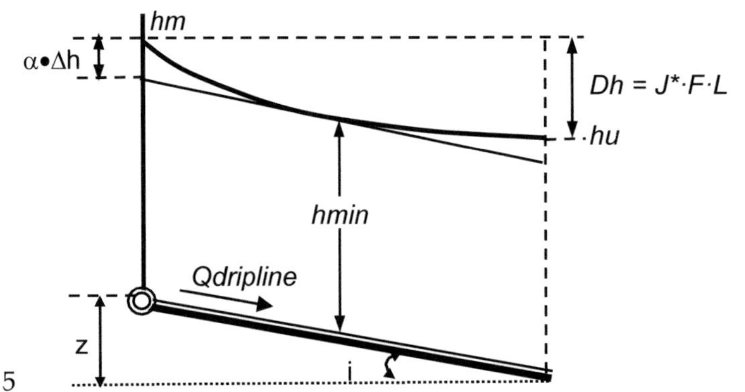

Fig. 2. Pressure distribution in a drip line fed by the extreme in a downward slope terrain.

In these figures, the maximum of pressure, hmax (m), coincides with the pressure in the beginning of the drip line, hm (m), which is determined by means of the eq. (5):

$$hm = ha + 0.75 \cdot Dh + 0.5 \cdot z \tag{5}$$

ha (m) is the average pressure in the drip line.
z (m) is the unevenness between the beginning and the end of the drip line. This value is obtained by the next equation (6), multiplying the slope i ($m \cdot m^{-1}$) by the pipe Length (m):

$$z = i \cdot Length \tag{6}$$

Fig. 1 illustrates the pressure distribution in an upward slope terrain. In this case, the minimum pressure, hmin (m), is the pressure in the last emitter, hu (m), which is determined by:

$$hu = hm - Dh - z = ha - 0.25 \cdot Dh - 0.5 \cdot z \tag{7}$$

Fig. 2 shows the pressure distribution in a downward slope terrain. For this case, there are two situations.

a. Strong slope, where the absolute value of the slope i ($m \cdot m^{-1}$) is larger or equal to J* ($m \cdot m^{-1}$) ($|i| \geq J^*$). In this situation, minimum pressure, hmin (m), of the drip line coincides with the pressure in the beginning of the drip line, hm (m) (eq. 5). Maximum pressure, hmax (m), is the pressure value in the last emitter, hu (m) (eq. 7).

b. Soft slope. For this situation, the absolute value of the slope i (m m^{-1}) is less to J* (m m^{-1}) ($|i|<J^*$). In a drip line with a descending soft slope, the minimum value of pressure hmin (m) is placed along the drip line. This value is obtained by the next expression:

$$h\min = hm - \alpha \cdot Dh = ha + (0.75 - \alpha) \cdot Dh + 0.5 \cdot z \quad (8)$$

where α depends of F and the ratio z/Dh, by means of this equation:

$$\alpha = 1 + \frac{z}{Dh} + 0.375 \cdot \left(-\frac{z}{Dh} \right)^{1.57} \quad (9)$$

Maximum value of pressure hmax (m) is the higher value between hm (m) and hu (m), determined by eqs. 5 and 7.
For all the slope situations in a drip line (horizontal terrain, rising slope terrain and descendent slope terrain) if the difference of pressure hmax-hmin is under the value hp (m), the commercial diameters are adequate. This value hp is the pressure tolerance and is a required data.

3. Software

The graphic interface of the developed software consists of three tabs:

a. In the tap "Home" at the top of the screen, the data for calculation is introduced, and at the lower part valid commercial diameters are shown in green colour by means of light emitting diodes (LED) (see Fig. 3).

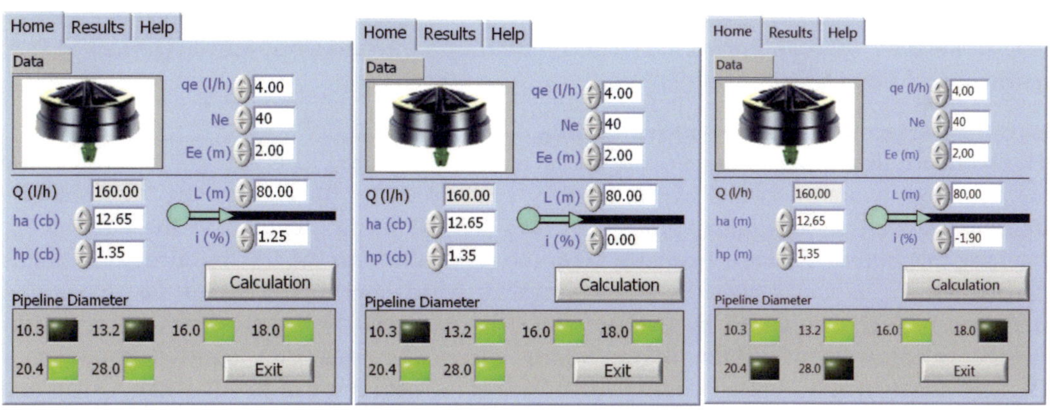

Fig. 3. "Home" tab for a horizontal terrain, an upward slope terrain and a downward slope terrain.

Required data are: nominal flow of the emitter qe (l h^{-1}), number of emitters Ne, drip line length Length (m), distance between emitters Ee (m), average pressure in the drip line ha in meter water column (m), pressure tolerance hp (m) and slope i, in percentage. After data introduction the button named "Calculations" has to be pressed in order to show the results in the frame. An example (Fig. 4) is developed with three slope values (i = 0.0%; i = 1.25%; i = -1.90%) and the same rest of the data (qe = 4 l h^{-1}; Ne = 40 emitters; Ee = 2 m; Length = 80 m; ha = 12.65 m; hp = 1.35 m).

In the example of Fig. 4, only the indicators of the adequate commercial diameters (see theoretical considerations) are coloured in green. In Fig. 4 the main results in three situations of a drip line are shown: no slope terrain (i = 0.0%), rising slope terrain (i = 1.25%) and descendent slope terrain (i = -1,90%).

b. The tab named "Results" (Fig. 4) shows, for every commercial diameter, the head losses in the drip line Dh (m), maximum pressure hmax (m) and minimum pressure hmin (m). At the lower part, it is shown a comparative vertical bar graphic that indicates the level of the allowed pressure tolerance hp (m), in blue, and, green in colour, the values of the difference hmax minus hmin in meters for every diameter. Moreover, as it is shown in Fig. 4, on the left of every screen, only the indicators of the adequate commercial diameters are again coloured in green, and all the result values are shown. Fig. 4 shows the results for the three examples detailed in a).

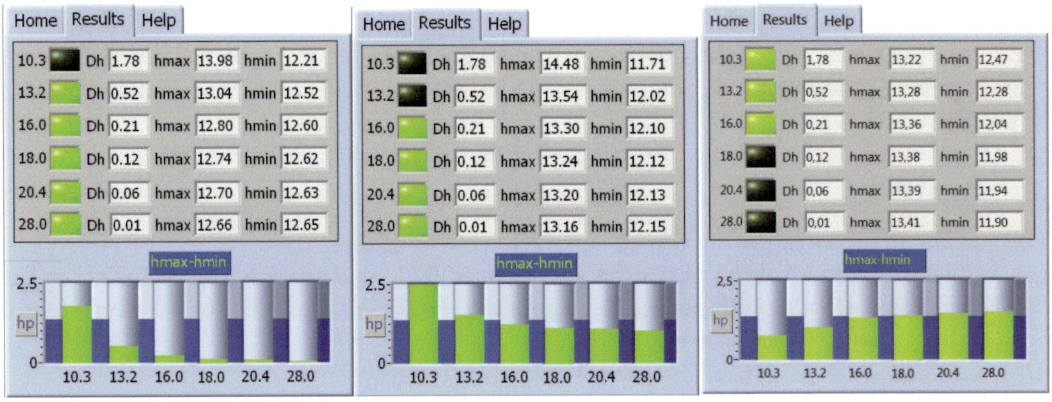

Fig. 4. "Results" tab for a horizontal terrain (i = 0.0%), a upward slope terrain (i =1.25%) and a downward slope terrain (i =-1,90%).

c. The last tab "Help" shows the contacting data for the authors.

The software flow chart is developed under a while loop structure that allows ending the software execution by means of the button "Exit" (see Fig. 3). The button "Calculation" determines the true and false values (TF) of a case structure included in the while loop. Pushing this button, the case structure takes the true value and the internal programming is carried out. Fig. 6 shows the software flow chart used to determine whether the pipe with a diameter of 13.2 mm could be used in the drip line considering general data entry. In parallel calculations are obtained: a) z (m) and i ($m \cdot m^{-1}$) values from required slope data, i (%), and the drip line length, Length (m); b) flow at the beginning of the drip line, Qdrip line ($l \cdot h^{-1}$) from nominal flow of the emitter qe ($l \cdot h^{-1}$) and the number of emitters Ne; c) Christiansen's reduction factor F, introducing eq. (2) in a "Express VI Formula" and taking as data input the number of emitters Ne; d) Dh, J*, hm and hu values using eqs. (1), (3), (5) and (7). The specific values for 13.2 diameter are expressed as Dh 13.2, J*(13.2), hm(13.2) and hu(13.2), respectively. These results are calculated with a double precision floating point (DBL) and showed in the screen (see Fig. 5).

The entry value hp is compared with the difference between hmax and hmin. In Fig. 4, the subtraction value is shown in the screen, in a vertical bar diagram (tap "Results"). Initially, the user has introduced hp value in the tap "Home". The software numerical control hp is joined to the vertical progress bar hp2 in order to show in the tap "Results" the previously introduced

value hp. (See part e) in Fig. 5). The corresponding LED is green in colour if this subtraction is less than hp. In the opposite case, LED is not coloured (true and false values, TF).
In the case structure has been used another one for selecting the necessary calculations if drip pipeline is on a horizontal, rising or descendent terrain. If slope i (%) is larger or equal to zero, is assigned a true value and will be executed the associated code for horizontal or rising terrains (Fig. 6). In the opposite case, if slope i (%) is minor than zero, will be assigned the false value and will be executed the associated code for descending terrains (Fig. 8).

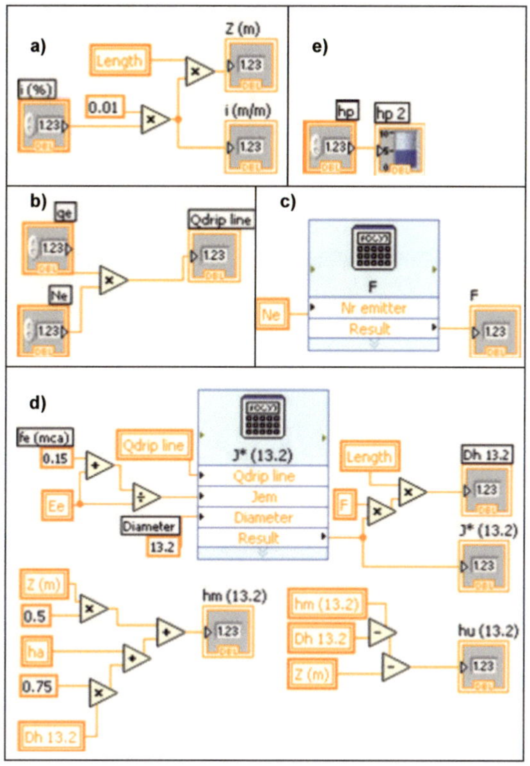

Fig. 5. Software flow chart.

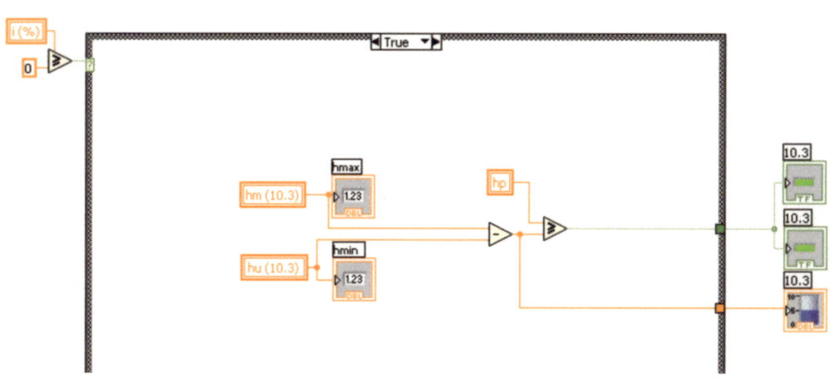

Fig. 6. Block diagram for drip lines in a horizontal or upward slope terrain. Pipe diameter of 10.3.

At the left-top corner of Fig. 6 the associated condition to the case structure is shown. Inside, is found the code that it would execute if the condition is true. Values hm and hu obtained previously will be shown in the indicators hmax and hmin of the tap "Results". The difference hmax minus hmin is obtained and it is compared with hp value fixed by the user. If hp value is larger than (hmax-hmin), then will be activated the LED diodes of the taps "Home" and "Results". (hmax-hmin) value will be shown in the graphic of the tap "Results". This last part of the calculation process is common for all the possible situations. Fig. 6 shows the cited process for a diameter of 10.3 millimeters.

When a descendent slope terrain is presented, a new case structure is executed. In this case, if the absolute value of the slope i (m m^{-1}) is larger or equal to J* (m.c.a. m^{-1}), exit value is true and the code associated to strong slope terrains it will be executed (Fig. 7). If this value is minor than J* (m.c.a. m^{-1}), then the code associated to soft slope terrains will be executed. In Fig. 7 and Fig.8 the processes for a diameter of 10.3 millimeters is shown.

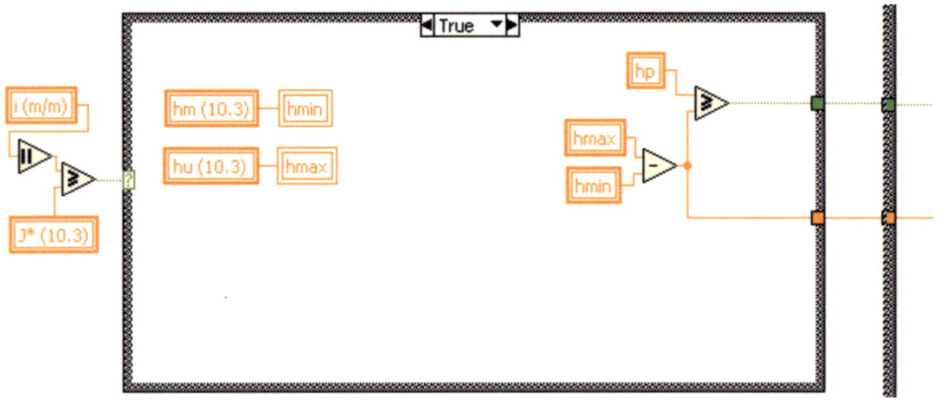

Fig. 7. Block diagram for drip lines in a strong downward slope terrain. Pipe diameter of 13.2.

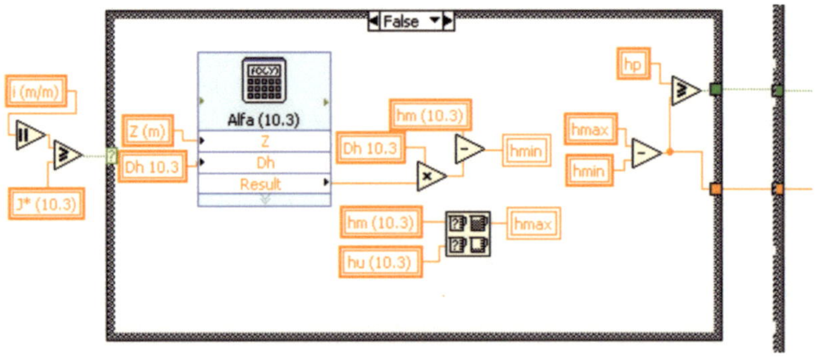

Fig. 8. Block diagram for drip lines in a soft downward slope terrain. Pipe diameter of 13.2.

A similar flow chart has been developed for the rest of every commercial diameter (10.3; 13.2; 16.0; 18.0; 20.4 and 28.0). These diagrams establish the algorithms to evaluate if the diameters of commercial pipes are adequate for the drip line, and the results are compared. All the results for every diameter could be shown in the console.

4. Case studies

In this Section two case studies considering upward and downwared slopes are presented to demonstrate the validity and usefulness of our application. In order to do this, has to be taking in account the theoretical considerations of Section 2. The obtained results has to be compared with the obtained by the proposed application.

4.1 Upward-slope terrain

In this case an upward-slope land was considered with 16 mm laterals with emitters spaced every 3 meters. We needed to determine if emitters could be placed every meter without changing the irrigation lateral. In order to solve this case, the irrigation drip line would have to be calculated using the following data:

a. The emitter data: qe= 3 l·h^{-1}, ha = 10 m (average pressure in the drip line is considered to be equal to the nominal pressure of the emitter).
b. The drip line data: Ne=90 (number of emitters), Ee=1 (distance between emitters), i=0.3 m·m^{-1} (upward slope). The pressure tolerance is hp = 1 m.

Head losses Dh (m) in the pipe of length Length (m), have been calculated with eq. 1:

$$Dh = F \cdot J^* \cdot Length = F \cdot J^* \cdot 90 \tag{10}$$

Using eq. 2 the Christiansen's reduction factor can be estimated as:

$$F = \frac{1}{1+\beta} + \frac{1}{2n} + \frac{\sqrt{\beta - 1}}{6n^2} = \frac{1}{1+1.75} + \frac{1}{2 \cdot 90} + \frac{\sqrt{1.75-1}}{6 \cdot 90^2} = 0.3692 \tag{11}$$

The value of β is 1.75 in Blasius formula for polythene pipes and n is the number of emitters in the drip line.

Unit head losses J*, have been determined using the empirical formula detailed in eq. 3:

$$J^* = J\frac{Ee + fe}{Ee} \tag{12}$$

Ee (m) is the distance between emitters and fe (m) is the equivalent length of the emitter that depends on the inner diameter Diameter (mm) of the drip line (Table 1) to estimate the minor head losses. This software version is only for on line emitters and standard dimensions of the emitter connection.

Ee has been extracted from Table 1. The results for each candidate diameter are shown in Table 2.

Unit major head losses, J (m·m^{-1}), have been determined using the Blasius's formula (with a standard temperature of 20° C) in polythene pipes (eq. 4).

$$J = 0.473\frac{(Qdripline)^{1.75}}{Diameter^{4.75}} \tag{13}$$

Where Diameter (mm) is the inner diameter of the drip line and Qdrip line (l·h^{-1}) is the flow in the beginning of the drip line. Qdrip line value is obtained multiplying the number of emitters Ne in the drip line by the nominal flow of the emitter qe (l·h^{-1}). The results for each drip line diameter are described in Table 3.

Diameter (mm)	J* (m m-1)
10.3	$J^* = J\frac{1+0.24}{1} = J \cdot 1.24$
13.2	$J^* = J\frac{1+0.15}{1} = J \cdot 1.15$
16.0	$J^* = J\frac{1+0.11}{1} = J \cdot 1.11$
18.0	$J^* = J\frac{1+0.08}{1} = J \cdot 1.08$
20.4	$J^* = J\frac{1+0.07}{1} = J \cdot 1.07$
28.0	$J^* = J\frac{1+0.04}{1} = J \cdot 1.04$

Table 2. Unit head losses J* (m m-1) for each candidate diameter.

Diameter (mm)	J (m m-1)
10.3	$J = 0.473\frac{(90 \cdot 3)^{1.75}}{10.3^{4.75}}$
13.2	$J = 0.473\frac{(90 \cdot 3)^{1.75}}{13.2^{4.75}}$
16.0	$J = 0.473\frac{(90 \cdot 3)^{1.75}}{16.0^{4.75}}$
18.0	$J = 0.473\frac{(90 \cdot 3)^{1.75}}{18.0^{4.75}}$
20.4	$J = 0.473\frac{(90 \cdot 3)^{1.75}}{20.4^{4.75}}$
28.0	$J = 0.473\frac{(90 \cdot 3)^{1.75}}{28.0^{4.75}}$

Table 3. Unit major head losses, J (m m-1) for each candidate diameter.

Hence, with the values of F, J* and J, head losses Dh (m) have been calculated from eq. 10 (see Table 4).

Diameter (mm)	Dh (m)
10.3	5.42
13.2	1.55
16.0	0.60
18.0	0.33
20.4	0.18
28.0	0.04

Table 4. Head losses Dh (m) for each candidate diameter.

The maximum pressure coincides with the pressure at the beginning of the drip line, hm (m), that is determined using eq. 5 for each drip line candidate diameter (see results in Table 5).

$$hm = ha + 0.75 \cdot Dh + 0.5 \cdot z \qquad (14)$$

Diameter (mm)	hm (m)
10.3	14.20
13.2	11.30
16.0	10.58
18.0	10.38
20.4	10.27
28.0	10.16

Table 5. Maximum pressure hm (m) for each candidate diameter.

Unevenness between the beginning an the end of the drip line, z (m), is by eq. (6):

$$z = i \cdot \text{Length} = 0.3 \cdot 90 = 2.7\text{m} \qquad (15)$$

In this case, the minimum pressure hmin is the pressure of the last emitter, hu (m), that is determined by eq. 7 and shown, for each drip line diameter, in Table 6.

Diameter (mm)	hu (m)
10.3	8.51
13.2	9.48
16.0	9.72
18.0	9.78
20.4	9.82
28.0	9.86

Table 6. Minimum pressure hmin for each candidate diameter.

Finally, the difference of pressure hmax-hmin, which coincides with hm-hu, is calculated in Table 7.

Diameter (mm)	hm - hu (m)
10.3	5.68
13.2	1.86
16.0	**0.87**
18.0	**0.60**
20.4	**0.45**
28.0	**0.31**

Table 7. Minimum pressure hmin for each candidate diameter.

Since the pressure tolerance hp has a value of 1 m, the commercial diameters 16.0, 18.0, 20.4 and 28.0 mm are adequate.

Thanks to the DH 2.0 application these data could be calculated in situ and provide instant feedback without making any manual calculation. The results obtained with the mobile device are shown in Fig. 9.

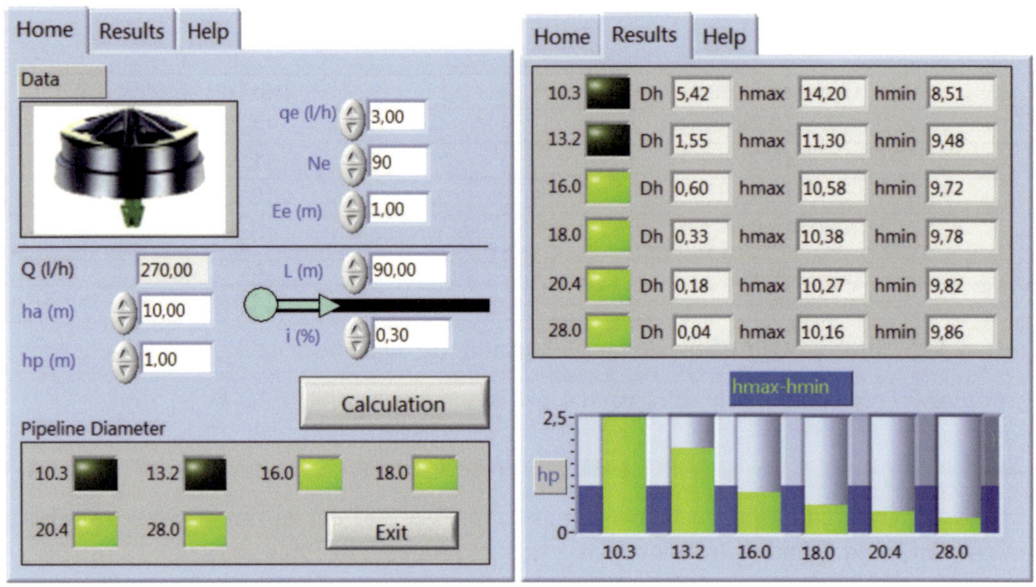

Fig. 9. Results for the case study obtained in situ with the mobile device.

4.2 Downward-slope terrain

In this case the diameter of a drip irrigation line had to be calculated to place it in a downward-slope land with a slope of $i = -0.034\ m\cdot m^{-1}$. Emitters with $qe = 4\ l\cdot h^{-1}$ had to be used, placed every 2 m (Ee), with a total line length of 80 m (which gives an amount of 40 emitters). The datasheet of the emitter allowed to know that the nominal pressure of the emitter (which is considered to be equal to the average pressure in the drip line) had a value of ha = 12.65 m, and the pressure tolerance is hp =1.35 m.

Diameter (mm)	fe (m)	J ($m\cdot m^{-1}$)	J* ($m\cdot m^{-1}$)	$\vert i \vert \geq J^*$?	Dh (m)	z/Dh (-)	α (-)
10.3	**0.24**	**0.0526**	**0.0589**	**No**	**1.78**	**-1.56**	**0.16**
13.2	0.18	0.0162	0.0177	Yes	0.52	0.00	0.00
16.0	0.11	0.0065	0.0069	Yes	0.21	0.00	0.00
18.0	0.08	0.0037	0.0039	Yes	0.12	0.00	0.00
20.4	0.07	0.0020	0.0021	Yes	0.06	0.00	0.00
28.0	0.04	0.0005	0.0005	Yes	0.01	0.00	0.00

Table 8. Calculated values for different commercial drip line diameters in a downward-slope terrain.

The values calculated using theoretical equations from Section 2 are detailed in Table 8 and Table 9 for the different commercial drip line diameters.
Hence only the 10.3 mm diameter drip line fulfils the pressure tolerance condition (hp) since hmax – hmin (1.25 m) is lower than hp (1.35 m).

Diameter (mm)	α·Dh = hm-hmin (m)	hm (m)	hmin (m)	hu (m)	hmax - hmin (m)
10.3	**0.27**	**12.59**	**12.33**	**13.58**	**1.25**
13.2	0.00	11.68	11.68	13.88	2.20
16.0	0.00	11.44	11.44	13.96	2.52
18.0	0.00	11.38	11.38	13.98	2.61
20.4	0.00	11.34	11.34	13.99	2.66
28.0	0.00	11.30	11.30	14.01	2.71

Table 9. Calculated values for different commercial drip line diameters in a downward-slope terrain.

As is shown in Fig. 10, these values coincide with those calculated with the DH V2.0.

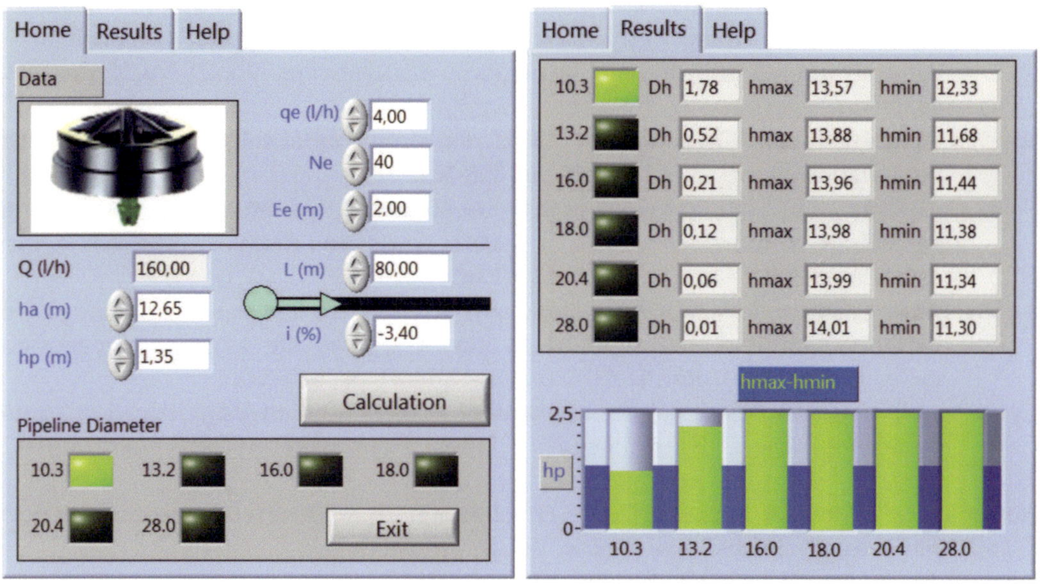

Fig. 10. Results for the case study obtained in situ with the mobile device.

5. Conclusions

This software allows users of drip irrigation systems to evaluate the sensibility to changing conditions (water needs, emitters, spacing, slope…) in all commercial polythene diameters of drip lines. These calculations are executed at once for every commercial diameter in a pocket PC. This allows to users makes these calculations immediately in the field without the need of moving to the office and using a PC.

Software has been developed with LabVIEW PDA®. This is an intuitive programming language and allows configuring several algorithms that compute in parallel at once.
This software version is limited to drip lines, with on line drippers, fed by the extreme with a slope terrain. It is an accessible freeware, contacting with authors or from the link (http://decibel.ni.com/content/docs/DOC-4771).
This software is limited but new tools are being implemented actually to develop the project and extend new calculations to the main parts of a pressurized irrigation system.
Finally, the validity and usefulness of the application have been verified with a case study.

6. Acknowledgments

The authors would like to express their gratitude to National Instruments for its help spreading the developed software in its website.

7. References

Anyoji H. & Wu I. P. (1994). Normal-distribution water application for drip irrigation schedules. *Transactions of the ASAE*, Vol.37, No.1, pp. 159-164.

Berg C.; Valdez, D.C.; Bergeron, P.; Mora, M.F.; Garcia, C.D. & Ayon, A. (2008). Lab-on-a-robot: Integrated microchip CE, power supply, electrochemical detector, wireless unit, and mobile platform. *Electrophoresis*, Vol.29, No.24, pp. 4914-4921.

Bracy, R.P.; Parish, R.L. & Rosendale, R.M. (2003). Fertigation uniformity affected by injector type. *HortTechnology*, Vol.13, No.1, pp. 103-105.

Cetin, O. & Uygan, D. (2008). The effect of drip line spacing, irrigation regimes and planting geometries of tomato on yield, irrigation water use efficiency and net return. *Agricultural Water Management*, Vol.95, No.8, pp. 949-958.

da Silva, C.R.; Folegatti, M.V.; da Silva, T.J.A.; Alves, J.; Souza, C.F. & Ribeiro, R.V. (2005). Water relations and photosynthesis as criteria for adequate irrigation management in 'Tahiti' lime trees. *Stientia Agricola*, Vol.62, No.5, pp. 415-422.

Gyasi-Agyei, Y. (2007). Field-scale assessment of uncertainties in drip irrigation lateral parameters. *Journal of Irrigation and Drainage Engineering, ASCE*, Vol.113, pp.512-519.

Holzapfel, E.A.; Jara, J. & Matta, R. (2001). Nivel de agua aplicado y fertirrigación bajo riego por goteo en cítricos, *Agro-Ciencia*, Vol.17, pp. 20-31.

Kang, Y.H. & Liu, W. (2004). Review of hydraulic analysis and design methods of microirrigation systems, In: *Land and Water Management: Decision Tools and Practices*, Vol. 1 and 2, pp. 914-924. *7th International Conference on Environment and Water*. Beijing.

Ko, J.H. ; Piccinni, G. & Steglich, E. (2009). Using EPIC model to manage irrigated cotton and maize. *Agricultural Water Management*, Vol.96, No.9, pp. 1323-1331.

Kuo, S.F. ; Merkley, G.P. & Liu, C.W. (2000). Decision support for irrigation project planning using a genetic algorithm. *Agricultural Water Management*, Vol.45, No.3, pp. 243-266.

Lajara, J.R. & Pelegri, J. (2007). *LabVIEW 8.20 Entorno Gráfico de Programación*, Marcombo, Barcelona.

López, J. R. (1996). *Riego localizado II. Programas informáticos*, Mundiprensa, Madrid.

Medina (1997). *Riego por Goteo*, Mundiprensa, Madrid.

Molina-Martínez, JM. & Ruiz-Canales, A. (2009). Pocket PC software to evaluate drip irrigation lateral diameters with on-line emitters. *Computers and Electronics in Agriculture,* Vol.69, pp. 112-115.

Narayanan, R ; Steele, D.D. & Scherer, T.F. (2002). Computer model to optimize above-ground drip irrigation systems for small areas. *Applied Engineering in Agriculture,* Vol.18, No.4, pp. 459-469.

Ortega, J.F. ; de Juan, J.A. & Tarjuelo, J.M. (2004). Evaluation of the water cost effect on water resource management: Application to typical crops in a semiarid region. *Agricultural Water Management,* Vol.66, No.2, pp. 125-144.

Pedras, C.M.G. & Pereira, L.S. (2001). A simulation model for design and evaluation of micro-irrigation systems. *Journal of Irrigation and Drainage, ASCE,* Vol.50, No.4, pp. 323-334.

Pedras, C.M.G. ; Pereira, L.S. & Gonçalves, J.M. (2008). MIRRIG: A decision support system for design and evaluation of microirrigation systems. *Agricultural Water Management,* Vol.96, No.4, pp. 691-701.

Pedras, C.M.G. ; Pereira, L.S. & Gonçalves, J.M. (2008). MIRRIG: A decision support system for design and evaluation of microirrigation systems. *Agricultural Water Management,* Vol.96, No.4, pp. 691-701.

Provenzano, G. & Pumo, D. (2004). Experimental analysis of local pressure losses for microirrigation laterals. *Journal of Irrigation and Drainage Engineering, ASCE,* Vol.130, No.4, pp. 318-324.

Ravikumar, V. ; Ranganathan, C.R. & Bosu, S.S. (2003). Analytical equation for variation of discharge in drip irrigation laterals. *Journal of Irrigation and Drainage Engineering, ASCE,* Vol.129, No.4, pp. 295-298.

Rodrigo, J. & Cordero, L. (2003). *Riego Localizado. Programas Informáticos para Windows,* Mundi-Prensa, Madrid.

Rodriguez-Diaz, J.A., Camacho-Poyato, E. & Lopez-Luque, R. (2004). Application of data envelopment analysis to studies of irrigation efficiency in Andalusia. *Journal of Irrigation and Drainage Engineering, ASCE,* Vol.130, No.3, pp. 175-183.

Valiantzas, J.D. (2003). Explicit hydraulic design of microirrigation submain units with tapered tanifold manifold and laterals. *Journal of Irrigation and Drainage, ASCE,* Vol.129, No.4, pp. 227-236.

Wu, I. P. & Gitlin, H.M. (1982). Drip irrigation lateral line network design. *Transactions of the ASAE,* Vol.25, No.3, pp. 675-685.

Wu, I.P. (1992). Energy gradient line approach for direct hydraulic calculation in drip irrigation design. *Irrigation Science,* Vol.13, No.1, pp. 21-29.

Yildirim, G. (2007). An assessment of hydraulic design of trickle laterals considering effect of minor losses. *Irrigation and Drainage,* Vol.56, No.4, pp. 399-421.

Yitayew, M. ; Didan, K. & Reynolds, C. (1999). Microcomputer based low-head gravity-flow bubbler irrigation system design. *Computers and Electronics in Agriculture*, Vol.22, No.1, pp. 29-39.

4

Application of Virtual Instrumentation in Nuclear Physics Experiments

Jiri Pechousek
Palacky University in Olomouc,
Czech Republic

1. Introduction

The new way in the design of computer-based measurement systems can be seen in the use of up-to-date measurement, control and testing systems based on reliable devices. Digital signal processing (DSP) is used in all engineering areas, such as in nuclear physics experiments, to in order replace conventional analog systems and to build measurement and test systems with an easy configuration, user-friendly interface, and possibility to run sophisticated experiments. DSP systems are applied in nuclear physics experiments for their performance in both energy and time domain. Different programming techniques and instrument solutions are employed, and many commercially available digital oscilloscopes can be used in DSP systems.

Nowadays, nuclear DSP systems are commonly realized by the virtual instrumentation (VI) technique performed in LabVIEW graphical programming environment. The advantages of this approach lie in the use of (a) ready-to-start measurement functions (DSP algorithms), (b) instrument drivers delivered with measurement devices, and (c) in the possibility to improve a particular system when new algorithms, drivers or devices are available. With these opportunities, a system using the VI techniques and based on commercially available devices (USB, PCI, PXI etc.) can be driven by any suitable developed application. This application is then nearly "hardware platform independent".

Many papers concerning nuclear physics experiments have been published so far and in many of them, LabVIEW has been successfully applied. This chapter focuses on the description of the nuclear systems, which use the VI concept as much as possible, and in which a large number of system functions are performed in the software form.

As the first example, it can be mentioned the development of a computer-based nuclear radiation detection and instrumentation teaching laboratory system (Ellis & He, 1993), where the sophisticated setup of various devices is presented. Simulation and analysis of nuclear instrumentation using the LabVIEW is performed in ref. (Abdel-Aal, 1993). The high-performance digitizer system for high-energy and nuclear physics detector instrumentation employed in ref. (Kirichenko et al., 2001), is a time digitizing system in the VXI system. An FPGA-based digital and elaboration system for nuclear fast pulse detection (Esposito et al., 2007) is used for the direct sampling of fast pulses from nuclear detectors. Virtual instrumentation in physics described in (Tłaczala, 2005) presents applications for γ-rays intensity analyzer, data analysis and presentation. Models of advanced nuclear physics experiments and measurements are presented as virtual laboratory with simulated nuclear physics experiments in (Tłaczala et al., 2008). The paper presents two simulated experiments that can be easily as well as remotely accessible (γ-energy determination and Mössbauer spectroscopy). Digital acquisition system (Belli et al., 2008) for digital pulse processing is applied to acquire data from n-γ detectors. It is based on FPGA. The description of a versatile, computer-based γ-ray monitor is presented in ref. (Drndarevic & Jevtic, 2008) and a similar concept using VI based α-particle spectrometer in ref. (Drndarevic, 2009). An auto-timing counts virtual instrument system with counter/timer module is presented in ref. (Yan et al., 2009). The development of an automated spectrofluorometer prototype, which is able to perform time-resolved fluorescence measurements, is described in ref. (Moreno et al., 2011). System is based on LabVIEW application and program controls the monochromator, and reads the information of the time-resolved detector signals measured by the digital oscilloscope. Fast pulse detection algorithms for digitized waveforms from scintillators (Krasilnikov et al., 2011) are implemented into the application that performs n-γ pulse shape discrimination.

In the LabVIEW powered DSP system (Pechousek et al., 2011) the VI technique has been applied to develop a system which provides nuclear spectroscopic measurements such as amplitude and time signal analysis. The system is based on a high-speed digitizer, acquires data from two simultaneously sampled channels, and is fast enough to capture the pulses from different types of nuclear detectors. The system finds its application in the time coincidence measurement where two channels are used for the start and stop nuclear events registration. The VI techniques were also applied for the development of the fully-LabVIEW powered Mössbauer spectrometer (Pechousek et al., 2005, 2007, 2010, 2011). This system is based on the phenomena of the nuclear resonance absorption and emission of the γ-rays.

2. Virtual instrumentation in nuclear physics instrumentation

There are several types of radiation spectroscopies, such as γ-ray, X-ray, spectroscopy of charged particles (alpha, electron, proton, etc.), neutron, mass, time and others, that utilize different properties of radiation to study materials and particles (Ahmed, 2007; Gilmore, 2008). Today, each of these spectroscopic measurements can be based on DSP technique. The differences consist in the type of used detector and overall data analysis process. On the other hand, low-level DSP algorithms and methods for signal/pulse analysis can be similar. The standard structure of the DSP γ-ray spectroscopy system is depicted in Figure 1. The DSP algorithms can replace most of analogue modules.

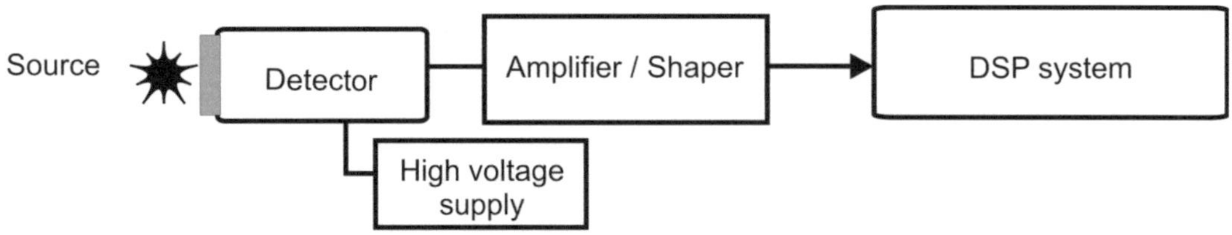

Fig. 1. Block diagram of standard DSP spectroscopy system.

Each DSP system has to use a device that digitizes an analog signal. A fast digital oscilloscope (digitizer) records the output signal from the radiation detector as an unprocessed signal or can acquire pulses coming through the signal amplifier or another preprocessing module. In the acquired signal, the pulse represents the nuclear event registration, and the amplitude of the peaks generally depends on the detected energy. The preamplifiers are used to amplify the low level signal and to match the detector and external circuit impedance. The typical acquired signal is shown in Figure 2.

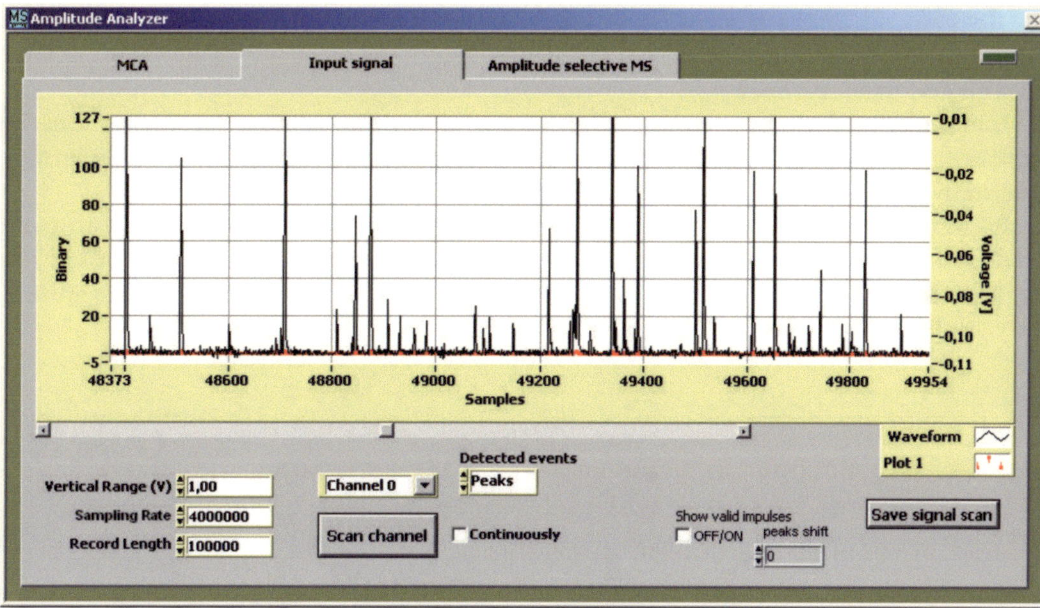

Fig. 2. Typical signal shape acquired from the nuclear detector.

2.1 Digitizing the signal from the detector

Data acquisition (DAQ) processes are performed digitally. There are two ways how to process data. Firstly, data are sampled (and transferred) by a digital oscilloscope, and acquired in a DSP program code. The second way is to sample data and acquire them by a programmable hardware (mostly by an FPGA) with DSP techniques implemented. Nowadays, many commercially available digitizers are frequently used either in the form of computer plug-in boards, or as stand-alone instruments connected to a computer via fast programming interface.

The digitizer discrimination properties are function of sampling rate and bit resolution. The 8-bit energy resolution is mostly used with very fast sampling rates in the order of GS s^{-1}. Today systems allow to use up to 16-bit resolution while achieving these sampling rates (Aspinall et al., 2009) for the best time resolution with fast detectors. The sampling rate used to digitize the detector output signal differs with the employed detector type. The sampling rates of about 100 MS s^{-1} are declared to be fast enough to capture the pulses from detectors for achieving the optimal pulse discrimination and to avoid the undersampling and signal aliasing. Hence, for most applications, a 10 ns time resolution is

sufficient to perform common time measurements (lifetime and other coincidence). Digitizer also produces accurate measurements if the analog bandwidth is wide enough and enables the signal to pass through without any attenuation (National Instruments, 2009a).
Currently, it is possible to increase the energy and time resolution by a fast digitizer or by a more advanced DSP technique. However, with increasing sampling rate and energy resolution, or using more robust algorithms, the dead-time of a spectrometer can increase due to a higher data transfer and processing, and, consequently, the overall counting rate can decrease.

2.1.1 Digital oscilloscopes

With up-to-date digitizers, special triggering and synchronization techniques can be exploited. These techniques allow to apply very sophisticated DAQ methods, where detector pulses can directly trigger DAQ process.
In this section, the use of technical and programming support for the NI-SCOPE instrument drivers and the National Instruments (NI) high-speed digitizers will be presented. The application of NI digitizers has been presented in ref. (Gontean & Szabó, 2011). In Figure 3, the types of NI digitizers applicable in various platforms are shown.

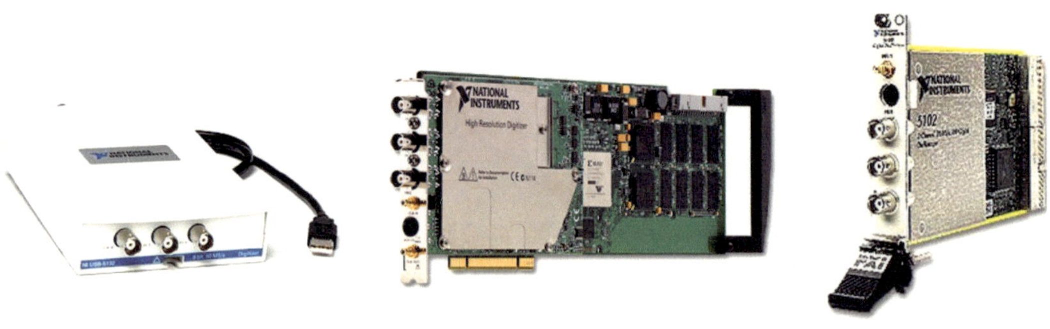

Fig. 3. USB, PCI, and PXI high-speed digitizers (National Instruments).

NI-SCOPE instrument driver is a set of software routines that control a programmable instrument. Each routine corresponds to a programmatic operation such as configuring, reading from, writing to, and triggering the instrument. Instrument driver functions can be divided in six categories—Initialize, Configuration, Action/Status, Data, Utility, and Close. As a part of this driver NI-SCOPE Soft Front Panel is also delivered, which is a software application for NI digitizers. When building a block diagram, it is necessary to apply several rules and recommendations, see NI-SCOPE Help (National Instruments, 2009a, 2010). Figure 4 shows the NI-SCOPE functions palette, where all subpalettes include the functions for digitizer control and data acquiring.
The function Initialize sets the driver and digitizer to a known state and establishes communication with the instrument. Configuration functions configure the instrument for performing a desired operation and, as a consequence, the instrument is ready to take measurements. Action functions cause the instrument to initiate or terminate the test and measurement operations. Status functions return the current status of the instrument. Data

functions include calls to transfer data to or from the instrument. Utility functions perform a variety of operations auxiliary to the most-used instrument driver calls. The Close function terminates the software connection to the instrument and deallocates system resources used during that instrument session (National Instruments, 2009a).

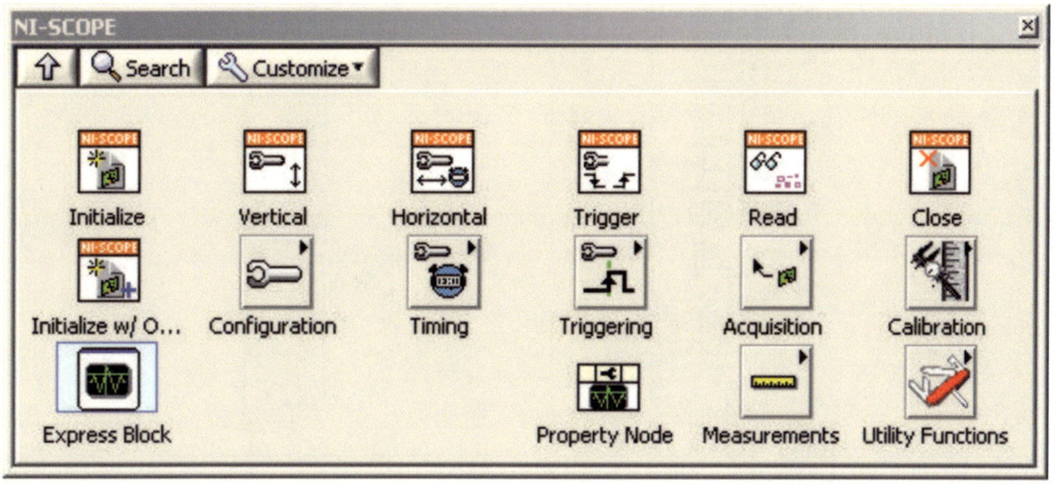

Fig. 4. NI-SCOPE palette.

The diagram in Figure 5 illustrates the basic programming flow for using NI-SCOPE functions in digitizer applications. The data flow is following. For any application, a session has to be open to establish the communication with the digitizer by using Initialize. After the initialization, the instrument is configured (vertical scale, horizontal scale, triggering options) and the DAQ process is started. Then, the data are read and transferred to DSP algorithms. When the program finishes, the DAQ process is aborted and the session has to be closed with Close.

The developed DSP module (depicted in Figure 5) was tested on PXI, PCI, and USB platforms, namely on NI PXI-5102 (8-bit, 20 MS s^{-1}), NI PCI-5124 (12-bit, 200 MS s^{-1}), and NI USB-5133 (8-bit, 100 MS s^{-1}) digitizers. In this example, the amplified pulse coming from a detector is acquired with the niScope Fetch (poly) function, which retrieves data that the digitizer has acquired and returns a one-dimensional array of binary 8-bit values.

2.2 Signal processing - pulse shaping and amplitude measurements

Detectors realize the detection and measurement of radiation. An electronic detector uses a detection medium to generate an electrical signal when radiation passes through it. There are different types of radiation detectors depending on the interaction of radiation with the matter (Ahmed, 2007). The DAQ processes will be demonstrated on the signals acquired from scintillation detectors which are based on photomultiplier tube (PMT) with a common NaI:Tl scintillator of two different thicknesses, fast YAP:Ce scintillator, and slow gas filled proportional counter (GPC).

The NaI:Tl scintillator has a high light yield and a relatively long decay time of 230 ns. The YAP:Ce scintillator has a much lower light yield and a short decay time of 28 ns.

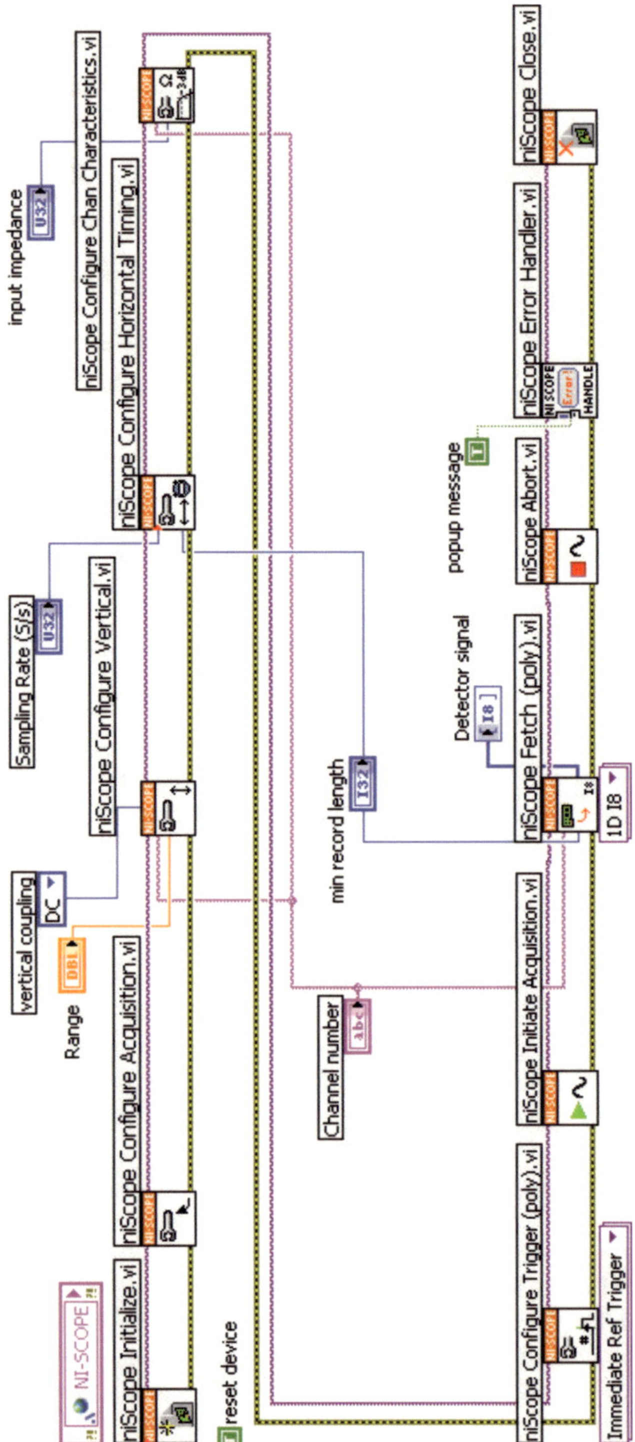

Fig. 5. LabVIEW code with NI-SCOPE driver functions.

It is suitable for the detection of a low energy γ-radiation. The optimal thickness for low energy γ-rays, 14.4 keV (emitted by ^{57}Co source), are 0.15 mm for NaI:Tl and 0.35 mm for YAP:Ce, respectively (Kholmetskii et al., 1997). The PMT is used to detect scintillation photons. The result is an electric output pulse with amplitude large enough to be easily measured by a digitizer. In both cases, the low energy detectors are laboratory made with an integrated high voltage supply (Figure 6). The high energy γ-ray detector is the commercial detector (Scionix) with a NaI:Tl scintillator, the thickness 51 mm and 38 mm in diameter (Figure 6). The GPC detector is the Xenon/Methane filled detector suitable mainly for X-ray detection.

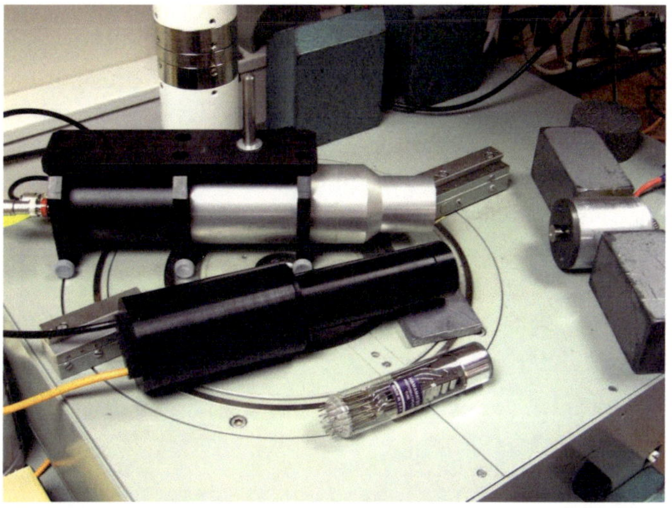

Fig. 6. High energy detector - upper, and low-energy detector - lower; and simply PMT.

The amplified signals acquired from two detectors with (a) YAP:Ce and (b) thick NaI:Tl scintillators are shown in Figure 7. The pulses from the particular detector are acquired, and the locations and magnitudes of their amplitudes can be obtained. The signals are obtained with the radioactive source ^{57}Co and sampling rate of 200 MS s^{-1}.

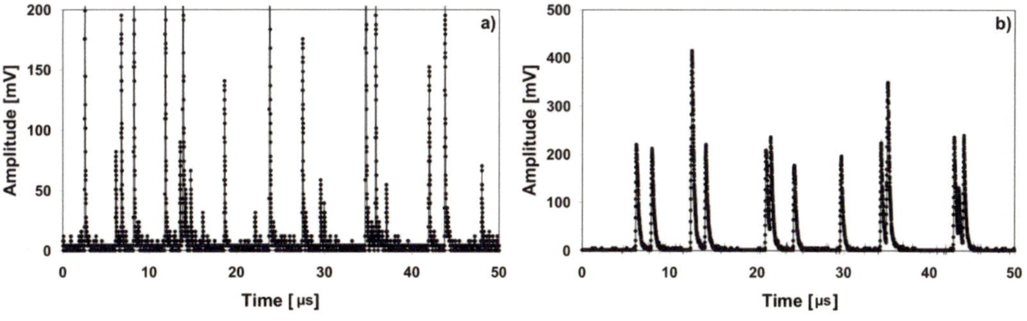

Fig. 7. Signals from a) YAP:Ce detector (14.4 keV) and b) thick NaI:Tl detector (122 keV).

Digitally implemented signal processing features (shaping, filtering, pulse validation, energy and time measurement, pulse shape analysis, noise reduction, pile-up rejection, amplitude multichannel analysis (MCA), etc.) can offer one DSP system for various types of detectors. At this time, there are many DSP systems for the pulse shape analysis/determination. They are namely applied in a high counting rate of X-ray, γ-ray and/or nuclear particles.

Pulse shaping is used for increasing the signal to noise ratio and also for increasing the pulse pair resolution, hence, the commonly applied DSP method is a pulse pile-up correction. In the case of nuclear detectors, when high activity sources and detectors with a long pulse decay time are used, two or more events can be recorded as a single event. Various methods are used for the detection and either the correction or rejection of these pulses (Cosulich et al., 1992; Belli et al., 2008). The pile-up affects the counting rate, energy and time resolution of the spectroscopy system. Fast scintillators may be used for a pile-up rejection; however then, fast DSP systems have to be used. The innovative DSP algorithms for an optimal filtering, rise-time discrimination, and proper pulses correction are also used.

The DSP based amplitude analysis in LabVIEW can be developed with LabVIEW function Waveform Peak Detection VI (WPkD). The amplitude analysis process is controlled by several input parameters of WPkD (Figure 8). The amplitude values of the detected peaks are used for the pulse height analysis.

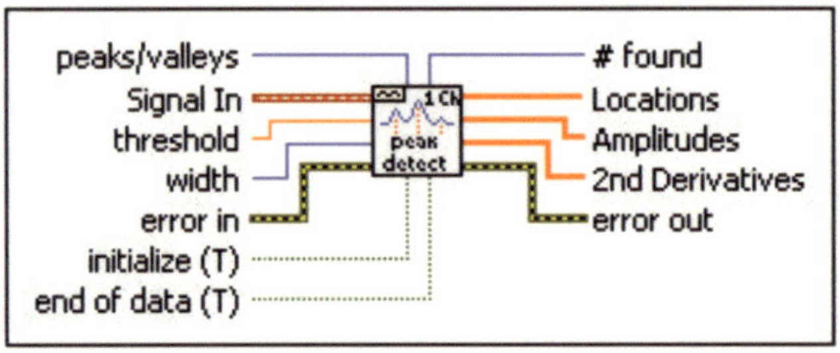

Fig. 8. Icon of Waveform Peak Detection VI.

WPkD function finds the location, magnitude of amplitude and the 2nd derivatives of the peaks in the detector signal. The threshold and width, input parameters, serve as separation tools of the true detector pulses from the noise. The threshold determinates the minimum value of the peak amplitude and the width determinates the minimum peak width according to the number of samples over the given threshold. WPkD is a software equivalent of the electronic pulse height analyzer, hence, the optimal treatment of the detector signal from the various types of detectors is achieved by DSP. The implementation of WPkD function in the block diagram is shown in Figure 9.

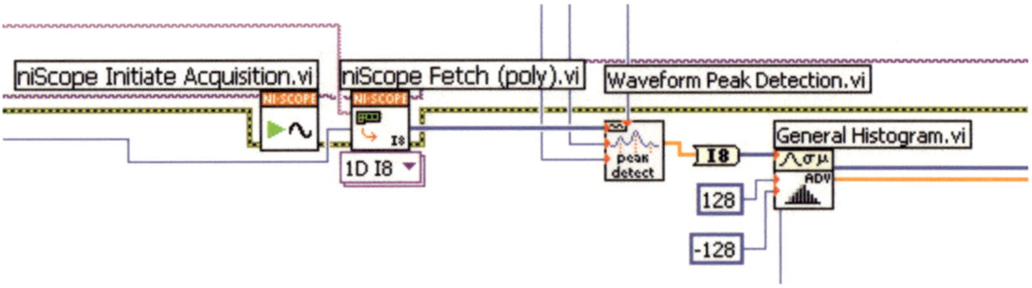

Fig. 9. Implementation of the WPkD function.

By changing the sampling rate, by means of the changes of the width and threshold parameters for peak validation in WPkD, the non-valid peaks rejection and signal noise reduction are performed. No pile-up correction/rejection is performed by this function. WPkD distinguishes the pile-up pulses, but their amplitudes are not corrected. In addition, few disadvantages of such function for the fast processing were found (Krasilnikov et at., 2011; Pechousek et al., 2007, 2011), and additional improvements, or new DSP algorithms were designed.

Another simple DSP module, called "discriminator", checks whether the analog output signal is above a predefined threshold or not, and produces a digital output. The threshold values (voltages) can be adjusted through a front panel.

2.3 Signal analyzer and MCA application

The main part of the presented system is the commercially available digitizer NI PCI-5124, which uses up to 200 MS s^{-1} real-time sampling. The digitizer is controlled by instrument drivers, as mentioned above, and called in the designed software application which performs all DSP functions. This digitizer was also used in γ-spectroscopy of high rate events (Yang et al., 2009) and in Mössbauer spectrometer designs (Pechousek et al., 2010).

The ^{57}Co radiation source is used and typical pulses sampled by 200 MS s^{-1} are displayed. The signals are acquired from the detectors connected with an amplifier. In Figure 10, the pulse shapes of three selected detectors are shown. The presented pulse shapes are the results of an average of one thousand pulses with the same amplitude.

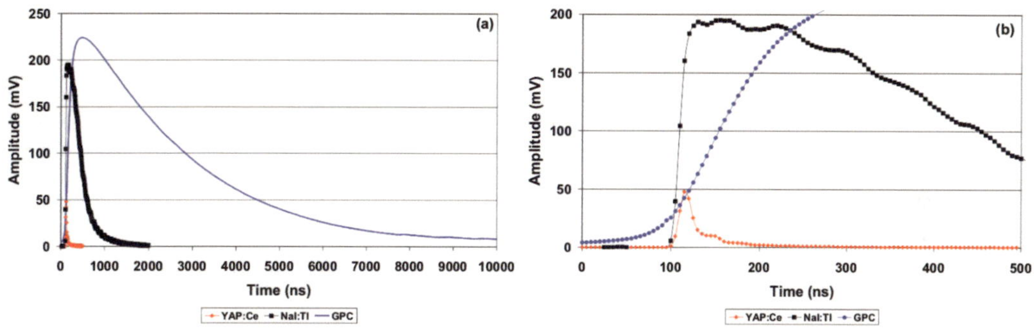

Fig. 10. a) The 14.4 keV pulses acquired from the detectors equipped with YAP:Ce scintillator (red) and GPC (blue) and 122 keV pulse acquired from the detector equipped with thick NaI:Tl scintillator (black), and b) the details of the rising parts of these pulses.

In Figure 10 (b), the common ringing in the pulses, mostly originating from the PMTs, is evident.

The most usual DSP method is the pulse height analysis preformed in MCA, which records the number of pulses in each pulse bin. In MCA, the channel number corresponds to the amplitude of a pulse, and the counting histogram is accumulated. Recently, DSP-MCA has been developed and system performance tested by us (Pechousek et al., 2011) on the nuclear detectors with very short time pulses (from 40 ns up to few microseconds), and in the range of low and high energies of X- and γ-rays. The front panel of the main application is shown in Figure 11, where negative pulses are acquired. The application code is based on the functions presented in Figures 5 and 9. Blue and red cursors in the MCA window (Figure 11) can be used to extract and analyze the pulses in a selected energy range. These cursors are also used as the discrimination levels for the additional processing included e.g. in Mössbauer spectrometers.

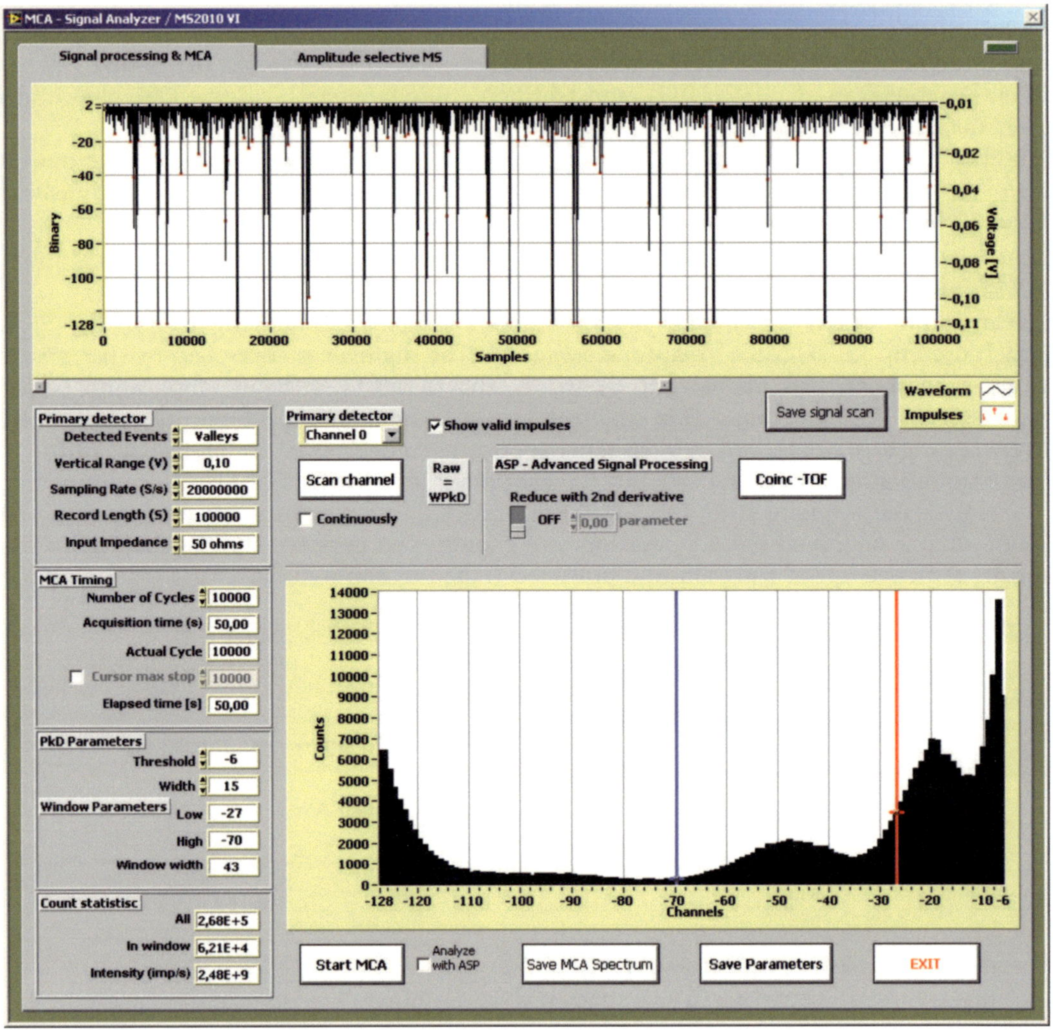

Fig. 11. Signal and Multichannel analyzer - front panel.

2.3.1 Improvement of MCA with high sampling rate

Four detectors employed for signal analysis and two γ-ray sources are presented in this part. For each detector, MCA was performed and the main photopeak positions were determined. In addition to ^{57}Co source, ^{137}Cs (γ-ray, 662 keV) source was also used. The MCA spectra were measured by means of the detector, amplifier, digitizer, and analyzed by the DSP with the WPkD.

As a first step, the detector signal was sampled with a low sampling rate (10 MS s^{-1}) for establishing the standard values. This sampling rate is usable in classic MCA and slow coincidence systems, but it is still low for a precise MCA spectrum recording. In fast lifetime measurements, it is necessary to use a maximal sampling rate (time resolution) and, therefore, the analysis with this sampling rate could be performed for the estimation of the influence on the MCA spectrum shape (energy resolution). Hence, the second value of the sampling rate was chosen to be of 200 MS s^{-1}. The MCA energy spectra of X- and γ-radiation emitted by ^{57}Co and ^{137}Cs sources are shown in Figure 12, where black line belongs to a low sampling rate and red line to a high sampling rate, respectively.

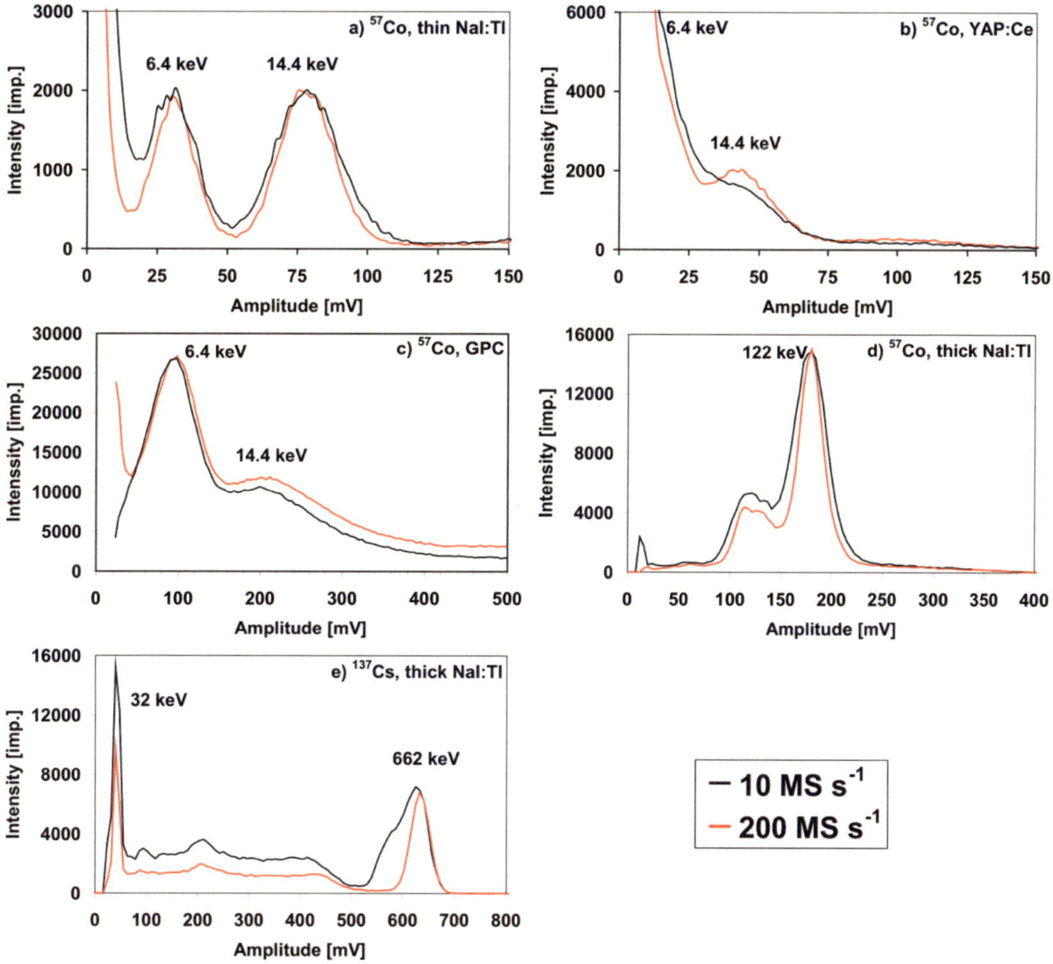

Fig. 12. ^{57}Co MCA spectra for a) thin NaI:Tl, b) YAP:Ce scintillators, c) GPC, d) thick NaI:Tl scintillator, and e) ^{137}Cs MCA spectrum for thick NaI:Tl scintillator. Signal is acquired at 10 and 200 MS s^{-1} sampling rate.

When the detector or source was changed from one to another, the distance was adjusted to achieve the reasonable counting rates and to minimize the occurrence of pile-up events. Figure 12 shows the energy resolution improvement for all photopeaks except the GPC detector, in which case a significant improvement is not evident. Furthermore, in the range of high energy impulses, another significant improvement is observed due to a better interleaving of the pulses. The 10 MS s^{-1} sampling rate is quite underlimited for the YAP:Ce coupled detector. Generally, the improvement for fast detectors and high energy regions is the most visible, due to the better recognition of the rising part of a observed pulse.

2.4 Time-of-flight and coincidence techniques

In common time-resolved coincidence nuclear systems, two different detectors are used in order to detect different photon energies emitted from the radioactive source, when a radioactive decay is studied. Similar methods are used i.e. in the time-resolved fluorescence system (Moreno et al., 2011) estimating the intrinsic fluorescence decay.

The system published in ref. (Pechousek et al., 2011) is suitable for nuclear coincidence measurements as the nuclear excited state half-life determination, where two DAQ channels are necessary. The first channel can detect the start nuclear events and the second channel the stop events. Both channels are sampled by the highest sampling rate. When the short-lived excited states are analyzed, time-of-flight (TOF) values has to be determined with the highest accuracy. The 200 MS s^{-1} sampling rate is used for precise MCA and time-resolving measurements and the system is then sensitive to decay lifetimes from tens of nanoseconds. In Figure 13, a block diagram of the above discussed system is shown.

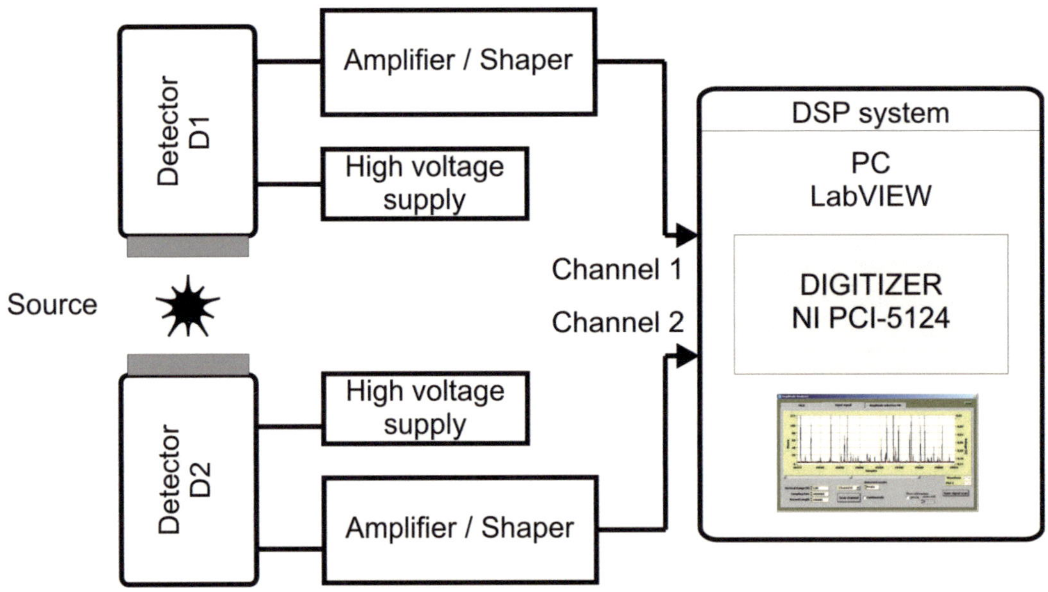

Fig. 13. DSP system for time-resolved nuclear spectroscopy.

In time-resolved spectrometry, the TOF value determines when a photon or particle arrives into the detector. The time accuracy of the measurement system depends on the properties of the detector and the type of electronics processing the signal. TOF measurement offers the possibility to perform coincidence and anticoincidence nuclear experiments. There are several analog timing methods (leading edge timing, crossover timing, constant-fraction timing, first photoelectron timing) implemented in DSP (Abdel-Aal, 1993; Aspinall et al., 2009). In one of them, the pulse starting time is interpolated from the samples of the pulse rise and a digital leading-edge discriminator (LED) determines the TOF value. The TOF then represents the time at which the pulse crosses the threshold (discrimination level). The LED is a simply implemented timing method usable mainly when similar pulses shapes in a signal stream occur. Therefore, the developed DSP system with the TOF-LED technique can be used with various types of detectors. The description of the LabVIEW LED is given in ref.

(Pechousek et al., 2011). The TOF algorithm development and its application in the coincidence measurement were carried out. The TOF calculation is depicted in Figure 14. The code has to distinguish between the maximum value position (from WPkD) and the beginning of the pulses.

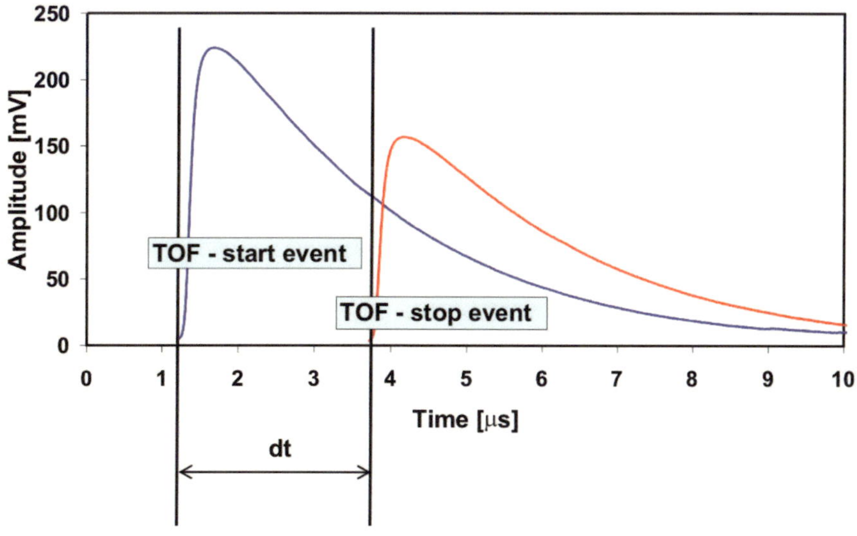

Fig. 14. Practical behavior of the TOF procedure.

As mentioned above, when using a code with the original WPkD function, only the valid peaks are recognized. However, problems arise for high-rate sampling and therefore, DSP-TOF improvement is necessary. With a high-rate sampling, the peak location is sometimes found out of the pulse-maximum position. This error-shift negatively affects time resolving measurements, and has to be reduced for a precise nuclear coincidence measurement by modifying the WPkD algorithm with adding the TOF determination. The presented modified TOF-resolving method is applicable for various detectors and is independent on the pulse rising time (Pechousek et al., 2011).

2.4.1 Lifetime coincidence measurement

The presented DSP system is typically applied in the coincidence measurement where the lifetime of the excited nuclear state can be measured by the registration of X-γ, or γ-γ cascade. In this section, the lifetime coincidence measurement of ^{57}Fe 14.4 keV excited state is presented. The registrations of two events are acquired with two different detectors optimized for given energies. In the case of ^{57}Co source, it decays by an electron capture to the excited state of ^{57}Fe (136 keV) which deexcites thorough the 122 keV and 14.4 keV states to the ground state. The 14.4 keV excited state has a half-life of 98.3 ns (Dickson & Berry, 1986).

In accordance with Figure 13, the first detector (D1) detects 122 keV γ-photons (thick NaI:Tl) as start events and the second detector (D2) detects 14.4 keV γ-photons (YAP:Ce or thin NaI:Tl) as stop events. The coincidence intervals, calculated with TOF code, have been accumulated into the histogram, and are shown in Figure 15.

Each channel of the DSP system was configured individually to detect relevant start and stop events. The value of the half-life was estimated to be 98.9 ± 0.3 ns.

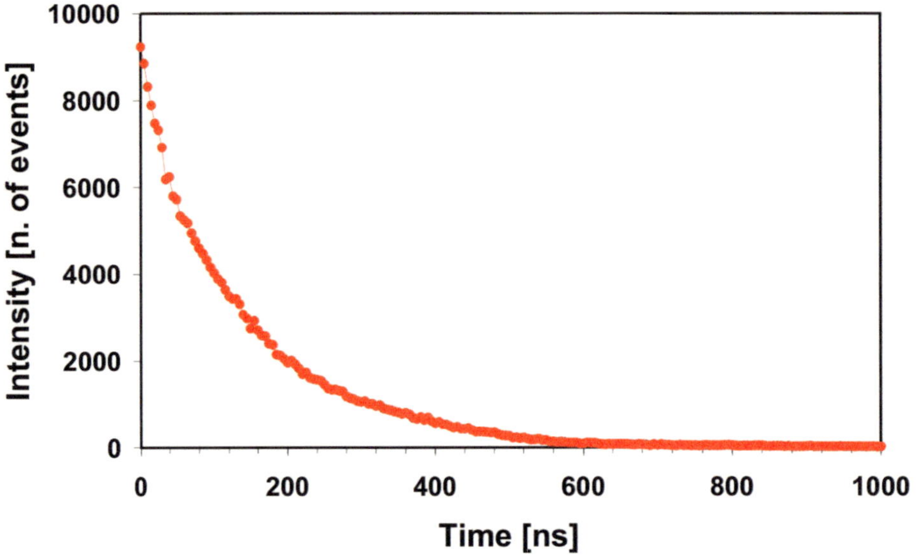

Fig. 15. Lifetime measurement of the 14.4 keV excited state in ^{57}Co source.

3. Additional DSP methods in nuclear systems performed by VI

Acquiring data from a detector is the most common process in the nuclear systems. Additionally, various methods are used in other different spectroscopies. For instance, one method can be the generation of an analog signal (waveform) for controlling a particular device. Hence, synchronizing such DAQ processes with detector signal digitizing becomes necessary. This is described in the text below.

3.1 Function generators

Different analog output devices are used. The function generator device with its instrument drivers delivered will be described. The examples presented below have been established with the NI 5401 (12-bit, 40 MS s^{-1} update rate) function generator. This function generator features also the Real-Time System Integration (RTSI) or PXI trigger bus for routing the trigger signals in the PCI or PXI system to synchronize other DAQ processes. The NI-FGEN instrument driver is used in NI 5401 applications and the Soft Front Panel (SFP) can be employed to interactively generate waveforms with NI the signal generators module, in a similar way as with stand-alone instruments.

The diagram in Figure 16 shows the general programming flow for applications using NI-FGEN driver. Details are presented in LabVIEW NI-FGEN Help (National Instruments, 2004, 2009b).

This instrument driver is used in a similar way as the above mentioned NI-SCOPE driver. After the initialization and configuration processes, the signal generation is started. At the end of the generation, the abort function is called and the instrument session is closed.

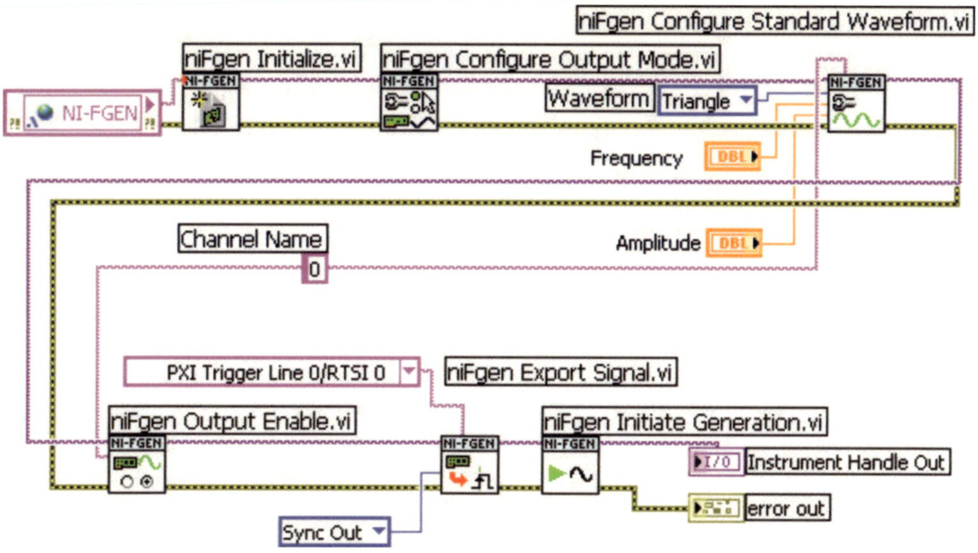

Fig. 16. Data flow for NI-FGEN application.

3.2 Synchronization and triggering techniques implemented via RTSI bus

If an application requires more than two DAQ devices, it is possible to synchronize these devices on all platforms using digital triggers.

RTSI (Real-Time System Integration) bus is employed to share and exchange timing and control signals between multiple boards. The RTSI bus cables are short, 34-conductor ribbon cables equipped with two to five connectors linking together a group of boards. Figure 17 shows an example of an extended five-board cable setup.

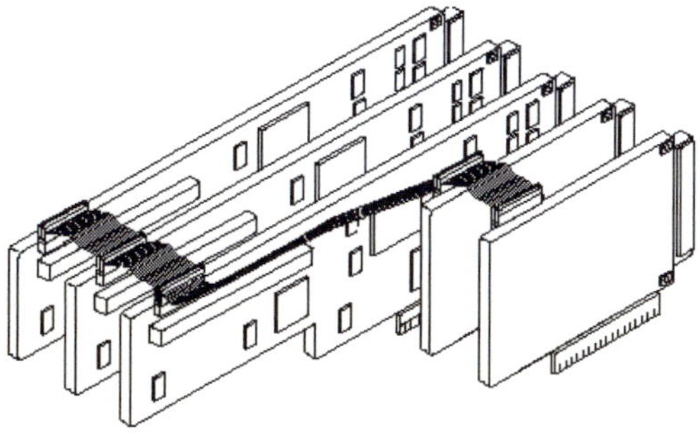

Fig. 17. RTSI bus used for synchronization of PCI devices (National Instruments, 2010).

The PXI system uses the PXI trigger bus that includes the RTSI bus and is linked to all slots in the chassis. Other devices can use the PFI (Programmable Function Interface) digital triggers on the I/O connector.

Synchronization and triggering are commonly used in more sophisticated measurements, where one or more DAQ processes relate with other processes. Such a type of combination is common in applications where one device works as a master (generates signals) and the other device works as a slave (waits for trigger). In the VI concept, it is easy to build such a system and the exchange the working mode of these devices.

A trigger is a signal that initiates one or more instrument functions. The trigger basic types are digital, software, or analog, and can be derived from the attributes of a signal being acquired, such as the level and slope of the signal. Triggers can be internal (software-generated) or external. External triggers allow synchronizing the hardware operation with an external circuitry or other devices. There are several types of triggering, and each kind of triggering uses a different NI-SCOPE or NI-FGEN Configure Trigger function (National Instruments, 2009b, 2010).

For instance, in the computer-based modular Mössbauer spectrometer (Pechousek et al., 2010), there are two main parts; the first one is a computer with the NI 5102 digitizer, and the second, the NI 5401 function generator controlled by VI. Their synchronization is provided by the RTSI bus or PXI Trigger bus. The function generator generates a velocity signal on its ARB OUT output. On the SYNC OUT output, a trigger signal is available for the synchronization of other devices (the routing of this signal is shown in Figure 16). This is used in the internal RTSI bus and triggers the DAQ process in the digitizer. In the case of USB devices, it can be generated externally by the digital output signal available in the multifunction devices.

3.2.1 Triggering with NI-FGEN

When triggering a signal generator, it is possible to select the type of the trigger, trigger source, and trigger mode. For instance, the function generator works as a master, and except the periodic analog signal, it generates the digital trigger signal with the same frequency on the SYNC OUT output. This signal will be routed on the RTSI bus line by the function of *niFgen Export Signal VI* (see Figure 18) to control other devices. This function routes signals (clocks, triggers, and events) to the specified output terminal, i.e. the RTSI connector.

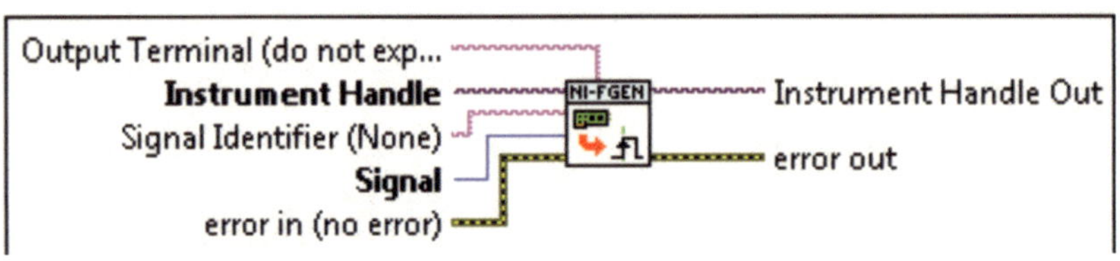

Fig. 18. Function *niFgen Export Signal VI* used to route the trigger signals.

The SYNC OUT signal is normally exported on the SYNC_OUT front panel connector.

3.2.2 Triggering with NI-SCOPE

With NI-SCOPE triggering functions, the trigger can transfer a device from a nonsampling into a sampling state, then the device starts acquiring data. The function which configures the digitizer for different types of triggering is *niScope Configure Trigger (poly)*, see Figure 19.

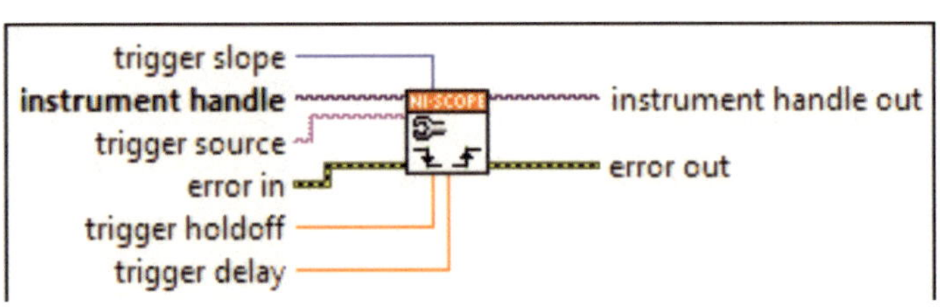

Fig. 19. Function *niScope Configure Trigger (poly)* used to trigger the digitizer.

After initializing an acquisition, the digitizer waits for the start trigger which is configured through the Start Trigger Source property. The default setting is "immediate". Upon receiving the start trigger, the digitizer begins sampling pretrigger points. After the digitizer finishes sampling pretrigger points, the digitizer waits for a reference (stop) trigger that is specified by a Configure Trigger VI. Upon receiving the reference trigger, the digitizer finishes the acquisition after completing posttrigger sampling (National Instruments, 2010). The configuration of the digital and analog triggers with NI-SCOPE is shown in Figure 20.

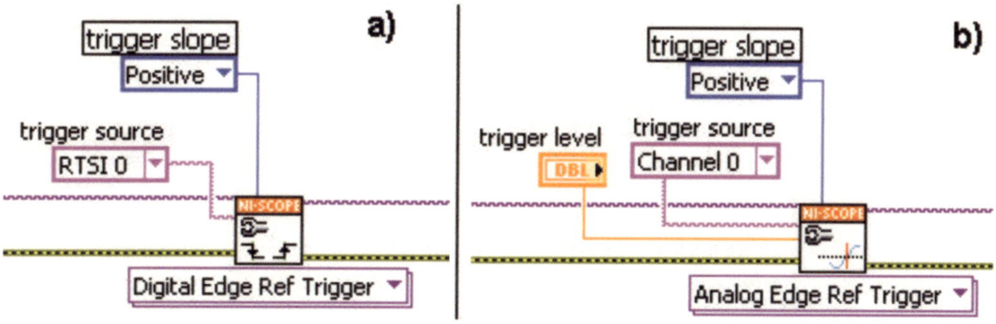

Fig. 20. Types of NI-SCOPE triggers a) digital and b) analog.

In the case of digitizers, analog triggers set at one DAQ channel can trigger the second channel (Figure 20 b), which is used in time resolved measurements. Analog triggers in digitizer applications are commonly used in time-resolved spectroscopies, in which two DAQ channels are used. This technique has been described in the previous section - the start event channel triggers the stop event channel.

4. Mössbauer spectroscopy

In this section, methods for pulse processing, movement control and DSP synchronization will be presented and demonstrated on the Mössbauer spectrometer construction. All the tasks use DSP abilities of LabVIEW system running in the main computer, and the former single-purpose spectrometer units were replaced by DAQ modules. Hardware solution is based on DAQ devices working on the USB, PCI or PXI platform controlled by the main application running on the personal computer or PXI controller. Final application allows, in addition to Mössbauer spectra accumulation, the detailed analysis of the acquired detector signal in energy and time domains, and also to tune the velocity driving system separately. This concept can be used with all common spectrometric benches with different velocity transducers, radioactive sources and γ-ray detectors.

Mössbauer spectroscopy represents an essential tool for the investigation of specific elements-containing materials (Fe, Sn, Au ...) as its local probing capability. It allows to determine and quantify different atomic surrounding, magnetic states and in-field magnetic arrangements of magnetic moments, conveying thus structural and magnetic information. In addition, Mössbauer spectroscopy is highly element selective and allows identifying the desired component even if it exists in a very small amount in the mixed sample.

The Mössbauer effect is based on recoilless nuclear emission and resonant absorption of γ-rays in the sample, and the Mössbauer spectra acquisition is performed by the γ-ray intensity measurement together with the precise radioactive source motion control. The Mössbauer spectrum is dependency between radioactive source velocity and the detected γ-ray intensity. This experimental technique is a frequently used tool in many areas of research such as physics, chemistry, biology, metallurgy etc.

4.1 Spectrometer configuration

The standard structure of the Mössbauer spectrometer is depicted in Figure 21, where most of these blocks could be replaced by the DSP algorithms. The LabVIEW programming environment allows realizing such system with minimum single purpose electronic devices. The typical Mössbauer spectrometric bench is shown in Figure 22 (for room temperature measurements).

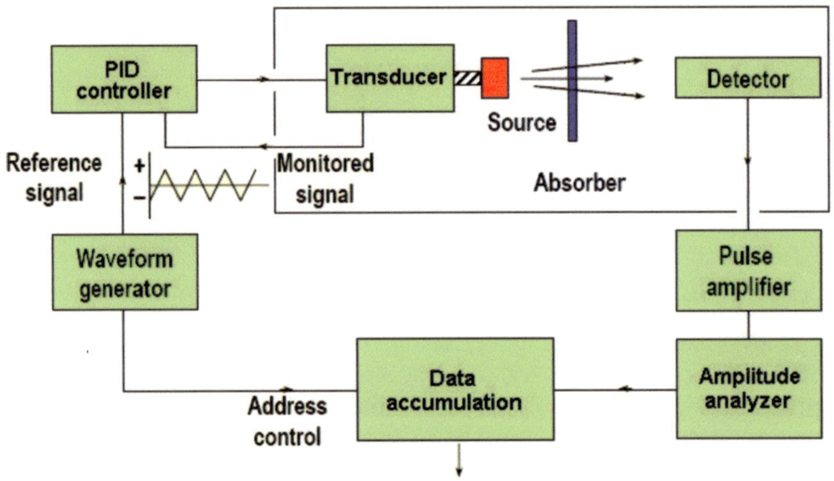

Fig. 21. Block diagram of the standard Mössbauer spectrometer.

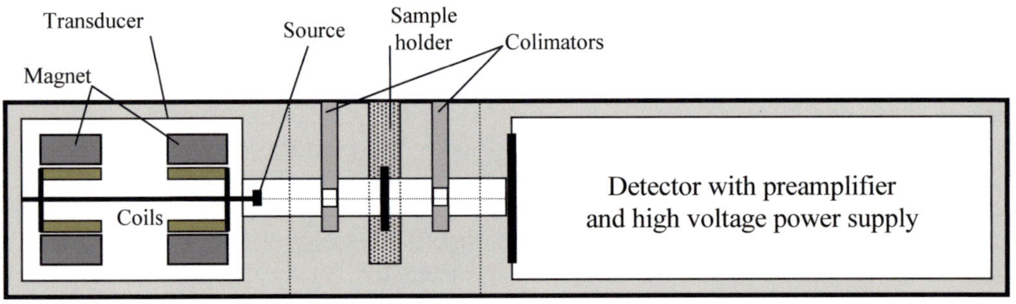

Fig. 22. Block diagram of the Mössbauer spectrometer

Various programming techniques and instrument solutions are used to develop Mössbauer spectrometers. However, traditional solutions are based primarily on stand-alone instruments or specific modular systems.

The spectrometer has to perform tasks such as γ-ray pulse-height analysis, reference velocity signal generation for the motion of the radioactive source, proportional integral derivative (PID) control of the relative velocity between the source and the absorber, and Mössbauer spectra accumulation. By using LabVIEW with NI PXI, PCI, USB devices, and CompactRIO, a Mössbauer spectrometer that is open and flexible enough to operate within multiple hardware setups was built (Pechousek et al., 2010).

4.2 Amplitude analyzer and spectra accumulation

The system's γ-ray detector and amplitude analyzer are based on an NI high-speed digital oscilloscope. The detector impulses represent registered nuclear events, the amplitude of which depends on the detected γ photon energy. The sampling rate of the detector output signal differs with the detector type (scintillation, gas-filled, semiconductor). The detection function was performed using NI PXI, PCI, and USB digitizers; the NI 5102 8-bit 20 MS s^{-1} modules, NI PCI-5124 12-bit 200 MS s^{-1} high-resolution digitizer, and NI USB-5133 8-bit 100 MS s^{-1} digitizer/oscilloscope.

The spectra accumulation process combines the radioactive source velocity data with the corresponding γ-ray intensity. Only some emitted photons with appropriate energy are affected by the specimen, and only relevant impulses are identified and recorded. The amplitude discriminator is based on the LabVIEW WPkD function. The other software component performs the multichannel analysis of the detector signal.

Figure 23 shows the basic concept of the spectrometer block diagram. This code synchronizes the DAQ process for the velocity signal generation and the detector signal processing.

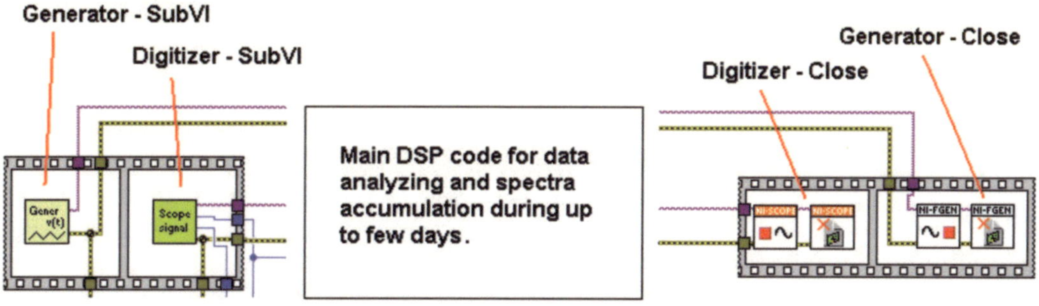

Fig. 23. The basic concept of the spectrometer block diagram..

Other SubVIs for data handling, measurement configuration, etc. are included in the application. The front panel of the main application is shown in Figure 24.

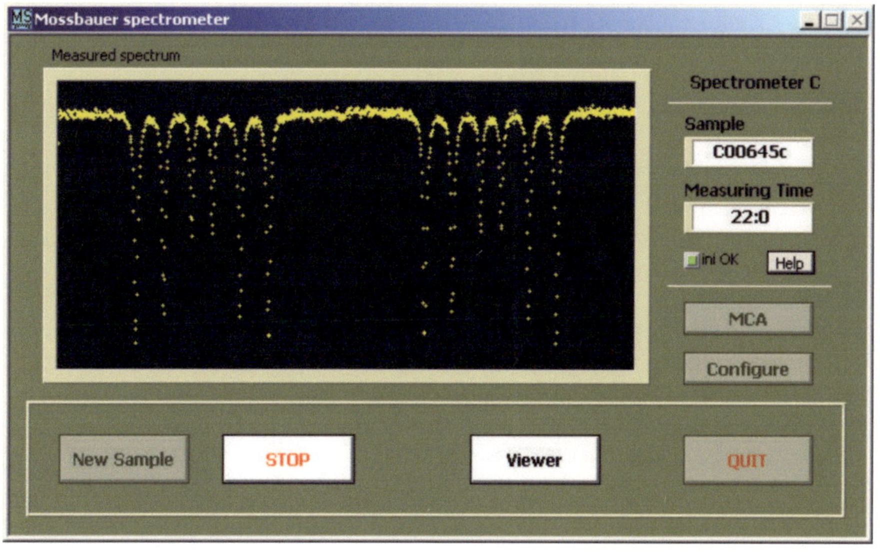

Fig. 24. Main application front panel.

4.3 Velocity-driving system

A common velocity-driving system for Mössbauer spectrometer consists of the velocity signal generator, PID controller, and the electromechanical linear transducer coupled with the Mössbauer source. The reference signal is lead through a PID controller to the drive coil of the transducer, and the pick-up coil signal is connected back into the PID controller. The common reference velocity a), drive b), and error c) signals are presented in Figure 25. The velocity signal frequency is mostly up to tens of Hz.

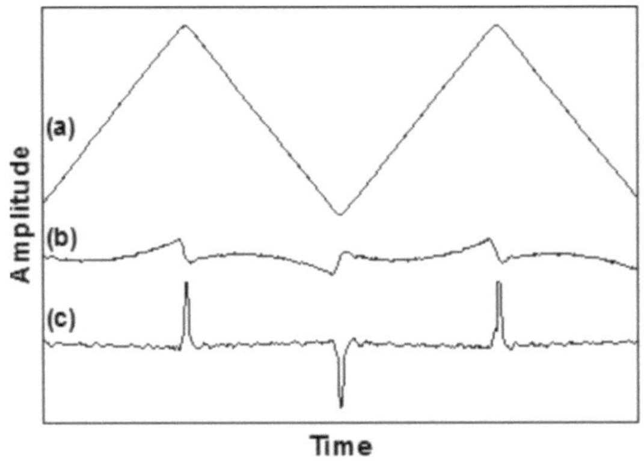

Fig. 25. Velocity a), drive b), and error c) signals used in the velocity unit.

NI analog output devices as velocity signal generators are coupled to the digital PID circuit. In addition, with the flexibility of the VI concept, generator can be replaced by the other multifunction card with proper analog and digital output on the USB, PCI or PXI platform. Limiting parameters are 12-bit resolution and the 150 kS s^{-1} update rate at the analog output as the minimum The selected devices are for instance the NI USB-6221 16-bit 833 kS s^{-1} and NI USB-6215 16-bit 250 kS s^{-1} multifunction DAQ modules. One advantage of using PXI and PCI modules is that the RTSI bus allows transferring of fast trigger signals, which must be generated to synchronize the spectra accumulation process.

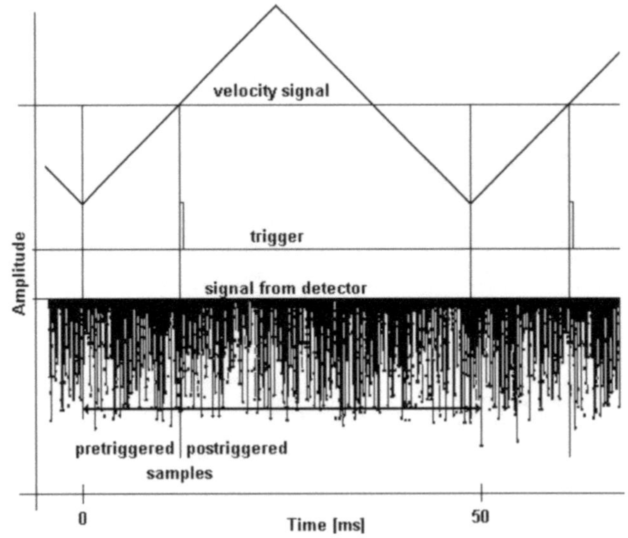

Fig. 26. DAQ processes synchronization.

In Figure 26, the basic principle of the DAQ processes synchronized with the techniques described above is depicted. The velocity signal is generated with given frequency and the trigger signal synchronizes the detector signal acquisition.
Each period of the source movement is divided into 2048 velocity/time intervals. The number of the detected photons accumulated during each time interval is saved into the relevant velocity channel. The spectra accumulation process is based on the periodical summation of the appropriate data from each repetitive movement period for hours or days. The spectra accumulation process is depicted in Figure 27.

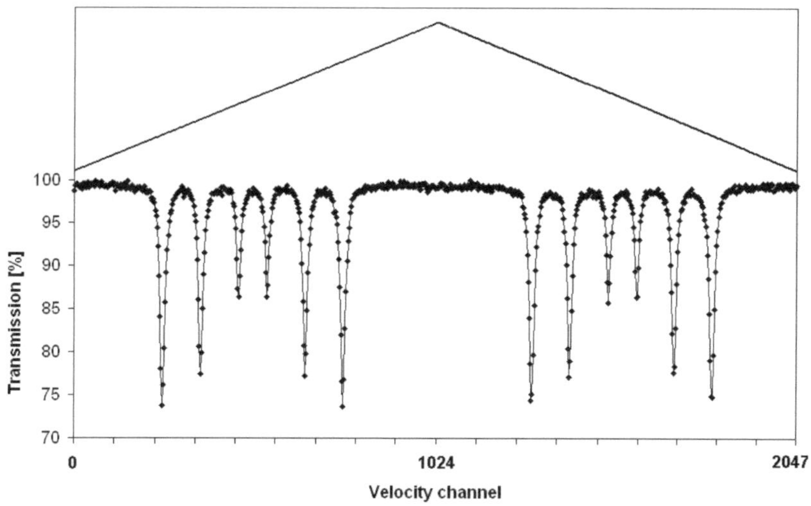

Fig. 27. Mössbauer spectrum accumulation

For the second available generator, NI CompactRIO was selected to build a digital PID controller and the reference velocity generator in the joint device (Pechousek et al., 2009). The cRIO real-time controller and cRIO chassis with an FPGA provide the digital PID algorithm based on discrete PID function in the LabVIEW FPGA Module. The analog input module acquires the transducer pick-up coil signal and the reference velocity signal when an external generator is used. The analog output module generates the drive signal, and the digital output module is used as a trigger source.

4.4 Spectrometer utilization

Currently, at the Regional Centre of Advanced Technologies and Materials, a part of Palacky University in Olomouc (www.rcptm.com), three VI spectrometers based on USB (multifunction card and high-rate digitizer), PCI (function generator and high-rate digitizer) and PXI (function generator and high-rate digitizer in the NI PXI-1033 5-slot chassis with integrated MXI-Express controller) are used.
The new digital PID system based on CompactRIO is used in the most important application in which it has achieved higher stability and system reliability in nonstandard working conditions, including vibrations coming from lab equipment and external magnetic forces. CompactRIO serves as a remote system, which allows to change the PID parameters at a safe distance from the radioactive source and the high magnetic field.

5. Conclusion

The measurement systems built with LabVIEW modular instrumentation offer a popular approach to nuclear spectrometers construction. By replacing the former single-purpose system units with universal data acquisition modules, it is achieved a lower-cost solution that is reliable, fast, and takes high-quality measurements. The result is a user-friendly application with high system flexibility.
Performances of the DSP systems were directly determined by spectroscopy application. The presented methods are simple in realization simultaneously with improvement in performance for nuclear experiments. Moreover, with VI open approach, it is easy to modify the configuration of the system in the future.

6. Acknowledgment

This work has been supported by the projects "Advanced Technologies in the Study of Applied Physics" (CZ.1.07/2.2.00/07.0018) and "Education of Research Workers in the Regional Centre of Advanced Technologies and Materials" (CZ.1.07/2.3.00/09.0042) in Operational Program Education for Competitiveness - European Social Fund. Author would also like to thank to Karolina Siskova for her help with this paper.

7. References

Abdel-Aal, R.E. (1993). Simulation and analysis of nuclear physics instrumentation using the LabVIEW graphical programming environment. *The Arabian Journal for Science and Engineering*, Vol. 18, No. 3, (July 1993), pp. 365-382, ISSN 1319-8025

Ahmed, S.N. (2007). *Physics and Engineering of Radiation Detection* (first edition), Academic Pres, ISBN 0-12-045581-1, London, Great Britain

Aspinall, M.D., Joyce, M.J., Mackin, R.O., Jarrah, Z., Boston, A.J., Nolan, P.J., Peyton, A.J. & Hawkes, N.P. (2009). Sample-interpolation timing: an optimized technique for the digital measurement of time of flight for γ rays and neutrons at relatively low sampling rates. *Measurement Science and Technology*, Vol. 20, (November 2008), 015104, 10pp, ISSN 0957-0233

Belli, F., Esposito, B., Marocco, D., Riva, M., Kaschuk, Y., Bonheure, G. & JET EFDA contributors (2008). A method for digital processing of pile-up events in organic scintillators. *Nuclear Instruments and Methods in Physics Research A*, Vol. 595, (July 2008), pp. 512-519, ISSN 0168-9002

Bettiol, A.A., Udalagama, C. & Watt, F. (2009). A New Data Acquisition System for Nuclear Microscopy based on a Field Programmable Gate Array Card. *Nuclear Instruments and Methods in Physics Research B*, Vol. 267, (June 2009), pp. 2069-2072, ISSN 0168-583X

Cosulich, E. & Gatti, F. (1992). A digital processor for nuclear spectroscopy with cryogenic detectors. *Nuclear Instruments and Methods A*, Vol. 321, (September 1992), pp. 211-215, ISSN 0168-9002

Dickson, D.P.E. & Berry, F.J. (1986) Mössbauer spectroscopy. Cambridge: Cambridge University press, ISBN 978-0521018104

Drndarević, V. (2008). A very low-cost alpha-particle spectrometer. *Measurement Science and Technology*, Vol. 19, (April 2008), 057007, 5pp, ISSN 0957-0233

Drndarevic, V. & Jevtic, N. (2008). A versatile, PC-based gamma ray monitor. *Radiation Protection Dosimetry*, Vol. 129, No. 4, (October 2007), pp. 478-480, ISSN 1742-3406

Ellis, W.H. & He, Q. (1993). Computer-Based Nuclear Radiation Detection and Instrumentation Teaching Laboratory System. *IEEE Transactions on Nuclear Science*, Vol. 40, No. 4, (August 1993), pp. 675-679, ISSN 0018-9499

Esposito, B., Riva, M., Marocco D. & Kaschuck Y. (2007). A Digital Acquisition and Elaboration System for Nuclear Fast Pulse Detection. *Nuclear Instruments and Methods in Physics Research A*, Vol. 572, (March 2007), pp. 355-357, ISSN 0168-9002

Gilmore, G. (2008). *Practical Gamma-ray Spectroscopy* (second eddition), Wiley, ISBN 978-0470861967,

Gontean, A. & Szabó, R. (2011). LabVIEW Remote Lab, In: *LabVIEW - Modeling, Programming and Simulations*, Riccardo de Asmundis, ISBN 978-953-307-521-1, InTech, Rijeka, Croatia

Green, D.P., Bruce J.B. & Thomas, J.L. (1996). Sensor Measurement and Experimental Control in Nuclear Magnetic Resonance Imaging. *Review of Scientific Instruments*, Vol. 67, No. 1, (January 1996), pp. 102-107, ISSN 0034-6748

Kholmetskii, A.L., Mashlan, M., Misevich, O.V., Chudakov, V.A., Lopatik, A.R. & Zak, D. (1997). Comparison of the productivity of fast detectors for Mössbauer spectroscopy. *Nuclear Instruments and Methods in Physics Research B*, Vol. 124, (April 1997), pp. 143-144, ISSN 0168-583X

Kirichenko, A.F., Sarwana, S., Mukhanov O.A., Vernik I.V., Zhang, Y., Kang, J. & Vogt, J.M. (2001). RSFQ Time Digitizing System. *IEEE Transactions on Applied Superconductivity*, Vol. 22, No. 1, (March 2001), pp. 978-981, ISSN 1051-8223

Krasilnikov, V., Marocco, D., Esposito, B., Riva, M. & Kaschuck, Y. (2011). Fast pulse detection algorithms for digitized waveforms from scintillators. Computer Physics *Communications*, Vol. 182, (October 2010), pp. 735-738, ISSN 0010-4655

Moreno, E., Reyes, P. & de la Rosa, J.M. (2011). Time-resolved fluorescence spectroscopy with LabView, In: *LabVIEW - Modeling, Programming and Simulations*, Riccardo de Asmundis, ISBN 978-953-307-521-1, InTech, Rijeka, Croatia

National Instruments. (2004). NI-FGEN Instrument Driver Quick Reference, 02.04.2011, Available from http://www.ni.com/pdf/manuals/371307e.pdf

National Instruments. (2009). NI High-Speed Digitizers Help, 02.04.2011, Available from http://digital.ni.com/manuals.nsf/websearch/349CC538026ACD5A862576E8004DB89D?OpenDocument&seen=1

National Instruments. (2009). NI Signal Generators Help, 02.04.2011, Available from http://digital.ni.com/manuals.nsf/websearch/6F0CB519A713D1E28625762000689402

National Instruments. (2010). Getting Started with NI-SCOPE, 02.04.2011, Available from http://zone.ni.com/devzone/cda/tut/p/id/3382

Nelson, M.A., Rooney, B.D., Dinwiddie, D.R. & Brunson, G.S. (2003). Analysis of digital timing methods with BaF2 scintillators. *Nuclear Instruments and Methods in Physics Research A*, Vol. 579, (June 2003), pp. 247-251, ISSN 0168-9002

Pechousek, J. & Mashlan, M. (2005). Mössbauer spectrometer in the PXI/CompactPCI modular system. *Czechoslovak Journal of Physics*, Vol. 55, No. 7, (July 2005), pp. 853-863, ISSN 0011-4626

Pechousek, J., Mashlan, M., Frydrych, J., Jancik, D. & Prochazka, R. (2007). Improving detector signal processing with Pulse Height Analysis in Mössbauer Spectrometers. *Hyperfine Interactions*, Vol. 107, (February 2007), pp. 1-8, ISSN 0304-3843

Pechousek, J., Prochazka, R., Mashlan, M., Jancik, D. & Frydrych, J. (2009). Digital proportional-integral-derivative controller of a Mössbauer Spectrometer. *Measurement Science and Technology*, Vol. 20, (November 2008), 017001, 4pp, ISSN 0957-0233

Pechousek, J., Jancik, D., Evdokimov, V. & Prochazka, R. (2009). Velocity driving system for an in-field Mössbauer spectrometer. *Nuclear Instruments and Methods in Physics Research B*, Vol. 267, (February 2009), pp. 846-848, ISSN 0168-583X

Pechousek, J., Prochazka, R., Jancik, D., Mashlan, M. & Frydrych, J. (2010). Universal LabVIEW-powered Mössbauer spectrometer based on the USB, PCI or PXI devices. *Journal of Physics: Conference Series*, Vol. 217, (May 2010), pp. 012006, ISSN 1742-6588

Pechousek, J., Prochazka, R., Prochazka, V. & Frydrych, J. (2011). Virtual instrumentation technique used in the nuclear digital signal processing system design: Energy and time measurement test. *Nuclear Instruments and Methods in Physics Research A*, Vol. 637, (February 2011), pp. 200-205, ISSN 0168-9002

Prochazka, R., Tucek, P., Tucek, J., Marek, J., Mashlan, M. & Pechousek, J. (2010). Statistical analysis And digital processing of the Mössbauer spectra. *Measurement Science and Technology*, Vol. 21, (January 2010), 025107, 7pp, ISSN 0957-0233

Tłaczala, W., Grajner, G. & Zaremba, M. (2008). Virtual Laboratory with Simulated Nuclear Experiments. *IEEE Transactions on Instrumentation and Measurement*, Vol. 57, No. 8, (August 2008), pp. 1766-1770, ISSN 0018-9456

Tłaczala, W. (2005). Virtual instrumentation in physics, In: *Handbook of Measuring System Design*, P. Sydeman & R. Thorn, (Eds.), 695-701, Wiley, ISBN 0-470-02143-8, Hoboken, NJ, USA

Yan, J., Liu, R., Li, Ch., Jiang, L., Lu, X., Zhu, T., Wang, M., Wen, Z. & Lin, J. (2009). LabVIEW-based auto timing counts virtual instrument system with ORTEC 974 Counter/Timer. *Nuclear Science and Techniques*, Vol. 20, (October 2009), pp. 307-311, ISSN 1001-8042

Yang, H., Wehe, D.K. & Bartels, D.M. (2009). Spectroscopy of high rate events during active interrogation. *Nuclear Instruments and Methods in Physics Research A*, Vol. 598, (October 2008), pp. 779-787, ISSN 0168-9002

Part 2

Hardware in the Loop Simulation

5

Real-Time Rapid Embedded Power System Control Prototyping Simulation Test-Bed Using LabVIEW and RTDS

Karen Butler-Purry and Hung-Ming Chou
Texas A&M University
United States of America

1. Introduction

When developing new control, protection, and stability methods for power systems, it is important to study the complex interactions of the system dynamics with the real-time operation of the new methods. Historically hardware prototypes were developed to study these interactions. With the recent introduction of the much cheaper rapid hardware and software prototyping tools, developers are choosing instead to use these tools to study dynamic interactions during real-time operation. This technology provides a cost effective option and flexibility in modeling and coding which allows use for versatile applications. Rapid prototyping technology is being widely used in many application areas for real-time data analysis and control such as avionics, power, acoustics, mechatronics, and automotive applications (Keunsoo et al., 2005; Postolache et al., 2006; Spinozzi, 2006; Toscher et al., 2006). Parallel digital signal processors (DSPs) (French et al., 1998; Lavoie et al., 1995) are also being used as rapid prototyping technology for real-time simulation and control.

To study real-time dynamic interactions of isolated power systems and control methods, a test bed is developed that uses rapid prototyping technology. This chapter discusses the real-time test bed which was developed more generally to study real-time issues, and validate and verify new designs of centralized and de-centralized control, protection, and wide-area monitoring methodologies for stand alone power systems, such as naval shipboard power systems, power transmission and distribution system and microgrids.

The National Instruments Compact RIO (*NI CompactRIO*, 2011)low cost reconfigurable control and acquisition system is used to implement the new control and protection methods in the test bed. The NI CompactRIO embedded system contains the NI reconfigurable technology and a real-time controller with an embedded (Pentium) floating-point processor. The 8-slot reconfigurable chassis contains an embedded user-programmable FPGA (field programmable gate array) chip providing direct access to hot swappable input/output (I/O) modules for precise control and flexibility in timing, triggering, and synchronization. The I/O modules contain built-in signal conditioning and isolation. The control and protection methods are implemented using the LabVIEW RT and FPGA Modules on a Host PC. The code is downloaded to the cRIO controller and FPGA for execution. LabVIEW Virtual Instruments (VIs) are used to remotely monitor and control (if desired) the RT Power System and Controller simulation. National Instruments data acquisition cards and hot swappable input and output analog and digital modules are used to pass signals between the cRIO controller

and the real time power system simulation. The inputs and outputs of the NI I/O modules were mapped in VIs. Further data acquisition settings for the I/O modules such as the number of channels, data type, sampling rate, and data buffer length were programmed in VIs.
The power systems are modeled using RSCAD software for a real time digital simulator (RTDS®) (*Real Time Digital Simlator - RTDS*, 2011) which is a unique integration of hardware and software specifically designed to perform electromagnetic transient simulation (EMTP) of AC and DC power systems with external hardware in the simulation loop. Based on its unique architecture, it is equally suitable for simulating large transmission and distribution systems or tightly coupled power systems such as ship systems, locomotives, airplanes, automobiles, and micro grids. The RTDS simulator architecture exploits the parallel computation nature of the mathematical model of large power systems using proprietary parallel processing hardware. The RSCAD run-time interface of the RTDS is interactive and is used to view the simulation results and provide user inputs while the simulation is in progress. RTDS is a modular system consisting of racks that are paralleled. Each rack consists of several processing cards which can be customized to provide the computational power of a specific power system problem. These racks can be used to run simultaneous simulations of multiple smaller systems or large simulations requiring multiple racks. RTDS provides high precision (16 bit) real-time input/output (I/O) interfaces of both analog and digital signals to interface with the external instrumentation in the simulation loop.
The implementation of an overcurrent relay protection scheme is discussed in this chapter to illustrate the operation of the test bed. A two-bus power system which has a generator at one bus, a load at the other bus, and a transmission line between them, is simulated on the RTDS. The overcurrent relay is implemented on the RT processor and FPGA. Measurements of the current flowing through the cable and the node voltages are measured. Further the results of several case studies are discussed.
This book chapter will focus on the concept of real-time rapid embedded control prototyping simulation and its implementation using LabVIEW. Section two will describe RTDS and cRIO as well as the proposed methodology for implementation of embedded controller-in-the-loop simulation. Section three will present the detailed implementation of the overcurrent relay case study, including the programs in RTDS and in cRIO. Also, a synchronization technique to synchronize the RTDS with the cRIO in real-time operation will be discussed. In section four, simulation results will be described. Lastly, the conclusions and some future work will be presented.

2. Real-Time Rapid Embedded Power System Control Prototyping Simulation Test Bed

There are two main components in the Real-Time Embedded Power System Control Rapid Prototyping Simulation Test Bed. One component uses the National Instruments CompactRIO (cRIO) Embedded Design Platform that allows users to rapidly build embedded control or acquisition systems. The other component uses the RTDS real-time digital simulator which allows real-time simulation of power systems and hardware-in-the-loop (HIL) studies with controllers, protective relays, and power system components. Figure 1 shows a high-level system diagram for the Real-Time Embedded Rapid Prototyping Simulation Test Bed which is used to test new embedded power system control and protection methods. Test power systems are implemented in the RTDS and new controller designs are implemented in the cRIO.

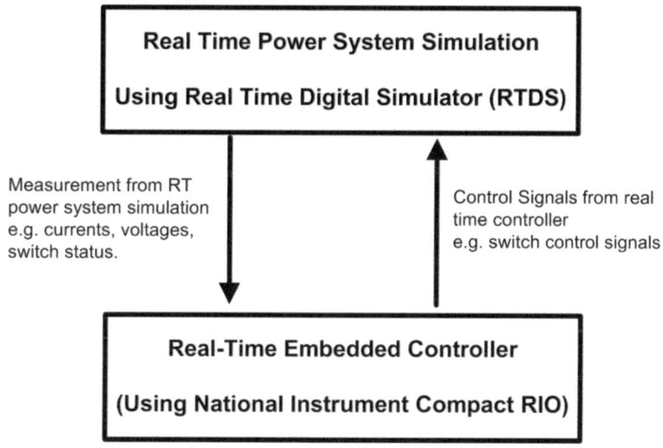

Fig. 1. System Diagram for the Real-Time Rapid Power System Control Prototyping Simulation Test Bed

The test bed is designed based on hardware-in-the-loop (HIL) simulation theory. Hardware-in-the-loop simulation is an approach that is used during the development and testing of complex real-time embedded controller. HIL simulation provides an effective platform by adding the complexity of the plant under control to the test platform. The embedded controller under test interacts with a plant simulation that is a mathematical representation of all related dynamic systems of the plant. HIL simulation includes electrical emulation of sensors and actuators which act as the interface between the plant simulation and the embedded controller under test. The value of each electrically emulated sensor is controlled by the plant simulation and is read by the embedded controller under test. Likewise, this embedded controller outputs actuator control signals based on its control algorithm. Changes in the control signals result in changes to variable values in the plant simulation.

There are several advantages of HIL (Isermann et al., 1999), including

- Designing and testing of the control hardware and software without the need to operate a real process.
- Testing of the effects of faults and failures of system.
- Operating and testing of extreme and dangerous operating conditions.
- Reproducible experiments, frequently repeatable.
- Saving of cost and development time.

For example, HIL simulation can be utilized during the validation of flight controllers (Karpenko & Sepehri, 2006). During the development of flight controllers, their functionality must be tested. The most realistic way is to put the flight controllers in an actual aircraft. In this setting, due to safety and cost issues, the extremely dangerous scenarios cannot be performed, such as engine failure and stalling. However, in HIL simulation, the actual aircraft can be modeled in a real-time simulator and the flight controllers can directly interact with the simulation in real-time. During HIL simulation, all possible scenarios can be performed to test the functionality of the flight controllers without worrying about safety and cost issues. Therefore, a primary benefit of HIL simulation is that by the time the controllers first operate

in the actual system, they will already have undergone a great deal of thorough testing in a realistic simulation environment (Ledin, 2001).
In the Real-Time Embedded Power System Control Rapid Prototyping Simulation Test Bed, a power system is simulated in real-time in RTDS while a controller under test is implemented in NI cRIO. Figure 2 shows the schematic of the major components in the test bed. The host machine has two functions. One is to allow users to write programs for RTDS with RSCAD and programs for cRIO with LabVIEW. The other function is to provide user interface and control of the program execution for RTDS and cRIO.

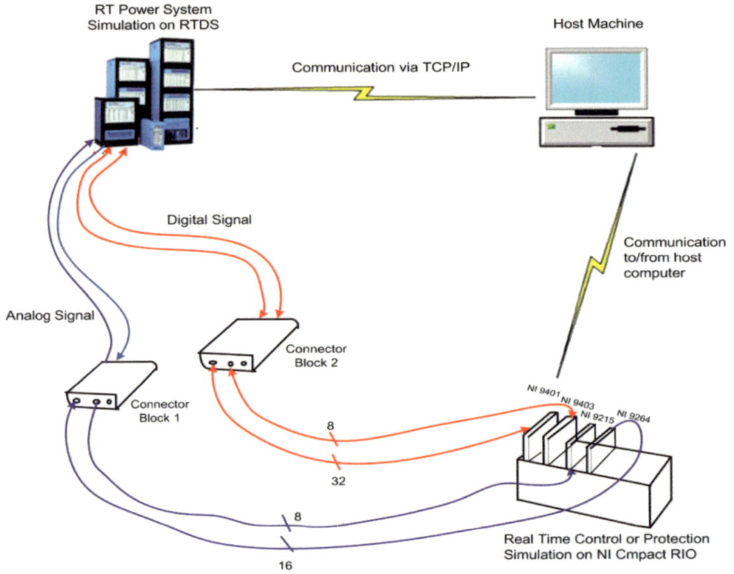

Fig. 2. Schematic of real-time rapid embedded control prototyping simulation test bed

2.1 Real time digital simulator for power system real-time simulation

Real time digital simulator (RTDS), shown in Figure 2, is used to model and simulate power systems in real time. RTDS (*Real Time Digital Simlator - RTDS*, 2011) is a unique integration of hardware and software specifically designed to perform electromagnetic transient simulation of AC and DC power systems. RTDS is a modular system consisting of racks that are parallel. Also it provides high precision real-time input/output interfaces of both analog and digital signals. Detailed information of the input/output module and the processor of RTDS are summarized in Table 1.
The RSCAD software package provides a graphical user interface to write and execute programs in RTDS. RSCAD provides numerous libraries of power system component models as well as control and protection models. RSCAD also provides an interactive run-time interface and allows users to view simulation results and enter or adjust user inputs while the simulation is in progress.

2.2 CompactRIO for rapid control prototyping

The National Instruments CompactRIO (cRIO) low cost reconfigurable control and acquisition system, shown in Figure 2, is an embedded hardware controller, which can be programmed to implement various control and protection methodologies for different applications (*NI*

Component	Detail
GPC × 3	GIGA Processor Card (Solve up to 54 nodes and 56 breakers)
GTDI	Digital Input Module (64 Channels, Sampling rate: 300 ns)
GTDO	Digital Output Module (64 Channels, Updated every time step)
GTAI ×2	Analog Input Module (12 Channels, Sampling rate: 6 μs)
GTAO ×2	Analog Output Module (12 Channels, Sampling rate: 1 μs)
WIF	Workstation Network Card

Table 1. Detailed RTDS hardware information

CompactRIO, 2011). The cRIO System contains four components: Reconfigurable chassis housing the user programmable FPGA; Hot swappable I/O modules; Real-time controller for communication and processing; and Graphical LabVIEW Software for rapid Real Time and FPGA programming.

The cRIO contains reconfigurable technologies (FPGA) and a real-time controller with an embedded floating-point processor (RT processor). The 8-slot reconfigurable chassis contains an embedded user-programmable FPGA (Field Programmable Gate Array) chip providing direct access to hot swappable I/O modules for precise control and flexibility in timing, triggering, and synchronization. In addition to I/O functionalities, FPGA has the computing power which performs integer math operation. Table 2 summarizes the detailed hardware information for the cRIO used in the test bed.

By using LabVIEW RT module and FPGA module, the user can write programs in the LabVIEW programming language on a host PC and then download these programs to the RT processor and the FPGA for execution. In this way, the cRIO can implement various types of new control methodologies with great flexibility.

Component	Detail
NI cRIO 9004	Real-Time Controller (195 MHz Pentium processor, 512 MB CompactFlash, 64 MB DRAM)
NI cRIO-9104	8-Slot, 3M Gate (FPGA) CompactRIO Reconfigurable Embedded Chassis
NI 9215	8 Channel Analog Input Module
NI 9264	16 Channel Analog Output Module
NI 9401	8 Channel Digital Input/ Output Module
NI 9403	32 Channel Digital Input/ Output Module

Table 2. Detailed cRIO hardware information

2.3 Methodology for implementation of embedded controller-in-the-loop simulation

A methodology for implementing controller-in-the-loop (CIL) simulation in the test bed was developed with the major aspects adapted from chapters 3 and 4 in Ledin's book (Ledin, 2001). Chapter 3 focuses on non-real-time simulation of dynamic systems, while Chapter 4 focuses on issues related to real-time hardware-in-the-loop simulation. The CIL simulation methodology has four phases: off-line simulation of full system, real-time implementation of full system, ride-alone (open-loop) simulation, and controller-in-the-loop simulation. Figure 3 shows a flowchart that conveys the steps for the four phases.

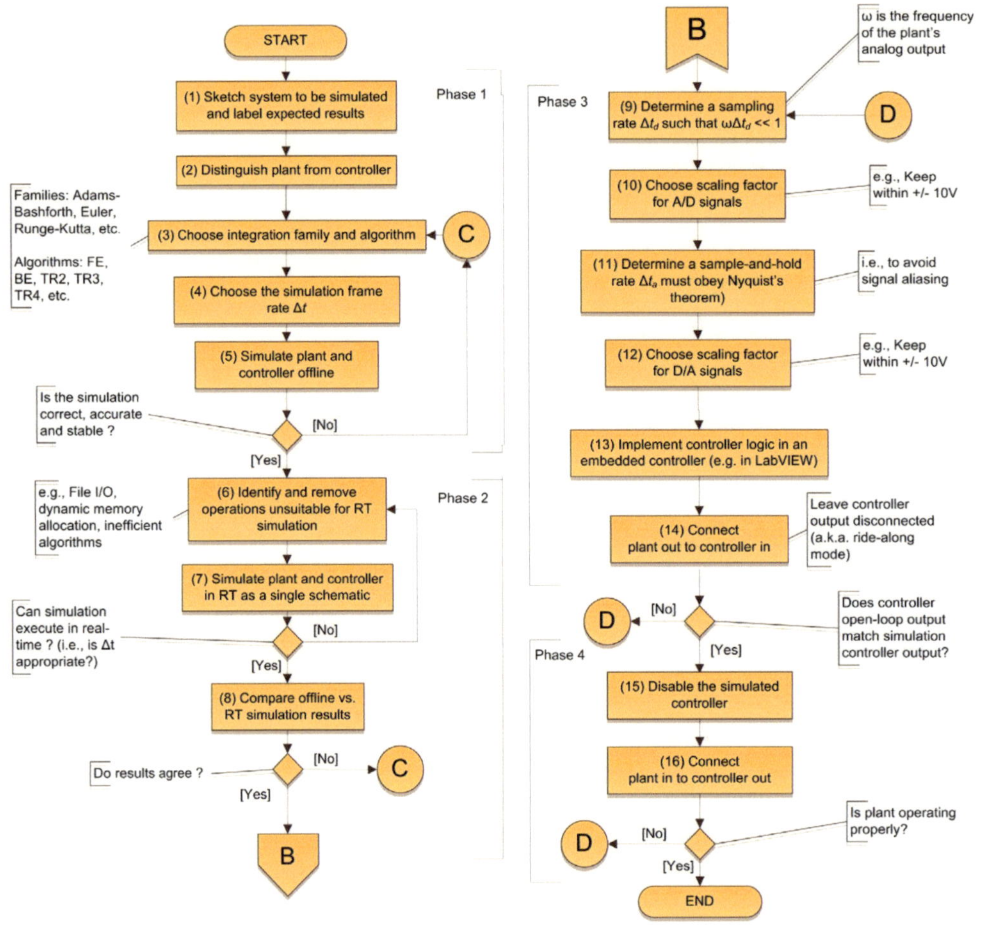

Fig. 3. Procedure of implementing embedded controller-in-the-loop simulation

2.3.1 Phase 1: Offline simulation of full system

In this phase, both the plant and the controller are simulated in a single schematic offline in non-real time by using commercially available software, such as Matlab or PSCAD. An appropriate integration algorithm and simulation step time should be chosen appropriately based on system dynamics. If the simulation results of Phase 1 are correct, the user proceeds to Phase 2.

2.3.2 Phase 2: Real-time implementation of full system

In this phase, both the plant and the controller are simulated in a single schematic in real time using the real-time digital simulation(RTDS) systems .

To convert a simulation from non-real time into real time, operations that are not appropriate for real-time simulation are identified. Some examples are reading or writing disk files, dynamic memory allocation, and inappropriate algorithms with indeterminate execution

time. In addition, the appropriate integration step time based on the system dynamics must be selected. If the time step is too short, the simulation will require more computing power to run in real-time. If the time step is too long, based on Nyquist's theorem, the simulation results will be inaccurate.
The results of Phase 2 and Phase 1 are compared. If the difference is acceptable, the user continues to Phase 3. If the difference is unacceptable, go back to Phase 1 to identify the source of the errors and revise accordingly.

2.3.3 Phase 3: Ride-along mode simulation

In this phase, the actual embedded controller, which was simulated in RTDS in phase 2, is connected to the real-time simulator that models the power system (plant). Input and output interface between the real-time simulator and the embedded controller is set up, including scaling factor, sampling rate, sample-and-hold rate, etc. The control signals from this embedded controller are inputs to the real-time simulator.
These control signals from the embedded controller are not input into the system modelled in the real-time simulator. Instead, the control signals from the simulated controller inside the real-time simulator are input to the modelled system. The purpose of this stage is to compare the control signals from the simulated controller in real-time simulator and that from the embedded controller.
Since the simulated controller will not perfectly represent the actual embedded controller; therefore, in the ride-along mode, we may observe that the response of the actual embedded controller is not actually close to the response of the simulated controller (Ledin, 2001). However, ride-along mode simulation should still give a very good idea of whether or not the controller is operating correctly in this environment. If the difference between these two control signals is acceptable for the application, go to the next and final phase, CIL mode simulation.

2.3.4 Phase 4: CIL mode simulation

With the successful completion of ride-along mode simulation, CIL mode simulation can be performed by using the control signal from the actual embedded controller as input to the real-time simulation. Often the closed loop simulation will work correctly on the first attempt.

3. Case study implementation

A digital protective relay is a protective relay that uses a microprocessor to analyze power system voltages and currents for the purpose of detection of faults in an electric power system. An overcurrent relay discriminates between normal operation and fault operation in a power system. When the current exceeds a specific pickup value, the relay will open the breaker to clear the fault (J. Duncan Glover, 2007). Some of the functions of an overcurrent digital protective relay that are implemented in this case study are listed below.

- The relay applies A/D (analog-to-digital) conversion processes to the incoming currents.
- The relay analyzes the A/D converter output to extract, at a minimum, magnitude of the incoming quantity, commonly using Fourier transform concepts (RMS and some form of averaging are used in basic overcurrent relays).
- The relay applies advanced logic in determining whether the relay should trip or restrain from tripping based on current magnitude, parameters set by the user, relay contact inputs, and the timing and order of event sequences.

A simple two-bus, three-phase power system, whose one-line diagram and detailed information are shown in Figure 4 and Table 3, is implemented in the RTDS. A microprocessor-based overcurrent relay controls the breakers: BRK_A, BRK_B and BRK_C. This overcurrent relay has three current transformers (CT) that measure line current in each of the three phases: $i_a(t)$, $i_b(t)$ and $i_c(t)$. Based on these measurements, the relay logic in the over-current relay will determine the correct value for the control signals that control the breakers. If the RMS value of the line current is higher than the pickup value, the relay logic will open the breaker in the corresponding phases to protect the power system. In this case study, the breaker and CTs are implemented in the RTDS and the relay logic is implemented in the cRIO.

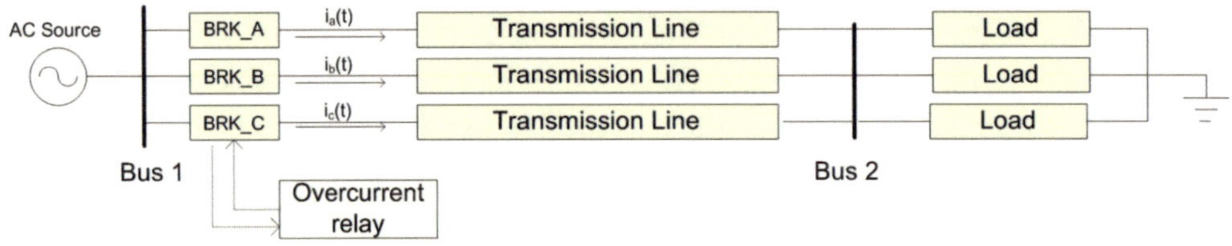

Fig. 4. One line diagram of two-bus, three-phase with overcurrent relay protection

Component	Detail
AC Source	3 Phase, 60 Hz, 2.45 kV (Hz: Hertz, V: Volt)
Transmission Line	66.6 mΩ + 5.3mH (Ω: Ohm, H: Henry)
Load Impedance	21.26mΩ + 10.1mH (Ω: Ohm, H: Henry)
Closed Resistance of Breaker	0.001 Ω
Pickup Value of Overucurrent Relay	0.1 kA (RMS) (A: Amp, RMS: Root Mean Square)

Table 3. Parameters of the simple power system

Figure 5 shows the functional blocks of RTDS and cRIO in CIL simulation. In the RTDS, the power system is modeled and simulated in real time. The RTDS sends to the cRIO three phase current measurements, $i_a(t)$, $i_b(t)$ and $i_c(t)$ via the RTDS analog output (AO) module and sends the triggering signal via the RTDS digital output (DO) module. Based on the current measurements, the RMS calculation block in the FPGA of the cRIO calculates the RMS values of these three current measurements. Based on these RMS values, the relay logic implemented in the RT processor in the cRIO determines the value of the breaker signals. Then the cRIO sends these three breaker signals (BRK_cRIO_A,BRK_cRIO_B,BRK_cRIO_C) back to RTDS via the cRIO digital output (DO) module to RTDS digital input (DI) module to control these three breakers of the simple power system simulation in RTDS.

The program in the FPGA runs at 50 us loop rate while that in the RT processor runs at 5 ms loop rate. The procedure for selecting the loop rates for the FPGA and RT processor will be discussed later in this chapter. Since the loop rates for the FPGA and the RT processor are different, a data buffer: DMA-FIFO is used to transfer data from the FPGA to the RT processor without losing data.

To have a higher chance of having successful CIL simulation, Ledin (Ledin, 2001) recommends that before implementing HIL simulation, it is better to implement ride-along mode simulation. To perform ride-along mode simulation, it requires implementation of identical RMS calculation blocks and over-current relay logic blocks in RTDS and cRIO. In this way, we can compare the breaker signals from RTDS (BRK_Rtds_A, BRK_Rtds_B, BRK_Rtds_C) and that from cRIO (BRK_cRIO_A,BRK_cRIO_B,BRK_cRIO_C). In the ride-along mode, the goal is to determine if the embedded controller simulation is accurate. Figure 6 shows the functional block of RTDS and cRIO in the ride-along mode simulation.

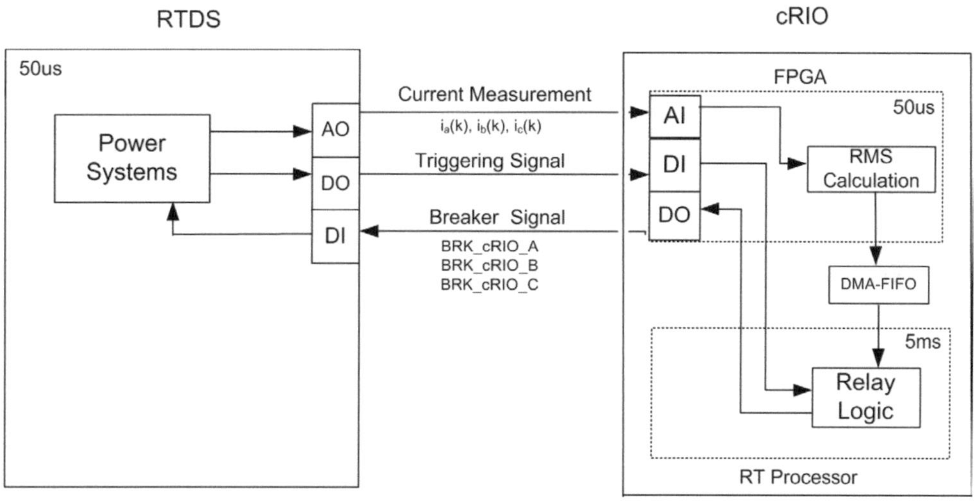

Fig. 5. Functional blocks of RTDS and cRIO in CIL simulation

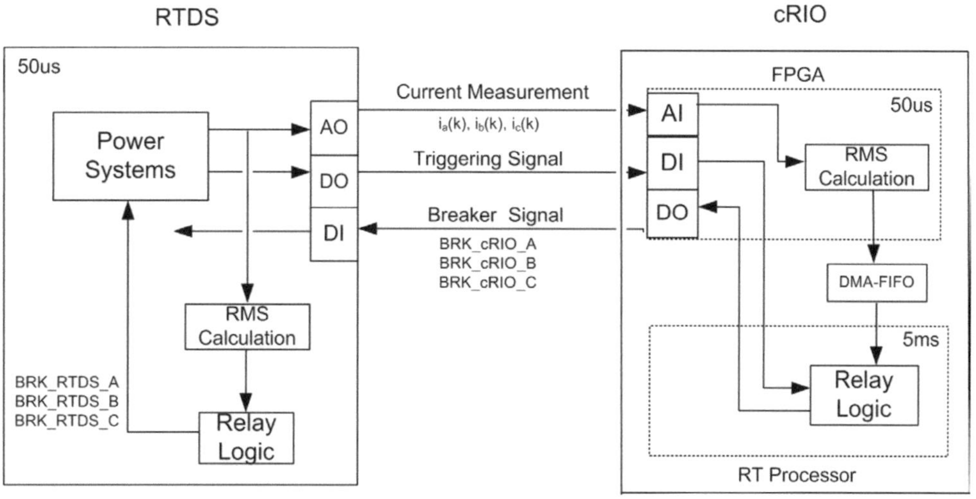

Fig. 6. Functional blocks of RTDS and cRIO in ride-along simulation

In the remainders of this section, a brief description of the implementation of the power system in RTDS will be given. After that, the implementation of overcurrent relay in cRIO, including the program in FPGA and RT processor will be described in detail.

3.1 Brief description of implementation in RTDS

In RTDS, the simulation time step is fixed at 50 us. Figure 7 shows the simple two-bus, three-phase power system implemented in RTDS, while Figure 8(a) shows the analog output module that sends the three current measurements to cRIO, (b) shows the digital input module that receives the breaker signals and one debugging signal from cRIO, and (c) shows the digital output module that sends the triggering signal and one cRIO program control signal to cRIO.

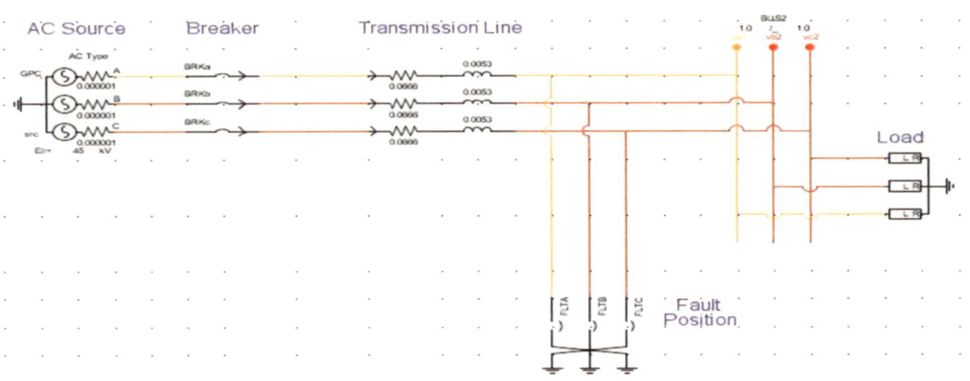

Fig. 7. Circuit diagram in RTDS

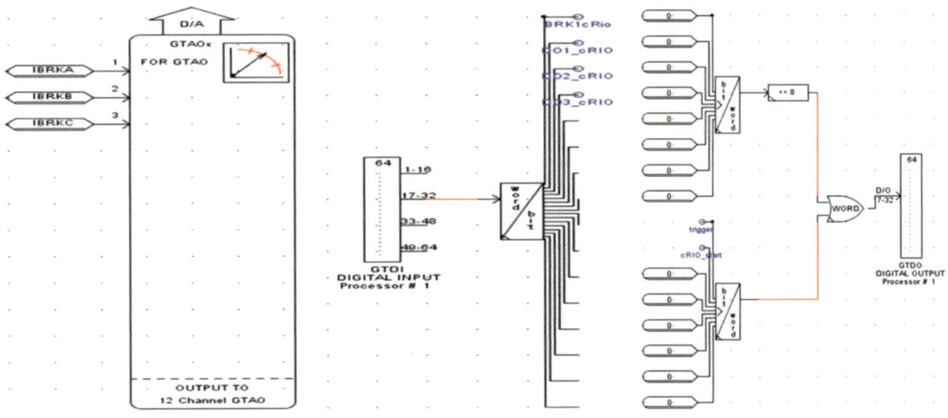

(a) Analog output (AO) (b) Digital input (DI) (c) Digital output (DO)

Fig. 8. Input and output modules in RTDS

Table 4 summarizes the detailed description and settings of the I/O modules of RTDS. In the setting of the analog output module, the value of scaling factor should be set according to the range of the current measurements. In this power system, the maximum fault current is found to be 2000A. To make best use of the whole range of the analog output module of RTDS, whose maximum voltage is 10V, the scaling factor should be "5 Volt for 1 Unit". This is because when the current is 2000A, the amp meter will read 2 units. Based on the specified scaling factor, the analog output module of RTDS will output its maximum voltage: 10 V. This scaling factor should be kept in mind when we write VI program for cRIO so that cRIO can interpret the voltage correctly.

I/O module	Variable	Setting
Analog Output	$i_a(t), i_b(t), i_c(t)$	GTAO Card Number:2 GPC GTIO Fiber Port Number:1 D/A Output Scaling: 5Volt for 1 Unit Oversampling Factor:1 Advance Factor:1
Digital Input	BRK_cRIO_A BRK_cRIO_B BRK_cRIO_C	GTDI Card Number:1 GPC GTIO Fiber Port Number:2
Digital Output	Trig	GTDO Card Number:1 GPC GTIO Fiber Port Number:2

Table 4. Settings of I/O module of RTDS

3.2 Description of implementation of over-current relay in cRIO

In the cRIO, there are two parts that have computing power: FPGA and RT processor. The VI programs in these two parts run simultaneously. The VI in the FPGA is responsible for input/output functions and the RMS calculation of the current measurement signals from the RTDS. The VI in the RT processor is responsible for the relay-logic implementation and user interface. The relay logic makes the decision based on the RMS calculation from the FPGA and updates the breaker signals that are sent to FPGA to be output at the digital output module. In the remainder of this section, detailed description of VIs in the FPGA and in the RT processor will be described.

3.2.1 FPGA

There are two tasks performed in the FPGA. One is the input/output functions, while the other is calculation of the RMS values of current measurements and writing of RMS values into FIFO. Figure 9 shows the flowchart of the program in FPGA. Some initialization (Step A1, A2 and B1) is performed before the execution of the main program (Step A3, A4 and B2). Figure 10 shows the VI implemented in the FPGA.

3.2.1.1 Calibrate analog input module (Step A1 in Figure 9)

Since the analog input module returns a binary value, which is the uncalibrated representation of the voltage as a signed 32-bit integer (I32), we need to convert this binary value into a calibrated nominal value. Therefore, before using the analog input module, we need to get the calibration data that is read from the input analog module. The calibration data includes LSB weight and Offset. These values are used to convert the binary value into the nominal value by Equation 1 (NI, 2004).

$$\text{Nominal value} = [(\text{Binary Value} \times \text{LSB Weight}) - \text{Offset}] \times 10^{-9} \quad (1)$$

3.2.1.2 Allocate FIFO_RMS (Step A2 in Figure 9)

An iterative algorithm of RMS calculation is used, so it is necessary to have one period of the three-phase current measurements. These measurements are stored in three FIFOs, which

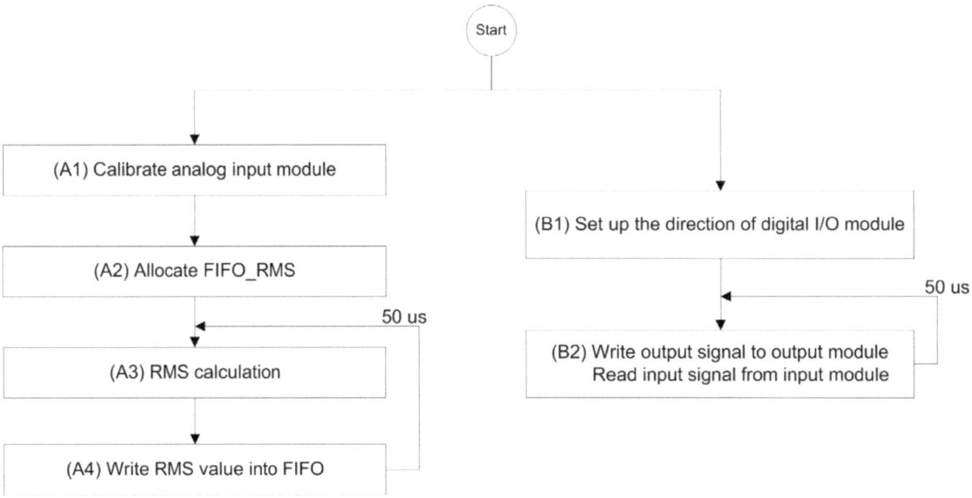

Fig. 9. Flowchart for FPGA VI, shown in Figure 10

are called FIFO_RMS_A, FIFO_RMS_B and FIFO_RMS_C. The following settings are used, including (1) memory type, (2) data representation, and (3) number of elements in FIFOs. The type of FIFO is a look-up table since it takes less space in FPGA. The representation of the FIFO is set to be I32 since the output of the analog input module is I32. Since the frequency of the current measurements is 60 Hz and the sampling rate is 50us, which is the same as the loop rate at which FPGA is running, the number of elements N in FIFO_RMS is determined by Equation 2.

$$N = \frac{\text{Period}}{\text{Sampling Rate}} = \frac{1/60}{50 \times 10^{-6}} = 333.333 \approx 334 \tag{2}$$

3.2.1.3 RMS calculation (Step A3 in Figure 9)

There are two steps in RMS calculation. The first step is to convert the voltage value read from the analog input module of the cRIO into the correct current value. The second step is to compute the RMS value of the current value using an iterative RMS calculation algorithm.

Step 1: Convert the voltage into current value

An uncalibrated binary value is read from the analog input module of cRIO. To convert this binary value into the nominal value, Equation 1 is used. To get the corresponding current value, the nominal value from Equation 1 is multiplied by a scaling factor, shown in Equation 3. The scaling factor in RTDS makes it output 10 V signal on its analog output module when the current measurement is 2 kA. Therefore 1 V sensed by the cRIO's analog input module means that the corresponding current is 200 A. In other words,the scaling factor of cRIO is 200.

$$\text{Current Value} = \text{Nominal Value} \times \text{Scaling Factor} \tag{3}$$

Since the maximum number for signed 32 bits representation is $2,147,483,647 \cong 2.147 \times 10^9$ (NI, 2004), it is important to make sure the mathematical operation does not overflow. If the operation overflows, the result of the mathematical operation will be incorrect. To make sure the operation does not overflow, LabVIEW provides some operations with an overflow flag. The flag, which can be connected to indicators, will be one if the operation overflows. It is a

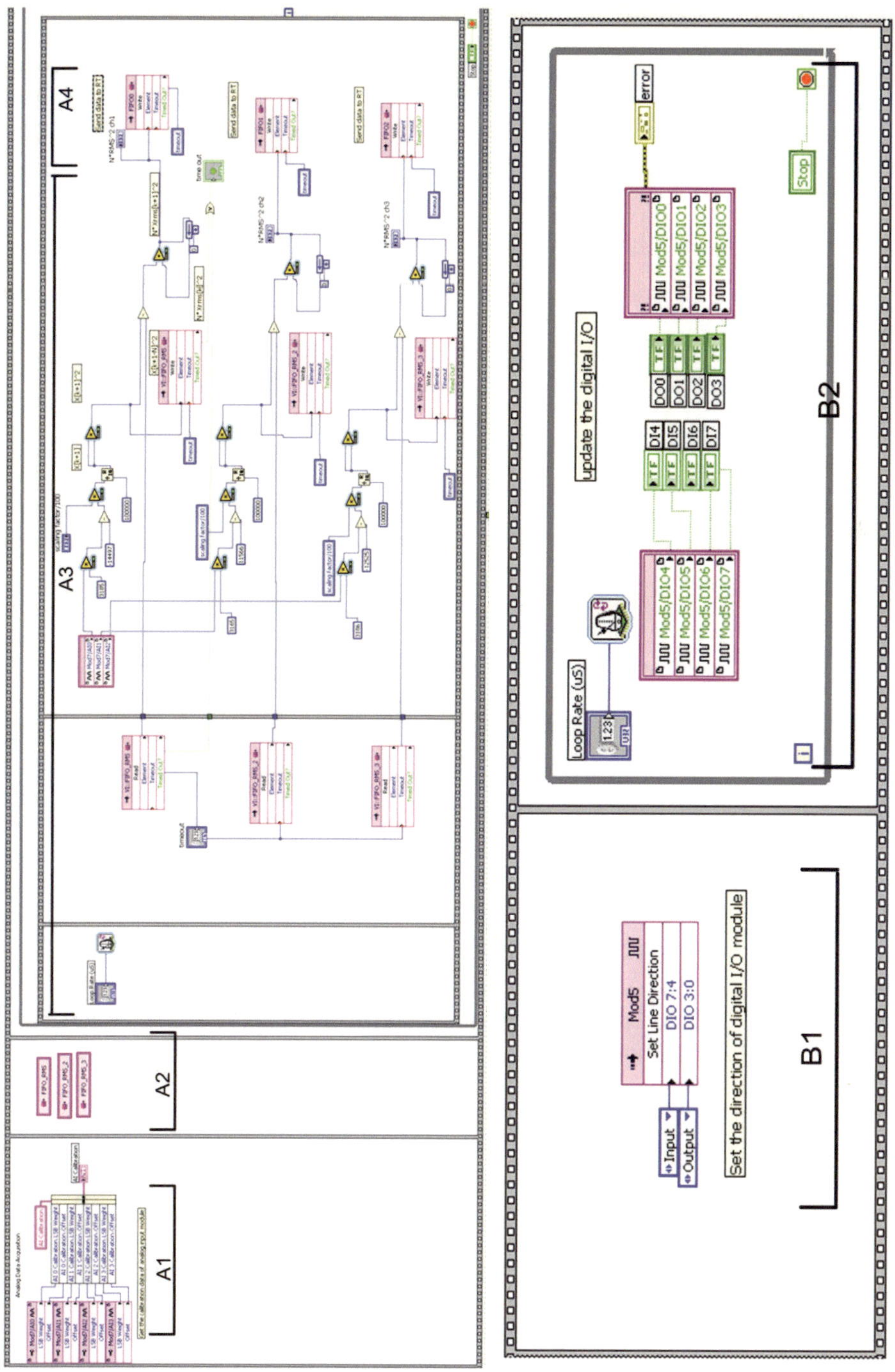

Fig. 10. VI in the FPGA

good practice to check this flag when implementing a program. When you are sure that there is no overflow from the mathematical operations, these overflow indicators can be removed to reduce the FPGA space.
The range of the current measurements is between 20A and 2000A in this simple power system; therefore, the output voltage of RTDS is from 0.1V to 10 V. The corresponding range of the binary value from the analog input module of cRIO is between 327.67 to 32767. To prevent the overflow when Equation 3 is implemented, some arrangements of this equation were made:

$$\begin{aligned}\text{Current Value} &= [\text{Binary Value} \times \text{LSB Weight} - \text{Offset}] \times 10^{-9} \times \text{Scaling Factor} \\ &= [\text{Binary Value} \times \text{LSB Weight} - \text{Offset}] \times 10^{-2} \times 10^{-7} \times \text{Scaling Factor} \\ &= [\text{Binary Value} \times \text{LSB Weight} - \text{Offset}] \times 10^{-2} \times 10^{-5} \times \frac{\text{Scaling Factor}}{100} \\ &= [\text{Binary Value} \times (\text{LSB Weight} \times 10^{-2}) - \text{Offset} \times 10^{-2}] \times 10^{-5} \times \frac{\text{Scaling Factor}}{100}\end{aligned} \tag{4}$$

Figure 11 shows the program that implements the last equation in Equation 4, where the value 318506 is the LSB weight while -1449794 is the offset, both of which are calibration data.

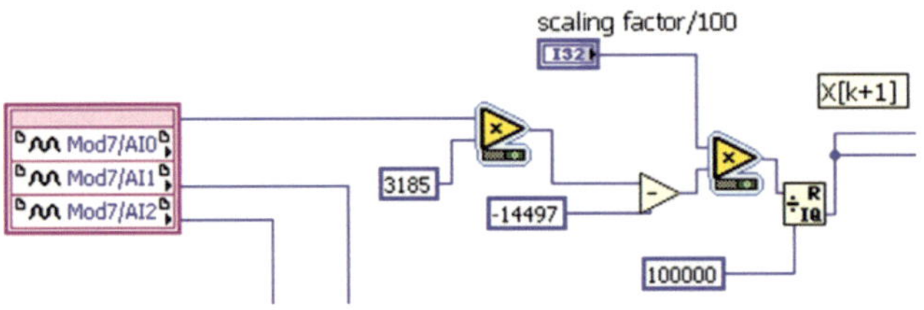

Fig. 11. Program to convert binary value into current value

Step 2: Iterative RMS Calculation

Equation 5 shows the iterative RMS calculation algorithm used in this program. N is the number of elements in the calculation window, x_{rms}^{k+1} is the new RMS value of next time step, x_{rms}^{k} is the present RMS value, x^{k+1} is the new current value, x^{k+1-N} is the current value that is N time steps ago. Since the division operation takes lots of space (slice) of FPGA and time to execute, the formula is converted from Equation 5 to Equation 6 to reduce the number of operations.

$$(x_{rms}^{k+1})^2 = \frac{(x^{k+1})^2 - (x^{k+1-N})^2}{N} + (x_{rms}^{k})^2 \tag{5}$$

$$N(x_{rms}^{k+1})^2 = (x^{k+1})^2 - (x^{k+1-N})^2 + N(x_{rms}^{k})^2 \tag{6}$$

From Equation 6, $N(x_{rms}^{k+1})^2$ is calculated and written into DMA-FIFO, which will be discussed next. So instead of using pickup value of x_{rms}^{k+1}, the pickup value of $N(x_{rms}^{k+1})^2$ is used in over-current relay logic, which is implemented in RT processor.
One point worth discussion is that the mathematical operation in FPGA is integer operation, so the fraction part of a number will be truncated, resulting in some errors. However, as seen from the formula implemented, the integer operation is operated on a large number (the smallest input voltage is 327.68), therefore, the error percentage is very low, less than 1%.

3.2.1.4 Write RMS value into FIFO (Step A4 in Figure 9)

As mentioned before, the speed of FPGA is much faster than that of RT processor. In this case, the loop rate of FPGA is 50 us while the loop rate of RT processor is 5 ms. In order to transfer data (RMS of current value) from FPGA to RT processor without losing data, another FIFO is used. FPGA will put one current RMS value into the FIFO every 50 us, while the RT processor will retrieve data from the FIFO every 5 ms. The number of data that the RT processor takes each time is 100 $[= (5ms)/(50us)]$.
The function of this FIFO is different from that of FIFO_RMS. FIFO_RMS is used to store one period of current values to calculate the RMS value of current measurements, while this FIFO is used as a buffer between the FPGA and the RT processor due to their different execution speeds. Since there are three RMS values of three-phase current value, three FIFOs are used.
To allocate these FIFOs, go to the "Project Explorer", right click on "FPGA Target", select "New"-> "FIFO". Then the properties of FIFO are set: "Target-to-Host DMA" is used and the depth is 255, which is the number of elements of FIFO in FPGA part. (The number of elements of FIFO in RT processor is set in RT program, which will be discussed later in this book chapter) DMA is the abbreviation of Direct Memory Access, which transfers data from the FPGA directly to the memory on the RT processor. A DMA-FIFO consists of two parts, an FPGA part and RT processor part. LabVIEW uses a DMA engine to connect these two parts. When the DMA engine runs, it transfers data between the two parts of the FIFO automatically so they act as one FIFO array. For more information on DMA-FIFO, please refer to Lesson 8, Section F in (NI, 2004). After the DMA-FIFO is set, the value to be passed into RT processor can be written into DMA-FIFO by using FIFO Write function.

3.2.1.5 Set up the direction of digital I/O module (Step B1 in Figure 9)

Because the channels in the digital I/O module (NI 9401 or NI 9403) can be set as either input or output, the input and output channels must be specified.

3.2.1.6 Update the value of digital I/O module (Step B2 in Figure 9)

A while-loop is used to update the value of the digital I/O module. Controllers (DO0, DO1, DO2, DO3) are connected to the output ports of the digital I/O module while indicators (DI4, DI5, DI6, DI7) are connected to the input ports of the digital I/O module.
To be able to run this FPGA VI, this VI needs to be compiled into FPGA code. For detailed information of FPGA compilation, please refer to Lesson 4, Section I in (NI, 2004). To start the execution of this VI, you can hit the RUN button in the LabVIEW window; however in this project, the VI in the RT processor controls the execution of this FPGA VI, including start, stop as well as parameter settings, such as loop rate and scaling factor.

3.2.2 RT processor

There are two functions implemented in RT processor. One function is overcurrent relay logic, shown on the left side of Figure 12. The other function is user interface and parameter settings via front panel communication, shown on the right side of Figure 12. The first function is in the time-critical loop while the second function is in a non-time-critical loop. The reason we separate the VI into two timed-loops is to prioritize these two different functions.

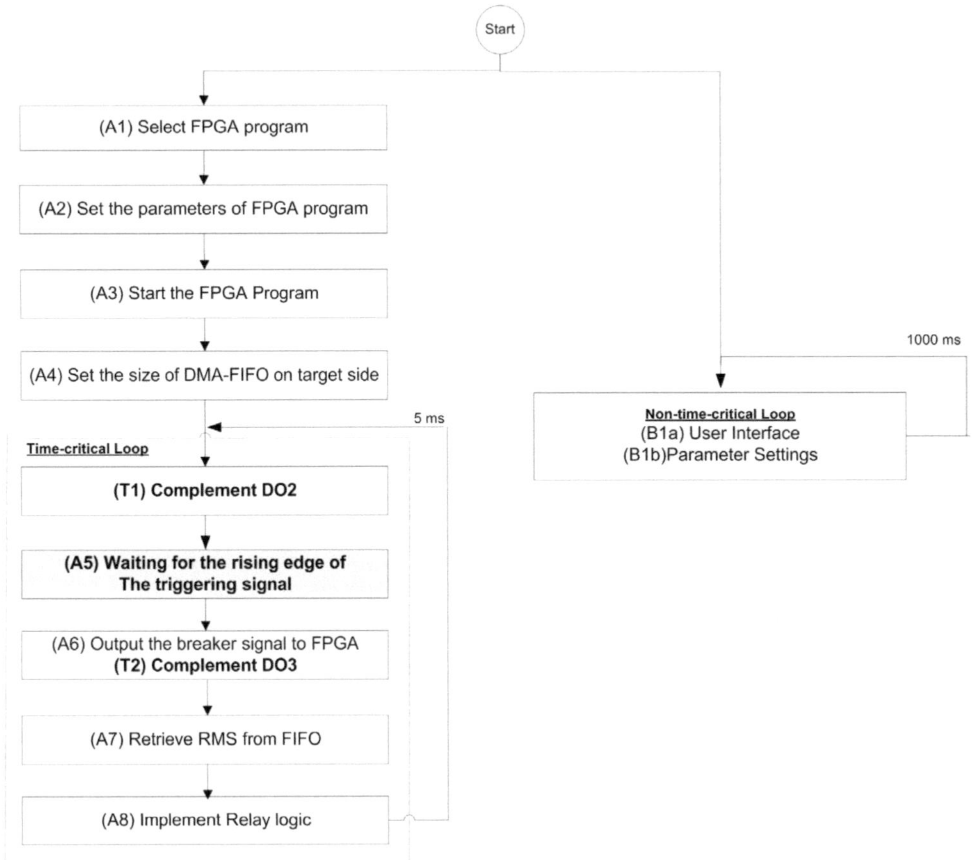

Fig. 12. Flowchart of RT processor VI, , shown in Figure 13

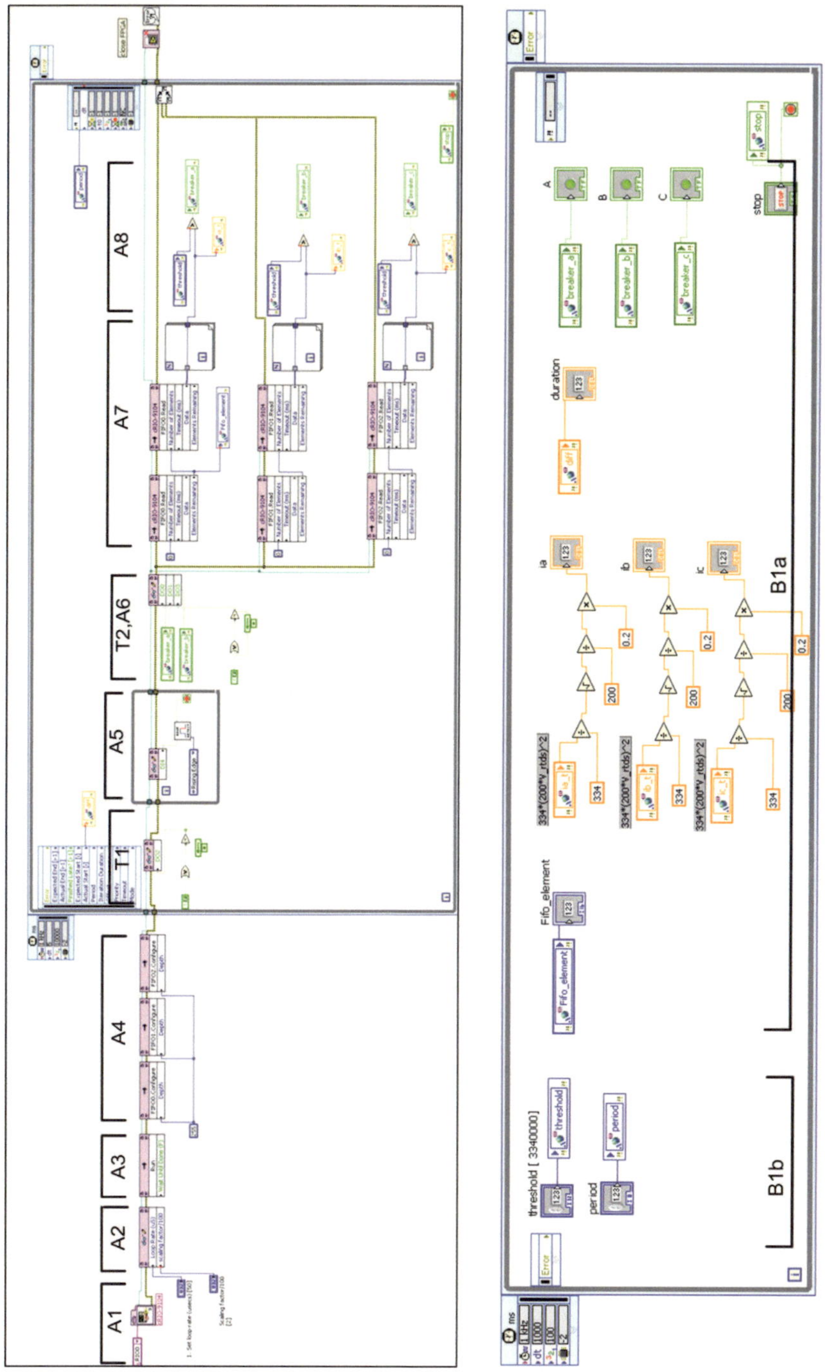

(a) Time-critical loop (b) Non-time-critical loop

Fig. 13. VI in the RT processor

It is possible to put the above two functions in the same timed-loop. However, since front-panel communication takes care of the user interface, such as displaying value in the host-PC screen and sending control value from host-PC to cRIO, it takes time to execute. More importantly, the time it takes is not deterministic. Therefore, to make the over-current relay logic deterministic, two timed-loops with different priorities are used. The time-critical loop with higher priority includes the over-current relay logic while the non-time-critical loop with lower priority includes user interface and parameter settings. Therefore, the RT processor resource will be given to the time-critical loop whenever this time-critical loop needs the resource. Only when time-critical loop doesn't need the resource, will the non-time-critical loop use the resource. In this way, the program implemented in the time-critical loop can be ensured to run deterministically. For more information about the concept of time-critical loop, please refer to Lesson 3 in (NI, 2009) .

Figure 13 shows the VI implemented in the RT processor. Part(a) is the program that includes the initialization and the time-critical loop while part(b) includes the non-time-critical loop.

3.2.2.1 Select FPGA program (Step A1 in Figure 12)

Figure 14(a) shows the program that selects the desired FPGA VI to be executed. The selected file is a FGPA bitfile, which is generated after the FPGA VI is compiled.

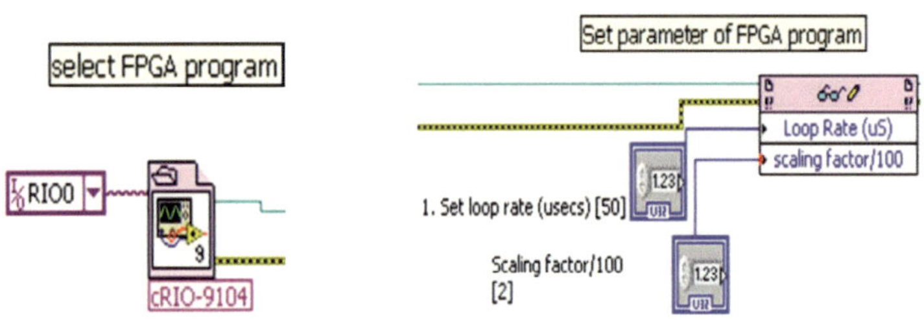

Fig. 14. (a)Select FPGA program, (b)set the parameters of FPGA VI

3.2.2.2 Set the parameters of FPGA program (Step A2 in Figure 12)

Some parameters of the FPGA VI, including the loop rate of FPGA and the scaling factor, are set by the program shown in Figure 14(b). Therefore, users can use the front panel to set these parameters of FPGA VI.

3.2.2.3 Start the FPGA program (Step A3 in Figure 12)

Figure 15(a) shows the program that starts the FPGA VI execution.

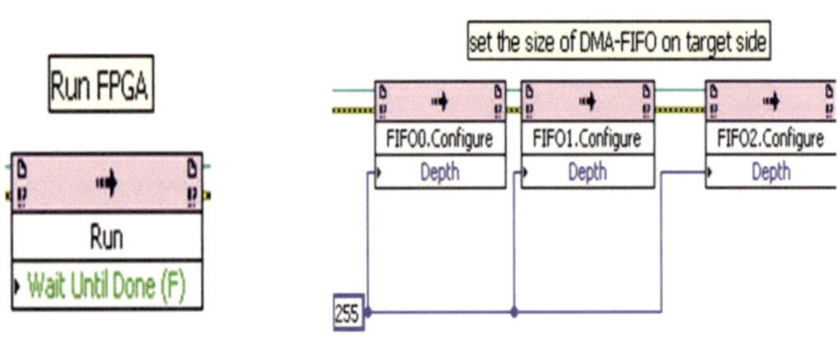

Fig. 15. (a)Run FPGA program, (b)set the FIFO size on target side

3.2.2.4 Set the size of DMA-FIFO on target side (Step A4 in Figure 12)

As mentioned, there are two parts of DMA-FIFO. One is in the FPGA and the other is in the RT processor. The size of DMA-FIFO in the FPGA is set in the FPGA program while the size of DMA-FIFO in the RT processor is set by using the function shown in Figure 15(b). If the size of DMA-FIFO in RT processor side is not specified, then the system will automatically set the size to be twice the size of the DMA-FIFO in the FPGA. Care must be made when determining the size of DMA-FIFO. If the size is too small, the DMA-FIFO tends to be full and data cannot be written into the DMA-FIFO. If the size is too big, it will waste memory space.

3.2.2.5 Waiting for the rising edge of the triggering signal (Step A5 in Figure 12)

Since the clock rates of RTDS and cRIO are different, there should be some mechanism such that the program in RTDS and the program in cRIO do not run out of step. In other words, there needs to be something used to make the two programs proceed together in time.
Using real-time programming concept, the time-critical loop can run in real-time and deterministically. So why do we need to use triggering signal? Because even if we can run the program in the RT processor deterministically, say it runs every 5 ms, it is still possible that in the time frame of RTDS, the program in RT processor runs every 5.001 ms. This is because the accuracy of clock rate of cRIO and RTDS are not exactly the same. Even though the difference is very small, in some applications, this difference may accumulate to cause some problems. Since RTDS is running in real time, the difference will accumulate quickly. Further discussion of triggering signal will be given in the last part of this section.
Figure 16(a) shows the rising edge detection. If the rising edge of the triggering signal is not detected, the program will stay in this while loop. When the rising edge of the triggering signal is detected, the program will leave the while loop and go to the next stage.

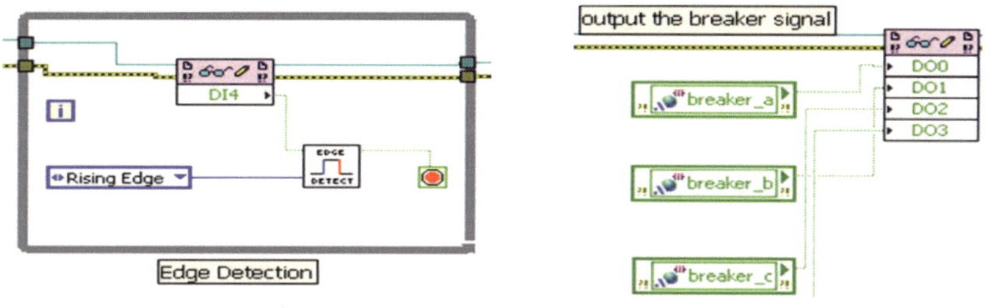

Fig. 16. (a)Rising edge detection of triggering signal, (b)output the breaker control signals

3.2.2.6 Output the breaker signal to FPGA (Step A6 in Figure 12)

Figure 16(b) shows that the breaker control signal is output to the digital output channel DO0, DO1 and DO2. This signal is based on the result of the previous iteration which is 5 ms ago, the loop rate of RT program.

3.2.2.7 Retrieve RMS data from DMA-FIFO(Step A7 in Figure 12)

Figure 17 shows the program of retrieving data (RMS of current value) from the DMA-FIFO. Since the execution speed of RT processor is much slower than that of the FPGA (the loop rate of RT processor is 5 ms while the loop rate of FPGA is 50 us), to prevent this DMA-FIFO from overflowing, the program in RT processor should retrieve all data in the DMA-FIFO each time.

There are two steps to retrieve all data in the DMA-FIFO. First, the left function block in the Figure 17(a) gets the number of elements in the DMA-FIFO and passes this number to the "Number of Elements" of the right function block. The right function block reads "Number of Elements" number of data from DMA-FIFO and transfers it to "Data" as an array. Since the data from DMA-FIFO is an array and only the latest data($N \times RMS^2$)is needed, a for-loop without the N value specified as shown in Figure 17(b) was used.

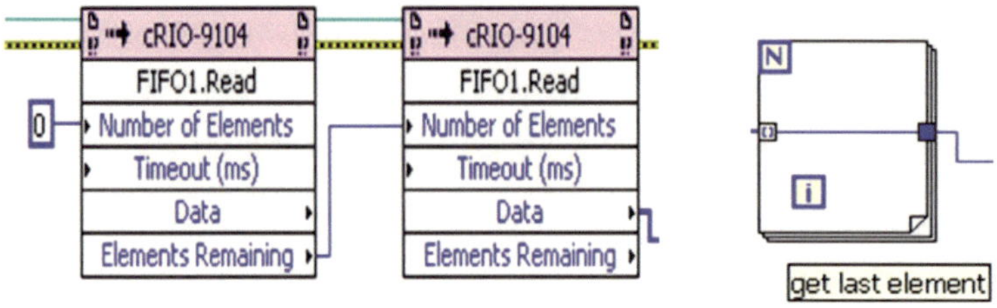

Fig. 17. (a)Retrieve data block in FIFO, (b)get the last element of data block

3.2.2.8 Implement relay logic (Step A8 in Figure 12)

Figure 18 shows the implementation of the overcurrent relay logic, which updates the breaker signal. The retrieved $N \times RMS^2$ value is compared with the threshold (pickup) value. Since the retrieved data is $N \times RMS^2$, the threshold value is also in the same format. In this example, the threshold current is 0.1 kA, so based on the scaling factor of RTDS, the output voltage is 0.5 V. Since the scaling factor of cRIO is 200 and N is 334., the threshold value is 3,340,000, which is equal to $334 \times (200 \times 0.5)^2$. If the retrieved $N \times RMS^2$ value is higher than the threshold value, the breaker signal will be equal to one (open value). Otherwise, the breaker signal will be zero (closed value). Note that this breaker signal is updated, but is not output to the digital output module via FPGA. The new breaker signal is output in the step A6 of next iteration of the time-critical loop.

Fig. 18. Comparison with threshold value

3.2.2.9 Implementation in non-time-critical loop (Step B1 in Figure 12)

Below are the tasks for non-time-critical loop:

1. Send the settings of VI from the host PC to the RT processor via front panel communication, including threshold value, period of time-critical loop, and loop rate of time-critical-loop.
2. Send the results of VI to the host PC, including breaker status, time duration of time-critical loop, RMS value of current, number of FIFO elements.
3. Convert $(N \times V_{RMS})^2$ to actual RMS value of current value.

3.2.2.10 Communication between time-critical and non-time critical loops

The signal passing between the time-critical loop and the non-time-critical loop is done via "Shared Variable". The type of this shared variable is set to be "Single-Process", since these two timed-loops are in the same single process.
Since the period of these two timed-loops is different, like the situation where there is FPGA and RT processor, to pass data without loss, FIFO mechanism should be used. Since we just care about the newest data, then FIFO with "single element" is used. To pass multiple data lossless, the FIFO with "multi-element" is used and the number of elements of this FIFO is based on the loop rate of these two timed loops. These settings are done in the "Properties Dialog" of shared variables.

3.2.2.11 How to measure the timing of signal (Step T1, T2 in Figure 12)

cRIO and RTDS execute in real time, so it is impossible to store all the simulation results, making it difficult to debug the program. To check whether the program is executed as expected, especially the timing of the program, we can take advantage of the digital output module of the cRIO as well as the RTDS plotting function.
Figure 19 shows one block of program in the RT processor. This block of program complements the digital output channel DO1 when it is executed. We can place this program around the place of which we want to check the timing. In this VI, we complement DO2 in the beginning of the time-critical loop and complement DO3 when the rising edge of the triggering signal is detected.
To measure these timing signals from the digital output module of the cRIO, we can use oscilloscopes that have limited numbers of channels. Another way is to use RTDS that can plot signals from its digital input module. In this way, we can overlay these numerous timing signals in the same plot and check the timing of the RT program. Moreover, it is possible to store a portion of data points in the plot of RTDS. RTDS greatly facilitates the investigation of these timing signals.

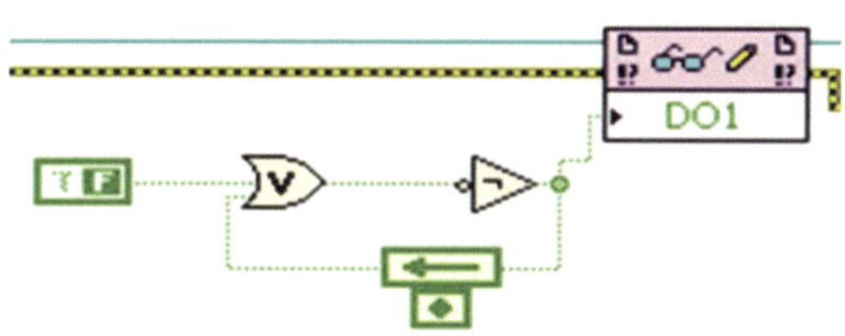

Fig. 19. Complement the digital output when executed

3.3 Discussion of synchronization of RTDS and cRIO

The benefit of outputting the breaker control signals at the rising edge of the triggering signal is that only at the rising edge of the triggering signal can the breaker control signals be output. The breaker control signal cannot be output at other times.
Even though there are some benefits of implementing this synchronization technique, there are some disadvantages. Since each iteration of the time-critical loop in RT processor needs to wait for the rising edge of the triggering signal, it slows down the response of the embedded controller. This amount of the time delay varies, depending on the phase difference between the triggering signal and the time-critical loop. It also depends on the frequency of the triggering signal. If this frequency is low, the time-critical loop will take longer time to wait

for the rising edge of triggering signal. However, if the frequency is too high, then EMI issues will occur. Therefore, the frequency of the triggering signal needs to be selected carefully. In this case study, 1 kHz is selected.
However, if this small time difference is acceptable and doesn't cause any problems for the application, it is not necessary to implement this synchronization technique. This embedded controller will have quicker response.

4. Case studies

In these case studies, a three-phase ground fault was applied at the end of the transmission line as shown in Figure 20. When this fault occurs, the value of the phase currents $i_a(t)$, $i_b(t)$ and $i_c(t)$, and corresponding RMS values increase. As soon as the RMS value was larger than the pickup value of the overcurrent relay, the overcurrent relay would open the breaker to protect the system.

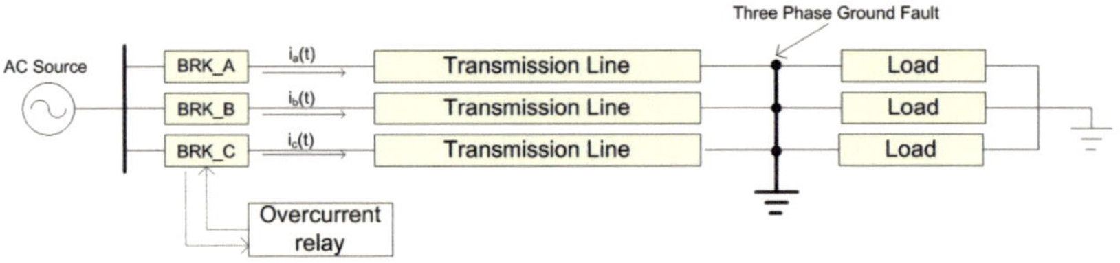

Fig. 20. One-line diagram of system with three-phase ground fault

The loop rate of FPGA was selected to be 50 us, which was the same as the time step in RTDS. The loop rate of the RT processor was selected to be as fast as possible, while at the same time permitting the time-critical loop to run deterministically. Therefore, this loop rate would depend on the computing power of RT processor as well as the complexity of the RT processor VI. In these case studies, three cases where the period of the RMS calculation window was half cycle, one cycle and two cycle, respectively, were compared. For the half cycle, a period is 8.33 ms, for one cycle, a period is 16.66 ms and for two cycle, a period is 33.33 ms. For the half-cycle and one-cycle case, the loop rate of RT processor was 5 ms while for the two-cycle case, the loop rate was 10 ms. This was because in the two-cycle case, the amount of data was larger, requiring more time for RT processor to execute.
The first case study was a modified ride-along mode. The overcurrent relay was implemented in the RTDS and the cRIO. The purpose of ride-along mode is to compare breaker control signals from each overcurrent relays program and see if they are equivalent for determining the accuracy of the implementation.
To ensure that both overcurrent relays observed the same dynamics, the breakers in the RTDS were always closed even when the fault was applied, which was a modified version of the ride-along mode shown in Figure 6. This was done because if one of the overcurrent relays responded first and opened the breaker, the current would decrease, making the other slower overcurrent relay unable to detect the fault. Therefore the breaker signals from this slower overcurrent relay remained closed. The comparison between these two breaker signals would not be right, invalidating the results of ride-along simulation. Therefore, a modified-ride-along mode was used, where the control signals from RTDS and cRIO were not used to control the breaker in RTDS. The breakers were always closed in these studies.
Figure 21 shows the response around the time when the fault was applied. Table 5 summarizes three cases where the window size of RMS calculation were different. The time difference

between the breaker signals from RTDS and cRIO was a little more than the loop rate of the RT processor. The loop rate was 5 ms for half cycle and one cycle windows while the loop rate was 10 ms for two cycle window. This was because when the window size of RMS calculation is two cycles, the number of elements in FIFO_RMS were twice the size of one cycle case, requiring more time to retrieve the data for cRIO computation. Therefore, the loop rate of RT processor had to be increased to ensure deterministic operation.

Another observation was that when the RMS calculation window was smaller, the time difference between fault and breaker signal was smaller since the RMS calculation was more sensitive if its calculation window was small.

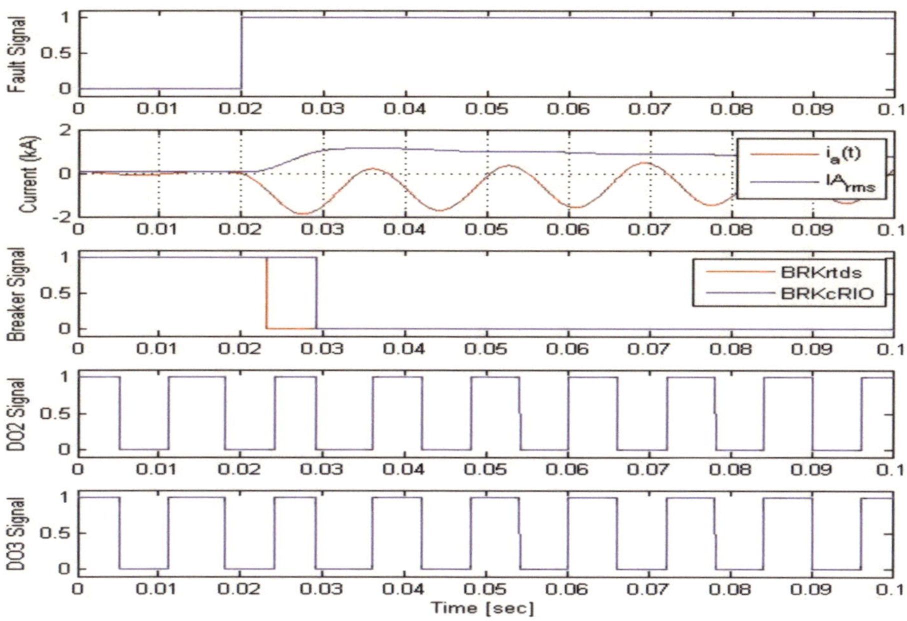

Fig. 21. Response in modified-ride-along mode to a fault scenario

Signals \ RMS window size	0.5 cycle	1 cycle	2 cycle
Fault and BRK_RTDS	0.0043 sec	0.0051 sec	0.0053 sec
Falut and BRK_cRIO	0.0104 sec	0.0102 sec	0.0159 sec
BRK_RTDS and BRK_cRIO	0.0060 sec	0.0051 sec	0.0106 sec

Table 5. Time difference among signals for three RMS calculation window in modified-ride-along mode

The second set of case studies was CIL mode. The overcurrent relay implemented in RTDS was disabled and the breaker signals from cRIO controlled the breakers implemented in RTDS. Figure 22 shows the waveform around the time when a three-phase ground fault was applied. It can be observed that the breaker signals from cRIO successfully opened the breakers after the fault occurred. The time difference between the fault occurrence and the opening of the breaker was approximately 10 ms in each phase which was two times the loop rate of RT processor. Like the first set of case studies, if the window size of RMS calculation was smaller, it took less time to open the breaker after fault was applied, which is shown in Table 6.

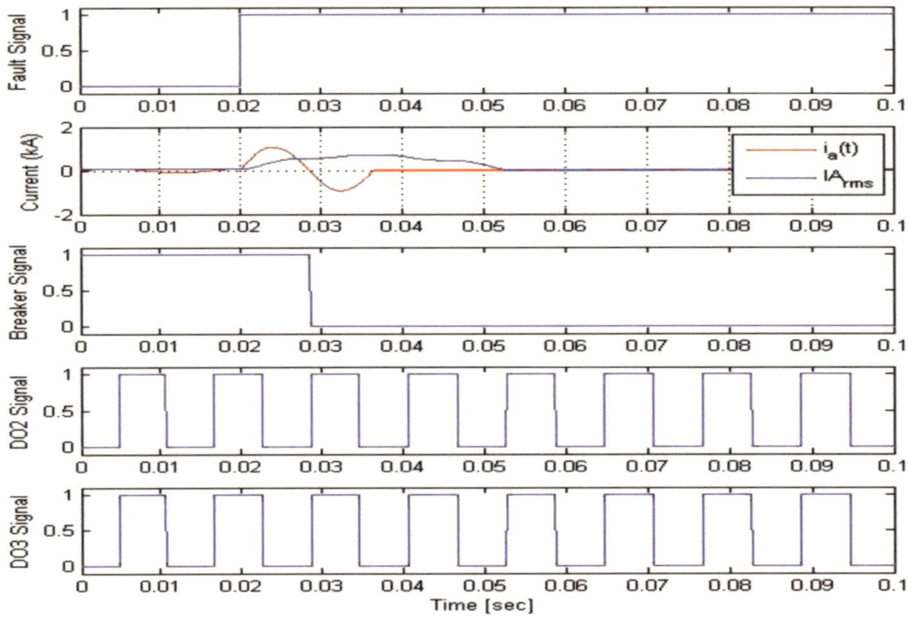

Fig. 22. Response in CIL mode to a fault scenario

RMS window size / Signals	0.5 cycle	1 cycle	2 cycle
Fault and BRK	0.01034 sec	0.0111 sec	0.016 sec

Table 6. Time difference among signals for three RMS calculation window in CIL

The results of a timing analysis of the measured signals from the modified-ride-along mode simulation are shown in Figure 23. Since the breaker signal (BRK_RTDS) from the overcurrent relay in RTDS is updated when the time-critical loop starts (when DO2 changes its polarity), the difference between the fault signal and BRK_RTDS is T_1. The breaker control signal from the overcurrent relay in cRIO (BRK_cRIO) is updated when there is a rising edge during the execution of time-critical loop (when DO3 changes its polarity), therefore the difference between the fault signal and BRK_cRIO is $T_1 + T_2$. Sometimes it may take an extra loop iteration for the RMS value to be greater than the pickup value, so the difference maybe $T_1 + T_2 + T_3$, where T_3 is close to T_{RT}. Therefore, the time difference between BRK_RTDS and BRK_cRIO is $T_2 + T_3$.The range of T_1 is between 0 and T_{RT}, range of T_2 is between 0 and to T_{tri} and the range of T_3 is between 0 and T_{RT}, where T_{RT} is the loop rate of the time-critical loop in RT processor and T_{tri} is the period of the triggering signal.

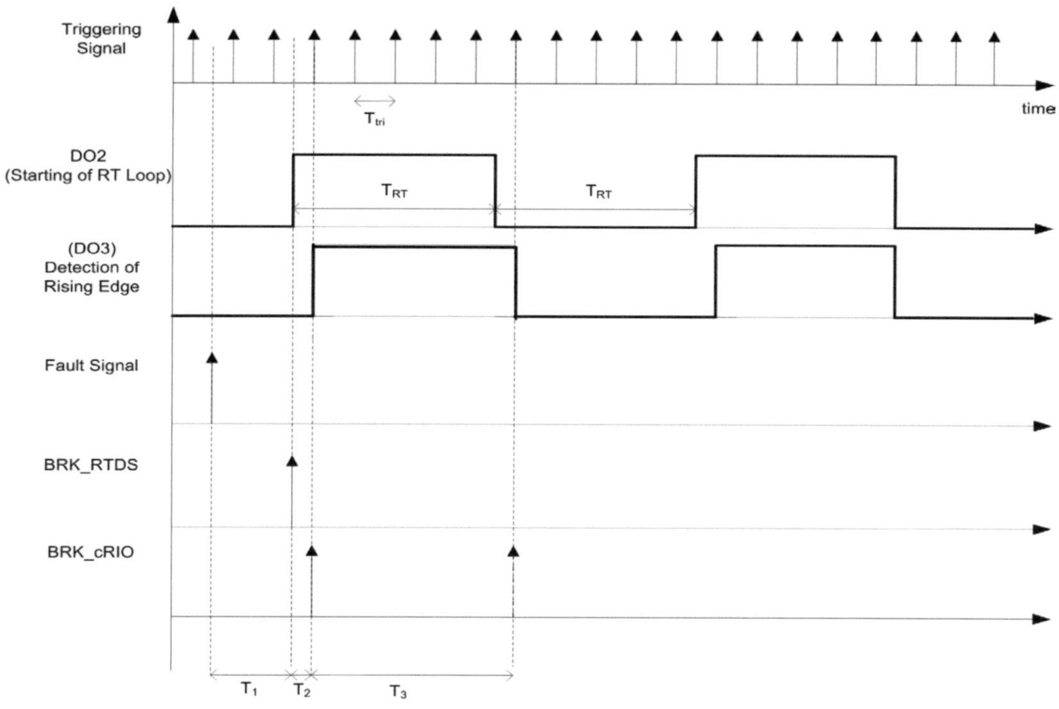

Fig. 23. Time analysis of simulation results in Figure 21

5. Conclusions and future work

In this book chapter, the concepts and the implementation of a real-time rapid embedded power system control prototyping simulation test bed were described. The methodologies for implementing embedded controller-in-the-loop simulation (CIL) was explained. To illustrate the functionality of the test bed, the detailed implementation of an overcurrent relay protection scheme for CIL simulation was described, including the settings and programming of RTDS, the programming in cRIO, which included the FPGA and RT processor, by using LabVIEW. Also, a synchronization approach for the RTDS and cRIO was discussed.

Additional studies are ongoing to refine the test bed design, such as studies to investigate the time delay and data synchronization and its relationship to system performance and stability. For example, in a power system, to be transient stable, a fault has to be cleared within a specific amount of time. If the response of the breaker is too late or incorrect, the system will become unstable.

Further the test bed is being utilized to study new control strategies and their performance. In power system applications, voltage regulation and load management are used to maintain the proper operation of power systems. These control strategies can be verified and validated using the test bed discussed in this chapter. Due to the real-time environment of RTDS and RT target, it is possible to observe the effectiveness of these control strategies in the real-time simulation environment.

6. Acknowledgment

The authors gratefully acknowledge the contributions of Tania Okotie and the funding from Office of Naval Research under grants N00014-09-1-0579, N0014-04-1-0404, and N00014-07-1-0939.

7. References

French, C. D., Finch, J. W. & Acarnley, P. P. (1998). Rapid prototyping of a real time dsp based motor drive controller using simulink, *Simulation, International Conference on*, pp. 284–291.

Isermann, R., Schaffnit, J. & Sinsel, S. (1999). Hardware-in-the-loop simulation for the design and testing of engine-control systems, *Control Engineering Practice* pp. 643–653.

J. Duncan Glover, Mulukutla S. Sarma, T. O. (2007). *Power System Analysis and Design*, 4 edn, CL-Engineering.

Karpenko, M. & Sepehri, N. (2006). Hardware-in-the-loop simulator for research on fault tolerant control of electrohydraulic flight control systems, *American Control Conference*, p. 7.

Keunsoo, H., Seok-Gyu, O., MacCleery, B. & Krishnan, R. (2005). An automated reconfigurable fpga-based magnetic characterization of switched reluctance machines, *Industrial Electronics, Proceedings of the IEEE International Symposium on*, pp. 839–844.

Lavoie, M., QuÃľ-Do, V., Houle, J. L. & Davidson, J. (1995). Real-time simulation of power system stability using parallel digital signal processors, *Mathematics and Computers in Simulation* pp. 283–292.

Ledin, J. (2001). *Simulation Engineering*, CMP Books, Lawrence, USA.

NI (2004). *CompactRIO and LabVIEW Development Fundamentals*.

NI (2009). *LabVIEW Real-Time Application Development Course Manual*.

NI CompactRIO (2011). Available at: http://www.ni.com/compactrio/.

Postolache, O., Dias Pereira, J. M. & Silva Girao, P. (2006). Real-time sensing channel modelling based on an fpga and real-time controller, *Instrumentation and Measurement Technology Conference, Proceedings of the IEEE on*, pp. 557–562.

Real Time Digital Simlator - RTDS (2011). Available at: http://www.rtds.com/.

Spinozzi, J. (2006). A suite of national instruments tools for risk-free control system development of a hybrid-electric vehicle, *American Control Conference, 2006* p. 5.

Toscher, S., Kasper, R. & Reinemann, T. (2006). Implementation of a reconfigurable hard real-time control system for mechatronic and automotive applications, *Parallel and Distributed Processing Symposium, IPDPS 20th International* p. 4.

6

The Development of a Hardware-in-the-Loop Simulation System for Unmanned Aerial Vehicle Autopilot Design Using LabVIEW

Yun-Ping Sun
Department of Mechanical Engineering, Cheng Shiu University, Taiwan

1. Introduction

This chapter describes a continuing research on design and verification of the autopilot system for an unmanned aerial vehicle (UAV) through hardware-in-the-loop (HIL) simulation. UAVs have the characteristics of small volume, light weight, low cost in manufacture, high agility and high maneuverability without the restriction of human body physical loading. Equipped with the on-board autopilot system an UAV is capable of performing out-of-sight missions that inspires scientists and engineers with a lot of innovative applications. Not only in the military but also in the civil, the applications of UAVs are in full bloom. Apparently one of the key challenge of UAV research and development is its autopilot system design.

For the purpose of designing an autopilot, the technology of hardware-in-the-loop simulation plays an important role. The concept of HIL simulation is that a stand-alone personal computer is used to simulate the behavior of the plant, several data-acquisition devices are exploited to generate the real signals, and the prototype controller can be tested in real-time and in the presence of real hardware. HIL simulation presents a new challenge of control engineering developers as the "correctness" of a real-time model not only depends upon the numerical computation, but the timelines with which the simulation model interacts with external control equipment that is the major difference between HIL simulation and numerical simulation. Due to the useful feature, HIL simulation is applicable to solve many problems in engineering and sciences effectively (Shetty & Kolk, 1997; Ledin, 2001).

HIL simulation provides an effective technique for design and test of autopilot systems. Using HIL simulation the hardware and software at subsystem level perform the actual input/output signals and run at real time so that the test target (e.g. prototype controller) is working as if in real process. This provides the ability to thoroughly test subsystems under different working loads and conditions; therefore, engineers can correct and improve their original designs early in the development process. The advantages of HIL simulation are reducing the risk in test and shortening the development time. Especially HIL simulation is suitable for critical or hazardous applications.

(Cosic et al., 1999) used TMS320C40 DSP to set up a HIL simulation platform for a semi-automatic guided missile system. (Carrijo et al., 2002) applied HIL simulation to test the on-board computer on a satellite launcher vehicle for motion and attitude control. (Sun et al., 2006; Sun et al., 2008a; Sun et al., 2009; Sun et al., 2010) developed the HIL simulation system to evaluate the performance of UAV autopilot that was employed different control laws.

Some valuable applications in traffic control (Bullock et al., 2004) and UAV design (Cole et al., 2006; Salman et al., 2006) using HIL simulation can be found.
The hardware arrangement of HIL simulation includes a personal computer used to simulate the behavior of an UAV plant, several plug-in data-acquisition (DAQ) devices used to acquire/generate the specific real input/output signals, and the embedded control system used to execute the control laws and send control signals to real hardware.
The software development environment for HIL simulation in this work is LabVIEW. LabVIEW is a graphical programming language widely adopted throughout industry and academia as a standard for data acquisition and instrument control software. LabVIEW provides an intuitive graphical programming style to create programs in a pictorial form called a block diagram that allows users to focus on flow of data within applications and makes programming easy and efficiency. Additionally, LabVIEW can command plug-in DAQ devices to acquire or generate analog/digital signals. In combination of LabVIEW and DAQ devices, a PC-based or embedded control system can communicate with the outside real world, e.g., take measurements, talk to an instrument, send data to another subsystem. These features are very helpful in building a HIL simulation system for UAV autopilot design. As a matter of fact, LabVIEW is not the only software development environment for HIL simulation, but based on the enumerated advantages it is certainly a nice choice.
In this chapter we are going to apply different control methods to accomplish the design of UAV autopilot, and compare their results in HIL simulations using LabVIEW. The chapter is organized as follows. Section 2 describes the dynamic model of an UAV. Section 3 outlines the HIL simulation system architecture and introduces hardware and software development environment LabVIEW. Section 4 focuses on stability augmentation system design. Section 5 focuses on autopilot system design including pitch attitude hold mode, velocity hold mode, roll attitude hold mode and heading angle hold mode. Section 6 concludes this chapter.

2. Dynamics model of an UAV

The MP2000UAV (Fig. 1) is a low-cost and small-volume unmanned aerial vehicle (UAV). Its physical properties are wingspan 1.75 m, length 1.4 m, wing area 0.5116 m^2, wing chord 0.29 m, and weight 3.84 kg. MP2000UAV equipped with a 40 in^3, 1 HP, 2 cycle glow engine and a miniature autopilot is capable to carry out autonomous operations.

Fig. 1. Unmanned aerial vehicle MP2000UAV

The dynamics of an aircraft obey the equations of motion derived by Newton's second law. The forces and moments resulting from lift and drag, the control surface, the propulsion system, and gravity govern the aircraft. A body-fixed coordinate system shown in Fig. 2 that is fixed to center of mass and rotating with the aircraft is used to express these forces and moments. The rigid body equations of motion in body-fixed coordinates can be derived as: (Bryson, 1994; Cook, 2007)

$$\begin{aligned} m(\dot{U} - RV + QW) &= X - mg\sin\theta + T\cos\kappa \\ m(\dot{V} + RU - PW) &= Y + mg\sin\phi\cos\theta \\ m(\dot{W} - QU + PV) &= Z + mg\cos\theta\cos\phi - T\sin\kappa \end{aligned} \tag{1}$$

$$\begin{aligned} I_{xx}\dot{P} - (I_{yy} - I_{zz})QR - I_{xz}(\dot{R} + QP) &= L \\ I_{yy}\dot{Q} - (I_{zz} - I_{xx})PR + I_{xz}(P^2 - R^2) &= M \\ I_{zz}\dot{R} - (I_{xx} - I_{yy})PQ + I_{xz}(QR - \dot{P}) &= N \end{aligned} \tag{2}$$

where

m = mass of the aircraft,
g = gravitational acceleration per unit mass,
I_{ii} = moments and products of inertia in body-fixed axes,
U, V, W = components of the velocity of c.m. (center of mass) in body-fixed frame,
P, Q, R = components of the angular velocity of the aircraft in body-fixed frame,
X, Y, Z = components of the aerodynamic force about the c.m. in body-fixed frame,
L, M, N = components of the aerodynamic moment in body-fixed frame,
T = thrust force,
θ, ϕ = Euler pitch and roll angles of the body axes with respect to horizontal,
κ = angle between thrust and body x-axis,

The equations of motion derived for a body-fixed coordinate system are nonlinear that is difficult for analysis and design. In order to proceed for analysis and design they have to be linearized using the small-disturbance theory (Nelson, 1998; Roskam, 2007). On the assumption that the motion of the aircraft consists of small deviations about a steady flight condition, all the variables in the equations of motion are replaced by a perturbation.

The linearized equations of motion for an aircraft that describe small deviations from constant speed, straight and level flight can be divided into two fourth-order uncoupled sets representing the perturbations in longitudinal and lateral motion as follows: (Nelson, 1998)

$$\begin{bmatrix} \dot{v} \\ \dot{p} \\ \dot{r} \\ \dot{\phi} \end{bmatrix} = \begin{bmatrix} Y_v & Y_p & -(u_0 - Y_r) & g \\ L_v & L_p & L_r & 0 \\ N_v & N_p & N_r & 0 \\ 0 & 1 & 0 & 0 \end{bmatrix} \begin{bmatrix} v \\ p \\ r \\ \phi \end{bmatrix} + \begin{bmatrix} 0 & Y_{\delta_r} \\ L_{\delta_a} & L_{\delta_r} \\ N_{\delta_a} & N_{\delta_r} \\ 0 & 0 \end{bmatrix} \begin{bmatrix} \delta_a \\ \delta_r \end{bmatrix} \tag{3}$$

$$\begin{bmatrix} \dot{v} \\ \dot{p} \\ \dot{r} \\ \dot{j} \end{bmatrix} = \begin{bmatrix} Y_v & Y_p & -(u_0 - Y_r) & g \\ L_v & L_p & L_r & 0 \\ N_v & N_p & N_r & 0 \\ 0 & 1 & 0 & 0 \end{bmatrix} \begin{bmatrix} v \\ p \\ r \\ j \end{bmatrix} + \begin{bmatrix} 0 & Y_{\delta_r} \\ L_{\delta_a} & L_{\delta_r} \\ N_{\delta_a} & N_{\delta_r} \\ 0 & 0 \end{bmatrix} \begin{bmatrix} \delta_a \\ \delta_r \end{bmatrix} \tag{4}$$

where

u, v, w = perturbations of the linear velocity in body-fixed frame (unit: m/s),
p, q, r = perturbations of the angular velocity in body-fixed frame (unit: deg/s),
δ_e = deflection of control surface, elevator (unit: deg),
δ_a = deflection of control surfaces, aileron (unit: deg),
δ_r = deflection of control surfaces, rudder (unit: deg),
δ_{th} = throttle setting,

and there are 13 dimensional stability derivatives in longitudinal model, including X_u, X_w, X_{δ_e}, $X_{\delta_{th}}$, Z_u, Z_w, Z_{δ_e}, $Z_{\delta_{th}}$, $\bar{M}_u$, $\bar{M}_w$, $\bar{M}_q$, $\bar{M}_{\delta_e}$, $\bar{M}_{\delta_{th}}$, and 14 dimensional stability derivatives in lateral model, including Y_v, Y_p, Y_r, Y_{δ_r}, L_v, L_p, L_r, L_{δ_a}, L_{δ_r}, N_v, N_p, N_r, N_{δ_a}, N_{δ_r} to be determined (Nelson, 1998; Roskam, 2007).

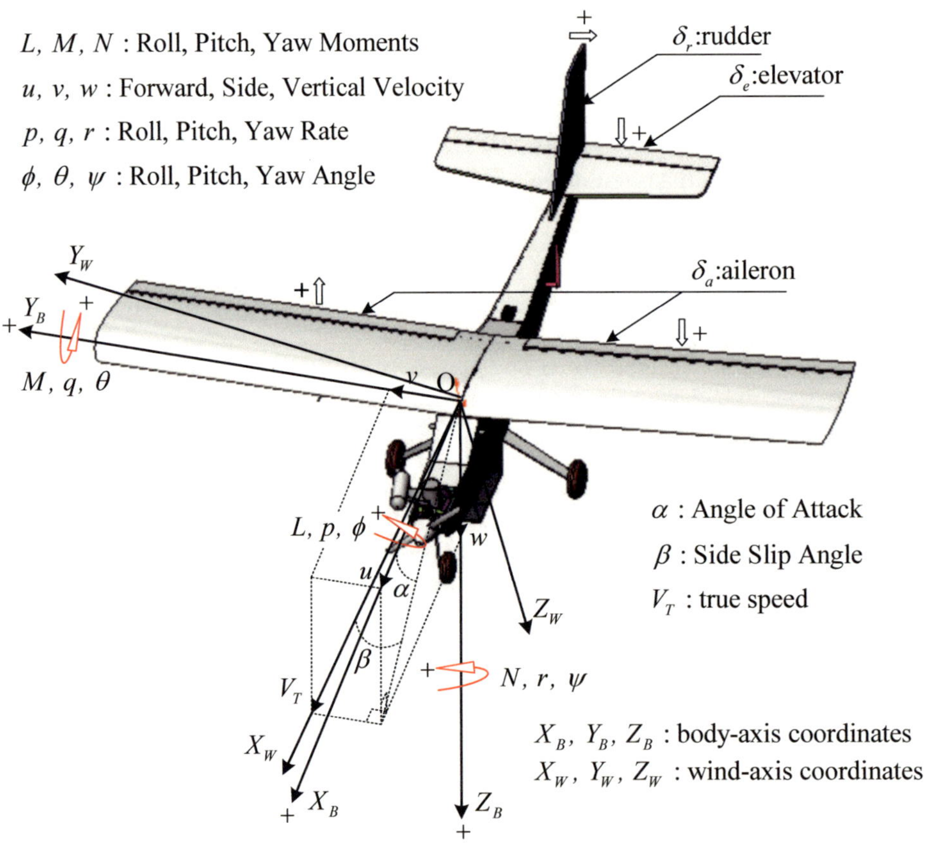

Fig. 2. Definition of aircraft coordinates

These stability derivatives of MP2000UAV are estimated from flight test data in a straight and horizontal flight condition, $u_0 = 16$ m/s at 80 m altitude and shown in Table 1 (Sun et al., 2008b).

X_u	X_w	X_{δ_e}	$X_{\delta_{th}}$	Z_u	Z_w	Z_{δ_e}	$Z_{\delta_{th}}$	$\bar{M}_u$
-6.114	0.789	-0.273	2.936	8.952	-9.220	3.919	143.24	1.275
$\bar{M}_w$	$\bar{M}_q$	$\bar{M}_{\delta_e}$	$\bar{M}_{\delta_{th}}$	Y_v	Y_p	Y_r	Y_{δ_r}	L_v
-1.291	-1.366	-1.699	-64.192	-0.374	-5.113	0.764	-1.264	-2.136
L_p	L_r	L_{δ_a}	L_{δ_r}	N_v	N_p	N_r	N_{δ_a}	N_{δ_r}
-2.656	-5.414	0.967	5.974	0.584	1.250	1.307	-0.191	-4.969

Table 1. Estimation results of dimensional stability derivatives

As a result, for the unmanned aerial vehicle MP2000UAV, the longitudinal equations of motion in state-space form are:

$$\begin{bmatrix} \dot{u} \\ \dot{w} \\ \dot{q} \\ \dot{\theta} \end{bmatrix} = \begin{bmatrix} -6.113 & 0.7889 & 0 & -9.8 \\ 8.952 & -9.220 & 16 & 0 \\ 1.2746 & -1.290 & -1.3656 & 0 \\ 0 & 0 & 1 & 0 \end{bmatrix} \begin{bmatrix} u \\ w \\ q \\ \theta \end{bmatrix} + \begin{bmatrix} -0.273 & 2.9361 \\ 3.9191 & 143.24 \\ -1.699 & -64.192 \\ 0 & 0 \end{bmatrix} \begin{bmatrix} \delta_e \\ \delta_{th} \end{bmatrix} \tag{5}$$

and the lateral equations of motion in state-space form are:

$$\begin{bmatrix} \dot{v} \\ \dot{p} \\ \dot{r} \\ \dot{\phi} \end{bmatrix} = \begin{bmatrix} -0.373 & -5.113 & -15.236 & 9.8 \\ -2.135 & -2.6564 & -5.4143 & 0 \\ 0.5837 & 1.2497 & 1.3069 & 0 \\ 0 & 1 & 0 & 0 \end{bmatrix} \begin{bmatrix} v \\ p \\ r \\ \phi \end{bmatrix} + \begin{bmatrix} 0 & -1.2636 \\ 0.9666 & 5.9744 \\ -0.191 & -4.9689 \\ 0 & 0 \end{bmatrix} \begin{bmatrix} \delta_a \\ \delta_r \end{bmatrix} \tag{6}$$

where the maximum deflection angles of elevator, aileron, and rudder are ±15°, ±6°, and ±10°.

3. HIL simulation system

Hardware-in-the-Loop (HIL) simulation is a kind of real-time simulation that the input and output signals shows the same time dependent values as the real process. It is usually used in a laboratory environment on the ground to test the prototype controller under different working loads and conditions conveniently and safely. Compared with numerical simulation, HIL simulation is more reliable and credible because numerical simulation is often operated in ideal circumstances, without considering noise, disturbance, and some practical problems often ignored which might result in fatal failure. HIL simulation has the advantages of reducing the risk, shortening the developing time, and being well suitable for critical and hazardous applications.

The concept of HIL simulation is described by Fig. 3. A typical HIL simulation system for UAV autopilot design is composed of a stand-alone embedded real-time control system, a personal computer, a servo unit, and a host PC. The hardware arrangement of HIL simulation system is shown in Fig. 4. The graphical programming language LabVIEW is the software development environment for data acquisition (DAQ) and instrument control in performing HIL simulation.

3.1 Embedded real-time control system (prototype controller)

The prototype controller is implemented by the National Instruments (NI) PXI real-time embedded control system which includes:

Real-time Controller NI PXI-8184 RT: It is a stand-alone embedded real-time control system. This system real-time computes the control output according to the implemented control law and the error between command signal and feedback signal from sensor.

Multifunction DAQ device NI PXI-6259: It takes the responsibility on (1) acquiring the analog feedback signal from the plant PC, (2) sending the analog control signal to the plant PC and the host PC, (3) receiving the digital signal from the host PC to start/stop the PXI system.

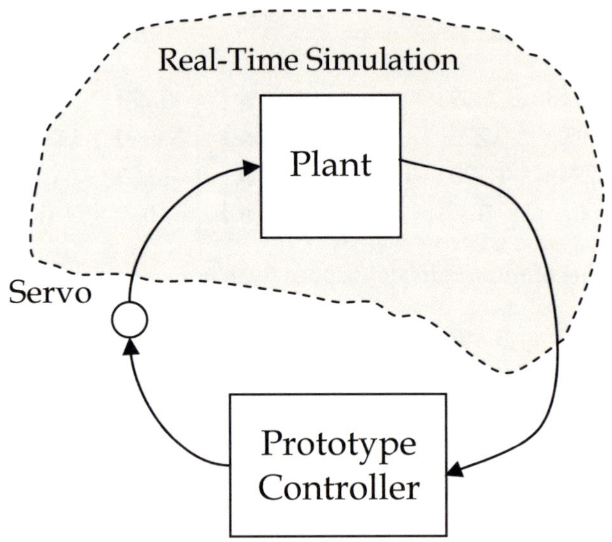

Fig. 3. The concept of HIL simulation

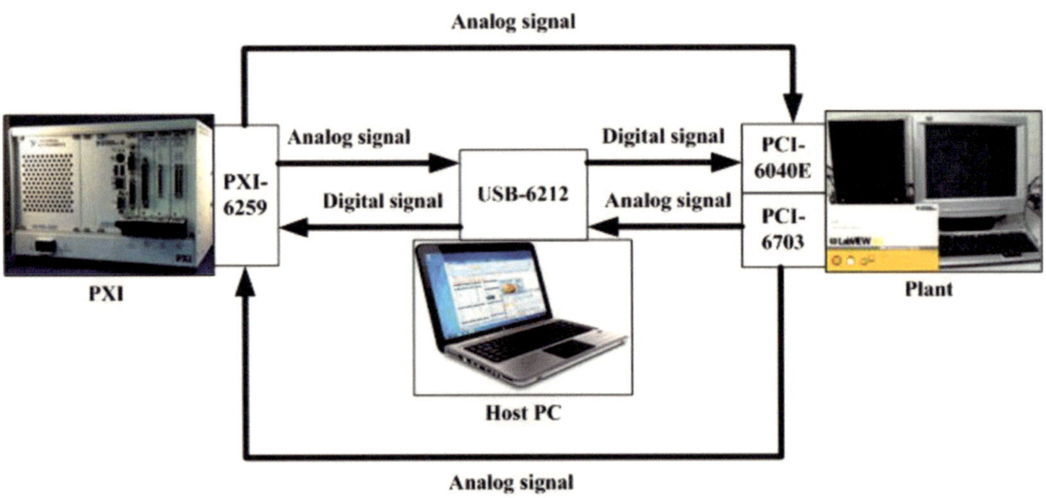

Fig. 4. The hardware layout of a typical HILS system

3.2 Personal computer (Plant)

The personal computer (PC) is used to simulate the dynamics of plant (UAV). The major specifications are Intel Pentium 4-3.0 GHz CPU and 1 GB SDRAM. The I/O interfaces include:

Multifunction DAQ device NI PCI-6040E: It takes the responsibility on (1) acquiring the analog control signal from the PXI system or from the potentiometer on the servo unit that represents the control surface angle, (2) receiving the digital signal from the host PC to start/stop the plant PC.

Multifunction DAQ device NI PCI-6703: It takes the responsibility on sending the analog state signal to the PXI system and the host PC.

3.3 Servo unit

Each servo unit contains two sets of servos, Futaba S3001, which is used to actuate the control surface in UAV to generate the corrective torque in order to keep the desired attitude. The rotational angle of servo is measured by potentiometer, model no. J50S, manufactured by Copal Electronics Co., Ltd. in Japan.

3.4 Host PC

The host PC or notebook is used to monitor, synchronously digitally trigger, and display the virtual aircraft instruments of UAV. The major specifications are Intel Core 2 Duo P8400-2.26 GHz CPU and 2 GB SDRAM. The I/O interfaces include:

Multifunction DAQ device NI USB-6212: It takes the responsibility on (1) acquiring the analog state signal from the plant PC, (2) acquiring the analog control signal from the PXI system, (3) and sending the digital signal to synchronously trigger the start/stop action of the plant PC and PXI system.

3.5 Software development environment LabVIEW

To develop a HIL simulation system is not an easy work. The graphical programming software LabVIEW streamlines the system building with a convenient environment to integrate hardware and software seamlessly. LabVIEW is a graphical programming language that has been widely adopted throughout industry and academia as the standard for data acquisition and instrument control software. While other text-based languages create lines of codes, LabVIEW provides an intuitive graphical programming style to create programs in a pictorial form called a block diagram. Graphical programming allows users to focus on flow of data within the applications that makes programming easy and efficiency.

A LabVIEW program, called virtual instrument (VI), has two main parts: a front panel and a block diagram. The front panel is the interactive user interface of a VI that the appearance and operation often imitates actual physical instruments. The block diagram is the VI's source code and is the actual executable program. The components of a block diagram are lower-level VIs, functions, constants, and program execution control structures. In addition, LabVIEW can command plug-in DAQ devices to acquire or generate analog and digital signals. You might use DAQ devices and LabVIEW to hook your computer up to the real world, for example, to take measurements, talk to an instrument, send data to another computer. It is very convenient to construct HIL simulation systems using LabVIEW. A lot of valuable books (Larsen, 2011; Travis & Kring, 2007) provide more foundations, programming skills, and applications for LabVIEW.

4. Stability augmentation system

In order to perform missions, the UAV has to be hold on or maneuvered to a specified cruising speed, altitude, and attitude. A typical feedback system providing desirable handling qualities for pilot/autopilot commands is called stability augmentation system (SAS). Especially for an aircraft flying throughout an extended flight envelope, the stability derivatives in Eq. (3) and (4) are expected to vary significantly. Because of the variation of stability derivatives, the handling qualities also are going to change. SAS can be designed to improve the handling qualities over its entire operational envelope (Nelson, 1998; Roskam, 2003; Kayton & Fried, 1969).
The stability augmentation system (SAS) is the inner loop of the flight control system (FCS) that provides the desirable handling characteristics for pilots. The design parameter in the SAS is the feedback gain that is determined by applying the root locus technique. The root locus technique is a simple and powerful tool in classical control theory for determining, by graphical plot, the detailed information about the stability and performance of a closed-loop system knowing only the open-loop transfer function. The root locus plot shows the poles of the closed-loop system in complex plane for every value of the feedback gain. The location of the closed-loop system poles determine two important quantities, damping ratio and natural frequency, that are closely related to the time-domain performance specifications (Cook, 2007; Nise, 2008). According to the linear mathematical models of longitudinal dynamics for the MP2000UAV, the SAS for pitch attitude control are at first designed by the root locus technique in MATLAB and then are tested in HIL simulation.

4.1 Design of SAS

The pitch angle, one of the state variables in Eq. (3), is an appropriate output variable for attitude control. Therefore the pitch angle is used as a feedback in SAS; it can be measured by vertical gyro or attitude and heading reference system (AHRS).
The negative pitch-attitude-to-elevator transfer function from Eq. (2) for the MP2000UAV is:

$$\frac{-\theta(s)}{\delta_e(s)} = \frac{1.699(s+4.7308)(s+13.7827)}{(s+0.0106)(s+8.854)(s+3.917 \pm j2.4488)} \tag{7}$$

The open-loop system has two real poles at -0.0106, -8.854, and a pair of stable complex poles at $-3.917 \pm j2.4488$. The corresponding damping ratios and natural frequencies are given in Table 2.

Poles	Natural frequency	Damping ratio
-0.0106	0.0106	1
-3.917+j2.4488	4.6195	0.8479
-3.917-j2.4488	4.6195	0.8479
-8.854	8.8540	1

Table 2. The natural frequency and damping ratio for open-loop poles

From the step response as shown in Fig. 5, it is obviously that the settling time is too long, approximately 300 sec. As a result, the maneuverability is very poor. It is necessary to design a SAS to enhance the handling quality. The block diagram for pitch-angle to elevator feedback of SAS is shown in Fig. 6. The elevator deflection is produced in proportion to the pitch angle and adding it to the pilot's control input as:

$$\delta_e = \delta_{e\_pilot} + K\theta \quad (8)$$

where δ_{e_pilot} is that part of the elevator deflection created by the pilot. The gain K is the design parameter.

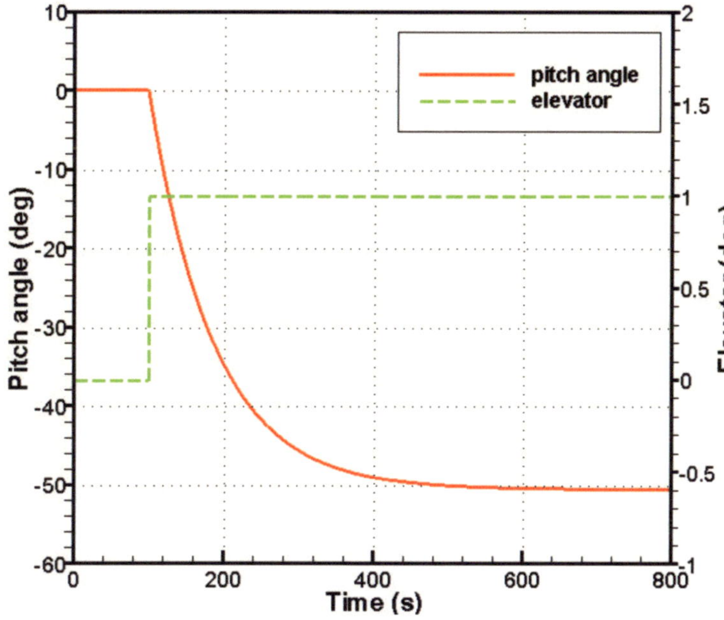

Fig. 5. Step response of open-loop system

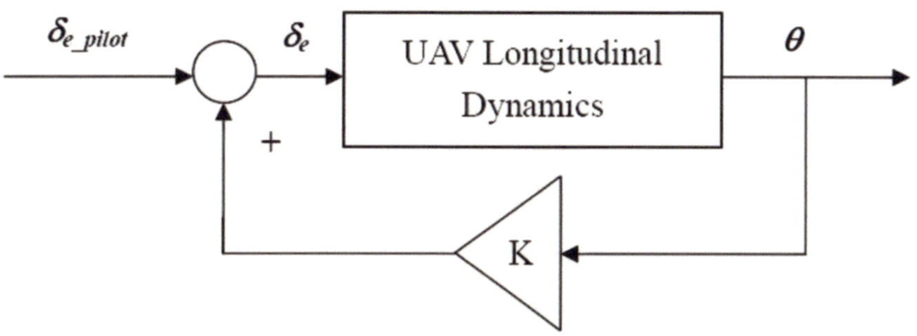

Fig. 6. The block diagram of SAS for pitch angle control

From classical control theory, the system response is determined by the pole location in complex plane. The time-domain performance specifications such as peak time, percent overshoot and settling time are functions of damping ratio and natural frequency of the dominant poles. The duty of SAS is, therefore, to modify the damping ratio and natural frequency by adjusting the value of feedback gain K so that the UAV is easier to control. Studies have shown that to obtain a desirable transient performance such as a smaller overshoot and a shorter settling time, the design specifications for damping ratio is approximately 0.6-0.7 and natural frequency is larger than 2 rad/s.

The root locus technique permits the designer to view the trajectories of the close-loop system poles as the design parameter (feedback gain K) is varied. It is very convenient to determine the value of K in SAS by applying the root locus technique. The root locus plot constructed by using MATLAB for the pitch-attitude-to-elevator transfer function, Eq. (7), is shown in Fig. 7.

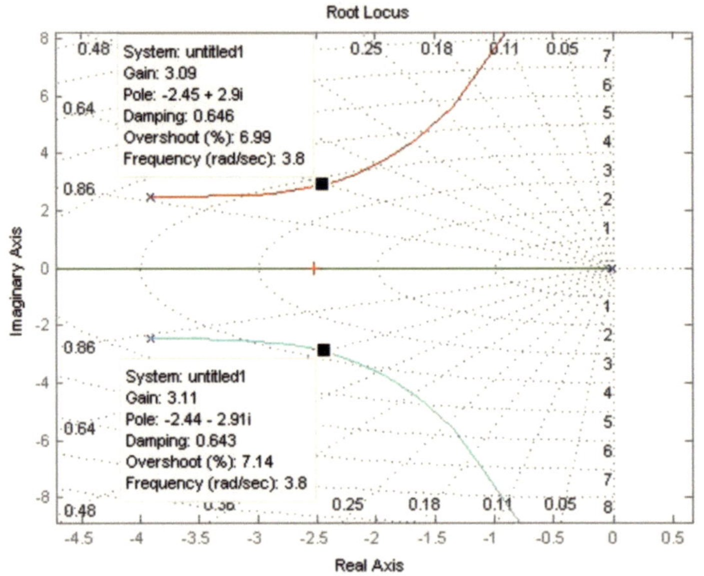

Fig. 7. Root locus plot for SAS

It is noted that at $K = 3$ the damping ratio and natural frequency of the dominant poles meets the specifications while the damping ratio is 0.6564 and natural frequency is 3.7915. All the closed-loop system poles and the corresponding damping ratios and natural frequencies are given in Table 3.

Poles	Natural frequency	Damping ratio
-2.5306	-2.5306	1
-2.489+j2.86	3.7915	0.6564
-2.489-j2. 86	3.7915	0.6564
-9.1904	9.1904	1

Table 3. The natural frequency and damping ratio for closed-loop poles

The dc gain (steady-state gain) of closed-loop system is -0.3313. It indicates that at steady state the ratio of pitch angle to pilot's control input is approximately one-third:

$$\frac{\theta(\infty)}{\delta_{e\_pilot}(\infty)} \text{»} -\frac{1}{3} \tag{9}$$

In Fig. 8 the transient response shows a significant improvement that the settling time is greatly reduced to 1.2 sec by employing SAS. At this stage, the performance of SAS is verified by computer simulation that the desired handling quality for pilot command is achieved.

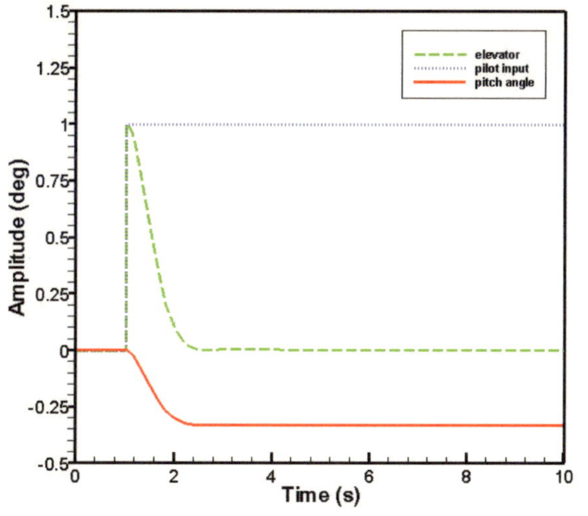

Fig. 8. Step response of closed-loop system

4.2 HIL simulation results

In this section the prototype SAS is realized and implemented by the PXI real-time control system, and the performance of SAS is examined by HILS experiment in real time and real signal.

4.2.1 Pilot input on time-table experiment

The pilot control input according to schedule is defined as:

$$\delta_{e\_pilot}(t) = \begin{cases} 0, 0 \le t < 1 \\ 5, 1 \le t < 2 \\ 0, \quad t \ge 2 \end{cases} \tag{10}$$

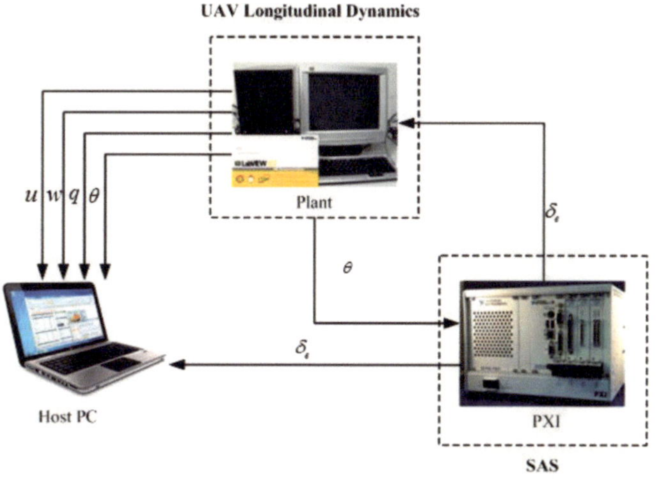

Fig. 9. The signal flow diagram of HIL simulation

The signal flow diagram of HILS system is shown in Fig. 9. The LabVIEW virtual instruments of the controller, plant, and host PC used to perform HILS experiment are presented in Figs. 10-14. The sampling rate is 50 Hz.

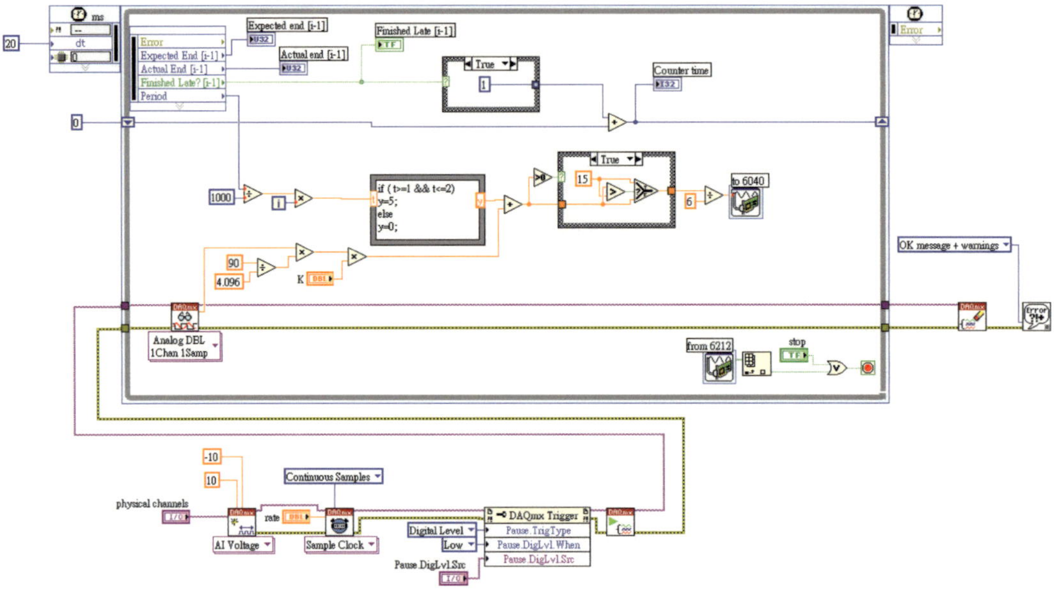

Fig. 10. The LabVIEW block diagram of controller.

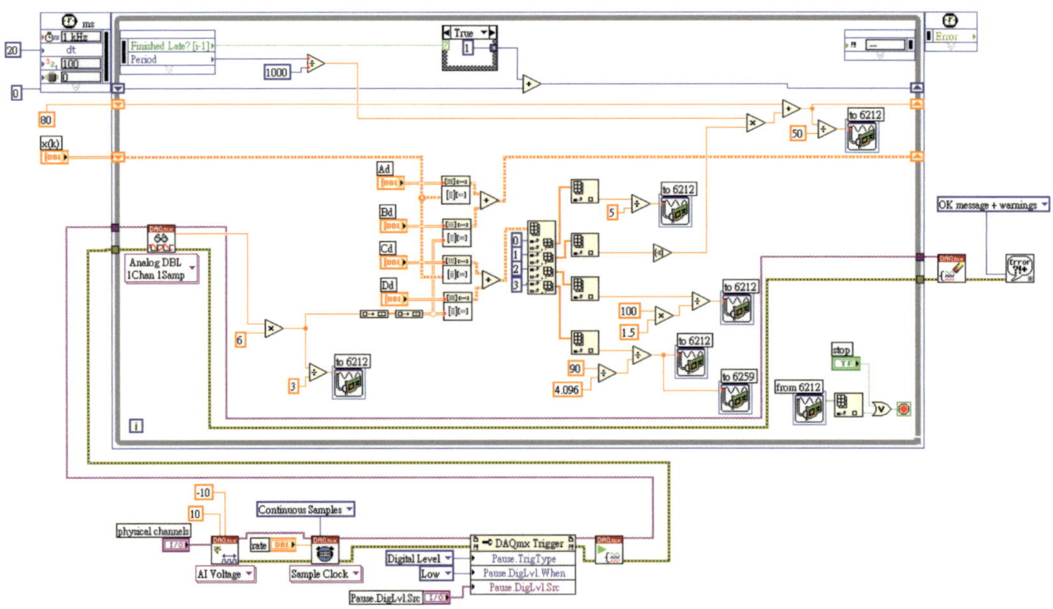

Fig. 11. The LabVIEW block diagram of plant

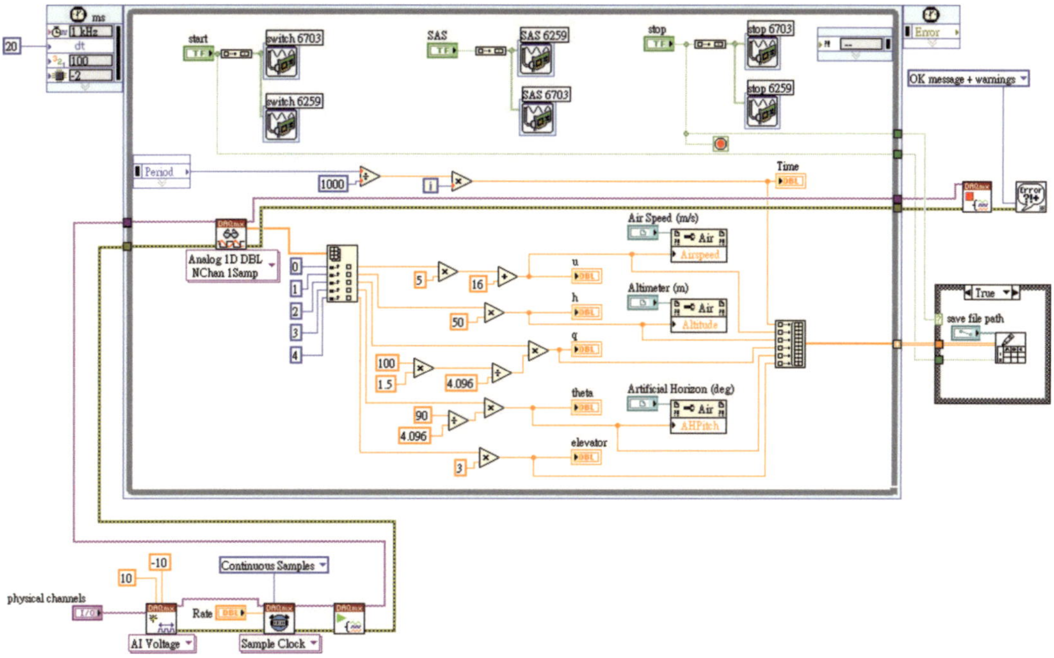

Fig. 12. The LabVIEW block diagram of host PC

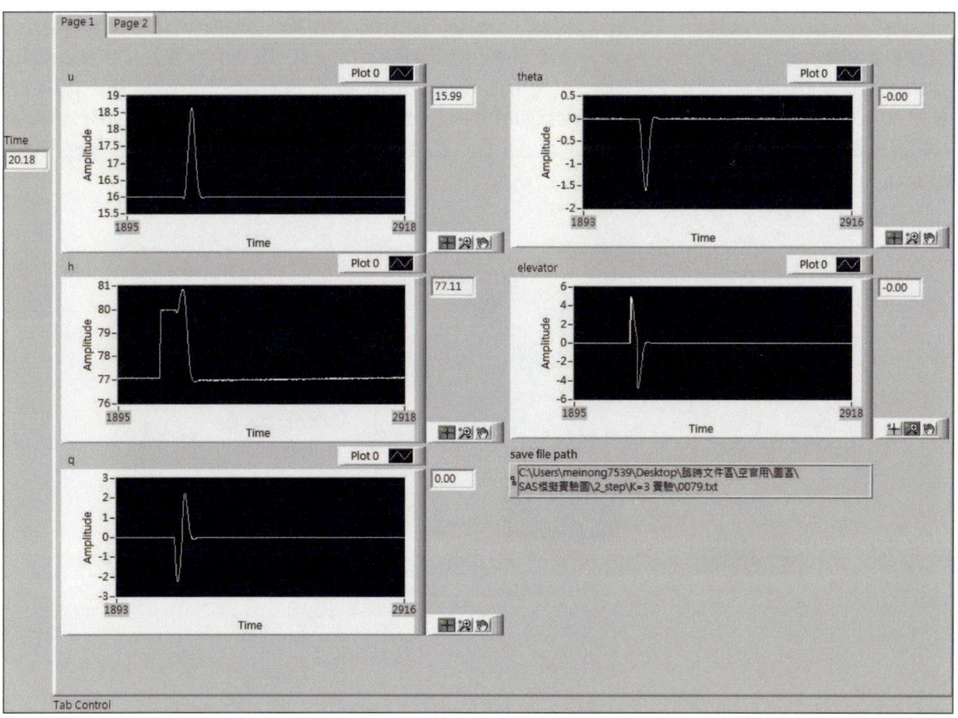

Fig. 13. The LabVIEW front panel of host PC (flight data)

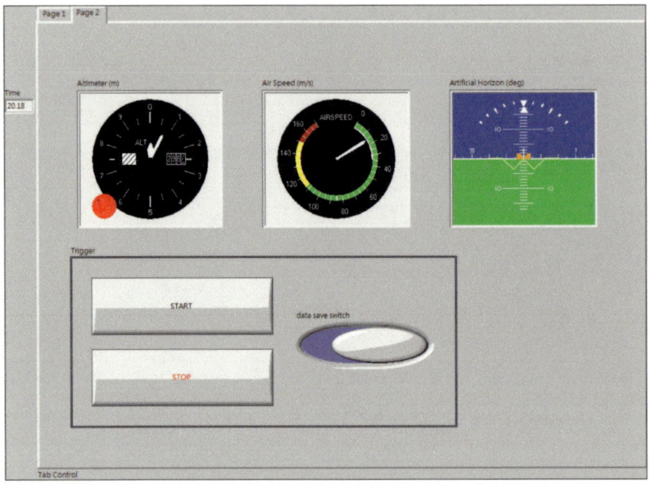

Fig. 14. The LabVIEW front panel of host PC (aircraft instruments)

4.2.2 Pilot-in-the-loop experiment

The pilot-in-the-loop (PIL) experiment is developed to test the performance of SAS when the human pilot joins in the control loop. The pilot's task is to control UAV pitch attitude to a desired angle. The pilot looks at the virtual aircraft instruments displayed in the host PC screen and tries to correct the error between the desired pitch angle and the actual pitch angle. This process of pilot in control can be expressed as follows: (1) the pilot's eyes watch the pitch angle on the screen, (2) the pilot's brain figures out the magnitude of the error, (3) the pilot's brain sends a signal to actuate the hand of pilot, (4) the pilot's hand manipulates the control stick to move the elevator, (5) the deflection of elevator changes the pitch angle of the UAV. The operation of PIL experiment depicted in Fig 15 describes a compensatory control situation: the pilot tries to maintain the desired pitch attitude by driving the pitch angle error to zero with the assistance of SAS.

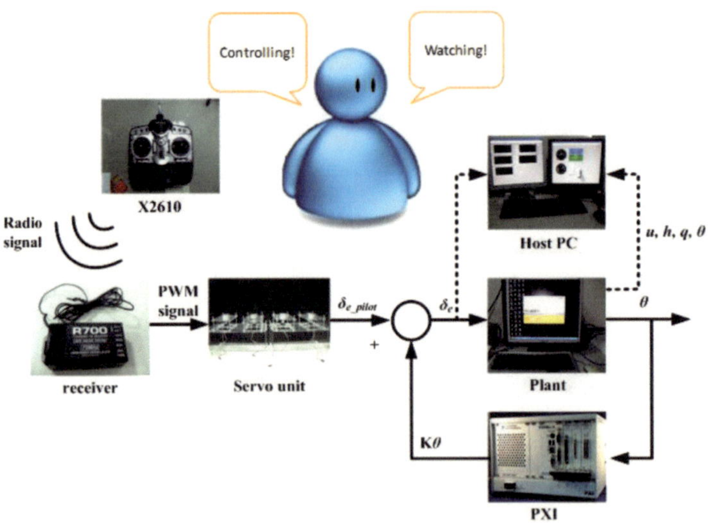

Fig. 15. The operation of pilot-in-the-loop experiment

From the HIL simulation results of PIL experiment in Fig. 16-17, pilot control using SAS demonstrates an excellent handling performance than that without using SAS. The effect of SAS on improving the handling qualities of UAV is confirmed.

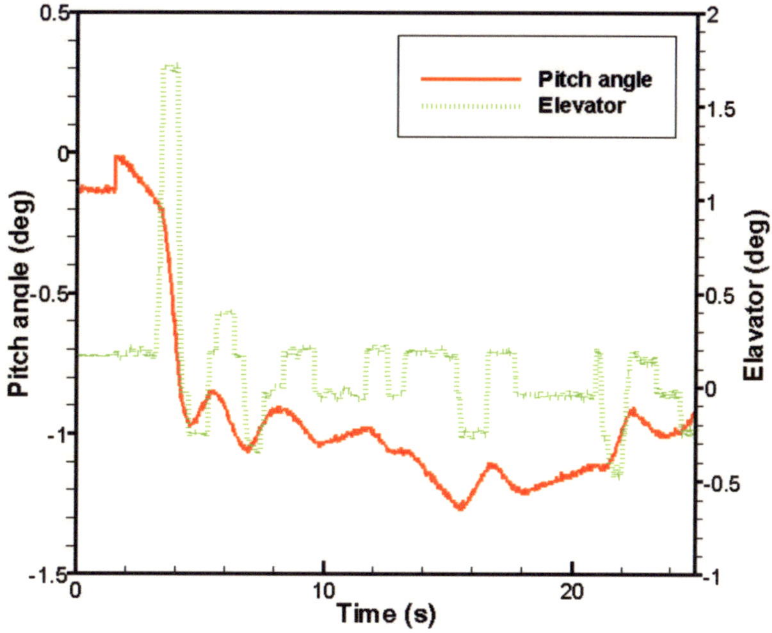

Fig. 16. PIL experiment without SAS

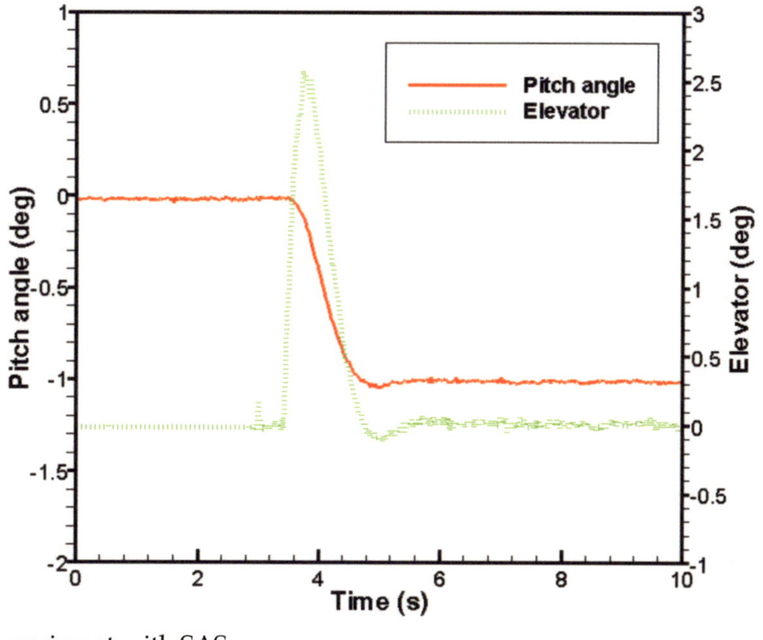

Fig. 17. PIL experiment with SAS

5. Autopilot system

The function of stability augmentation system is to improve the flying qualities of an airplane for pilot manual control. To lower pilot workload, particularly on long-range flights or out-of-sight flights of UAV, most airplanes or UAVs are equipped with automatic flight control systems or autopilots. The basic autopilot modes include pitch attitude hold mode, airspeed hold mode, bank angle (roll attitude) hold mode and heading angle hold mode.
Normally pitch attitude is controlled by the elevator, airspeed is controlled by the engine throttle, roll attitude is controlled by the aileron, and heading is controlled by the rudder. Thus there are four feedback loops to achieve four different autopilot modes. Fig. 18 shows the block diagram of pitch attitude hold mode in HILS experiment.

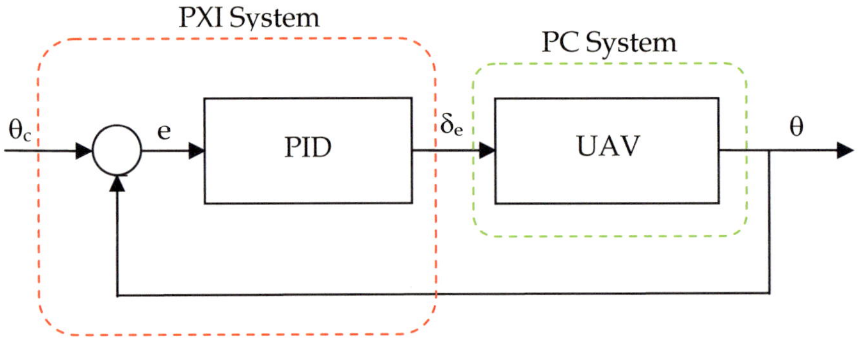

Fig. 18. The block diagram of pitch attitude control for autopilot in HILS experiment

5.1 PID controller design

The proportional-integral-derivative (PID) controllers are frequently used in practical control systems owing to their simple structures and quite clear physical senses. Usually the PID controller is described by the transfer function:

$$K_{PID}(s) = K_p + \frac{K_i}{s} + K_d s \tag{11}$$

where K_p, K_i, and K_d are gains to be determined to meet design requirements. Specifically, the PID controller can be expressed by the form in time domain as:

$$u(t) = K_p\left(e(t) + \frac{1}{T_i}\int_0^t e(\tau)d\tau + T_d\frac{de(t)}{dt} \right) \tag{12}$$

where u is the controller output, e is the error between desired and actual output, T_i is integral time, and T_d is derivative time. Three important characteristics of PID controller are described as follows: it provides feedback; it eliminates steady-state error through integral action; it improves transient response by anticipating the future through derivative action. In order to meet the design specifications on transient and steady-state response, PID control is an ideal choice for autopilot design.
The PID controllers are designed by two phases. At first, the coarse PID gains are obtained according to the well-known Ziegler Nichols tuning rules that provide an acceptable closed-

loop response. Next, let the coarse PID gains be the initial guess, the Nonlinear Control System Toolset in MATLAB/Simulink is applied to optimally determine the fine PID gains to meet time domain specifications such as rise time, overshoot, settling time, steady state error, and actuator constrain. The resulting PID gains in four feedback loops of autopilot are listed in Table 4.

	K_p	T_i	T_d
Pitch Altitude Loop	-11.99	0.001118	0.005657
Velocity Loop	0.07506	0.03649	0.004805
Roll Attitude Loop	0.2571	0.003650	0.01531
Heading Loop	-1.9058	0.07574	-0.04379

Table 4. The PID Gains in Four Feedback Control Loops of UAV Autopilot.

5.2 HIL simulation results

In this section the prototype PID controller for each mode of autopilot is implemented by the PXI real-time control system, and the performance is explored in HIL simulation. The hardware arrangement of HIL simulation system is shown in Fig. 19. Figs. 20 and 21 represent the LabVIEW front panel and block diagram of UAV plant.

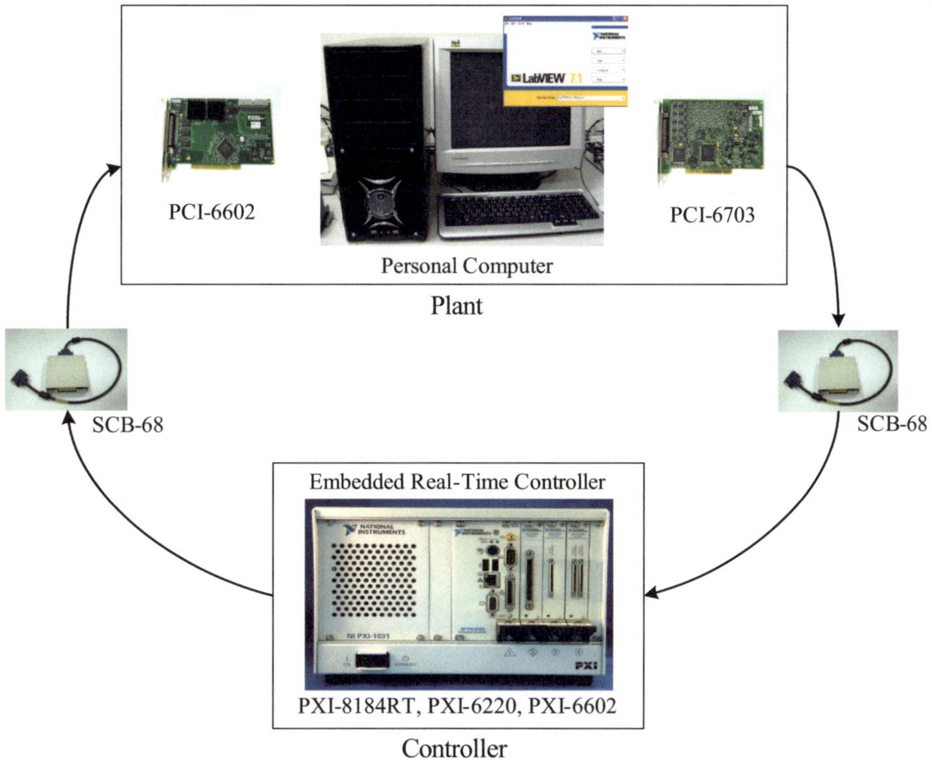

Fig. 19. The Hardware Setup of HIL simulation for UAV autopilot

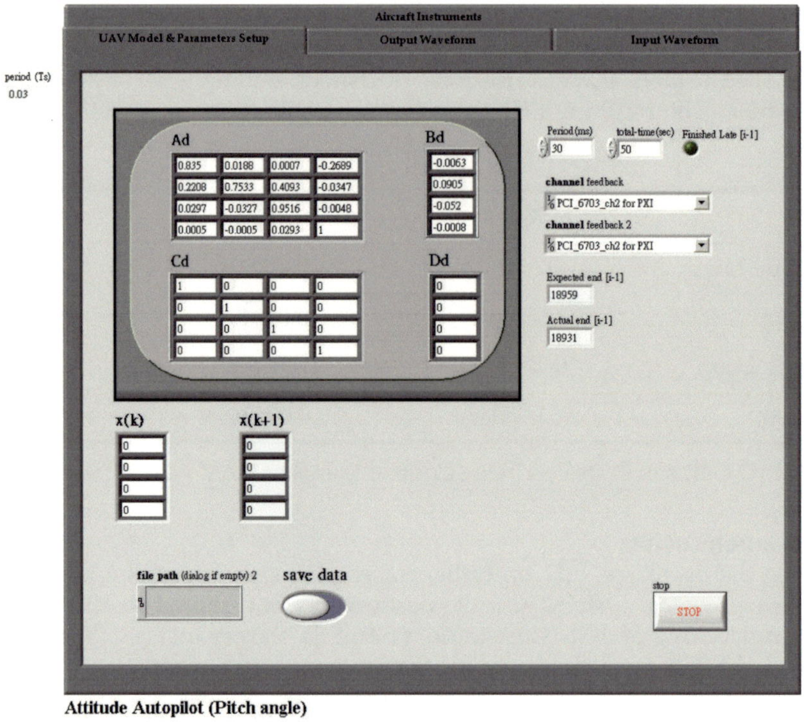

Fig. 20. LabVIEW front panel of UAV plant

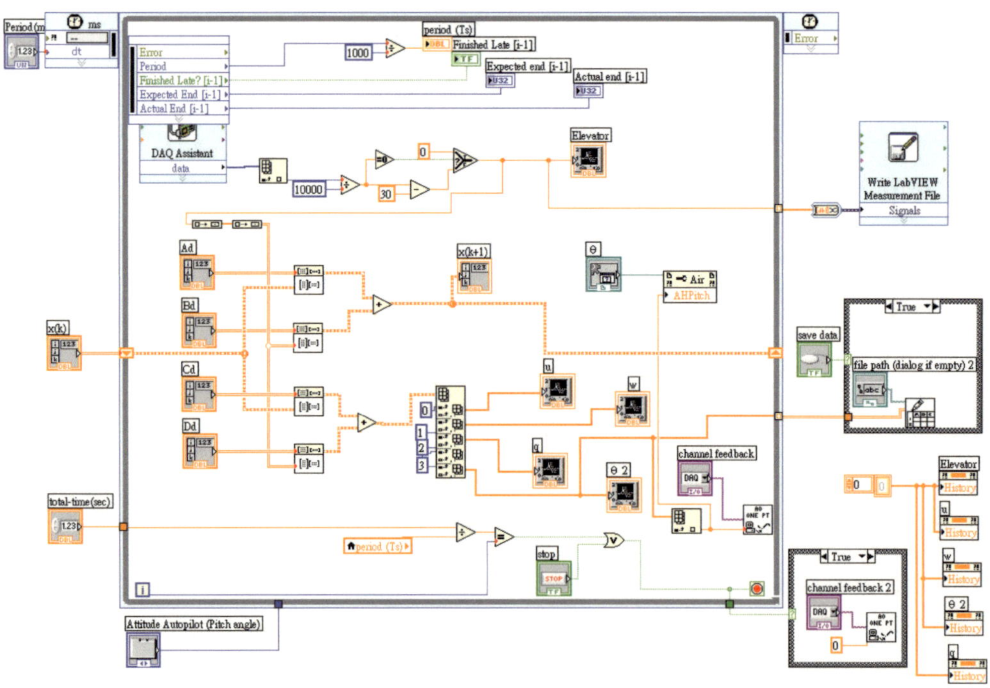

Fig. 21. LabVIEW block diagram of UAV plant

The following LabVIEW front panel and block diagram windows shown in Fig. 22 represent the prototype PID controller in pitch attitude hold mode of autopilot. It is noticed that the values of PID gains in front panel are from Table 4 where the integral time T_i and the derivative time T_d are in minute available for LabVIEW PID function.

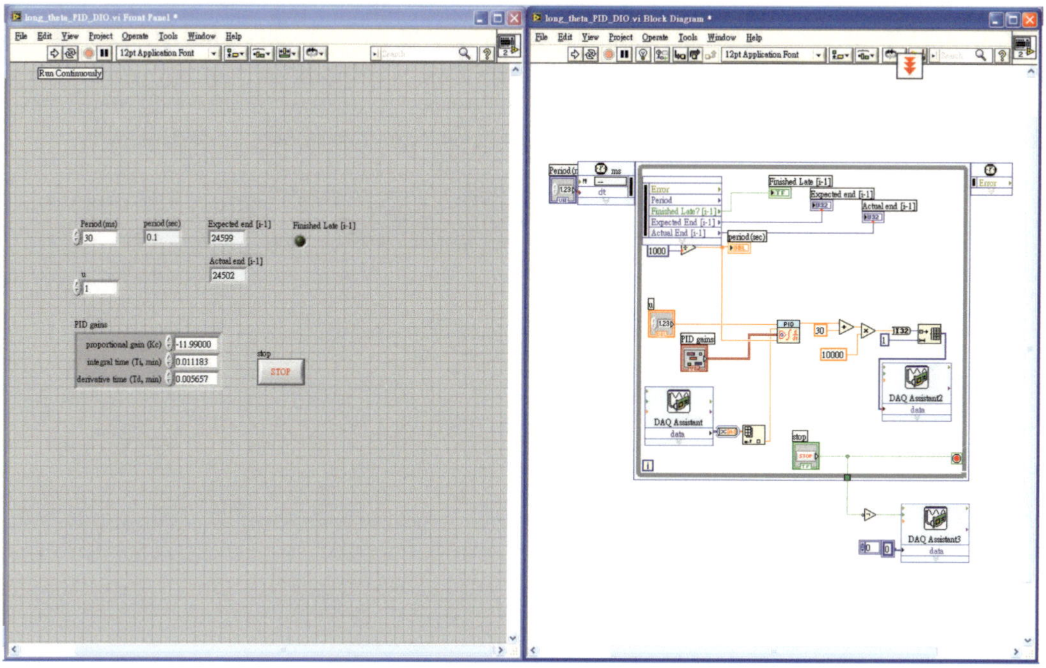

Fig. 22. LabVIEW front panel and block diagram window of PID controller

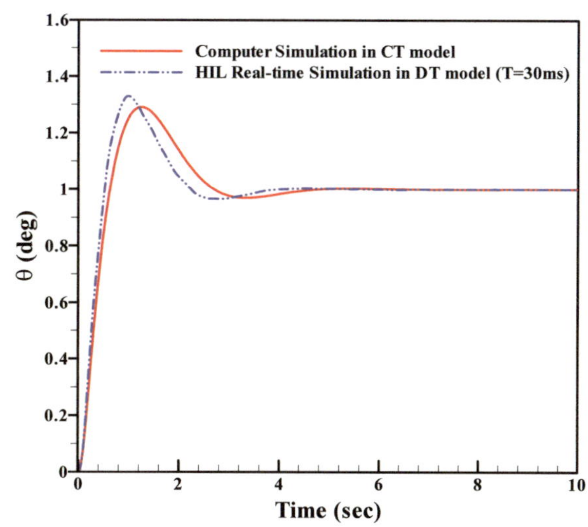

Fig. 23. The unit-step response of PID controller in pitch attitude hold mode

Figs. 23-26 show the closed loop unit-step time response of PID controllers in pitch attitude hold mode, velocity hold mode, bank angle hold mode and heading angle hold mode for

UAV autopilot. Apparently, the results of HIL simulation and computer simulation are very close to each other. Fig. 23 exhibits an underdamped response in pitch control with 4 sec. settling time, 30% overshoot, and no steady-state error; Fig. 24 also exhibits an underdamped response (a little increase in damping ratio) in velocity control with 6 sec. settling time, 35% overshoot, and no steady-state error; Fig. 25 also exhibits an underdamped response (a bigger time constant) in roll control with over 25 sec. settling time, 5% overshoot, and still no steady-state error; Fig. 26 exhibits an overdamped response in heading control with 14 sec. settling time, no overshoot, and no steady-state error. From the results in HIL simulation, PID controllers demonstrate very good performance.

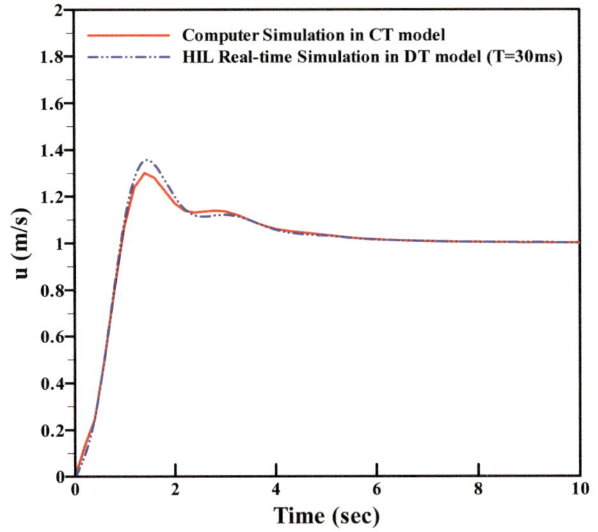

Fig. 24. The unit-step response of PID controller in airspeed hold mode

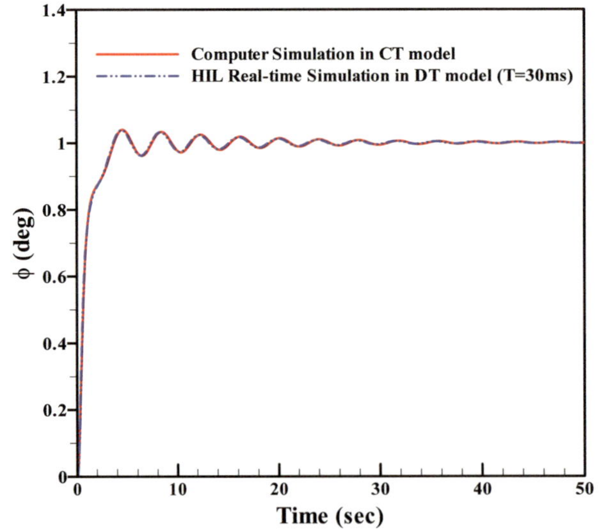

Fig. 25. The unit-step response of PID controller in bank angle hold mode

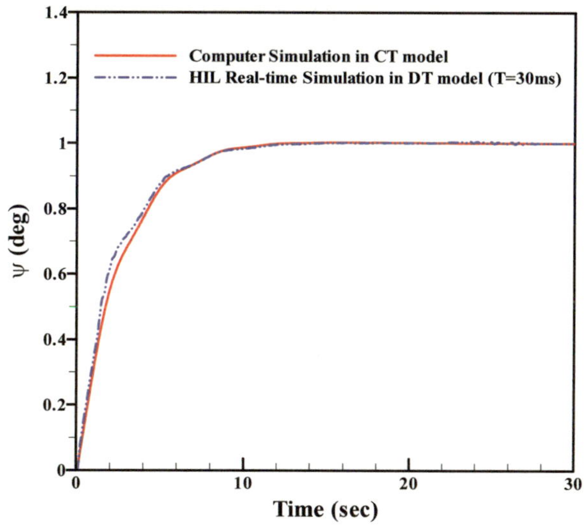

Fig. 26. The unit-step response of PID controller in heading angle hold mode

5.3 HIL simulation system including a servo unit

In this subsection the HIL simulation system with servo unit is taken into consideration. The servo unit is described in section 3.3. The HIL simulation system with servo unit is composed of three major parts: a Pentium 4 desktop personal computer (PC) system, a National Instrument (NI) real-time PXI system, and a servo unit. The hardware arrangement is shown in Fig. 27.

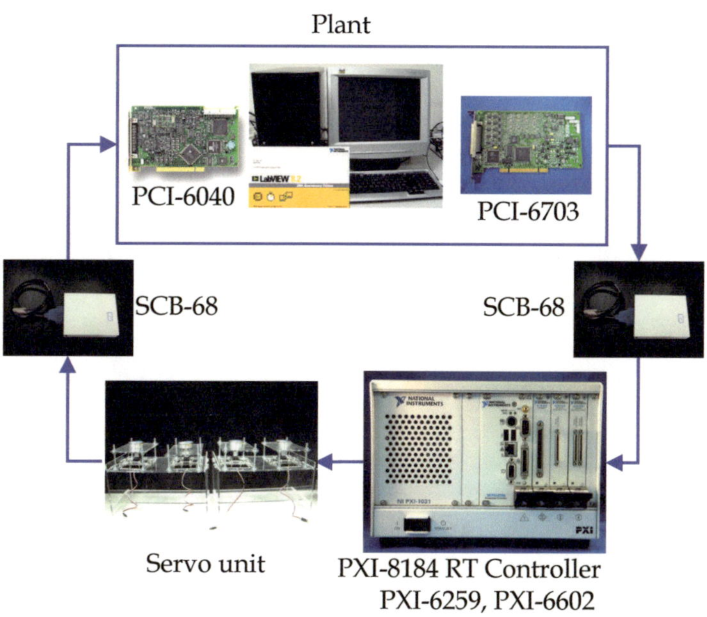

Fig. 27. The hardware arrangement of HIL simulation system with a servo unit

After receiving feedback signals by DAQ PXI-6259 from plant (PC system) that represent UAV actual states, the real-time PXI system carries out the proportional-integral-derivative (PID) algorithm, computes the control effort (control surface deflection angle and throttle setting) for UAV flight control, and then generates pulse-width-modulation (PWM) signals by DAQ PXI-6602 to control a real servo. Each servo unit consists of two Futuba-S3001 servos and two accurate potentiometers. The servo receives PWM signals from PXI system and rotates to a specific angle. The resulting angle is measured by a potentiometer and fed back to the plant through DAQ PCI-6040. Finally the PC system computes the dynamical states of UAV based on the state-space model and outputs these analog signals to the PXI system by DAQ PCI-6703. As a whole the PC system, PXI system, and servo unit constitute a real-time closed-loop control system for UAV autopilot HIL simulation.
The HIL simulation results of PID controller for system including servo is denoted by the solid line in Fig. 28. Apparently the performance becomes a little worse because the real servo and potentiometer involved in HILS system result in so called unmodelled dynamics that is not taken into consideration in controller design. This deterioration of controller performance is revealed by HIL simulation not by numerical simulation. The PID controller has to be tuned to obtain an acceptable performance. It clearly demonstrates that HIL simulation is indispensable to controller design and verification.

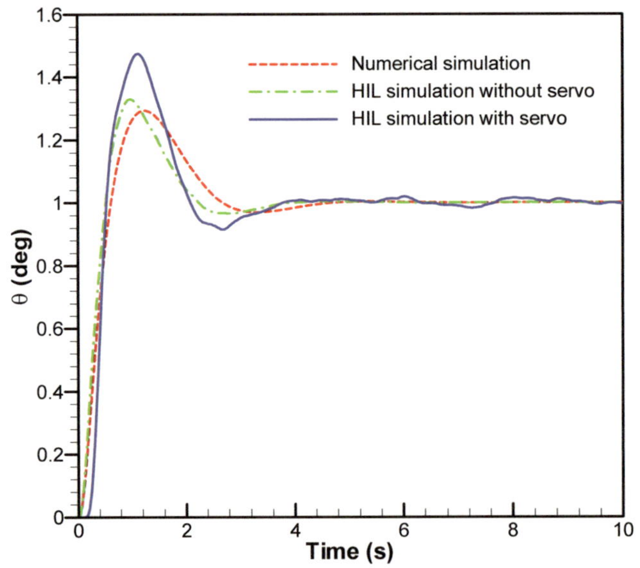

Fig. 28. The performance of PID controller for HIL simulation system including servo

6. Conclusion

With the growing importance of autonomous vehicles for industry, science, aerospace and defense applications, engineers are encouraged to use HIL simulation methodology to shorten development cycle, lower total cost and improve functional performance of the vehicles. LabVIEW features an easy-to-use graphical programming environment and an intuitive data flow programming style that makes the work of HIL simulation to be easier and more efficiency. This chapter not only provides LabVIEW solutions to HIL simulation but also presents a complete analysis, design and HILS verification of UAV stability augmentation system and autopilot.

7. References

Bullock, D., Johnson, B., Wells, R. B., Kyte, M. & Li, Z. (2004). Hardware-in-the-Loop Simulation. *Transportation Research Part C: Emerging Technologies,* Vol. 12, No. 1, (February 2004), pp. 73-89, ISSN 0968-090X

Bryson, A. E., Jr. (1994). *Control of Spacecraft and Aircraft,* Princeton University Press, ISBN 0-691-08782-2, Princeton, New Jersey, USA

Carrijo, D. S., Oliva, A. P. & W. de Castro Leite Filho (2002). Hardware-in-the-Loop Simulation development. *International Journal of Modeling and Simulation,* Vol. 22, No. 3, pp. 167-175, (July 2002), ISSN 0228-6203

Cole, D. T., Sukkarieh, S. & Goktogan, A. H. (2006). System Development and Demonstration of a UAV Control Architecture for Information Gathering Missions. *Journal of Field Robotics* , Vol. 26, No. 6-7, (June-July 2006), pp. 417-440, ISSN 1556-4967

Cook, M. V. (2007). *Flight Dynamics Principles* (2nd Ed.), Elsevier, ISBN 978-0-7506-6927-6, Oxford, UK

Cosic, K., Kopriva, I., Kostic, T., Samic, M. & Volareic, M. (1999), Design and Implementation of a Hardware-in-the-Loop Simulator for a Semi-Automatic Guided Missile System . *Simulation Practice and Theory,* Vol. 7, No. 2, (April 1999), pp. 107-123, ISSN 1569-190X

Kayton, M. & Fried, W. R. (Editors). (1969). *Avionics Navigation Systems,* John Wiley & Sons, ISBN 471-46180-6, New York, USA

Larson, R. W. (2011). *LabVIEW for Engineers,* Prentice-Hall, ISBN-13 978-0-13-609429-6, New Jersey, USA

Ledin, J. (2001). *Simulation Engineering,* CMP Books, ISBN 157-820-0806, Lawrence, USA

Nelson, R. C. (1998). *Flight Stability and Automatic Control* (2nd Ed.), McGraw-Hill, ISBN 0-07-115838-3, Boston, Massachusetts, USA

Nise, N. S. (2008). *Control Systems Engineering* (5th Ed.), John Wiley & Sons, ISBN 978-0-470-16997-1, New Jersey, USA

Roskam, J. (2007). *Airplane Flight Dynamics and Automatic Flight Controls,* Part I, DARcorporation, ISBN-13 978-1-884885-17-4, Kansas, USA

Roskam, J. (2003). *Airplane Flight Dynamics and Automatic Flight Controls,* Part II, DARcorporation, ISBN 1-884885-18-7, Kansas, USA

Salman, S. A., Puttige, V. R. & Anavatti, S. G. (2006). Real-Time Validation and Comparison of Fuzzy Identification and State-Space Identification for a UAV Platform. *Proceedings of the 2006 IEEE International Conference on Control Applications,* pp. 2138-2143, ISBN 0-7803-9797-5, Munich, Germany, October 4-6, 2006

Shetty, D. & Kolk, R. A. (1997). *Mechatronics System Design,* PWS Publishing Company, ISBN 053-495-2852, Boston, USA

Sun, Y. P., Wu, L. T. & Liang, Y. C. (2006). System Identification of Unmanned Air Vehicle and Autopilot Verification via Hardware-in-the-Loop Real-time Simulation. *Proceedings of International Forum on Systems and Mechatronics,* ISBN 986-688-904-1, Tainan, Taiwan, December 6-8, 2006

Sun, Y. P., Chu, C. Y., & Liang, Y. C. (2008a). Using Virtual Instruments to Develop an Actuator-Based Hardware-in-the-Loop Test-Bed for Autopilot of Unmanned Aerial Vehicle. *Proceedings of SPIE-Fourth International Symposium on Precision Mechanical Measurements*, Vol. 7130, Part I, pp. 71301J-1-6, ISBN 9780819473646, Anhui, China, August 25-29, 2008

Sun, Y. P., Wu, L. T. & Liang, Y. C. (2008b). Stability Derivatives Estimation of Unmanned Aerial Vehicle. *Key Engineering Materials*, Vol. 381-382, pp. 137-140, ISSN 1013-9826

Sun, Y. P., Tsai, C. H. & Liang, Y. C. (2009). Fuzzy Logic Control Design and Verification of Unmanned Aerial Vehicle Autopilot via Hardware-in-the-Loop Simulation. *Proceedings of the 2009 International Symposium on Mechatronic and Biomedical Engineering and Applications*, pp. 156-164, ISBN 978-986-7339-508 , Kaohsiung, Taiwan, November 5, 2009

Sun, Y. P., Tsai, C. H. & Liang, Y. C. (2010). Design and Implementation of a Stability Augmentation System for an Unmanned Aerial Vehicle Using Hardware-in-the-Loop Simulation. *Proceedings of the 2010 International Symposium on Mechatronic and Biomedical Engineering and Applications*, pp. 183-193, ISBN 978-986-7339-62-1, Kaohsiung, Taiwan, November 9, 2010

Travis, J. & Kring, J. (2007). *LabVIEW for Everyone: Graphical Programming Made Easy and Fun* (3rd Ed.), Prentice Hall, ISBN 0-13-185672-3, New Jersey, USA

7

Equipment Based on the Hardware in the Loop (HIL) Concept to Test Automation Equipment Using Plant Simulation

Eduardo Moreira[1], Rodrigo Pantoni[1,2] and Dennis Brandão[1]
[1]*University of São Paulo,*
[2]*Federal Institute of São Paulo,*
Brazil

1. Introduction

Considering the difficulties to test a real control system at a learning laboratory, related to equipment acquisition or physical installation, it is necessary to develop a simulation system that will act as parts of the real system.

In this scenario, through the use of recent computational resources in hardware and software, it is possible to explore the concept named Hardware in the Loop (HIL), which consists on well known technique mostly employed on the development and testing of electronic, mechanical and mechatronic real equipments by the use a data and signal interface between the equipments and computational real-time systems.

This work proposes a HIL-based system where a Foundation Fieldbus control system manages the simulation for a generic plant in an industrial process. The simulation software is executed in a PC, and its purpose is the didactic use for engineering students to learn to control a process similar to the real system.

The plant is simulated in a computer, implemented in LabVIEW and part of the fieldbus network simulator named FBSIMU (Mossin et al., 2008). Foundation Fieldbus physical devices are configured to operate in a control strategy and interact with the simulated environment.

Results demonstrate it is a feasible technique that can be extended to more complex and elaborate control strategies.

2. Works related to hardware in loop for industrial networks

HIL concept is well-known and used in the research area. For this reason, this section cites the most recent works related to HIL applied to industrial networks.

(Godoy & Porto, 2008) suggest the use of HIL technique to develop Networked Control Systems (NCS) with CAN (Controller Area Network) networks, presenting the structure for HIL usage and evaluating the benefits of using this tool to develop NCS with CAN.

Huang & Tan (2010) proposed a HIL simulator that provides an efficient development and test platform for real-time systems used in assembling lines of automation factories.

Fennibay et al. (2010) introduced the HIL technique for hardware and software shared in embedded systems. This technique reduces the need for developing models for existing hardware platforms and increases system accuracy and performance.

Li & Jiang (2010) performed a study using a physical system with steam generation together with HIL simulation, inside a training simulator of an industrial nuclear plant. The purpose is the study of fieldbus networks for steam systems. Results showed that some existent delays could be eliminated, according to the authors' suggestions.

The next chapters describes some important details of the Foundation Fieldbus protocol as well as its simulator named FBSIMU, which includes a simulation module for the dynamics of industrial plants, developed over LabVIEW and used in an HIL experiment with a real fieldbus network.

3. The foundation fieldbus protocol

The term FOUNDATION Fieldbus indicates the protocol specified by the Fieldbus Foundation. It is a digital, serial, bidirectional, and distributed protocol which interconnects field devices such as sensors, actuators and controllers. Basically, this protocol can be classified as a LAN (Local Area Network) for instruments used in process and industrial automation, with the ability to distribute the control application through the network.

This protocol is based on the ISO/OSI (International Organization for Standardization/Open System Interconnection) seven-layer reference model (International Organization For Standardization, 1994). Although being based on the ISO/OSI model, the FF does not use the network layer, the transport layer, the section layer, neither the presentation layer, because it is restricted to local applications. The entire network structure of the FF concentrates on the physical layer, the data link layer (DLL) and the application layer. Besides these three implemented layers, the protocol defines an additional layer called User Application Layer.

The FF Physical Layer, named H1, uses shielded twisted pair cable as a communication medium. The H1 specifies a 31.25 KBit/s baud rate with Manchester bit codification over a bus powered channel. The network topology configuration is flexible: it is typically configured with a trunk and several spurs, attending certain physical and electrical limitations regarding maximum lengths and number of transmitters.

The DLL carries the transmission control of all messages on the fieldbus and its protocol grants to the FF network temporal determinism. The communication is based on a master-slave model with a central communication scheduler (master), named Link Active Scheduler or LAS. This node performs the medium access control (MAC).

Two types of DLL layer are standardized: Basic and Link Master. A Basic DLL transmitter does not have LAS capabilities, it operates passively as a communication slave. A Link Master DLL transmitter, on the other hand, can execute LAS functions and thus, if the active LAS node fails, become the LAS node.

The FF Data Link Layer supports two transmission policies: one addressed to scheduled cyclic data and another to sporadic (unscheduled) background data. These two communication policies share the physical bus but they are respectively segmented in cyclic time slots or periods. In the scheduled communication period, most process variables generated by periodic processes are transmitted cyclically according to a static global schedule table loaded on the LAS node. This cyclic transmission mode has higher priority over acyclic transmission modes.

A periodic process can be defined as a process initiated at predetermined points in time, also called a time-triggered process. The period for this class of process is typically some milliseconds, and it is mandatory to consider that the generated data must be delivered before the next data is available. This type of periodic data is usually related to measurement and control variables (Cavalieri et al., 1993).

The sporadic or unscheduled communication is used to transmit non periodic, or aperiodic, data generated by sporadic processes not directly related to the control loop cycles, but to configuration actions and data supervision efforts. The unscheduled transmissions are dispatched under a token pass scheme. A token that circulates among all active nodes on the bus is used in FF protocol. Once a transmitter receives the token, it has granted the right to send pending aperiodic messages with a minimum priority for a specific time period.

Non periodic (or event-triggered) processes are initiated as soon as specific events are noted (Pop et al., 2002). The event-triggered processes are unpredictable and usually related to alarm notifications, configuration data and user commands as cited before. Although the acyclic traffic is less frequent than the cyclic one, the acyclic data should be delivered also prior to a certain time deadline, according to the system requirements.

For a description of the MAC operation on both cyclic and acyclic phases, refer to (Hong & Ko, 2001) (Wang et al., 2002) (Petalidis & Gill, 1998).

The FF User Layer is directly related to the process automation tasks themselves and it is based on distributed control or monitoring strategies of Function Blocks. Function Blocks (FBs) are User Layer elements that encapsulate basic automation functions and consequently make the configuration of a distributed industrial application modular and simplified (Chen et al., 2002). Distributed among the transmitters, the FBs have their inputs and outputs linked to other blocks in order to perform distributed closed control loop schemes. When blocks from different transmitters are linked together, a remote link is configured and mapped to a cyclic message. Considering that all cyclic messages should be released in a predetermined instant defined on a schedule table, and that they carry data generated by the FBs, it is adequate to synchronize the execution of the FB set on the system with the referred cyclic transmissions schedule table. This solution leads to the concept of joint scheduling (Ferreiro et al., 1997).

The Foundation Fieldbus standardized a set of ten basic function blocks (Fieldbus Foundation, 1999a), a complementary set of eleven advanced control blocks (Fieldbus Foundation, 1999b), and a special flexible function block intended to be fully configurable, i.e., internal logic and parameter, by the user (Fieldbus Foundation, 1999c). The standard and advanced block sets provide mathematical and engineering calculations necessary to configure typical industrial control loops strategies, while the flexible function block can be applied to custom or advanced controls or to complex interlocking logics based on ladder nets. It is important to state, however, that the standard is open at this point, permitting the integration of "user-defined" custom function blocks in order to enhance the capabilities of FF control system and make the integration of novel control techniques possible.

4. FBSIMU architecture

The basic concept of the FBSIMU architecture is to map each Function Block, as well as the plant, in an independent LabVIEW application, also named Virtual Instrument (VI). The configuration of the whole system is centralized in the FBSIMU.CONF module. This module's front panel (GUI) is inspired by commercial fieldbus configuration tools.
As mentioned before, the FBSIMU is focused on the function block application layer and it is composed exclusively of software according to a modular and extensible architecture. The simulator was developed in LabVIEW using the G graphical programming language, "native" language in this environment. Each FBSIMU module or software unit simulates an element or a structure of a real FOUNDATION Fieldbus system (Mossin et al., 2008).

4.1 Function block simulation

The Function Block modules are programmed into the FBSIMU according to the FF specifications directions and, consequently, the usage and configuration of a simulated control loop on the FBSIMU environment is identical to a real FF system.
A VI library has been developed (Pinotti & Brandão, 2005) to provide a range of typical Foundation Fieldbus control and acquisition functions according to the standards. Another VI functionality facilitates the development and integration of standard and custom FBs to the system. These functions encapsulate different FF calculations and data type manipulations necessary to build Function Blocks, configuring a "LabVIEW Foundation Fieldbus Tool Kit". A Function Block seed module is also used to facilitate the process of developing and integrating new projects. The seed has the whole FB module structure (an empty structure) and directions to proceed with a FB project from the design to the final test procedures.
Each FB module is built as two different versions that share the same FB core: stand-alone and process. The stand-alone FBs are executed by user commands and controlled by its front panel. Its execution can be performed independently of any other module, so the user is able to test the FB and simulate its operation under a controlled condition of inputs and outputs. The graphical user interface is intuitive and enables the user to execute the FB continually or in a step-by-step mode.
The process version of a FB, on the other hand, is controlled remotely likewise real FBs. Each process FB has a unique identification and its operation is controlled by the user through the following commands:

- FB_Read: this service allows the value associated with a block parameter to be read.
- FB_Write: this confirmed service allows the value associated with a block parameter to be written.
- FB_Exec: this service triggers the block algorithm to be executed.
- FB_Reset: this service allows default values associated with all block parameters to be written.

Process FBs do not have front panels; they are instantiated by the FBSIMU.CONF in each simulation process. The communications between process FBs and the FBSIMU.CONF are performed programmatically and dynamically by the LabVIEW function "Call by Reference Node". It is important to note that the industrial transmitters are not considered in the FBSIMU architecture, i.e., function blocks are instantiated on the simulation without being allocated in specific "virtual" transmitters. The FBSIMU.CONF module front panel for fieldbus configuration is shown in Figure 1.

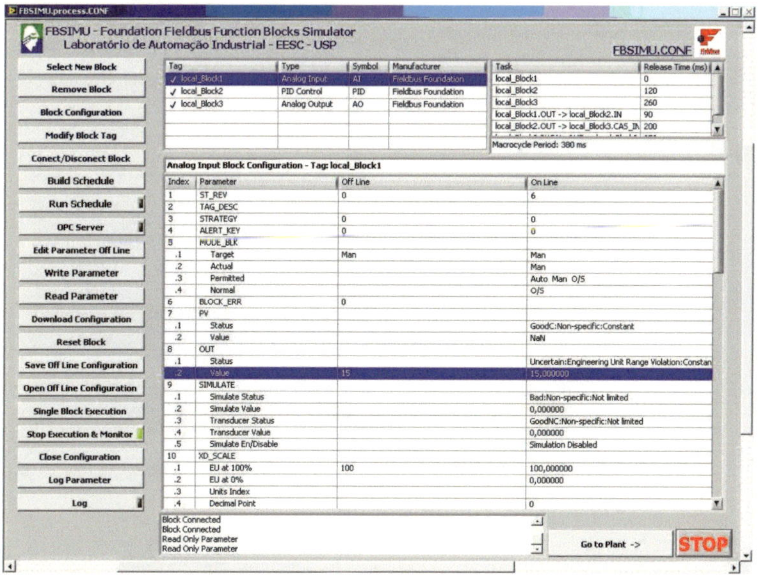

Fig. 1. FBSIMU front panel for fieldbus configuration

4.2 Physical plant simulations

The plant module cyclically executes a discrete single variable (SISO) linear ARX (Auto-Regressive with Exogenous Inputs) mathematical structure (Ljung, 1999), according to equation 1. This module is configured by the FBSIMU.CONF and simulates the controlled plant. The adopted ARX structure is represented by equation (1), where k is the discrete time instant, Y is the output vector, U is the input vector, i is the number of MIMO plant inputs and outputs, na is the number of output regressors, and nb is the number of input regressors. In the current version, i is set to 1 (one) to reflect a SISO model.

$$Y_{ix1}(k) = \sum_{s=1}^{na} As_{ixi} \otimes Y_{ix1}(k-s) + \sum_{s=1}^{nb} Bs_{ixi} \otimes U_{ix1}(k-s) \tag{1}$$

The simulated plant dynamic behavior is modeled on the dynamic matrixes A and B. It must be observed that the number of regressors limits the model dynamic order - in the actual version it is limited to third order systems - and that all regressors must be initialized prior to starting the simulation. A white noise generator function adds a simulated acquisition noise to each plant output bounded by user configurable amplitude.

As the user chooses the plant order (1st, 2nd or 3rd) and dynamics (gain for 1st and 2nd order systems, damping ratio, natural frequency and time constant), the selected plants' Bode Magnitude Chart, Pole-Zero Map, Root Locus Graph and the Step Response are instantly presented on the front panel. The third order system is composed of a first order system in series with a second order one, both adjustable by the user, as stated.

A white noise signal can be also introduced with configurable absolute amplitude over the plant output. Figure 2 shows the FBSIMU.CONF module front panel for plant configuration.

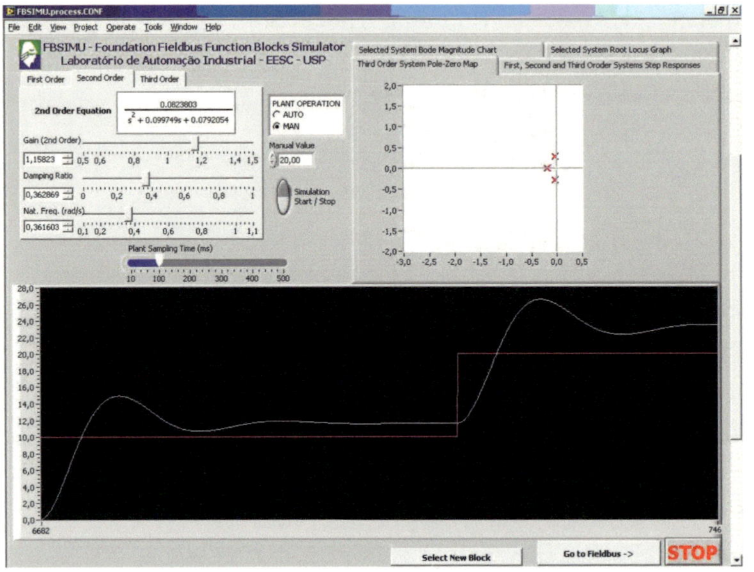

Fig. 2. FBSIMU front panel for plant configuration

4.3 Simulation architecture

The proposed execution model for the fieldbus simulation on FBSIMU can be considered hybrid, because some tasks are event-driven while other tasks are time-triggered. All tasks related to the user interface are event-driven, they are executed after a user action such as selecting a new block, configuring schedule table, saving a configuration or starting the execution.

On the other hand, the tasks related to executing FBs according to a schedule table, plant simulation, and online monitoring of FBs are time-triggered.

Due to the fact that all tasks are performed on a single microprocessor they are, naturally, concurrent. The proposed solution for preventing unexpected delays of time-triggered tasks (considered critical) due to executing event-driven tasks (considered non-critical) is adopting priority levels for each task and preemptive execution mode.

In the preemptive execution mode, a higher priority task that is ready to execute preempts all lower priority tasks, which are also ready to execute or actually during execution.

Table 1 summarizes the FBSIMU task set and its timing and execution characteristics.

Module	Priority	Execution	Timeout	Determinism
GUI & User commands	Low-Low	Event driven	1 sec.	No
FB Schedule	High-High	Time triggered according to the schedule table	No	Yes
Plant Execution	High	Periodic with configurable period	No	Yes
Online FB Parameters Monitoring	Low	Periodic with period = 500ms	No	Yes

Table 1. FBSIMU task set

5. Proposed hardware in loop

This section presents the topics related to developing a process automation system based on the HIL concept: the architecture, variables and equipments dimensioning, materials used, and application tools used. The goal is to prove the efficiency of using the HIL concept to create a process automation didactic kit with analog measuring for a simulated plant.

5.1 Architecture

The simplest architecture of a device using the HIL concept consists of two components: the system simulator and the related control. It is important to consider the communication interface of the devices, since the interaction between them is not really common from the point of view of the applications they were designed for.

The project development is divided based on these components, because from the HIL applications viewpoint these areas are modular and, apart from few restrictions, their components can be replaced without compromising the quality of the tests. However, this is just one path to start researching the devices to be used.

To reach the final architecture, intermediate steps decide the types of components necessary for the proper operation of the device. Available resources were analyzed at each step, considering some restrictions, such as: device availability, architecture requirements and simplicity (only one input and one output).

The diagram, illustrated in Figure 3, was defined after the final step, and it contains all types of devices necessary for proper operation.

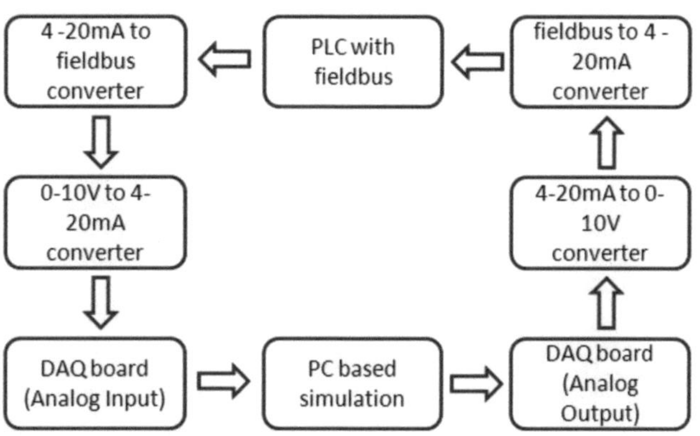

Fig. 3. View of the architecture

5.2 Materials and dimensioning

After defining the final architecture, it is possible to select the components available for the kit. Table 2 lists all physical components used in the project as well as the corresponding description, including the device model and manufacturer. Components with the description "---" are accessories to the device operation, but they do not perform a role related to control/simulation.

Role in Architecture	Device Model	Manufacturer
Bridge	DF51 1x10 Mbps, 4xH1 - FF	SMAR
---	PS302 - DC Power Supply for DF51	SMAR
---	DF53 - Power Supply Impedance for FF - H1 network	SMAR
---	BT302 Bus Terminator	SMAR
Converter FF -> 4-20mA	FI302 – Triple Channel Fieldbus to Current Converter	SMAR
Converter 4-20mA -> FF	IF302 – Triple Channel Current to Fieldbus Converter	SMAR
---	BT302 – Bus Terminator	SMAR
Converter 4-20mA -> 0-10V	TCA1100 – 1-Channel Current to Voltage Converter	TECNATRON
Converter 0-10V -> 4-20mA	TCA1100 – 1-Channel Voltage to Current Converter	TECNATRON
---	24 V DC Power Supply for TCA1100	TECNATRON
Data Acquisition Boards	NI-DAQmx 6221	NATIONAL INSTRUMENTS
PC	Personal Microcomputer with two NIC	Not available
Software Programs	LabVIEW®8.2 – for simulation Syscon 7 – for bridge configuration	NATIONAL INSTRUMENTS & SMAR

Table 2. Physical components

Devices were installed according to the corresponding datasheets and manuals. Figure 4 shows the electrical installation schema among the devices listed in Table 2.

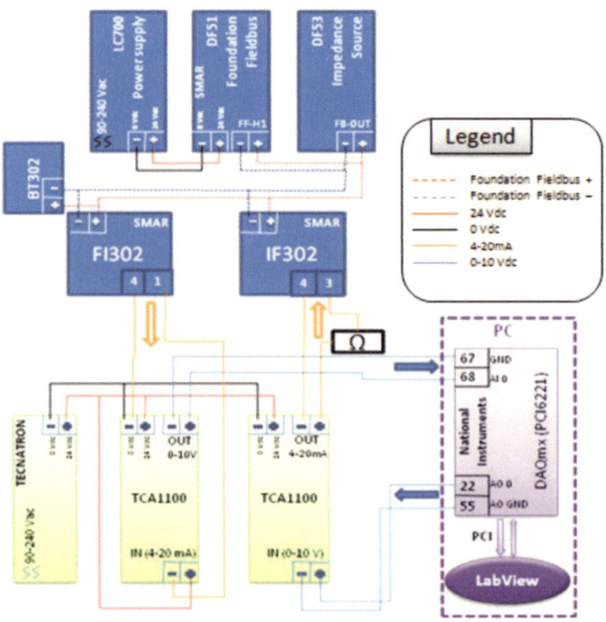

Fig. 4. Electrical installation among components

5.2.1 Communication interface

Automation systems are developed to operate with real systems and not computer simulations, therefore it is necessary to develop an interface that packs the signals and assures a coherent signal conversion.

The interface is composed by devices that connect simulation to control instruments. The interface is used when conforming input and output signal from the virtual plant created, so the field devices are able to read those signals.

National Instruments Data Acquisition board - NI-DAQmx PCI 6221 (National Instruments, 2003) - was chosen as the communication interface to assure compatibility and signal quality, because the virtual plant is configured by LabVIEW, software product from the same manufacturer. However, since this board generates signals by varying the 0-10 volts voltage, it was necessary to add transducers because field devices read and write 4-20 mA standard signals.

Figure 5 shows the electrical installation schema for the interface to pack signals. The box on the right represents the Analog Digital Converter NI-DAQmx PCI 6221 connected to the PCI slot in the computer executing simulation. The other boxes are components for the 0-10 volts to 4-20 mA standard converter (s).

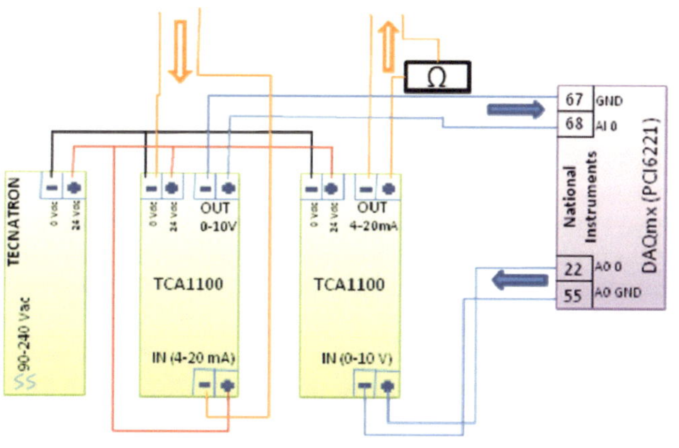

Fig. 5. Interface electrical installation

The interface operation is very simple. The control signal from the FI302 transmitter, from SMAR, is sent to the 4-20 mA converter input, and then converted to the 0-10 volts standard, so the National Instruments data acquisition board can read and send the signal to the simulator.

On the other way around, the simulator sends the signal converted to the 0-10 volts standard by DAQ 6221, straight to the transducer to be then converted to a 4-20 mA signal. After that, the signal is read by IF302.

A system that reads many variables and operates several instruments is clearly more complex because it requires a large amount of transducers, but, it would be only necessary to repeat basic transducer units describe here. A boiler, for instance, may request reading from the internal pressure, temperature, or internal liquid flow. Control operation for this system may involve liquid input and output flow control, pressure valves, etc.

5.3 Software

After installing the physical instruments of the project, simulation and FF instruments configuration are implemented. LabVIEW® is used as a development environment to configure the simulator, and Syscon (Smar Syscon, 2011), configures and monitors the Foundation Fieldbus network.

5.3.1 LabVIEW®

In this project, the FBSIMU simulation environment is a software tool developed using LabVIEW®, from National Instruments. The advantage of this environment is the fact that it is a platform for creating virtual instruments (VIs), with emphasis to the external signal acquisition.

The Simulator was developed to be intuitive and simple to use. Simply define the parameters intrinsic to the transfer function that represents an industrial process, and the user will view the response to this function in a graphical screen. This functionality was designed considering three main areas: the response chart, the fundamental analysis chart, and parameter inputs. In order to manually control the input, a scroll button was implemented to enable the user to visualize the plant reaction (transfer function) according to the input alteration.

Function H(s) may represent first-order, second-order, and third-order functions. Parameters can be altered according to the user's need on the same tab showing the function. There are three tabs: the first-order, second-order, and third-order. Besides showing the parameters to be configured, these tabs also show Function H(s) - response to the unitary impulse - related to the selected tab, and the user can understand how altering the parameters can affect the function.

Select the tab related to the function to be used to activate the function, and then, execute the function.

While the parameters values of the transfer function vary, the user can analyze the function in several ways. For instance, when the fundamental frequency bar varies, the impulse response chart indicates the function behavior according to each unitary impulse on the function.

For a real time system, input and output information must be updated constantly. During implementation, it was necessary to discretize the transfer function, then it would be possible to add a parameter (sampling time) to reduce processing costs. This fact would contribute to the veracity of the simulation, if the measuring devices were digital, which is not the case in this project, based on analog measuring.

After the discretization of the transfer function, the function output is calculated and sent to the data acquisition board output. This result is also plotted on a chart, in the software screen.

Input and output processing requires three steps to be executed:

I. Read the value the controller is sending to the input function, directly from the data acquisition board;
II. Process the input value according to the applied function - discretization and output calculation;
III. Write the value directly to the data acquisition board so the controller can read it and make a decision.

Similarly, this process can also be applied to other analysis charts in the simulator. Therefore, system designers, as well as control theory students, will have a clear view, quickly calculated, of several graphical analyses of the simulated transfer function.

The NI-DAQmx 6221 data acquisition board has VIs (or Virtual Instruments, which represent several function blocks) for control and communication ready to be used in LabVIEW®. These functionalities enable the simulator to connect directly to the world outside the computer. Input and output acquisition blocks were connected direct to the input and output of the simulator's transfer function. Thus the information cycle is closed, as indicated in Figure 6.

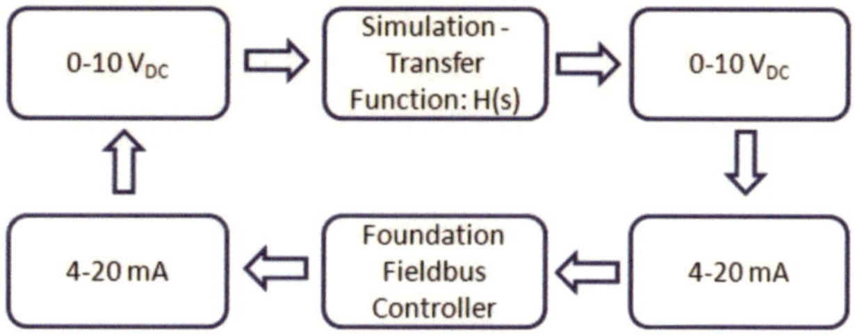

Fig. 6. Connection between simulation and devices

LabVIEW programming is implemented with blocks connected through "lines" where the information travels. Each line can carry information in different formats, from a single Boolean variable to a status matrix. There also loops for cyclic processes, created by the programmer. Figure 7 shows the logical project for the FBSIMU Fieldbus network simulator.

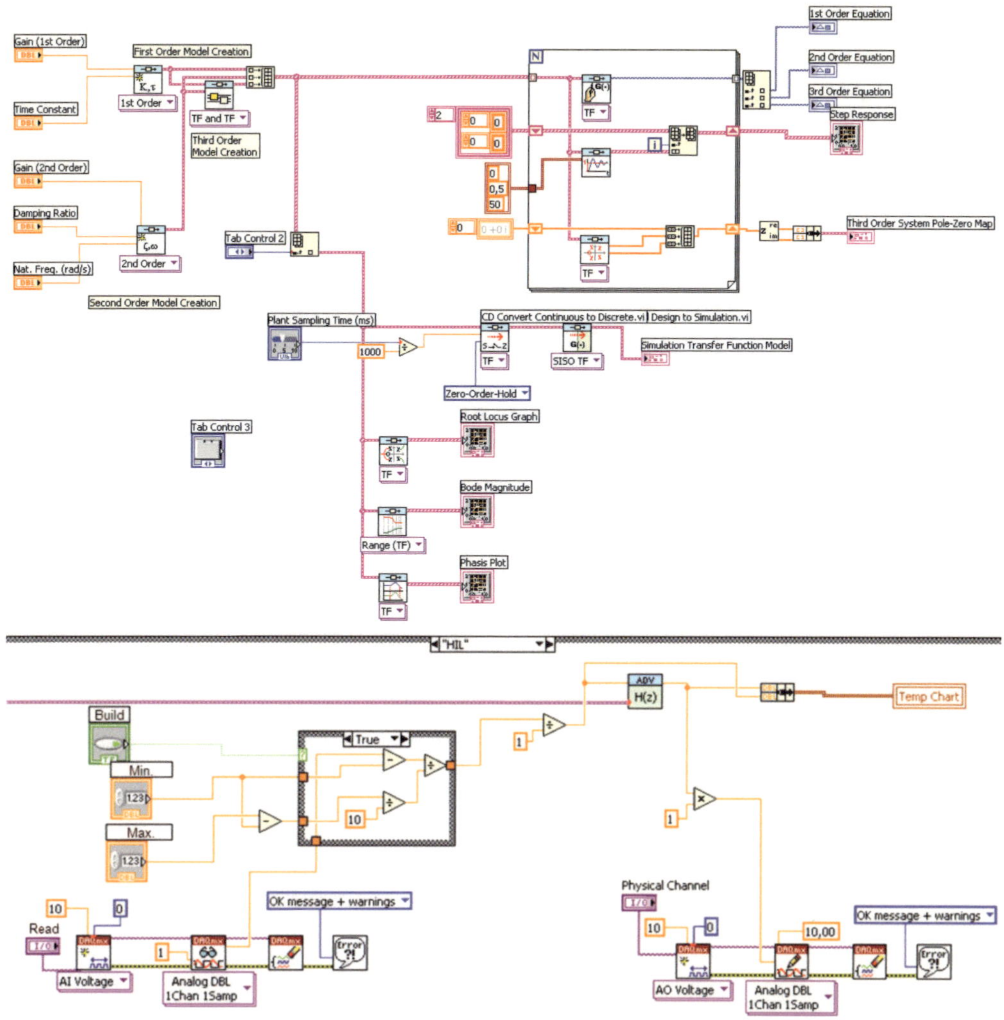

Fig. 7. Instruments and simulation connections

5.3.2 SYSCON

Syscon, a software tool developed by Smar, configures and maintain FF Networks.
In this project, Syscon is responsible for configuring and maintaining the following devices:

- SMAR DF51 - Bridge Foundation Fieldbus
- SMAR FI302 - Foundation Fieldbus to 4-20mA Transducer
- SMAR IF302 - 4-20mA to Foundation Fieldbus Transducer

Considering the list of all blocks available, the most convenient blocks are selected for the application. In this project, the following blocks are configured:

- Analog Input - IF302 function block that converts the analog current signal to Foundation Fieldbus standard selected during configuration;
- Analog Output - FI302 function block that converts the Foundation Fieldbus standard signal to current;
- PID Control - FI302 function block that executes Proportional Integral Derivative control.

The Tests and Results section describes the blocks involved in the control strategies and their corresponding parameterizations, on which the tests and results from this work are based.

6. Tests and results

This section describes how the simulator and its control operation were started, which tests were performed, and results from the tests. Information generated in this phase will be a base to conclude the project. Two tests were performed: Loop test and PID Control test.

6.1 Loop test

The loop test measures all process variables and may indicate how the system behaves, as for response time or error range, for example. In addition, this test usually calibrates instruments. The following paragraphs reports the steps to perform this test.
Initially, the Fieldbus network must be created using Syscon. The bridge (DF51) is added to this network, and the slave devices for measuring and reading (IF302 e FI302) are added to this bridge.
Since no processing is really executed in the devices during this test, only the input and output blocks need to be configured for the IF302 and FI302 devices. Therefore, the next step is to configure parameters for the devices.
The Analog Input block is added to IF302, because the device's internal transducer will only have to convert the 4-20mA signal to the Foundation Fieldbus standard. Figure 8 illustrates Syscon window showing the devices and the blocks configured for IF302. TR, RS, DSP and AI blocks are configured according the parameters and related values listed in Table 3.

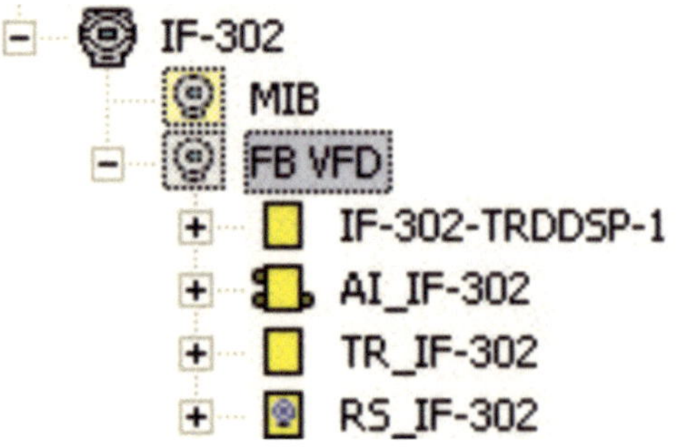

Fig. 8. Syscon window and IF302

Block	Parameter		Value
TR	MODE_BLK TARGET		AUTO
	TERMINAL_NUMBER		3
RS	MODE_BLK TARGET		AUTO
DSP	MODE_BLK TARGET		AUTO
	BLOCK_TAG_PARAM_1		AI_IF-302
	INDEX_RELATIVE_1		8
	MNEMONIC_1		CUR_FIELD
	ACCESS_1		MONITORING
	ALPHA_NUM_1		MNEMONIC
	DISPLAY_REFRESH		UPDATE DISPLAY
AI	MODE_BLK TARGET		AUTO
	XD_SCALE	EU_100	20
		EU_0	4
		UNITS_INDEX	mA
	OUT_SCALE	EU_100	100
		EU_0	0
		UNITS_INDEX	%
	CHANNEL		3
	L_TYPE		INDIRECT

Table 3. Function block configuration for IF302

FI302 contains the Analog Output block, because this device will have to convert Foundation Fieldbus standard signals to 4-20 mA signals. Figure 9 illustrates Syscon window showing the devices and the blocks configured for FI302. TR, RS, DSP and AO blocks are configured according the parameters and corresponding values listed in Table 4.

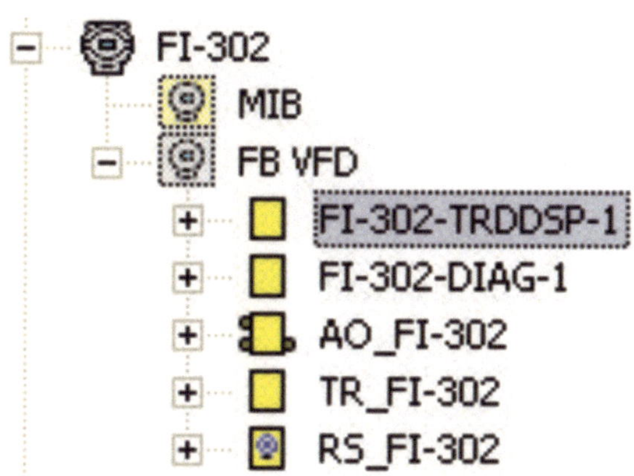

Fig. 9. Syscon window and FI302

After configuring the devices, it is necessary to create the control strategy. In loop test, data travels in loop with no alterations, and the control strategy simply connects an input block to an output block, as indicated in Figure 10.

Block	Parameter		Value
TR	MODE_BLK TARGET		AUTO
	TERMINAL_NUMBER		1
RS	MODE_BLK TARGET		AUTO
DSP	MODE_BLK TARGET		AUTO
	BLOCK_TAG_PARAM_1		AO_FI-302
	INDEX_RELATIVE_1		9
	MNEMONIC_1		CUR_FIELD
	ACCESS_1		MONITORING
	ALPHA_NUM_1		MNEMONIC
	DISPLAY_REFRESH		UPDATE DISPLAY
AO	MODE_BLK	TARGET	CAS_AUTO
		NORMAL	CAS_AUTO
	PV_SCALE	EU_100	100
		EU_0	0
		UNITS_INDEX	%
	XD_SCALE	EU_100	20
		EU_0	4
		UNITS_INDEX	mA
	CHANNEL		1

Table 4. Function block configuration for FI302

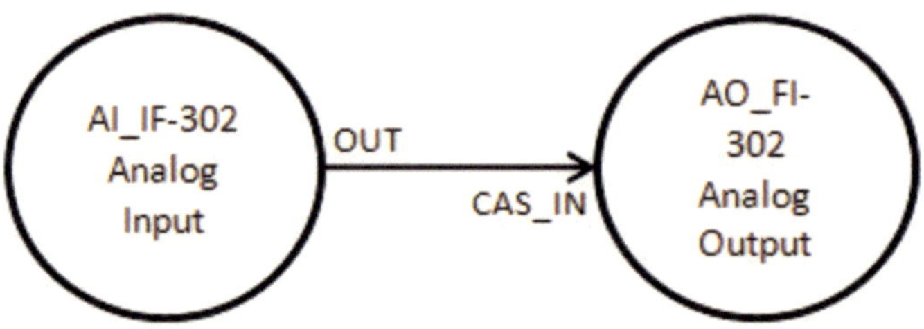

Fig. 10. FF strategy control for I/O test

Once devices are configured and the control strategy is implemented, the plant must be commissioned, and after that, the configuration and the strategy must be downloaded. Finally, the physical control plant is ready to operate.

The next step is using a software tool to complete the prototype data loop. Therefore, a new VI is configured for the test. In this VI, the user can set a value - using the scroll bar - to the loop. If the implementation is correct, this value should appear on a second bar with a slight variation. For example, if value "7" is set on the scroll bar, a sequence close to this value should appear during the loop execution, as indicated in Figure 11.

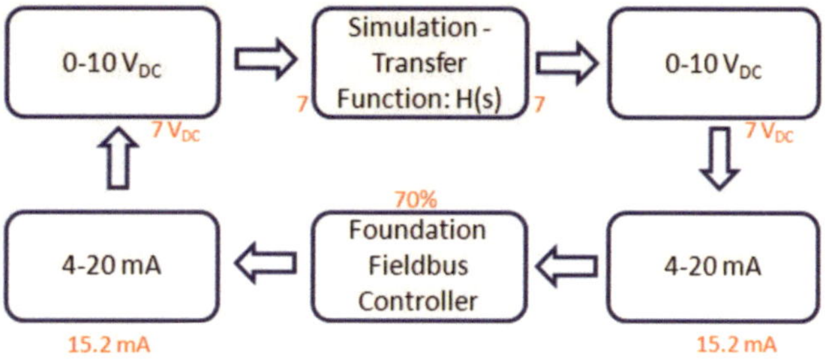

Fig. 11. Loop values for the first test

Figure 12 exemplify the VI specially developed to execute the test, with value "7" being written and read.

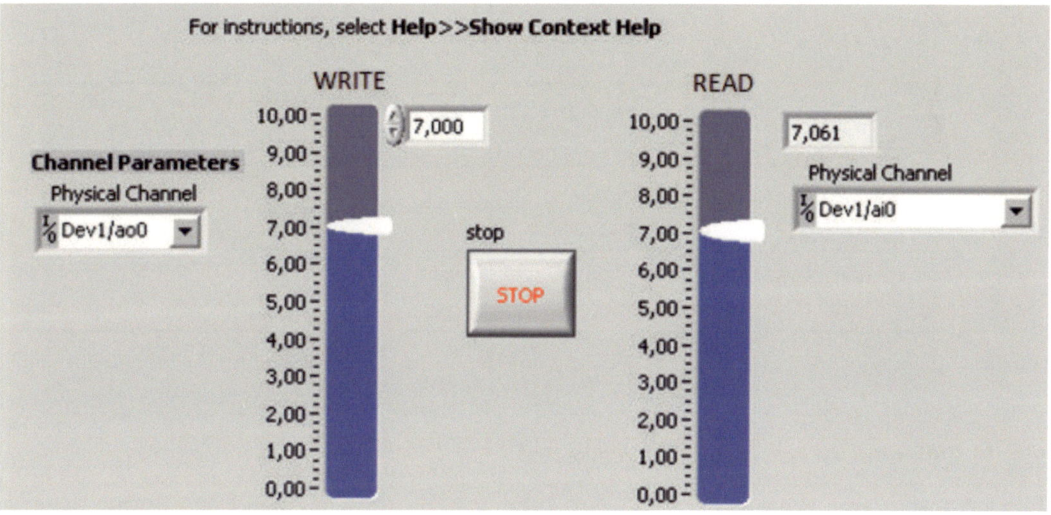

Fig. 12. Screen capture for the VI developed for the test

Figure 13 represents the logic applied to develop the VI from Figure 9.

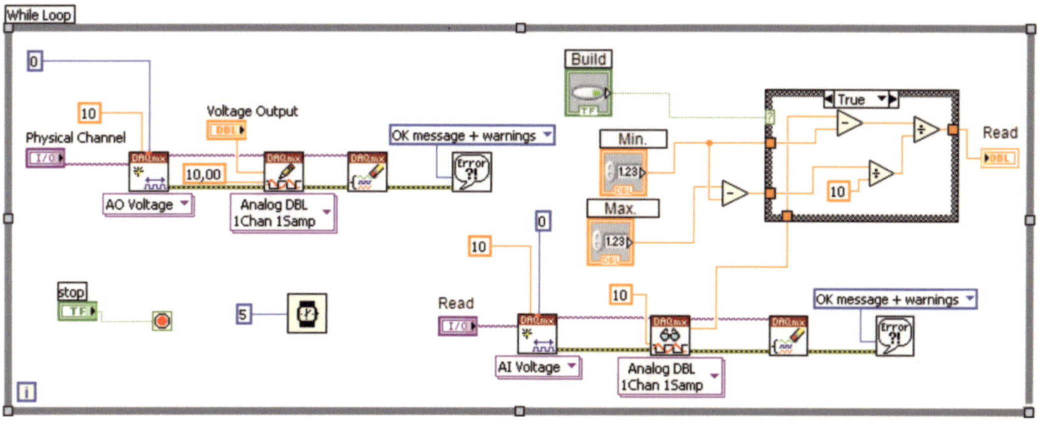

Fig. 13. Logic developed on the VI for the test

During the cycle tests, a difference on the voltage values the controller sends to the simulated plant was detected. Several tests were performed to evaluate this problem and the conclusion is that somehow the analog input from NI-DAQmx 6221 was sampling values different from the values measured externally (with multimeters, for example). Other analog inputs were used, but they all showed the same problem. Several attempts to calibrate the board were made, but none was successful.

Since a more complex calibration would demand more time, it was decided to adopt a mathematical solution by changing the coordinates, so there would be a better signal adequacy. Differences in values are according to the chart in Figure 14.

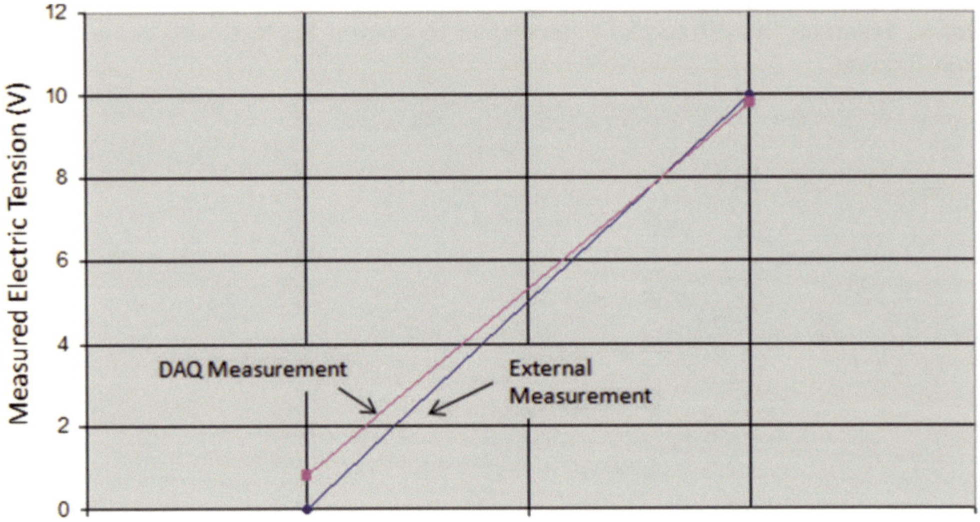

Fig. 14. Difference in values read and corrected

The next step was measuring the delay time for the data to travel the entire loop. A maximum value (10) was set on the scroll bar, and the time the second bar took to get to a very close value was then measured. The results indicated in Table 5 were obtained.

Procedure	No. of Measurings	Average Time
Maximum ascent variation (0 → 10)	10	2,33 s
Maximum descent variation (10→ 0)	10	2,70 s

Table 5. Average delay time for the complete loop

These results are just qualitative and do not accurately represent the reality of the system. However, they give an idea of the delay that occurs while actuating the plant. Delays are caused by processing and conversions the signal undergoes during the cycle.

6.2 PID control test

After the loop test was finished successfully, the plant PID control test is executed. The simulator can be finally executed to test external control. Only the alterations made on the previous item (the changes in coordinates) are included to the program for proper operation. The control diagram is according to the representation in Figure 15.

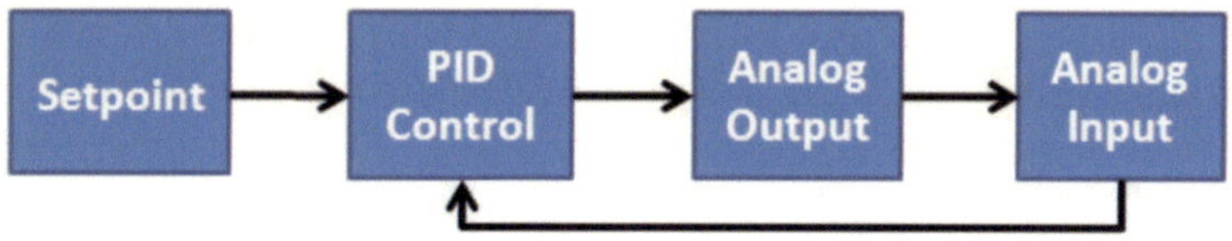

Fig. 15. Control diagram

Unlike the Pure I/O test, the PID Control test requires a control block, therefore the "PID" block was added to the strategy used in the previous test, between the AI and AO blocks, creating a cascade control strategy as illustrate in Figure 16.

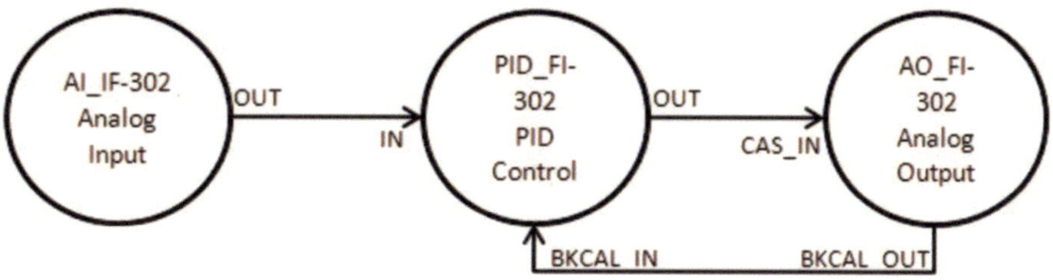

Fig. 16. FF control strategy for PID test

Since the IF302 and FI302 devices were already configured for the previous test, only the new PID control block - from FI302 - must be configure for the operation. Table 6 indicates the configuration for the PID block from FI302.

Block	**Parameter**		**Value**
PID	MODE_BLK.	TARGET	AUTO
	PV_SCALE	EU_100	100
		EU_0	0
		UNITS_INDEX	%
	OUT_SCALE	EU_100	100
		EU_0	0
		UNITS_INDEX	%
	GAIN		0.5
	RESET		1
	RATE		0

Table 6. PID Function block configuration

Parameters GAIN, RESET and RATE are Kp, Ki and Kd, respectively.
The control can finally actuate the simulated plant on LabVIEW once the configuration is ready. A first-order function is selected on the simulation environment because it is visually easier to understand the control actuation with this function. Equation (2) is used in domain "s" for the experiment.

$$H(s) = \frac{1}{4s+1} \tag{2}$$

On the first attempt to control via PID, only the Proportional parameter was selected, because the response curve should be very close to the step response curve of the function above. The expected response is a reaction of the plant to the input that varies around the PID set point. The chart in Figure 17 shows the excitation and response curves related to the function, for a proportional gain equals to 0.5.

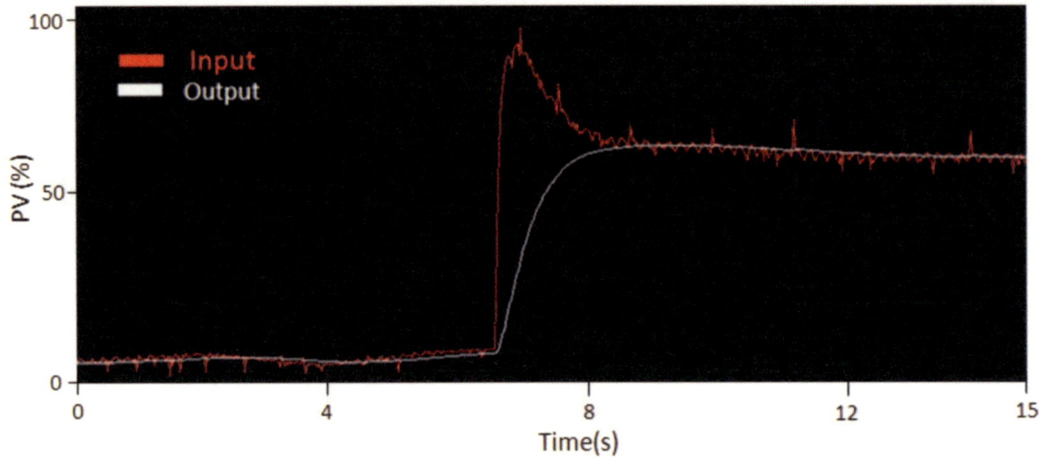

Fig. 17. Step response chart for Kp = 0.5

The control system actuation can be clearly noted in Figure 17, increasing the input value so the function can quickly reach the stationary value configured on the PID set point.
The Proportional control actuation was successful, and then the Integral parameter (Ki) was added with value set to 1 on the control loop of the simulated plant, keeping the proportional gain set to 0.5. Figure 18 shows the chart with the result from this experiment, a chart in response to the set point variation induced on the plant. The set point was initially at 70%, then it was altered to 10% and, right after that, it was altered to 80%. On the chart, these values are proportional to 7, 1, and 8, respectively. Observe quite an undulation due to the Integral parameter actuation mainly, which adds one magnitude to the function.

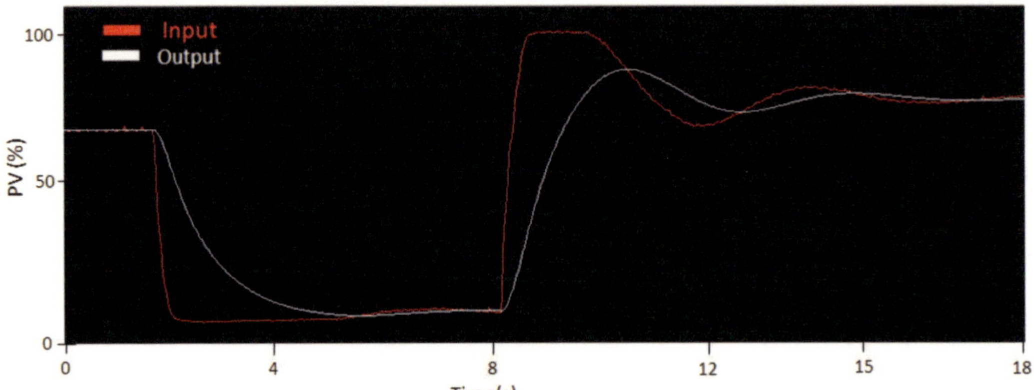

Fig. 18. Step response chart for Kp = 0.5 and Ki = 1

7. Conclusions

Considering the experiments described in the previous section, all tests for the project were performed successfully. Even with the problem related to the signal reading on the data acquisition board, the procedure for signal adequacy was successful as well, allowing the tests to continue.

An interesting fact occurred during the PID controller test: contrary to the pure I/O test, it was not necessary to correct the signal reading probably because, due to the use of a feedback control, the controller assumes the error is part of the plant's characteristics. Therefore, the signal is controlled according to the specified set point value for the PID controller.

This project intended to develop a device that could provide control and automation students the access to a variety of case studies for process automation in a learning laboratory that does not have access to a real process plant, and also provide engineers the possibility to test control strategy configurations before actuating a real plant.

Tests demonstrated the proper operation of the controllers and the anticipated functionality. Control systems are totally independent from the simulator and can be replaced, when needed.

Fine-tuning for devices and control strategies is not on the scope of the project, since all tests had a qualitative aspect. System and equipments hereby described will be used in automation classes, and students will be able to program and tune strategies by themselves.

In conclusion, the project fulfils its purpose, because even considering the signal acquisition problem on the NI-PCI 6221, the PID tests were successful.

8. References

Cavalieri, S.; Di Stefano, A.; Mirabella, O. (1993). Optimization of Acyclic Bandwidth Allocation Exploiting the Priority Mechanism in the Fieldbus Data Link Layer. *IEEE Transactions on Industrial Electronics*, Vol. 40, No. 3, 1993, pp. 297-306.

Chen, J.; Wang, Z.; Sun, Y. (2002). How to Improve Control System Performance Using FF Function Blocks, Proceedings of IEEE International Conference on Control Application, Glasgow, Scotland, 2002.

Ferreiro Garcia, R.; Vidal Paz, J.; Pardo Martinez, X. C.; Coego Botana, J. (1997). Fieldbus: preliminary design approach to optimal network management, Proceedings of IEEE International Workshop on Factory Communication Systems, Barcelona, Spain, 1997.

Fieldbus Foundation (1999a), *Foundation Specification Function Block Application Process Part 1: FF-890-1.3.* Austin, USA, 1999.

Fieldbus Foundation (1999b*). Foundation Specification Function Block Application Process Part 3: FF-892 – FS1.4.* Austin, USA, 1999.

Fieldbus Foundation (1999c). *Foundation Specification Function Block Application Process Part 5: FF-894 – DPS0.95.* Austin, USA, 1999.

Fennibay, D.; Yurdakul, A.; Sen, A. (2010). Introducing Hardware-in-Loop Concept to the Hardware/Software Co-design of Real-time Embedded Systems, Proceedings of IEEE IEEE 10th International Conference onComputer and Information Technology (CIT), 2010.

Godoy, E. P. ; Porto. A.J.P. (2008). Proposal of hardware-in-the loop in Control Systems Using CAN Networks. Proceedings of IEEE International Conference on Industry Applications, 2008.

Hong, S. H.; Ko, S. J. (2001). A Simulation Study on the Performance Analysis of the Data Link Layer of IEC/ISA Fieldbus, *Simulation*, 2001, pp. 109-118.

Huang, S.; Tan, K.K. (2010). Hardware-in-the-Loop Simulation for the Development of an Experimental Linear Drive. *IEEE Transactions on Industrial Electronics*, Vol. 57, No.4, 2010, pp. 1167-1174, ISSN: 0278-0046.

International Organization For Standardization (1994). *ISO/IEC 7498-1: Information technology - open systems interconnection - basic reference model: the basic model.* Switzerland. CD-ROM.

Li, Q.; Jiang, J. (2010). Evaluation of Foundation Fieldbus H1 Networks for Steam Generator Level Control. *IEEE Transactions on Control Systems Technology*, Vol. 99, september 2010, pp. 1-12 ISSN: 1063-6536.

Ljung, L. (1999). *System Identification- Theory for the User*, Prentice Hall, 1999, Englewood Cliffs.

Mossin, E ; Pantoni, R.P. ; Brandão, D. (2008). A fieldbus simulator for training purposes. *ISA Transactions*, Vol. 48, p. 132-141, 2008.

National Instruments (2003). LabVIEWTM Basics I e II Introduction: Course Manual Course Software Version 7.0, june 2003.

Pinotti Jr, M. ; Brandão, D. (2005) . A flexible fieldbus simulation platform for distributed control systems laboratory courses, *The International Journal Of Engineering Education*, 2005, Dublin, Vol. 21, No. 6, p. 1050-1058.

Petalidis, N.; Gill, D.S. (1998) The formal specification of the fieldbus foundation link scheduler in E-LOTOS. Proceedings of International Conference on Formal Engineering Methods, Brisbane, Australia, 1998.

Pop, T.; Eles, P.; Peng, Z. (2002). Holistic Scheduling and Analysis of Mixed Time/Event-Triggered Distributed Embedded Systems, Proceedings of 10th international symposium on Hardware/software codesign, Estes Park, USA, 2002.

Smar Syscon (2011). Smar International Corporation, In: *Smar International Coorporation WebSite*,01abril2011,Availablefrom:<http://www.smar.com/products/syscon.asp>

Wang, Z.; Yue, Z.; Chen, J.; Song, Y.; Sun, Y. (2002). Realtime characteristic of FF like centralized control fieldbus and it's state-of-art, Proceedings of IEEE International Symposium On Industrial Electronics, L´Aquila, Italy, 2002.

Part 3

eHealth

8

Sophisticated Biomedical Tissue Measurement Using Image Analysis and Virtual Instrumentation

Libor Hargaš, Dušan Koniar and Stanislav Štofan
University of Žilina, Faculty of Electrical Engineering, Slovakia

1. Introduction

Modern medical diagnostic and measurement methods are situated in the intersection of conventional science and industry branches: physics, electronics, informatics, telecommunications and medicine. This fact supports mutual cooperation between medical and technical institutes for research purposes.

Some of the last medical conferences which took place in Slovakia and focused on respiratory system diagnostics brought information about missing workstations for cinematic analysis of respiratory epithelium.

In 2009 started European projects Centre of Experimental and Clinical Respirology I and II, and Measurement of Respiratory Epithelium Cilium Kinematics between Jessenius Medical Faculty in Martin and University of Žilina (both Slovakia). The main goal of these projects is design and verification of experimental workstation with high speed camera linked with light microscope.

From the technical point of view, the most important is that analyzed microscopic objects in motion have high frequency (ca. 18-30 Hz) and they are too small to be equipped with conventional sensors of cinematic parameters. These facts puts accent for conception using means of image signal processing (software tools - virtual instrumentation LabVIEW) and move solution from spatial to frequency (time) domain.

The main topics are frequency measurement and control with high speed video camera and microscope using LabVIEW. The system is designed as phantom and real measurement. Phantom is realized with linear motor and controlled by DSP processor. The motor frequency is measured using image acquisition. This acquisition is done by high speed video camera. The sequences of captured images are processing with image analysis. Image analysis and other algorithms are done by virtual instrumentation using LabVIEW. The parameters of measured objects give relevant information about frequency and trajectory. This system can be used in sophisticated measurements in many educational, research and industrial applications where moving objects of investigation can't be equipped with sensors of cinematic parameters.

2. Structure and function of respiratory epithelium

The human respiratory apparatus is characterized by large surface in continual interaction with outer environment. Many foreign particles are inhaled to this apparatus in the inbreath phase, but we know some defence mechanisms: surface moisturizing or particles removing by mucociliary transport.

The respiratory mucous membrane is created from glandular epithelium (covering the layer producing mucus) and ciliated epithelium of various types, which moves mucus with foreign particles out of the respiratory apparatus (Jelinek, 2003).

One phase of cilia movement is called effective stroke, when cilia pike (end) shifts mucus in oral direction (out of the respiratory apparatus). In the healthy respiratory epithelium, the movements of cilias are synchronized (in one direction) and the mucus is normally transported. Inherited or obtained defects in cilia structure cause immovability or bad synchronization. These structural changes underlie mucus stagnation and continuous infections of the respiratory apparatus. In case of inherited defects, we can talk about PCD (Primary Ciliary Dyskinesis) syndrome or cystic fibrosis.

Objects investigated by light transmission microscopy usually can't be highlighted using reflection marks or equipped with sensors of kinematics parameters. In this case we often use advantages of image analysis and signal processing. Some methods for frequency measurement (using photodiode and photomultiplier) of biomechanical or microscopic objects can't do the correct analysis of structure pathologies. The most progressive method is high speed digital video method, which brings relatively good results in formation of mathematical and mechanical model of structure movement (Eyman, 2006).

On the other side, optimal light conditions in microscope can be achieved using various types of regulators (dimmers). Quality of obtained and analyzed digital images depends on acquisition system and its settings. Tissue measurement in modern medical praxis needs mutual cooperation of medicine, electronics and signal processing.

As example of moving biomechanical system we can consider cilium of respiratory epithelium cell (Fig. 1). Each ciliated cell of respiratory epithelium contains ca. 200 cilias (6 µm long) beating with frequency up to 30 Hz.

Cilias are synchronized with metachronal waves propagated in periciliar liquid. From the basic position cilium folds down to the epithelium cell (recovery stroke - 75% of beating cycle) and then rapidly darts up to move mucus with its tip (effective stroke) (Javorka, 2001). Relatively high frequency of cilium movement leads to high requirements for the parts of acquisition system - microscope, camera, acquisition computer and others.

3. Currently used methods for CBF (Ciliary Beat Frequency) diagnostics

Ciliated cells are obtained from nose using a cytological brush; after being put into saline, they perform their physiological functions for a short time (max. 20 minutes). Currently, we can investigate the kinetic and structural parameters of cilia by light and electron microscopy. Thanks to good discrimination ability (10-9 m), electron microscopy is used mainly for structural parameters investigation. Light microscopy has smaller discrimination ability (10-6 m) than electron microscopy, but it is a sufficient method for movement analysis; in addition, light microscopy is cheaper and less time-consuming.

There are some advanced methods, such as high-speed cinematography, laser light spectroscopy, photoelectrical measurements and stroboscopy. These methods often need expensive and sophisticated equipment and in many cases cannot reveal the primary cause of dyskinesis. Another problem is frequency analysis: frequency seems to be normal if a significant number of cilia are not damaged.

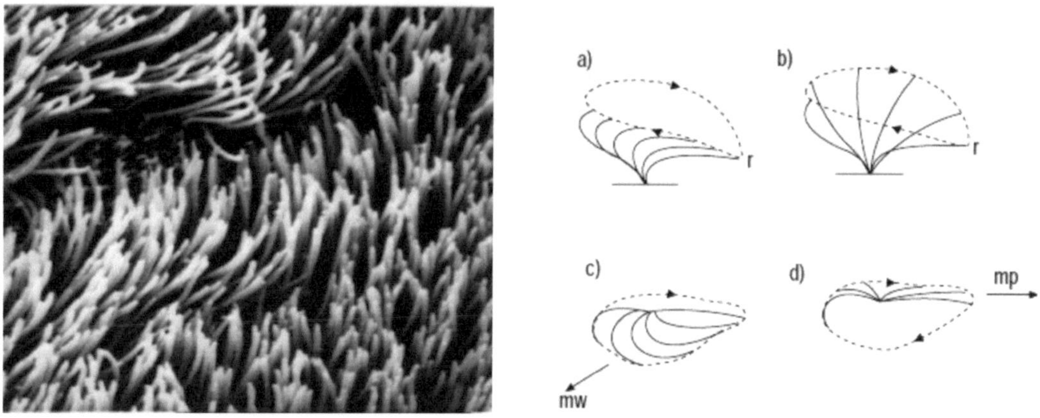

Fig. 1. Ciliated respiratory epithelium in electron microscopy imaging mode and phases of cilia movement

In these days, in clinical praxis, light and electron microscopy are used in many research centres for structure and movement study of biological objects. Electron microscopy has bigger resolution power (1 nm) than light microscopy (1 µm), so we can use it for structure study, but this diagnostics is more expensive. Light microscopy (usually using phase contrast typical for biology measurements) is used for movement study.
In case of cilia movement study, there are some sophisticated and expensive methods based on fast and quality hardware components like high speed digital cameras, stroboscopes, photo multipliers and many others. These methods require long time training and we can find them in few research centres in the world.
Some methods for frequency measurement (using photodiode and photomultiplier) can't do the correct analysis of object structure pathologies. The most progressive method is high speed digital video method, which brings relatively good results in formation of mathematical and mechanical model of cilia movement (or other biological objects) (Eyman, 2006).

3.1 High speed video method

In this method the motion of object is recorded with high frame ratio (400 FPS or more). High speed sequence is the basic key for analysis of the selected motion and structural parameters of moving objects. Sequence is then processed frame after frame. At the beginning, frequency or object trajectory were measured manually: specialists were counting the number of frames necessary for one object motion cycle and they were doing statistical measurements. High speed video method needs relatively quick memory storage components for its big dataflow. In the time of origin of this method, there was one main aim: to design some algorithms for automated and real-time analysis of movement kinetics.
CBF is measured manually by counting of number of frames needed for 1 ciliary cycle or using formula for better accuracy:

$$CBF = \frac{FPS}{N \cdot 10} \tag{1}$$

where FPS is actual frame ratio of sequence, N is number of frames for 10 object movement cycles (Chilvers & O'Callaghan, 2000).
High speed record is previewed in slow mode or frame after frame.

3.2 Photodiode and photomultiplier method

Videosequence is viewed on high resolution display (screen). Photosensitive device (diode, multiplier) is placed near the display surface and focused on the area of beating cilium or periodically moving object. The aperture size is ca. 2,2 μm2. Movement of object modifies intensity values in the relevant image region of interest in the place of photosensitive device. Photodiode or multiplier generates voltage signal, which is processed with the tools of spectral analysis, such as FFT (Fast Fourier Transformation) or PSD (Power Spectral Density).

Study (Chilvers & O'Callaghan, 2000) is the first to compare directly two of the most commonly used methods of estimating ciliary beat frequency of respiratory cilia with high speed imaging. The photomultiplier and photodiode techniques recorded ciliary beat frequencies that were significantly slower than those measured using the digital high speed video method.

The limits of agreement for both methods were wide, which confirms that results obtained using the different techniques cannot be used interchangeably. These results emphasise the need for normal reference ranges of ciliary beat frequency to be established for each technique if it is to be used as a diagnostic test for primary ciliary dyskinesia.

4. Tissue measurement design by virtual instrumentation

Frequency of moving object(s) is measured from a waveform that is generated by the variation in grey-level intensity of the phase-contrast image that results from the repetitive motion of object (cilia). Intensity variance curve from high speed video recording is processed using various methods (Zhang & Sanderson, 2003).

The key elements of designed workstation concept are high speed camera and acquisition computer. Camera must have sufficient frame ratio to make analysis more accurate. High frequency of recording specifies usage of powerful computer due to amounts of image data. High frequency also requests higher microscope illumination, which can be adaptive controlled (in spectrum and in intensity). This task belongs to power electronics: to find optimal light source and its topology with suitable type of supply and ability of automatic control.

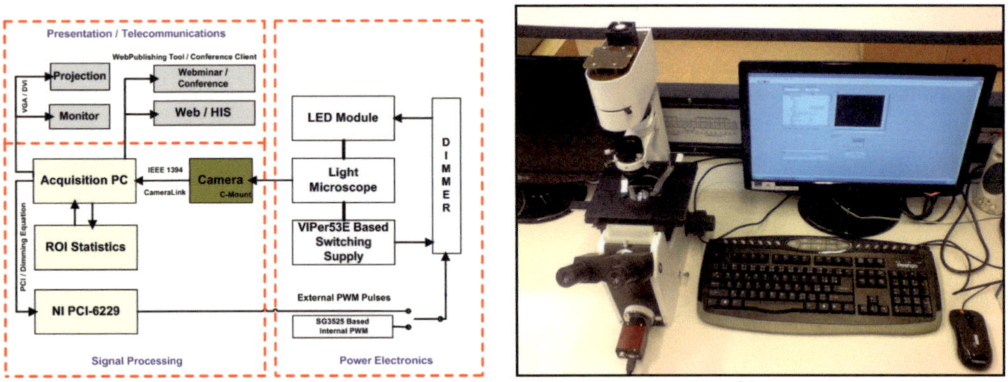

a) b)

Fig. 2. a) Block diagram of hf (high frequency) video workstation – main components and relations between them, b) Inverse microscope MODEL IM 1C

Recording, preprocessing and analysis of obtained video sequences are done on acquisition computer. Computer communicates with microscope illumination source (this regulation is based on statistical analysis of recorded image). This computer is also connected to the Ethernet / Internet to share analyzed information to secured clinical information systems (HIS). This functionality also enables to control whole experiment through Internet or make "webminars" using conference client.
Some of the main parts of workstation (Fig. 2a) is composed from changeable modules, what creates variability of system. Detailed description and possibility analysis of most important parts is done in the tables in following chapters.

4.1 Videosequence acquisition system

The first real measurements (in Clinic of pathological physiology, Jessenius Faculty of Medicine, Martin, Slovakia) were taken after algorithm debugging on phantoms. Because the ciliary beating frequency 'in vitro' goes down from ca. 18 Hz to a half value, primary we used acquisition system with slower camera. In the first approach, we have generated beating frequencies 3 Hz and 9 Hz. Phantoms were recorded with camera AVT Marlin F-046B using 60 FPS recording modes (Fig. 3a). AVT Marlin F-046B camera was connected to inverse biological light microscope MODEL IM 1C via C-mount adaptor. Sequences from camera were stored on acquisition computer through IEEE 1394 (FireWire) as uncompressed sequences with parameters: 8 BPP / 640 x 480 pxl / 60 fps.
In designed system we can use two cameras: AlliedVision AVT Marlin F-046B (60 fps) and Basler A504kc (500+ fps) (Fig. 3b). Both cameras (Fig. 3) are linked directly to microscope via C-Mount or F-to-C-Mount adaptor.

a) b)

Fig. 3. a) Camera AVT Marlin F-046B, b) Basler A504kc

4.2 Light microscopy

The issue of kinetic analysis of ciliated cells can be divided into few basic steps: image (video) acquisition, image pre-processing, kinetic parameters analysis (frequency and trajectory).
Hardware acquisition equipment is: inverse biological light microscope and monochrome camera connected to PC through IEEE 1394 (FireWire). LabVIEW application is the software platform for videosequence acquisition. The acquisition system and camera connection with microscope are shown in Fig. 2b.
Phase-contrast transmission light microscopy was described by F. Zernik in 1935 for increasing contrast for details in biology objects. Differences in light refraction in the case of constant absorption of light in object are not visible. Phase-contrast method converts phase

difference of transmitted or reflected light waves to intensity difference, which is good visible (Jandoš & Říman & Gemperle, 1985).
Fig. 4a shows light transmission through phase object: this object modifies only the phase, not intensity. Phase contrast then converts dλ to intensity value.

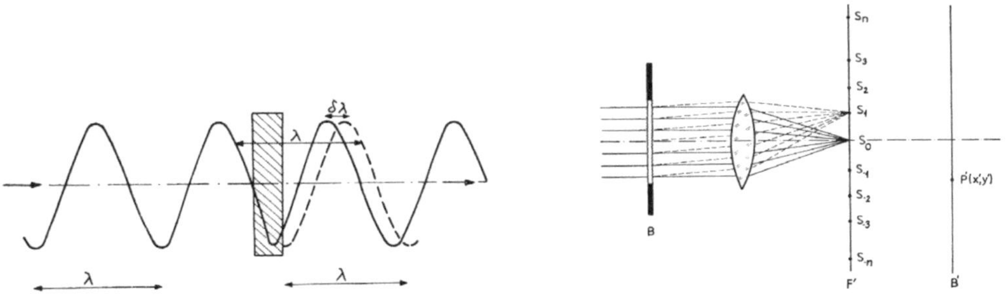

a) b)

Fig. 4. a) Light transmission through phase object, b) Optical system with diffraction spectrums in focal plane, B - object, F′ - focal plane, B′ - imaging plane, P′(x′;y′) - projected point

Abbe's optical theorem says that each object is diffracting, so in the focal plane object creates spectrums from 0-th to N-th order (Fig. 4b.). It is necessary to hold the light from the maximum number of spectrums in the imaging plane for true imaging.
Consider plane light wave with unit amplitude:

$$e^{i2\pi \vec{k}\vec{r}} \tag{2}$$

where $\vec{k}$ is wave vector in the wave direction and $|\vec{k}| = 1/\lambda$; $\vec{r}$ is positional point vector in optical system.
Also consider coordinate system parallel with optical axis of system, then in plane z = 0 we can write formula (without object in optical system):

$$V_0(x;y) = e^{i2\pi(k_x \cdot x + k_y \cdot y)} \tag{3}$$

Then relation:

$$F(x;y) = \frac{V(x;y)}{V_0(x;y)} \tag{4}$$

is transfer function of object in optical system. If F(x;y) ∈ R, then the object is amplitude object (modifies intensity of transmitted light). If |F(x;y)| = 1, then the object is phase object, Φ is phase shift and:

$$F(x;y) = e^{i\Phi(x;y)}, \quad \Phi(x;y) \in \mathrm{R}. \tag{5}$$

Intensity of light in P′(x′;y′) corresponding to point P(x;y) in object (Fig. 4b) in optical imaging system is:

$$\mathrm{I} = \mathrm{C2}.|\mathrm{F}|2, \tag{6}$$

where C is characteristic constant of optical system and F is transfer function. In the case of pure phase object and intensity is constant. In the case of weakly phase object $\Phi(x;y) << 1$ and we can expand $F(x;y)$ to series with ignoring elements up from 3-th order:

$$F(x;y) = 1 + i\Phi(x;y) \tag{7}$$

The first element of series corresponds to light concentrated in diffraction spectrum of 0-th order and the rest of series corresponds to light from higher order spectrums.
We can place phase or absorption plate in the place of 0-th spectrum, which changes the phase of light wave $\pm(\pi/2)$. This plate modifies first element in the series by multiplying it with factor:

$$a.e^{\pm i\frac{\pi}{2}} = \pm ia \tag{8}$$

where a represents absorption ratio. Then the series transforms to:

$$G(x;y) = \pm ia + i\Phi(x;y). \tag{9}$$

Intensity in true imaging is:

$$I = C^2|G|^2 \approx a^2 \pm 2a\Phi(x;y) \tag{10}$$

if expression $\Phi^2(x;y) << 1$ is neglected. Image contrast is then increased and equals:

$$\frac{\pm 2\Phi(x;y)}{a}. \tag{11}$$

Sign "+" in formula for contrast expresses positive contrast: regions with high optical density are bright and placed on dark background. Sign "-" expresses negative contrast, what is inversion of first state.
In practical solution in phase-contrast light microscopes annulus aperture is used. This fact and basic structure of phase-contrast optical system is shown in Fig. 5.

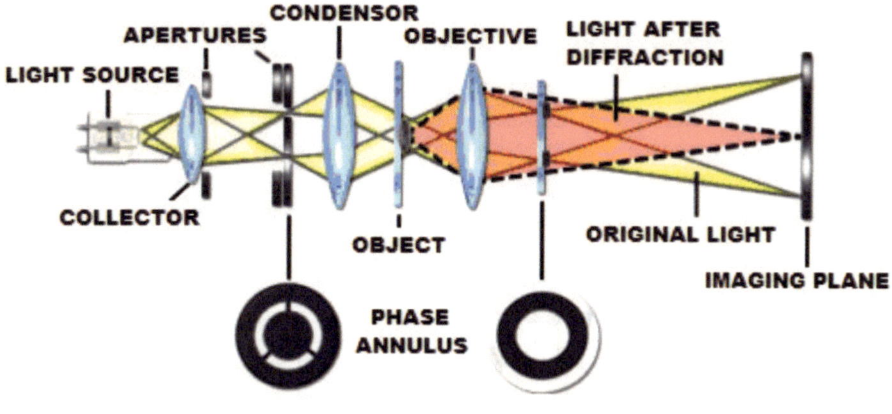

Fig. 5. Structure of phase-contrast light microscopy; position of phase-contrast annulus aperture plates

4.3 Illumination control by videosequence acquisition process

The reliability of kinematics analysis depends on frame rate of used camera. Higher frame rate (500fps and high) brings more information for analysis but also brings more volume of irrelevant data. Higher frame rate in camera required fast electronic elements used in camera for reading, buffering and data streaming. The reading process from image chip is taken in short time interval. Due to this fact, exposure time is too short, so it is necessary to use lighting source with higher optical (illumination) efficiency.

Our present microscope used as light source the halogen lamp with electrical power 120 watts. The efficiency in this case is very low (10 – 25%). We search the solution, which will provide enough optical power with higher energy efficiency. We have therefore decided to focus on the use of the light source based on LEDs. This group of light sources growth in last time. They have higher energy efficiency, better spectral performance and better geometrical radiating characteristic. The other conditions were a good possibility to the output power control.

It is very important set the illumination conditions by acquisition process and hold their on constant value during all process. We try developing the algorithm that can regulate a soft change of illumination conditions during the acquisition process. The main control loop computes the main value of histogram in current image frame. When has the value changed the algorithm adjusts the change via power regulator of light source.

The block diagram of regulator is on Fig. 6. The flyback converter converts the input voltage from value 230 V AC to 15V DC. It isolates galvanic also the other components. The output current can be maximal 2A. The DC voltage is coming into current source block. The output source is adapted for LED module conditions. We use few variation of value output power (0,1A/0,4A/1A). It is depend on LED module. The current source is based on circuit L200. The output current is switched with MOSFET transistor. The switching is controlled with LabVIEW application. The output power is controlled with change of duty cycle of input PWM signal. The signal is coming from I/O card from computer (for example NI-PCI6229).

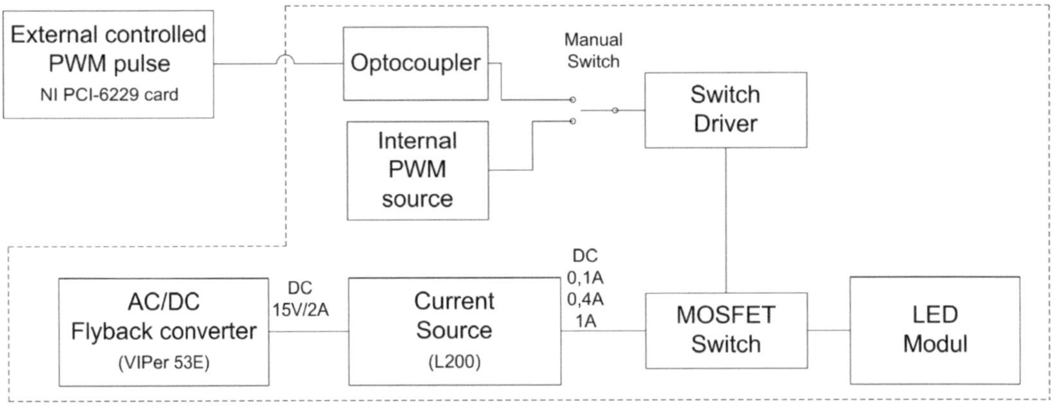

Fig. 6. Illumination regulation block diagram

Fig. 7 shows the illumination dependences on electrical power. The characteristic was measured on LED PG1N-3LXC-SD (ProLight). This LED should replace the previous halogen lamp. It was used in microscope as light source. Now we can take the better energy efficiency (Špánik et. al, 2010).

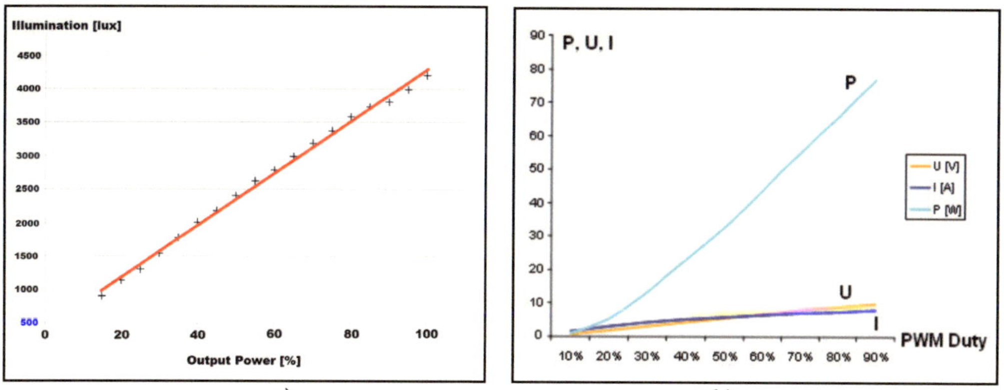

a) b)

Fig. 7. Illumination dependences on electrical power - a) LED diode, b) halogen lamp

In the case of usage high speed camera system (Basler), microscope illumination is very important. We have changed microscope condenser light source and made some measurements of intensity by Lutron LX-1102 luxmeter.

In case of ultra high frame ratio of camera we can meet these essential problems: if the illumination of specimen is too low, frames in video sequence are underexposed and dark; if the illumination of specimen is too high, frames are overexposed and too bright (Fig. 9a-d); high frame ratio causes growth of data for storage, so we must consider optimal connection between camera and acquisition computer. These non-optimal conditions causes same „faults" in intensity curve.

Original maximal value of illumination (measured between condenser optics and specimen) changed from 8,6 klx to ca. 80 klx after replacing 20W halogen lamp for 120W halogen lamp. Heat from condenser must have been removed using active CPU cooler mounted onto microscope or using intelligent dimming tool.

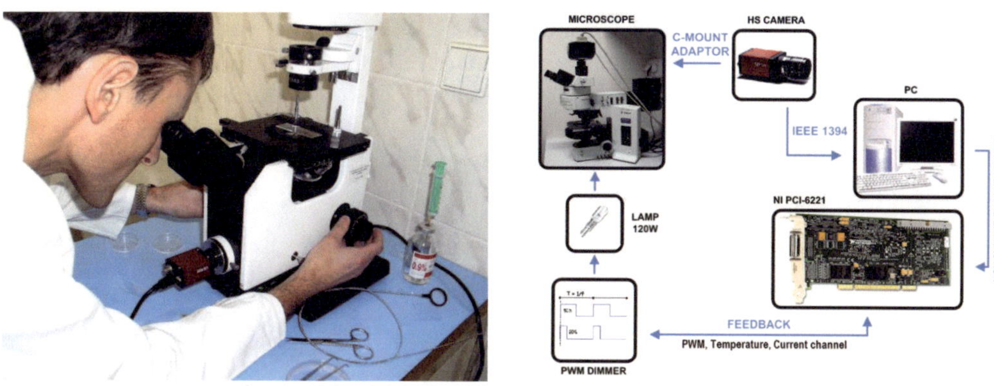

a) b)

Fig. 8. a) Experimental workstation - microscope connected to digital camera, b) block scheme of whole acquisition scheme -processing

The intelligent dimmer was designed based on simulations. The power supply is made directly from the main supply 230V via input transformer (Frivaldsky et al, 2009). Dimming feature is provided through one PWM channel, which generates driving impulses of switching transistor (Drgoňa et al, 2009). PWM signal is generated in NI PCI-6229 LabVIEW measurement card and is isolated from power circuit through optocoupler and amplified in transistor driver. PWM has constant frequency of 50 kHz and regulation is done through duty cycle of impulses. This regulation part of acquisition system uses software regulation feedback included in acquisition virtual instrument and will be described later. Power regulation in dependency on duty cycle and its influence on image histogram is shown in Fig. 9e-h.

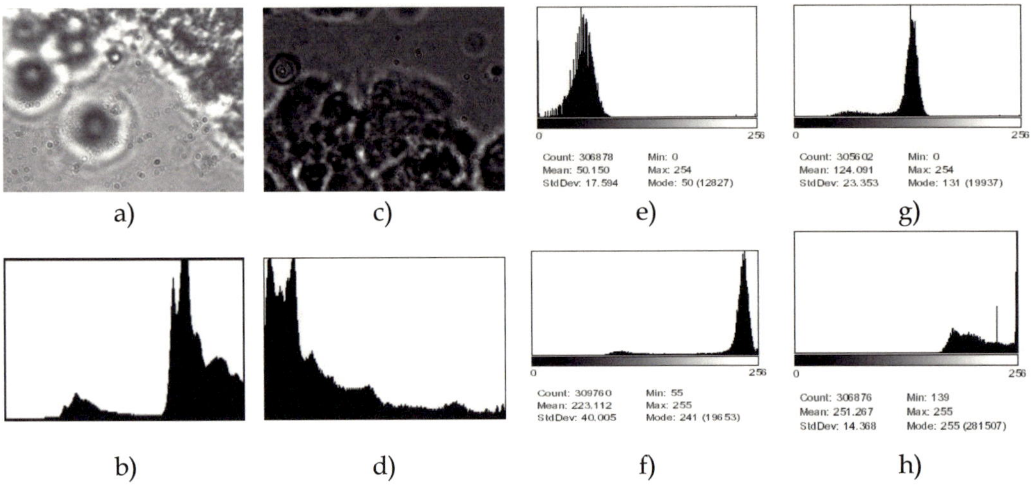

Fig. 9. a) Overexposed image, b) Overexposed image histogram, c) Underexposed image, d) Underexposed image histogram, e) PWM 20%, f) PWM 30%, g) PWM 25%, h) PWM 40%

4.4 Illumination regulation feedback

In process of sequence acquisition, a ROI (Region Of Interest) placed into image extracts important image feature: average image intensity and histogram distribution. Overexposed image has its histogram concentrated to high intensity values and underexposed image to low values (Fig. 9a-d). Histogram distribution is used as regulation parameter for setting up the PWM for halogen lamp dimmer. Dependency of histogram mean (μ) on duty cycle (dc) for actual frame ratio (fps) of video system can be described by kvasi-linear characteristics (Fig. 10).

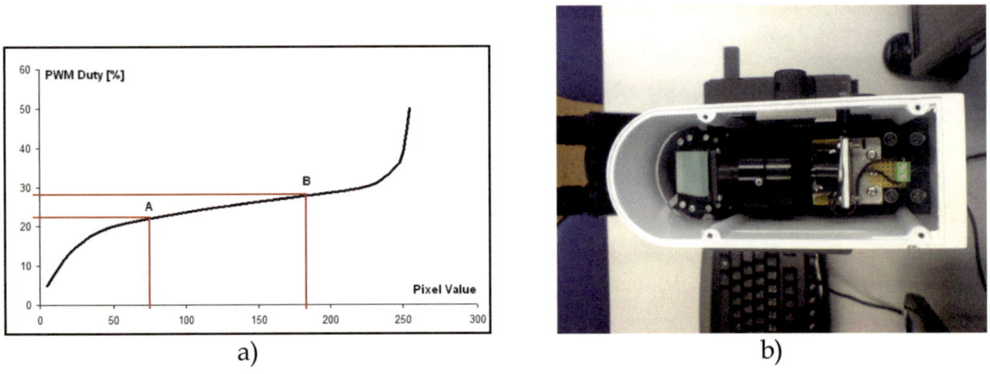

Fig. 10. a) Illumination characteristics for 60 fps framing. Optimal μ_0 corresponds with $d.c_0$ = 25%. Acceptable duty cycles lies in range 20-30%, all duty cycles under or over this interval brings underexposed or overexposed image, b) microscope illumination module

Regulation algorithm approximates this characteristic with a line using two or more known points:

$$y = ax + b \tag{12}$$

$$A = [\mu_1, dc_1];\ B = [\mu_2, dc_2] \tag{13}$$

$$a = \frac{dc_2 - dc_1}{\mu_2 - \mu_1} \tag{14}$$

$$b = dc_1 - \frac{dc_2 - dc_1}{\mu_2 - \mu_1}\mu_1 \tag{15}$$

$$y = \frac{dc_2 - dc_1}{\mu_2 - \mu_1}x + dc_1 - \frac{dc_2 - dc_1}{\mu_2 - \mu_1}\mu_1 \tag{16}$$

and calculates Δ dc for setting histogram $\mu_0 \approx 128$, what is half of grayscale range 0 - 255; dc_0 - duty cycle corresponding to μ_0:

$$\pm\Delta dc = dc_i - dc_0 \tag{17}$$

Delay of the regulation algorithm depends on framing ratio of camera and is 1/fps [s].

5. Analysis and evaluation of videosequence

One of the intensity variance curve analysis methods is described in methods (Zhang & Sanderson, 2003). Researchers from this study saved digital images directly to an array of SCSI (Small Computer System Interface) hard drives configured as a stripped drive; the data storage rate is determined by the speed and number of the individual drives. The data rate is often ca. 120 MB/s.

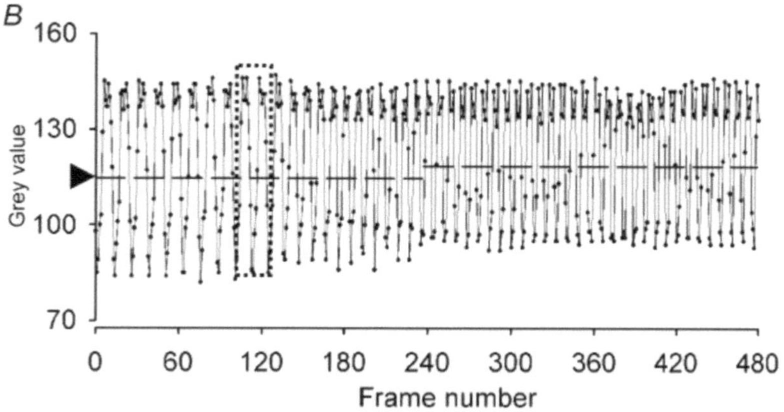

Fig. 11. Intensity variance curve with highlighted beating cycle

Basic problem is to select suitable ROI (Region Of Interest) in image. The best placement is in the end of beating object. Size of ROI underlies optimal signal-to-noise ratio. Researchers from methods (Zhang & Sanderson, 2003) used ROI ca. 3x3 pixels (0,87µm x 0,80µm gap of photo sensitive device).
Fig. 11 shows example of intensity variance curve generated by photo sensitive device captured from oscilloscope and normalized for 8 BPP grayscale image palette.
Used technique computes object beating frequency by searching points of intersection with "threshold line". This helps us to indicate starts and ends of each beating cycle. For more accuracy, this technique recalculates analysis parameters after each second.
Consider intensity variance curve like discrete function G(n) (Fig. 12a), where time quantization is done by FPS. For each second we can compute arithmetic mean value of G(n) and call it G_{cross}:

$$G_{cross} = \frac{1}{N}\sum_{n} G(n), \tag{18}$$

where N is number of frames for 1 second of recording (N = FPS).
Algorithm searches time between two frames F_n and F_{n+1}, where F_n is frame when $G(n) < G_{cross}$ and F_{n+1} is frame when $G(n) > G_{cross}$. This time expresses beating period of periodical motion.
In consequence of noise processes, we can check intersection with G for more than 2 points: $G(n) < G(n+1) < G_{cross} < G(n+2) < G(n+3)$.
Because the intensity variance curve is discrete, accurate intersection time T_{cross} (Fig. 12b) usually lies between two discrete frame times. Providing intensity variance function linear and continuous, we can interpolate T_{cross} with formula:

$$T_{cross} = \frac{F_n + \dfrac{G_{cross} - G(n)}{G(n+1) - G(n)}}{FPS} \tag{19}$$

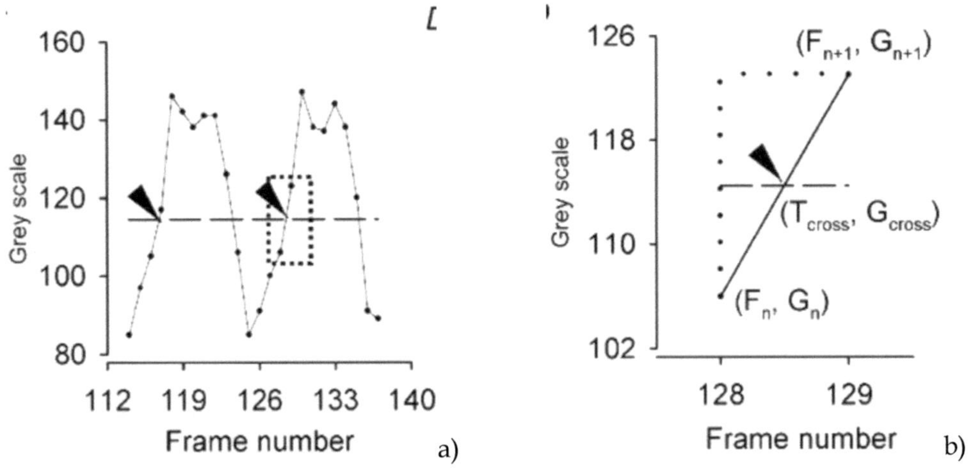

Fig. 12. Object beating cycle; a) starting intersections of each cycle; b) computing of the cross time

5.1 Videosequence preprocessing

Preprocessing has two goals: to shorten analysis time and improve kinetic parameters analysis. Grayscale videosequences are sufficient for further analysis as many LabVIEW tools are applicable only on grayscale image. The given acquisition system can be easily built in medical or laboratory environment. In order to test the applications for sequence pre-processing and kinetic parameters analysis some phantom sequences were acquired (without microscope or using microscope - microscopic grid movement).

Fundamental function for image (videosequence) acquisition is LabVIEW express function for communication with the device on IEEE 1394 port and control items enabling to set up the camera shutter, format, FPS, brightness and gain, number of frames (sequence length). Final videosequence is written as raw video file (*.avi) (Fig. 13a).

The time needed for analysis can be reduced by cutting off of the regions or frames (redundant time intervals) which do not contain relevant information. In this aspect we can talk about time reduction (e.g. frames selection from 7 to 153 of the whole sequence) or spatial reduction (selection of ROI containing isolated cell). Script is very simple and its output is time or spatial (or both) reduced videosequence.

An important phase is improving intensity levels in the whole image. Fig. 13b shows the Front Panel of application for image (sequence) pre-processing. After videosequence opening the following operators and tools can be applied:

- extraction of single color plane,
- lookup Table (LuT) operators,
- convolution (spatial) filtering,
- equalization,
- histogram.

The pre-processing application has many degrees of freedom for user. Filters and tools can be fully combined, so the application can be used in various cases. After the pre-processing phase, the kinetic parameters are analyzed.

- *Extraction of single color plane* - this tool extracts 8-bit gray plane from color image, because many LabVIEW tools and operators work only with grayscale images. The most important is Luminance 8-bit plane (from HSL model, which is RGB derivate). Luminance plane contains information about objects position and minimizes information stored in textures, which is more important for movement detection.
- *Lookup Table (LuT) operators* - Lookup Table is a transfer characteristic (linear, linear in parts, nonlinear) between an original image and a processed image. They enhance and improve intensity relations in the whole image, change brightness and contrast. The kind of LuT operator is BCG Correction. The Lookup exponent is the variable which gives the final curving of the base curve. LuT range is intensity interval on which the LuT curve is applied. While often effective, employing a lookup table may nevertheless result in a severe penalty if the computation that the LUT replaces is relatively simple. Memory retrieval time and the complexity of memory requirements can increase application operation time and system complexity relative to what would be required by straight formula computation. The possibility of polluting the cache may also become a problem.
- *Convolution (spatial) filtering* - convolution filtering belongs to linear filtering. Filter uses a kernel. Kernel moves through the image, convolution between original image and kernel array is calculated on each position and result is written on the central pixel position. Result can be divided with normalization factor N, which is the sum of kernel values or 1.

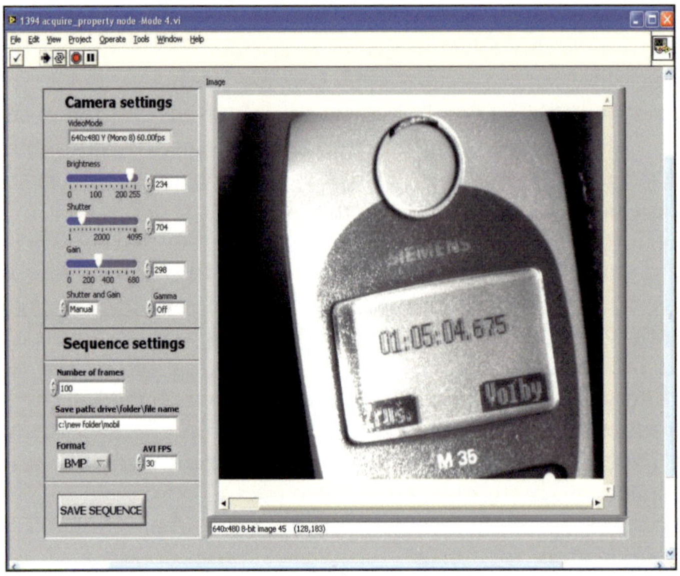

a)

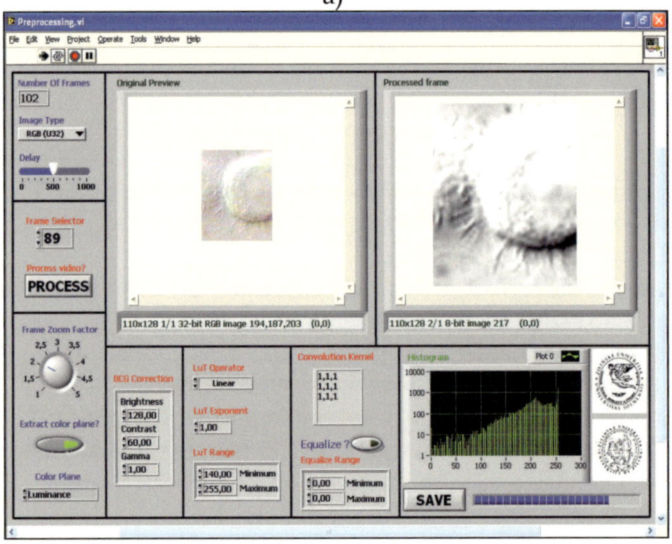

b)

Fig. 13. a) Acquisition application Front Panel, b) Pre-processing application Front Panel - videoseqence pre-processing

- *Equalization* - equalization enhances pixel intensities. Equalization range is the value interval on which the transformation is done; this interval will be remapped on 0-255 interval, so we can reveal details from this interval only.
- Consider a discrete grayscale image {x} and let n_i be the number of occurrences of gray level i. The probability of an occurrence of a pixel of level i is:

$$p_x(i) = p_x(x = i) = \frac{n_i}{n}, 0 \le i < L \tag{20}$$

L being the total number of gray levels in the image, n being the total number of pixels in the image, and $p_x(i)$ being in fact the image's histogram for pixel value i, normalized to [0,1]. Let us also define the cumulative distribution function corresponding to p_x as

$$cdf_x(i) = \sum_{j=0}^{i} p_x(j) \tag{21}$$

which is also the image's accumulated normalized histogram.
We would like to create a transformation of the form y = T(x) to produce a new image {y}, such that its CDF will be linearized across the value range, i.e.

$$cdf_x(i) = iK \tag{22}$$

for some constant K. The properties of the CDF allow us to perform such a transform, it is defined as

$$y = T(x) = cdf_x(x) \tag{23}$$

Notice that the T maps the levels into the range [0,1]. In order to map the values back into their original range, the following simple transformation needs to be applied on the result:

$$y' = y \cdot (\max\{x\} - \min\{x\}) + \min\{x\} \tag{24}$$

In the case, that the cdf must be normalized to [0,255], the general histogram equalization formula is:

$$h(v) = round\left(\frac{cdf(v) - cdf_{\min}}{(M \times N) - cdf_{\min}} \times (L-1) \right) \tag{25}$$

where cdf_{min} is the minimum value of the cumulative distribution function (in this case 1), M × N gives the image's number of pixels and L is the number of grey levels used (in most cases, 256).

- *Histogram* - histogram shows the dependency between intensity value and number of pixels of this gray value. Histogram gives us the complex view on the image and facilitates us the noise removal or segmentation.

In a more general mathematical sense, a histogram is a function mi that counts the number of observations that fall into each of the disjoint categories (known as bins), whereas the graph of a histogram is merely one way to represent a histogram. Thus, if we let n be the total number of observations and k be the total number of bins, the histogram m_i meets the following conditions:

$$n = \sum_{i=1}^{k} m_i \tag{26}$$

Cumulative histogram - a cumulative histogram is a mapping that counts the cumulative number of observations in all of the bins up to the specified bin. That is, the cumulative histogram M_i of a histogram m_j is defined as:

$$M_i = \sum_{j=1}^{i} m_j \tag{27}$$

Number of bins and width - There is no "best" number of bins, and different bin sizes can reveal different features of the data. Some theoreticians have attempted to determine an optimal number of bins, but these methods generally make strong assumptions about the shape of the distribution. The number of bins k can be assigned directly or can be calculated from a suggested bin width h as:

$$k = \left\lceil \frac{\max x - \min x}{h} \right\rceil \tag{28}$$

The braces indicate the ceiling function.
The preprocessing application has many degrees of freedom for user, filters and tools can be fully combined, so application can be used in various cases. The kinetic parameters are analyzed.

5.2 Phantom acquisition system design

Measurement method designed by our team is based on frequency analysis of intensity variance curve. This curve is obtained from video sequence by capturing intensity variation in selected region of interest (ROI). Curve is then analyzed with FFT algorithm, measurement is verified using curve thresholding and envelope analysis. Whole algorithm is shown in Fig. 14.

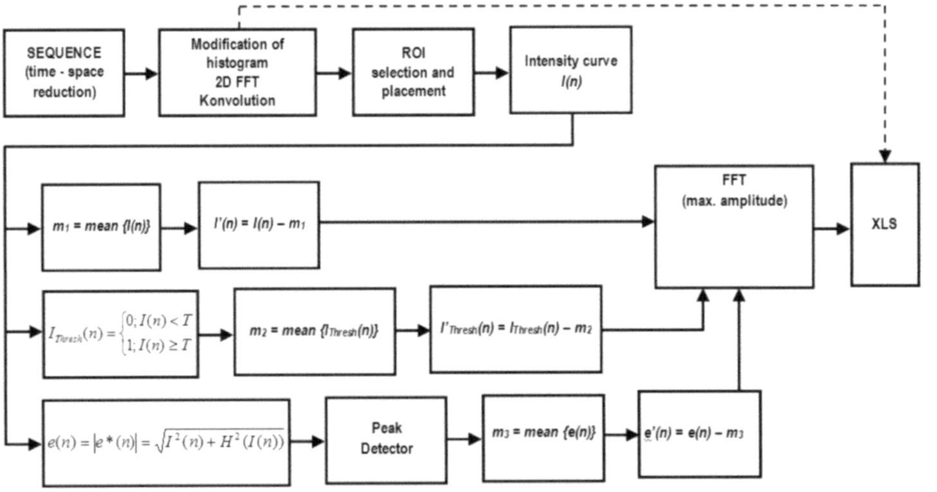

Fig. 14. Frequency measurement algorithm

Measurement is done in graphical development system NI LabVIEW as virtual instrument and results are written as Microsoft Excel XLS file. This component helps to integrate results of investigation to laboratory or clinic information systems. Next advantage of LabVIEW virtual instrument is called Web Publishing Tool. Using this tool we can provide control of whole application through Internet.

To generate an accurate object beating frequency, we used DSP controlled stepping motor with reflection mark on the vane of its propeller (Fig. 15a). Phantoms with defined parameters are common and useful parts in design process of new diagnostic or measuring method.

5.3 Recording of intensity variance curve

On reference frame of videosequence we can interactively select ROI (region of interest) which contains beating object (Fig. 15b). Consider ROI size k * l pixels with left top corner coordinates (L;T). Then mean intensity value for ROI for N-th frame is:

$$I_{avg}(N) = \frac{1}{k.l}\sum_{i=1}^{k}\sum_{j=1}^{l} f(i+T;j+L)_N \tag{29}$$

where $f(i;j)_N$ is intensity value of pixel (i;j) in ROI. Formula (29) is 2-D transformation of (18). Algorithm then creates intensity variance curve from each mean value for all frames. Basic curve is then relation between intensity means and number of frame. If FPS of videosequence is known, we must transform frame axis to time axis using transformation formula:

$$t[\text{sec.}] = \frac{N}{FPS}. \tag{30}$$

Size of ROI underlies the shape of main repetitive pattern of intensity variance curve. Smaller ROIs are more sensible for intensity variance and the curve pattern have bigger differences between maximum and minimum value. On the other hand, bigger ROIs have better "signal-to-noise ratio".

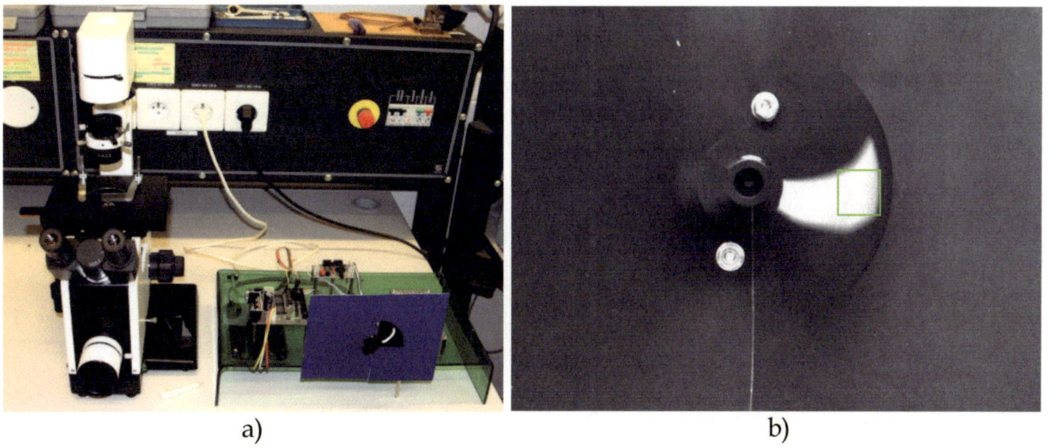

a) b)

Fig. 15. a) Generator of accurate object beating frequency, b) Frame from phantom videosequence with selected ROI

Curve fineness depends on FPS and used video compressor. Next measurements were taken on raw (uncompressed) AVI file with 60 FPS. Each frame is grayscale bitmap with 8 BPP depth.

In the case of rotating phantom (whole circle or partial circle movement) measured beating frequency would not depend on the ROI placement on the object (base, middle part or end), because angle speed of object isn't a function of distance from the axis of rotation. Even though (Zhang & Sanderson, 2003) recommends placement of ROI on the end of object, because in the case of cilia, base is joint with epithelial cell and cilia spike movement is relevant part for frequency analysis.

Measurements 1-4 (Fig. 16 and Fig. 17) confirm facts above. ROI size in measurement 1 and 2 influences value differences in beat pattern. Placement of ROI to the base or to the end of object gives equivalent results.

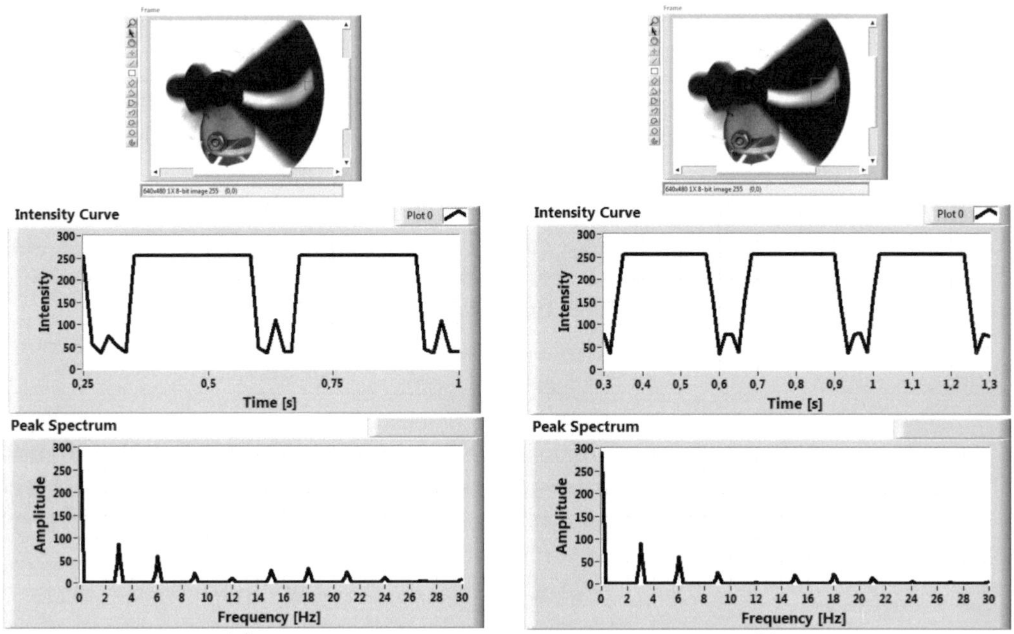

a) b)

Fig. 16. a) Measurement 1: 3 Hz / ROI size: 15 x 15 (px) / bright background, b) Measurement 2: 3 Hz / ROI size 45 x 45 (px) / bright background

In the case when (FPS/BF) is integral number, we can't see any "floating" in variance curve, because the number of frames needed for one beating cycle of object is integral number too (Fig. 18a). In measurement 1 and 2 the contribution:

$$\frac{FPS}{BF} = \frac{60}{3} = 20 \tag{31}$$

is integral number.

In the measurement 3 and 4, this contribution is 60/9 = 6,67, what isn't integral number and we can see floating of variance curve (Fig. 18b). This floating is caused by fact that number of frames needed for one beating cycle isn't an integral number.

The more efficient and quick way to do spectral analysis of variance curve is FFT (Fast Fourier Transform). FFT decomposes a sequence of values into components of different frequencies. For discrete signal FFT uses formula (Brigham, 1988):

$$X_k = \sum_{n=0}^{N-1} x(n).e^{-i2\pi k\frac{n}{N}} \tag{32}$$

where X_k is complex spectral component, k = 0,…,N-1, x(n) is element of discrete function, N is number of samples used for computing, $N = 2^m$, m is integral number. Computed spectral components are complex number, we can split this complex spectrum to magnitude spectrum (amplitudes) and phase spectrum.
Detailed description of variance curve from measurement 3 and 4 is shown in Fig. 19a.
Applying this signal processing tool on variance curve, we can create spectrum and plot it into the spectral graph (Fig. 19b, Fig. 20b). Beating pattern in the curve creates the main spectral component: first harmonic component with maximal peak (amplitude).
Because the mean value of intensity curve isn't zero, in the spectrum we can see DC component (in the position of 0 Hz). DC component does not contain any information about object movement, so we can reject it.

5.4 Measurement of frequency (CBF)

Healthy cilia make continuous and synchronized moves. The frequency is often called CBF (Cilia Beat Frequency). This parameter can be measured using the intensity method. In this method, the ROI is created in near surrounding of beating cilia. Passing of cilia across the ROI causes intensity variations in it. The average ROI intensity is recording in time and this periodical curve is processed with tools of frequency analysis. The frequency spectrum of beating can be displayed by application of FFT (Fast Fourier Transform). The PSD graph (Power Spectral Density) can be also displayed, which is FFT of curve autocorrelation. In Fig. 20a is shown graph of intensity variations and in Fig. 20b PSD of this curve. We can also see (Fig. 20b) that Measured frequency is in the range of 17 - 20 Hz and this fact is shown in Fig. 20b. This measured frequency is the physiological value.

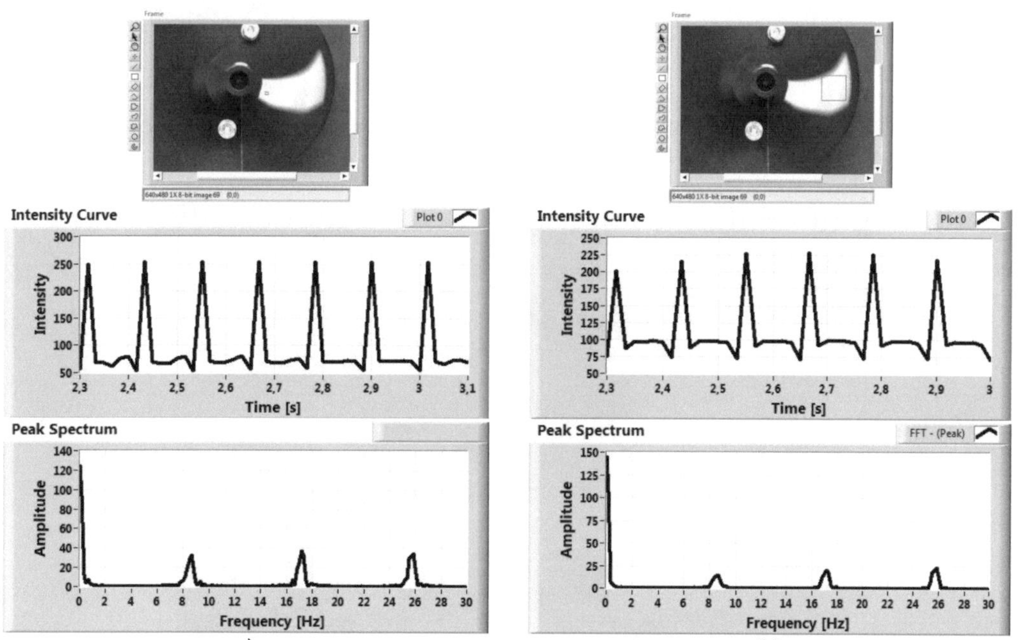

a) b)

Fig. 17. a) Measurement 3: ~9 Hz / ROI size 5 x 5 (px) / dark background, b) Measurement 4: ~9 Hz / ROI size 45 x 45 (px) / dark background

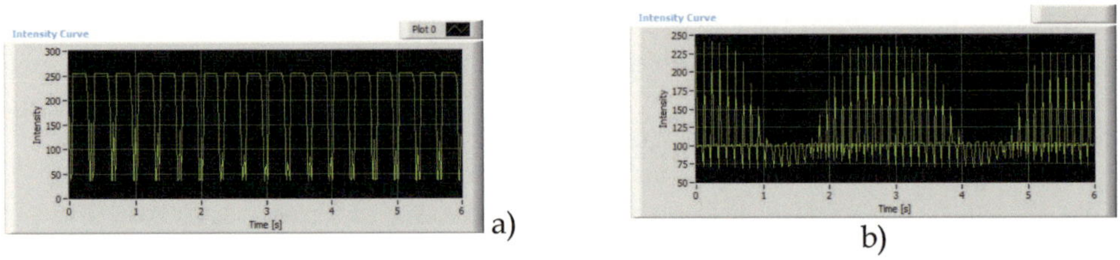

Fig. 18. a) Intensity variance curve for 3 Hz phantom without "floating", b) Intensity variance curve for 9 Hz phantom with "floating"

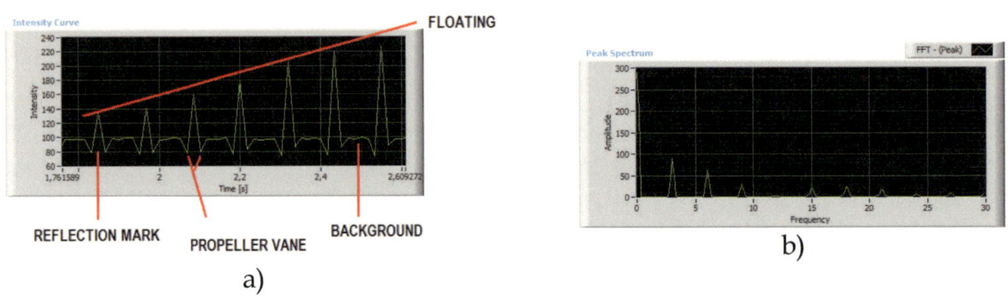

Fig. 19. a) Detailed show of intensity variance curve, b) Magnitude FFT spectrum for 3 Hz phantom

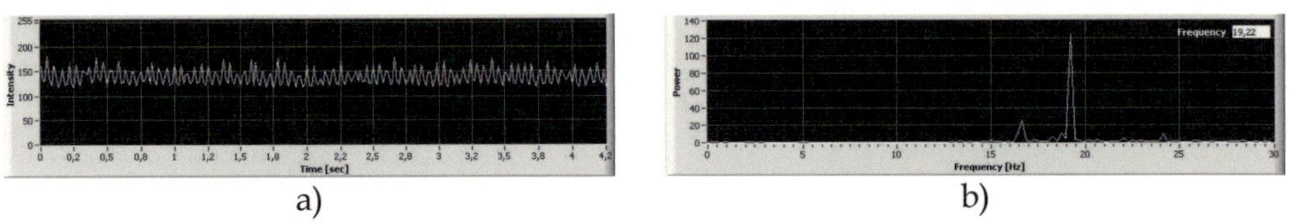

Fig. 20. a) Average ROI intensity variance graph, b) Power spectral density of variance graph

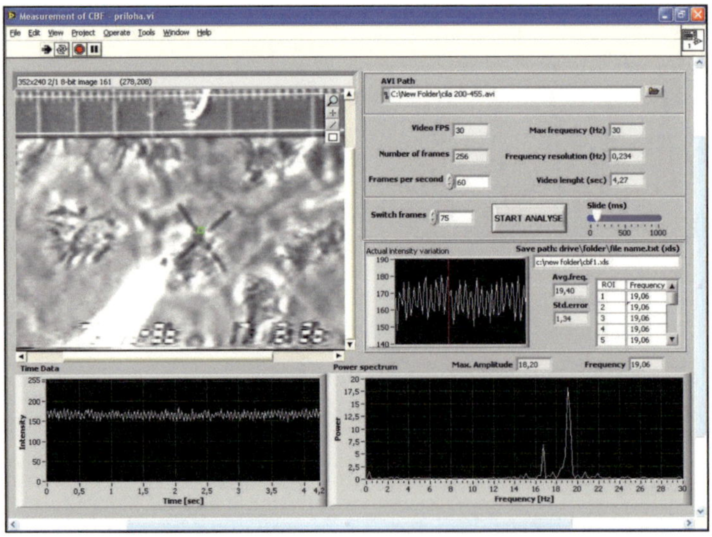

Fig. 21. CBF analysis Front Panel

LabVIEW contains components working with MS Office, so measurement results can be stored in Excel table. There is Front Panel of application for frequency analysis in Fig. 21.
Second parameter - trajectory (or object position in the frame) is analysed by algorithms of object detection.

5.5 Analysis of cilia trajectory

The main tool in this phase of work is Pattern Matching. This tool searches a defined template on each frame of videosequence. Pattern Matching is a set of algorithms based on many techniques. The best known algorithm is cross correlation computing between an original image and a template. Computing of correlation consists of many elementary multiplications and it is very time-consuming; cross correlation cannot find rotated objects (rotation against the template max. 5 - 10°) and scaled objects (bigger or smaller than objects in the template) (NI, 2010). In practice we often use techniques working in frequency domain, pyramidal matching or other intelligent techniques.
Pattern Matching and trajectory detection were tested on phantom videosequence with circular movement of the object. In Fig. 22, is shown the Front Panel of the application for trajectory detection. The Pattern Matching settings is shown in Fig. 23. The matching process is shown in Fig. 24 - Fig. 26. The frame to frame from videosequence is processing and trajectory and angle trajectory is calculated.

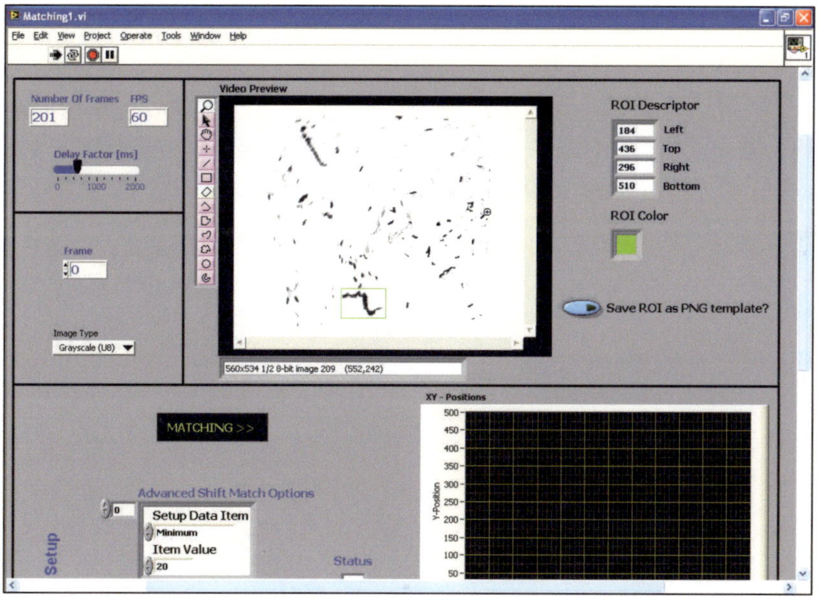

Fig. 22. Pattern Matching detection Front Panel

Designed workstation for high speed digital camera has several possibilities in many points of view partially mentioned above. Smart illumination lights created by LED modules are energy saving, directive sources with changeable emitting spectrums without need of cooling. This fact determinates usage of this hf digital microscopy not only for motion analysis of epithelial cilia. (This system was successfully used for analysis of small PCB traces.)

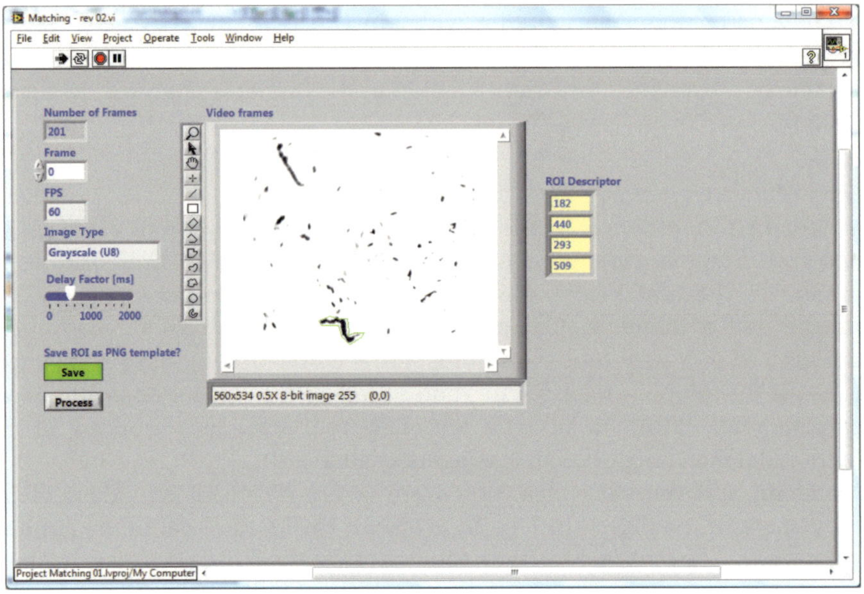

Fig. 23. Pattern Matching setting Front Panel

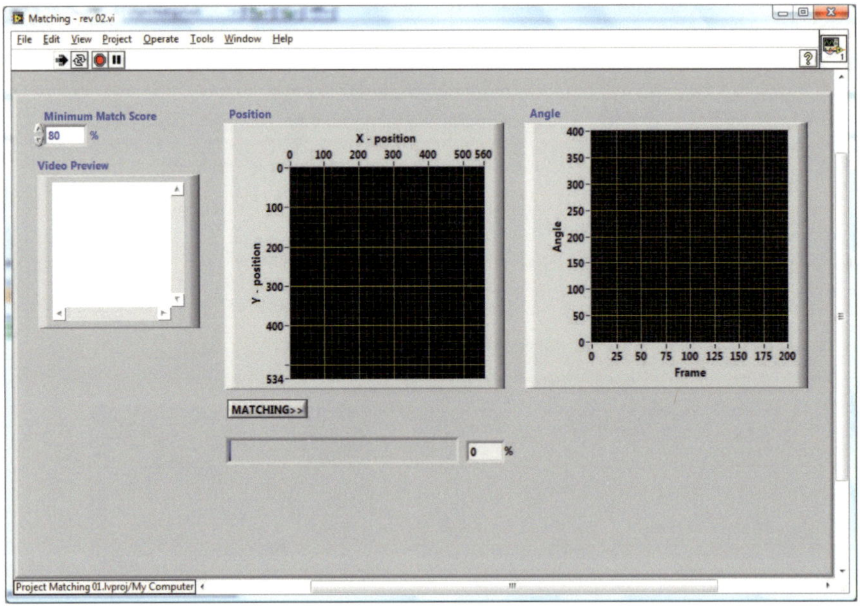

Fig. 24. Pattern Matching processing window "Matching Start"

Another possibilities result from LabVIEW Web Publishing tool usage. Acquisition computer with running virtual instruments is set as server and these scripts can be remote controlled from client computers linked through Ethernet / Internet network. Measurement can start e.g. in Martin hospital and recording or signal processing of recorded sequences can be fully controlled from Žilina or other cooperative clinics. But this remote control needs high speed Internet connection.

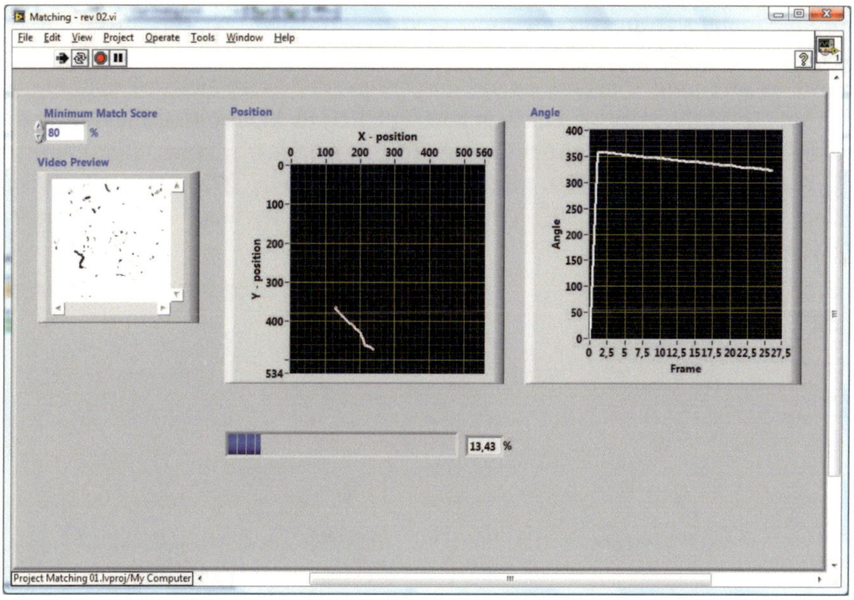

Fig. 25. Pattern Matching processing window - matching is in process (14%)

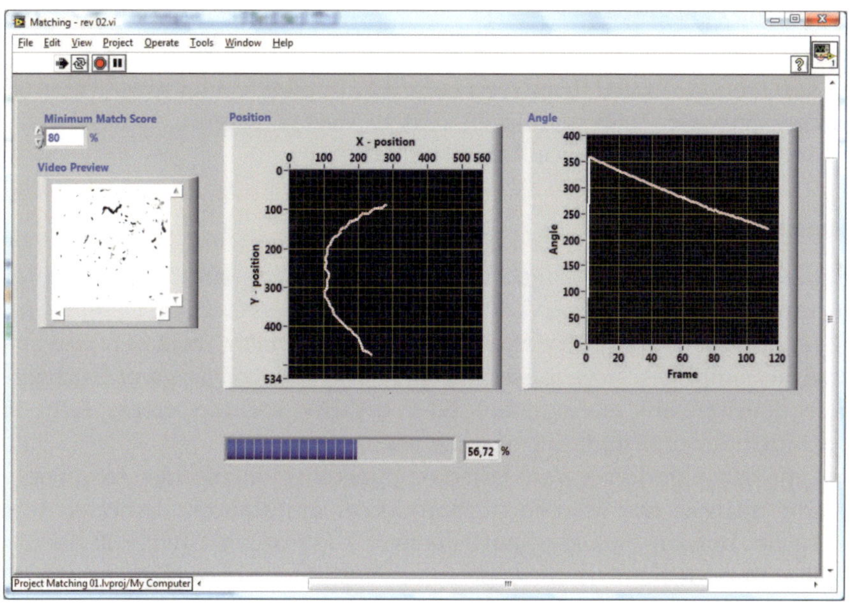

Fig. 26. Pattern Matching processing window - matching is in process (57%)

Acquisition computer is also via Ethernet connection linked with central server, where obtained video sequences are stored on hard drives in secured databases. LabVIEW analysis application generates Excel table (*.xls) with main analysis presets and results (Fig. 27a), which can be distributed on selected e-mail, server folder or directly to HIS (hospital / clinic information system). These LabVIEW tools for network communication speed up distributions of materials and results for analysis between cooperating clinics and institutes.

Video data and images from camera connected to light microscope can be projected from projector. In this mode specialists can do consilium and discuss about any problem. Measurement, results and discussions may be presented with help of suitable conference client. Our team in University of Žilina is testing Click to Meet client for online discussions and webminars, where logged users can share media files, images, documents and web pages, talk together through video and audio channel (Fig. 27b). This client runs on the same server (secured port 8080), where is clinical database with video sequences, applications and analysis results.

LuT transfer char.	y = 3x + (-128)		
Histogram min. (M)	37		
Histogram max. (N)	111		
Convolution kernel	0	2	0
	2	1	2
	0	2	0
2D FFT filter type	DP		
Cutoff frequency [%]	90		
Brightness	128		
Contrast	50		
Gamma	0,8		
Frame width	266		
Frame height	140		
Frames per second (FPS)	60		
Compression	None		
Frame number	361		
ROI type	3		
ROI position [x;y]	130;69		
ROI resolution w x h [pxl]	4 x 8		
Analysis time [s]	1,95 [0:00.17 - 0:02.12]		
Frequency (var. curve)	8,48		
Frequency (PWM curve)	8,57		
Frequency (envelope)	3,03		

a)

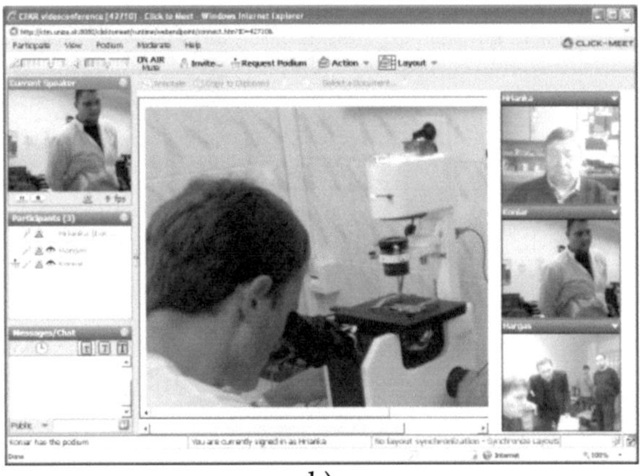

b)

Fig. 27. a) Excel table generated in analysis LabVIEW application for given video sequence stored in server database / HIS analysis, b) Click to Meet conference client; discussion on experiment took in Jessenius medical faculty in Martin

6. Conclusion

In medical praxis - especially in diagnostics of respirathory apparatus - CBF represents very important parameter for describing various pathologies of epithelium. Designed solution for measuring object beating frequency from video sequence using tools of image analysis and spectral analysis simplifies present used methods and reduces usage of hardware devices. Using some development environment NI LabVIEW we can create fully automated application with interactive inputting of some parameters.

In the first approach, algorithms were tested on phantoms with defined frequency. Intensity variance curve analysis can be used in many other applications dedicated to frequency measurement not only in biological environment. Designed hardware acquisition system can be used with or without microscope in applications, where placement of kinematics parameters sensors is not able. Intelligent regulation of condenser illumination through image features extraction and histogram analysis enables fully automated approach to video sequence acquisition.

Biomedical solution of high speed camera workstation is composed from medical, power electronics, signal processing and telecommunications tasks. Software modules represented by LabVIEW enables remote control of experiments and offline analysis and do whole work more effective. Due to changeable modules and open architecture, it is easy to change any module and upgrade the workstation.

After a series of experimental measurements, system is ready for use in clinical environment (clinic of children and youth or institute of pharmacology). First clinical measurements will create useful feedback for technical support for final debugging of system parts.

7. Acknowledgment

Results of these experiments were made with support of grant agency VEGA, project No. 1/0320/10,, they are parts of project "Centre of Experimental and Clinical Respirology", IMTS code: 26220120004, "Centre of Experimental and Clinical Respirology II", IMTS code: 26220120034, "Measurement of Respiratory Epithelium Cilium Kinematics", IMTS code: 26220120019 funded by European Community, also for financial support to Slovak Research.

Európska únia
Európsky fond regionálneho rozvoja

Agentúra
Ministerstva školstva, vedy, výskumu a športu SR
pre štrukturálne fondy EÚ

Operačný program
VÝSKUM a VÝVOJ

„We supported the research activities in Slovakia/Project is co-financed from EU sources"

8. References

Brigham E. O. (1988): *The Fast Fourier Transform and Applications*, Prentice-Hall, ISBN: 0133075052, New York

Chilvers M. A., O'Callaghan Ch. (2000): Analysis of ciliary beat pattern and beat frequency using digital high speed imaging: comparision with the photomultiplier and photodiode methods, *Thorax 2000*, Vol. 55, pp. 314-37, BMJ Publishing Group Ltd & British Thoracic Society (April)

Drgoňa P. - Bobek V. - Dobrucký B. - Frívaldský M. (2009): Performance analysis of equation computation for real time model of PMSM for VHFIM control of PMSM position drive, *International Conference on ELECTRICAL DRIVES and POWER ELECTRONICS*, Dubrovnik, October 2009

Duchoň, F., Štrenger, M. (2008): Microsoft Robotics Studio, *AT&P Journal Plus*, Vol. 10, No. 1, pp. 18-23., ISSN 1336-5010

Eyman S. (2006): Ultrastructural Studies of the Airway Epithelium in Airway Diseases (Digital Comprehensive Summaries of Uppsala Dissertations from the Faculty of Medicine 123), *Acta Universitatis Upsaliensis*, ISBN 91-554-6492-0, Uppsala, 2006

Frivaldsky M., Drgoňa P., Príkopová A. (2009): Design and modeling of 200kHz 1,5kW LLC power semiconductor resonant converter, *IEEE International conference on applied electronics*, Pilsen, September 2009

Gheber L., Priel Z. (1997): Extraction of cilium beat parameters by the combined application of photoelectric measurements and computer simulation, *Biophysical Journal*, Vol. 72, No. 1, ISSN 1542-0086

Jandoš F., Říman R., Gemperle A. (1985): *Využití moderních laboratorních metod v metalografii*, SNTL Praha (in Czech)

Javorka, K. et al (2001).: *Medical Physiology*, Osveta, ISBN 80-8063-023-2, Martin (in Slovak)

Jelinek R. et al (2003): Histologie embryologie, In: *Charles University*, 16. 02. 2011, http://old.lf3.cuni.cz/histologie/materialy/doc/skripta.pdf

National Instruments (2010): NI Vision Concepts Manual

Špánik P., Frivaldsky M., Drgoňa P., Kandráč J. (2010): Efficiency increase of switched mode power supply trough optimization of transistor´s commutation mode, *Electronics and electrical engineering,* No. 9 (105), pp. 49-52, ISSN 1392-1215

Zhang, L., Sanderson, M. J. (2003): Oscillations in ciliary beat frequency and intracellular calcium concentration in rabbit tracheal epithelial cells induced by ATP, *The Journal of Physiology*, Vol. 546, No. 3, ISSN: 0022-3751

9

Instrument Design, Measurement and Analysis of Cardiovascular Dynamics Based on LabVIEW

Wei He[1], Hanguang Xiao[1,2], Songnong Li[1] and Delmo Correia[1]
[1]Chongqing University,
[2]Chongqing University of Technology,
China

1. Introduction

With the increasing aging of population, cardiovascular diseases have become one of the most common diseases. It has been recognized as the leading killer of the 21st century by World Health Organization (He & Yu 2010). It is believed that one-third of deaths around the world result from cardiovascular disease, but many of them died from absence of timely detection of the diseases (Mark 2003). Therefore, timely and accurate detection and diagnosis of this kind of diseases are of great significance for prophylaxis and treatment. For this purpose, more powerful instruments are needed to be developed.

In recent years, LabVIEW have been wildly used in various fields as a powerful development environment and platform based on graphical and dataflow programming language (Johnson & Jennings 1997; Whitley & Blackwell 2001; Klinger 2003; Bitter et al. 2007). LabVIEW-based research and development of medical instruments is one of the most outstanding representatives in the R&D of virtual instruments (He & Yu 2010).

In this chapter, we will introduce the design of our independently developed product, which is named as YF/XGYD atherosclerosis detection system developed by LabVIEW. Three aspects of the system will be mainly described, namely overall design of the hardware system, the brief design and LabVIEW realization of the software system, and the clinical measurement and analysis of hemodynamic parameters of cardiovascular system, such as pulse wave velocity (PWV) and arterial stiffness index (ASI).

In the first part of the chapter, we will mainly described the overall design of the hardware system, such as the measure method of analog signals of blood pressure, the design and realization of the signal processing circuit, the design of digit circuit and loop of aeration and deflation, and the circuit of motor control.

In the second part of the chapter, the overall framework of the software system will be displayed in a block diagram. Then, the interface design of the software system is described, for example the main interface, test interface and record interface. In addition, we will show how to build and manage the patient database of the software system.

Finally, the basic principle, measurement and analysis of two key parameters are introduced, namely PWV and ASI. We would like to apply the system to clinical test and discuss the performances of the system.

2. Design of a cardiovascular dynamics parameters measuring instrument

The cardiovascular dynamics parameters measuring instrument is mainly composed of two parts: the hardware system and the software system. In what follows, the overall design of hardware and software systems of YF/XGYD Artery Stiffness Measuring Instrument (YF/XGYD) developed by Chongqing University are mainly described in this chapter.

2.1 Design of hardware system

The hardware circuit and gas path system of YF/XGYD is mainly composed of three parts: analog signals detecting circuit; digital control circuit; charge-discharge gas loop of electromotor. The overall design of hardware system is displayed in the following block diagram (Fig. 1).

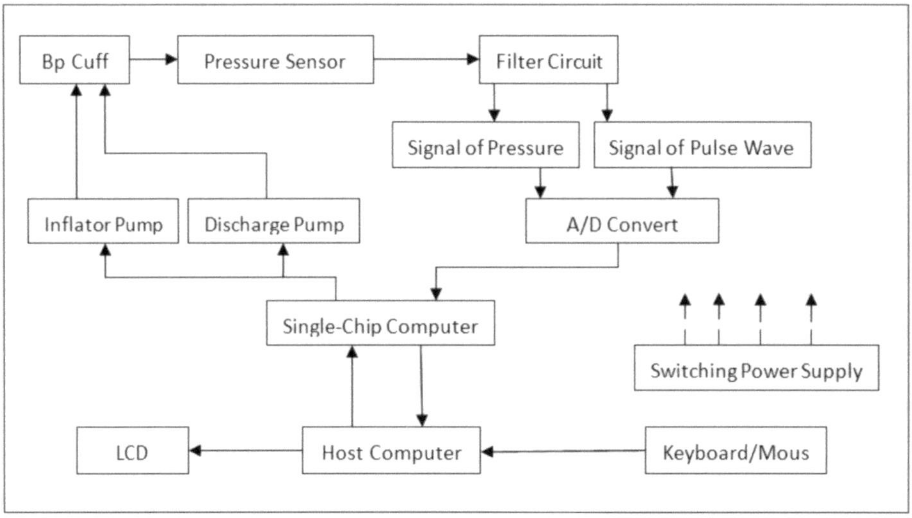

Fig. 1. The overall design of hardware system

In testing, place the object in sitting position, the brachial cuff is used around the left upper arm, near elbow joint, and the wrist cuff is used around the radial artery. The cuff is inflated by air pump under the control of single-chip computer. Simultaneously, pressure pulse signals in the cuff are collected through pressure sensors. When pressure of cuff reaches the preconcert set point, inflation of cuff is stopped. In the same time, pulsation of brachial artery stops because of the pressure of cuff. Then pressure of cuff decreases gradually when the deflation valve is working slowly according to programs in the single-chip computer. Brachial artery begins pulsing when pressure of cuff decreases below systolic pressure, and the pulsation increases as pressure of cuff decreases. Through pressure sensors, pulsation signals of cuff pressure, brachial artery and radial artery are converted into voltage signals. After these voltage signals are amplified and under filtering processing, we get three signals of appropriate amplitude. These signals include one signal of cuff pressure and two signals of pulse wave. Then these three signals are A/D converted into digital signals, with these digital signals to be analyzed and processed in single-chip computer. These digital signals can be sent to and then analyzed and processed thoroughly in host computer through RS232 series communication by single-chip computer. These contents of analysis and processing in

host computer include that: real-time displays and records pressure waves of brachial artery, radial artery and cuff pressure; calculates parameter values through existing algorithm; saves tester's information, parameter values and waveforms; evaluates the artery's health condition of the object.
The YF/XGYD artery stiffness measuring instrument and the field testing can be seen in Fig. 2.

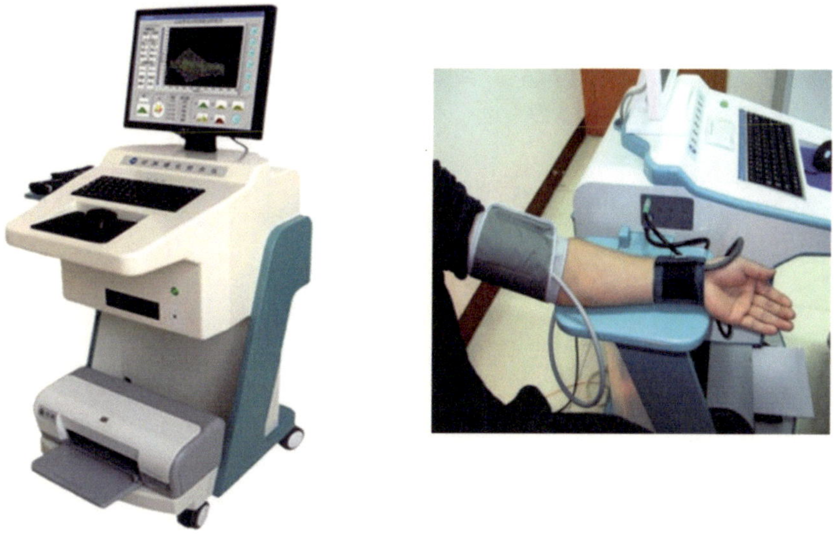

Fig. 2. The YF/XGYD artery stiffness measuring instrument and the field testing

2.2 Design of software system

2.2.1 The overall block diagram of software system

The software system of YF/XGYD is based on virtual instrument LabVIEW 8.5. It is mainly used to collect and preprocess data signals, analyze and calculate blood flow parameters, and store, replay and print test results. The whole block diagram can be seen in Fig. 3. Through utilizing the powerful function of data acquisition and digital signal processing of LabVIEW 8.5, we can collect and process these signals of pulse wave and cuff pressure. In addition, LabVIEW 8.5 has well function of database management and many kinds of tools and methods. So it can manage many different types of database. Users can utilize data control to access, add, delete and inquire existing different types of database. And users can utilize Visual System Manager (VSM) to establish and maintain many different types of database and generate database application program. Because those well functions of database management in LabVIEW 8.5, through programming we achieved storage management of patient file, including: database maintenance, query answering, statistical analysis and printing.

2.2.2 User interface design of software system

The user interface is very important component in interactive software system. A good user interface should have the advantages, such as perfect performance, simplified operation, reliable operation and accurate interpretation of results. Every part of the architecture block diagram of software system (Fig. 3) corresponds with function module and user interface in software system, respectively.

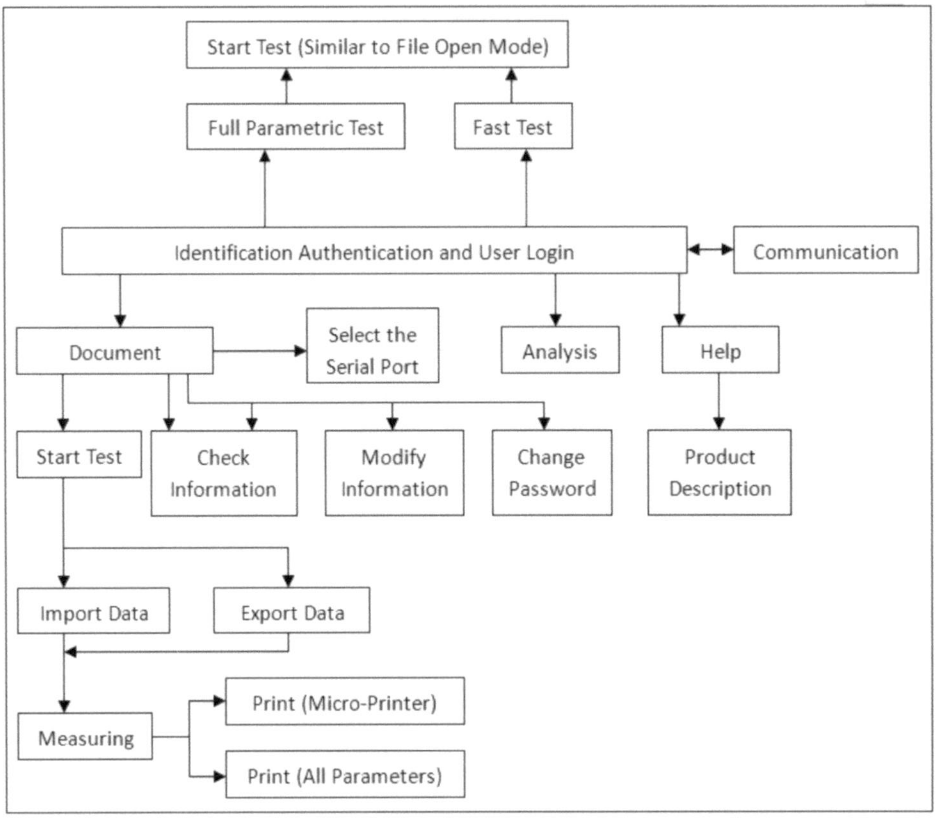

Fig. 3. The architecture block diagram of software system

1. Main window of the software system

To ensure the security of the software system, users could set a password in the secret code dialogue window which will be popped out when user starts the system. Only after entering the correct password, user can enter the main window.

Users could utilize the function menus in the main window to achieve a variety of processing operations. The window interfaces in the system be generated by menu tool (Menu Editor) in LabVIEW 8.5 are all standard Windows pull-down menu system. To make the system easy to operate and make users easy to master, we take into account the following principles in the design of the menu: in design, organize system menu on the basis of functions, so users could know clearly structure and function of the system when they browse the menu; to give a meaningful title to menu against the specified function; to set hotkeys for these staple menus; to organize menu item according to frequency of utilization.

The main window and its LabVIEW program code of YF/XGYD can be seen in Fig. 4 and Fig. 5, respectively. The main window is relatively simple; in addition, in terms of function set-up, it includes three pull-down menus (the File, the Analysis and the Help) and three function-buttons (the Fast Test, the Full Parametric Test and the Exit).

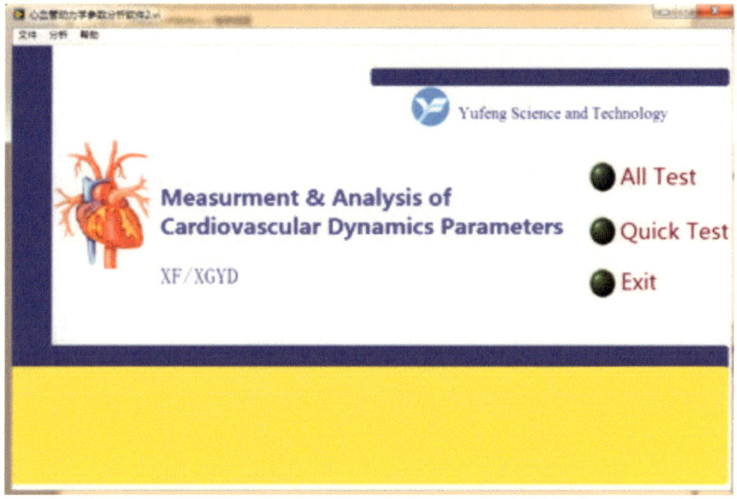

Fig. 4. Main window of YF/XGYD system

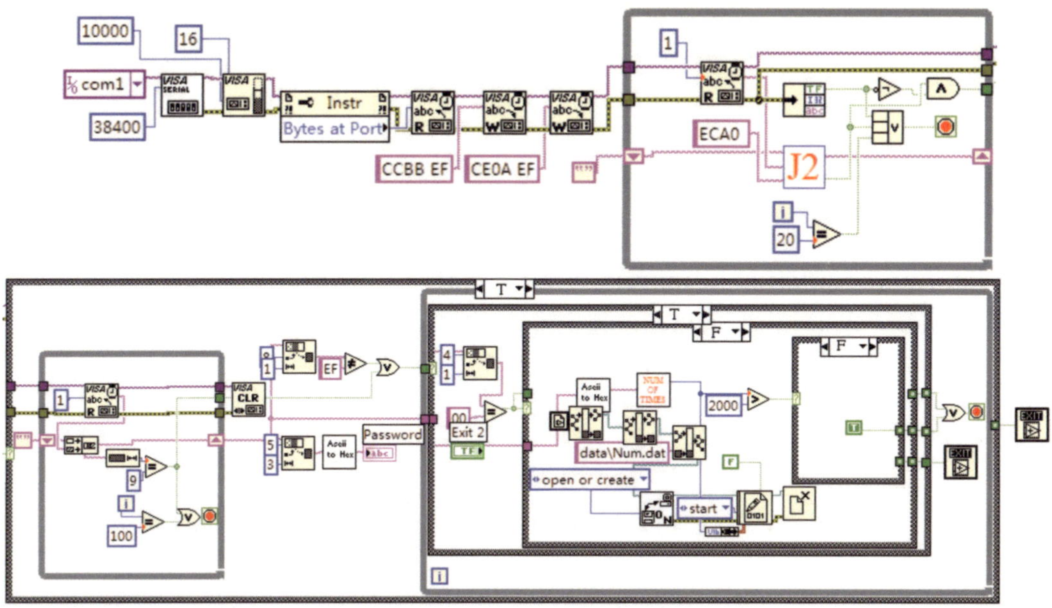

Fig. 5. LabVIEW program code of the main window

2. Test window of the software system

When the YF/XGYD system measures the cardiovascular active state of human, the system software will carry out data communications and synchronously draw graphics of these measuring signals. Furthermore, to visually and intuitively describe the process of inflation and deflation in cuff, the system can utilize progress bar control to dynamically simulate rising and falling of mercury column in sphygmomanometer when charging and discharging gas in blood press measurement by the stethoscope. The full parametric test window and its LabVIEW program code of YF/XGYD can be seen in Fig. 6 and Fig. 7, respectively.

The interface (shown in Fig. 6) can be divided into three areas, such as the Function Button Area, the Test Waveform Display Area, and the Personal Data and Test Results Display Area.

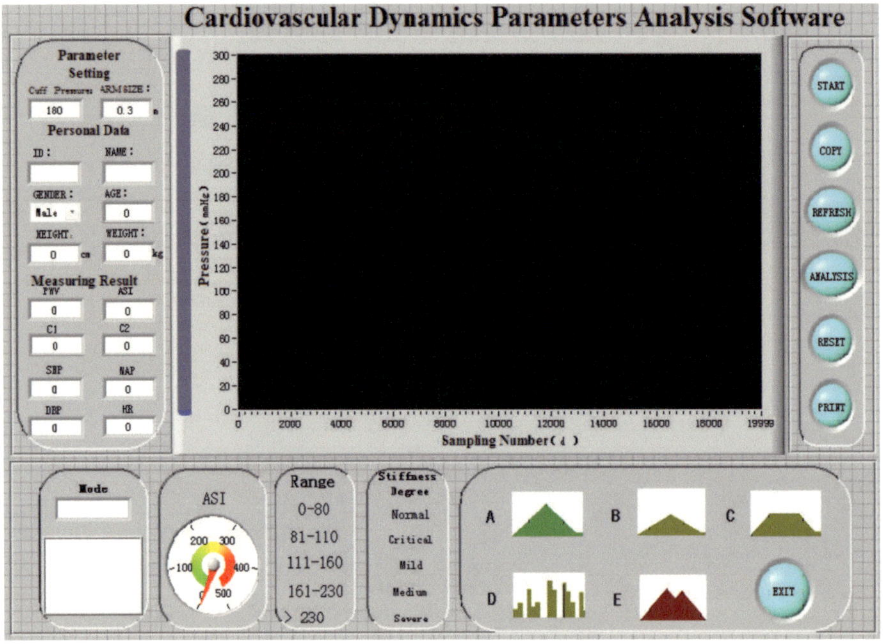

Fig. 6. The full parametric test window

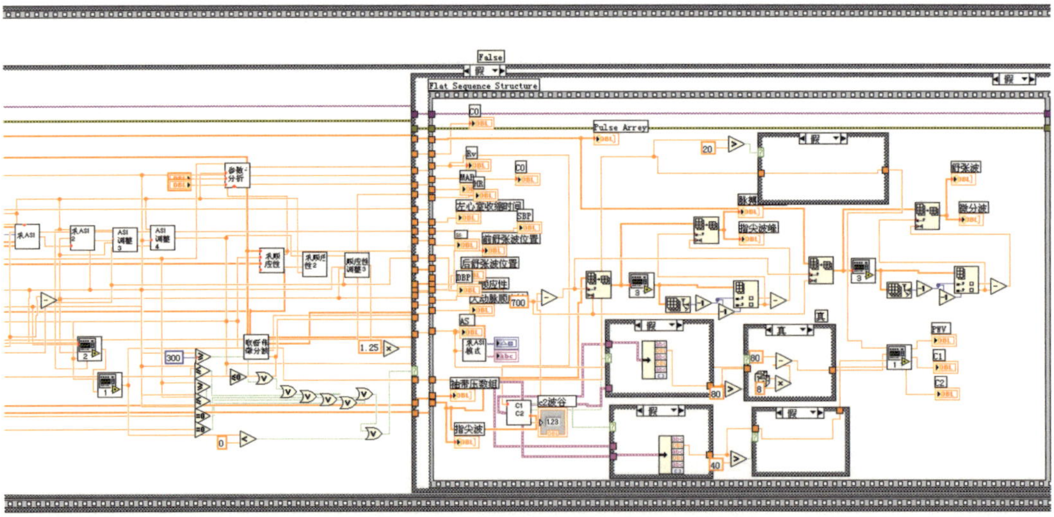

Fig. 7. A part of LabVIEW program code of the full parametric test window

According to the needs of testing procedure, users could choose the Measuring Button, the Save Button, the Refresh Button, the Analysis Button, the Reset Button and the Print Button, respectively. When user clicks the Measuring Button, YF/XGYD system enters testing status. In this state, the host computer begins to communicate with the slave computer; in the meantime, cuffs are inflated; then the system displays real-time waveform variation value of three-way signals in the Test Waveform Display Area. These waveforms can be seen in Fig. 8.

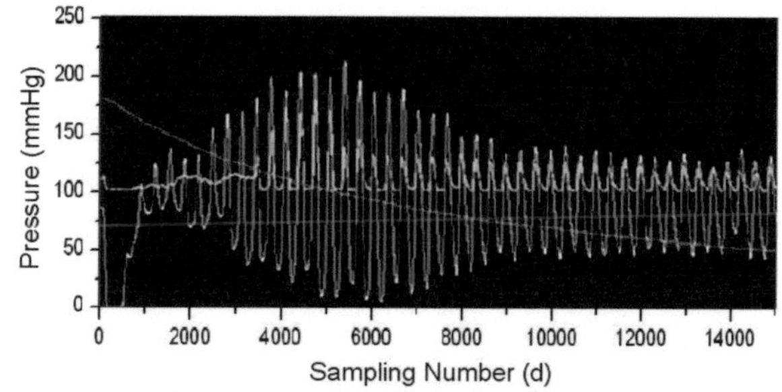

White -----Pulse Wave Curve of Brachial Artery

Green -----Pulse Wave Curve of Radial Artery

Red -----Curve of Cuff Pressure

Fig. 8. Graphs of pulse wave and cuff pressure

The roles of function buttons are: the Measuring Button, to begin testing; the Save Button, to save measuring results, personal data, measuring waveforms, etc.; the Reset Button, to eject the Input Tester Data Sub Interface and re-input tester basic information (including ID, name, gender, age, height and weight) in this sub-interface; the Refresh Button, to empty personal data and measuring waveforms and wait for next test; the Analysis Button, to enter the Parametric Analysis Interface of Patient who have been tested (the interface and its LabVIEW program code can be seen in Fig. 9 and Fig. 10, respectively), and to look over Diastolic initiation wave, Systolic decent wave and other cardiovascular parameters of patients; the Print Button, to print measuring results.

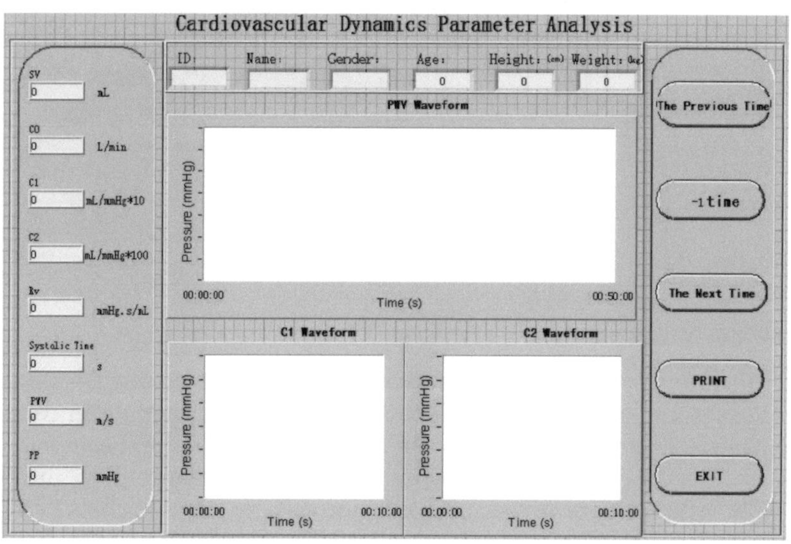

Fig. 9. Parametric analysis interface

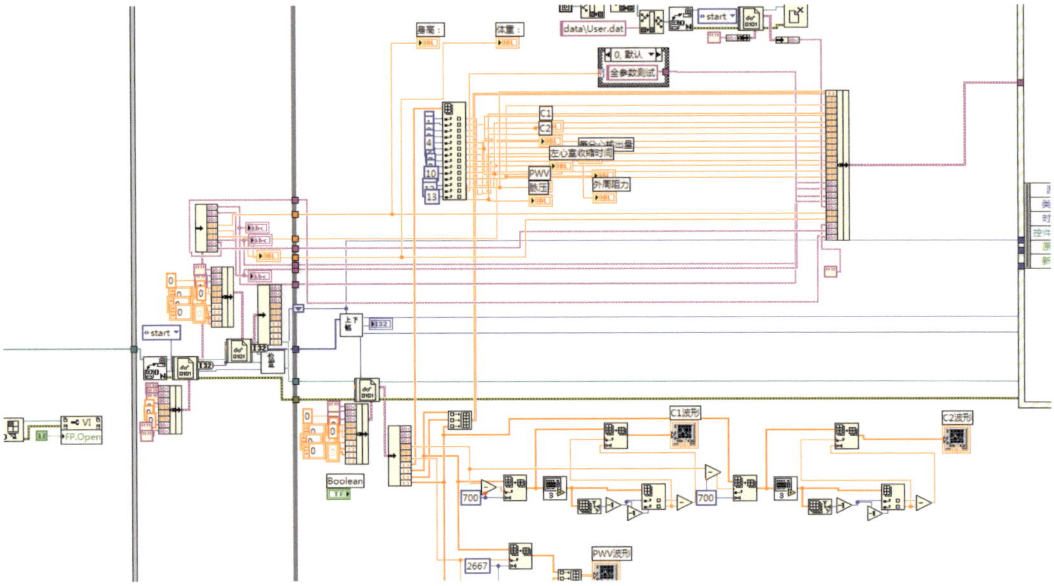

Fig. 10. A part of LabVIEW program code of the parametric analysis interface

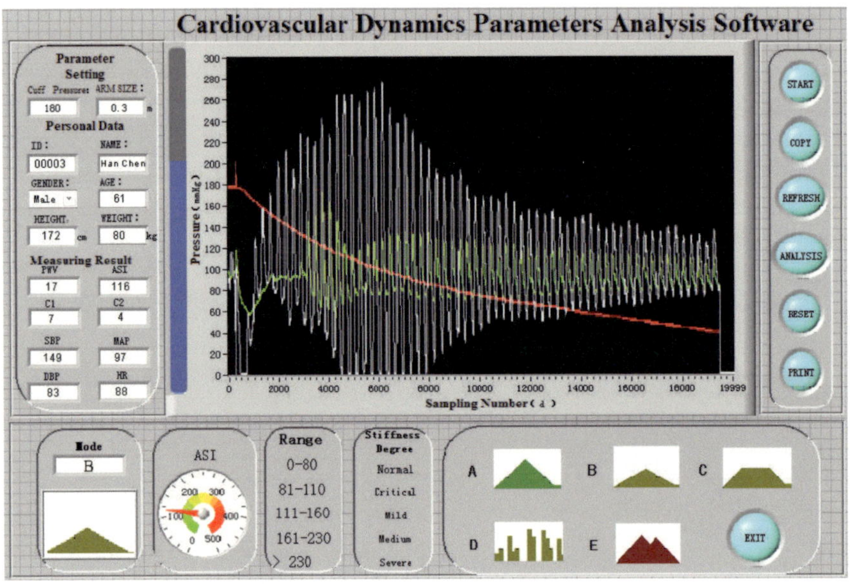

Fig. 11. Measuring results interface

These test results are displayed in the Personal Data and Test Results Display Area. These results include personal data, such as ID, name, gender, age, height and weight, and test results, such as systolic pressure, diastolic pressure, mean pressure, heart rate, pulse wave velocity [PWV], artery stiffness index [ASI], large artery compliance [C1], and small artery compliance [C2]. According to measured values of each parameter, the YF/XGYD system can estimate the cardiovascular status of the object. For example, the system can utilize vivid Graphic Correlation method to estimate the range of ASI value; waveform envelope shape

of pulse wave is divided into five types (A, B, C, D, and E), so the system can synthetically estimate general situation of artery elasticity. In Fig. 11, we can clearly see a 61-year-old patient's test result: systolic pressure is 149mmHg, ASI is 116, and waveform type of pulse wave is B, and so on. The test result indicates that the patient whose arteries are already mild stiffness has the tendency of potential artery disease.
In addition, the system software has the Test Waveform Display Area interface. User can utilize the interface to examine, delete, recover and print patient's personal data and waveforms and results of each record. In order to facilitate contrastive analysis, different parametric results of every test are all displayed on the interface. Fig. 12 showes a patient's two test records (ASI is 200 in the first time and 190 in the second time) which reflect that the patient's arteries are moderately stiff.

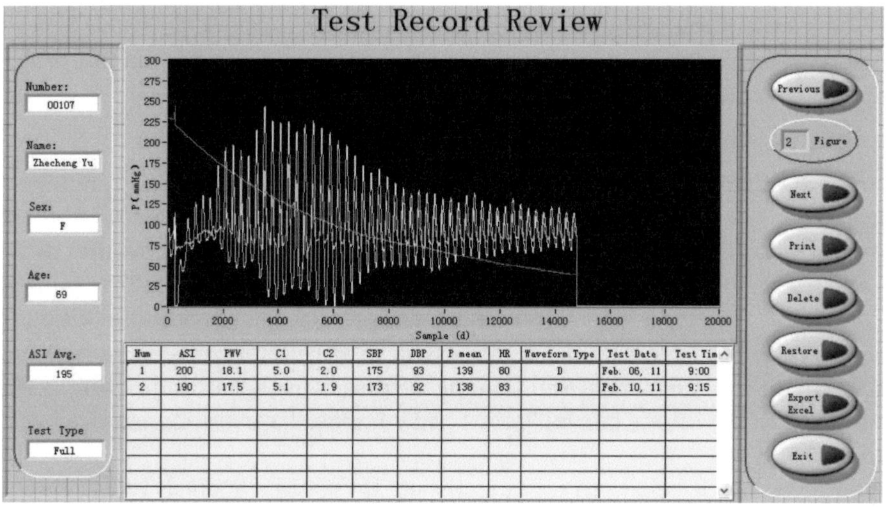

Fig. 12. Test waveform display area interface

2.2.3 Database of software system

1. Establishment of database

The medical signal database with three data tables is created strictly in accordance with the relational model of database. The tables are: the table of patient's basic information, including ID, name, gender, age, height and weight; the table of patient's basic parameter, including pulse wave, cuff wave, heart rate, systolic pressure, diastolic pressure, mean pressure and stroke volume; the table of diagnostic results, to save the corresponding results in the field of diagnostic results.

2. Operation of database

The operation of database includes data browsing, data query and database editor that adds, modifies and deletes patient data. Inquiry statistic is a very important function in management system. The YF/XGYD system utilizes LabVIEW 8.5 well database management function to achieve the inquiry and statistics of relevant data. It takes a great of convenience to clinical and scientific researches. The edit function of database can achieve these operations to add, modify and delete patient records. Choosing the corresponding option in the menu, user can achieve the maintenance of patient records. According to the actual need, user can choose the print option in the menu to print patient records. It takes a great of convenience to analysis of patient's condition.

3. Data management module

Data store can be divided into file store and database store in LabVIEW 8.5. Database store can overcome the constraints imposed by file store which is proven unfavourable to data query and management, so the YF/XGYD system utilizes database to store data in the development of virtual instrument system. This improves running efficiency of the system. Through Open Database Connectivity (ODBC), LabVIEW communicates with the database. User needs to name database and install drivers in ODBC. Through third-party software (LabSQL), software communication interface between LabSQL and LabVIEW database is created. Users can utilize the interface to log in local or network database and establish, store, modify and manage this database. Data exchange between application program and database is achieved by calling the SQL execution module.

4. Data storage module

Users can respectively choose the independent storage and the statistics storage to store measuring data. Users can look over measuring waveforms, parameters and results of patient by the independent storage ways or save patient's measuring results to LabVIEW tables in the manner of statistical model by the statistics storage ways. At the same time, the system can create a homonymous Excel electronic spreadsheet. On account of large amount of waveform data, the method of examining data in Excel is inconvenient. The method of examining data in LabVIEW table will become necessary means for improving performance of examining data. And users can look over and compare large categories of waveforms by this method.

Users can directly call Excel electronic spreadsheet for statistic analysis by SPSS software. A set of clinical test results after being evaluated and saved is shown in Fig. 13, which is displayed under the LabVIEW environment. Excel electronic spreadsheet and this LabVIEW table have same file name and path, but different formats. Users can choose to analyze the whole measuring data or a certain measuring data or multiple measuring data to contrast and analyze by statistical method. Users can analyze in term of the repeatability these data which are gained by repeated measuring the same people. These measuring results of multiple hospitals can be saved as the same document and displayed synchronously. By and large, the efficiency of clinical analysis is greatly improved through the improvement of database.

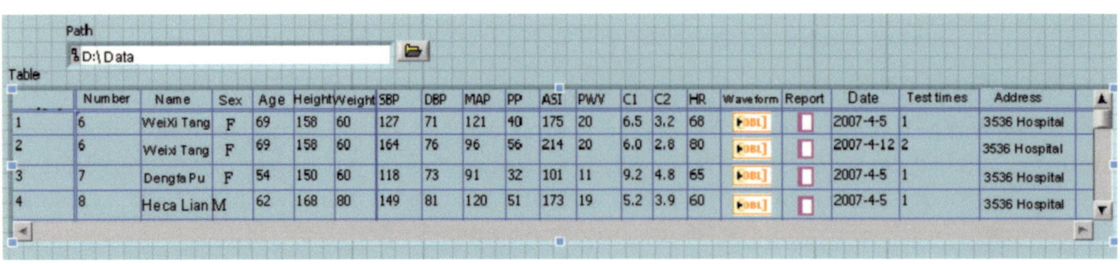

	Number	Name	Sex	Age	Height	Weight	SBP	DBP	MAP	PP	ASI	PWV	C1	C2	HR	Waveform	Report	Date	Test times	Address
1	6	WeiXi Tang	F	69	158	60	127	71	121	40	175	20	6.5	3.2	68			2007-4-5	1	3536 Hospital
2	6	Weixi Tang	F	69	158	60	164	76	96	56	214	20	6.0	2.8	80			2007-4-12	2	3536 Hospital
3	7	Dengfa Pu	F	54	150	60	118	73	91	32	101	11	9.2	4.8	65			2007-4-5	1	3536 Hospital
4	8	Heca Lian	M	62	168	80	149	81	120	51	173	19	5.2	3.9	60			2007-4-5	1	3536 Hospital

Fig. 13. A set of clinical test results

3. Algorithm, encoding and measurement of arteriosclerosis parameter

Many parameters of artery system can be measured by YF/XGYD system. PWV and ASI are the two most commonly used parameters among them. We mainly introduced the method of calculation, the programming of LabVIEW and the process of measurement of the two parameters.

3.1 Pulse wave velocity (PWV)

3.1.1 Definition of PWV

The systole and diastole of heart lead to the periodic change of blood pressures in whole arterial system, and the periodic contraction and dilatation of arterial wall, which force the pulse wave to propagate along blood vessels from heart to whole body(McDonald 1974; Qiao & Wu 2000). PWV is mainly decided by the arterial physical parameters, such as arterial wall thickness and Young's modulus of elasticity. Therefore, PWV can reflect the changes of these parameters, and judge whether arteriosclerosis or not (Takenaka & Kobayashi 2004).

3.1.2 Calculation of PWV

In the system, a noninvasive method is used to measure the brachial-radial PWV (commonly abbreviated as BRPWV) by detecting, collecting and analyzing the pulse signals at brachial artery and radial artery simultaneously. BRPWV is commonly used for the degree assessment of human arteriosclerosis (Zhang et al. 2005).
Because pulse wave propagates from heart to peripheral arteries, pulse wave arrive at brachial artery firstly, then radial artery (McDonald 1974; Qiao & Wu 2000; Mark 2003). We can measure the time difference Δt of wave arriving at two measure point at brachial and radial artery, and the distance ΔL of two measuring points, namely the distance of two pressure sensors in two cuffs. Then we can calculate BRPWV as Eq. 1.

$$PWV = \frac{\Delta L}{\Delta t} \tag{1}$$

In order to obtain Δt , the foot of the pulse wave need to be detected, namely the takeoff point D. Because of the existence of interference factors, the ideal pulse wave is hard to be obtained, namely the takeoff point D is not the trough location of pulse wave. In Fig. 14, point A is the trough of pulse wave, and point D is the takeoff point which is needed to detect. Obviously, the two points are not the same point, so the point D is needed to calculate using a special algorithm.
The algorithm of detecting the takeoff point D:
Step 1. find the trough A (x_1, y_1) and peak B (x_2, y_2) of the pulse wave;
Step 2. establish the equation of line AB:

$$(y_1 - y_2)x + (x_2 - x_1)y + (x_1y_2 - x_2y_1) = 0 \tag{2}$$

Step 3. calculate the distance from a point on the waveform between A and B to the line AB, and find the maximal distance from a point which is the takeoff point D.

After detecting the takeoff points of the brachial and radial pulse wave, the x coordinate different value of the two points is the time difference Δt . The schematic figure of calculating Δt is showed in Fig. 14.

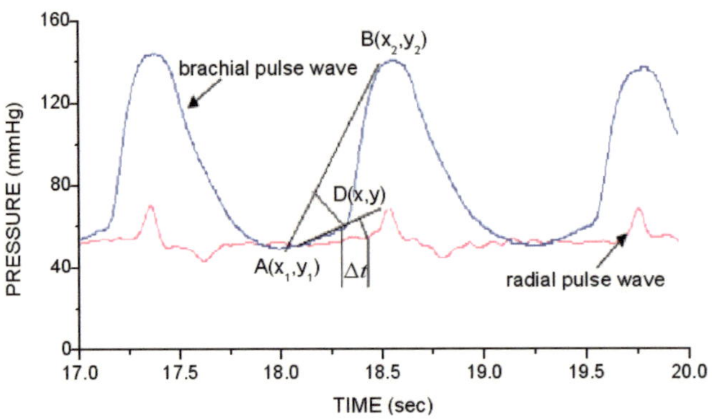

Fig. 14. The schematic figure of calculating Δt

3.1.3 LabVIEW code of calculation of PWV

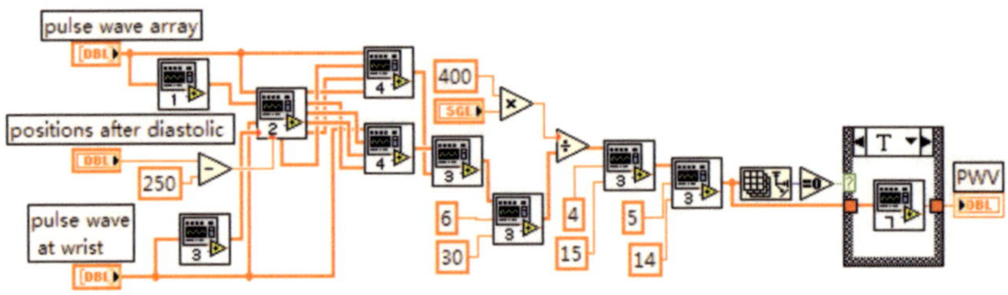

Fig. 15. LabVIEW graphical code of calculation of PWV

The LabVIEW graphical code of calculating PWV is showed as Fig. 15. There are four subprograms called by the main program in Fig. 15. The subprogram 1 and 3 are used for finding the trough and peak of the pulse wave, respectively. The subprogram 2 is used to establish the equation of the line AB. The takeoff points of the brachial and radial artery and the time difference are calculated by the subprogram 4 and 5. In order to improve the accuracy, the subprogram 6 and 7 are used to find several time differences of lower relative error and calculating the mean of them. The LabVIEW graphical codes of the subprogram 2 and 4 are showed in Fig. 16 and 17.

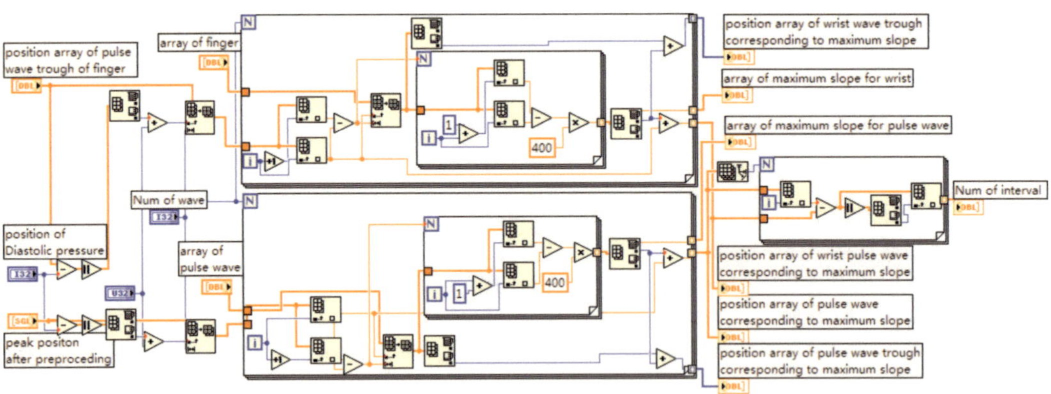

Fig. 16. The LabVIEW graphical codes of the subprogram 2

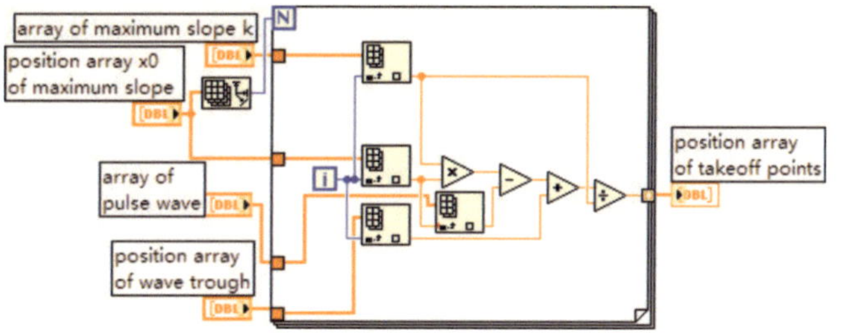

Fig. 17. The LabVIEW graphical codes of the subprogram 4

3.2 Arterial stiffness factor (ASI)

3.2.1 Definition of ASI

ASI is an important nondimensional parameter which represents the degree of blood-vessel stiffness (Sunthareswaran 2003; Quan et al. 2006). ASI can indicate arterial wall elasticity, and serve as an independent predictor of cardiovascular diseases. It is also an important parameter of YF/XGYD system.

3.2.2 Calculation of ASI

In the system, we use the whole pulse waveform and the pressure curve of cuff to calculate ASI (Yao et al. 2007). Generally, we find out two peaks at the front and back of the maximum peak, which are closest approach to 80% of the maximum peak. Then, two cuff pressures corresponding to the two peaks can be obtained by a subprogram. Finally, ASI is calculated by multiplying the difference of the two cuff pressures by a special factor.

In the measurement of ASI, the maximum peak P_{Max} of the whole pulse wave is obtained firstly, namely the MAP of the pulse wave. Secondly, we need to find out two peaks of pulse wave whose values are the most approach to $P_{Max} * 80\%$ at the front and back of the maximum peak. The difference of two cuff pressures corresponding to the two peaks multiplies a special factor to get ASI. The schematic diagram of calculating ASI is showed as Fig. 18. The equation of calculation is as follows:

$$ASI = K * (P_1 - P_2)$$

Where, K is the correction factor which is relate to the particular case of tester, such as smoking, sex, age, and health.

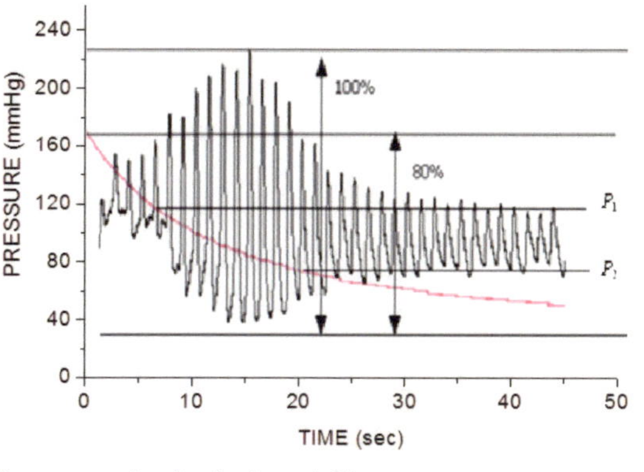

Fig. 18. The schematic diagram of calculating ASI

In LabVIEW, we use a subprogram VI to realize the calculation of ASI. The graphical code of the subprogram is showed as Fig. 19.

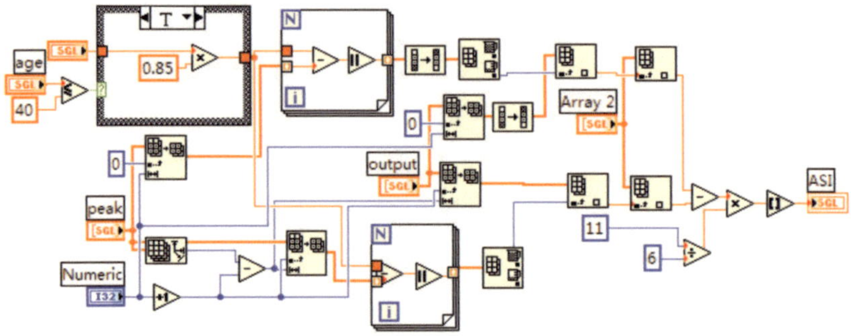

Fig. 19. The graphical code of calculating ASI

3.2.3 Singular wave processing in actual measurement of ASI

In actual measurement of ASI, the pulse wave signal is greatly influenced by environment around the tested body (Quan, He et al. 2006; Quan et al. 2006; Yao, He et al. 2007). For example, the saltation of respiration and the body shaking may product a few singular waveforms. This kind of interferences will not only influence the data collection, and may even generate invalid data. In order to remove the influence of singular waveform, we need to conduct a series of signal processing, such as filtering processing of moving average, deleting adjacent-wave, high peak and low peak, etc.

1. Deleting adjacent wave processing

In measurement, there are some adjacent waves generated from interference as shown in Fig. 20. Pulse adjacent wave likely cause the detecting error of the systolic blood pressure and diastolic blood pressure. So we need to remove these pulse adjacent waves. Through a lot of waveform analysis, we summarize a method for detecting adjacent wave: if the time difference of two adjacent peaks is less than 100 sampling points, the two waves corresponding to the two adjacent peaks are judged to be adjacent wave. Fig. 21 showed the graphical code of adjacent wave processing.

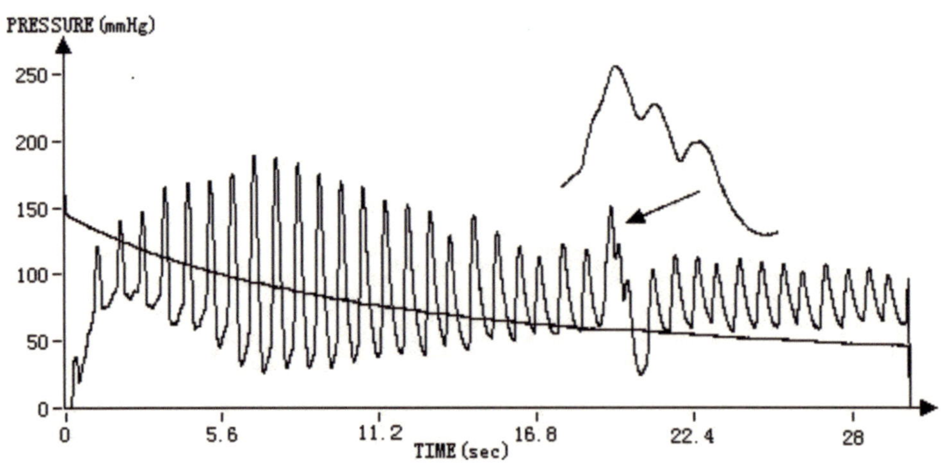

Fig. 20. Processing adjacent wave

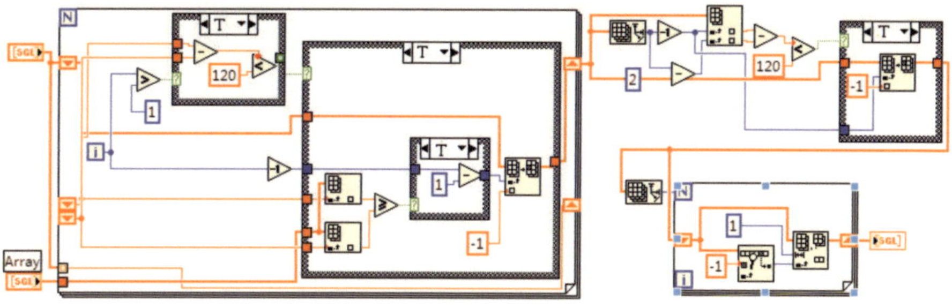

Fig. 21. The graphical code of adjacent wave processing

2. Deleting sharp peak processing

In measurement, a vibration of a part of body or other reasons probably cause the phenomenon of sharp peak in pulse wave as shown in Fig. 22. If the system applies the singular sharp peak in analysis, the singular wave will be misjudged to be the position of mean blood pressure. So system must delete these singular sharp peaks.

Through a lot of waveform analysis, we summarize a method for detecting singular sharp peak: (1) if the value of a certain point A of all pulse peaks surpasses 30 of front and back point of the point A; (2) if the value of a certain point A of all pulse peaks is more than 30 of front point, 10 of back point and 30 of back two points of the point A; (3) if the value of a certain point A of all pulse peaks is more than 30 of back point,10 of front point and 30 of front two points of the point A; we judge the point A is a singular peak when anyone condition is right. Fig. 23 shows the graphical code of sharp peak processing.

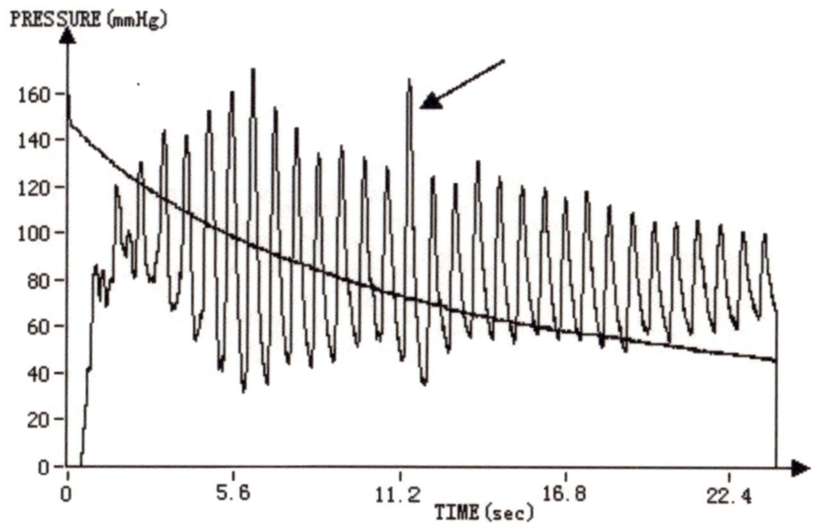

Fig. 22. Processing sharp peak

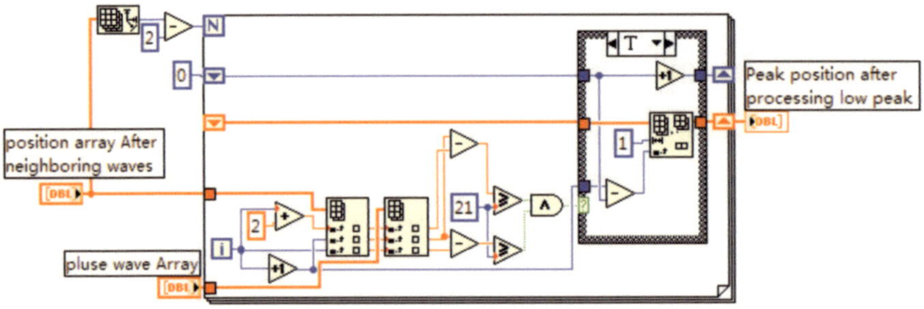

Fig. 23. The graphical code of sharp peak processing

3. Deleting low peak processing

Singular low peak cause measurement error of the systolic blood pressure and diastolic blood pressure easily. So we must detect and remove them from pulse wave for the performance of the system. An example of singular low peak is shown in Fig. 24. Through a lot of waveform analysis, we summarize a method for detecting singular low peak: if a certain peak A of pulse peaks is lower than 15 of the front and back peaks of the peak A, the peak A is judged to be a wrong peak.

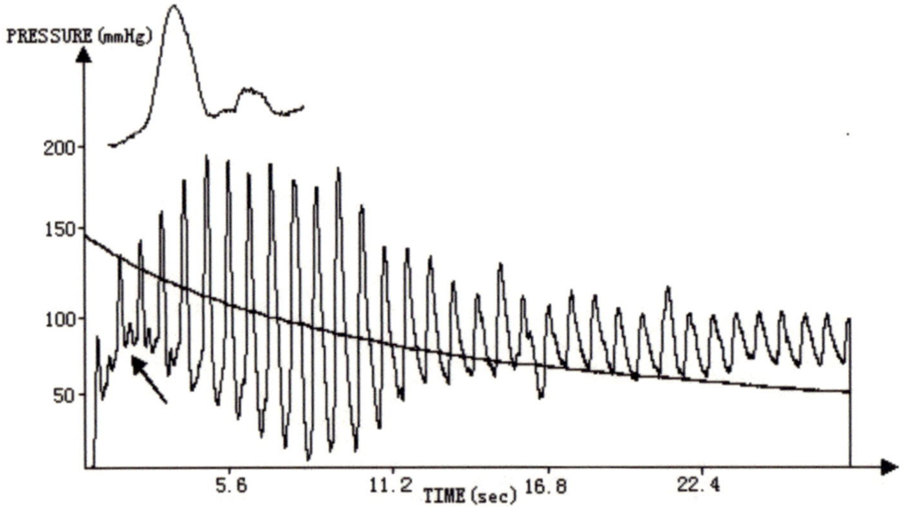

Fig. 24. Processing low peak

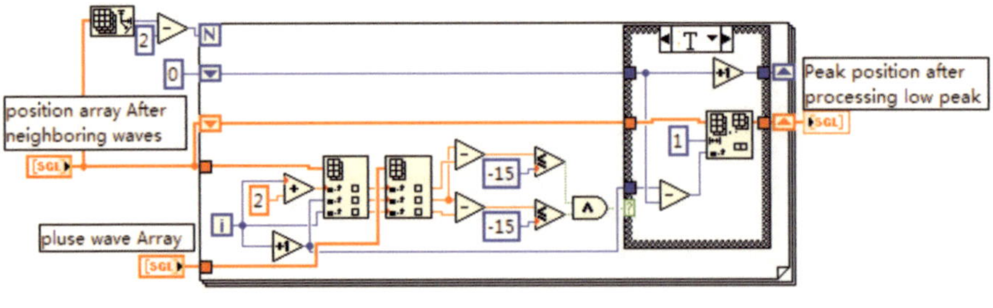

Fig. 25. The graphical code of singular low peak processing

3.2.4 The display of ASI diagnose result

ASI is usually divided into five types corresponding to the five status of vessel: normal, critical, arteriosclerosis, arrhythmia and arteriosclerosis, and cardiac function defect and arteriosclerosis. For different types, there are five intervals of ASI and five basic pulse waveforms corresponding to the five vessel types as shown in Table 1.

type	ASI	Basic type of pulse waveform	pulse waveform	diagnosis
A	0-70			normal
B	71-120			critical
C	121-180			arteriosclerosis
D	181-300			arrhythmia and arteriosclerosis
E	300-			cardiac function defect and arteriosclerosis

Table 1. Pulse waveform and diagnosis corresponding to different ASI

4. Clinical research

4.1 PWV clinical research

For validating the effectiveness and reliability of the system in PWV measurement, we conducted clinical trials with cardiologists in the second affiliated hospital Chongqing medical university. In clinical trials, we selected 199 participants without diabetes, coronary heart disease and hyperlipidemia, and divided them into three groups according to the result of blood pressure measurement and Chinese hypertension guidelines, which is shown in Table 2.

Group	Type	Case number	DBP(mmHg)	SBP(mmHg)
1	Normal	123	<120	<80
2	Normal but high	30	120-139	80-89
3	hypertension	45	≥ 140	≥ 90

Table 2. The definition of blood pressure levels and sub-table

In measurement, participants were in sitting posture and tranquillization with two different size cuffs around the brachial and radial artery. After recording the personal profile of participant, a test begins with an auto inflation of the two cuffs. The front panel of LabVIEW of the system shows the pressure curves of the two cuffs. At the end of deflation, all parameters of artery elasticity are calculated and displayed on the software of upper computer, which spends only two minutes. The measurement results are saved as Excel. Then, the statistic software SPSS11.5 was used to analysis the results. The difference among groups was analyzed with mean. The statistic result of PWV of each group is shown in Table 3. T test was used to analyze the difference significance as shown in Table 4.

	Group	Mean	Standard deviation	Standard error
PWV	1	14.63	4.59	0.63
	2	17.01	6.09	1.52
	3	18.99	5.37	0.89

Table 3. Statistics of PWV in each group

Among Group	t	Degree of freedom	P	Mean difference	Standard deviation of mean difference	95% confidence interval	
						low	high
1 and 2	-3.092	151	0.003	-4.378	1.4161	-7.2047	-1.552
2 and 3	0.008	74	0.994	0.0139	1.7409	-3.4649	3.522
3 and 4	-3.914	167	0.000	-1.364	1.1151	-6.5823	-2.145

Table 4. Independent samples t test

From Table 4, we can see that P equals to 0.003 between group 1 and 2, and 0.000 between group 3 and 4, which means both differences were statistically significant. But P equals to 0.994 for group 2 and 3, which means the difference was not statistically significant. It might be relative to the small size of the samples.

The clinical trial demonstrates that PWV can reflect the difference among borderline hypertension, hypertension and normal group, and can be used as auxiliary hint for the diagnosis of hypertension.

4.2 ASI clinical trial

In order to validate the effectiveness of ASI, a clinical trial was conducted on 420 healthy adults. The participants were divided into four groups according to their age: 20 to 29, 30 to 45, 46 to 59, 60 to 75. The test result of ASI is shown in table 5 for each group.

age	male		female		P
	number	ASI	number	ASI	
20～29	36	78.55±12.71	34	71.29±10.47	>0.05
30～45	69	82.32±14.39	40	80.15±15.94	>0.05
46～59	42	85.34±13.12	61	83.29±11.94	>0.05
60～75	83	102.06±10.52	55	109.36±14.11	>0.05
P		<0.05		<0.05	

Table 5. The results of ASI measurement

Table 5 indicates that ASI is increasing with age gradually. The difference of ASI is very small about 75~85 in the group of age less than 60. But the difference of ASI is higher obviously in the group of age between 60 and 75. ASI of male and female subgroup reaches to 102 and 109 (P<0.05), respectively. The ASI difference of male and female subgroup in the other groups is small and not statistically significant (P>0.05). In addition, the repeatability of ASI measurement is better when the time interval of two measurements is more than 5 minutes.

5. Conclusion

In this chapter, the hardware and software design of the arterial elasticity measurement system were mainly introduced. According to the oscillography principle and pulse wave theory, two cuffs were used to collect the pulse signals of brachial and radial artery in the system and realized an invasive, easy and quick measurement of PWV and ASI. The effectiveness and reliability of the system were demonstrated by a lot of clinical trial and data. The system can diagnose the condition of arterial elasticity and the degree of arteriosclerosis. The study results have certain application value for epidemiological survey, disease prevention and early detection of cardiovascular diseases.

6. References

Bitter, R.; Mohiuddin, T. & Nawrocki, M. (2007). *LabVIEW advanced programming techniques*, CRC Press, ISBN 0849333253, Florida, USA

He, W. & Yu, C.X. (2010). *Measurement principle and clinical application of cardiovascular dynamic parameters*, Science Press, ISBN 9787030262813, Beijing, China

Johnson, G.W. & Jennings, R. (1997). *LabVIEW graphical programming: practical applications in instrumentation and control*, McGraw-Hill Professional, ISBN 007032915X, New York USA

Klinger, T. (2003). *Image processing with LabVIEW and IMAQ Vision*, Prentice Hall, ISBN 0-13-047415-0, New Jersey, USA

Mark, O.B. (2003). *Atlas of Cardiovascular Monitoring*, Science Press, ISBN 703010952, Beijing, China

McDonald, D.A. (1974). *Blood Flow in Arteries*, Edward Amold, ISBN 0713142138, London, England

Qiao, A. & Wu, S. (2000). Theories of Pulse Wave in Arteries. *Journal of biomedical engineering*, Vol.17, No.1, pp. 95-100, ISSN 1001-5515

Quan, X.; He, W. & Gu, L. (2006). Measurement and clinical study of atherogenic index *Chinese Medical Equipment Journal* . Vol.27, No.2, pp. 1-2, ISSN 1003-8868

Quan, X.; He, W. & Zhang, W. (2006). A New Algorithm for Oscillometric Blood Pressure Measurement *Space Medicine & Medical Engineering*, Vol.19, No.1, pp. 71-73, ISSN 1002-0837

Sunthareswaran, R. (2003). *Cardiovascular System*, Science Press, ISBN 703009689, Beijing, China

Takenaka, T. & Kobayashi, K. (2004). Pulse wave velocity as an indicator of arteriosclerosis in hemodialysis patients. *Atherosclerosis* Vol.176, No.2, pp. 405-409., ISSN 0021-9150

Whitley, K.N. & Blackwell, A.F. (2001). Visual programming in the wild: A survey of LabVIEW programmers. *Journal of Visual Languages & Computing*, Vol.12, No.4, pp. 435-472, ISSN 1045-926X

Yao, J.; He, W. & Quan, X. (2007). One Method of Removing Thorax Impedance Baseline Wander by Cubic Spline Interpolation. *Chinese Journal of Medical Physics*, Vol.6, No.5, pp. 371-374, ISSN 1005-202X

Zhang, W.; He, W. & Quan, X. (2005). Improvement and realization of blood pressure determination based on oscillation method. *Chinese Medical Equipment Journal*, Vol.26, No.11, pp. 5-6, ISSN 1003-8868

10

ECG Ambulatory System for Long Term Monitoring of Heart Rate Dynamics

Agustín Márquez-Espinoza, José G. Mercado-Rojas,
Gabriel Vega-Martínez and Carlos Alvarado-Serrano
CINVESTAV,
México

1. Introduction

Poor eating habits, a sedentary life style, and smoking have made acute coronary syndrome a disease characteristic of modern life, that it is expected to be the primary cause of death in the world by the year 2020, in spite of the development of reperfusion therapy and the use of defibrillators (Fuster, 2002). At the present time, cardiovascular diseases (CVDs) are the number one cause of death globally, and according to World Health Organization (WHO), an estimated 17.1 million people died of CVDs in 2004, representing 29% percent of all global deaths. Of these deaths, an estimated 7.2 million were due to coronary heart disease (CHD) (WHO, 2011). In Mexico, CVDs are the main cause of death, and the most frequent form is the ischemic heart disease (Instituto Nacional de Estadística, Geografía e Informática [INEGI], 2010).

CHD involves a reduction in the blood supply to the myocardium by narrowing or blocking of the coronary arteries, so the cells in the region served by the vessel will behave abnormally due to hypoxia (myocardial ischemia) or may die (myocardial infarction). These abnormalities due to neuronal damage and metabolic derangements cause alterations in sympathetic and parasympathetic flow to the heart, leading to increased heterogeneity of ventricular repolarization and to the development of terminal arrhythmias (Metha, 1997).

Therefore, the use and development of noninvasive techniques as electrocardiography, that records the electrical activity generated by the muscles of the heart in the surface on the body, opens a useful perspective for diagnosis and treatment in patients with heart diseases as the ischemia and infarction. The electrocardiogram (ECG) is the waveform produced by this electrical activity of the heart and its generation depends of four electrophysiological processes: the formation of electrical impulse in the main heart pacemaker (sinoatrial node), the transmission of this impulse through specialized fibers in the conduction, the activation (depolarization) and the recovery (repolarization) of the myocardium.

The electrical activity generated by the heart can be modeled as a vector whose magnitude and direction changes throughout the cardiac cycle. To record the different projections of this vector, several electrodes are attached to the body in different locations known as leads.

Because each lead measures the ECG between two points from different directions, amplitudes, polarities, times and durations of the ECG components vary between leads, so these have been standardized. The lead system most accepted in clinical practice is the standard 12 lead system, that is the combination of the bipolar limb leads I, II and III, the augmented unipolar limb leads aVR, aVL and aVF, and the six unipolar precordial leads V1-V6. Limb leads (I, II, III) derive signals from the left arm (LA), the right arm (RA) and the left leg (LL). The right leg (RL) electrode is the common reference in the amplifier.

The augmented signals (aVR, aVL, aVF) were proposed by Goldberger and derive signals from the limb leads. The unipolar chest leads were proposed by Wilson, and derive signals from six different chest locations, in where the common reference is the Wilson central terminal, that is formed by a resistive network that contributes equally weighted signals from each of the LA, RA and LL electrodes (Thakor 1988). Waves, segments and intervals of the ECG are shown in the Fig. 1.

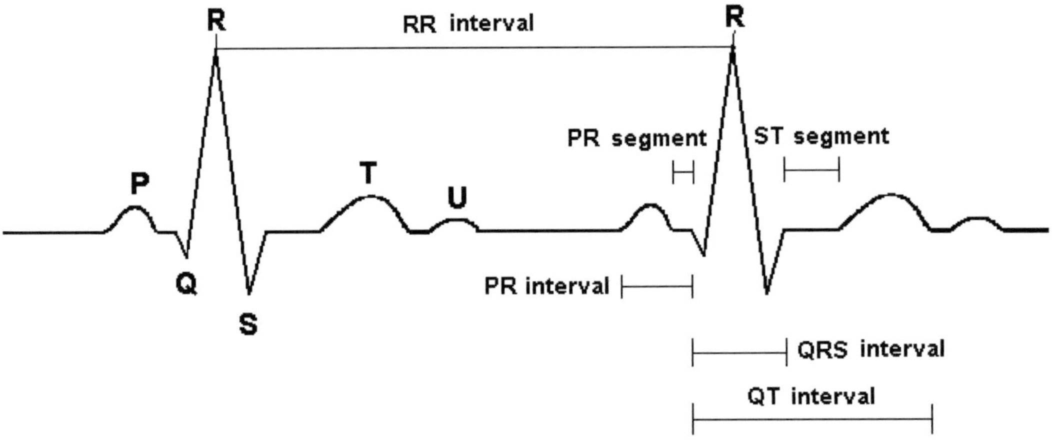

Fig. 1. Waves, intervals and segments of the ECG

The P, QRS, and T waves reflect the rhythmic electrical depolarization and repolarization of the myocardium associated with the contractions of the atria and ventricles. The P wave represents depolarization of the atrial musculature. The QRS complex is the combined result of the repolarization of the atria and the depolarization of the ventricules, which occur almost simultaneously. The T wave represents repolarization of the ventricles, whereas the U wave, if present, is believed to be the result of after-potentials in the ventricular muscle. Time intervals defined by the onsets and ends of these waves are important in electrocardiographic diagnosis because reflect electrophysiological processes of heart and autonomic nervous system (ANS), and carry clinical implications when they lie outside the range of the normal variation.

The most important intervals are the PQ interval, the QRS interval, the ST segment, the QT interval and the RR interval. The PQ interval reflects in part the atrioventricular conduction time. The QRS interval is a measure of the total duration of depolarization of ventricular tissue. The ST segment represents the end of ventricular depolarization and the onset of ventricular repolarization. The QT interval reflects the total period of ventricular depolarization and repolarization. The RR interval is the interval between consecutive heart beats and determines heart rate.

The intervals that detect the following pathological conditions: slowed conduction (QRS interval), heterogeneities in ventricular repolarization (QT interval and QT dispersion [maximal difference of QT intervals between leads]), and imbalance in autonomic tone (temporal variation in the RR intervals named heart rate variability [HRV]), are considered as noninvasive risk stratification parameters for identifying patients with coronary artery disease who are at risk for sudden cardiac death (Goldberger et al., 2008).

Because a standard ECG provides only a fixed picture of 12 leads portraying cardiac electrical events over a brief duration, there is a need for continuous ECG recording over long periods of time, due to certain abnormalities may occur only during sleep or with mental, emotional, or exercise-induced changes in cardiac oxygenation or function. The technique of continuous ECG recording or long term ECG (typically used for 24 to 48 h) with ambulatory ECG monitors (also termed Holter monitors), is used in clinical practice to detect, document, and characterize occurrences of abnormal cardiac electrical behavior of the heart during ordinary daily activities (Kadish et al., 2001).

The major uses of long term ECG are in the diagnosis and assessment of cardiac symptoms, the prognostic assessment or risk stratification of cardiac disease populations and the evaluation of therapeutic interventions. The use of Holter recordings for risk stratification of cardiac populations has used parameters like ST segment changes (for myocardial ischemia), RR interval changes (for HRV) and QT interval measurements [for repolarization abnormalities] (Kennedy, 2004).

This chapter describes the development of a prototype of a telemetry ambulatory system of long-term of 3-lead ECG and algorithms for detection of R wave peak of ECG and processing of RR intervals implemented in LabVIEW® for the study of heart rate dynamics.

2. Methodology

The basic requirements considered for the ECG telemetry ambulatory system design are:

- RF Wireless communication
- Low power consumption
- Small size
- Battery operated for a minimum continuous operation of 24 h
- Low battery voltage detection
- Simultaneous acquisition of three ECG leads: DI, aVF and V2, and battery information
- Recording, display and storage in real time of three ECG leads and battery information in a PC with an interface developed in Lab VIEW

The proposed system is composed of two blocks: a transmitter and a receiver (Fig. 2). Tasks of the transmitter are conditioning, digitalization, processing, encoding and simultaneous RF transmission of 3 ECG leads and battery information to the receiver. In the receiver, the transmitted ECG signals are detected, decoded, and sent to USB port or serial port in the PC for recording, storage and display.

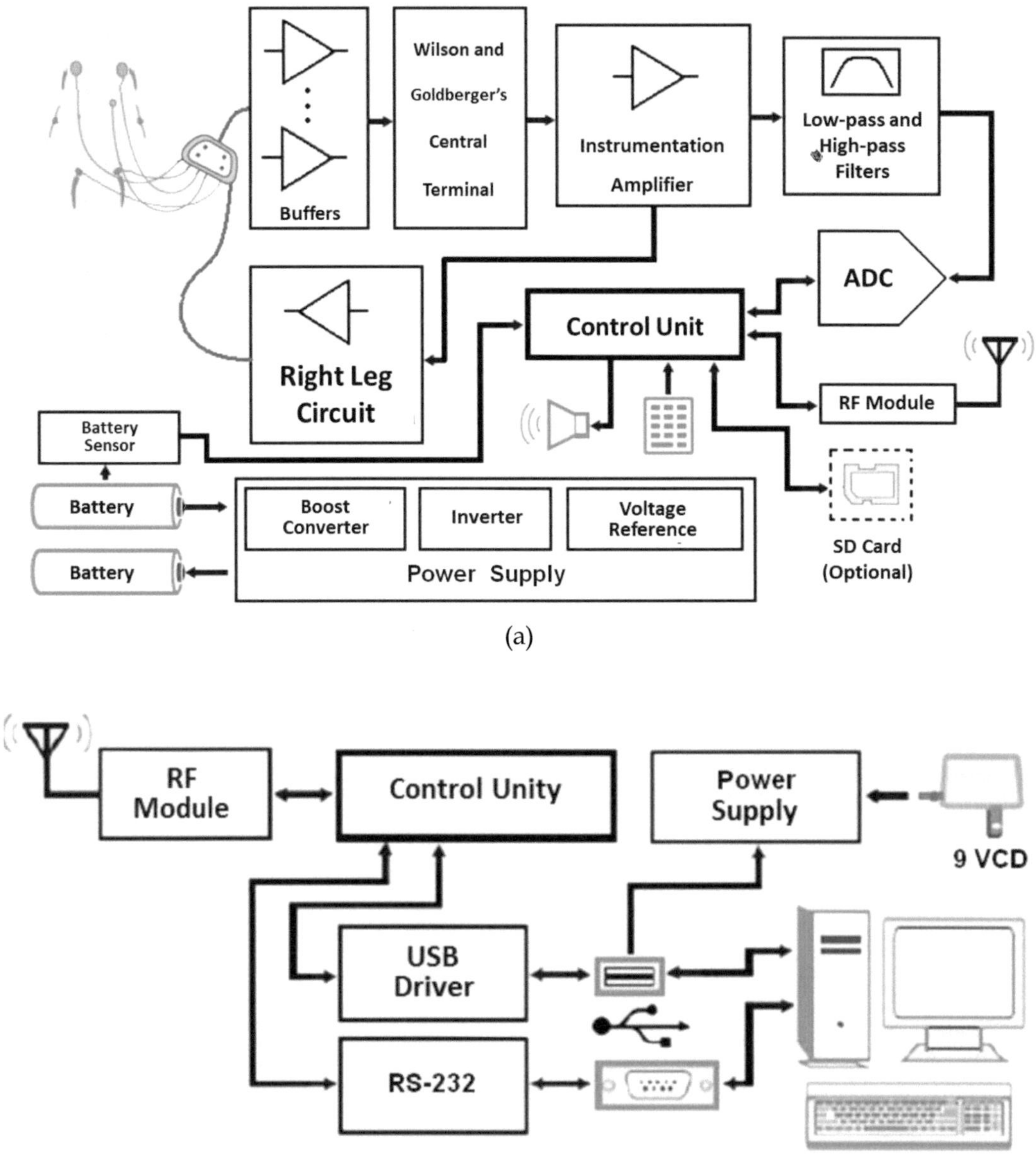

(a)

(b)

Fig. 2. ECG telemetry ambulatory system block diagram (a) Transmitter. (b) Receiver.

2.1 Transmitter

2.1.1 Conditioning stage

The main function in this stage is to amplify ECG signal in selected leads without distortion, and to minimize noise and interference, because an inadequate low-frequency response of ECG amplifier introduces artificial distortion in the level of ST segment (Christov et al. 1997).

This stage consists of the buffers section, the resistors network of central terminals of Wilson and Goldberger and three ECG amplifiers for three leads. Lead system used is of 5 electrodes, where 4 electrodes are placed in the LA, RA, LL and RL positions, and 1 electrode can be placed in any of the standard V1 to V6 locations. Therefore it allows the recording of any of the 6 limb leads (leads I, II, III, aVR, aVL, or aVF) plus 1 precordial lead. To represent the cardiac vector, we use quasi-orthogonal leads: D1, aVF, and V2, due to these leads are equivalent to orthogonal leads: X, Y and Z respectively (Glancy et al. 1995).
To increase the input impedance and thus reduce the effect of variations of a imperfect mechanical contact in the skin-electrode interface that causes high and unpredictable impedances that can contribute to distortion in the ECG, we use four buffer amplifiers for the signals from electrodes LA, RA, LL and V2 [Spach et al. 1966]. For the implementation of the reference input to the amplifier for the required leads, a network of 10 kΩ resistors was used to create the central terminals of Wilson for V2 lead, and of Goldberger for aVF. Definition of required leads is:

$$\mathrm{D1} = \mathrm{LA} - \mathrm{RA} \tag{1}$$

$$\mathrm{aVF} = \mathrm{LL} - \left(\frac{\mathrm{RA} + \mathrm{LA}}{2} \right) \tag{2}$$

$$\mathrm{V}_2 = \mathrm{v}_2 - \left(\frac{\mathrm{RA} + \mathrm{LA} + \mathrm{LL}}{3} \right) \tag{3}$$

The specifications for the ECG amplifier design based in standard requirements are (Bailey et al., 1990, Association for the Advancement of Medical Instrumentation [AAMI], 1999):

- Amplifier input impedance: differential > 2.5 MΩ and common-mode > 100 MΩ
- Input range: ± 5 mV
- DC offset range: ± 300 mV
- Resolution: 10 µV
- Gain: 1000
- CMRR minimum: 80 dB
- Bandwidth: 0.05 Hz to 100 Hz

Fig. 3 shows the ECG amplifier used for a single supply operation of 5 V with a balanced AC coupled front end proposed by Spinelli et al., that has been implemented with low noise operational amplifiers TLC2274 (U2) and LMC60421 (U8).
The front end provides AC coupling for differential signals and a DC path for amplifier bias currents, which drain to ground through the RL common ECG electrode, and because the input network is not grounded, a large common mode rejection ratio (CMRR) is achieved (Spinelli et al., 2003). Because the AC coupling network is a fully differential circuit, differential and common-mode voltages define four transfer functions, so the main transfer function G_{dd} is the quotient between the Laplace transforms of the differential output voltage V_{od} and the differential input voltage V_{id} (Pallàs-Areny & Webster, 1999). Then if $R_{10}C_3 = R_{11}C_4 = \lambda_1$, and $R_{12}C_3 = R_{13}C_4 = \lambda_2$, Gdd reduces to:

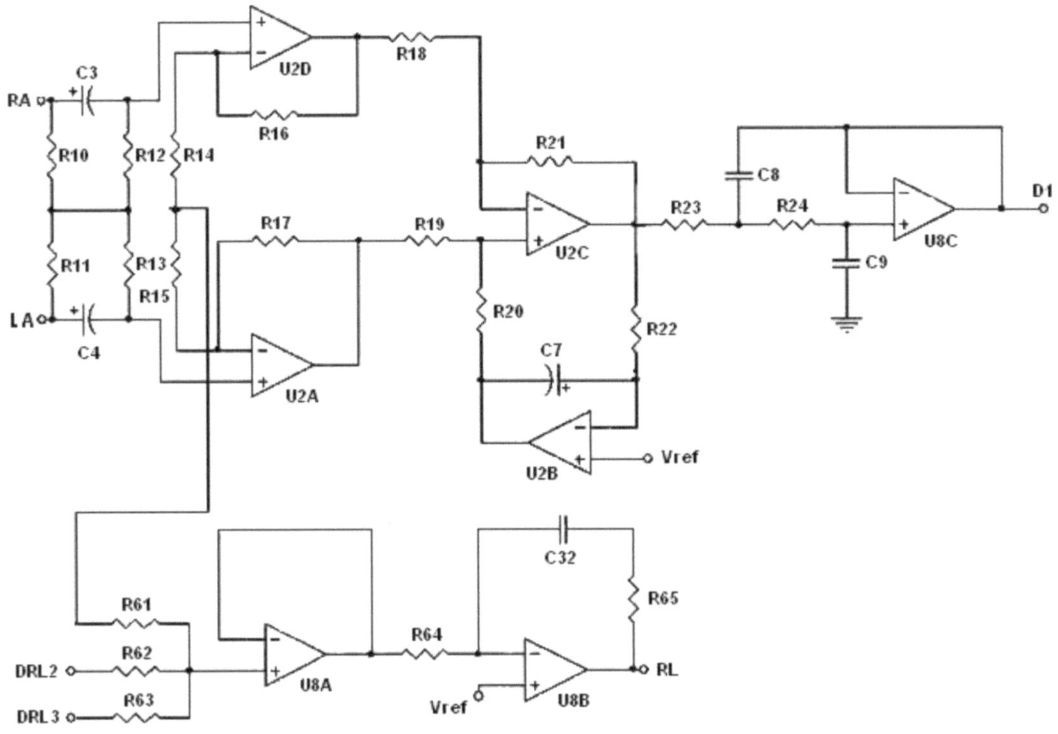

Fig. 3. ECG amplifier for D1 lead

$$Gdd(s) = \frac{s\lambda_2}{1+s\lambda_2} \tag{4}$$

G_{dd} corresponds to a first-order high pass filter. If the time constants are not matched, the circuit has two poles and two zeros, but using passive components with a reasonable tolerance yields a transfer function similar to (4). Because G_{dd} does not depend on R_{10} and R_{11}, high values are selected in order to avoid loading effects on the input signal and also to simplify design $R_{10}=R_{11}=R_{12}=R_{13}$. Then according to AAMI standard, it is necessary an input impedance > 2.5 MΩ at 10 Hz, so $R_{10}=R_{11}=R_{12}=R_{13}$= 4.7 MΩ.

To remove input offset voltages of the op. amps, thermal noise of R_{12} and R_{13} and op-amp input voltage noise, including 1/f noise, amplifier circuit uses an integrator in a feedback loop around the difference amplifier (Pallàs-Areny & Webster, 1999). The amplifier circuit has two AC coupled stages: the front differential AC coupling network and the high pass difference amplifier, so the overall transfer function is:

$$T(s) = \frac{s\lambda_2}{(1+s\lambda_2)} \frac{s\lambda_i A_{V0}}{(1+s\lambda_i)} \tag{5}$$

Where: $\lambda_i = R_{22}\,C_7$ and $A_{V0} = 1+ 2\,R_{17}/R_{14} + R_{15}$.

The amplifier gain A_{V0} of 1001 is obtained with R_{17}= 200 kΩ and R_{14} + R_{15} =400 Ω. The first factor in equation (2) corresponds to the passive AC coupling network and the second factor corresponds to the amplifier and DC restoration circuits.

Time constants λ_2 and λ_i define low frequency behavior of the amplifier and, are designed to obtain the desired transient response which is given in terms of responses to rectangular or triangular pulses. For a rectangular pulse of 1 mV amplitude and 60 ms duration, amplifier shall not produce and offset on the ECG record from the isoelectric line greater than 20 μV, so the two AC stages contribute to that offset, whose amplitude will be:

$$y(60\text{ms}) = \frac{1\text{mV}}{\lambda_2 - \lambda_i}\left[(\lambda_i - \lambda_2) + \lambda_2 e^{\frac{-60\text{ms}}{\lambda_i}} - \lambda_i e^{\frac{-60\text{ms}}{\lambda_2}}\right] \quad (6)$$

Selected values for time constants are λ_2 = 4.7 s and λ_i = 10 s that yields $y(60\text{ ms})$ = 18.6 μV. From λ_2, we determine C_3 and C_4:

$$C_{3,4} = \frac{\lambda_2}{R_{12,13}} = \frac{4.7\text{s}}{4.7\text{x}10^6\Omega} = 1\mu\text{F} \quad (7)$$

From λ_i, for a proposed value for R_{22}= 10 MΩ, C_7 will be:

$$C_7 = \frac{\lambda_i}{R_{22}} = \frac{10\text{s}}{10\text{x}10^6\Omega} = 1\mu\text{F} \quad (8)$$

For bandwidth limiting in high frequency and to avoid overshoot in the amplifier response, a second order low pass filter type Sallen-Key was used. To obtain the -3 dB cutoff frequency at 100 Hz, a value of Q=0.5 for damping was selected. This value of Q corresponds to an attenuation of 6 dB at 150 Hz in the standard second order response. Therefore, in these conditions f_0=150 Hz, R_{23}=R_{24}=R, C_8=C_9=C, and proposing R=100 kΩ, then C will be:

$$C = \frac{1}{2\pi R f_0} = \frac{1}{(2\pi)(100\text{x}10^3\,\Omega)(150\,\text{Hz})} = 10.6\text{ nF} \quad (9)$$

The complete transfer function with the designed time constant values results in:

$$T(s) = \frac{s4.7}{(1+s4.7)}\frac{sA_{V0}10}{(1+s10)}\frac{1}{(1+s0.001)^2} \quad (10)$$

In the ECG amplifier, the voltage of the patient with respect to the amplifier's common is called the common mode voltage (V_c) that is mainly due to power line interference. Since V_c can be transformed by the amplifier into an interfering differential signal and combines with ECG, it is desirable minimize it. This voltage can be controlled by a Driven Right Leg Circuit (DRL), which uses negative feedback of common mode voltages and feeds it back to the body via the RL electrode (Winter & Webster, 1983).

In the circuit, V_c is picked up by means of averaging resistors R_{14} and R_{15} = 200 Ω, and coupled by R_{61}=10 kΩ and a buffer amplifier. After it is compared to a reference voltage (V_{REF}=V_{cc}/2), and fed back to the body with R_{64}= 10 kΩ and C_{32}= 10 nF, driving it to a V_{REF} potential. To protect the patient from amplifier faults, R_{65}= 510 kΩ limits the DC output current of DRL circuit to 10 µA. To enable single supply operation in the ECG amplifier circuits, V_{REF}=2.5 V is connected to the noninverting input of the op-amp of the DRL (U8B) and the integrator (U2B) circuits (Spinelli et al., 2001).

2.1.2 Digitalization stage

Analog-to digital conversion parameters should be adequate to maintain fidelity criterion for visual reading of the ECG, for morphological diagnosis by digital program and for digital transmission and storage of data. To meet these requirements, a minimal sampling rate of 500 Hz with minimal resolution of 10 µV of the ECG is recommended (Bailey et al., 1990). In order to select the analog to digital Converter (ADC), it is necessary to know the characteristics of the ECG that define the required dynamic range (DR) for the ADC. The desired dynamic range for the ECG amplifier will be:

$$DR = \frac{\text{input range}}{\text{resolution}} = 20\lg\frac{[+5-(-5)]\,\text{mV}}{10\,\mu\text{V}} = 20\lg(1000) = 60\ \text{dB} \tag{11}$$

Therefore, DR for ADC must have a minimum DR of 60 dB, then the number of bits n for the ADC is:

$$n \approx \frac{DR(dB)}{6} \approx \frac{60}{6} \approx 10\ \text{bits} \tag{12}$$

As the system is of 4 channels (3 ECG leads and 1 for low battery voltage detection), and the sampling frequency required for each channel is 500 Hz, then we sample 4 channels at 2 kHz. The ADC that meets these requirements is incorporated into microcontroller Microchip PIC18F252, which we use to perform the control tasks of the system. This ADC is of successive approximation, it has 5 inputs multiplexed, 10-bit resolution and a conversion time of 120 µS (Microchip, 2010). The block diagram of the A/D module is shown in Figure 4, and it shows connection of each channel to the ADC, D1 is connected in AN0, aVF in AN1, V2 in AN2 and battery sensor BAT in AN3. The objective of battery sensor is to detect low voltage with a voltage divider in order to avoid errors because an inadequate recording of the ECG signals.

Digital conversion of the 4 channels is implemented by the microcontroller using the ADC module and Timer 0 (TMR0) of 16 bits. To operate the TMR0 is necessary to define some parameters. The clock used in the microcontroller is 40 MHz so that the machine cycle is equal to 0.1 µs (Microchip, 2010). If we use TMR0 without prescaler then we have a resolution of 0.1 µs. In 16-bit TMR0 overflows each 6.5535 ms, so it will be necessary to initialize TMR0 with a value to obtain the 2 ms we need, the required value is:

$$\text{TMR0H:TMR0L} = 65535 - 20000 = 45535 = \text{0XB1DF} \tag{13}$$

Then, TMR0 registers are loaded with this value (TMR0H = 0XB1 and TMR0L = 0XDF). Subsequently microcontroller is configured to cause an interrupt whenever TMR0 overflows, in the interrupt service routine digital conversion is achieved of each channel and thus sampling frequency of 500 Hz.

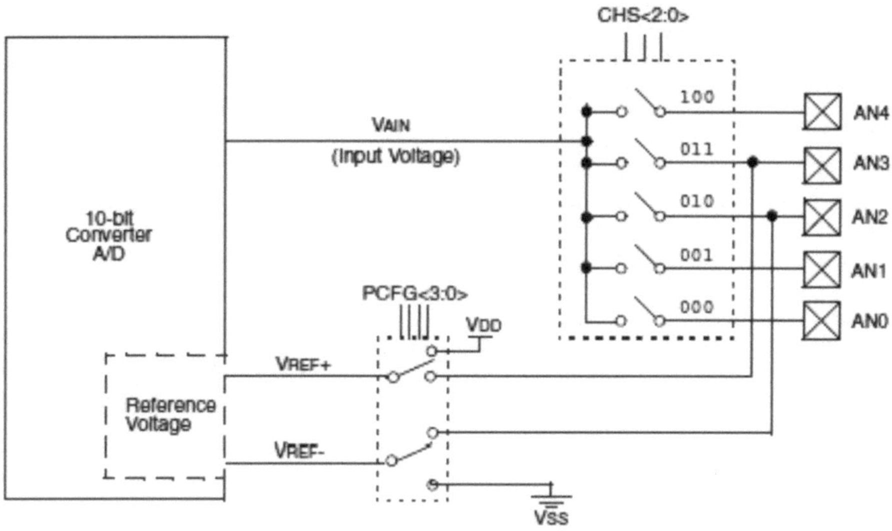

Fig. 4. A/D block diagram

2.1.3 Radiofrequency module

The device used for transmitter and receiver of the telemetry system is the nRF24L01 of Nordic Semiconductor. It is a single chip transceiver with an embedded baseband protocol engine named Enhanced ShockBurst™ (ESB), designed for ultra low power wireless applications, and for operation in the world wide Industrial-Scientific-Medical (ISM) frequency band at 2.400 - 2.4835 GHz (Nordic Semiconductor, 2007). ESB enables the implementation of ultra low power, high performance communication with low cost host microcontrollers (MCU).

The nRF24L01 is configured and operated through a Serial Peripheral Interface (SPI), in which the register map is available. The register map contains all configuration registers in the nRF24L01 and is accessible in all operation modes of the chip. The radio front end uses GFSK (Gaussian Frequency Shift Keying) modulation, and has user configurable parameters like frequency channel, output power and air data rate. Its internal voltage regulators ensure a high Power Supply Rejection Ratio (PSRR) and a wide power supply range.

2.1.3.1 Control of the nRF24L01

The nRF24L01 has a built-in state machine that controls the transitions between the different operating modes of the chip. The state machine takes input from user defined register values and internal signals. The nRF24L01 can be configured in four main modes of operation:

- Power down mode: In this configuration nRF24L01 is disabled with minimal current consumption.
- Standby modes: Standby-I mode is used to minimize average current consumption while maintaining short start up times, and part of the crystal oscillator is active. In standby-II mode extra clock buffers are active compared to standby-I mode and much more current is used compared to standby-I mode.

- Rx mode: In this mode the receiver demodulates the signals from the RF channel, constantly presenting the demodulated data to the baseband protocol engine, which constantly searches for a valid packet.
- Tx mode: In this mode the device transmits a data packet previously loaded by the control stage (MCU).

Transmitter and receiver are programmed with the same RF channel frequency and the same air data rate to be able to communicate with each other. Then, a RF channel frequency of 2.4 GHz, a bandwidth of 2 MHz and an air data rate of 2 Mbps were used. This air data rate provides lower average current consumption and reduced probability of on-air collisions. The PA control was used to set the output power from the nRF24L01 power amplifier (PA) to 0 dBm with a DC current consumption of 11.3 mA. In the nRF24L01 receiver the gain in the Low Noise Amplifier (LNA) is controlled by the LNA gain setting, which it is possible to reduce the current consumption in RX mode with 0.8 mA at the cost of 1.5 dB reduction in receiver sensitivity.

2.1.3.2 Communication protocol

The embedded baseband protocol engine (ESB) is based on packet communication and supports various modes from manual operation to advanced autonomous protocol operation, which it is a desired characteristic in this application. It has internal FIFOs registers that ensure a smooth data flow between the radio front end and the system's MCU, so it reduces system cost by handling all the high-speed link layer operations, and firmware and required memory in the MCU. The format of the ESB packet contains a preamble field, address field, packet control field, payload field and a cyclic redundancy check (CRC) field (Figure 5).

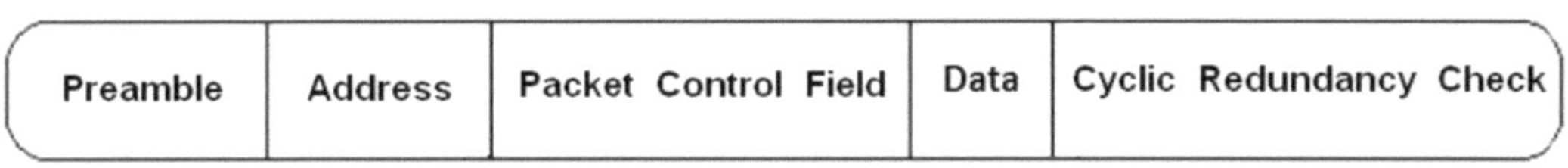

Fig. 5. Format of the Enhanced ShockBurst™ (ESB) packet

- Preamble: The preamble is a bit sequence used to detect 0 and 1 levels in the receiver. The preamble is one byte long and is either 01010101 or 10101010. If the first bit in the address is 1 the preamble is automatically set to 10101010 and if the first bit is 0 the preamble is automatically set to 01010101. This is done to ensure there are enough transitions in the preamble to stabilize the receiver.
- Address: In this field address for the receiver is defined, and ensures that the correct packet are detected by the receiver. The address field can be configured to be 3, 4 or, 5 bytes long.
- Packet Control Field: This field consists of 9 bits. The most significant 6 bits are used to specify the size in bytes of the data field, which can be from 0 to 32 bytes. The 2 bit PID (Packet Identity) field is used to detect if the received packet is new or retransmitted, this prevents the MCU receives the package more than once. The PID field is incremented at the TX side for each new packet received through the SPI. The PID and CRC fields are used by the PRX device to determine if a packet is retransmitted or new. The last least significant bit is used for a special feature of the nRF24L01 called auto acknowledgement.

- Data: This field is the user defined content of the packet. It can be 0 to 32 bytes wide and is transmitted on-air as it is uploaded (unmodified) to the device.
- CRC: This field is used as the error detection mechanism in the packet. It may either be 1 or 2 bytes and its calculation is based on the contents of the fields of address, Packet Control Field, and Data. No packet is accepted by ESB if the CRC fails. The polynomial for 1 byte CRC is X8 + X2 + X + 1. The polynomial for 2 byte CRC is X16+ X12 + X5 + 1.

ESB provides automatic packet handling and timing. In transmission, ESB assembles the packet and clocks the bits in the data packet into the transmitter for transmission. In reception, ESB constantly searches for a valid address in the demodulated signal. When ESB finds a valid address, it processes the rest of the packet and validates the packet by CRC. If the packet is valid the payload is moved into the RX FIFO. The high speed bit handling and timing is controlled by ESB.

2.1.3.3 Data and control interface

The data and control interface gives access to all the features in the nRF24L01. The data and control interface consists of the following six 5 V tolerant digital signals:

- IRQ: this signal is active low and is controlled by three maskable interrupt sources
- CE: this signal is active high and is used to activate the chip in RX or TX mode
- CSN: SPI enable signal
- SCK: SPI clock signal
- MOSI: SPI serial data input signal
- MISO: SPI serial data output signal

The SPI is a standard SPI with a maximum data rate of 8 Mbps. In this application, IRQ pin is used mainly to carry out the monitoring of device.

2.1.3.4 nRF24L01 transceiver circuit

The complete nRF24L01 transceiver circuit of 2.4 GHz with the recommended components according to the manufacturer's data sheet is shown in Figure 6 (Nordic Semiconductor, 2007). The ANT1 and ANT2 output pins provide a balanced RF output to the antenna. The pins must have a DC path to VDD_PA, through a RF choke, and a recommended matching network for 50 Ω load impedance is used in the circuit. To achieve a crystal oscillator solution with low power consumption and fast start-up time a crystal with a low load capacitance specification C_L must be used (typically 12 pF), and also with a lower equivalent parallel capacitance C_0 (typically C_0=1.5pF), but may increase the cost of the crystal.

With respect to PCB layout of the circuit is necessary a good design to achieve good RF performance.

A PCB with a minimum of two layers including a ground plane is recommended for optimum performance. The nRF24L01 DC supply voltage should be decoupled as close as possible to the VDD pins with high performance RF capacitors, and it should be filtered and routed separately from the supply voltages of any digital circuitry. Long power supply lines on the PCB should be avoided. Full swing digital data or control signals should not be routed close to the crystal or the power supply lines. A fully qualified RF-layout for the nRF24L01 and its surrounding components, including matching networks, is given by the manufacturer (Nordic Semiconductor, 2007).

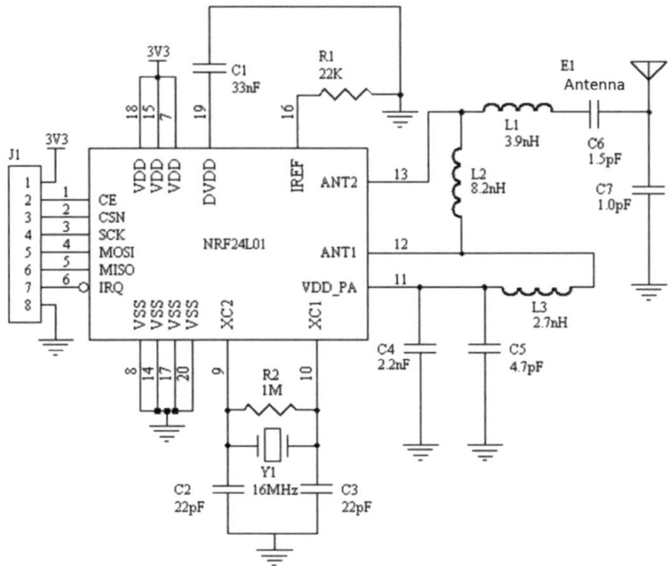

Fig. 6. nRF24L01 transceiver circuit with single ended 50 Ω RF output

2.1.4 Control unit

The control unit is the most important part of the transmitter, because this unit receives data of digitized ECG, battery monitoring and transmission and reception via radio frequency. To perform these tasks a microcontroller Microchip PIC18F252 with RISC architecture was used. Figure 7 shows the PIC18F252 connected to all its peripherals.

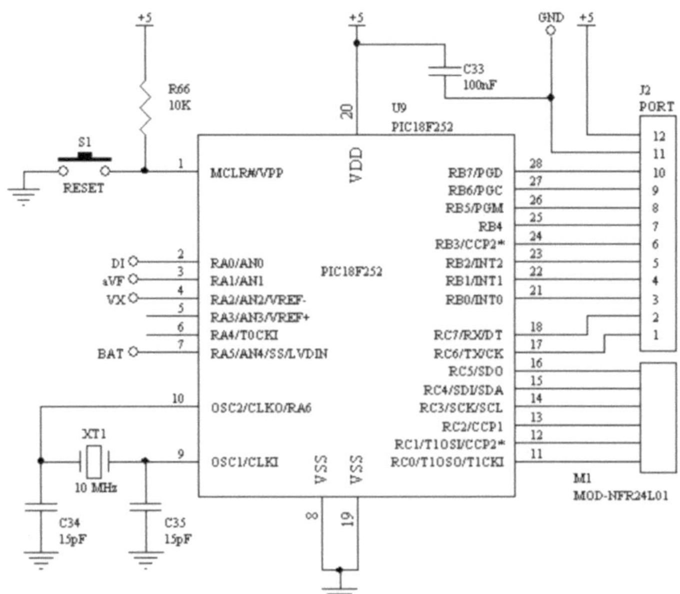

Fig. 7. PIC18F252 as main controller of the transmitter

The MCU operates at a speed of 10 MIPs with a 10 MHz crystal and the PLL (Phase-Locked Loop) enabled. Analog signals from DI, aVF, Vx and BAT are digitized by the internal ADC, in where the TMR0 sets the sampling rate and the conversion is controlled by TMR0 interrupt. Once digitized the signals are sent to nRF24L01 through the SPI port, where the control of all radio functions are performed. The RB7 pin of the port B is used only to show system status through a LED. The port B is reserved for future expansions, being able to connect an optional SD memory card, LCD screen etc. The MCLR pin is used for MCU Reset and for development purposes only.
The figure 8 shows the flowchart of the algorithm implemented in the firmware of the PIC18F252. The language used for development is the C compiler using MPLAB C Compiler for PIC18 MCUs in professional version 3.00, and the development environment is the MPLAB version 8.00 both of Microchip, Inc.

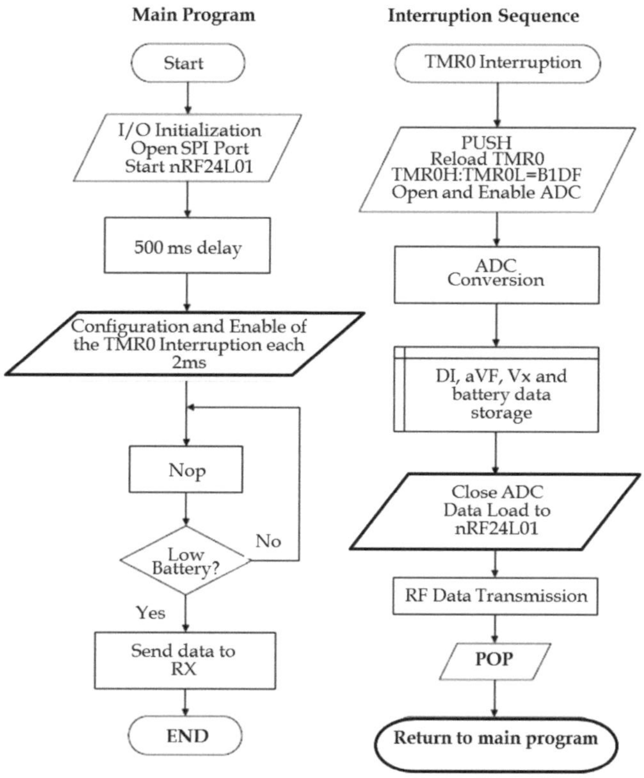

Fig. 8. Flowchart of the algorithm implemented in the PIC18F252 firmware as transmitter

2.1.5 Power supply

The general characteristics required of the power supply are:

- Supply with type AA batteries
- Regulated voltage outputs of ± 5 V and 5 V
- Maximum current of 100 mA
- Low ripple
- High efficiency

As first stage of the power supply, the high efficiency step-up DC to DC converter NCP1400 is used to generate a regulated voltage of 5 V with 100 mA of output current to generate a voltage of -5 V from a +5 V a switched capacitor voltage inverter MAX828 is used which has high efficiency and low operating current. To obtain the reference voltage of 2.5 V required to shift ECG baseline and the matching with ADC range of 0 to 5 V, a micropower voltage reference diode LM385 is used which provides a current of 15 µA to 20 mA with a resistor of 200 kΩ.

2.2 Receiver

The block diagram is shown in the figure 2b, and it is composed of a control unit, a RF module, two communication ports and a power supply.

2.2.1 Radiofrequency module

The design of this section is identical to the RF transmitter module but now the transceiver is configured as receiver. Due to both modules use the same MCU, driver that is used in the firmware of both modules is the same. At the reception, data are received first in the lowest layer referring to the protocol explained previously and inversely on the transmission (Fig. 5). Unpacked data are put into the internal registers of the microcontroller to be processed later. The electric circuit is also identical to the transmitter (Fig. 6).

2.2.2 Control unit

To perform all tasks in this stage, the same PIC18F252 microcontroller is used. Connection of the PIC18F252 with its peripherals is shown in Figure 9. The PIC18F252 has connected in pin MCLR a push button to reset if it is necessary and for development purposes, in pins RA0, RA1 and RA2, three LEDs for general indication of the system status (red = power, green = reception and orange = transmission), a 10 MHz crystal for MCU clock, the RF module connected to the port SPI and in the UART lines (RX and TX) the interface RS232 formed by integrated circuit MAX232 necessary to match voltage levels or the USB controller only one at a time.

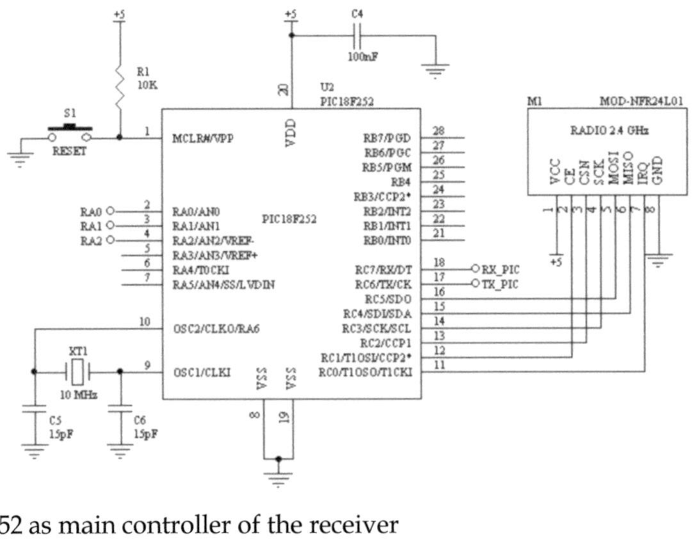

Fig. 9. PIC18F252 as main controller of the receiver

The PIC18F252 firmware is also written in C using the compiler MPLAB C Compiler for PIC18 MCUs in its professional version 3.00 and the development environment is the MPLAB version 8.00 both of Microchip, Inc. In the figure 10 shows the flowchart of the algorithm implemented in the firmware of the PIC18F252.

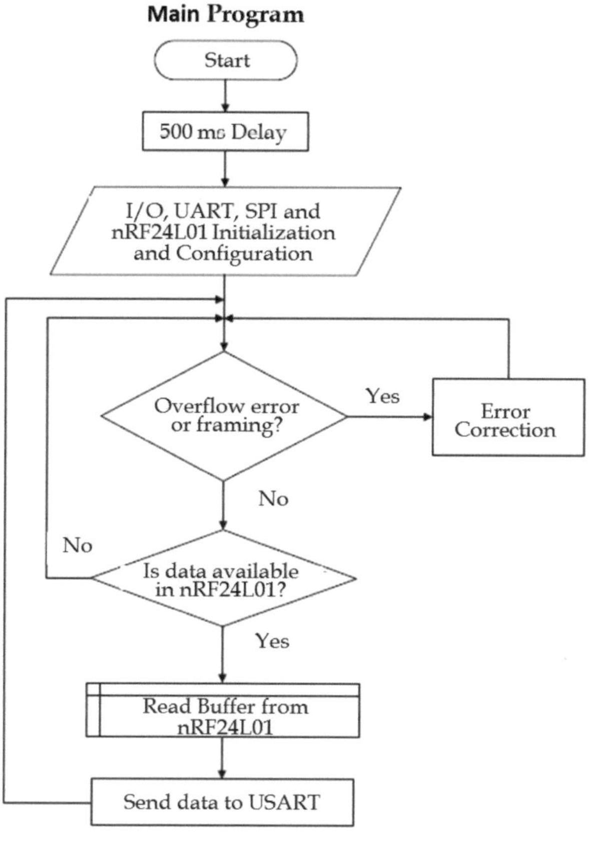

Fig. 10. Flowchart of the algorithm implemented in the PIC18F252 firmware as receiver

2.2.3 RS-232C Interface

The communications port uses the USART interface of PIC18F252. The configuration and control of USART is performed by the MCU firmware. The device used that conditions MCU and RS-232C voltage levels is the MAX232. MCU and computer must be configured to operate to 115,200 Bauds, without parity, 8 bits data and 1 bit stop. A power supply with a regulated voltage of 5 V is used in this interface.

2.2.4 Acquisition, display, storage, conditioning and processing of data

The format used to transmit the packet of each digitized sample to the RS-232C interface is shown in figure 11. The data are sent in hexadecimal and each parameter consists of 1 byte if we use ADC in 8-bit mode, and 2 bytes if we use the maximum 10 bit allowed for the digitization of each sample.

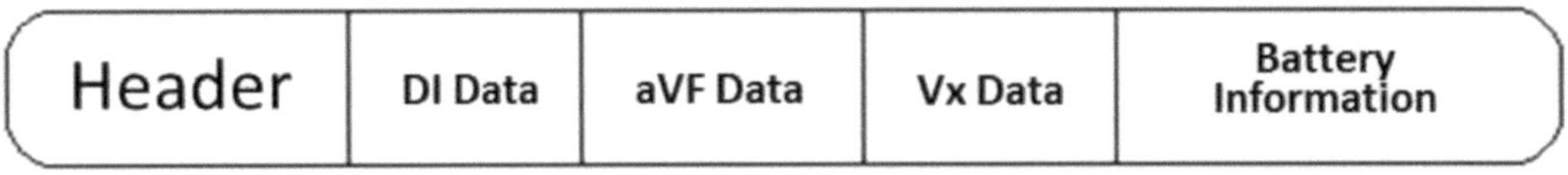

Fig. 11. Format of the data packet sent by the receiver to the RS-232 interface

The software implementation of this equipment was performed in LabVIEW®. The software purposes are the acquisition, display and storage of data, and the development of an R wave peak detection algorithm. In order to achieve these objectives different sub-VIs gathered together into two different main VIs were realized. The general structure of the first program (Acquisition VI) is described in Figure 12.

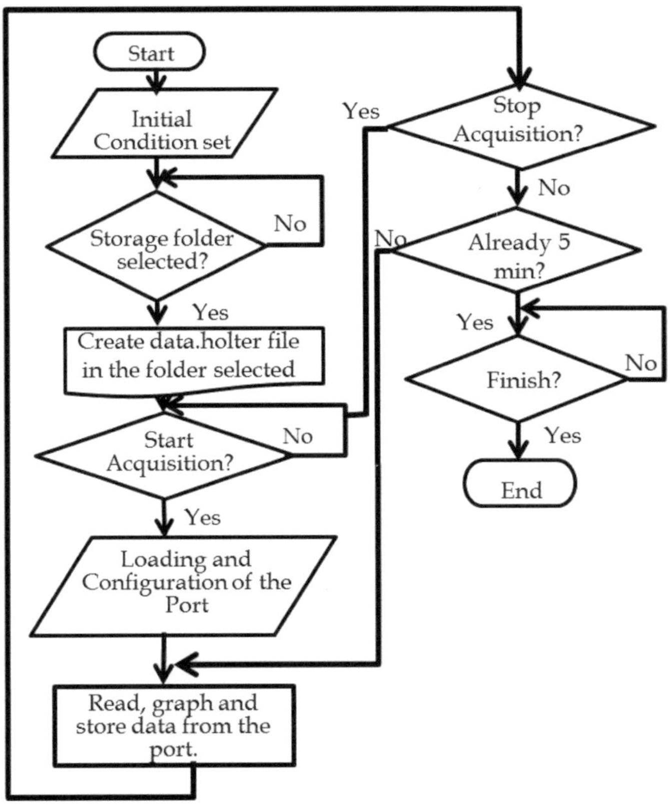

Fig. 12. General block diagram for acquisition VI

In this VI is where the acquisition of data is realized. As shown in the preview diagram when the VI starts, initial conditions as the position of frontal panel (FP) (Fig. 13) and button initialization are implemented. Then the user must select a folder in the CPU in order to continue. Once selected the folder where the data will be stored the program automatically generates appropriate files for the signal storage. At this point, user must indicate at which port is connected the equipment and ensure the configuration in the CPU is the correct one. Start acquisition's button will be available after this and the user will define when to start the acquisition. When the initial button is pressed the acquisition process starts during 5 minutes. There is also the option of stopping the acquisition process in this stage by pressing the stop button. Until the acquisition process is finished, exit button is allowed. At this phase user can choose between two options. One is to start a new acquisition overwriting previewed data acquired. Or user can choose to finish the acquisition VI program.

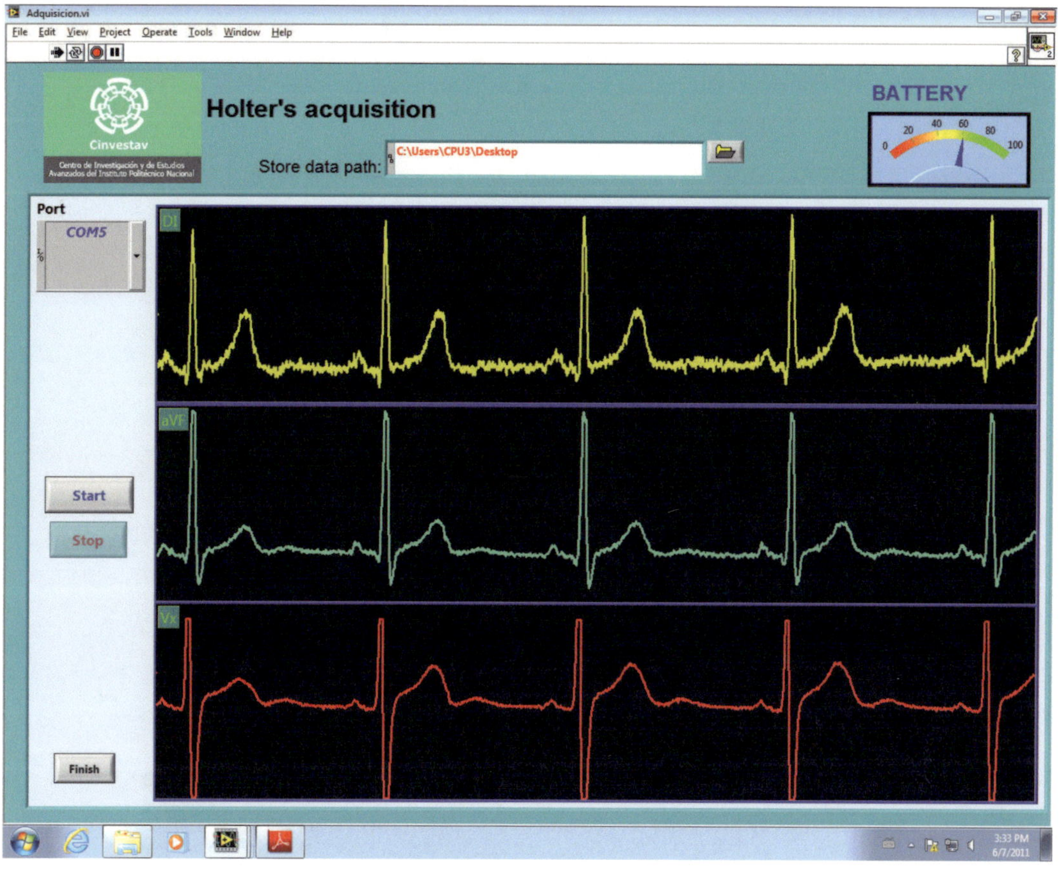

Fig. 13. Acquisition VI program frontal panel

Then the program automatically starts the second VI (conditioning VI) where the signal previously acquired will be processed. General structure of the conditioning VI is shown in Figure 14. When this VI starts it sets the initial conditions for the graphs charts, the buttons, and the FP position. The VI knows where the data was previously stored, so when the user presses the start button it automatically starts to takeoff from the original signal the trend, the noise and it process this information to obtain the R wave peak detection.

Detrending process performed in this VI is implemented with the LabVIEW® Wavelet Analysis Detrend VI. It considers the energy in the ECG signal to remove baseline wander due to low frequency artifacts (Weng et al., 2006). The denoising process is realized with the Wavelet Analysis Denoise VI. This VI performs noise reduction using the undecimated wavelet transform (UWT) for the elimination of high-frequency component due to noise.

At the end, the R wave peak detection is performed using a self-programmed variation of the LabVIEW® Wavelet Analysis Multiscale Peak Detection. This variation allowed the program a complete and correct detection of all the R wave peaks in the ECG signal. Figure 15 shows the final FP of the conditioning VI.

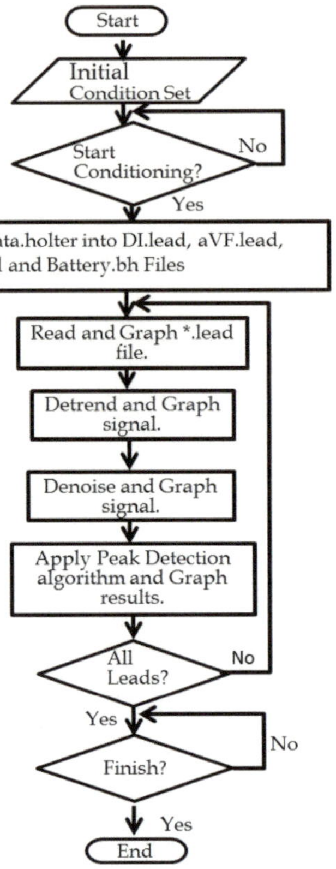

Fig. 14. General block diagram for conditioning VI

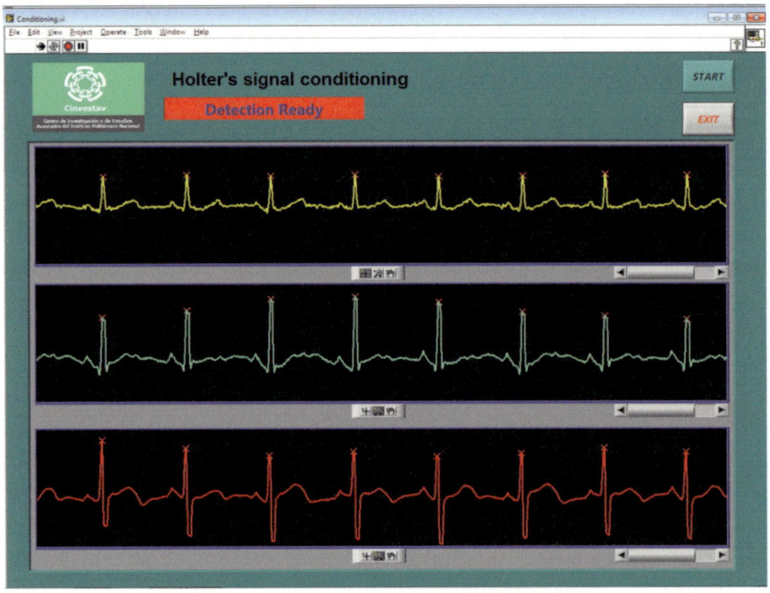

Fig. 15. Conditioning VI frontal panel after complete R wave peak detection

The programming process of both VI was realized with Queued State Machine-Producer Consumer architecture (QSM-PC). This architecture is used for event structures that send commands for asynchronous processes. The different tasks inside the VI (e.g. initializations, acquisition, and storage) are the consumers or commands handler in the QSM-PC. These commands are triggered by events or producers (e.g. button pressing, status changes, and user's actions) which controls the states of the QSM-PC. These states can be sequentially assigned by the programmer in order to achieve certain structure (Fig. 16).

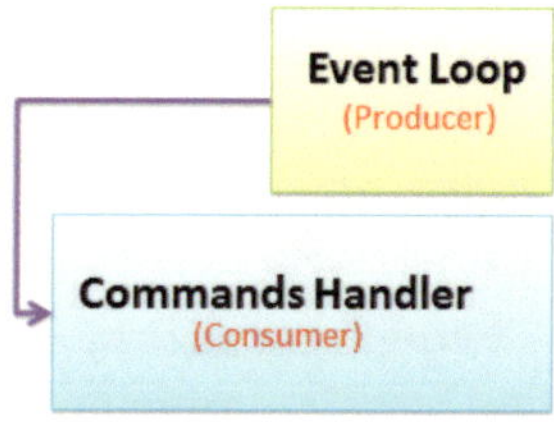

Fig. 16. Queued State Machine-Producer Consumer architecture used for the VI's programming

The acquisition VI program consists of 6 commands handlers and three producers (Fig. 17).

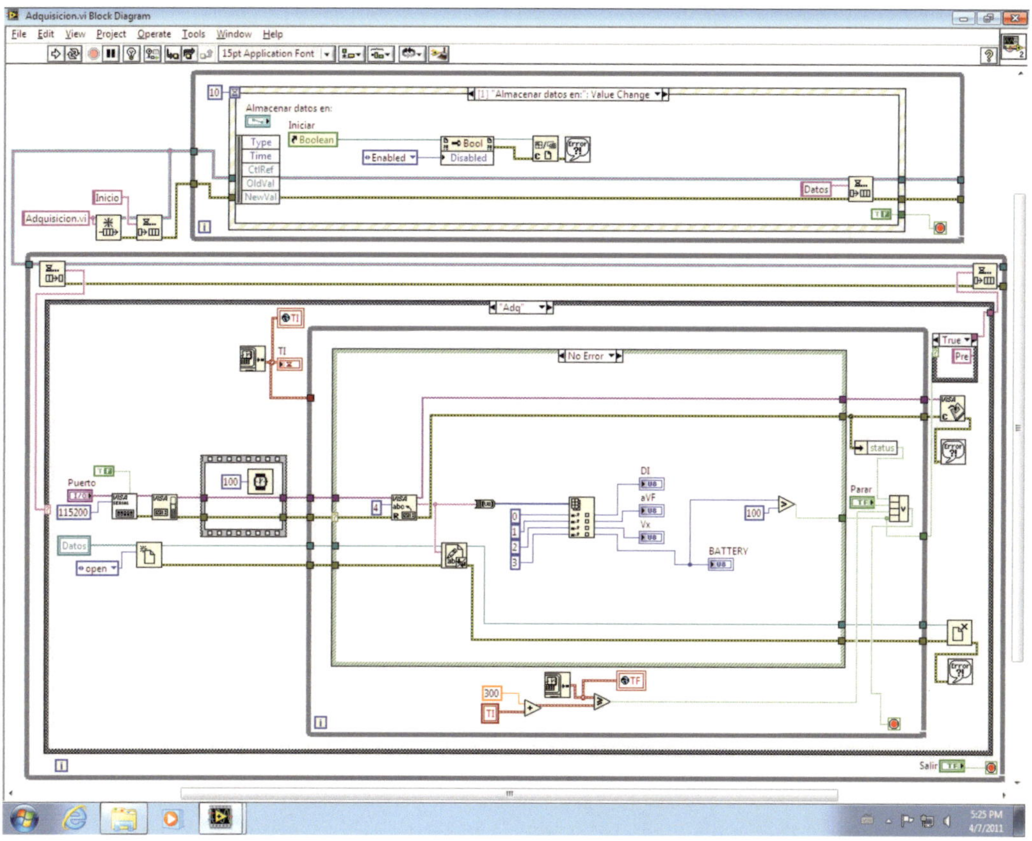

Fig. 17. Diagram block of the acquisition VI in acquisition's handler and path's change value producer

The first command handler is the one that sets all the initial condition such as button conditions, window position, path conditions and the graphs initial set. The second handler is to create the file where data will be saved. The next handler is a pre-setting for showing the data while it is obtained and after this the acquisition handler begins. Once finished the acquisition the next handler is in charge of setting initial conditions again for a new acquisition or the end of the program. At least all programs must have a default handler. This handler is just a loop in the program that waits for a producer to be triggered. For the producers as stated before there are three. One is for the path's change value event that assures the place where data will be stored. The second producer is for the beginning of data acquisition. This producer is triggered by pressing the start button. At least, the third producer is for exiting the program. This occurs when the Finish button is pressed.

Figure 18 shows the Conditioning VI which consists of 6 commands handlers and two event producers. Just as the first VI, the first handler implements the initial conditions. The second handler is pre-setting condition where data is arranged. This arranging is made by a sub-VI constructed for decoding the data previously acquired and stored. After this the conditioning handler starts.

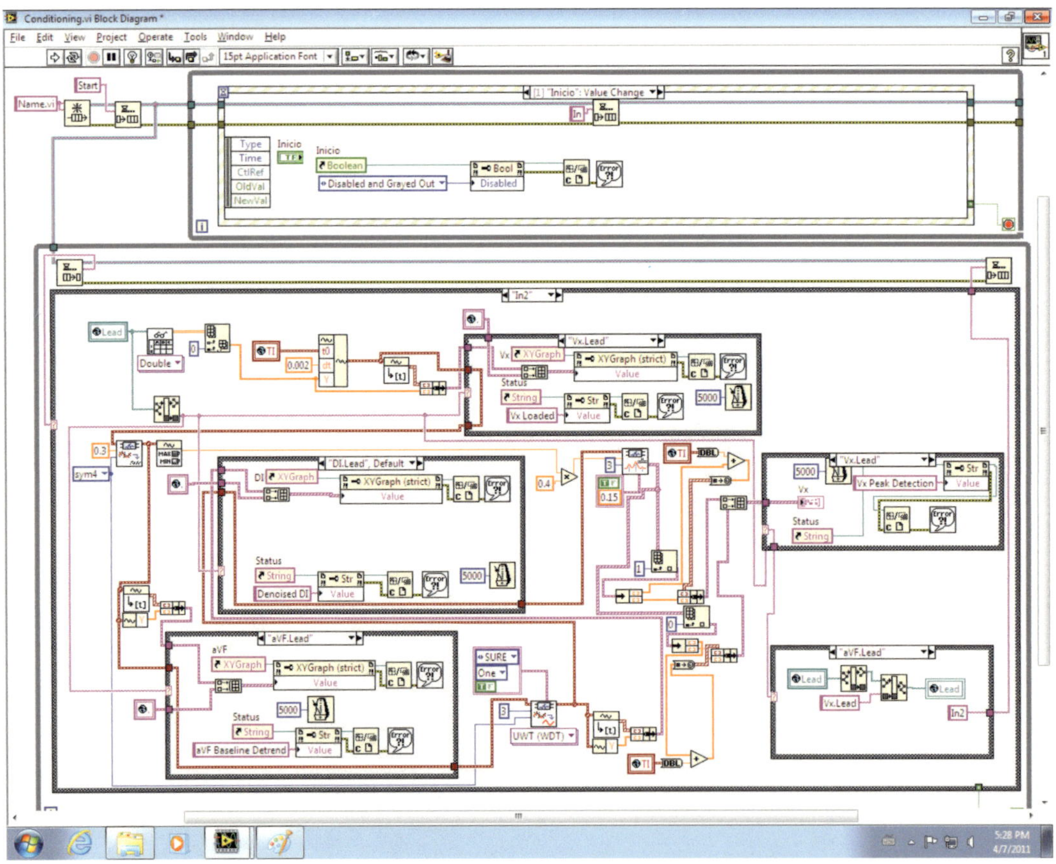

Fig. 18. Diagram block of the conditioning program in the conditioning handler and the start event producer

This handler has inside a sub-VI in which the detrending, denoising, and peaks detection are integrated. Then after conditioning is finished, the next handler is the post-conditioning. This handler configures a display alarm indicating that the conditioning is finished. At least there is an exit handler that finishes the program. This program also has a default handler that waits for an event's producer action. The event producers for this program are just two. One is for beginning the conditioning, and the other for finishing the program.

3. Results

To quantify the rejection of common mode interferences of the ECG amplifiers, we measured its Common Mode Rejection Ratio (CMRR), which is the quotient between the differential mode gain *Ad* and the common mode gain *Ac*, and it can be expressed in decibels where CMRR (dB)=20 lg (*Ad*/*Ac*). Initially, we measured the frequency response of the differential gain with one input of ECG amplifier grounded, and later, the common mode gain with both inputs of ECG amplifier short-circuited. Obtained values were: *Ad*= 1000, bandwidth=0.05 to 100 Hz and CMRR of 88 dB at 60 Hz with a mean of 84 dB in all bandwidth. Similar results were obtained in the other two amplifiers. Figure 19 shows the frequency response of the *Ad* and CMRR of the ECG amplifier.

With respect to the maximum value of DC voltage that ECG amplifier can tolerate in its input, the measured value was of ± 500 mV.

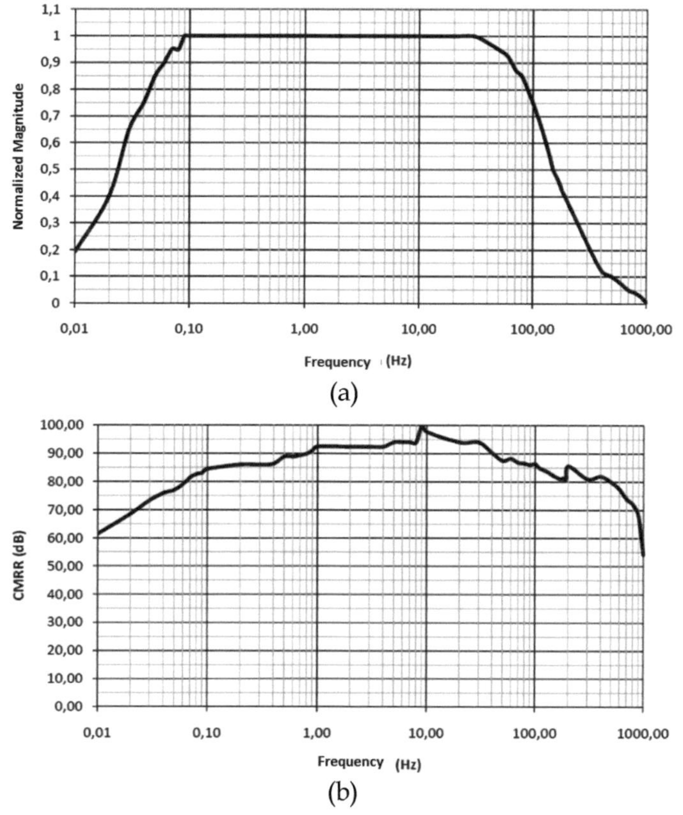

Fig. 19. Frequency response of ECG amplifier (a) *Ad*. (b) CMRR.

As power supply for the system, two AA rechargeable batteries of 2500 mAh were used to provide power to all circuits of the transmitter at 0 dBm output power. The maximum current consumption under normal operation was of 115 mA with a battery life-time minimum of 24 hours as required. To measure the distance of the RF link of the whole system, we tested the system in different sites using the maximum power of RF transmitter module at 0 dBm with a small ceramic chip antenna resulting from 10 m in indoors and 30 m in outdoors.

One of the developed applications implemented in LabVIEW® analyzes the variations in the RR intervals named HRV, using statistics methods with a record of 24 hours of the RR series (Fig. 20). The first stage covers the elimination of artifacts within the RR series; these are caused by the omission of R waves or the detection of nonexistent R waves (Fig. 21). In the second stage, statistics indexes are calculated and grouped in 5 minutes records according to standards of measurement of HRV (Task Force of the European Society of Cardiology and the North American Society of Pacing and Electrophysiology, 1996). The third stage reports 7 statistics indexes accompanied of a histogram (Fig. 22).

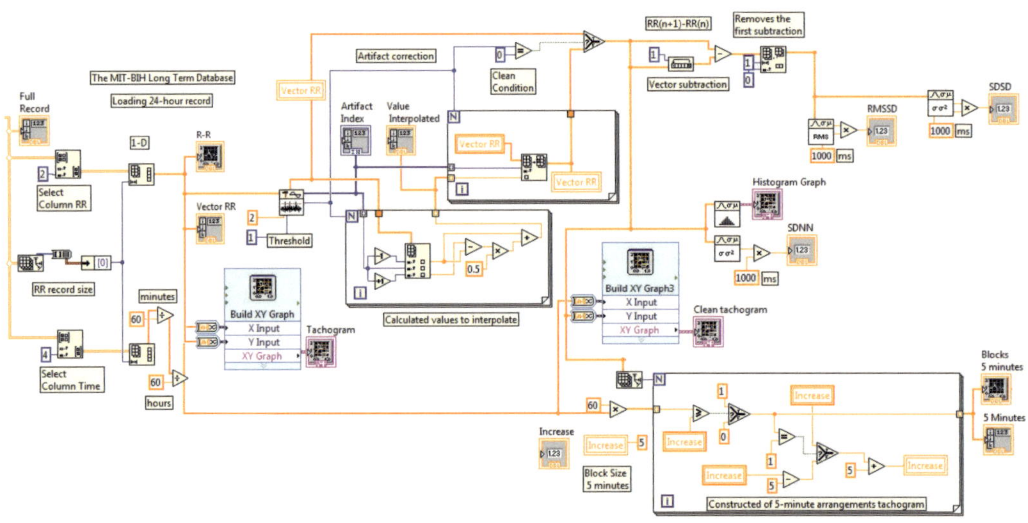

Fig. 20. Elimination of artefacts and segmentation of the record in blocks of 5 minutes

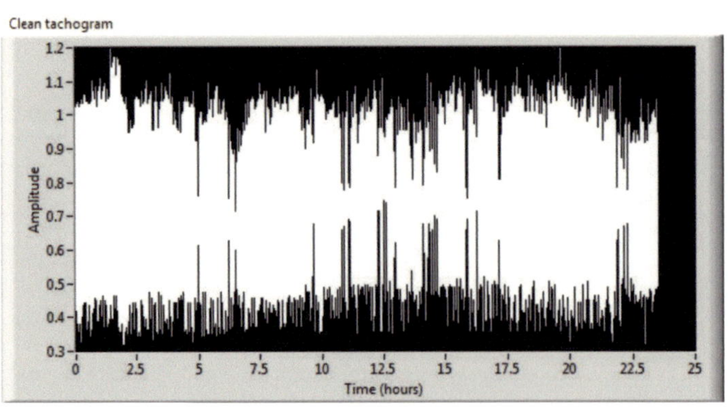

Fig. 21. Clean tachogram

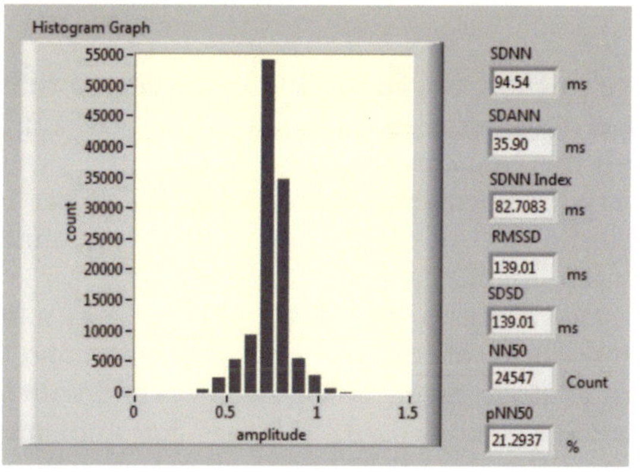

Fig. 22. Histogram and statistics indexes.

The printed circuit boards of the transmitter and receiver are shown in figure 23. Dimensions of the system are: transmitter (11 cm x 14 cm x 4 cm), receiver (8 cm x 7.5 cm x 3 cm). The telemetry ambulatory system is shown in figure 24.

(a) (b)

Fig. 23. Printed circuit boards (a) Transmitter. (b) Receiver.

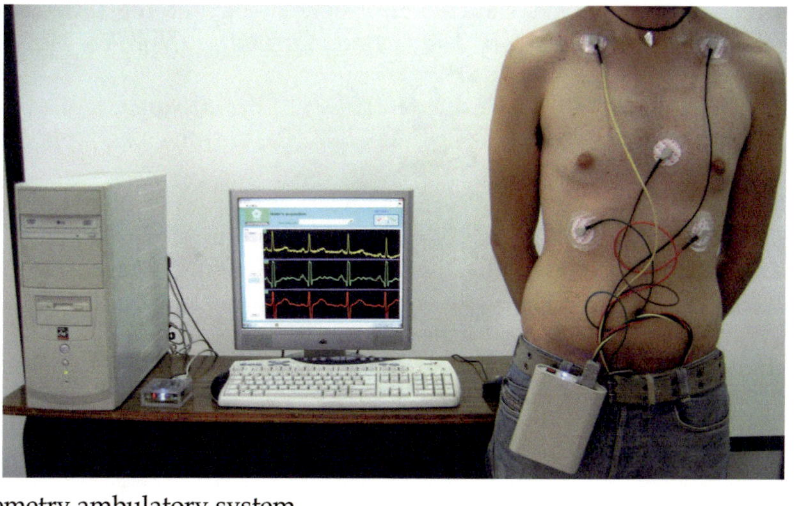

Fig. 24. Telemetry ambulatory system

4. Conclusion

The prototype of ECG telemetry ambulatory system developed fulfills the requirements of real time transmission of long term records, low power consumption and low cost. In agreement with standard requirements to ensure accurate diagnosis, ECG amplifiers meet important features of input impedance, input range, DC offset range, resolution, gain, CMRR, bandwidth, reduction of movement artifacts and baseline drift, and ADC with sampling frequency and resolution.
With respect to digital stage of the system, high integration in transmitter and receiver is achieved using two integrated circuits, a microcontroller and a RF transceiver. RF communication is robust to electromagnetic interferences and with low probability of error due to the communication protocol used. Software for implementation of acquisition, display and storage of the 4 signals (3 ECG leads and battery voltage), detection of R wave peak of ECG and processing of R-R intervals based in LabVIEW® was developed for the study of heart rate dynamics.
This system will be used to create a database of long-term records of normal subjects and patients that it will allow the clinical research of new indexes to assess risk of malignant ventricular arrhythmias, and analyse dynamics of other important electrophysiological variables like ST segment changes, QT interval (duration and dispersion) and T-wave alternans. Future work will be performed to reduce the size of the transmitter using surface mount devices.

5. References

Association for the Advancement of Medical Instrumentation (AAMI). (1999). *American National Standard ANSI/AAMI EC38:1998, Ambulatory Electrocardiographs*, AAMI, ISBN 1-57020-115-3, Arlington, VA

Bailey, J.J., Berson, A.S., Garson Jr., A., Horan, L.G., Macfarlane, P.W., Mortara, D.W., & Zywietz, C. (1990). Recommendations for standardization and specifications in automated electrocardiography: bandwidth and digital signal processing. A report for health professionals by an ad hoc writing group of the Committee on Electrocardiography and Cardiac Electrophysiology of the Council on Clinical Cardiology, American Heart Association. *Circulation*, Vol. 81, No. 2, (February 1990), pp. 730-739, ISSN 1524-4539

Daskalov, I., Christov, I., & Dotsinsky, I. (1997). Low frequency distortion of the electrocardiogram. *Med. Eng. Phys.*, Vol. 19, No. 4, (June 1997), pp. 387-393, ISSN 1350-4533

Fuster, V. (2002). Investigación cardiológica aplicada. Retos en el nuevo milenio. *Revista Española de Cardiología*, Vol. 55, No. 4, (Abril 2002), pp. 327-332

Glancy, J.M., Garratt, C.J., Woods, K.L. & De Bono, D.P. (1995). Three-lead measurement of QTc dispersion. *J. Cardiovasc. Electrophysiol.*, Vol. 6, No. 11, (November 1995), pp. 987-992

Goldberger, J.J., Cain, M.E., Hohnloser, S.H., Kadish, A.H., Knight, B.P., Lauer, M.S., Maron, B.J., Page, R.L., Passman, R., Siscovick, D., Stevenson, W.G. & Zipes, D.P. (2008). American Heart Association/American College of Cardiology Foundation/Heart Rhythm Society scientific statement on noninvasive risk stratification techniques for identifying patients at risk for sudden cardiac death: a scientific statement from the American Heart Association Council on Clinical Cardiology Committee on Electrocardiography and Arrhythmias and Council on Epidemiology and Prevention. *Circulation*, Vol. 118, No. 14, (September 2008), pp. 1497–1518, ISSN 1524-4539

Instituto Nacional de Estadística, Geografía e Informática (INEGI). (April 2010). Defunciones generales totales por principales causas de mortalidad 2008, In: *Estadística, Demografía y Población, Mortalidad, Causas de defunción*, 03.03.2011, Available from: http://www.inegi.org.mx/sistemas/sisept/Default.aspx?t=mdemo107&s=est&c=23587

Kadish, A.H., Buxton, A.E., Kennedy, H.L., Knight, B.P., Mason, J.W., Schuger, C.D. & Tracy, C.M. (2001). ACC/AHA clinical competence statement on electrocardiography and ambulatory electrocardiography: a report of the American College of Cardiology/American Heart Association/American College of Physicians-American Society of Internal Medicine Task Force on Clinical Competence (ACC/AHA Committee to Develop a Clinical Competence Statement on Electrocardiography and Ambulatory Electrocardiography). *Circulation*, Vol. 104, No. 25, (December 2001), pp. 3169–3178, ISSN 1524-4539

Kennedy, H.L. (2004). Use of long-term (Holter) electrocardiographic recordings, In: *Cardiac Electrophysiology: From Cell to Bedside*, Zipes D.P., Jalife J., pp. 772-787, Saunders, ISBN 0721603238, Philadelphia, USA

Metha, D., Curwin, J., Gomes, J.A. & Fuster, V. (1997). Sudden death in coronary artery disease: acute ischemia versus myocardial substrate. *Circulation*, Vol. 96, No. 9, (November 1997), pp. 3215–3223

Microchip. (November 2010). PIC18FXX2 Datasheet, In: *Home, Products, 8-bit PIC® Microcontrollers*, 10.11.2010, Available from: http://www.microchip.com/wwwproducts/devices.aspx?ddocname=en010276

Nordic Semiconductor. (July 2007). nRF24L01 Single Chip 2.4 GHz Transceiver Product Specification, In: *Home, Products, 2.4 GHz RF*, 16.8.2009, Available from: http://www.nordicsemi.com/eng/Products/2.4GHz-RF/nRF24L01

Pallàs-Areny, R. & Webster, J. G. (1999). *Analog Signal Processing*, Wiley, ISBN 0471125288, New York, USA

Spach, M. S., Barr, R. C., Havstad, J. W. & Long, E. C. (1966). Skin-electrode impedance and its effect on recording cardiac potentials. *Circulation*, Vol. 34, No. 4, (October 1966), pp. 649–656, ISSN 1524-4539

Spinelli, E. M., Martinez, N. H., & Mayosky, M. A. (2001). A single-supply biopotential amplifier. *Med. Eng. Phys.*, Vol. 23, No. 3, (April 2001), pp. 235-238, ISSN 1350-4533

Spinelli, E.M., Pallás-Areny, R. & Mayosky, M.A. (2003). AC-coupled front-end for biopotential measurements. *IEEE Transactions on Biomedical Engineering*, Vol. 50, No. 3, (March 2003), pp. 391-395, ISSN: 0018-9294

Task Force of the European Society of Cardiology and the North American Society of Pacing and Electrophysiology. (1996). Heart rate variability: standards of measurement, physiological interpretation and clinical use. *European Heart Journal*, Vol. 17, No. 3, (March 1996), pp. 354-381, ISSN 0195-668X

Thakor, N.V. (1988). Electrocardiographic monitors, In: *Encyclopedia of Medical Devices and Instrumentation*, J.G. Webster, pp. 1002-1017, Wiley, ISBN 0471629693, USA

Weng, B., Blanco-Velasco, M., Barner, K.E. (2006). Baseline wander correction in ECG by the empirical mode decomposition. Bioengineering Conference, 2006, Proceedings of the IEEE 32nd Annual Northeast, 2006, pp. 135-136, ISBN 0-7803-9563-8, May 2006

Winter, B.B. & Webster J.G. (1983). Driven-right leg circuit design. *IEEE Transactions on Biomedical Engineering*, Vol. 30, No.1, (January 1983), pp. 62-66, ISSN: 0018-9294

World Health Organization (WHO). (January 2011). Cardiovascular diseases (CVDs), In: *Media centre, Fact sheet No. 317*, 04.03.2011, Available from: http://www.who.int/mediacentre/factsheets/fs317/en/index.html

Part 4

Test and Fault Diagnosis

11

Acoustical Measurement and Fan Fault Diagnosis System Based on LabVIEW

Cao, Guangzhong
Shenzhen University,
P.R.China

1. Introduction

It is difficult to diagnose the reasons of fan fault because of lacking mapping relationship between fault and symptom. Current fault diagnosis methods for rotating machinery such as vibration detection, temperature detection and so on, have to use contact measurement. However, those methods cannot be available for many important field devices.

Either in time domain or in frequency domain the local characteristics of wavelet are good in extracting time-varying signal characteristics. Neural network has a strong capability to identify the multi-dimensional and non-linear model. Therefore, it is possible to improve the accuracy of diagnosis system by combination of wavelet and neural network. In this chapter, an intelligent fan fault diagnosis system is presented where the noise produced by fan is considered the diagnosis signal, a non-contact measurement is adopted and the non-linear mapping from feature space to defective space using the wavelet neural network is performed.

2. Basic concept and theory

2.1 Acoustical measurement basis

2.1.1 Basic acoustical parameters

Analysis of sound and acoustics plays a role in such engineering tasks as product design, production test, machine performance, and process control. In order to perform analysis of sound and acoustics, we should know the parameters and process for acoustical measurement. In general, there are many physical parameters that should be measured in acoustical measurement such as sound pressure, sound intensity, sound power and others. The most common acoustical measurement parameters are as follows:

1. Sound pressure (acoustic pressure) P

Sound pressure is the local pressure deviation from the ambient atmospheric pressure caused by a sound wave. The value of the rapid variation in air pressure due to a sound wave, measured in pascals. *Instantaneous* sound pressure is the peak value of air pressure and its value reflects the intensity of sound. Usually, *sound pressure* is the effective sound pressure for short. *Effective sound pressure* is the RMS value of the instantaneous sound pressure taken at a point over a period of time as:

$$P = \sqrt{\frac{1}{T}\int_0^T P^2(t)dt} \qquad (2\text{-}1)$$

where $P(t)$ is instantaneous sound pressure, T is the time interval averaging.

2. Sound pressure level L_P

Sound pressure level L_P is a logarithmic measure of the effective sound pressure of a sound relative to a reference value. It is measured in decibels (dB). For sound in air, it is customary to use the value $2\times10^{-5}\ pa$. The formula for calculating the sound pressure level is defined as (Cao & Ruan, 2002; Donald & Hall, 1987) :

$$Lp = 10\lg\frac{P^2}{P_0^2} = 20\lg\frac{P}{P_0} \tag{2-2}$$

where Lp is sound pressure level(dB), P_0 is the reference sound pressure ($2\times10^{-5}\ pa$), P is effective sound pressure.

3. Sound level L and A-weighted sound level L_A

Sound pressure level only reflects the sound intensity of human feeling of loudness, but the human ear's sensitivity is strongly dependent on frequency. Loudness level and loudness of the sound that reflect people's subjective feelings are too complex, so the concept of sound level, i.e. the concept of the weighted sound pressure level is proposed. Sound level is the sound pressure level obtained by weighting with some weighted networks. To simulate the human ear's sensory characteristics of loudness, the weighting network classifications are divided into A, B and C-weighted networks. The simplest and probably most widely used measure of noise is the A-weighted sound level, expressed in dBA. A-weighting assigns to each frequency a "weight" that is related to sensitivity of the ear at that frequency (Kinsler et al., 2000).

4. Equivalent continuous sound level L_{eq}

For rolling or discontinuous noise, the equivalent continuous sound level is needed to evaluate the impact of noise on people. Equivalent continuous A-weighted sound pressure level is widely used as an index around the world. It is defined as "the A-weighted sound pressure level of a noise fluctuating over a period of time T, expressed as the amount of average energy." It is expressed as:

$$L_{eq} = 10\lg(\frac{\Delta t}{T}\sum_{i=1}^{n}10^{0.1L_{Ai}}) = 10\lg(\frac{1}{n}\sum_{i=1}^{n}10^{0.1L_{Ai}}) = 10\lg(\sum_{i=1}^{n}10^{0.1L_{Ai}}) - 10\lg(n) \tag{2-3}$$

where T denotes the length of sampling, Δt is the sampling interval, n is the sampling number, L_{Ai} is instantaneous A-weighted sound level, L_{eq} is equivalent continuous sound level.

5. Statistical sound level L_N

Because environmental noise often fluctuates over a wide range of time and space, no single value describes the noise accurately. Another useful set of parameters is needed, which are statistical sound levels by using probability or cumulative probability to indicate the appearance of different sound level. Statistical sound level L_N indicates that the probability of appearance of the sound level greater than this sound level is N%. The most common levels used are L_{10}, L_{50} and L_{90}. L_{10} is equivalent to the average noise level of peak, L_{50} is equivalent to median noise level, and L_{90} is equivalent to background noise.

2.1.2 Sound level meter

Sound level is a fundamental physical quantity of acoustical measurement. Sound level meter (SLM) is a basic instrument for measuring noise and sound levels in a specified manner. There are many categories of sound level meters due to different classification criteria. In terms of different uses, sound level meter can be classified into ordinary sound level meter, pulse sound level meter, integrating sound level meter, statistical-integral sound level meter and others. In terms of accuracy level, SLM can be divided into type 0 SLM (as in a laboratory, a standard SLM with an accuracy of ±0.4 dB), type-I SLM (a precision SLM with an accuracy of ±0.7 dB), type-II SLM (a general purpose SLM with an accuracy of ±1.0 dB), type-III SLM (a universal SLM with accuracy of ±2.0 dB); According to different size of volume, a SLM can be divided into desktop SLM, portable SLM, pocket-size SLM and so on.

Although there are many types of SLM, the working principle of all categories of SLM is identical in nature. The difference is some additionally special features which enable SLM to carry out various measurements such as adding integral circuit can help to measure the equivalent continuous sound level. In acoustics, a SLM usually consists of a microphone, amplifiers, an attenuator, frequency weighted networks, detector, indicator and power supply, etc (Cao & Ruan, 2002; Cao et al. 2004; Donald & Hall, 1987; Kinsler et al., 2000; Ruan & Cao, 2006). The working principle of the SLM is shown in Fig.2.1.

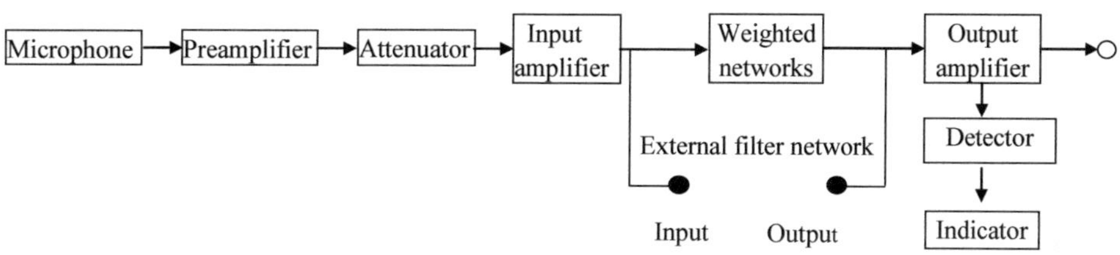

Fig. 2.1. SLM composition

In this figure, the microphone is the most critical element for acoustical measurement which is an acoustic-to-electric transducer or sensor that converts sound pressure signal into an electrical signal. In terms of different principles for conversion of mechanical signals into electrical signals, the types of microphone are divided into three main categories: dynamic microphone, piezoelectric microphone and condenser or capacitor microphone. The microphone applied in SLM requires a wide frequency and high dynamic range, low distortion, high sensitivity, small temperature coefficient and so on. Dynamic microphone has larger volume with uneven frequency response. Therefore it is vulnerable to electromagnetic interference. Piezoelectric microphone is susceptible to temperature changes with poor stability. Thus, the use of the above microphones in SLM is limited. The condenser microphone overcomes the above shortcomings and is usually employed in acoustic measurement field. However, it has the disadvantage of high internal resistance which requires an impedance converter, amplifier and attenuator with some designated voltage supplier.

Preamplifier is needed to meet the requirements of using capacitor microphone because the capacitor microphone has high internal resistance, low capacitance (usually only tens of picofarad (pF), and even several pFs). If a capacitor microphone is connected to an amplifier whose input capacitance is similar to the capacitor microphone, it may reduce the sensitivity of the microphone. If the amplifier input resistance is too low, then the low frequency sensitivity of the capacitor microphone will be reduced, that is, the frequency range of the capacitor microphone is limited. Therefore, suitable preamplifier is needed for the SLM with a capacitor microphone.

Amplifier: Capacitor microphone converts sound into electrical signal. The signal is generally very weak, not enough to drive display in an indicator, thus, amplifier circuit is needed to amplify the electrical signal to drive detector circuit and indicating instrument. The amplifier of a SLM requires a certain amplifier factor, a certain dynamic range, a wide frequency range and small level of non-linear distortion.

Attenuator: The SLM measures not only the weak signal but also the strong one. It should have the large dynamic measurement range. However the detector and the indicator of a SLM may not have wide measurement range, so we should use the attenuator to attenuate the input signal, acquire the appropriate command from the indicator, and enlarge measurement range.

Weighted network: Weighted network of a SLM is a set of electric networks which undertake frequency filtering according to certain weighted characteristics, usually formed by a multi-stage RC network. Because 'A' sound level is widely used, almost all SLMs have A-weighted network. Athough some of SLMs also have B-weighted network and C-weighted network. Even some of SLMs also have "linear" frequency response, which is used to measure the non-weighted sound pressure levels.

Detector and indicator: Detection circuits used to change the output signal of the amplifier into a DC signal to gain proper instructions in the indicating instrument. Usually the size of the signal is measured by the peak, average and RMS. In the measurement of sound level, the most commonly used is the RMS.

2.2 Wavelet theory and Mallat algorithm

2.2.1 Wavelet theory

A wavelet is a "small wave", which has its energy concentrated in time to give a tool for the analysis of transient, non-stationary, or time-varying phenomena (Burrus, 2005). It still has the oscillating wave-like characteristic and the ability to allow simultaneous time and frequency analysis.

As a new mathematical branch, wavelet theory has made an important breakthrough and development in a lot of research fields such as signal processing, image processing, pattern recognition, and so on.

The concept of wavelet transform was first introduced by a France geologist J. Morlet when he analyzed geological data in 1970s. He applied it successfully in seismic signal analysis. Later a famous France mathematician Y.Meyer carried out a series of theoretical researches on wavelet. In 1986, based on the multi-resolution analysis, S.Mallat proposed the dyadic wavelet transform and its fast algorithm—Mallat algorithm, which established the foundation for wide area applications of wavelet analysis. Wavelet analysis is a kind of mathematical method that can carry out partial analysis of signal in time and frequency domain at the same time. Its sampling step length in time domain for signal with different frequency is diverse from each other, that is, there is higher frequency resolution and lower time resolution for lower frequency signal, and vice versa. That is why wavelet analysis has adaptability to signal and wavelet transform is regarded as mathematical microscope.

2.2.2 Wavelet transform

Wavelets consist of a family of mathematical functions used to represent a signal both in time and frequency domain. A wavelet transform (WT) decomposes a temporal signal into a set of time-domain basis functions with various frequency resolutions. The WT is computationally similar to the windowed short-term Fourier Transform (WFT). However, unlike the sine and cosine functions used in the WFT, the wavelet functions used in the WT are localized in spaces. Thus, the wavelet transform can decompose a signal into two sub-signals: *approximations* and *details* (Adeli & Jiang, 2009). The *approximations* represent the high-scale, low-frequency components of the signal, while the details represent the low-scale, high-frequency components. Therefore, compared with the Fourier transform, the wavelet transform provides a more effective representation of discontinuities in signals and transient functions.

If the time series with *N* measured data points, *f(t)*, is considered to be a square integrable function (i.e., the integral of its square is finite),both continuous wavelet transform(CWT) and discrete wavelet transform(DWT) can be used to analyze the time series data. The CWT of *f(t)* is defined as(Mallat, 1989):

$$W_f(a,b) = \int_{-\infty}^{\infty} f(t)\psi_{a,b}dt \qquad (2\text{-}4)$$

The two-dimensional wavelet expansion functions $\psi_{a,b}$ are obtained from the basic function (also known as mother or generating wavelet) $\psi(t)$ by simple scaling and translation:

$$\psi_{a,b}(t) = \frac{1}{\sqrt{|a|}}\psi\left(\frac{t-b}{a}\right), a,b \in R, \psi \in L^2(R) \qquad (2\text{-}5)$$

where $\in$ denotes membership, t is the time variable, the parameters a ($\neq 0$) and b denote the frequency (or scale) and the time (or space) location, respectively, and R is the set of real numbers. The notation $L^2(R)$ represents the square summable time series space of the data, where the superscript 2 denotes the square of the modulus of the function.

To avoid intensive computations for every possible scale *a* and dilation *b*, the dyadic values are often used for both scaling and dilation in discrete wavelet transform as follows:

$$a_j = 2^j, b_{j,k} = k2^j, j,k \in Z \qquad (2\text{-}6)$$

where k and j denote the time and frequency indices, respectively, and Z is the set of all integers.

Substituting Equation (2-6) into Equation(2-5), the following wavelet expansion function is obtained:

$$\psi_{j,k}(t) = 2^{-j/2}\psi\left(2^{-j}t-k\right), j,k \in Z, \psi \in L^2(R) \qquad (2\text{-}7)$$

So Equation (2-4) is rewritten as:

$$W_f(j,k) = 2^{-j/2}\int_{-\infty}^{\infty} f(t)\psi\left(2^{-j}t-k\right)dt, j,k \in Z, \psi \in L^2(R) \qquad (2\text{-}8)$$

which is the DWT of the time series *f(t)*.

The DWT represented by Equation (2-8) aims to preserve the dominant features of the CWT from Equation (2-4) in a succinct manner. Conceptually, the DWT can be considered as a judicious sub-sampling of CWT coefficients with just dyadic scales (i.e., $2^{j-1}, j = 1,2,...,L$, where L is the maximum number of the decomposition level). Compared with the DWT, the CWT can represent the physical system more accurately as it makes very subtle information visible, but it requires more intensive computations for integrating over every possible scale, *a*, and dilation, *b*.

The time series can be reconstructed by inverse of the CWT of Equation (2-4) in the double-integral form or the DWT of Equation (2-5) in the double-summation form. In terms of DWT, the time series *f(t)* is reconstructed by:

$$f(t) = \sum_j \sum_k a_{j,k} \psi_{j,k}(t) \tag{2-9}$$

where the coefficients of the series $\{a_{j,k}\}$ are calculated as follows:

$$a_{j,k} = < f(t), \psi_{j,k}(t) > \tag{2-10}$$

in which $< f(t), \psi_{j,k}(t) >$ represents the inner product of two functions $f(t)$ and $\psi_{j,k}(t)$.

2.2.3 Mallat algorithm

The role of the fast algorithm of wavelet transform Mallat is the same as Fast Fourier Transform in Fourier transform. It decomposes signals orthogonally and effectively into different independent wave bands. The nature of Mallat algorithm is that there is no need to know the specific structure of scaling function and wavelet function and signal decomposition and reconstruction can be achieved by the coefficients of Mallat algorithm. Furthermore the length of the coefficients can be reduced in half for each decomposition, thus the calculated amount of wavelet transform is significantly decreased. Thus the application and development of wavelet is greatly pushed forward (Mallat,1992).

Suppose the discrete sample sequence of the signal $f(t)$ is expressed by $f(n)$, $n = 1,2,...N$, if $f(n)$ is the approximation of signal at scale $j = 0$, it is marked by $c_0(n) = f(n)$. Therefore, the decomposing formula can be described by:

$$c_{j+1}(n) = \sum_{m \in z} c_j(m) h(m - 2n) \tag{2-11}$$

$$d_{j+1}(n) = \sum_{m \in z} c_j(m) g(m - 2n) \tag{2-12}$$

The reconstruction formula can be represented by:

$$c_j(n) = \sum_{m \in z} \left(c_{j+1}(m) h(n - 2m) + d_{j+1}(m) g(n - 2m) \right) \tag{2-13}$$

In Equation (2-11)-(2-13), $m = 0,1,2 \cdots, N-1$, and N is the length of the input sequence, c_j is the approximate coefficient at j th layer; d_j is the detail coefficient at j th layer, h is the low-pass filter coefficients of the used wavelet; g is the high-pass filter coefficients of the applied wavelet.

2.3 BP neural network

2.3.1 Artificial neural networks

An Artificial Neural Networks (ANN) is a nonlinear large-scale adaptive system based on numerous processing units. It is proposed and developed from the results of scientific research in the modern neuro-physiology to simulate the simple model of human neural cell with capability of generalization and learning. It is essentially a simple mathematical model representing a nonlinear mapping function from a set of input X to output Y, i.e., $f: X \rightarrow Y$.
The most commonly used ANN model is the feedforward neural network (Adeli,2009 & Rumelhart et al., 1986). This network usually consists of input, hidden, and output layers. The information moves only in the forward direction, from the input nodes, through the hidden nodes to output nodes. There are no loops in the network.
For example, Fig.2.2 shows a widely used three-layer feedforward ANN model, with arrows depicting the dependencies between variables at each layer. Its single output $\hat{y}$ (i.e., model prediction) is the nonlinear weighted sum of the inputs X. In Fig.2.2, the input vector X consists of P variables $x_i(i=1,...,p)$. The parameter $a_{ij}(i=1,...,p; j=1,...,K)$ represents the weight of the link connecting the input node i to node j in the hidden layer, in which K is the number of nodes in the hidden layer. The parameter W_j represents the weight of link connecting the hidden node j to the node in the output layer, and the variable d represents the weight of the bias. The bias term (a constant value, typically one) allows the neural network to return a nonzero value at the origin. a_{ij}, W_j and d are parameters needed to be estimated using a learning algorithm which will be discussed later.
Let $\theta = \{a_{ij}, W_j, d\}$ represent the group of parameters to be estimated. The model output $\hat{y}$ is conceptually expressed as(Rumelhart et al., 1986):

$$\hat{y} = f(x, \theta) \quad (2\text{-}14)$$

In training an ANN model, a measure of the error e is often used as a model -quality index. The error is defined as the difference between the actual and predicted values, expressed as:

$$e = y - \hat{y} \quad (2\text{-}15)$$

A well-trained model should yield small prediction errors, which is often used to assess the validity of the trained model.

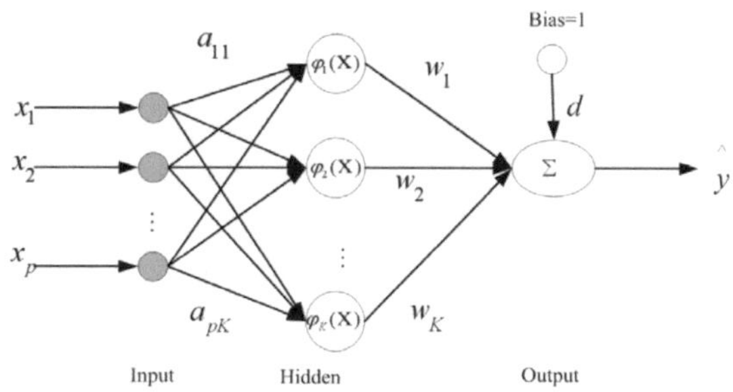

$x = [x_1, ..., x_p]$ = Input vector containing P variables.
a_{ij} = Weight of the link connecting the input node i to node j in the hidden layer.
W_j = Weight of the link connecting the hidden node j to the node in the output layer.
d = Weight of the bias.
y = Model output.
Fig. 2.2 An illustrative example for feedforward three-layer ANN model

The ANN is suitable particularly for problems that are too complex to be modeled and solved by classical mathematics and traditional procedures, such as engineering design and image recognition. Typical ANN models include back-propagation (BP) neural network, radial basis function (RBF) neural network, Boltzmann neural network and dynamic neural network. One of the reasons for popularity of the neural network is the development of the error back-propagation training algorithm, which is based on a gradient descent optimization technique. The principle of BP network will be introduced briefly in the following section.

2.3.2 Principle of BP network

The error back-propagation neural network is called BP network for short. This algorithm makes training sample outputs and target outputs as a nonlinear optimization problem. By using gradient descent method, the weights can be obtained between nodes (Hagan & Menhaj, 1994). Actually, BP network reflects the mapping relationship between the input and output in the form of weights.
The structural model of a BP network is shown in Fig.2.3 which consists of an input layer, a hide layer and an output layer (Ripley, 1996). First the input layer receives characteristic parameter information, then the hide layer studies and processes input information and connects the input layer and the output layer by weights, last the output layer compares with target value continually and propagates the error back.

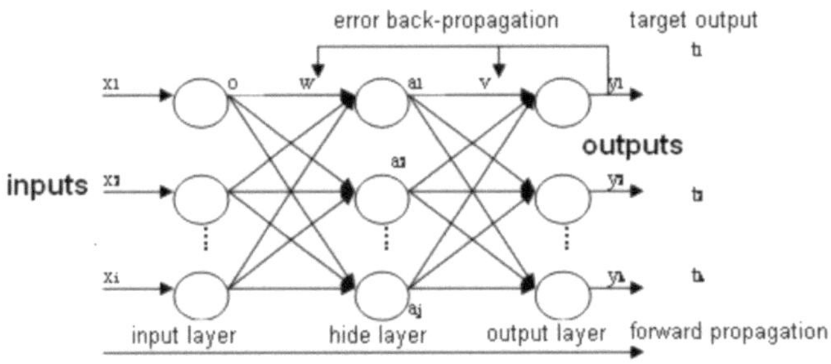

Fig. 2.3. The structure model of BP network

The weight from input layers to hide layers and the one from hide layers to output layers are corrected continually by forward propagation and back propagation. The inherent law of input samples can be found afterwards. In Fig.2.3, x is the input characteristic parameter; i is the number of input nodes; w is the weight from input layers to hide layers; a is the output of the hide layer; j is the number of hide layer nodes; v is the weight from hide layers to output layers; y is the output of output layers; k is the number of output layer nodes; t is the target value of the network.
Process of forward propagation can be described as follows: Input layer: Adopt the linear input function and equal any output o_i to its input x_i; Hide layer: Any input net_j is the weighted sum of forward outputs o_j, $net_j = \sum w_{ji}o_j + \theta_i$, here θ_i is the threshold of hide layer nodes. The output is $a(j) = f(net_j)$; f can be represented by the *sigmoid* function as $f(net_j) = 1/(1+\exp(-net_j))$; Output layer: the weighted sum of hide layer outputs is the input of output layer. Adopting linear output function makes the kth output y_k be $y_k = \sum_j v_{kj}a_j$, where k is an integral number.

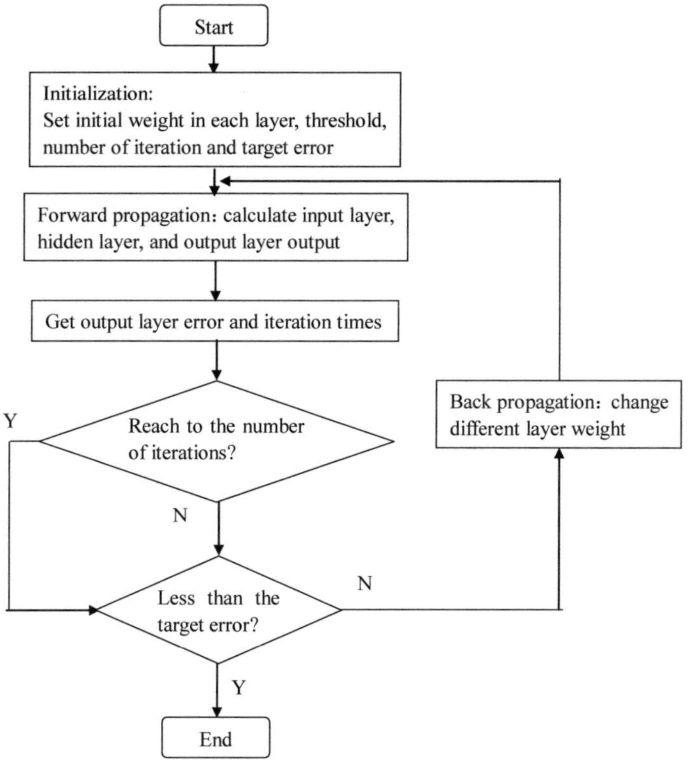

Fig. 2.4. BP network learning process

During processing of back propagation, the error function E_P is defined by $E_P = \frac{1}{2}\sum_k (t_k - y_k)^2$; if the output error is not satisfied with the requirement, the network propagates errors back to modify the weight.

For weight correction, the learning algorithm of BP network adopts gradient descent method to adjust the weight value. Adjusted quantity is fixed as $\Delta W_{kj} = -\eta \frac{\partial E_p}{\partial W_{kj}}$. From this formula we can obtain the weight correction between hide layers and output layers as $\Delta_{kj} = \eta \xi_k a_j$. Here η is learning rate, and $\xi_k = y_k(1-y_k)(t_k - y_k)$; the weight correction between input layer and hide layer is $\Delta w_{ji} = \eta \xi_j o_i$, here $\xi_j = a_j(1-a_j)\sum_k \xi_k v_{kj}$. The BP network learning process is shown in Fig.2.4.

3. Design of the virtual SLM

3.1 Structure of the virtual SLM

The overall structure of the virtual SLM is decided to adopt PC plug-in virtual instrument mode, namely "A/D + PC + software" which is shown in Fig.3.1 (Pedro & Fernando, 2010). The microphone is the device to convert the measured source of sound signal to electrical signal. The A/D card inserted in PC slot is used to convert the analog electrical signal into digital signal. The Personal computer is applied to carry out the signal analysis and processing. Here the PXI-4472 A/D card from National Instruments Company is chosen. LabVIEW platform is used to develop the software of the virtual SLM to read the converted A/D signal and complete the signal analysis, computation, storage and display (Cao & Luo, 2007).

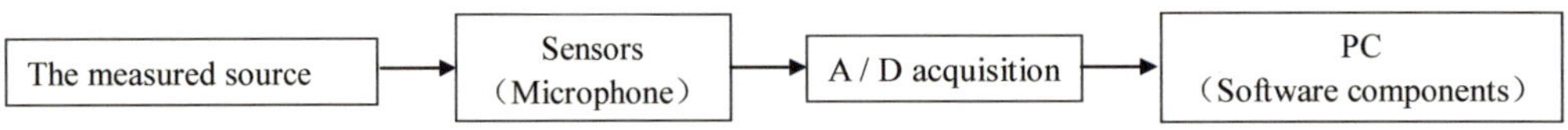

Fig. 3.1. Hardware structure of virtual SLM

3.2 Software structure

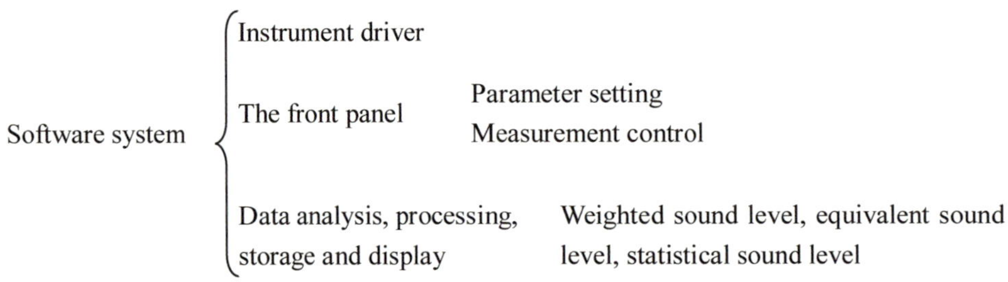

Fig. 3.2. Software structure of virtual SLM

As shown in Fig.3.2, the front panel is mainly responsible for the configuration of measured parameters, display of the measured results, etc. The function of data collection, analysis and processing are realized in the block diagram program.

3.3 Front panel control program

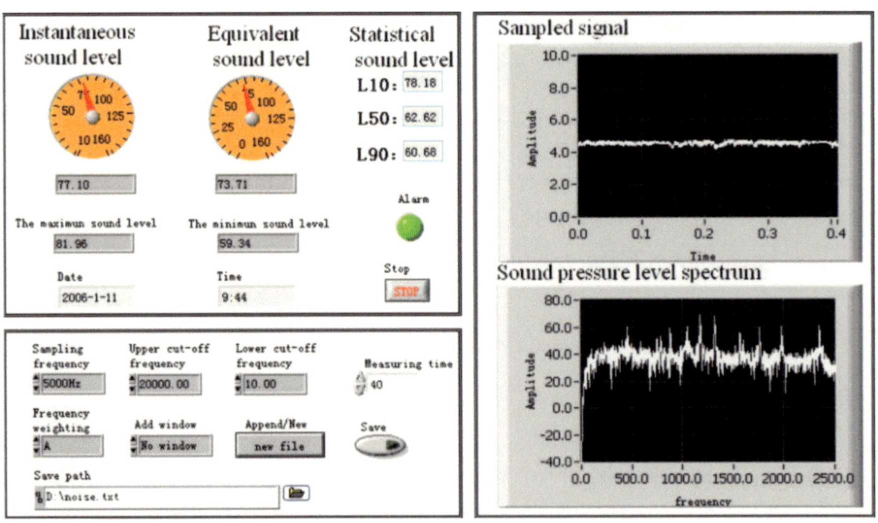

Fig. 3.3. The front panel of the virtual SLM

As shown in Fig.3.3, the front panel is mainly divided into three modules: result display module, parameter setting module and waveform display module. It is necessary to configure the measuring parameters that mainly include sampling frequency, add window type, filter fluctuation cut-off frequency, measuring time and frequency of weighted pattern (A, B and C), file path and preservation method. The measurement results mainly include the instantaneous sound level, equivalent continuous sound level, statistical sound level, the maximum- minimum sound level, alarm lamp, and the current date time, etc.

3.4 Procedure of signal processing of the virtual SLM

As shown in Fig.3.4, LabVIEW first reads the signal from A/D channel, and then processes adding window, filtering and other preprocessing to suppress the interference composition, next calculates unilateral power spectrum, converts the signal to frequency domain. After effective value transform, calculation of each frequency sound pressure, frequency weighting from instantaneous sound level at each sampling period are fulfilled. Finally based on instantaneous sound level, maximum/minimum sound level, statistical sound level and continuous equivalent sound level can be calculated (Luo et al., 2008)

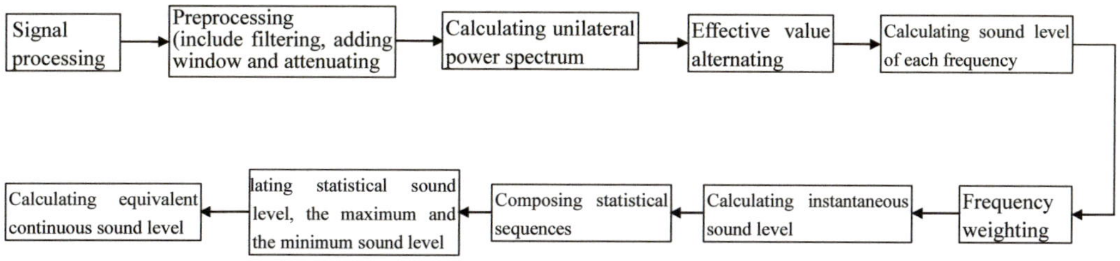

Fig. 3.4. Procedure of signal processing of the virtual SLM

3.5 Preprocessing

Signal often contains undesired noise, especially electrical noise signal. So filtering is needed for preprocessing. The bandpass filter is applied since upper and lower cutoff frequency can be dynamically adjusted according to requirement. In order to reduce the spectrum leakage due to signal truncation, adding windows processing is applied. The window function can be Hanning windows, Hamming windows, or Blackman windows, etc. The program is shown in Fig.3.5.

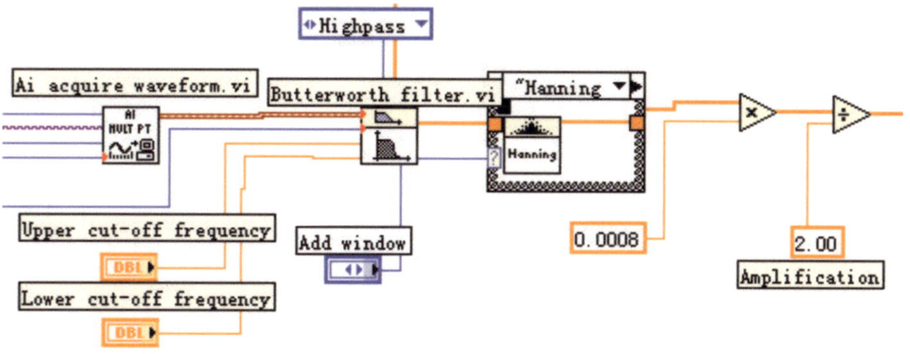

Fig. 3.5. Preprocessing program

3.6 Frequency weighting

1. Least squares

In scientific experiment data processing, it is a common task to seek out the function relationship between independent variable x and dependent variable y as $y = f(x;a_0,\cdots,a_n)(n < m)$, here a_i is undetermined parameters from a set of experimental data as $(x_i,y_i), i = 0,1,\cdots m$. In general, observation data have errors and the undetermined parameter number is less than that from experiment. This kind of problem is different from interpolation and function $y = s(x) = s(x;a_0,\cdots,a_n)$ is not required to pass through the data points (x_i,y_i), and only requires that the sum of squares $\sum_{i=0}^{m}\delta_i^2$ of $\delta_i = s(x_i) - y_i \ (i = 0,1,\cdots m)$ is smallest at the given data points. This is the so-called least-square approximation. The least-square fitting curve $y = s(x)$ can be obtained thereby. This approach is called curve fitting least-square method. Frequency weights at each frequency are obtained by using the least-square method in the frequency weighting module.

2. Frequency weighting

Weighted network is an important part of SLM which directly affects the accuracy of various sound levels. As shown in Fig.3.6, the approach is to fit the frequency weighted value of A, B, C provided by IEC651 "sound level meter" into curves using least-squares polynomial fitting method in MATLAB. According to the curves, the required frequency weighting correction values are calculated and stored in array x, the unilateral power spectrum sequence of the input signal are calculated and stored in array L. Then the sum of L and x is the corresponding frequency weighting result of the signal. According to the frequency weighted signal, sound pressure level is calculated for one sampling period. That is the value of the instantaneous sound level.

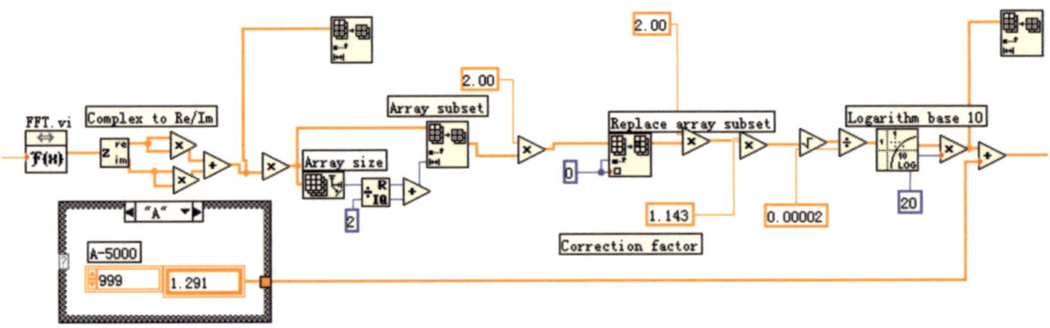

Fig. 3.6. Frequency weighting

3.7 Statistical analysis

As shown in Fig.3.7, in order to perform statistical analysis of sound level, the instantaneous sound level is input to a statistical array in a loop and then sort operating is carried out. It is easy to get the statistical sound levels L_{10}, L_{50}, L_{90} the largest and smallest sound level L_{max}, L_{min}. In addition, the time of statistical analysis is changed by adjusting the length of the statistical array.

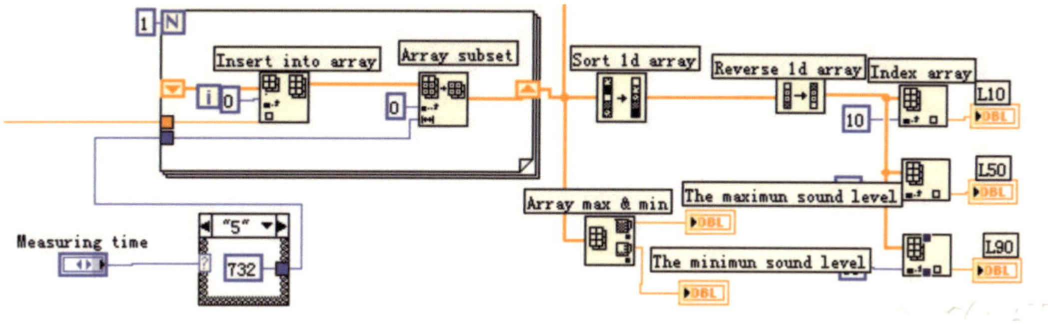

Fig. 3.7. Statistical analysis

3.8 Equivalent continuous sound level

Calculation of equivalent continuous sound level is carried out according to Equation (2-3). The program is implemented as shown in Fig.3.8. The control of the equivalent time namely measurement time is achieved by varying the length of statistical sequence.

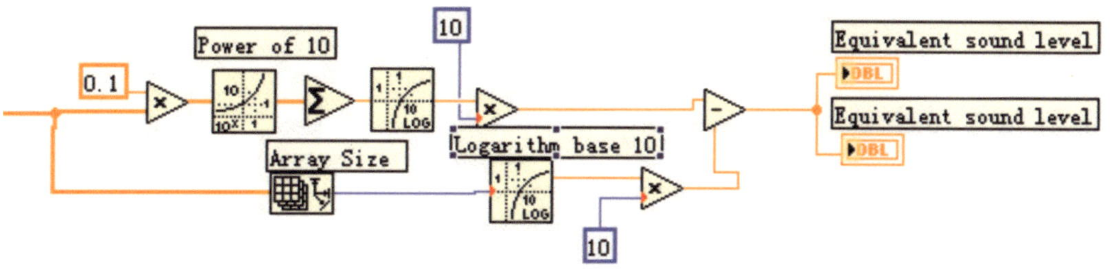

Fig. 3.8. Calculation of equivalent continuous sound level

3.9 Frequency spectrum analysis, preservation and alarm

Spectrum analysis, preservation and alarm function etc. are realized by calling the appropriate controls in LabVIEW.

3.10 Calibration of the system magnification

TES-1356 sound pressure calibrator from Taishi Company, Taiwan is selected to calibrate the virtual SLM system. The output frequency of TES-1356 is 1000HZ (±4%). The two standard output sound pressure levels are 94dB and 114dB with accuracy within ±0.5dB respectively. Calibration experiments have been carried out. The measured sound pressure levels are compared with the standard pressure levels to get the errors when the magnification factor is varied from 1.0 to 2.2. The experimental data are given in Table 3-1. In the table, $\Delta x1 = \frac{L_x - 94}{94} \times 100\%$, $\Delta x2 = \frac{L_x - 114}{114} \times 100\%$. Lx is the actual sound level and $\Delta x1$ 、 $\Delta x2$ respectively represent the error rate under 94dB and 114dB standard value. Considering the values of $\Delta x1$ and $\Delta x2$, the system magnification factor is determined to be 1.9. Since the calibrator generates a pure tone at 1000Hz, the calibration at this frequency means calibrating the entire system at all frequencies excluding the frequency weighting model. Moreover the applied A-weighted correction values fall into the tolerance range of 0-type sound level meter specified by the IEC651 standard "sound level meter".

Multiple / Sound pressure	1.0	1.2	1.4	1.6	1.7	1.74	1.76	1.78	1.80	1.90	2.0	2.1	2.2
94dB	99.48	97.88	96.52	95.38	94.84	94.63	94.49	94.42	94.32	93.89	93.41	92.99	92.58
$\Delta x1$	5.83	4.13	2.68	1.47	0.89	0.67	0.52	0.45	0.34	-0.12	-0.63	1.07	-1.51
114dB	119.92	118.33	116.99	115.83	115.32	115.10	115.02	114.88	114.80	114.32	113.86	113.48	113.06
$\Delta x2$	5.1	3.8	2.62	1.61	1.16	0.96	0.89	0.77	0.7	0.28	-0.12	-0.46	-0.82

Table 3-1. The experimental data of system calibration

3.11 Comparative experiment

Time(s) / Sound level A	5	10	15	20	25	30	35	40	45	50
Sound level（dB）	59.3	59.7	59.4	59.0	59.6	59.7	59.8	59.0	59.2	59.4
Time(s) / Sound level A	55	60	65	70	75	80	85	90	95	100
Sound level (dB)	59.7	59.1	59.6	59.3	59.3	59.6	60.0	59.4	59.3	59.6

Table 3-2. The instantaneous sound level A (L_A) Measured by TES—1357 per 5 seconds

Comparative experiments between the virtual SLM and a commercial SLM TES-1357 with an accuracy of ±1.5dB from Taishi Company of Taiwan have been carried out. In the relatively quiet and closed environment, generate a stable sound field with PXI-1002 from NI is generated, and then the microphone of TES-1357 and the microphone of this system are placed into the same location of the stable sound field. Experiment is performed and data are given in Table 3-2 and Table 3-3.

Time (s)	5	10	15	20	30	40	50	100	150
The average value of sound level A during N seconds (dB)	59.31	59.50	59.04	59.90	59.25	59.59	59.50	59.52	59.55

Table 3-3. The average value of instantaneous sound level A(L_A) measured by the virtual SLM during N seconds

As shown in Table 3-2, the average value ($\overline{L}_A$) of 20 instantaneous sound level A is 59.45dB. The average value of instantaneous sound level A is 59.52dB within 100 seconds and the average value is 59.55dB within 150s as shown in Table 3-3. Compared with the average value 59.45dB measured by TES-1357 within 100s, the errors of the virtual SLM are +0.07dB, +0.1dB respectively. TES-1357 is a precise sound level meter with an accuracy of ± 1.5 dB. The comparative experiment verifies that the accuracy of the virtual SLM is acceptable.

The maximum error between A-weighted correction value in this system and the value specified by IEC651 is 0.3113dB which implies that the tolerance requirement of type-0 SLM is met. The sound level meter is calibrated by a standard sound level calibrator. The errors of the virtual SLM compared with the calibrator at 94dB, 114dB are 0.11dB, 0.32dB, respectively. It indicates the measurement error of the developed virtual SLM is under ± 0.5dB and thus the precision achieves the requirements of type-1 SLM.

4. An online fan fault diagnosis system based on wavelet and neural network under LabVIEW platform

4.1 Implementation of wavelet de-noising on LabVIEW

4.1.1 Wavelet decomposition for signal with noise in each layer

As shown in Fig.4.1, original signal "*signal*" is convolved with "*wfiters*" which denote low-pass and high-pass filter coefficients. Then the result is down-sampled to get approximate coefficients ca_n and detailed coefficients cd_n respectively. At the same time, the length (*size*) of the approximate coefficients in each layer is returned. "*level*" denotes the number of decomposition layer. "*wname*" denotes the used wavelet name, and "*wfiters*" denotes the corresponding filter coefficients used by the wavelet which are computed by "*wfiters*" function in MATLAB. The program is shown in Fig.4.1.

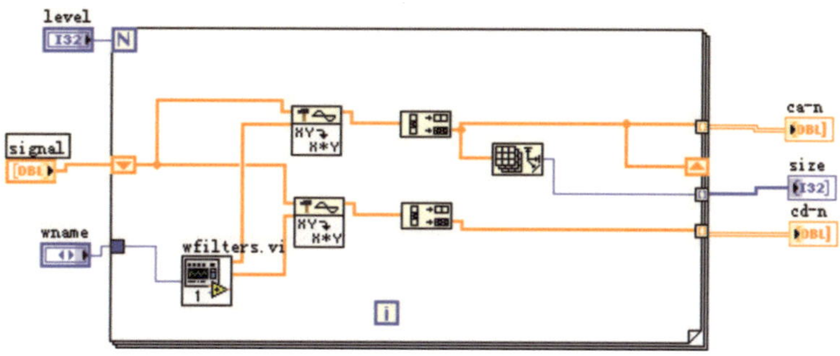

Fig. 4.1. Block diagram of wavelet decomposition

4.1.2 Thresholding for high frequency coefficients

1. Determination of threshold

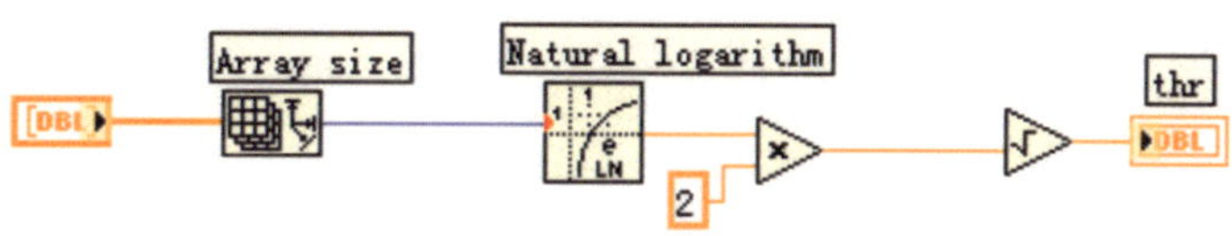

Fig. 4.2. Determination of threshold

Determination of threshold is a key step in signal de-noising based on wavelet since threshold selection has direct impact on the effect of de-noising. The determination of threshold can be realized by *Thselect* command in MATLAB. As shown in Fig.4.2, '*sqtwolog*' in *Thselect* command is adopted, so $thr = \sqrt{2\ln N}$, where N denotes the length of high frequency coefficient. This program is shown in Fig.4.2.

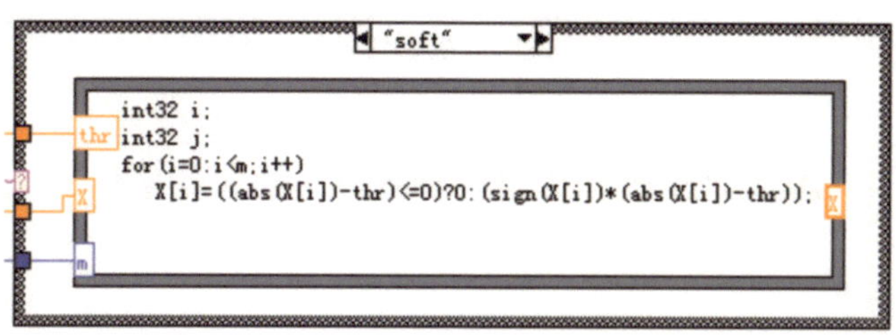

Fig. 4.3. Threshold processing

2. Thresholding

Modes of thresholding action are divided into hard thresholding and soft thresholding. Soft thresholding can be expressed as a mathematical formula:

$$X_{thr} = \begin{cases} sign(x)(|x| - thr) & |x| > thr \\ 0 & |x| < thr \end{cases} \tag{4-1}$$

Hard thresholding can be expressed as:

$$X_{thr} = \begin{cases} x & |x| > thr \\ 0 & |x| < thr \end{cases} \tag{4-2}$$

In Equation(4-1) and (4-2), x denotes the element of high frequency coefficient, thr denotes the selected threshold, and X_{thr} denotes a sequence after thresholding. Here threshold processing of the high frequency coefficients is achieved by utilizing Formula Node control as shown in Fig.4.3.

4.1.3 Reconstruction of low frequency coefficients and high frequency coefficients processed by thresholding

As shown in Fig.4.4, the process of reconstruction is as follows (Cao et al., 2009):

1. The N-layer approximate coefficient ca_n is up-sampled, then the result is convolved with the low-pass filter coefficients of the applied wavelet to get ca_conv. While the n-layer detail coefficient cd_n_thr is processed in the same way, cd_conv is obtained and high-pass filter coefficients of the same wavelet are used when carrying out convolution.
2. ca_ret is obtained by extracting ret elements from the sequence ca_conv starting at the kth element. The calculation of ret is expressed as, ret_w = the length of ca_n*2-the length of filter+1. If ret_w is odd, then ret= ret_w+1; If ret_w is even, then ret= ret_w. k= (the length of ca_n-the length of ret)/2. cd_ret can be obtained while the thresholded n-layer detail coefficient cd_n_thr is processed in the same way.
3. The de-noised signal ca_n-1 is obtained from adding ca_ret with cd_ret.
4. Then the (n-1)th wavelet reconstruction is made by use of ca_n-1 and cd_n-1_thr. Repeat until the first layer.

The program for one layer wavelet de-noise of a signal is shown in Fig.4.5, where $wname$ is the name of the used wavelet, and $mode\_opera$ denotes the mode of threshold action $hard$ or $soft$.

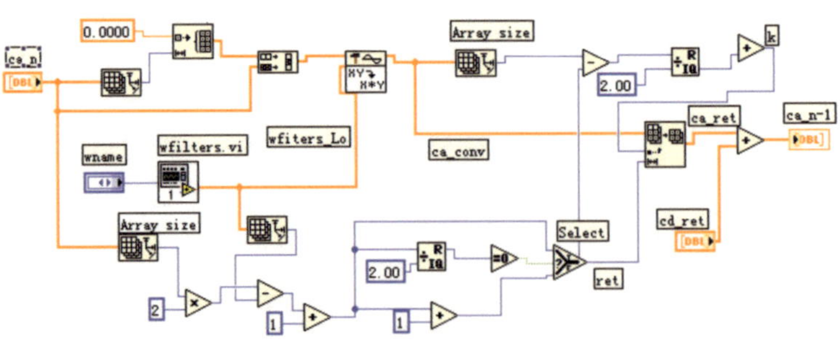

Fig. 4.4. Reconstruction of single-layer wavelet

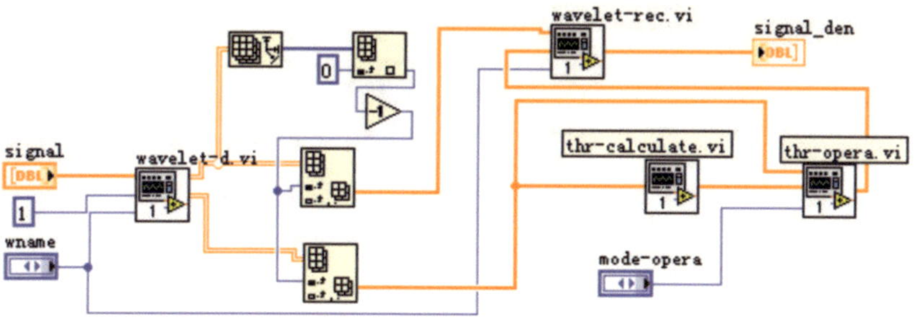

Fig. 4.5. Signal single-layer de-noising

4.2 Feature extraction based on wavelet

Since it is different that system faults suppress or enhance the noise signal energy with distinct frequency, the proportional relationship of the signal energy with different frequency contains abundant fault information. Proportion of certain frequency band energy represents certain fault feature. Therefore it is an important method based on wavelet feature extraction by using the diagnosis method of "energy ---fault". The realization steps are as follows (Cao et al., 2009):

1. Wavelet decomposes the collected signal to obtain each layer's details and approximate coefficient, and thresholdly process high frequency coefficients.
2. Reconstruct the low-frequency coefficients and high frequency coefficients after thresholdly processing, and obtain corresponding frequency signal.
3. Calculate frequency band energy corresponding to the square of frequency signal.
4. Create feature vector. Creating feature vector is based on relevant frequency band energy for the elements.

Whether you find an accurate vector that represents fault plays a key role for successful diagnosis or not. It is very important to choose the feature vector in fault diagnosis.

4.3 Fault diagnosis based on neural network

Fault diagnosis based on neural network includes the following steps (Cao et al., 2009):

1. Data acquisition and feature extraction for feature vector.
2. Network structure design. According to dimension number of the input feature vector and equipment fault status, the node number of the input and output layers of neural network can be determined. The node number of the hidden layer is selected on experience.
3. Network training. The extracted feature vectors are input vectors. Collect a certain amount of input data as training samples to train the network. When the network output error is less than the goal error, exit and save the network parameters.
4. Fault diagnosis. Input the sample data into the neural network and get the diagnosis result for the fault status.

4.4 Design of the online fan fault diagnosis system

4.4.1 Structure of the hardware system

The structure of the hardware system of an online fan fault diagnosis system is shown in Fig.4.6 which consists of the diagnosed object, microphone, amplifying circuit, A/D converter card, and a personal computer with LabVIEW platform. The microphone converts the signal produced by fan into voltage signal. The amplifying circuit conditions the signal to a required scope. The A/D converter card PXI-4472 from NI Company acquires the signal and converts it to digital signal. Then the digital signal is accessed to LabVIEW by the software of the online wavelet neural network fan fault diagnosis system.

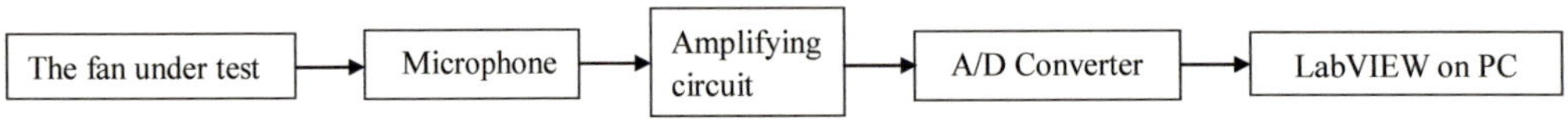

(a) Structure of the hardware system

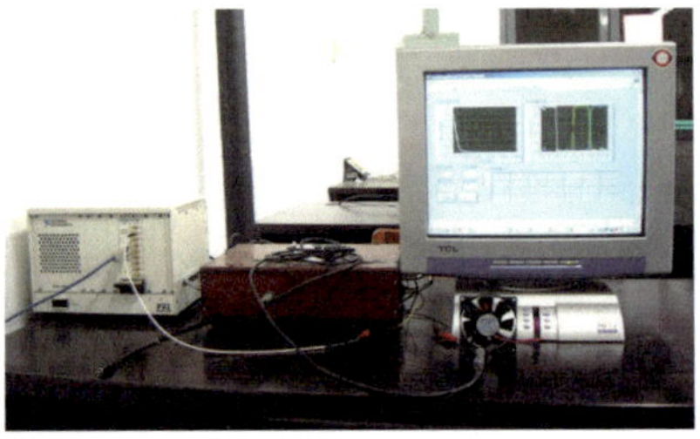

(b)Photo of the hardware system

Fig. 4.6. Structure of the hardware system

4.4.2 Design of the software system

As shown in Fig.4.7, the software system comprises three parts of training sample, network training and on-line diagnosis. The function of each part is described as follows.

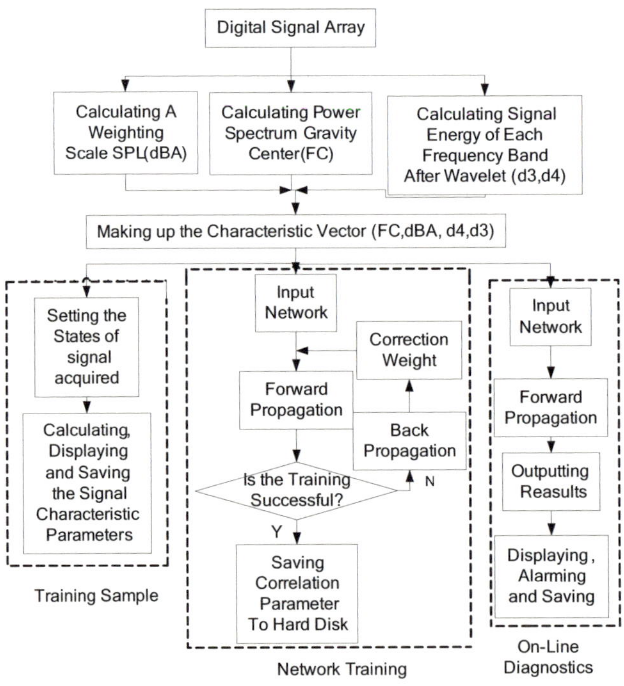

Fig. 4.7. Structure of the software system

Training sample: relying on the target under test sets frequency of sampling, number of samples, sample size, state of sampling signal such as normal state, paper choking, eccentric blade, blade breaks, and so on, acquire a certain number of samples of signal in different states. Then, calculate the feature vector of each state and save the vector to a specified location.
The function of network training: set the node number of input layer, hide layer and output layer; initialize the weights and threshold values of each layer; train network and save the correlation parameter for calling.
On-Line diagnostics: acquire the noise signal of fan; calculate the feature vector; input the trained network; output and save the fault probability and alarm message.

4.4.3 Extracting the feature vector

How to choose characteristic parameters directly affects the performance of diagnosis system. In the proposed system, the feature vector consists of A-weighted sound level, power spectrum gravity centre and signal energy of each frequency band after wavelet decomposition.
The power spectrum gravity center (FC) is calculated by:

$$FC = \frac{\sum_{i=1}^{N} f_i p_i}{\sum_{i=1}^{N} p_i} \tag{4-3}$$

where, f_i is the frequency, p_i is the magnitude and i is the order of the power spectrum line.
If fault occurs, the magnitudes of some frequency will change and affect the position of power spectrum gravity center, the energy distribution of different frequency band after wavelet decomposition and the measuring results of A-weighted sound level.

4.4.4 Experiments

Four fans RDM8025S made by RUILIAN SCIENC company of China, are used for the fault diagnosis experiment. One fan is normal, the other three are paper choking, eccentric blade, and blade breaks respectively.

1. Network structure design

Suppose FC stands for the frequency power spectrum gravity center. A-weighted sound level is dbA. d3 and d4 respectively stand for the energy distribution of the third and fourth frequency band after wavelet decomposition. The feature vector $x = (FC, dBA, d4, d3)$ is input of the network. The fault modes such as normal y_1, paper choking y_2, eccentric blade y_3 and blade breaks y_4 are composed of the output vector $y = (y_1, y_2 y_3 y_4)$. For example, $y = (0,1,0,0)$ shows that the fan fault is paper choking.
The node number of input layer equals four which is the dimension of x. Similarly, the node number of output layer equals the dimension of y. The node number of hide layer is empirically two. Linear action function is chosen at input and output layer. The action function of hide layer is the *sigmoid* function.

2. Signal acquisition

Set the sampling frequency as 5000 *Hz* and the number of samples as 2048. *db2* is used by wavelet and the decomposition level is four. Under each one of four states, we acquire ten sets data in which two sets are selected to calculate the feature vector. The results are shown in Table4-1.

Number of Samples	x1	x2	x3	x4	Mode
1	200.170	78.350	46.306	27.273	Normal
2	190.829	77.913	44.669	23.890	Normal
3	300.180	83.114	61.277	32.537	Paper choking
4	295.919	82.746	59.160	33.841	Paper choking
5	132.724	80.684	65.717	28.857	Eccentric blade
6	134.868	81.450	83.176	38.774	Eccentric blade
7	113.926	74.022	31.793	18.459	Blade breaks
8	122.163	75.550	36.515	19.621	Blade breaks

Table 4-1. Characteristic value of training sample acquired and the corresponding fault modes

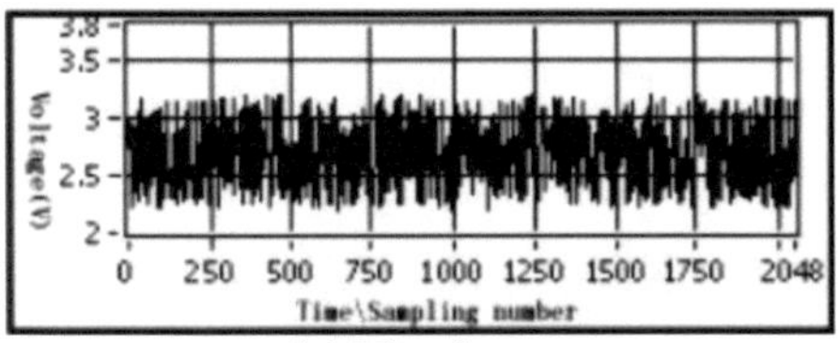

(a) The first group

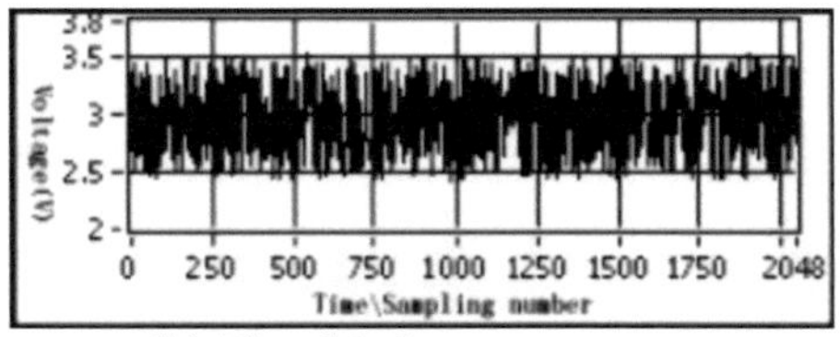

(b) The third group

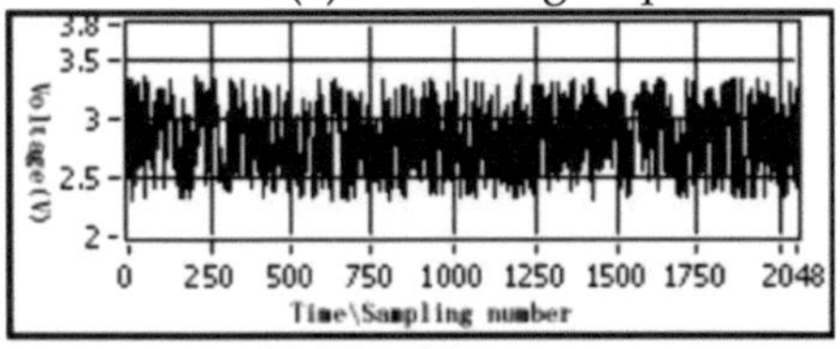

(c) The fifth group

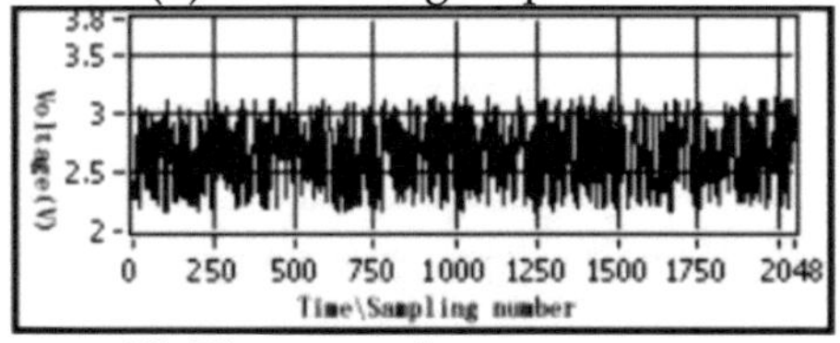

(d) The seventh group

Fig. 4.8. Time-domain waveforms of signal sample

For the first, third, fifth, and seventh set of signal samples time domain waveforms are respectively listed in Fig.4.8. The front panel of acquisition process is shown in Fig.4.9.

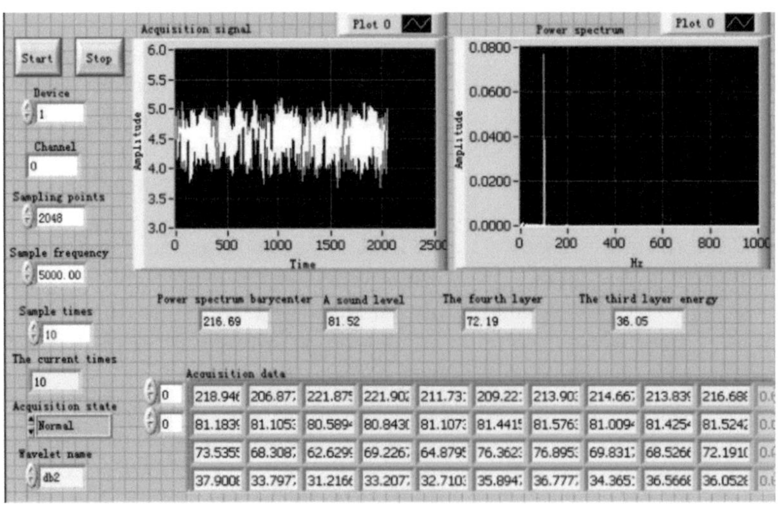

Fig. 4.9. The front panel of signal acquisition module

3. Network training

To keep a stable learning rate and avoid network oscillation, the learning rate, weight and the error of target should be selected suitably while executing the network training. If the learning rate is too fast, there will be a constant oscillation in the network that makes it difficult to achieve the target value. If the error of target is too small, the requirement of specified iteration number can not be achieved. The initial weight and threshold value are set as the random number between 0 and 1. In experiment, the error of target and the maximal iteration number are set as 0.05 and 5000 respectively.

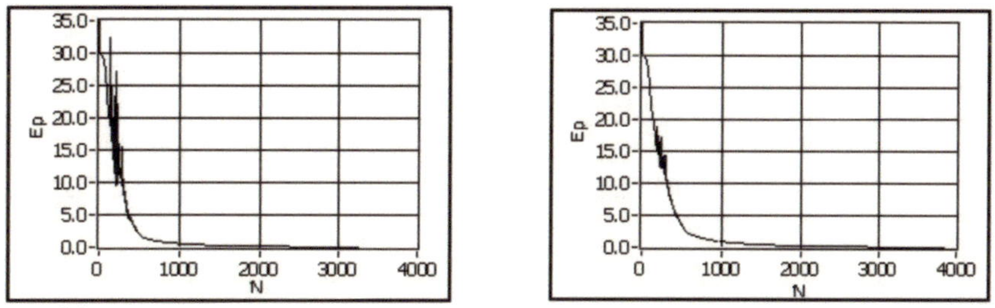

(a) Learning rate is 0.3 (b) Learning rate is 0.2

Fig. 4.10. Relationship between output error Ep and iteration number N

After the network is trained, the relationship between actual output error Ep and iteration number N is shown in Fig.4.10. In the figure (a), the learning rate is 0.35. A large oscillation occurs during training. In the figure (b), the learning rate is 0.2. However, the oscillation during the training is small. When the output error is decreased from 31.2 to 0.049997 and the required value is reached, the iteration number is 3677. The fault mode of training sample (t1, t2, t3, t4) and the actual output of network (y1, y2, y3, y4) is listed in Table4-2. It can be seen from Table4-2 that the fault mode of acquired samples has already been recognized accurately by the network. Last, the related parameters of this network are stored in the specified location. The front panel of the training process is shown in Fig.4.11.

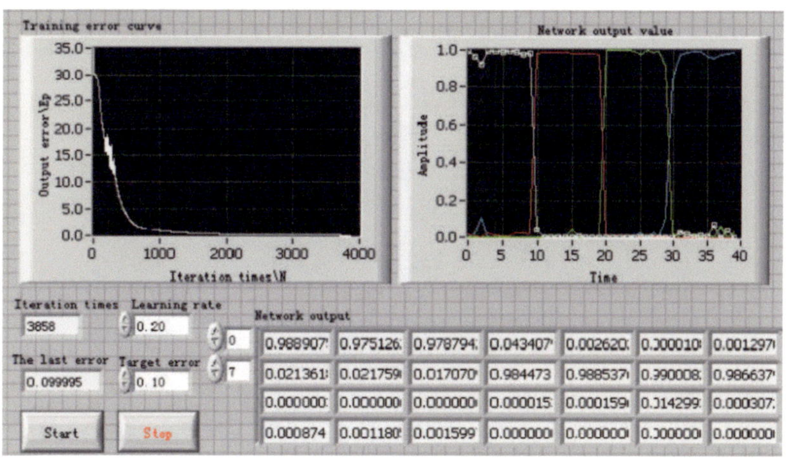

Fig. 4.11. The front panel of network training module

4. On-line diagnosis

The well trained network is used to diagnose the fan under test to acquire the noise signal produced by fan working at each mode. Using the sampling value, the corresponding feature vector is calculated for input to the well trained network in order to perform on-line diagnosis. Table4-3 lists the characteristic parameters and the corresponding network outputs.

Number of samples	Fault modes				Outputs of network			
	t1	t2	t3	t4	y1	y2	y3	y4
1	1	0	0	0	0.9695	0.0104	0.0002	0.0005
2	1	0	0	0	0.9769	0.0087	0.0001	0.0009
3	0	1	0	0	0.0567	0.9804	0.0007	0.0000
4	0	1	0	0	0.0441	0.9754	0.0021	0.0000
5	0	0	1	0	0.0003	0.0000	0.9921	0.0054
6	0	0	1	0	0.0005	0.0000	0.9434	0.0236
7	0	0	0	1	0.0268	0.0000	0.0325	0.9194
8	0	0	0	1	0.0299	0.0000	0.0146	0.9858

Table 4-2. Fault modes of training samples and outputs of network

Testing sample	Characteristic parameters				Outputs of network			
	x1	x2	x3	x4	y1	y2	y3	y4
1 (Normal)	221.104	79.039	46.127	24.898	0.976	0.047	0.001	0.000
2 (Paper hoking)	273.696	81.797	54.367	31.075	0.016	0.980	0.005	0.000
3 (eccentric lade)	135.684	78.717	60.857	26.812	0.003	0.060	0.994	0.010
4 (balde breaks)	110.927	74.364	31.303	17.032	0.002	0.000	0.044	0.997

Table 4-3. Characteristic parameters of testing sample and outputs of network

Compared to Table 4-3 with Table 4-2, we can find that although the feature vectors of fan under test are different with the training samples, the proposed system can diagnose the fault accurately. The front panel of online diagnosis module is shown in Fig.4.12.

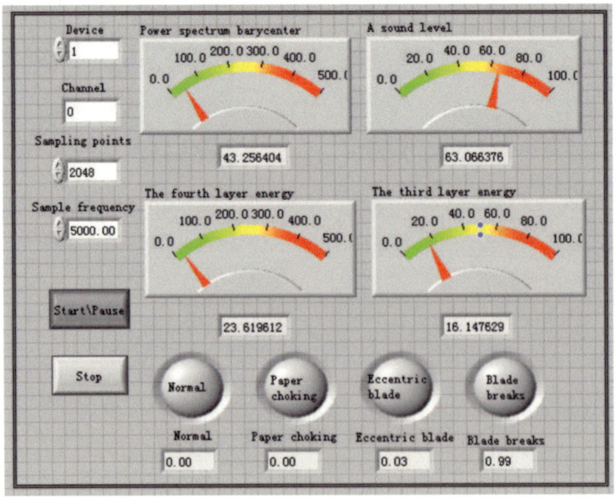

Fig. 4.12. The front panel of no-line diagnosis module

5. Conclusion

The proposed virtual SLM is calibrated by using TES-1356 sound level calibrator. Its accuracy is verified by the comparative experiment with TES-1357. The results indicate the measurement error is within 0.5 dB and the precision meets the requirements of the type I sound level meter.

In the proposed intelligent fault diagnosis system, the noise produced by fan is diagnosis signal, non-connect measurement is adopted and using the wavelet neural network performs the non-linear mapping from feature space to defective space. Modular programming is adopted in this system, so it is easier to extend and change the characteristic parameters of fault and structure parameters of the network. Utilizing the learning, memory and reckoning abilities diagnoses the fault adaptively. The designed system has the better capacity of learning, deducing and fault tolerant. The diagnosis results are reliable and accurate.

6. References

Adeli, H. & Jiang, X.J. (2009). *Intelligent Infrastructure: Neural Networks, Wavelets, and Chaos Theory for Intelligent Transportation Systems and Smart Structures,* CRC Press, ISBN 978-1-4200-8536-5, Boca Raton, FL

Burrus, C.S. (2005). *Introduction to Wavelets and Wavelet Transforms.* China Machine Press, ISBN 7-111-15911-X, Beijing

Cao, G.Z. & Ruan, S.C.(2002).Design of New Instrument Based on DSP for Measuring Car's Noise Combined with Rotating Speed. *Instrument Technique and Sensor(in Chinese),* No.08, pp. 11-13, ISSN 1002-1841

Cao, G.Z.; Wu, W. & Ruan, S.C. (2004). A New Method for Measuring the Rotary Speed of a Car's Engine Based on the Spacing Measurement of Its Noise and Its Implementation. *Journal of Xi'an Shiyou University(Natural Science Edition, in Chinese)* ,Vol.19, No.05, pp. 81-86, ISSN 1001-5361

Cao, G.Z. & Luo, C.G. (2007). Design of Virtual Sounnd Level Meter in LabVIEW. *Instrument Technique and Sensor (in Chinese),* No.06, pp. 16-18, ISSN 1002-1841

Cao, G.Z.; Lei X.Y. & Luo C.G. (2009). Research of a Fan Fault Diagnosis System Based on Wavelet and Neural Network. *2009 3rd International Conference on Power Electronics Systems and Applications,* Digital Reference: K210509062, ISBN 978-1-4244-3845-7, Hongkong

Donald, E. & Hall (1987). *Basic Acoustics,* Harper & Row, Publishers Inc. ISBN 0-06-042611-X, New York

Hagan, M. T. & Menhaj, M.B. (1994). Training FeedForward Networks with the Marquardt Algorithm. *IEEE Trans on Neural Networks,* Vol.05, No.06, pp. 989-993, ISSN 1045-9227

Kinsler, L.E.; Frey, A.R.; Coppens, A.B. & Sanders, J.V. (2000). *Fundanmentals of Acoustics.* Wiley, John & Sons Inc. Pub., ISBN 0-471-84789-5, New York

Luo, C.G.; Cao, G.Z. & Pan J.F. (2008). Design of a Fan Fault Diagnosis System Based on Wavelet and Neural Network. *Applied Acoustics(in Chinese),* Vol.27, No.3, pp. 181-187, ISSN 1000-310X

Mallat, S.G. (1989). A Theory for Multiresolution Signal Decomposition: the Wavelet Representation. *IEEE Pattern Analysis and Machine*, Vol.11, No.07, pp. 674-693, ISSN 0162-8828

Mallat, S.G. & Hwang, W.L. (1992). Singularity Detection and Processing with Wavelet. *IEEE Trans on Inform Theory*, Vol. 38, No.02, pp. 617-643, ISSN 0018-9448

Pedro, P.C. & Fernando, D. (2010). *Intelligent Control Systems with LabVIEW*, Springer, ISBN 978-1-84882-683-0, London

Rumelhart, D.E.; Hinton, G.E. & Williams, R.J. (1986). Learning Representations by Back-propagating Errors. *Nature,* Vol.03, No.23, pp. 533-536, ISSN: 0028-0836

Ripley,B.D. (1996). *Pattern Recognition and Neural Networks,* Cambridge University Press, ISBN0-521-46086-7, Cambridge

Ruan, Z.K. & Cao, G.Z. (2006). An Acoustic Signal Data Acquisition System Based on DSP. *Electric Instrumentation Customer(in Chinese)*,Vol.13, No.05, pp. 44-46, ISSN 1671-1041

12

Condition Monitoring of Zinc Oxide Surge Arresters

Novizon[1,2], Zulkurnain Abdul-Malek[1], Nouruddeen Bashir[1] and Aulia[1,2]
[1]*Universiti Teknologi Malaysia (UTM),*
[2]*University of Andalas (UNAND),*
[1]*Malaysia*
[2]*Indonesia*

1. Introduction

Over voltages in power system may occur due to lightning, fault or switching operation. These overvoltages could reach dangerous amplitudes for power system apparatus. To protect the system electrical equipment and to guarantee an economic and reliable operation, surge arresters are applied in almost all types of electrical power network. Gapless zinc oxide (ZnO) surge arresters are widely used. The surge arresters are usually connected between the phase and ground terminals. They limit the voltage level in equipments such as transformers below the withstand voltage level.

Figure 1 shows the values of overvoltage which can be reached without the use of arrester in per units. The time axis is divided into the range of lightning overvoltage in microsecond, switching overvoltage in millisecond and temporary overvoltage in second. In the lightning overvoltage and switching overvoltage range, the magnitude of overvoltage can reach several per unit if the system is without arrester protection. Arrester could limit overvoltage below withstand voltage of equipment. This phenomenon clearly shows the importance of arresters for lightning overvoltage protection.

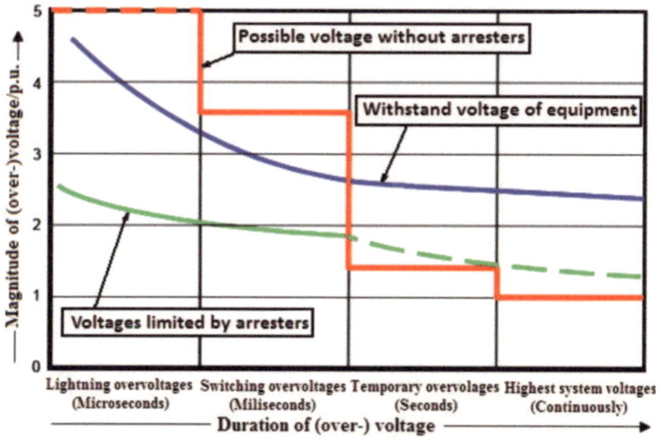

Fig. 1. Schematic representation of the magnitude of overvoltage

In this chapter, signal processing using LabVIEW is presented to separate the resistive leakage current from ZnO arrester leakage current using a novel technique called the Shifted Current Method for the purpose of monitoring the degradation of ZnO surge arrester.

1.1 Zinc oxide surge arrester

The construction of ZnO surge arresters consist of a very simple structure. They basically consist of an insulating housing which is made of porcelain or polymeric material, and the inner active column, composed of the ZnO varistors as shown in Figure 2.

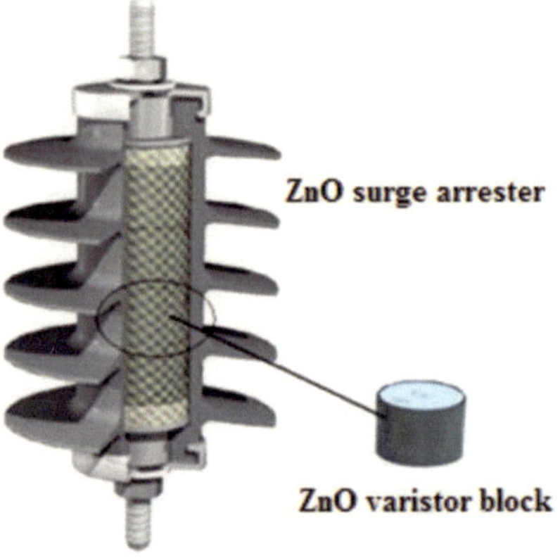

Fig. 2. The cross-section view of a polymeric insulated distribution class ZnO surge arrester

The ZnO varistor block elements are the main component of the ZnO surge arrester. They provide the desired non-linear characteristics and present a strong relation with the temperature (low current range). The non-linear resistivity is an inherent bulk property of the composite ceramic resistor, which consists of mainly ZnO with relatively small amount of several additives of other metal oxides such as $Bi_2 O_3$, CoO_2, MnO3, and Sb_2O_3 (Eda, 1989). These additives essentially determine the electric properties of the block arresters element.

1.2 Voltage current characteristics of ZnO varistor block

The ZnO surge arrester element is composed of high-purity ZnO, which is the major constituent, and also slight amounts of some oxides of bismuth (Bi), cobalt (Co), manganese (Mn), antimony (Sb), and etcetera. These are thoroughly mixed, granulated, formed (pressed into a disc), specially treated to produce high-resistance layers on all sides of the element and finally sintered at a high temperature of more than 1000°C.
The blend ratio of ZnO surge arrester and additives is not constant but is about 9:1 (Kobayashi, 1986). The microstructure of this element is clarified by a secondary electron image taken by EMPA (Electron Probe Micro Analyzer). Figure 3 shows the secondary-electron image of the element. As shown in Figure 3, fine ZnO grains of 1 to 10 µm size can be seen.
The intergranular layer comprises mainly of Bi_2O_3 and spinel ($An_7Sb_2O_{12}$) distributed in the grain boundary. The excellent voltage-current nonlinear characteristics of the element may be attributable to the junction of the ZnO grain and the intergranular layer consisting mainly of Bi_2O_3. While the specific resistivity of ZnO grain is 1 to 10 Ωcm, that of the intergranular layer is as high as 10^{10} Ωcm and therefore almost all of the voltage applied to the element is concentrated on this high-resistivity intergranular layer. This layer possesses such a non ohmic characteristic that its resistance decreases suddenly at a certain voltage as the applied voltage rises.

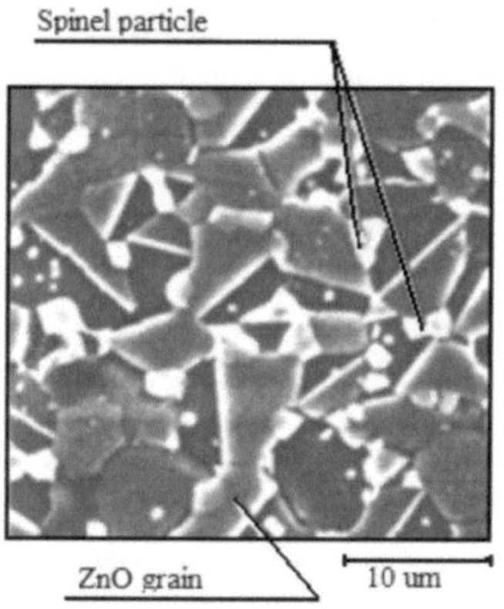

Fig. 3. Secondary-electron image of the ZnO element (Kobayashi, 1986).

The voltage-current characteristic of this layer shows an excellent non linearity throughout the range of 10^{-6} to 10^{4} A. The nonlinearity of this element is attributable to the combination of insulator (intergranular layer) and ZnO grain. Figure 4 shows the V-I characteristics of ZnO element which are divided into three regions, being low current region (I), operating region (II) and high current region (III).

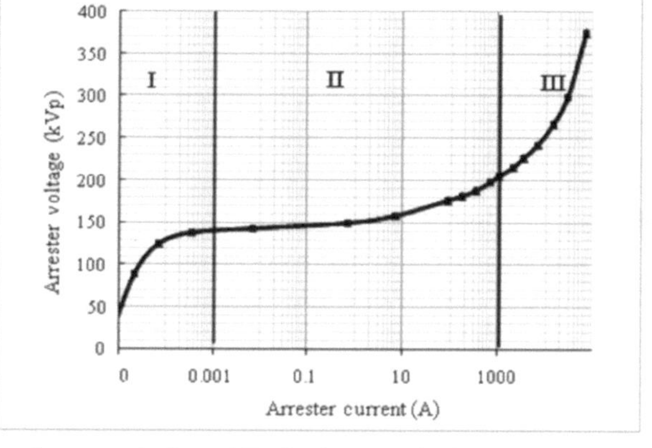

Fig. 4. Voltage-current characteristics of ZnO element (Eda, 1980)

The current density-electric field J-E, relationship in region I is expressed from the physical point of view as follows:

$$J = J_0 \exp\left\{-\frac{\phi - \beta E^0.5}{kT}\right\} \tag{1}$$

where $\beta = (e^{0.75}\, \pi\, \varepsilon\varepsilon_o)$, ϕ is the potential barrier (Â), E the electric field intensity (V/m), k the Boltzmann constant, T the absolute temperature (K), e the electron charge (C), ε_o the vacuum dielectric permittivity, and ε is the relative permittivity of the barrier substance.

Equation 1 clearly shows that, in low current region (I), the characteristics vary considerably with the temperature T. This region is located at a point where the line-frequency voltage is applied in applications for metal oxide arresters and it becomes important to pay attention particularly to the characteristic change with energized time and the temperature dependence.

In operating region (II), the current density is considered to be proportional to a power a of the electric field intensity and is explained by the Fowler-Nordheim tunnel effect:

$$J = J_0 \exp\left(\frac{\gamma}{E}\right) \tag{2}$$

where $\gamma = \frac{4(2m)^{\frac{1}{2}}}{3he}$, m is the electron mass, and h=ĥ/2π , with ĥ being the Planck's constant.

The nonlinearity is generally given by the following experimental expression:

$$I = CV^{\alpha} \tag{3}$$

where α = nonlinear exponent and C is a constant.

In applications of ZnO surge arrester this second region relates to protective characteristics when a lightning impulse current has flowed through the arrester. The greater the value of α, the better is the protective characteristics.

In high current region (III), the resistivity of ZnO grain is dominant and the characteristic is given by:

$$V \approx KI \tag{4}$$

where K is the resistivity of the ZnO grain.

1.3 ZnO arrester model

The non-linear voltage current characteristic of ZnO arrester in low current region (I) is generally represented by the equivalent circuit shown in Figure 5 (Lee, 2005). The resistor R_1 represents the non-linear resistance of the granular layers, where the resistivity ρ changes from 10^8 Ωm for low electric field stress to just below 0.01 Ωm for high stress. The equivalent capacitor C represents the capacitance between the granular layers with relative dielectric constant between 500 and 1200 depending on manufacturing process. R_z is the resistance of the ZnO grains with a resistivity of about 0.01 Ωm. To account for rate of rise effects, an inductor is included as shown in Figure 5. The inductance L is determined by the geometry of the current flow path.

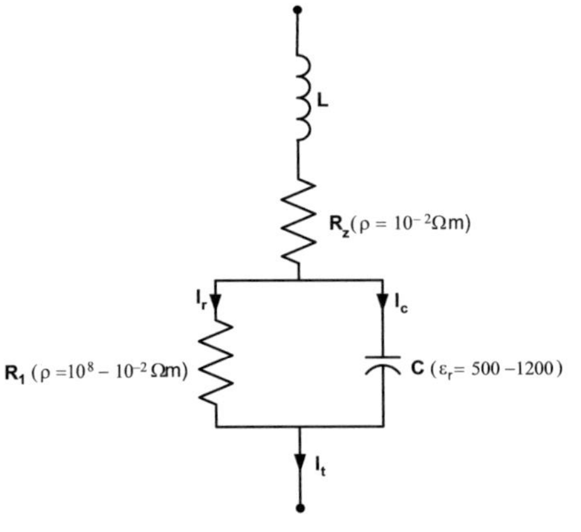

Fig. 5. Equivalent electric circuit of ZnO element

When R_1 and C changes, the capacitive current (I_c), and the resistive current (I_r) also change. The arrester's leakage current, in particular, the third harmonic component of the resistive leakage current, is known to be directly related to the degree of degradation of the ZnO arrester (Lundquist et al., 1990; Spellman et al., 1997; Zhou et al., 1998; Tang et al., 1999). In this work, in order to extract the resistive component from the total leakage current, the shifted current method (Abdul-Malek, et al. 2008) was used. The algorithm to extract the resistive component was implemented using the LabVIEW software.
The proposed method focuses on the ZnO arrester characteristic in low current region (I). In the low current region, R_z is much less than R_1 and the inductance L may be neglected. Therefore, in the continuous operating voltage region, the ZnO surge arrester is modelled as a non-linear resistor with a linear capacitive element in parallel as shown in Figure 6 (Haddad, et al. 1990).

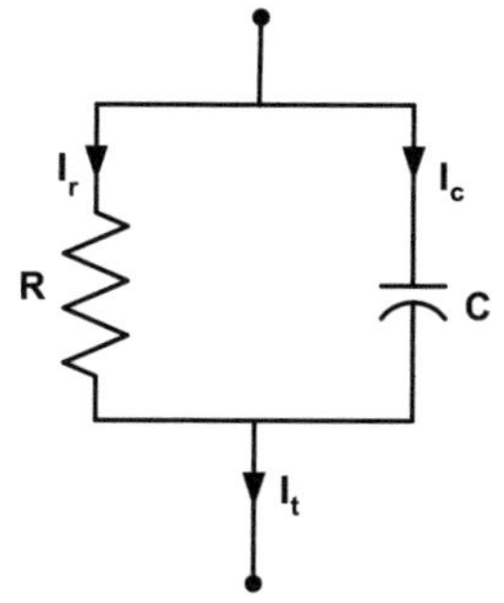

Fig. 6. Simplified equivalent model of a typical ZnO arrester

The total leakage current (I_t) of the arrester is given by a vector sum of a capacitive component (I_c) which does not vary with degradation of the arrester, and the resistive leakage current component (I_r) which varies with the degradation of the surge arrester. Figure 7 shows the typical phasor relationship of all these currents.

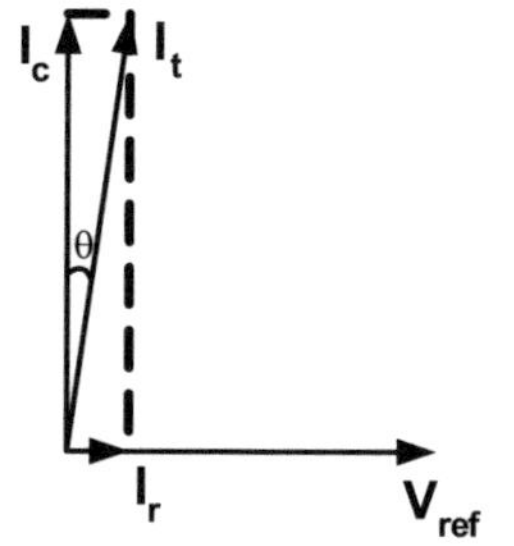

Fig. 7. Vector diagram of I_t, I_c, I_r and reference voltage.

All currents are time dependent, so I_t, I_c and I_r can be written as:

$$I_t(t) = I_r(t) + I_c(t) \tag{5}$$

The resistive current component can be obtained simply by subtracting the capacitive current component from the total leakage current as shown below:

$$I_r(t) = I_t(t) + I_c(t) \tag{6}$$

When system voltage is applied on the surge arrester at continuous operating voltage, about 80% of the rated voltage, the arrester experiences some leakage current. The amplitude of the leakage current depends on the condition of the surge arrester. The leakage current consists of the capacitive and the resistive current component. The typical specific capacitance of ZnO varistor block is 75 pF kV/cm². Typical values of the capacitive current range from 0.5 to 3 mA depending on the varistor diameter. For a complete surge arrester, the capacitive current depends on the number of varistor columns in parallel, the stray capacitances and actual operating voltage.

2. Shifted current method algorithm

One of the most common and straight forward techniques for extracting the resistive leakage current (LC) for the purpose of condition monitoring is the compensation technique (Shirakawa et al., 1998). In order to extract the resistive component from the total leakage current, the voltage across the arrester terminals is usually measured and used as a reference so that, based on the phase difference, the capacitive current component can be established. The resistive component is then obtained by just subtracting the capacitive component from the total leakage current. Other techniques to discriminate the resistive leakage current with the need of voltage as reference for the purpose of arrester condition monitoring have also been reported (Huijia et al., 2009; Kannus et al., 2007; Lira et al., 2007; Wenjun et al., 2008; Vitols et al., 2009).

Traditionally, measurement of total leakage current in substations or other installations was easily done using current shunts or current transformers, but the measurement of applied voltage to obtain the resistive LC make these techniques more appropriate in the laboratory rather than onsite due to the difficulty of measuring the voltage.

In this work, a new technique called the Shifted Current Method (SCM) is presented. This technique does not require knowledge of the applied voltage for the resistive leakage current to be obtained. The method is totally based on the manipulation of the total leakage current waveform. If the total leakage current is given by Equation 7 and the corresponding phase shifted (by a quarter of period) current by Equation 8, then the summation of these two waveforms can be written as Equation 9 below:

$$I_t(t) = I_t \cos(\omega t) \tag{7}$$

$$I_{tshifted}(t) = I_t \cos\left[\omega\left(t - \frac{1}{4f}\right)\right] \tag{8}$$

$$I_{sum}(t) = I_t\left[\cos(\omega t) + \cos\left\{\omega\left(t - \frac{1}{4f}\right)\right\}\right] \tag{9}$$

where $I_t(t)$ is the total leakage current, $I_{tshifted}$ is the shifted total leakage current (by a quarter of period of waveform), and I_{sum} is the summation of the total leakage current and the shifted current wave form. By signal manipulation technique, from this summation current, the capacitive component of total leakage current can be determined, and thereafter the resistive component of the leakage current can also be obtained by subtracting the capacitive component from the total leakage current.

Based on the above proposed technique, the algorithm to separate the resistive leakage current from the total leakage current was built. The algorithm for the shifted current method could be summarized as follows. Firstly, the arrester total leakage current is measured, and then a new waveform is introduced by shifting the measured arrester total LC by a quarter period of its operating frequency. Next, both the two total leakage currents are summed together and their peak time determined. The amplitude of summed total leakage currents at time T_P, where T_P is the time corresponding to the peak value of the summation waveform, is the peak value of the resistive current. The peak time obtained is used to determine the peak time of the capacitive current component which is equal to a quarter of period before or after the peak time of the resistive component. The peak value of the capacitive component is also determined from the original leakage current waveform. The capacitive leakage current is then generated based on the peak time, the peak value and the frequency detected. Finally, the resistive leakage current is obtained by subtracting the capacitive leakage current from the total leakage current. The block diagram of the algorithm for calculating the resistive leakage current using the shifted current method is shown in Figure 8.

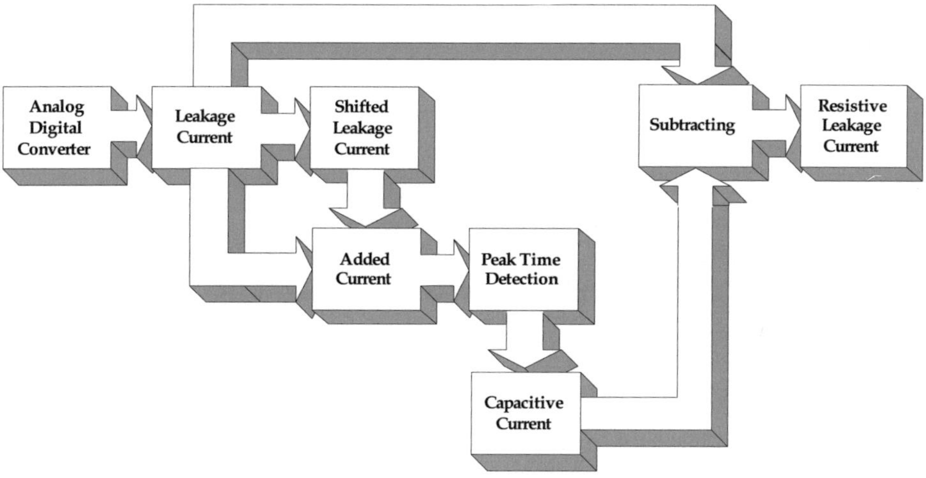

Fig. 8. Block diagram of the shifted current method algorithm

3. Implementation of method in LabVIEW

The shifted current method was implemented in NI LabVIEW 8.5 software. Each block was created and after that combined together to build an arrester monitoring system based on the SCM algorithm. The subsequent subsections explain the implementation of the SCM in LabVIEW.

3.1 LabVIEW-picoscope interface

Picoscope is a device that resembles the functions of an oscilloscope but runs on computer. Usually, Picoscope comes with software that turns it into a PC oscilloscope. In order to connect with LabVIEW, a VI (virtual instrument) interface was developed. LabVIEW Picoscope VI program links the Picoscope with LabVIEW software. The block diagram of the program is shown in Figure 9. The interface indicator shows a graph in front panel of the block diagram as shown in Figure 10.

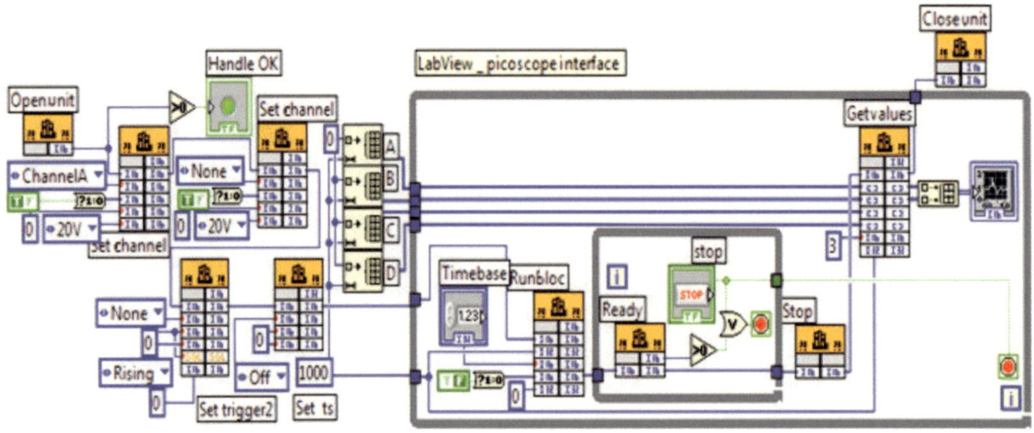

Fig. 9. NI LabVIEW-Picoscope VI interface block diagram

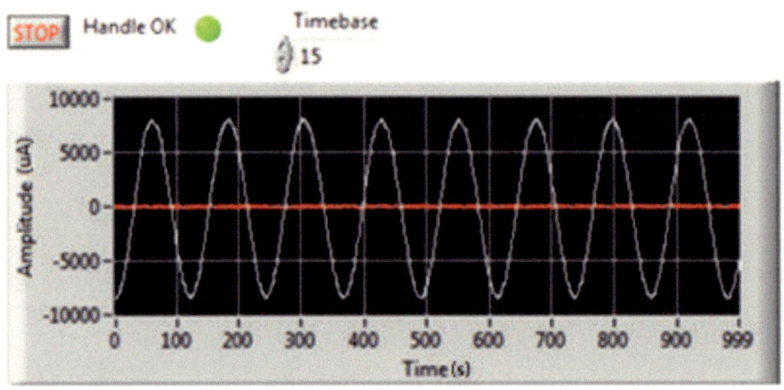

Fig. 10. Front panel of NI LabVIEW-Picoscope interface

3.2 Frequency detector block

The frequency detector block is a VI in the LabVIEW library as shown in Figure 11, used to detect the frequency, amplitude and phase of the surge arrestor total leakage current being measured. Figure 12 shows a typical output of the block in the form of front panel with the measured frequency, current and phase.

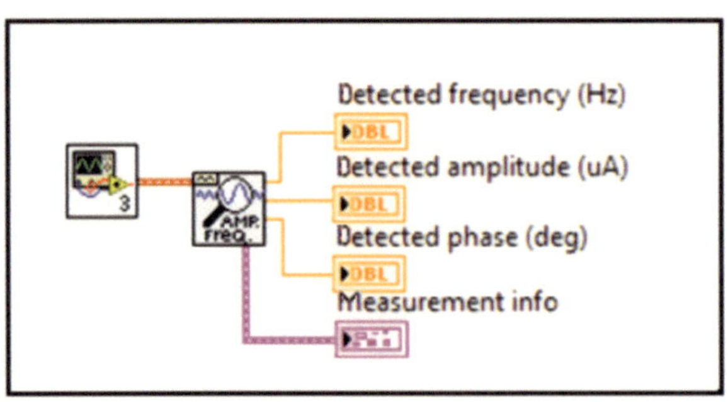

Fig. 11. Function of NI LabVIEW library for detecting frequency

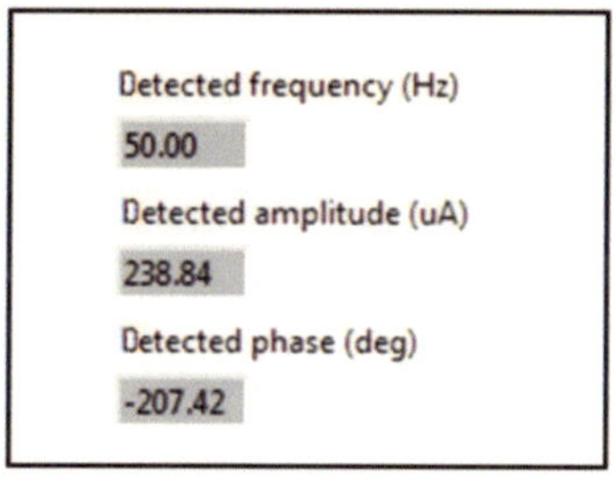

Fig. 12. NI LabVIEW front panel of frequency detector

3.3 Shifted signal block

This block was used to shift the total leakage current. In this block the total leakage current was generated and shifted to a quarter period of frequency. The frequency was detected using the frequency detector. It was then used as an input to the shifted signal block to shift the leakage current as shown in Figure 14. The time t to shift the total leakage current signal is given by

$$t = \frac{1}{4f} \tag{10}$$

where f is the signal frequency.

The frequency for this simulation is 50 Hz, so using Equation 10 the time to shift the current is 0.005 second. The signal was changed to array and shifted using NI LabVIEW Y[i-n].vi function as shown in Figure 13. The block diagram and front panel to shift the signal are shown in Figure 14 and Figure 15 respectively.

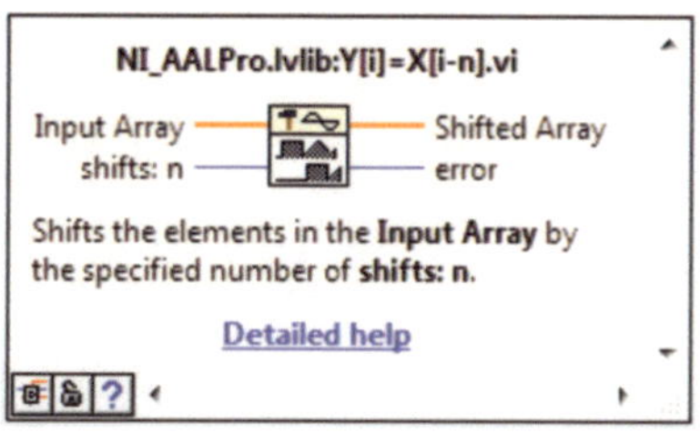

Fig. 13. Function of NI LabVIEW library for shifted array

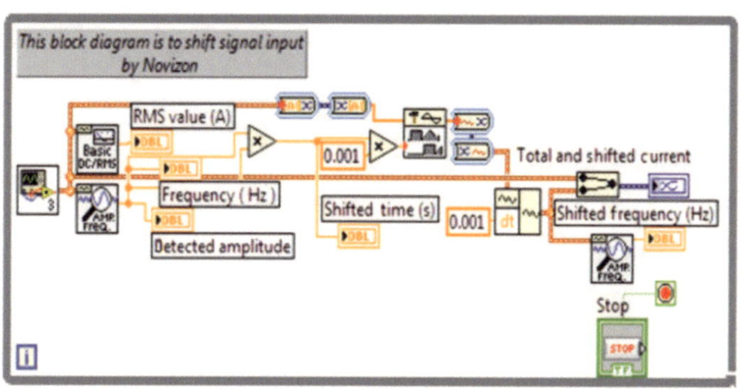

Fig. 14. The LabVIEW current shifting block diagram

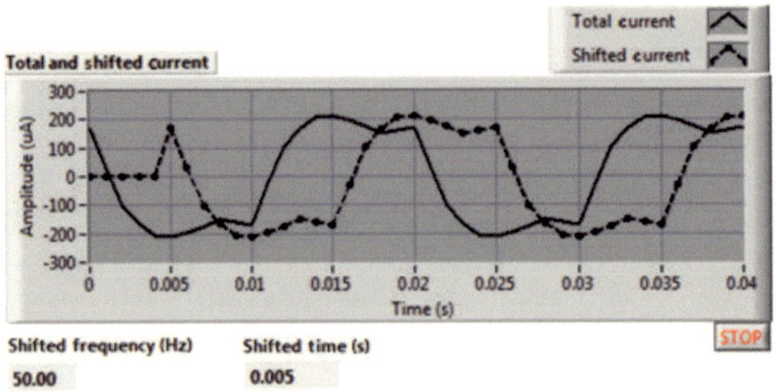

Fig. 15. Front panel of the current shifting

3.4 Adding signal block

The total leakage current and the shifted current were added using the adding block as shown in Figure 16. The result of the summation can be seen in Figure 17. The adding block is a simple block which was also available in LabVIEW library.

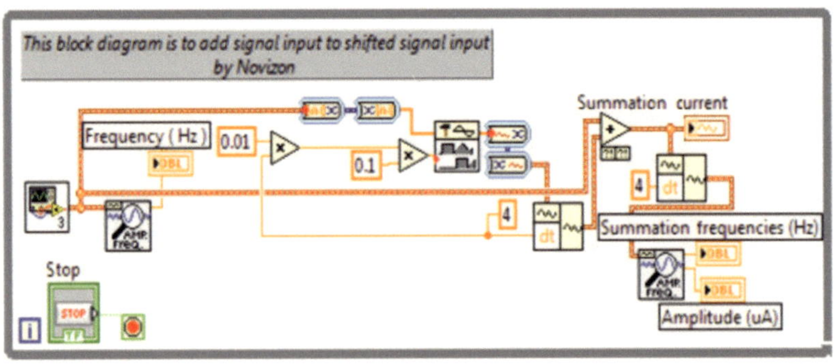

Fig. 16. LabVIEW block diagram of added signals

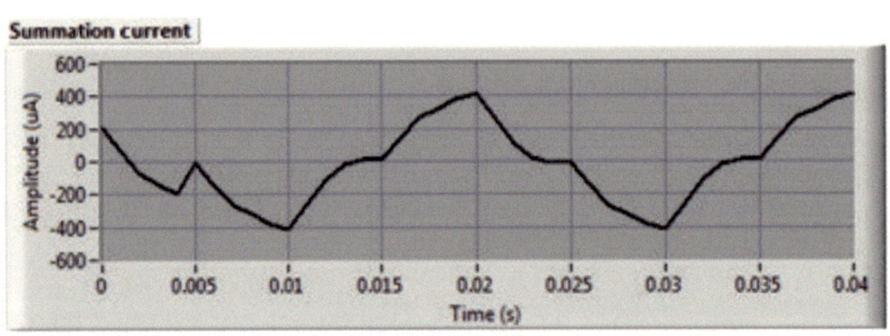

Fig. 17. Front panel of summed total LC signals

3.5 Peak time detector block

The peak of the summed total LC currents was detected using the peak detector shown in Figure 18. The time T_p was also detected. The block diagram of the peak signal detection consists of the peak amplitude and the corresponding time detection. Figure 19 shows the block diagram while Figure 20 shows the front panel indicating the peak and value of the parameter displayed on the front panel.

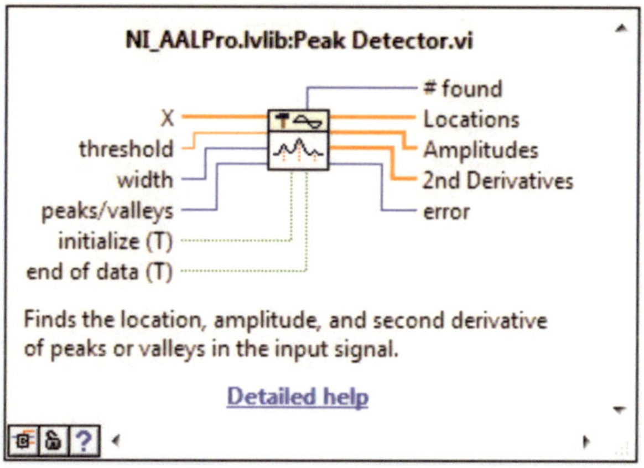

Fig. 18. Function of NI LabVIEW library for peak detector

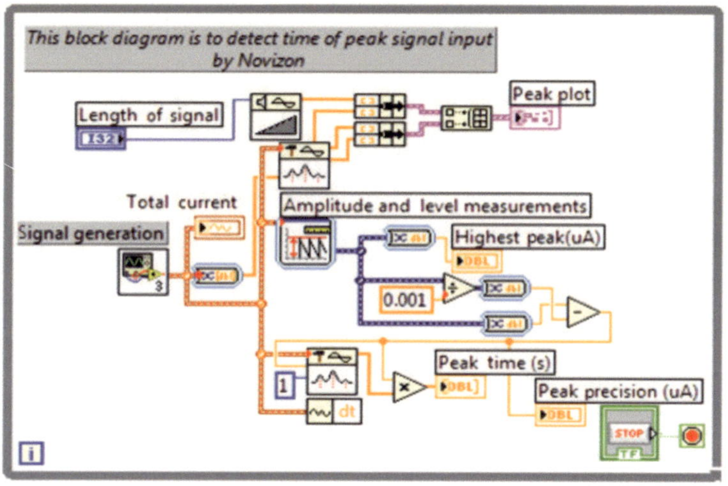

Fig. 19. LabVIEW diagram of peak detector

In the front panel, some easy-to-read parameters were also displayed. The parameters include the highest peak, the precision and the peak time. All parameters will be used in the xy determination block.

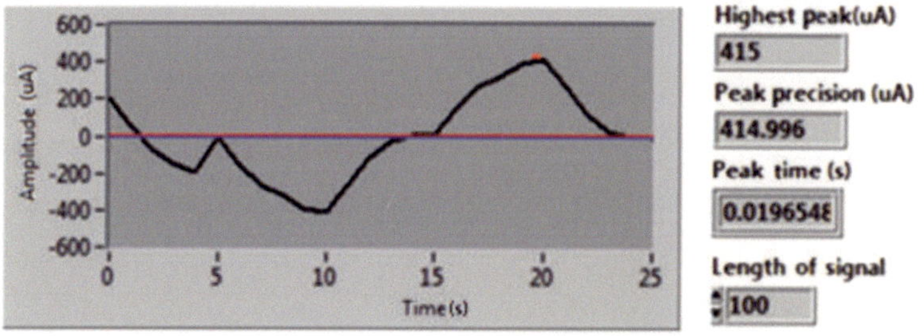

Fig. 20. Front panel of peak time detector

3.6 XY determination block

The peak value of the capacitive LC corresponds to the peak value of the summed total LC when a quarter of period of signal frequency is added to T_p. To do so, after the peak time T_p of the summed total LC was obtained, the value was then added with a quarter of period of the signal frequency. The XY determination block was then used to determine the peak value at that instant of time. Figure 21 shows the xy determination block.

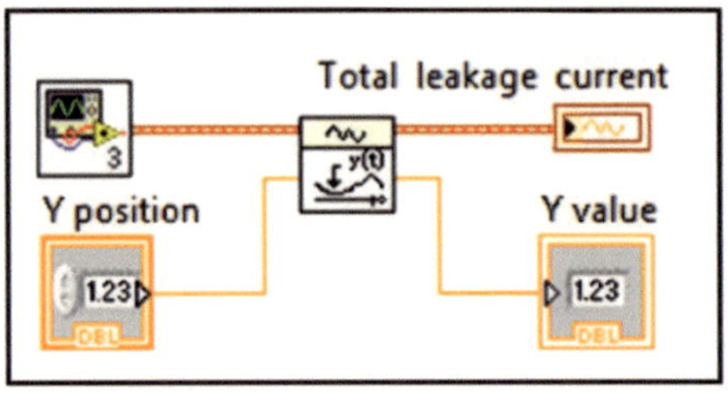

Fig. 21. LabVIEW diagram of XY determination

3.7 Signal generation block

After detecting the amplitude of the capacitive component of the total LC which corresponds to the y value of the XY determination block, together with the frequency of the total LC, a signal generator block shown in Figure 22 was used to generate the capacitive LC. The y value, the frequency and phase, were the inputs to this block and the output was a sinusoidal waveform as shown in Figure 23 and Figure 24.

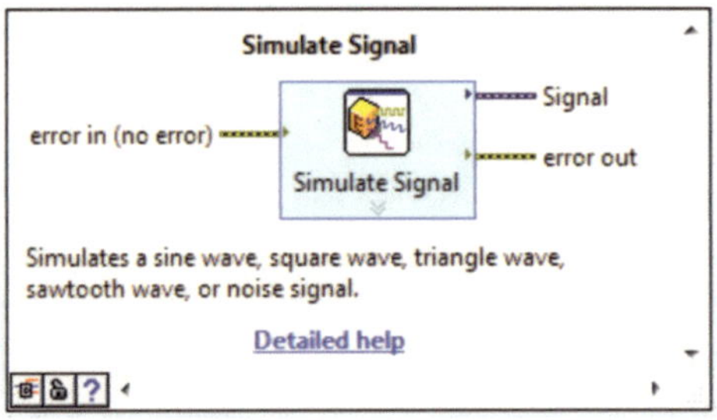

Fig. 22. Function of NI LabVIEW library for simulate signal

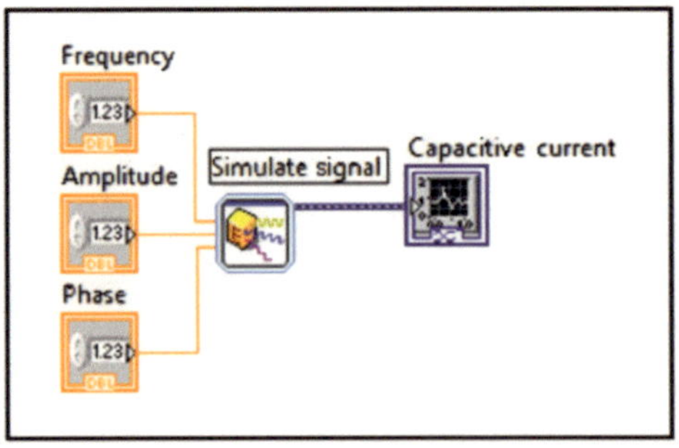

Fig. 23. LabVIEW diagram of capacitive signal generation

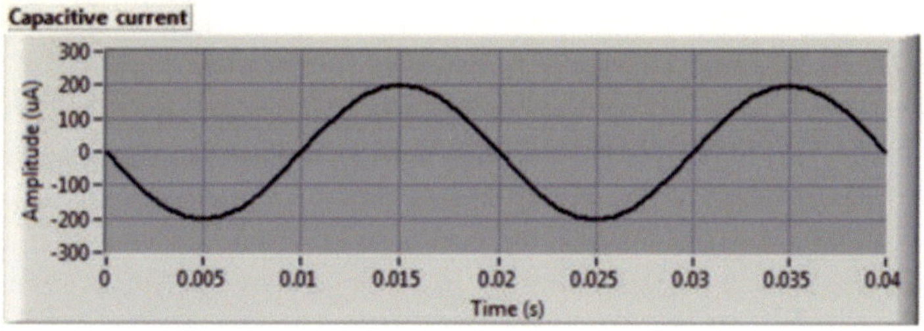

Fig. 24. Front panel of capacitive generation block

3.8 Resistive current extraction block

With the generation of the capacitive current obtained from the total LC, the resistive LC can be obtained by subtracting the total LC from the capacitive signal obtained using the signal generating block. This was achieved by simply using the LabVIEW subtracting block. Figure 25 shows the complete block diagram of this process. Figure 26 shows that capacitive and total leakage currents.

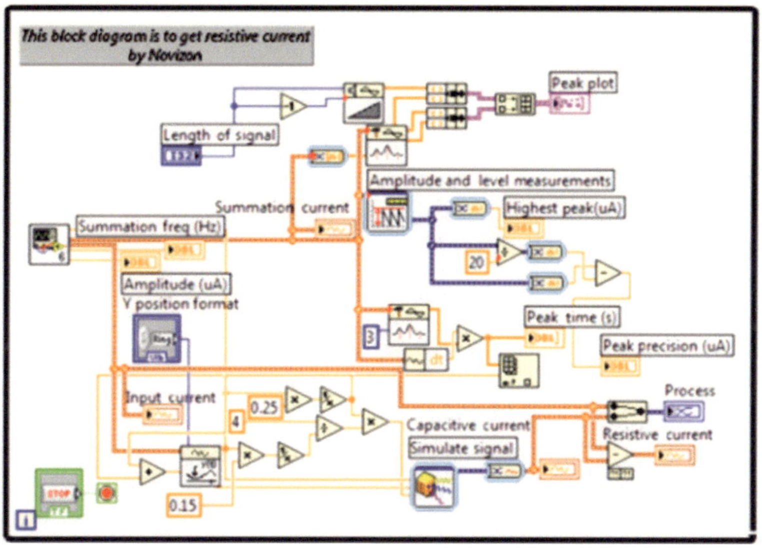

Fig. 25. LabVIEW block diagram of capacitive current discrimination

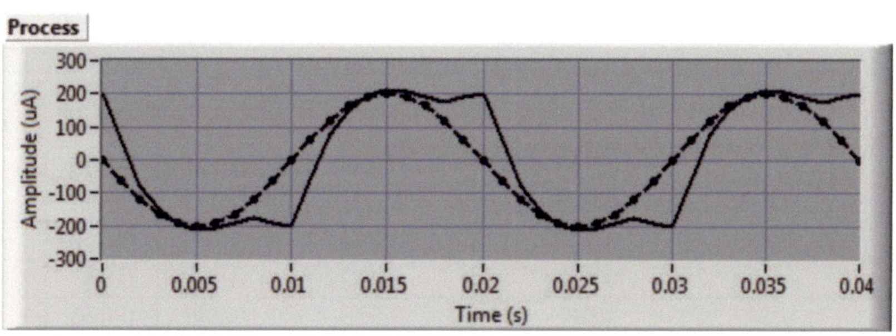

Fig. 26. Capacitive and total leakage currents

The result of this process which is the resistive component of the total leakage current can be seen in Figure 27. This resistive current contains harmonics because of the non linear characteristic of the ZnO material as well as the ageing effects. The third order harmonic of this resistive leakage current could be extracted using the Fast Fourier Transform (FFT).

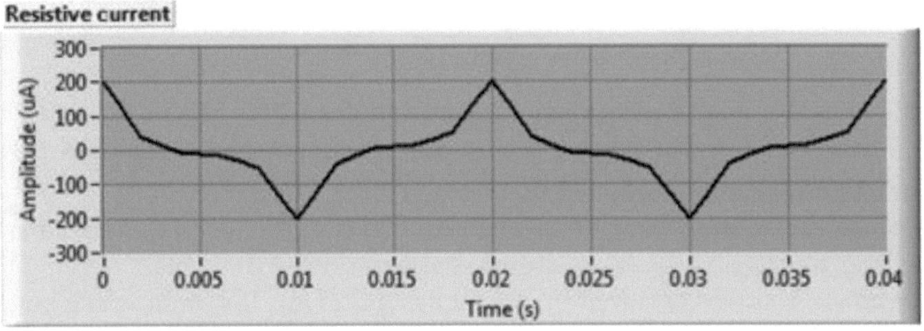

Fig. 27. The resistive leakage current

3.9 ZnO surge arrester monitoring system

All blocks which have been described above were combined to give a complete surge arrester monitoring system. The complete block diagram is shown in Figure 28.

4. Experimental results

Experimental work was conducted on a new zinc oxide (ZnO) arrester block in the laboratory. The ZnO arrestor block had a diameter and thickness of 40 mm and 21 mm respectively. Its rated voltage and discharge currents were 3 kV_{rms} and 10 kA. The arrester block's maximum continuous operating voltage (MCOV) was 2.55 kV_{rms}.
The total leakage current of the arrester block was measured using a 10 kΩ resistive shunt (power resistor) and the voltage using a capacitive divider with a ratio 686:1.
The total leakage current of surge arrester block or element that has not deteriorated will be dominated by capacitive LC thus having small resistive LC. When the zinc oxide element or block starts to experience degradation, the resistive LC gradually increases. In this study, for the zinc oxide block sample to experience increased resistive LC, voltages above the MCOV were applied (Shirakawa et al., 1998). The applied voltage was increased from 1 kV to 3.5 kV in steps of 0.5 kV. The results of measurement are presented in Table 1 and Figure 29 shows the graphical result for 3 kV displayed by the LabVIEW program.

Applied Voltage (kV)	I_T (mA)	Resistive Current (mA)	Leakage Current Harmonics			
			Fundamental	Third	Fifth	Seventh
1	0.150	0.065	0.053	0.021	0.005	0.003
2	0.165	0.075	0.061	0.032	0.006	0.005
2.5	0.288	0.137	0.094	0.059	0.032	0.018
3	0.53	0.458	0.512	0.117	0.063	0.041
3.5	0.707	0.512	0.558	0.239	0.076	0.054

Table 1. Measurement result using ZnO surge arrester monitoring system

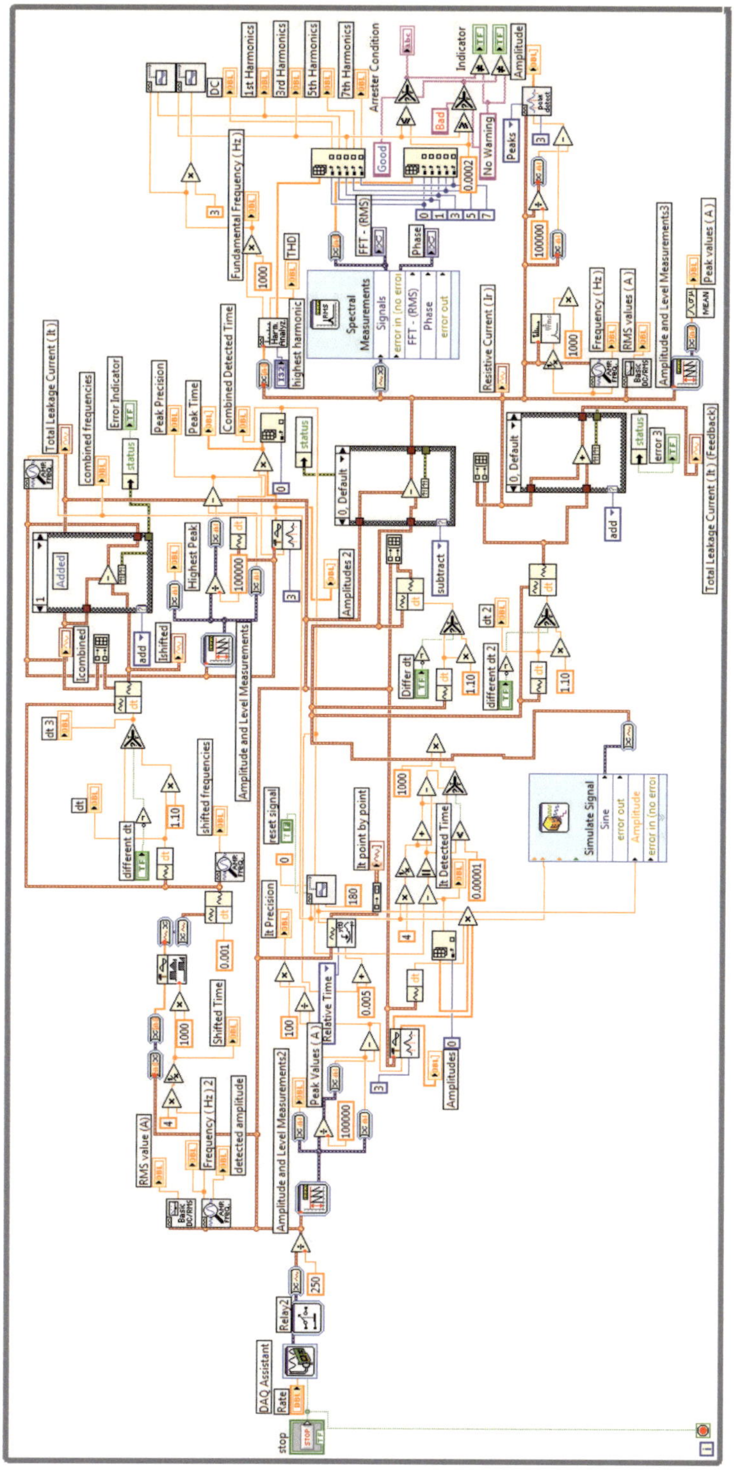

Fig. 28. LabVIEW block diagram of ZnO arrester monitoring system

It can be seen from Table 1 that the resistive current of the arrester block had low harmonics within nominal operating voltage (1 - 2.5 kV), suggesting it had not undergone degradation. As the voltage was increased beyond MCOV, the resistive LC as well as the LC harmonics especially the third harmonic increased exponentially indicating degradation.

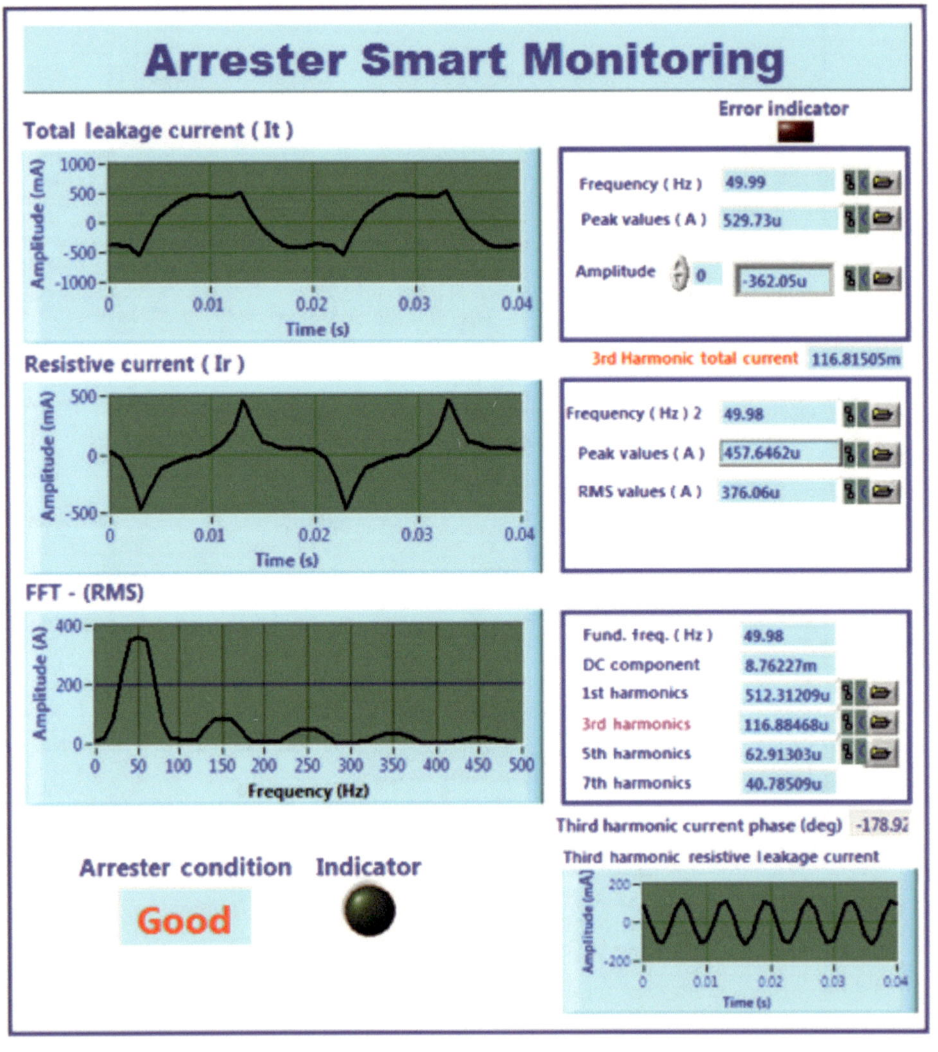

Fig. 29. Front panel of ZnO surge arrester monitoring system (applied voltage 3kV)

5. Conclusion

The new shifted current method technique to determine ZnO ageing was successfully implemented in LabVIEW software and proven useful for on-site measurement purposes. Field tests on the whole measuring and analysing system was successfully carried out. The developed program provides not only convenience in system management but also provides a user-friendly interface.

6. Acknowledgement

The authors would like to thank Ministry of Science, Technology and Innovation (MOSTI) Malaysia and Research Management Centre (RMC), Universiti Teknologi Malaysia, for the financial and management support.

7. References

Abdul-Malek Z. et al. (2008). A New Method to Extract The Resistive Component Of The Metal Oxide Surge Arrester Leakage Current, Proceedings of Power and Energy Conference (PECon), Johor Bahru, Malaysia, December 2008.

Abdul-Malek Z. et al. (2008). Portable Device to Extract Resistive Component of The Metal Oxide Surge Arrester Leakage Current, Proceedings of Australian Universities Power Engineering Conference (AUPEC), Australia, December 2008.

Eda, K. et al. (1980). Degradation Mechanism Of Nonohmic Zinc Oxide Ceramics, J. Appl. Phys., vol. 51, no. 5, pp. 2678–2684

Eda, K. et al. (1989). Zinc Oxide Varistors, IEEE Electrical Insulation Magazine; Vol. 5; No. 6; Nov-Dec 1989, pp. 28-41.

Haddad, A. et al (1991). Characterization of ZnO Surge Arrester Elements With Direct and Power Frequency Voltages, *IEE Science, Measurement and Technology*, vol. 137, No. 5, September 1991, pp. 265 - 272.

Huijia, L. et al. (2010). Development of Tester of the Resistive Leakage Current of Metal Oxide Arrester, Proceedings of Asia Pacific Power Engineering Conference, Chengdu, China, March 2010.

Kannus, K. et al. (2007). Laboratory Investigations of the Electrical Performance of Ice-covered Insulators and a Metal Oxide Surge Arrester, *IEEE Trans. Diel. Elect. Insul.*, Vol. 14, No. 6, December 2007, pp. 1357 - 1372.

Kobayashi, M. et al. (1986). Metal Oxide Surge Arrester, IEEE Transactions on Electrical Insulation Vol. EI-21 No.6, December, 1986, pp. 989 – 996.

Lee, B.H. and Sung, M.K, (2005). A New On-Line Leakage Current Monitoring System of ZnO Surge Arresters, *Journal of Material Science and Engineering B*, Vol.119,Issue 1, No. 15, May 2005, pp. 13 - 18.

Lira, J. G. A. et al. (2007). ZnO Surge Arresters Diagnosis Using Microcontroller, Proceedings of Instrumentation and Measurement Technology Conference Warsaw, Poland, May 2007.

Lundquist, J. et al. (1990). New Method For Measurement Of The Resistive Leakage Currents Of Metal-Oxide Surge Arresters In Service, IEEE Transactions on Power Delivery, Vol. 5, No. 4, November 1990, pp. 1811 - 1822.

Spellman, C.A. et al. (1997), A Technique for on-Line Monitoring of ZnO Surge Arrester, Proceedings of the 10th International Symposium on High Voltage Engineering, Canada, August 1997.

Tang, J. et al. (1999). Study of Multi-Coefficient Compensation Method on Resistive Current Passing Trough MOA, *High Voltage Engineering*, Vol.25, No.1, March 1999.

Vitols, A. P. et al. (2009). Condition Monitoring of Post Insulators and Surge Arresters, Proceedings of IEEE Electrical Insulation Conference, Montreal, Canada, May 2009.

Wenjun, Z. et al (2008). Design of on-line monitoring device for MOA used in 10kV distribution network, Proceedings of International Conference on Condition Monitoring and Diagnosis, Beijing, China, April 2008.

Zhou, L. et al. (1998). A Study on Variable Coefficient Compensation Method and Performance Diagnosis of Metal Oxide Arrester's Operating State Detection, Electric Technology Transaction, Vol. 13, No.6.

Part 5

Practical Applications

13

Remote Instrumentation Laboratory for Digital Signal Processors Training

Sergio Gallardo, Federico J. Barrero and Sergio L. Toral
University of Seville, Spain

1. Introduction

The development of computing and networking applications based on Internet has opened a new way to understand control and instrumentation systems. Information and communication technologies make possible the use of telecommunication networks, such as the Internet, to design remote applications applied to different fields, such as, telecontrol, measurement instrumentation, telemedicine, embedded systems, teaching and so on. Furthermore, remote control of measurement instrumentation for real experiments via the Internet is a growing topic of interest for many researchers (Chirico et al. 2005). This is especially noticeable in Digital Signal Processors (DSP) training, where practical training is absolutely essential to assure good knowledge transfer to educate good professionals (Hercog et al., 2007).

A growing interest has been experienced on recent decades in the development of DSP-based devices. DSP technology is commonly employed nowadays in devices such as mobile phones, multimedia computers, video and DVB recorders, CD and MP3 players, hard disc drive controllers, modems, and will soon replace analog circuitry in TV sets, telephones and other circuits (Poornachandra and Sasikala, 2010). In fact, the sales of DSP devices exceed the sale of general-purpose microprocessors by almost 10:1 (Hong et al., 2004).

The architecture of a DSP chip is designed to carry out operations incredibly fast, processing up to tens of millions of samples per second, to provide real-time performance, that is, the ability to process a signal "live" as it is samples and then output the processed signal, for example, to a loud speaker or video display. All the practical applications DSP mentioned earlier, such as disc drives and mobile phones, demand real-time operation and the design of such DSP solutions requires to the professionals a concurrent knowledge of signal processing methods and technology (Poornachandra and Sasikala, 2010). This fact has promoted the inclusion of DSP and DSP devices in the electronic engineering undergraduate curriculum. This tendency also appears in Instrumentation and Measurement courses. High quality DSP based instrumentation equipment has proliferated during the last years. Furthermore, one of the most demanded job profiles in the Information and Communications Technology (ICT) sector is related to the design of DSP applications, as it is claimed in the Career Space initiative (Office for Official Publications of the European Communities, 2001; Toral et al, 2006). The DSP Applications Designer is involved in requirement studies, simulations and performance analysis, and participates in the design and optimization of algorithms for signal modulation, detection and channel coding/decoding, compression and decompression, and implementation with digital signal processors. For instance, high-quality DSP based equipments have proliferated during the last years. Most of these equipments are based in the popular Texas Instruments TMS320C6711 or TMS320C6713 DSP devices and their starter kits, DSK6711 or DSK6713.

In this context there have been important changes in engineering education, especially in electrical and computer engineering (ECE) education, both in terms of content (curriculum) and what it is taught or how it is taught (delivery of material), (Carleyet al., 2000; Felder et al., 1998; Milliken et al., 2002; Roppel, 2002; Taylor et al., 2003; Wilson et al., 2000).

On the one hand, emphasis in the electrical engineering field has shifted significantly to the design of digital systems. On the other hand, technology that is around everything we do, has taken a place in the classroom and hypermedia tools, web-based educational support, simulation environments, and so on, have dramatically increased, (Aedo et al., 2000; Almeida et al., 2003; Bagui, 1998, Conole et al., 2004; Christian et al., 2001; Metzger et al., 2003; Pahl, 2003)

In this context, Telecommunication Engineering Studies at the University of Seville was first organized in 1991. The DSP course is an intermediate undergraduate digital electronic subject based on the design of advanced embedded digital systems and DSPs. The lack of enough lab work in the original organization motivated a change in the studies in 1998, searching for an increment in the practical work. This fact, together with the necessity of improving the teaching methodology in classrooms with more than 300 students per year, was the starting point to develop new teaching methods using computer-based educational tools (Martinez-Torres et al., 2005). The new European Area for Higher Education and ECTS (European Credit Transfer System) will shortly modify the teaching and learning processes, (Communiqué of Higher Education, 2003; Joint declaration, 1999) and the creation of this new area supposes a complete turnabout in the teaching and learning processes. Until now, these processes have been driven by the teaching activity, adapting the learning processes to the lecturer profile. But in the near future, the teaching and learning processes will be focused on the learning activity and on the learner profile. As a consequence, it is necessary to know the learner preferences and the variables with a significant relevance in the learner behaviour.

Learning through computer-mediated environments will contributed to create this new reality and novelty learning methodologies based on the active roll of students (Aedo et al., 2000; Bagui, 1998; Pahl, 2003; Schodorf et al., 1996; Taylor et al., 2003; Wilson et al., 2000).

Although these computer-based training solutions are satisfactory to support systems for subjects with a strong theoretical component, face-to-face lab learning methodologies continue playing an important role in subjects with an important experimental load (Bose, 1994; Felder et al., 1998; Milliken et al., 2002; Roppel, 2000). However, the cost in time and money required for planning and implementing scientific laboratories is outside the scope of many institutions. It can be noted that the high number of students enrolled in subjects with a strong practical component or the insufficient economic resources are the main restrictions for face-to-face laboratory training methodologies (Guimarães et al., 2003; Sánchez et al., 2002). This is the case of DSP learning.

Therefore, limitations of a traditional laboratory structure are well-known: - high price of the equipment and devices under test; - small physical space available inside the laboratory rooms, - limiting the number of users at a time; laboratory availability limited to office hours, and so on (Chirico et al. 2005; Davoli et al., 2006). Remote laboratories allow for much more efficient use of laboratory equipment and give users the opportunity to conduct experiments from the comfort of an Internet browser (Davoli et al., 2006).

Within this context, the idea of a remote and interactive laboratory arises from the necessity of a suitable educational tool capable of supporting a face-to-face laboratory training methodology. It would complement, but not remove, the student access to the traditional lab, with the possibility of being used for distance and asynchronous education. The amount of students' practical work is then increased (students have the possibility of accessing DSP boards and electronic equipments at any timetable and outside the laboratory building), without increasing available resources (lab equipments).

Web-based remote and interactive laboratories to be implemented can be classified into two categories based on the nature of the final equipment (or user access in an experiment): - Remote simulations, based on the possibility of simulating the dynamic behaviour of a system, but non physical hardware under test is used and, - remotely accessed equipment, based on real equipment which can be remotely handled and controlled by a user interface. Remote simulations support a whole gamut of capabilities and offer several advantages, such as low cost of implementation, absence of real equipment, easiness of integration (Spanias, A. et al., 2005). Nevertheless, remote simulations are not adequate when real-system control is required such as embedded systems control (Hercog et al., 2007) and DSP programming. The complexity of DSP internal architecture makes almost impossible the simulation of DSP internal blocks and functionalities.

Although many remote labs and e-learning tools can be found in the literature (Canfora et al., 2004; Casini et al., 2003; Ferrero et al., 2003; Kikuchi et al., 2004), it is worth mentioning the lack of in depth scientific studies devoted to validate this kind of tools. The majority of them are usually limited to one-dimensional post-training perceptions of learners (Abdel-Qader, 2003), for instance, "happy sheets" which ask learners to rate how satisfied they were with their overall learning experience. A remote instrumentation laboratory named eDSPLab has been implemented and recently used (academic years 2004-2005 and 2005-2006). As opposed to these previous approaches, this paper considers eDSPLab as a new technology for users, applying an information system theory called Technology Acceptance Model (TAM) as a novel method to validate its use (Lee et al., 2003). Using TAM, the causal antecedents or external variables which have a significant influence in the use of eDSPLab are identified. The obtained results show the external variables motivating the use of eDSPLab, allowing the inclusion of the remote lab in a wider e-learning tool based on a Learning Management System (LMS) to obtain an improved performance. This new e-learning tool combines a large variety of commercial software packages and Web oriented languages (Shockwave™, Macromedia Director™, HTML —Hypertext Markup Language—, VRML —Virtual Reality Modeling Language—), which improve the detected effectiveness of eDSPLab. All the desirable features of multimedia systems with utility in educational environments have been applied according to the European Higher Education Area (EHEA) and European Credit Transfer System (ECTS), devoting particular attention to the interactive features and their impact in the learning process.

In order to prove the benefit of eDSPLab, non-opinion-based assessment of outcomes is also provided and End User Quality of Service, defined as the quality perceived by the end user, is expressed in terms of satisfaction and technical terms. Objective and subjective

measurement parameters, as network performance parameters, user test, listening and interviews are proposed and employed to characterize system performance.
In short, based on these fundamental aspects, a remote measurement laboratory based on LabVIEW has been projected and implemented. It provides the users with access to remote measurement instrumentation and DSP embedded board, delivering different activities related to digital signal processing and measurement experiments. Novelty aspects of the proposed solution are the integration of an embedded system based on a DSP with measurement instrumentation for remote training and both integrates on a Web based environment which provides remote access to control different didactic setups related to DSP devices and their applications is shown. The environment, named eDSPLab, allows asynchronous and off-campus learning, and avoids some of the problems caused by the high number of enrolled students and the insufficient economical resources, the advantages of the LMS which integrates workflow and data management and tools for user collaboration and includes the ability to track very detailed information about individual learners, making the system highly beneficial to large online environments and a powerful server monitor to closely monitor the remote measurement laboratory, Fig. 1.

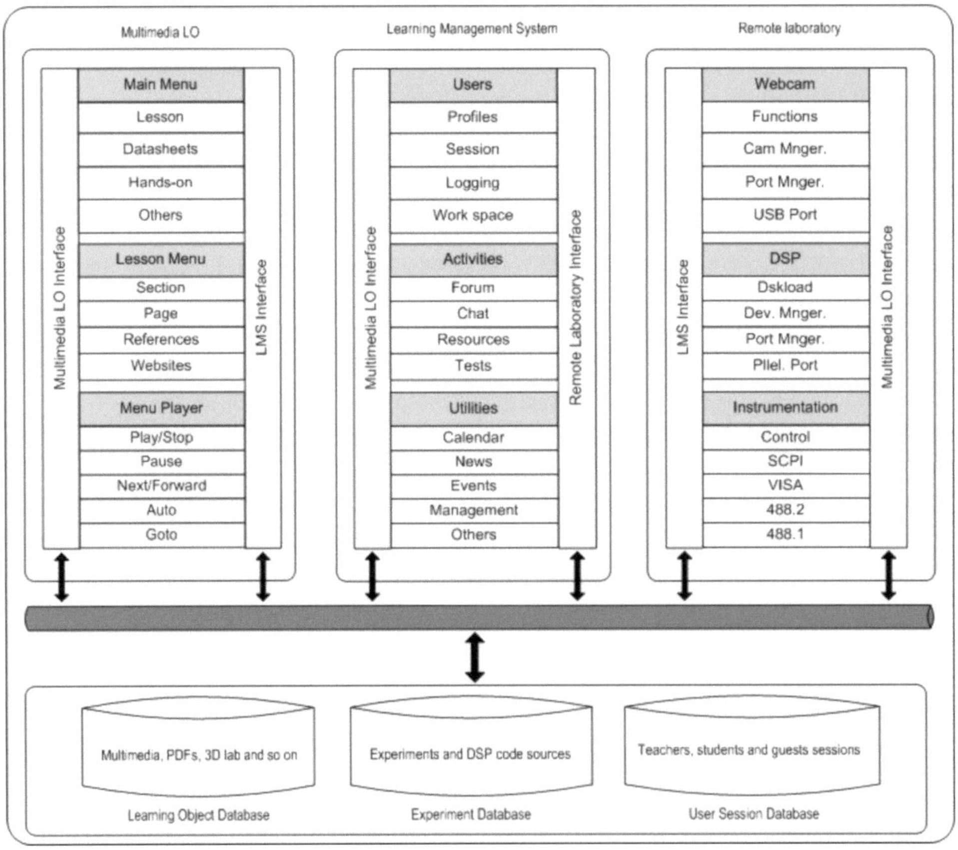

Fig. 1. Projected Web environment: Measurement laboratory based on LabVIEW, Learning Management System based on Moodle and Macromedia Director Learning objects.

2. Laboratory architecture and experimental setup

eDSPlab has been successfully implemented in an Advanced Microprocessor course and in an Instrumentation and Measurement course at the Telecommunication Engineering degree at the Electronic Engineering Department of the University of Seville, Spain, Fig. 2. It has been designed for real lab work using the DSP starter kits without a physical attendance to the real lab. Students interact with the DSK boards using the Web and eDSPLab for debugging real DSP experiences in the physical lab.

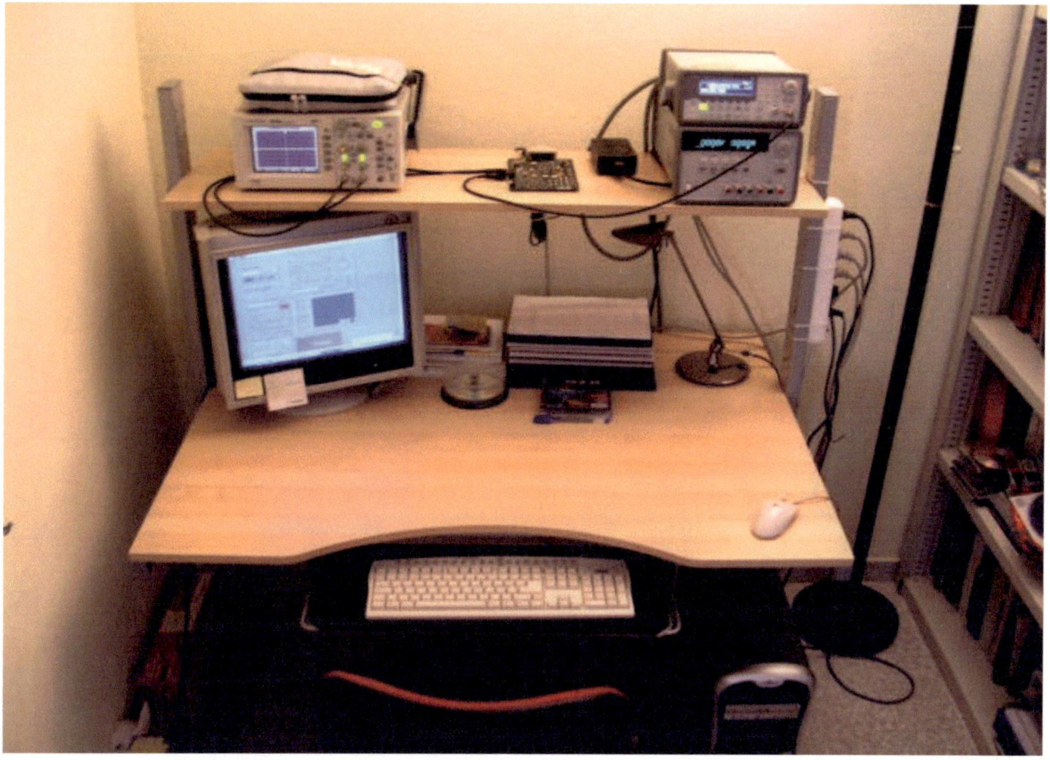

Fig. 2. eDSPlab test bench overview.

Both, the Advanced Microprocessor course and the Instrumentation and Measurement course are taught as part of the students' curricula in order to provide some DSP professional skills and measurement instrumentation skills, respectively. In this way, students are trained for eventual industrial work in companies using DSP technologies in their products. The real lab attendance is complemented by offering a distance and asynchronous learning methodology. In groups (2 to 3 students), students must implement predefined DSP exercises started in the real lab and completed using eDSPLab. The evaluation of the practical work (notice that the mark for the practical work has a contribution of 25% on the overall qualification) depends on the accomplishment of specific lab exercises at the end of the academic year.
eDSPlab architecture can be divided into three elements, the measurement instrumentation and embedded DSP board, the server framework, which is the core of the remote laboratory, and the client side, with thin client or fat client possibilities, Fig. 3.

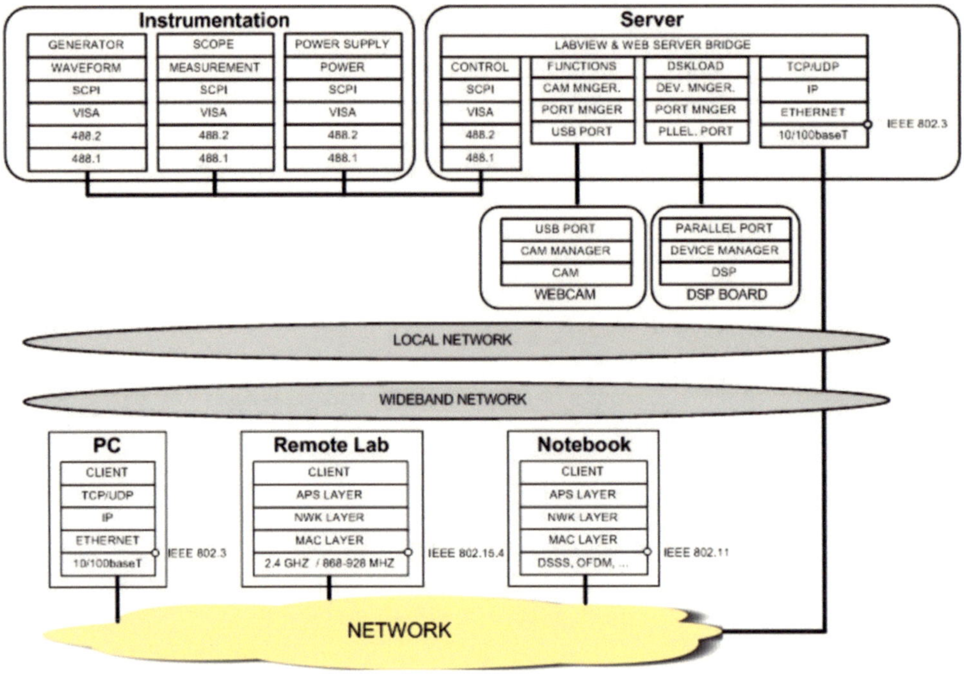

Fig. 3. eDSPlab architecture.

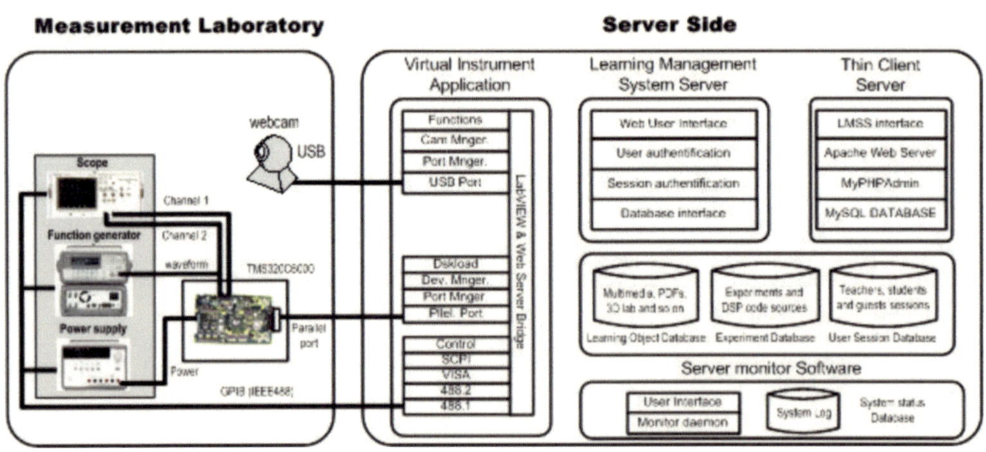

Fig. 4. Server architecture.

Furthermore, the server architecture can be structured into four components, Fig. 4:

- The Virtual Instrumentation Application (VIA). The VIA manages both, the flow of data between GPIB devices (an oscilloscope, a power supply, and an arbitrary waveform generator), and the DSK (Developer Starter Kit) communication, to load the remote user binary code onto the embedded device or DSK.
- The Thin Client Server (TCS). The TCS manages the thin client-server interaction. The thin client depends primarily on the central server for processing activities, and mainly focuses on conveying input and output between a user and a remote server.

- The Learning Management System Server (LMSS). The LMSS interfaces to users via Web and manage learning interventions. It provides Learner self-service, training workflow, the provision of on-line learning, on-line assessment, management of Continuous Professional Education (CPE), collaborative learning, and so on.
- Server Monitor Software (SMS). The SMS is used to closely monitor the remote measurement laboratory, notify the failures or performance problems and run actions, analyze network protocols, and so on.

2.1 Virtual instrumentation application (VIA)

In the last decade, personal computers evolution has boosted several engineering sectors. Among them is Instrumentation and Measurement discipline. This evolution has promoted the apparition of the term virtual instrumentation, referring to a combination of hardware and software elements whose functionality is beyond the one immediately available with the hardware used. Those instrumentation systems that integrate one or several virtual instruments and have the software as its major component, are presently used both in industrial and laboratorial applications (Geirinhas, 1998).

The instrumentation and measurement hardware which implements virtual instrumentation is practically unlimited, a whole gamut of possibilities can be found in the market to solve our necessities and the customization of a VI, its limitations and its overall performance depend on software framework, including languages and development tools (Geirinhas, 1998).

The VIA has been designed using LabVIEW™, a National Instrument graphical development environment designed for creating flexible and scalable test, measurement and control applications (National Instruments, 2003 & 2005). The VIA manages both, the flow of data between GPIB devices and the DSK communication.

The measurement instrumentation bench is composed by an Agilent E3631A Programmable DC Power Supply with GPIB and RS-232 interfaces to program both voltage and current, an Agilent 33220A function generator which offers 11 standard waveforms plus pulse and arbitrary waveforms, 20 MHz sine and square waveforms, 14-bit, 50 MSa/s, 64 Kpoint arbitrary waveforms, AM, FM, PM, FSK, and PWM modulation types and USB, GPIB and LAN interfaces and a digital scope HP 54603B with two channels, 60 MHz bandwidth and add-on modules to interface for remote control output to RS-232 and HP-IB. The bench is connected to the server via a GPIB board. All the electronic equipment (Agilent 54603B, Agilent E3631A and Agilent 33220A) are GPIB talkers and listeners (send and receive information through the GPIB bus) while the Personal Computer is the GPIB controller (manage the flow of data between the GPIB devices). The embedded board is connected to the server through its parallel port and it is based on the Texas Instruments TMS320C6711 DSP Starter Kit (DSK).

The VIA front panel, that is, the user interface of the VI, can be observed in Fig. 5. Different controls and indicators are implemented, which are the interactive input and output terminals of the VI, respectively. Controls simulate instrument input devices and supply data to the block diagram of the VI. Indicators simulate instrument output devices and display data the block diagram acquires or generates. The user interface of the VI is composed of eight sections: Three consoles which support the user interface of the virtual instruments, two interfaces associated with the DSK and a Web cam to real time monitoring, system status control and restricted-access section.

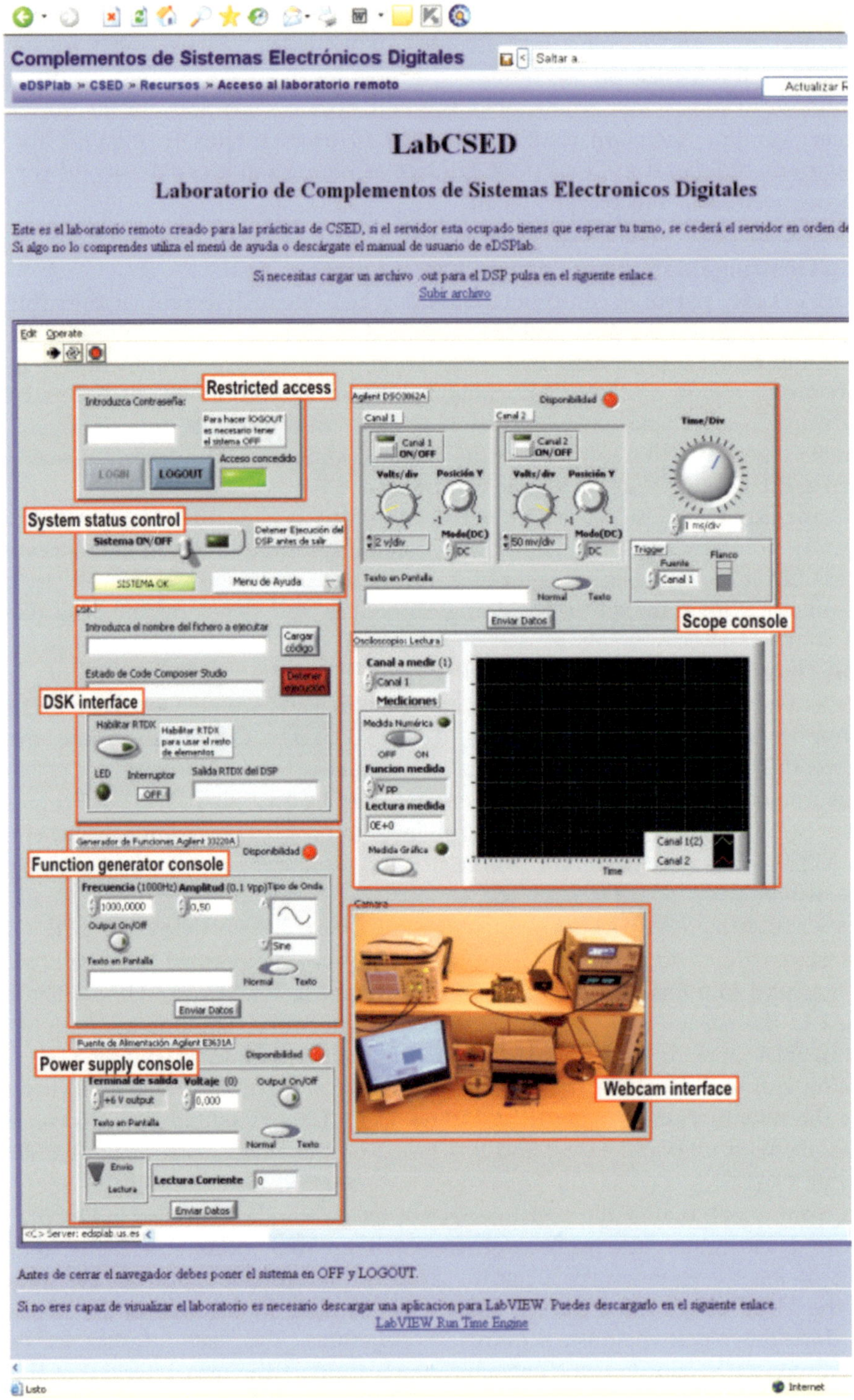

Fig. 5. Virtual Instrumentation Application (VIA) front panel.

The user interface of the VI is composed of three consoles: Function Generator, Power Supply and Scope. The different controls simulate instrument inputs and supply data to the block diagram of the VI. On the other hand, the indicators simulate instrument outputs and display data the block diagram acquires from the GPIB bus.

The DSK interface provides the users with access to the DSP embedded board, delivering different activities related to digital signal processing, Fig. 5. The integration of the LMSS allows controlling source code uploads to the server. The LMSS interfaces to users via Web and manage upload interventions. The source code to be loaded on the DSP embedded board is selected by the user. One time the source code to be executed is loaded, the DSP starts working. A text-based console interface informs the user of downloading and execution process.

eDSPlab also provides a real time monitoring application, based on a low cost 640x480 resolution Web-cam. The Web-cam offers visual real-time feedback of the remote measurement laboratory.

System status control and restricted-access section allows a user to request eDSPlab control. After the login process, it is possible to set a time limit on how long a remote client can control a VI when multiple clients are waiting to control the VI. The server spares a slot of time to this remote user and the eDSPlab control is assigned. The user controls the measurement laboratory during this slot of time, enabling virtual instrument and DSP operation. Instruments control and DSP programming works just the slot time expires: At this moment, the system queries its remote connection-table and extends (or not) the slot time.

2.2 Thin Client Server (TCS)

The TCS manages the thin client-server interaction. A thin client in client-server architecture networks depends primarily on the central server for processing activities, and mainly focuses on conveying input and output between the user and the remote server.

In designing client-server applications, there is a decision to be made as to which parts of the task should be done on the client, and which on the server. This decision can crucially affect the cost of clients and servers, the robustness and security of the application as a whole, and the flexibility of the design for later modification or porting.

One design question is how application-specific the client software should be. Using standardized client software such as a Web browser, remote panel or X11 display can save on development costs, since one does not need to develop a custom client—but one must accept the limitations of the standard client.

A lot of thin clients run only web browsers or remote desktop software, meaning that all significant processing occurs on the server (Andria et al., 2007).

Web applications are popular due to the ubiquity of a client. The ability to update and maintain Web applications without distributing and installing software on potentially thousands of client computers is a key reason for their popularity.

The view and control of a LabVIEW-VI front panel remotely can be made, either from within LabVIEW or from within a Web browser, by connecting to the LabVIEW built-in Web Server. When a front panel is open remotely from a thin client, the Web Server sends the front panel to the client, but the block diagram and all the subVIs remain on the server computer. A user can interact with the front panel in the same way as if the VI were running on the client, except the block diagram executes on the server. Its feature enables to publish entire front panels or to control remote applications safely, easily, and quickly

Thin clients have to use LabVIEW Run-Time Engine to be able to view and control a front panel remotely using a Web browser. The LabVIEW Run-Time Engine includes a LabVIEW browser plug-in package that installs in the browser plug-in directory. Clients install the LabVIEW Run-Time Engine and the user at the server computer creates an HTML file that includes an <OBJECT> and <EMBED> tag that references the VI that clients want to view and control. This tag contains a URL reference to a VI and information that directs the Web browser to pass the VI to the LabVIEW browser plug-in. Clients navigate to the Web Server by entering the Web address of the Web Server in the address or URL field at the top of the Web browser window. The plug-in displays the front panel in the Web browser window and communicates with the Web Server so the client can interact with the remote front panel. Clients request control by selecting Request Control of VI at the bottom of the remote front panel window in their Web browser or by right-clicking anywhere on the front panel and selecting Request Control of VI from the shortcut menu. If no other client is controlling the VI at this moment, a message appears indicating that the user has control of the front panel. If another client is currently controlling the VI, the server queues the request until the other client relinquishes control or until the control time limit times out.

2.3 Learning Management System Server (LMSS)

eDSPLab has been integrated into a more powerful educational environment and several applications currently operate in the server side. The LMSS interfaces to users via Web and manage learning interventions. It provides Learner self-service, training workflow, the provision of on-line learning, on-line assessment, management of Continuous Professional Education (CPE), collaborative learning, and so on. eDSPLab has been integrated into this powerful educational LMS environment, based on Moodle. Moodle has been selected as the LMS because it has been developed as an Open Source Software (OSS) project, with all the advantages of an OSS, such as increased cost effectiveness in the market (reducing the cost of production and avoiding the expensive royalties of commercial software), and the easy resolution of problems within the Open Source Community. The LMSS is able to manage learners, keeping track of their progress and performance across all types of training activities, and learning resources such as content, registration, classroom and instructor availability, instructional material fulfillment, and on-line learning delivery. Students can access the teaching material and they can also download data files containing reference material and class notes in pdf format. Student auto-evaluation tools, FAQ, notice and mark boards, quality survey to provide asynchronous feed back of the teaching process, and chat service to discuss about the concepts of the course are also easily implemented, Fig. 6.

The VI's have been integrated in the Moodle-based LMS, enabling remote users to get control of the measurement instruments. Therefore, the students' activities can be tracked at the Learning Object (LO) level.

Furthermore, students can also access to additional teaching material. Different LO have been designed, including reference material and class notes in .pdf format and multimedia learning tools (Lillo et al., 2005; Toral et al., 2007). The multimedia LOs are made up of a tight coupling of text, tutorials, illustrations, video segments and animations designed with Macromedia Director Software, Fig. 7, and they allow a virtual visit programmed using VRML to the real lab, Fig. 8 (Toral et al., 2007; Lillo et al., 2004; Gallardo et al., 2006; Gallardo et al., 2005).

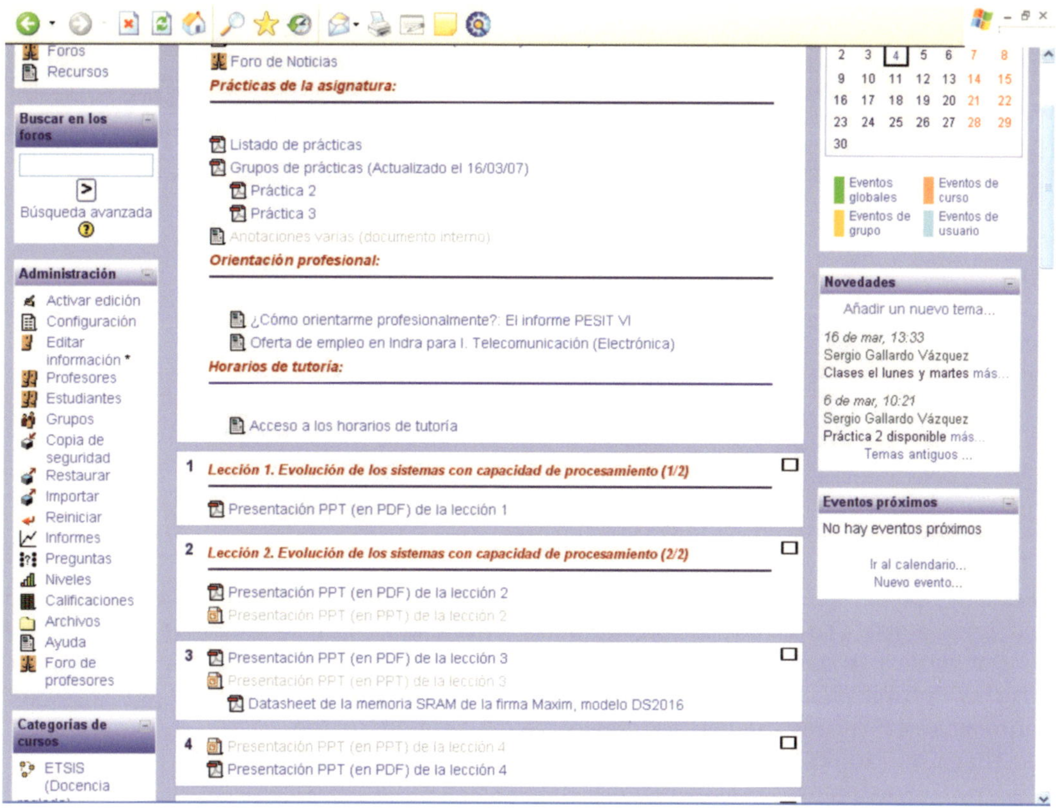

Fig. 6. LMS main menu overview.

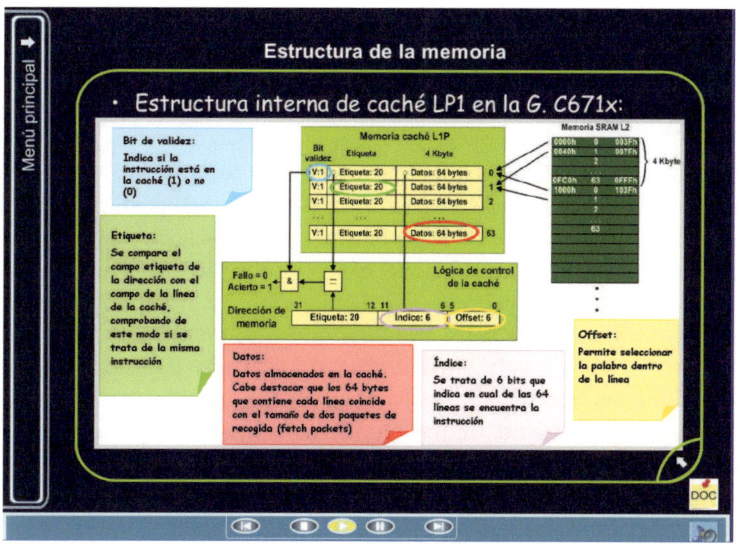

Fig. 7. Learning Object designed with Macromedia Director.

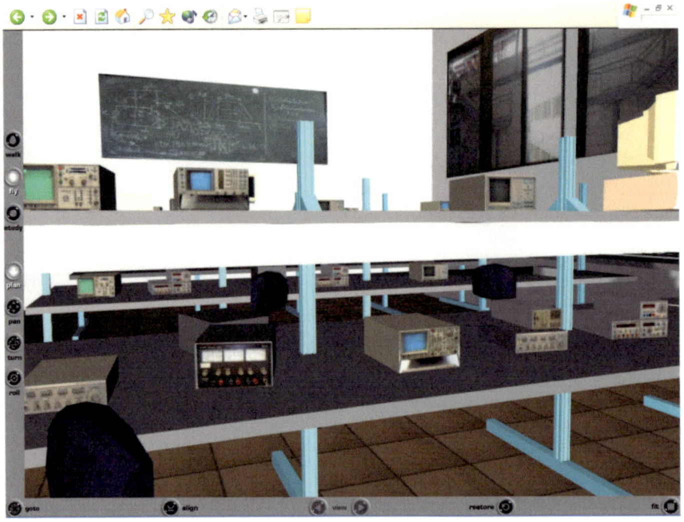

Fig. 8. 3D virtual visit to the real lab based on VRML.

Different users' profiles are managed by the system: "student", "teacher", and "administrator". The "student" profile allows the use of LO including the experiment control service (a complete eDSPLab access for probing specific DSP experiences), the "teacher" profile includes remote handling (creation, updating, removal) of LO, while the "administrator" is responsible for the correct operation of the overall system and for handling user profiles.

2.4 Server Monitor Software (SMS)

The Service Monitor Software (SMS) functionality is related with the capacity to monitor the remote measurement laboratory, notify the failures or performance problems and run actions, analyze network protocols and bandwidth occupation. It has been implemented using different OS tools and commercial applications.

3. Performance analysis

In the fields of packet-switched networks and computer networking, the traffic engineering term Quality of Service, abbreviated QoS, refers to resource reservation control mechanisms. However, the term Quality of Service is sometimes used as a quality measure, with many alternative definitions, rather than referring to the ability to reserve resources. Quality of Service sometimes refers to the level of Quality of service, i.e. the guaranteed service quality. This definition of QoS, used especially in telephony and streaming video, is a metric that reflects or predicts the subjectively experienced quality, for example the "user perceived performance", the "degree of satisfaction of the user", the "number of happy customers", the Mean Opinion Score (MOS) value, or the Quality of Experience (QoE) subjective business concept. In this context, QoS is the cumulative effect on subscriber satisfaction of all imperfections affecting the service. This definition includes the application and the human in the assessment, and demands an appropriate weighting of diverse objective measures such as response time, interrupts, noise, cross-talk, loudness levels, frequency response, noticeable echoes, and so on, and also includes grade of service (ITU-T, Rec E.800 & X.641).

EuQoS (End-user Quality of Service), defined by ITU-T as a collective effect of service performances, which determine the degree of satisfaction of a user of the service, has been measured. EuQoS is the quality perceived by the user, expressed in both, terms of satisfaction or technical terms. It can be viewed from different perspectives. Objective and subjective measurement methods can be employed, as network performance parameters, user test, listening and interviews.

The eDSPlab quality of service measurement and characterization is based on the comparison between both, the proposed thin client model, eDSPlab, and a fat client model. The fat client model is based on the possibility to control a front panel remotely from LabVIEW (installed in both, the client and the server side). In this case, LabVIEW is used as a client to view the remote front panel of the virtual instrument.

A reference experiment has been chosen to compare both proposals. The experiment is related with the implementation of a 4 KHz low-pass FIR (Finite Impulse Response) filter on the DSP embedded board. The integration of the LMSS allows source code uploads to the server. The source code to be loaded on the DSP embedded board is selected by the user (the FIR filter implementation). One time the source code to be executed is loaded, the DSP starts working. A text-based console interface informs the user of downloading and execution process. The remote user generates a sine waveform in the Agilent 33220A function generator, connected to the CODEC input of the DSP. Both, the CODEC output and the CODEC input are connected to scope channels A and B, respectively. The sine waveform input frequency is changed by the remote user between 2 KHz and 6 KHz.

3.1 Objective EuQoS

The SMS monitors the remote measurement laboratory based on the thin client paradigm and the remote measurement laboratory based on the fat client paradigm. Additionally, it will serve as an auxiliary tool for monitoring and troubleshooting.

In order to perform the comparison and to evaluate the performance of the approaches based on the thin client model and the fat client model, the CPU time, CPU usage, I/O Writes, I/O Reads and bandwidth of the involved processes in each approach have been measured, Fig. 9, Fig. 10 and Fig. 11.

"CPU time" parameter represents the amount of time that the processes involved in the remote access use the CPU. On the other hand, "CPU usage" refers to the percentage of time that the processes use the CPU. These parameters, "CPU time" and "CPU usage", are improved in the thin client approach, that is, thin clients only use the exact amount of CPU resources required by the current task, Fig. 9.

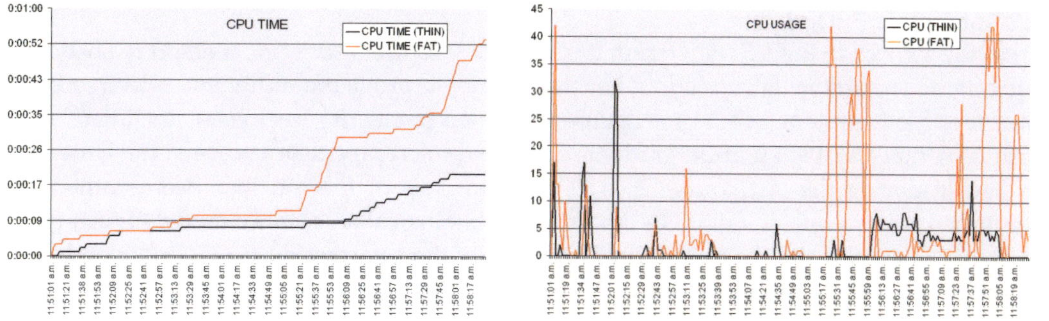

Fig. 9. Measured parameters: CPU time and CPU usage in both, thin client and fat client approaches.

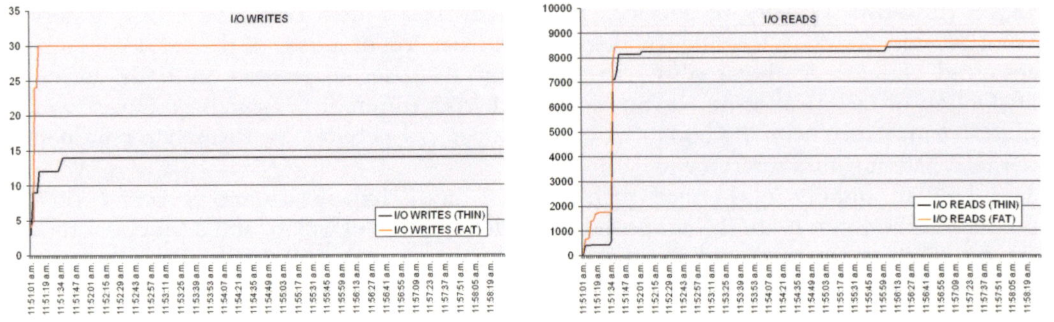

Fig. 10. Measured parameters: I/O Writes and I/O Reads.

Furthermore, "I/O writes" and "I/O reads" parameters are also reduced, Fig. 10. The importance of "I/O writes" lies in it is a statistic value signifying amount of write input/output operations generated by the remote access, including file, network, and device I/Os. Equally, "I/O reads" is the statistical value signifying amount of read input/output operations generated by the remote access (including file, network, and device I/Os).

Finally, the bandwidth occupation has been measured in both approaches. A significant bandwidth occupation reduction can be observed in thin client approach.

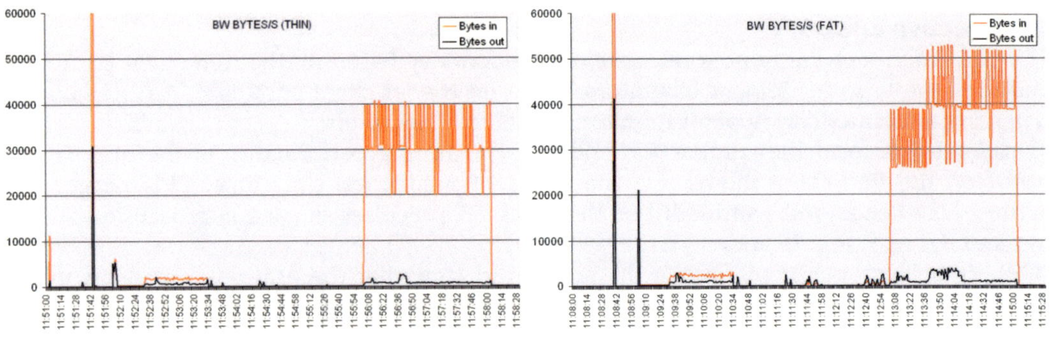

Fig. 11. Bandwidth occupation of both, thin client and fat client approaches.

3.2 Subjective EuQoS

From the subjective EuQoS viewpoint, it is necessary to use a scientific method to ensure the subjective measurements validation. For this reason, to prove the utility and effectiveness of the proposed system from the subjective viewpoint, it has been included as a complementary tool in an undergraduate advanced microprocessor course at the University of Seville during the last course 2004/05. An analysis of the tool has been studied and confirmed using a questionnaire to develop a technological acceptance model (TAM) (Toral et al., 2005). This model has been developed using the information provided by end users for guaranteeing the use of the tool. The obtained result also provides general information about the relationships among the variables involved in the acceptance of the tool and about the indicators used to measure each variable or dimension and guarantee its maximum effectiveness and usefulness, Fig. 12.

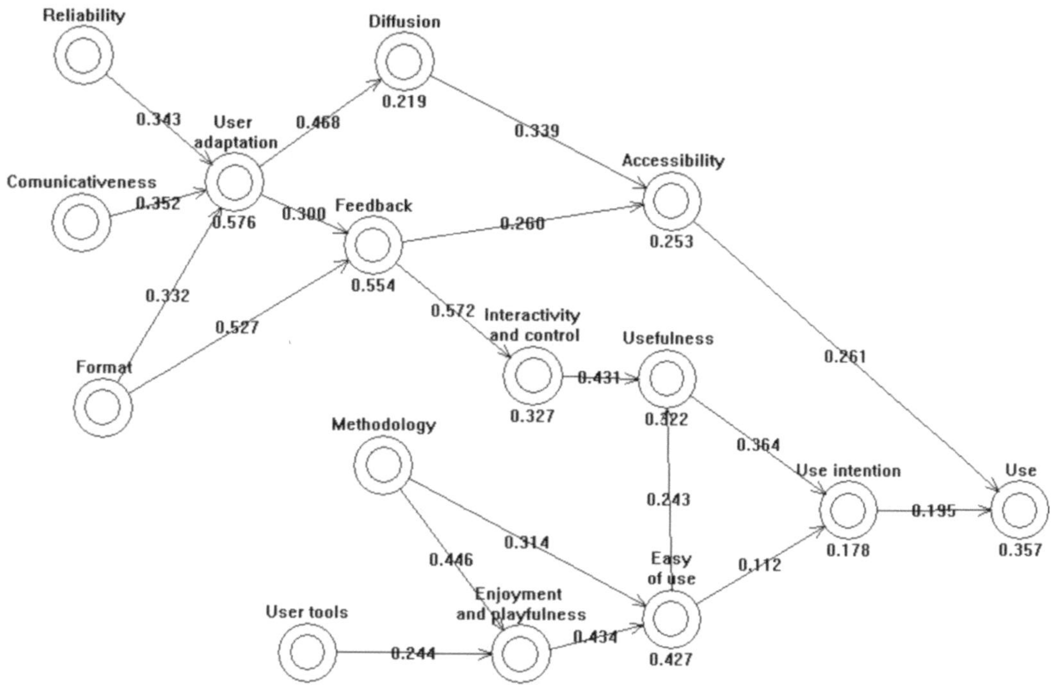

Fig. 12. Final acceptance model.

Learning through computer-mediated environments has dramatically increased. Some researchers state the validity, even the necessity, of these educational tools, but other authors are more sceptical about them. Sometimes, the use of computer simulation has replaced hardware-based laboratory courses. In this cases, students miss what can only be learned in a traditional lab. It seems as if computer-based educational environment has been used without any scientific criteria or, what it is worse, without real necessity. In fact, not much attention has been paid to scientific analysis for improving the teaching process which is normally empirically evaluated and improved.

In order to avoid this lack of scientific criteria in validating educational tools, TAM has been applied to the eDSPlab remote instrumentation laboratory and its LMS platform, to guarantee its maximum effectiveness and usefulness.

A questionnaire was prepared, validated, using the Cronbach's alpha (Toral et al., 2005) and distributed among 47 students of an undergraduate Advanced Microprocessor course to check the use of the tool and identify the external variables with a sensible influence in its use, Table 1. It consisted of 59 statements or indicators using 1-7 Likert type scale (1=strongly disagree, 7=strongly agree). Each dimension can be measured using a set of these statements or indicators which have been previously reported in the literature (Martínez-Torres et al., 2005).

Then, a principal components analysis was applied to reduce the number of variables. Each new generated variable (principal component) is a linear combination of the original indicators of Table 1 with the orthogonal property, so there is no redundant information. Table 2 depicts the results obtained from this analysis: the second column shows the number of principal component while the third one, the variances explained by these components.

Dimension (Reliability)		Item (Correlation item-dimension)
Format (0.7554)	I1	The instructional material is presented in a flexible order (0.3953)
	I2	Ease of readability/understandability of the text (0.5766)
	I3	The information provided by the tool is presented in a useful format (0.5668)
	I4	Clarity of the instructional material (0.6949)
Methodology (0.7601)	I5	The scope and the goals of the tool are clearly defined (0.6706)
	I6	The length of the content blocks are appropriate (0.4696)
	I7	The tool is adapted to the teaching content (0.6403)
Feedback (0.7849)	I8	Useful feedback from the tool (0.5135)
	I9	Receipt of timely feedback from the system (0.7431)
	I10	Feedback from the system stimulates the use of the tool (0.5782)
User adaptation (0.7537)	I11	The tool allows supervising the activity of users (0.4689)
	I12	The users have the possibility of choosing to solve the problems they like (0.4515)
	I13	The tool is adapted to different user profiles (0.5543)
	I14	The tool has different levels of complexity (0.4314)
	I15	The tool allows users to develop their own initiatives (0.5543)
	I16	Ability to control the sequence of instruction (0.4860)
	I17	The e-learning system enables you to learn the content you need (0.3511)
Communicativenes s (0.8763)	I18	The e-learning system makes it easy for you to discuss questions with your teachers (0.6845)
	I19	The e-learning system makes it easy for you to discuss questions with other students (0.8117)
	I20	The e-learning system makes it easy for you to share the learned content with other students (0.7964)
Diffusion (0.8562)	I21	Before using the tool, I know all its features (0.7507)
	I22	I know the technical requirements for using the tool (0.7187)
	I23	I know the formative requirements for using the tool (0.7606)
	I24	Lecturers promote the use of the eLearning tool (0.5673)

Table 1. Validation of a questionnaire using Cronbach's alpha. (Part 1 of 3).

The number of indicators was reduced considering the minimum number of components which could explain, at least, a 70% of the variance of each dimension. Using the data of Table 2, the correlations between these principal components and the use of the eDSPlab environment can be evaluated, to show those ones that have a significant influence in it. These correlations were used to hypothesize the relationships among dimensions. To validate this hypothesis, PLS (Partial Least Squares) technique was used (Chin, 1998). A partial least squares regression is an extension of the multiple linear regression models. In its simplest form, a linear model specifies the (linear) relationship between a dependent variable (the use of the tool), and a set of predictor variables (external variables previously obtained). The objective in PLS is to maximize the explanation variance R2. Thus, R2 and the significance of relationships among dimensions or constructs are measures indicative of how well a model is performing. The conceptual core of PLS is an iterative combination of principal component analysis relating indicators to dimensions, and path analysis allowing the construction of a model. The hypothesizing of relationships between indicators and dimensions, and dimensions and other dimensions is guided by the results of the obtained correlations. The estimation of the parameters representing the measurement and path relationships is accomplished using Ordinary Least Squares (OLS) techniques.

Accessibility (0.7980)	I25	Accessibility of the eLearning tool (0.6379)
	I26	The communication channel is appropriate for accessing the tool (0.6319)
	I27	The communication channel for accessing the tool is easy to use (0.6519)
Interactivity and control (0.8244)	I28	Ability to use a variety of methods (menu, button,2) to interact with the system (0.2490)
	I29	Extent to which the system enables the subjects to actively interact with it (0.6742)
	I30	Ability to control the pace of instruction (0.7968)
	I31	Ability to control the sequence of instruction (0.7333)
	I32	Ability to select components or modules of instruction needed to acquire the various concepts (0.7251)
Enjoyment and playfulness (0.8661)	I33	Using the eLearning tool is pleasant (0.6580)
	I34	I have fun using the eLearning tool (0.7010)
	I35	The content of the tool is showed in an amusing way (0.7540)
	I36	The graphic design is attractive to users (0.6085)
	I37	Using the eLearning tool excites my curiosity (0.6922)
	I38	Using the eLearning tool arouses my imagination (0.5579)
Reliability (0.8361)	I39	The tool is robust and works properly (0.6310)
	I40	The tool is reliable (0.6114)
	I41	Whenever I use the tool, it works properly (0.7482)
	I42	I am confident about the security of the tool (0.6789)
User's tool (0.6178)	I43	The tool includes a search tool (0.4228)
	I44	The tool shows the different events of my learning process (0.4731)
	I45	The tool includes forums and chats (0.3691)
Easy to use (0.9081)	I46	I find it easy to get the eLearning tool to do what I want it to do (0.8029)
	I47	My interaction with the eLearning tool is clear and understandable (0.8246)
	I48	I find the eLearning tool easy to use (0.8905)
	I49	Interacting with the eLearning tool will not require a lot of my mental effort (0.6683)

Table 2. Validation of a questionnaire using Cronbach's alpha. (Part 2 of 3).

Utility (0.9366)	I50	Using the eLearning tool would improve my performance in this course (0.7983)
	I51	Using the eLearning tool would increase my productivity in this course (0.8915)
	I52	Using the eLearning tool would enhance my effectiveness in this course (0.8243)
	I53	I find the eLearning tool would be useful in this course (0.7731)
	I54	Using the eLearning tool in my job would enable me to accomplish tasks more quickly (0.7705)
	I55	Using the eLearning tool would make it easier to do my task (0.8085)
Use intention (0.8248)	I56	I intend to review some concepts using the eLearning tool frequently (0.7018)
	I57	I intend to compare some theoretical and practical concepts explained in classes with the point of view of the eLearning tool (0.7018)
Use (0.8008)	I58	How many times per week have you used the eLearning tool? (Average value) (0.6678)
	I59	How many hours per week have you used the eLearning tool? (Average value) (0.6678)

Table 3. Validation of a questionnaire using Cronbach's alpha. (Part 3 of 3).

Dimension	Principal components	Explained variance
Format (FOR)	3	0.7797
Methodology (MET)	3	0.8582
Feedback (FED)	3	0.8716
User adaptation (UA)	5	0.7372
Communicativeness (COM)	2	0.8588
Diffusion (DIF)	3	0.8967
Accessibility (AC)	1	0.7223
Interactivity and control (IC)	3	0.8189
Enjoyment and Playfulness (EP)	3	0.7227
Reliability (R)	2	0.8162
User tool (UT)	3	0.8854
Easy of use (EOU)	2	0.8378
Usefulness (U)	1	0.7599
Use intention (UI)	1	0.8523
Use (US)	1	0.8710

Table 4. Reduction of items or questions using principal components analysis.

Figure 12 shows the final model obtained using PLS. The bottom right side of the figure is based on the typical dimensions of TAM (use, use intention, easy of use, and usefulness), while external variables of the model are placed on the top left side. Several combinations have been analyzed, using different relative positions for the external dimensions and according to the correlations of the principal components of Table 2.

The model shows the important role of variables such as accessibility, user adaptation, feedback, interactivity and control, and enjoyment and playfulness. All of them have a direct or indirect incidence in the four major variables of the classical acceptance model. In turn, they are affected by the five independent variables of the model: reliability, communicativeness, format, methodology, and user tools. These independent variables can be considered as design variables but they must take into account the incidence in other variables. For instance, the format of the e-learning tool should take into account its positive incidence over feedback and user adaptation. That means that the designer should provide a format adapted to different user profiles and complexity levels, stimulating the use of the tool with an appropriated feedback to users.

3.3 Academic results

Additionally, and from an academical point of view, some important conclusions have been obtained from the numerical analysis of the course results evolution.
eDSPLab, has been designed to improve the students' practical work taking into account the traditional limited economic resources of educational institutions, which usually entails one of the main problems in real lab training: the low number of laboratory working places in relation to the high number of enrolled students. The practical work has a contribution of a 25% on the overall qualification in the analyzed subject. Therefore, a comparison with academic years previous to its use has been performed to estimate the improvement that the new teaching tool provides. The abandoned and failed rate of the course was reduced from 20% to 16% after the introduction of the eDSPlab, Fig. 13. This fact is more evident during the second year after the introduction of this novel learning tool. Also, Fig. 14 shows how the students' mark distribution was improved. To obtain the rated student mark, a range from -1 to 4 has been used, with -1 being "a student who has abandoned the course", 0 being "a student who has not passed the course", and 4 being "a student who has exceptionally passed the course". The numbers in between refer to intermediate scores. Note that this scoring penalizes for abandonment of the course. The obtained result is prorated using the number of students during the academic year.

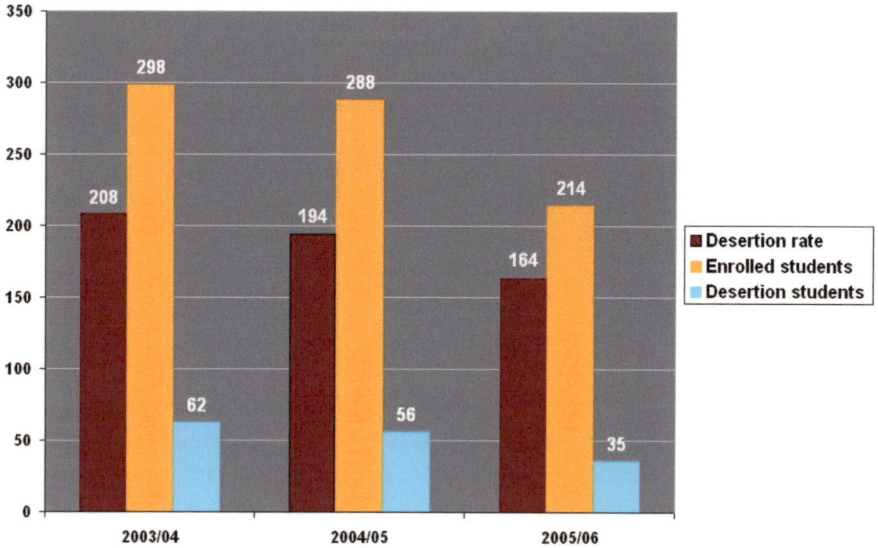

Fig. 13. Desertion plus failed rate showed in ‰.

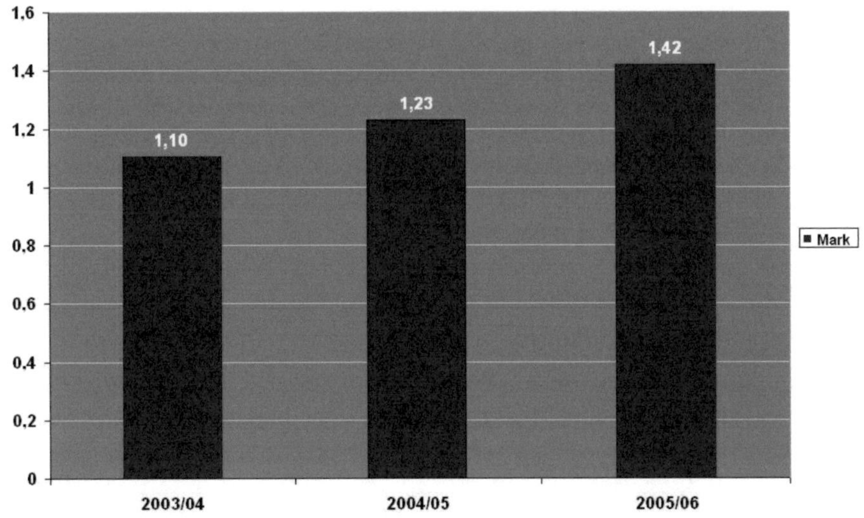

Fig. 14. Prorated students' mark distribution during the last academic years.

The first version of eDSPLab was introduced during academic year 2004-2005, and the final version, which was improved using the TAM results, was applied during the last academic year (2005-2006). It can be observed (Fig. 13) that the abandon and failed rate in the course before the introduction of eDSPLab was about 21%. Figure 13 also shows that the abandon rate during academic year 2004-2005 was about 19%. The use of the first version of eDSPLab poorly improved the abandon rate or, at least, improved the abandon rate less than expected. However, the abandon rate was reduced during the academic year 2005-2006 about a 20%, from 19 or 20% to 16%, after the evaluation of the tool using TAM. This fact corroborates that the efficiency of an e-learning tool like eDSPLab must be assured to validate its educational use. Notice that the students' lab work has increased using eDSPLab although the real lab attendance has decreased, which is confirmed by the increasing value of the students´ mark measurement, Fig. 14.

Academic Course	Enrolled Students	Desertion (-1) (Lowest Mark)	Passed	Remarkable	Excellent	Distinction (4) (Highest Mark)
2003/04	298	62	127	78	16	15
2004/05	288	56	82	126	20	4
2005/06	214	35	53	98	22	6

Table 5. Distribution of student marks since academic course 2003/04 to 2005/06.

Finally, an additional and important magnitude to be considered is the percentage of students that take the exam at first time and they pass it. This magnitude has been increased from 91,76 % to the 99.4 % during the course 2005/2006, that is, there is a significant improvement in the continuous assessment and, therefore, in the teaching-learning process.

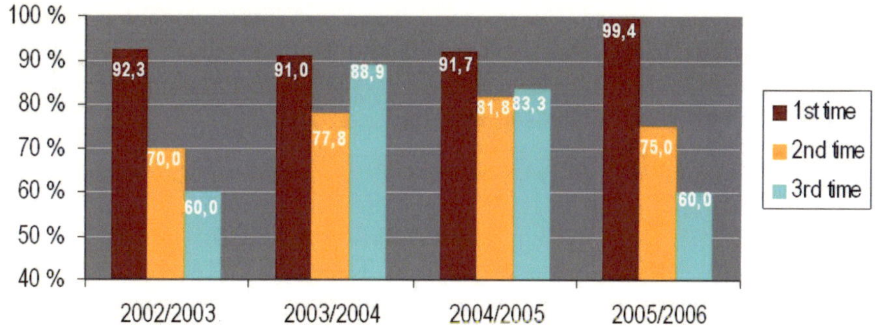

Fig. 15. Percentage of students that take the exam at first time, second time and third time and they pass it.

4. Conclusions

This paper concerns a Web-based measurement laboratory which provides access to remote control of DSPs and measurement instrumentation. eDSPLab, designed using LabVIEW™ and integrated on an LMS, has been presented. The educational tool which provides access for remote control of different didactic setups related to DSP has been used as a practical training tool in Undergraduate courses regarding advanced microprocessors architectures and their applications. Using eDSPLab students can work with the real lab equipment to test DSP applications without being physically present in the lab.

In order to optimize the remote access architecture, the thin client paradigm is used, contributing to improve speed, bandwidth and processor overload parameters of the system.

End-user Quality of Service has been measured and expressed in both, terms of satisfaction or technical terms. The technical measurement and characterization is based on the comparison between, the proposed thin client model, eDSPlab, and a fat client model, Fig. 9, Fig. 10 and Fig. 11. The results highlight improvements in terms of CPU time, CPU usage and I/O read/write operations.

As opposed to frequently reported e-learning tools, the eDSPLab has been evaluated in accordance with typical variables included in technological acceptance model. A questionnaire that measures the different variables or dimensions involved has been developed, and its reliability has been computed using Cronbach's alpha index. Using this questionnaire, a structural and measurement model for the use of the proposed tool has been deduced using PLS. Several results have been obtained. The current use of eDSPLab and the scores of the variables with a direct influence over its use, prove the effectiveness of eDSPLab as a teaching tool. Nevertheless, the derived model have shown the causal relationship among all the variables considered and have also guided some improvements of eDSPLab to increase its use. Particularly, the necessity of integrating eDSPLab into a more complex learning site has been deduced. User tools have been demonstrated to be an antecedent of easy of use and, as a consequence, the remote lab must be accomplished by new tools covering other theoretical and practical content of the subject.

The validity of the improved version of eDSPLab, modified taking into account the TAM analysis, has been also verified by non-opinion-based assessment data which compares the outcomes of the course with the previous years. The results show that the use of eDSPLab encourages students, reducing the abandonment rate registered during the last academic year, and improving academicals results. Academical statistics have been carried out, Fig. 14 and Fig. 15, which highlights an abandoned and failed rate of the course reduction, students' mark distribution improvement and a significant improvement in the continuous assessment and, therefore, in the teaching-learning process.

5. References

Abdel-Qader, I. M., Bazuin, B. J., Mousavinezhad, H. S., and Patrick, J. K. (2003). Real-Time Digital Signal Processing in the Undergraduate Curriculum, *IEEE Transactions on Education*, Vol. 46, No. 1, 2003, pp. 95-101, ISSN 0018-9359.

Andria, G., Baccigalupi, A., Borsic, M., Carbone, P., Daponte, P., De Capua, C., Ferrero, A., Grimaldi, D., Liccardo, A., Locci, N., Lanzolla, A. M. L., Macii, D., Muscas, C., Peretto, L., Petri, D., Rapuano, S., Riccio, M., Salicone, S., Stefani, F. (2007). Remote Didactic Laboratory "G. Savastano," The Italian Experience for E-Learning at the Technical Universities in the Field of Electrical and Electronic Measurement: Architecture and Optimization of the Communication Performance Based on Thin Client Technology, *IEEE Transactions on Instrumentation and Measurement*, Vol. 56, No. 4, August 2007, pp. 1124-1134, ISSN 0018-9456.

Andria, G., Baccigalupi, A., Borsic, M., Carbone, P., Daponte, P., De Capua, C., Ferrero, A., Grimaldi, D., Liccardo, A., Locci, N., Lanzolla, A. M. L., Macii, D., Muscas, C., Peretto, L., Petri, D., Rapuano, S., Riccio, M., Salicone, S., Stefani, F. (2007). Remote Didactic Laboratory "G. Savastano," The Italian Experience for E-Learning at the Technical Universities in the Field of Electrical and Electronic Measurements: Overview on Didactic Experiments, *IEEE Transactions on Instrumentation and Measurement*, Vol. 56, No. 4, August 2007, pp. 1135-1147, ISSN 0018-9456.

Aedo P. et al. (2000). Assessing the utility of an interactive electronic book for learning the Pascal language, *IEEE Transactions Education*, Vol. 43, No. 3, Aug. 2000, pp. 403-413, ISSN 0018-9456.

Almeida S. F., Piazzalunga R., Ribeiro V. G., Casemiro, M. B., Moreno R. (2003). Combining interactivity and improved layout while creating educational software for the Web, *Computers & Education* Vol. 40, 2003, pp. 271-284. ISSN: 0360-1315.

Bagui, S. (1998). Reasons for increased learning using multimedia, *Journal of Educational Multimedia and Hypermedia*, Vol. 7, 1998, pp. 3-18. ISSN: 1055-8896.

Bose T. (1994). A Digital Signal Processing Laboratory for Undergraduates, *IEEE Transaction on Education*, Vol. 37, No. 3, August 1994, pp. 243-246. ISSN 0018-9359.

Canfora G., Daponte P., Capuano S. (2004). Remotely accessible laboratory for electronic measurement teaching, *Computer Standards & Interfaces*, No. 26, 2004, pp. 489–499. ISSN: 0920-5489.

Carley L., Khosla P., Unetich R. (2000). Teaching 'Introduction to Electrical and Computer Engineering' in context, *Proceedings of the IEEE* , Vol. 88, pp. 8-22. ISSN: 0018-9219.

Casini, M., Prattichizzo D., Vicino A., (2003). The Automatic Control Telelab: A User-Friendly Interface for Distance Learning, *IEEE Transactions on Education*, Vol. 46, No. 2, May 2003, pp. 252-257, ISSN 0018-9359.

Chin, W. (1998). The partial least squares approach for structural equation modelling. In G.A. Marcoulides (Ed.), Modern methods for business research. Mahwah, NJ, Erlbaum, pp. 295-336. 1998.

Chirico, M., Scapolla, A.M., Bagnasco, A. (2005). A new and open model to share laboratories on the Internet, *IEEE Transactions on Instrumentation and Measurement*, Vol. 54, No. 3, (June 2005), pp. 1111-1117, ISSN 0018-9456.

Christian W. and Belloni M. (2001) Physlets: Teaching Physics with Interactive Curricular Material. Englewood Cliffs, NJ: *Prentice-Hall*, 2001. ISBN: 0130293415.

Communiqué of the Conference of Ministers responsible for Higher Education, "Realising the European Higher Education Area", Berlin, September 19th, 2003.

Conole G., Dyke M., Oliver M., Seale J. (2004). Mapping pedagogy and tools for effective learning design, *Computers & Education* Vol. 43, 2004, pp. 17–33. ISSN: 0360-1315.

Davoli, F. Palazzo, S., Zappatore, S. (2006). *Distributed Cooperative Laboratories: Networking, Instrumentation, and Measurements*, Springer-Verlag ISBN 978-0-387-29811-5, New York.

Felder R. M., Felder G. N., Dietz J. (1998). A longitudinal study of engineering students performance and retention v. comparisons with traditionally-taught students, *Journal of Engineering Education*, Vol. 98, no. 4, pp. 469-480, 1998. ISSN: 0949-149X.

Gallardo, S., F. Barrero, S.L Toral, (2005). Virtual instrumentation laboratory based on LabVIEW. A case study: A DSPs course, *ICECE, International Conference On Engineering And Computer Education*, ISBN 84-609-8149-5, Madrid, November 2005.

Gallardo S., Molina E., Barrero F., Toral, S.L., Duran, M., "Aplicación de tecnologías multimedia para el aprendizaje asíncrono de instrumentación electrónica", TAEE: Tecnologías Aplicadas a la Enseñanza de la Electrónica, vol. 1, Madrid, España, 2006.

Gallardo S., Barrero F., Toral, S.L. (2005). Building a Web-based virtual laboratory with VRML. A case study: An electronic instrumentation subject, *ICECE: International Conference On Engineering And Computer Education*, ISBN 84-609-8149-5, Madrid, November 2005.

Geirinhas Ramos, H.M.; Silva Girao, P.M. "Software environments for the implementation of virtual instrumentation", Electrotechnical Conference, 1998. MELECON 98.

Guimarães E., Maffeis A., Pereira J., Russo B., Cardoso E., Bergerman M., Magalhães M.F. (2003). REAL: A Virtual Laboratory for Mobile Robot Experiments, *IEEE Transactions on Education*, Vol. 46, No. 1, February 2003, pp.37-42, ISSN 0018-9359.

Ferrero, S. Salicone, C. Bonora, M. Parmigiani (2003). ReMLab: A Java-Based Remote, Didactic Measurement Laboratory, *IEEE Trans. Instrumentation and Measurement*, Vol. 52, No. 3, June 2003. ISSN 0018-9456.

Hercog, D., Gergic, B., Uran, S., Jezernik, K., (2007). A DSP-Based Remote Control Laboratory, *IEEE Transactions on Industrial Electronics*, Vol. 54, No. 6, (December 2007), pp. 3057-3068, ISSN 0278-0046.

Hong, P.S., Anderson, D.V., Williams, D.B., Jackson, J.R., Barnwell, T.P., Hayes, M. H., Schafer, R.W., Echard, J.D. (2004). DSP for Practicing Engineers: A Case Study in Internet Course Delivery, *IEEE Transactions on Education*, Vol. 47, No. 3, pp.301-310. ISSN 0018-9359.

ITU-T Rec E.800: Terms and definitions related to quality of service and network performance including dependability

ITU-T Rec X.641: Information Technology - Quality of Service: Framework

Joint declaration of the European Ministers of Education, "The European Higher Education Area", Bologna, June 19th, 1999

Kikuchi T., Fukuda S., Fukuzaki A., Nagaoka K., Tanaka K., Kenjo T., Harris D. A. (2004). DVTS-Based Remote Laboratory Across the Pacific Over the Gigabit Network, *IEEE Transactions on Education*, Vol. 48, No. 4, pp. 26-32, Feb. 2004. ISSN 0018-9359.

Lee, Y., Kozar, K.A. and Larsen, K.R.T. (2003) The Technology Acceptance Model: Past, Present, and Future", *Communications of the Association for Information Systems*, 12, 752-780, 2003. ISSN: 15429-3181.

Lillo J., et al. (2005). Implementation of a web-based educational tool for digital signal processing teaching using the technological acceptance model. *IEEE Transactions on Education*, Vol. 48, No. 4, December 2005, pp. 632–641, ISSN 0018-9359.

Lillo A., Gallardo S., Toral S.L. Barrero F. (2004). Laboratorio multimedia de procesamiento digital de señal usando en TMS320C3X DSP Starter Kit, *TAEE: Tecnologías Aplicadas a la Enseñanza de la Electrónica*, Vol. 1, Valencia, España, 2004

Martínez-Torres, M. R., Barrero, F., Toral, S. L., Gallardo, S. (2005). A Digital Signal Processing Teaching Methodology Using Concept Mapping Techniques, accepted for publication in the *IEEE Transactions on Education*. ISSN 0018-9359.

Metzger, M. J. , Flanagina A. J., Zwarun L. (2003). College student Web use, perceptions of information credibility, and verification behaviour, *Computers & Education*, Vol. 41, 2003, pp. 271–290. ISSN: 0360-1315.

Milliken J., Barnes L. P. (2002). Teaching and technology in higher education: student perceptions and personal reflections, *Computers & Education*, Vol. 39, 2002, pp. 223-235. ISSN: 0360-1315.

National Instruments Corporation, "LabVIEW TM User Manual", April 2003

National Instruments Corporation, "LabVIEW Fundamentals", August 2005

Office for Official Publications of the European Communities (2001), "Generic ICT Skills Profiles", Career-Space Project.

Pahl C. (2003). Managing evolution and change in web-based teaching and learning environments, *Computers & Education*, Vol. 40, 2003, pp. 99–114. ISSN: 0360-1315.

Roppel T. (2000). An Interdisciplinary Laboratory Sequence in Electrical and Computer Engineering: Curriculum Design and Assessment Results, *IEEE Transaction on Education*, Vol. 43, May 2000, pp. 143-152. ISSN 0018-9359.

Sánchez J., Morilla F., Dormido S., Aranda J., Ruipérez P. (2002). Virtual and Remote Control Labs Using Java: A Quality Approach, *IEEE Control Systems Magazine*, April 2002, pp. 8-20. ISSN: 0272-1708.

Schodorf J.B., Yoder M.A., McClellan J.H., Schafer R.W. (1996). Using Multimedia to Teach the Theory of Digital Multimedia Signals, *IEEE Transaction on Education*, Vol. 39, No. 3, Aug. 1996, pp. 336-341. ISSN 0018-9359.

Taylor R. L., Heer D., Fiez T. S. (2003). Using an Integrated Platform for Learning to Reinvent Engineering Education, *IEEE Transaction on Education*, Vol. 46, No. 4, November 2003, pp. 409-419. ISSN 0018-9359.

Toral, S.L., Barrero, F., Martínez-Torres, M. R., Gallardo, S., Lillo, A. J., (2005). Implementation of a web-based educational tool for digital signal processing teaching using the technological acceptance model, *IEEE Transaction on Education*, Vol. 48, Nº 3, August 2005, pp. 632-641, ISSN 0018-9359.

Toral, S.L., Martínez-Torres, M.R., Barrero, F., Gallardo, S., Vargas, E., González, V. (2006), Planning a Master Curriculum according to Career Space Recommendations using Concept Mapping Techniques, *International Journal of Technology and Design Education*, Vol. 16, No. 3, pp. 237-252. ISSN 0018-9359.

Toral S. L., Barrero F., Martínez-Torres, M. R., Gallardo S. (2007). Interactive multimedia teaching of digital signal processors, *Computer Applications in Engineering Education*, vol. 15, no. 1, pp. 88-98, 2007. ISSN 1099-0542.

Spanias A., Atti V., (2005). ShareMe: Running a Distributed Systems Lab for 600 Students With Three Faculty Members, *IEEE Transactions On Education*, Vol. 48, Nº 3, (August 2005), pp. 430-437, ISSN 0018-9359.

Poornachandra S. and Sasikala B., (2010). *Digital Signal Processing* (Third edition), Tata McGrawHill, ISBN(13): 978-0-07-067279-6, New Delhi.

Wilson J., Jennings W. (2000). Studio Courses: How Information Technology is changing the way we teach, on campus and off, *Proceedings of the IEEE*, Vol. 88, pp. 72-80, January 2000. ISSN: 0018-9219.

14

Digital Image Processing Using LabView

Rubén Posada-Gómez,
Oscar Osvaldo Sandoval-González, Albino Martínez Sibaja,
Otniel Portillo-Rodríguez and Giner Alor-Hernández
Instituto Tecnológico de Orizaba, Departamento de Postgrado e Investigación, México

1. Introduction

Digital Image processing is a topic of great relevance for practically any project, either for basic arrays of photodetectors or complex robotic systems using artificial vision. It is an interesting topic that offers to multimodal systems the capacity to see and understand their environment in order to interact in a natural and more efficient way.

The development of new equipment for high speed image acquisition and with higher resolutions requires a significant effort to develop techniques that process the images in a more efficient way. Besides, medical applications use new image modalities and need algorithms for the interpretation of these images as well as for the registration and fusion of the different modalities, so that the image processing is a productive area for the development of multidisciplinary applications.

The aim of this chapter is to present different digital image processing algorithms using LabView and IMAQ vision toolbox. IMAQ vision toolbox presents a complete set of digital image processing and acquisition functions that improve the efficiency of the projects and reduce the programming effort of the users obtaining better results in shorter time. Therefore, the IMAQ vision toolbox of LabView is an interesting tool to analyze in detail and through this chapter it will be presented different theories about digital image processing and different applications in the field of image acquisition, image transformations.

This chapter includes in first place the image acquisition and some of the most common operations that can be locally or globally applied, the statistical information generated by the image in a histogram is commented later. Finally, the use of tools allowing to segment or filtrate the image are described making special emphasis in the algorithms of pattern recognition and matching template.

2. Digital image acquisition

We generally associate the image to a representation that we make in our brain according to the light incidence into a scene (Bischof & Kropatsc, 2001). Therefore, there are different variables related to the formation of images, such as the light distribution in the scene. Since the image formation depends of the interaction of light with the object in the scene and the emitted energy from one or several light sources changes in its trip (Fig. 1). That is why the

Radiance is the light that travels in the space usually generated by different light sources, and the light that arrives at the object corresponds to the Irradiance. According to the law of energy conservation, a part of the radiant energy that arrives to the object is absorbed by this, other is refracted and another is reflected in form of radiosity:

$$\phi(\lambda) = R(\lambda) + T(\lambda) + A(\lambda) \qquad (1)$$

Where $\phi(\lambda)$ represents the incident light on the object, $A(\lambda)$ the absorbed energy by the material of the object, $T(\lambda)$ the refracted flux and $R(\lambda)$ the reflected energy, all of them define the material properties(Fairchild, 2005) at a given wave length (λ) . The radiosity represents the light that leaves a diffuse surface (Forsyth & Ponce, 2002). This way when an image is acquired, the characteristics of this will be affected by the type of light source, the proximity of the same ones, and the diffusion of scene, among others.

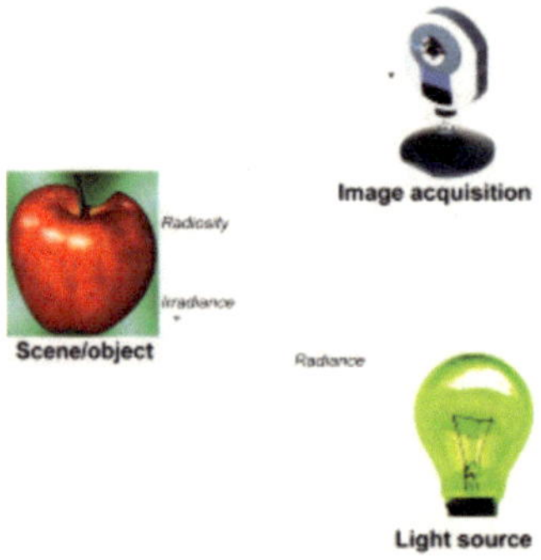

Fig. 1. Light modification at acquisition system.

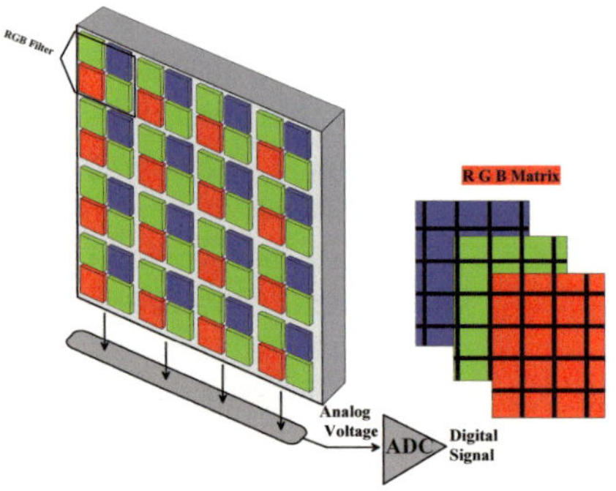

Fig. 2. Colour image acquisition with a CCD.

In the case of the digital images, the acquisition systems require in the first place alight sensitive element, which is usually constituted by a photosensitive matrix arrangement obtained by the image sensor (CCD, CMOS, etc.). These physical devices give an electrical output proportional to the luminous intensity that receives in their input. The number of elements of the photosensitive system of the matrix determines the spatial resolution of the captured image. Moreover, the electric signal generated by the photosensitive elements is sampled and discretized to be stored in a memory slot; this requires the usage of an analog-to-digital converter (ADC). The number of bits used to store the information of the image determines the resolution at intensity of the image.

A colour mask is generally used (RGB Filter) for acquisition of colour images. This filter allows decomposing the light in three bands, Red, Green and Blue. The three matrixes are generated and each one of them stores the light intensity of each RGB channel (Fig. 2).
The next example (presented in Fig. 3) show to acquire video from a webcam using the **NI Vision Acquisition Express**. This block is located in Vision/Vision Express toolbox and it is the easiest way to configure all the characteristics in the camera. Inside this block there are four sections: the first one corresponds to the option of "select acquisition source" which shows all the cameras connected in the computer. The next option is called "select acquisition type" which determines the mode to display the image and there are four modes: single acquisition with processing, continuous acquisition with inline processing, finite acquisition with inline processing, and finite acquisition with post processing. The third section corresponds to the "configure acquisition settings" which represents the size, brightness, contrast, gamma, saturation, etc. of the image and finally in the last option it is possible to select controls and indicators to control different parameters of the last section during the process. In the example presented in Fig. 3 it was selected the continuous acquisition with inline processing, this option will display the acquired image in continuous mode until the user presses the stop button.

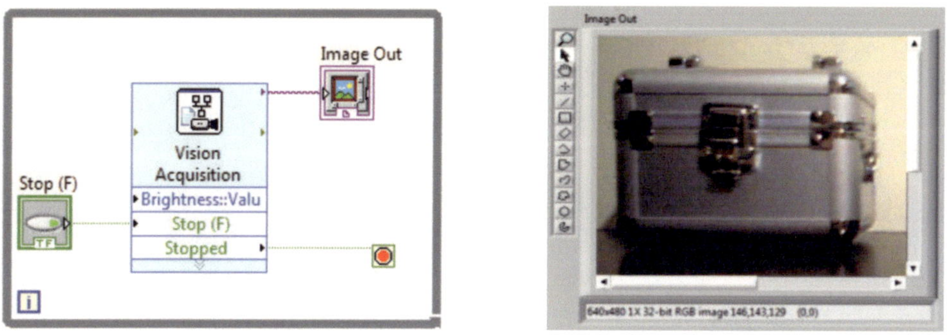

Fig. 3. Video Acquisition using IMAQ Vision Acquisition Express.

3. Mathematical interpretation of a digital image

An image is treated as a matrix of *MxN* elements. Each element of the digitized image (pixel) has a value that corresponds to the brightness of the point in the captured scene. An image whose resolution in intensity is of 8 bits, can take values from 0 to 255. In the case of a black and white image images it can take 0 and 1 values. In general, an image is represented in a bidimensional matrix as shown in (2).

$$I = \begin{pmatrix} x_{11} & x_{12} & \cdots & x_{1n} \\ x_{21} & x_{22} & \cdots & x_{2n} \\ \vdots & \vdots & \ddots & \vdots \\ x_{m1} & x_{m2} & \cdots & x_{mn} \end{pmatrix} \tag{2}$$

Since most of the devices acquire the images with a depth of 8 bits, the typical range of levels of gray for an image is from 0 to 255 so that the matrix elements of the image is represented by $x_{ij} \in [0...255]$.At this point it is convenient to say that even if the images are acquired at RGB format, it is frequently transformed in a gray scale matrix and for achieving the transformation from RGB type to gray Grassman level (Wyszecki & Stiles, 1982)is employed:

$$I_{gray} = I_R(0.299) + I_G(0.587) + I_B(0.114) \tag{3}$$

In the example presented in Fig. 4 shows how to acquire a digital image in RGB and grayscale format using the IMAQ toolbox. In this case there are two important blocks: The first one is the **IMAQ Create block** located in Vision and Motion/Vision Utilities/Image Management, this block creates a new image with a specified image type (RGB, Grayscale, HSL, etc.), the second block is the **IMAQ Read Image** which is located in Vision and Motion/Vision Utilities/Files/, the function of this block is to open an image file which is specified previously in the file path of the block and put all the information of this opened image in the new image created by **IMAQ Create**. In other words, in the example presented in Fig. 4 (A) the file picture4.png is opened by the **IMAQ Read Image** and the information this image is saved in a new image called imageColor that corresponds to a RGB (U32) image type.It is very simple to modify the image type of the system, in Fig. 4 (B) the image type is changed to Grayscale (U8) and the image is placed in imageGray.

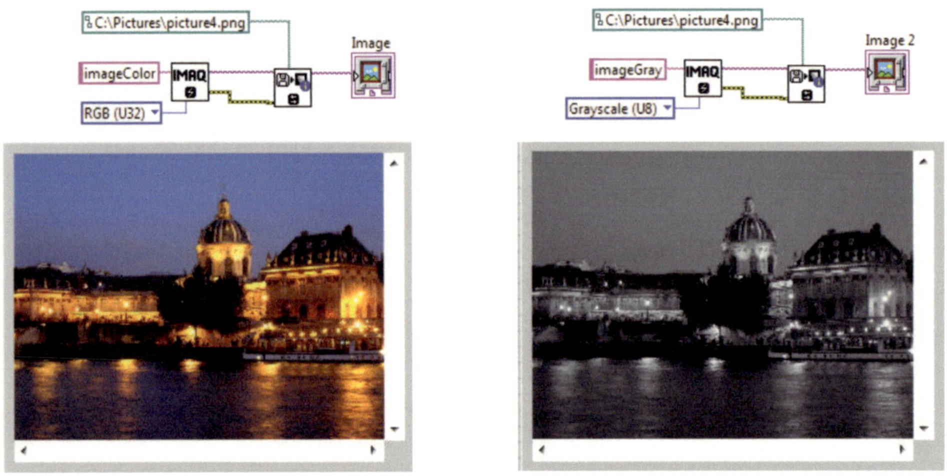

Fig. 4. RGB and Grayscale Image Acquisition.

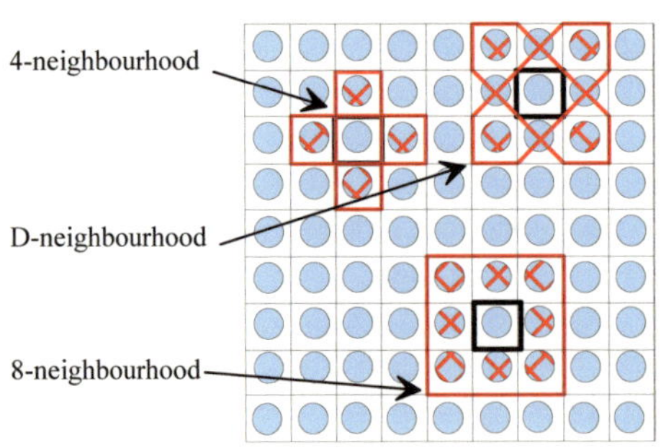

Fig. 5. Neighbourhood of a pixel.

Another important characteristic in the image definition is the neighbourhood of pixels, that could be classified in 3 groups described in (Fig. 5), if the neighbourhood is limited at the four adjacent pixels is named call 4-neighbourhood, the one conformed by the diagonal pixels is the D- neighbourhood and the 8 surrounding pixels is the 8-neighbourhood, the last one includes the 4- and the D-neighbourhood of pixel.

4. Image transformations

The images processing can be seen like a transformation of an image in another, in other words, it obtains a modified image starting from an input image, for improving human perception, or for extraction of information in computer vision. Two kinds of operations can be identified for them:

- Punctual operations. Where each pixel of the output image only depends of the value of a pixel in the input image.
- Grouped operations. In those that each pixel of the output image depends on multiple pixels in the input image, these operations can be local if they depend on the pixels that constitute its neighbourhood, or global if they depend on the whole image or they are applied globally about the values of intensity of the original image.

4.1 Punctual operations

The punctual operations transform an input image *I*, in a new output image *I'* modifying a pixel at the same time without take in account the neighbours pixels value, applying a function *f* to each one of the pixels of the image, so that:

$$I' = f(I) \tag{4}$$

The *f* functions most commonly used are, the identity, the negative, the threshold or binarization and the combinations of these. For all operations the pixels *q* of the new image *I'* depends of value of pixels *p* at the original *I* images.

4.1.1 The identity function

This is the most basic function and generates an output image that is a copy of the input image, this function this defined as:

$$q = p \tag{5}$$

4.1.2 The negative function

This function creates a new image that is the inverse of the input image, like the negative of a photo, this function is useful with images generates by absorption of radiation, that is the case of medical image processing. For a gray scale image with values from 0 to 255, this function is defined as:

$$q = 255 - p \tag{6}$$

In Fig. 6 is shown how to inverse the image using the toolbox of Vision and Motion of LabView. As it is observed in Fig. 6 b), the block that carry out the inverse of the image is called IMAQ inverse located in Vision and Motion/Vision Processing/Processing. This block only receives the source image and automatically performed the inverse of the image.

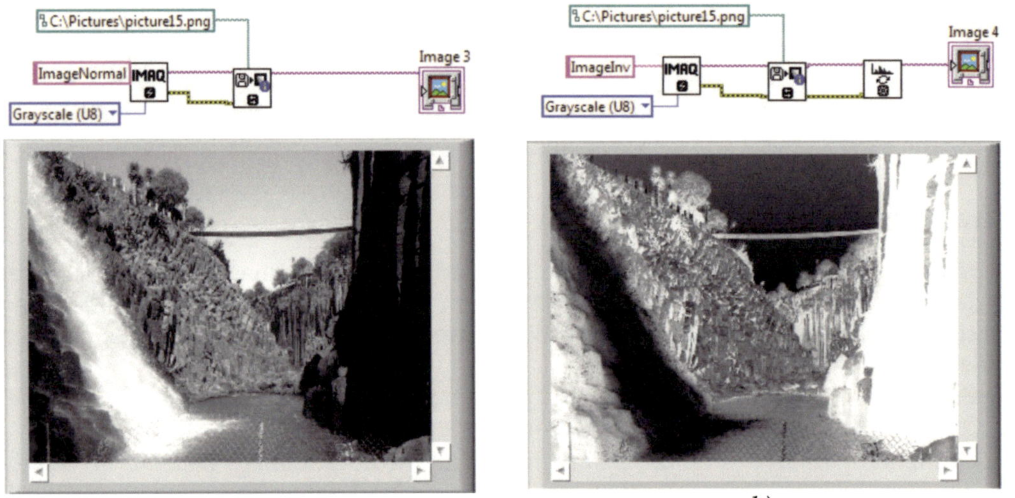

a) b)

Fig. 6. a) Gray scale image and b) Inverse grayscale image.

4.1.3 The threshold function

This function generates a binary output image from a gray scale input image; the transition level is given by the threshold value *t*, this function this defined as:

$$q = \begin{cases} 0 & if \quad p \le t \\ 255 & if \quad p > t \end{cases} \tag{7}$$

Fig. 7 b) shows the result of applying the threshold function to image in Fig. 7 a) with a *t* value of 150.

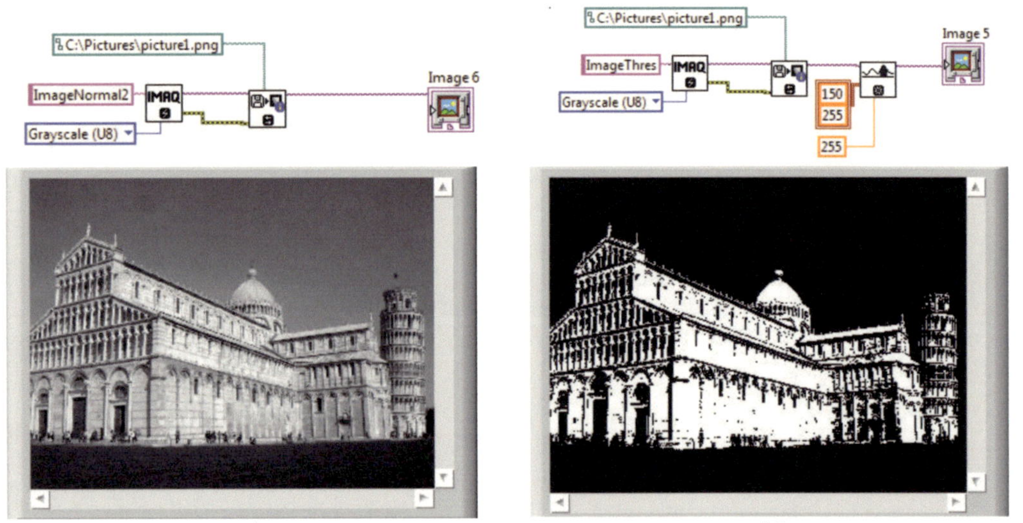

a) b)

Fig. 7. a) Original Image and b) Thresholding Image (150-255).

A variation of threshold function is the gray level reduction function, in this case, some values of threshold are used, and the number of gray levels at the output image is reduced as is shown in (8)

$$q = \begin{cases} 0 & if \quad p \le t_1 \\ q_1 & if \quad t_1 < p \le t_2 \\ q_2 & if \quad t_2 < p \le t_3 \\ \vdots & \vdots \quad \vdots \\ q_n & if \quad t_{n-1} < p \le 255 \end{cases} \tag{8}$$

4.2 Grouped operations

The grouped operations correspond to operations that take in consideration a group of points. In the punctual operations, a pixel q of the output image, depends only of a pixel p of the input image, however in grouped operations, the result of each pixel q in the image I' depends on a group of values in the image I, usually given by a neighbourhood.

So, if an 8-neighbourhoodis considered, a weighted sum must be done with the 8 neighbours of the corresponding pixel p and the result will be assigned to the pixel q.

To define the values of weight, different masks or kernels are generally used with constant values; the values of these masks determine the final result of the output image. For example if the mask is done as:

$$\begin{bmatrix} -1 & 0 & 1 \\ -2 & 1 & 2 \\ -3 & 0 & 3 \end{bmatrix} \tag{9}$$

The value of the pixel q in the position x,y will be:

$$\begin{aligned} & \left(-1 * p(x-1,y-1)\right) + \left(0 * p(x,y-1)\right) + \left(1 * p(x+1,y-1)\right) \\ q(x,y) = + & \left(-2 * p(x-1,y)\right) + \left(1 * p(x,y)\right) + \left(2 * p(x+1,y)\right) \\ + & \left(-3 * p(x-1,y+1)\right) + \left(0 * p(x,y+1)\right) + \left(3 * p(x+1,y+1)\right) \end{aligned} \tag{10}$$

Since the pixels at border of input image does not have 8 neighbours, the output image I' is smaller that the original image I.

Inside of grouped operations, a special mention must be done about the image filter. Similar to one-dimensional signal filters, two kinds of filters could be depicted: the high-pass filter and the low-pass filter. They let to pass the high or low frequencies respectively. In the case of the images, the high frequencies are associated to abrupt changes in the intensity of neighbouring pixels, and low frequencies are associated to small changes in the intensity of the same pixels.

A classic mask for a high-pass filter is done by (11):

$$High - pass \equiv \begin{bmatrix} \frac{1}{9} & \frac{1}{9} & \frac{1}{9} \\ \frac{1}{9} & \frac{1}{9} & \frac{1}{9} \\ \frac{1}{9} & \frac{1}{9} & \frac{1}{9} \end{bmatrix} \tag{11}$$

In the same way a low-pass filter is done by (12):

$$Low - pass \equiv \begin{bmatrix} -1 & -1 & -1 \\ -1 & 9 & -1 \\ -1 & -1 & -1 \end{bmatrix} \tag{12}$$

5. Image histogram

The histogram is a graph that contains the number of pixels in an image at different intensity value. In a 8-bit greyscale image a histogram will graphically display 256 numbers showing the distribution of pixels versus the greyscale values as is shown Fig. 8.

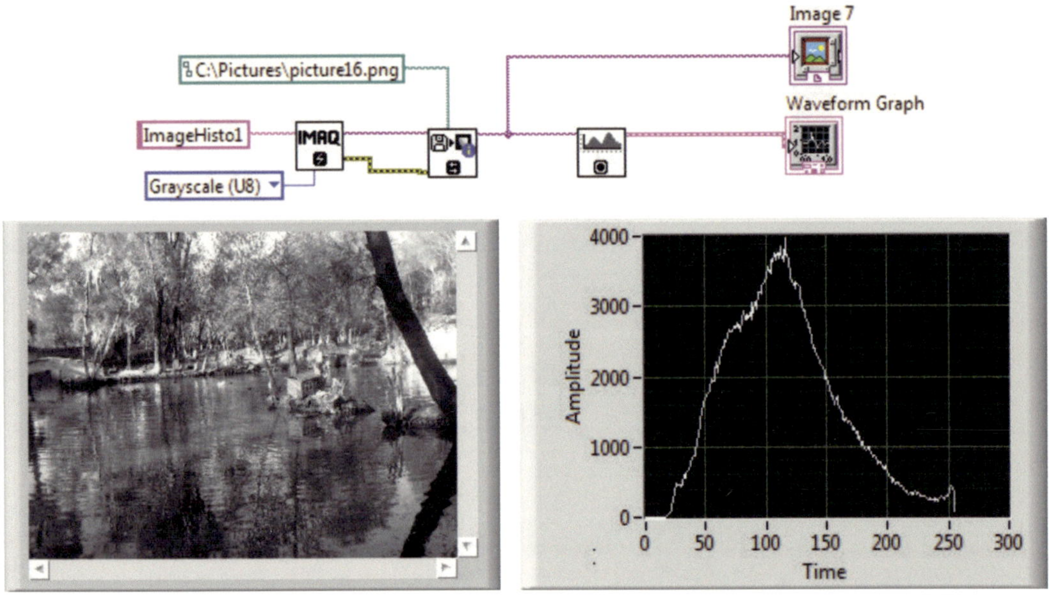

Fig. 8. Histogram Grayscale Image.

Fig. 9. Histogram RGB Image.

Fig. 8 and Fig. 9 shows the results of the greyscale histogram and RGB histogram using **IMAQ histograph** block located in Image Processing/Analysis. The output of the **IMAQ**

Read Image Block is connected to the input of the **IMAQ histograph** block and then a waveform graph is connected in order to show obtained results.

6. Image segmentation

Prewitt Edge Detector: The prewitt operator has a 3x3 mask and deals better with the noise effect. An approach using the masks of size 3x3 is given by considering the below arrangement of pixels about the pixel *(x , y). In Fig. 10 is shown an example of the Prewitt Edge Detector.*

$$Gx = (a_2 + ca_3 + a_4) - (a_0 + ca_7 + a_6) \tag{13}$$

$$Gy = (a_6 + ca_s + a_4) - (a_0 + ca_1 + a_2) \tag{14}$$

$$Gx = \begin{bmatrix} -1 & 0 & 1 \\ -1 & 0 & 1 \\ -1 & 0 & 1 \end{bmatrix} \quad Gy = \begin{bmatrix} 1 & 1 & 1 \\ 0 & 0 & 0 \\ -1 & -1 & -1 \end{bmatrix} \tag{15}$$

Fig. 10. Prewitt Edge Detector. (a) Grayscale image, (b) Prewitt Transformation.

Sobel Edge Detector: The partial derivatives of the Sobel operator are calculated as

$$Gx = (a_2 + 2a_3 + a_4) - (a_0 + 2a_7 + a_6) \tag{16}$$

$$Gx = (a_6 + 2a_s + a_4) - (a_0 + 2a_1 + a_2) \tag{17}$$

Therefore the Sobel masks are

$$Gx = \begin{bmatrix} -1 & -2 & -1 \\ 0 & 0 & 0 \\ 1 & 2 & 1 \end{bmatrix} \quad Gy = \begin{bmatrix} -1 & 0 & 1 \\ -2 & 0 & 2 \\ -1 & 0 & 1 \end{bmatrix} \tag{18}$$

In Fig. 11 and Fig. 12 is shown the image transformation using the Sobel Edge Detector.

Fig. 11. Sobel Edge Detector. (a) Grayscale image, (b) Sobel Transformation.

Fig. 12. Sobel Edge Detector. (a) Grayscale image, (b) Sobel Transformation.

7. Smoothing filters

The process of the smoothing filters is carried out moving the filter mask from point to point in an image; this process is known like convolution. Filter a *M*x*N* image with an averaging filter of size *m*x*n* is given by:

$$h(x,y) = \frac{\sum_{s=-a}^{a}\sum_{t=-b}^{b} d(s,t)\, f(x+s,y+t)}{\sum_{s=-a}^{a}\sum_{t=-b}^{b} d(s,t)} \tag{19}$$

In Fig. 13 is shown a block diagram of a smoothing filter. Although IMAQ vision libraries contain the convolution blocks, this function is presented in order to explain in detail the operation of the smoothing filter. The idea is simple, there is a kernel matrix of *mxn* dimension, these elements are multiplied by the each element of a sub-matrix (mxn) contained in the image of *M*x*N* elements. Once the multiplication is done, all the elements are summed and divided by the number of elements in the kernel matrix. The result is saved in a new matrix, and the kernel window is moved to another position in the image to carry out a new operation.

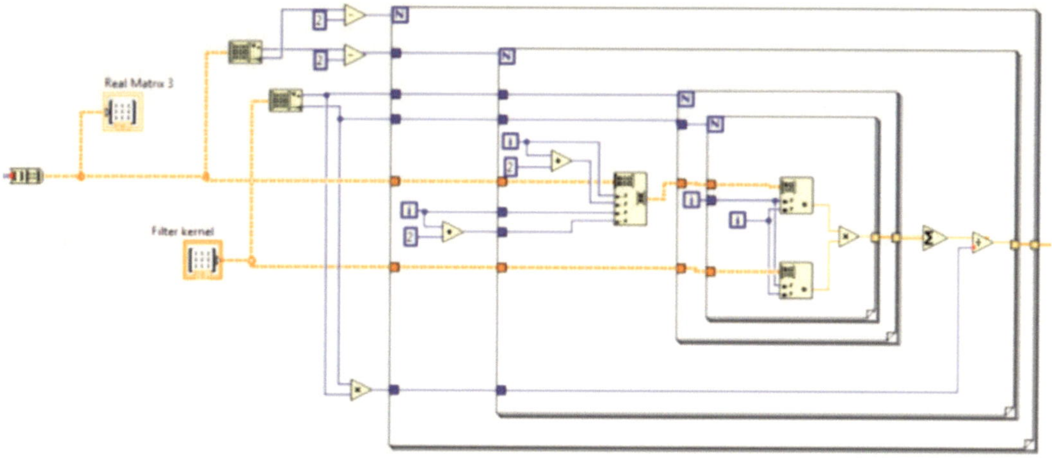

Fig. 13. Block diagram of a Smoothing Filter.

Fig. 14 shows the implementation of smoothing filters using the **Vision Assistant Block**. The image was opened using the **IMAQ Read Image block** and after this was connected to the **Image In** of the Vision Assistance Block. Inside the vision assistant block in the Processing Function Grayscale was chosen the Filters option. In the example of Fig. 14 the filter selected was the **Local Average filter** with a kernel size of 7x7.
In Fig. 14 (d) is observed the effect of the average filter in the image. In this case the resultant image was blurred because the average filters.

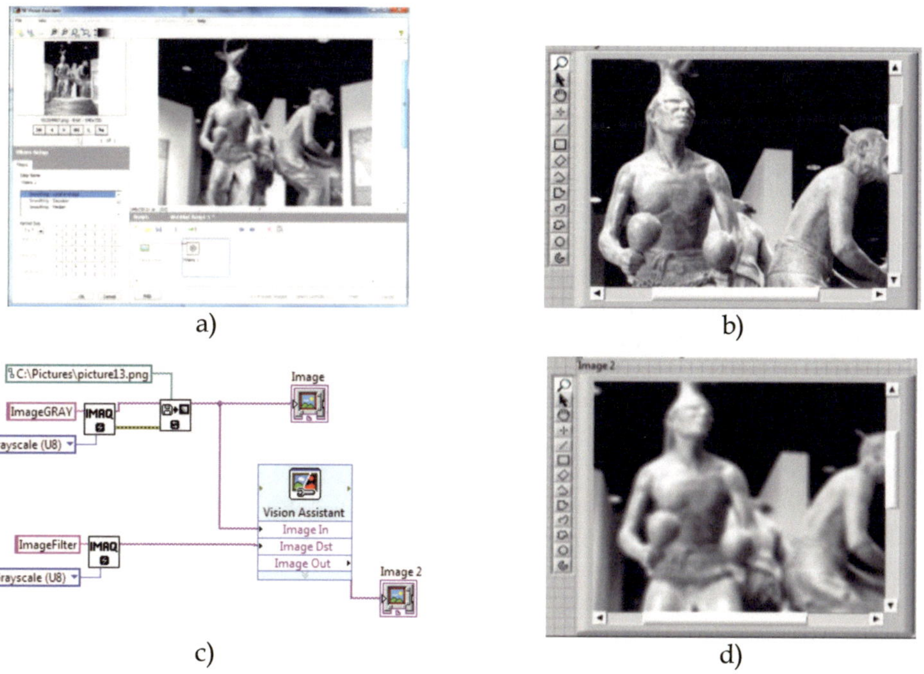

Fig. 14. Local Average Filter, a) Vision Express, b) Original Image, c) block diagram, d) smoothed image.

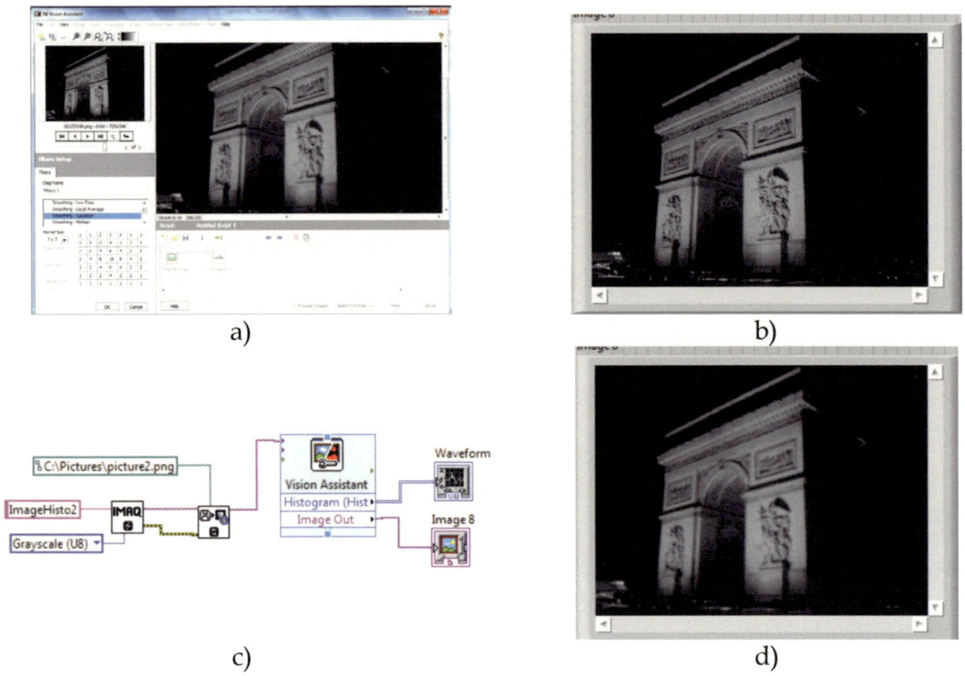

Fig. 15. Gaussian Filter, a) Vision Express, b) Original Image, c) block diagram, d) smoothed image.

8. Pattern recognition

Pattern recognition is a common technique that can be applied for the detection and recognition of objects. The idea is really simple and consists into find an image according a template image. The algorithm not only searches the exact apparition of the image but also finds a certain grade of variation respect to the pattern. The simplest method is the template matching and it is expressed in the following way:

An image *A* (size (*W*x*H*) and image *P* (size *w*x*h*), is the result of the image *M* (size (*W-w+1*)x(*H-h+1*)), where each pixel *M(x,y)* indicates the probability that the rectangle *[x,y]-[x+w-1,y+h-1]* of *A* contains the Pattern.

The image *M* is defined by the difference function between the segments of the image:

$$M(x,y)=\sum_{a=0}^{w}\sum_{b=0}^{h}\left(P(a,b)-A(x+a,y+b)\right)^2 \tag{20}$$

In the literature are found different projects using the template matching technique to solve different problems. Goshtasby presented an invariant template matching using normalized invariant moments, the technique is based on the idea of two-stage template matching (Goshtasby, 2009). Denning studied a model for a real-time intrusion-detection expert system capable of detecting break-ins, penetrations, and other forms of computer(Denning, 2006). Seong-Min presents a paper about the development of vision based automatic inspection system of welded nuts on support hinge used to support the trunk lid of a car(Seong-Min, Young-Choon, & Lee, 2006). Izák introduces an application in image analysis of biomedical images using matching template (Izak & Hrianka).

8.1 Pattern recognition example

In the next example, a pattern recognition system is presented. In Fig. 16 shows the block diagram of the video acquisition and the pattern recognition system. A continuous acquisition from the webcam with inline processing was used, therefore there is a while loop inside the blocks of video acquisition and pattern recognition system. One important parameter is to transform the format of the image in the acquired video into intensity values. One of the methodologies to change RGB values to intensity values is through **IMAQ extract single color plane** located in vision utilities/color utilities/. Once the image has been converted into intensity, this image will be the input for the pattern recognition function.

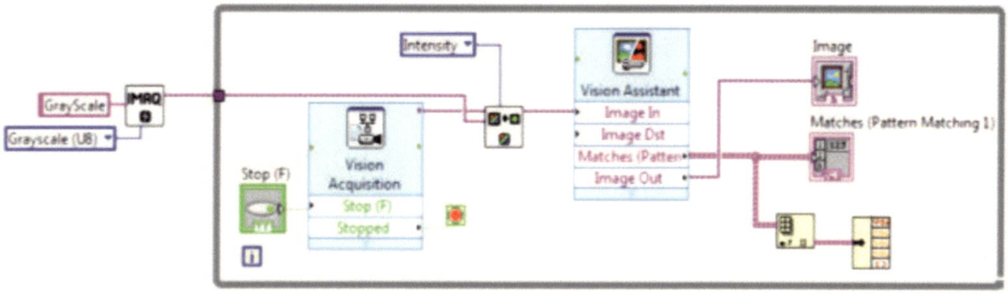

Fig. 16. Block Diagram of Pattern Recognition System.

The vision Assistant was used for the pattern recognition section. A machine vision located in processing function option was selected (Fig. 17 a). The next step is to create a new template clicking in the option new template and select in a box a desired image that will be the object that the algorithm will try to find (Fig. 17 b).

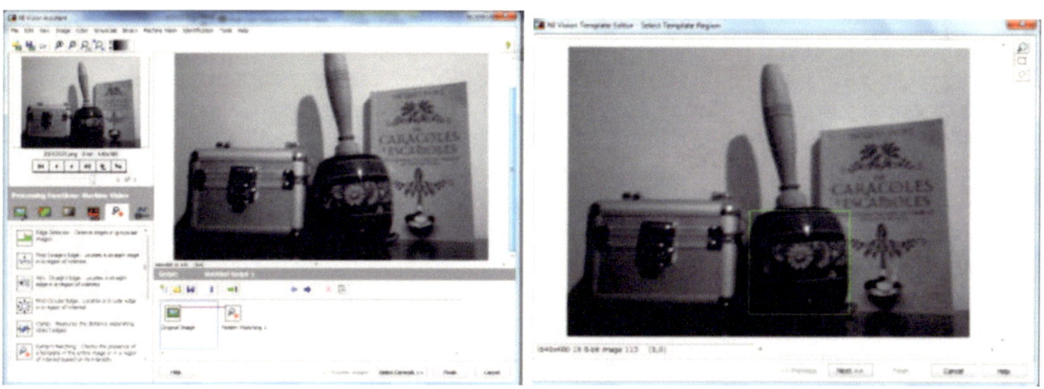

a) b)

Fig. 17. a) Selection of pattern matching, b) creation of new template.

In the last step of the configuration the vision assistant carries out the pattern matching algorithm and identifies the desired object in the whole (Fig. 18 a). Finally when the program is executed in real-time, each frame of the camera identifies the desired object in the scene (Fig. 18 b).

It is important to remark that in order to obtain the output parameters of the recognized matches, it must be selected the checking box Matches inside the control parameters. The output matches is a cluster that contains different information. In order to acquire certain parameters of the cluster is necessary to place an index array block and the unbundle block located in programming/cluster.

a) b)

Fig. 18. a) Recognition of the template in the whole image, b) real-time recognition.

8.2 Machine vision used in a mobile robot

In this section is presented the integration of machine vision algorithms in a mobile robot. This example uses a mobile robot with differential drive and with a robotic gripper mounted in its surface. The principal task of this mobile robot is to recognize objects in the scene through a webcam, when an object is recognized the robot moves through the recognized object and the gripper grasps it. This simple technique produces a kind of artificial intelligence in the system, generating that the robot can know its environment and make decisions according to the circumstances of this environment. This robot can be operated in manual and automatic form. In the manual way a joystick controls all the movements of the robot and in automatic way the digital image processing algorithms obtain information to make decision about the motion of the robot.

A mobile robot with two fixed wheels is one of the simplest mobile robots. This robot rotates around a point normally placed between the two driving wheels. This point is called instantaneous center of curvature (ICC). In order to control this kind of robot, the velocities of the two wheels must be changed producing a movement in the instantaneous center of rotation and different trajectories will be obtained.

In the literature are found different researches about mobile robots using differential drive. Greenwald present an article about robotics using a differential drive control (Greenwald & Jkopena, 2003). Chitsaz presents a method to compute the shortest path for a differential-drive mobile robot(Chitsaz & La Valle, 2006). The odometry is an important topic in mobile robotic,in this field Papadopoulus provides a simple and cheap calibration method to improve the odometry accuracy and to present an alternative method (Papadopoulos & Misailidis, 2008). In the field of control Dongkyoung proposes"a tracking control method for differential-drive wheeled mobile robots with nonholonomic constraints by using a backstepping-like feedback linearization (Dongkyoung, 2003).

The left and right wheels generates a specific trajectories around the ICC with the same angular rate $\omega = \frac{d\vartheta}{dt}$.

$$\omega * R = V_c \tag{21}$$

$$\omega * \left(R - \frac{D}{2}\right) = v_1 \tag{22}$$

$$\omega * \left(R - \frac{D}{2}\right) = v_2 \tag{23}$$

Where v_1 and v_2 are the wheel's velocities, R is the distance from ICC to the midpoint between the two wheels.

$$R = \frac{v_2 + v_1}{v_2 - v_1} * \frac{D}{2} \tag{24}$$

$$\omega = \frac{v_2 - v_1}{D} \tag{25}$$

The velocity in the C Point is the midpoint between the two wheels and can be calculated as the average of the two velocities

$$Vc = \frac{v_1 + v_2}{2} \tag{26}$$

According to these equations if v_1=v_2 the robot will move in a straight line. In the case of different values in the velocities of the motors, the mobile robot will follow a curved trajectory. Brief description of the system: A picture of the mobile robot is shown in Fig. 19. The mobile robot is dived in five important groups: the mechanical platform, the grasping system, the vision system, the digital control system and power electronics system.

- In mechanical platform were mounted 2 DC motors, each one of the motors has a high torque and a speed of 80 RPMs. Obtaining with these two parameters a high torque and acceptable speed of the mobile robot.
- The grasping system is a mechatronic device with 2 DOF of linear displacements, there are two servos with a torque of 3.6 kg-cm and speed of 100 RPMs.
- The Microsoft webcam Vx-1000 was used for the Vision System section. This webcam offers high-quality images and good stability.
- The digital control system consists in a Microcontroller Microchip PIC18F4431. The velocity of the motors are controlled by Pulse Wide Modulation, therefore, this microcontroller model is important because contains 8 PWMs in hardware and 2 in software (CCP). Moreover, all the sensors of the mobile robot (encoders, pots, force sensors, etc.) are connected to the analog and digital inputs. The interface with the computer is based on the protocol RS232.
- The power electronic system is carried out by 2 H-Bridges model L298. The H-Bridge regulates the output voltage according to the Pulse Wide Modulation input. The motors are connected to this device and the velocity is controlled by the PWM of the microcontroller.

The core of the system remains in the fusion of the computer-microcontroller interface and the vision system. On one hand, the computer-microcontroller interface consists in the serial communication between these two devices, therefore it is important to review how a serial communication can be carried out using LabView. In the other hand, the vision consists in the pattern matching algorithm which find the template of a desired object in an acquired image.

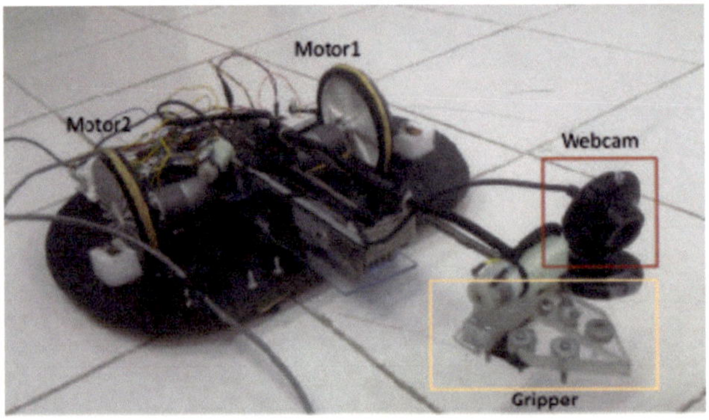

Fig. 19. Mobile Robot.

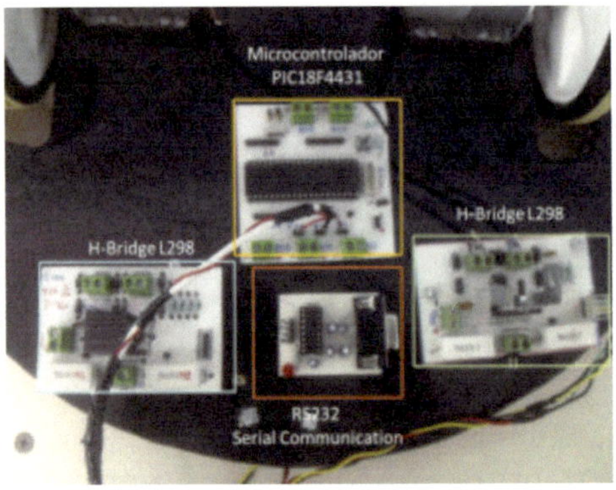

Fig. 20. Electronics Targets.

Fig. 21 presents an example about RS232 communication (write mode). There is an important block for serial communication called VISA configure serial port located in Instrument IO/Serial/. In this block is necessary to place the correct information about the COM, the baudrate, data bits, parity, etc. For this example COM4 was used, with a baudrate of 9600, 8 bits of data and none parity. A timed loop structure was selected to write information in determined time, in this case the timed loop was configured in a period of 50msec. It is important to remark that the data in serial communication is transmitted like string of characters, therefore it is important to convert any numerical value in a string value. The block used for this task is: numeric to decimal string, located in programming/string/string conversion/, this block convert a decimal number into a string and contains two input parameters, the first one is the decimal number to be converted and the second one is the width of this decimal number, all the string conversion outputs are concatenated using the concatenate string block and this information is sent to the write buffer input of the VISA write block. The VISA write block is the responsible to write the string information in the specified serial port. Normally a termination character is very important in the serial communication, in this case it was used the termination character \r. The block VISA property node is the responsible to add a termination character. In this block must be chosen the option TermChar, TermChar En and ASRL End Out. For this example was written 13 in Termchar that corresponds to \r, the TermChar En was activated with a True value and in ASRL end Out was chosen the TermChar option.

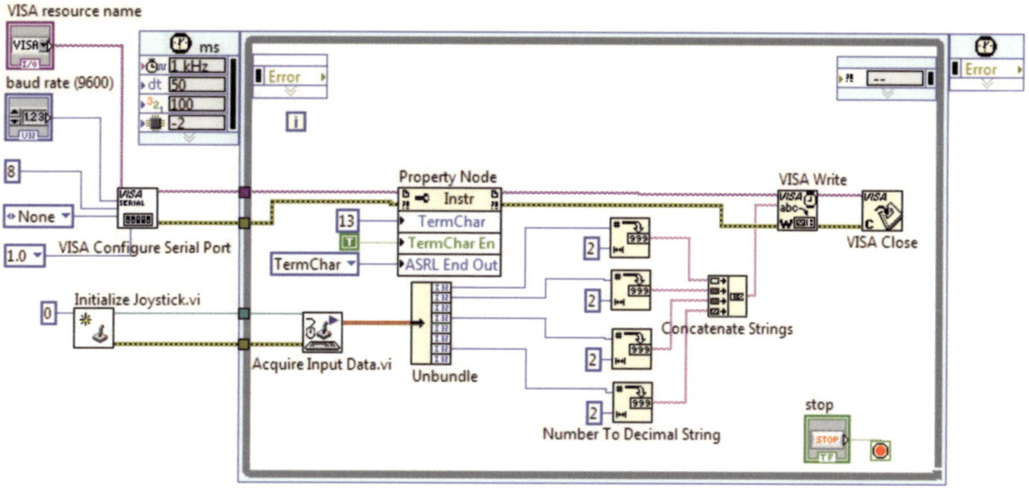

Fig. 21. Serial Communication and Joystick configuration/control.

The mobile robot can work in automatic and manual way, in the manual way the mobile robot can be manipulated through a joystick. The configuration of the joystick is a simple task, there is a block called Initialized Joystick located in connectivity/input device control/. This block needs the index parameter, in this case there is only one joystick connected and the index is 0. Once the joystick is configured, the second step is to acquire the data through the block Acquired Input Data. In data is presented in a cluster format. Therefore an unbundle block is necessary to obtain the parameters in an individual form.

Fig. 22. Mobile robot observing the scene.

The aim of the mobile robot is to recognize a specific object for the environment using machine vision. In order to do this task, a specific object was selected like the pattern image (in this case was the red box Fig. 23) using the Vision Assistant toolbox. Once the pattern image was selected, the algorithm can identify the location of the box in real-time. Fig. 22 shows the mobile robot observing the environment and looking for the desired object. The searching algorithms are inside the microcontroller, if the pattern matching does not recognize any match, the robot moves in different position until a match is recognized. Once the match is recognized the algorithms gives the x,y position of the match in the image. This position is important because the robot will try to center the gripper according to the x,y position of the desired object. There is an infrared sensor that obtains the distance from the gripper to the desired object and the microcontroller moves the gripper to the correct position and grasps the object.

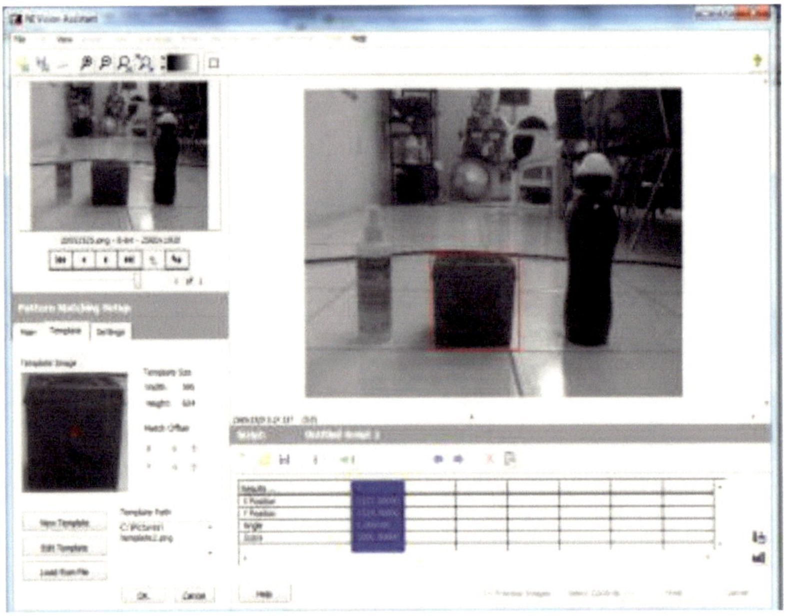

Fig. 23. Pattern Matching configuration.

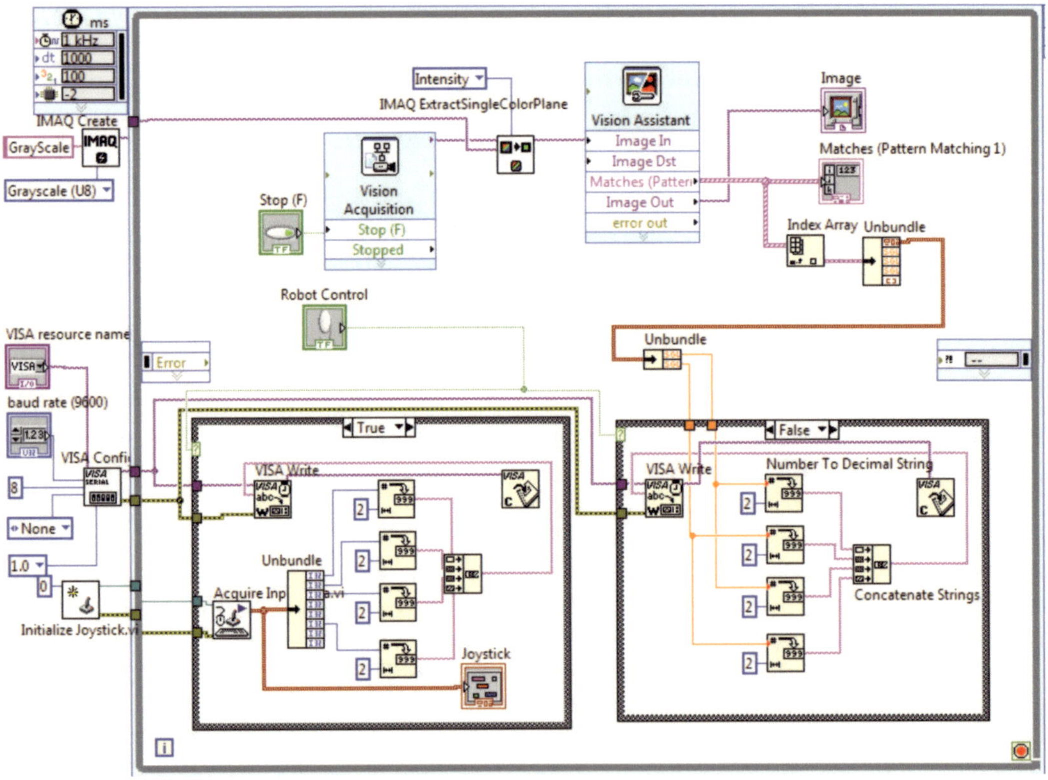

Fig. 24. Block Diagram of the Mobile Robot System.

Fig. 24 shows the complete block diagram of the mobile robot, there is a timed loop where the joystick and serial transmission are performed in a specific interval of time in the same time the vision algorithms are carried out in the same loop. Moreover, there is a selector to switch from manual to automatic control. In the automatic way, the coordinates of the match are sent to the microcontroller and this device runs special routines to orientate the robot in a correct position. In the manual way, the control is carried out by the user using a joystick.

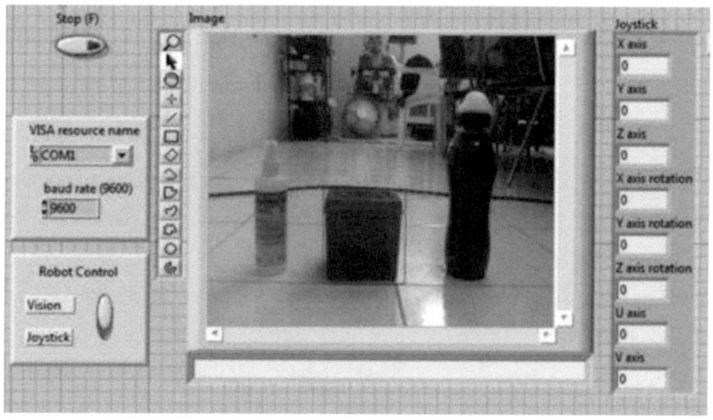

Fig. 25. Front Panel of the Mobile Robot System.

Fig. 25 shows the results of the pattern recognition algorithm, the robot was capable to observe its environment and recognize the desired object. This final project presents the integration of different algorithms that were presented and explained in previous sections of this chapter. The block diagram presents the initial configuration of the joystick and the serial port using the Initialize joystick block and the VISA configuration block. In the timed loop is executed the vision algorithms for the object recognition and the serial data transmission using the joystick or using automatic form. In the automatic form the microcontroller receives the x-y position of the object and the carries out all the algorithms of path planning inside the microcontroller to arrive to this object and grasp it.

9. Conclusions

Different basis techniques of digital image processing using LabView have been boarded in this chapter. At the beginning some theoretical concepts about the image generation were discussed for standing out the effects of illumination, scene and acquisition system in the results of image processing.

Then the stages of a classic system of image processing were described as well as the necessary tools of the LabView platform to achieve each stage, from the acquisition of the image to a control of a mobile using the image matching template. The image transformation leave to know how the output image is generated from an input image with the use of punctual and grouped operations, some examples were presented of most comment image transformations.

Finally the pattern recognition section shows how to use an image into a computer vision application, through an example of object detection and the use of other functionalities of LabView suggest that the use of LabView as an excellent platform to develop robotic projects as well as vision and image processing applications. The versatility provided by the software LabView and the capability of IMAQ toolbox increase the possibility to improve the use of digital image processing in any application area.

10. Acknowledgement

This work is supported by the General Council of Superior Technological Education of Mexico (DGEST).
Additionally, this work is sponsored by the National Council of Science and Technology (CONACYT) and the Public Education Secretary (SEP) through PROMEP.

11. References

Chitsaz, H., & La Valle, S. (2006). Minimum Wheel-Rotation Paths for Differential Drive Mobile Robots Among Piecewise Smooth Obstacles. *Robotics and Automation, 2006. ICRA 2006. Proceedings 2006 IEEE* , 1616 - 1623.

Denning, D. (2006). Software Enginnering. *IEEE Transaction on , SE-13*, 222-232.

2001 Digital Imiage AnalysisNew YorkUSASpringer-Verlag

Dongkyoung, C. (2003). Tracking Control of Differential-Drive Wheeled Mobile Robots Using a Backstepping-Like Feedback Linearization. *IEEE transactions on systems, man, and cybernetics – part a: systems and humans* , 1-11.

Fairchild, M. (2005). *Color Apperance Modeles.* Chichester, UK: Wiley-IS&T.

Forsyth, D., & Ponce, J. (2002). *Computer Vision: A Modern Approach.* New Jersey: Prentice Hall.

Frery, L. V., Gomes, A., & Levy, S. *Image Processing for Computer Graphics and Vision.* New York, USA: Springer-Verlag.

Goshtasby, A. (27. Enero 2009). Pattern Analysis and Machine Intelligence. *IEEE transactions on* , 338-344.

Greenwald, L., & Jkopena, J. (2003). Mobile Robot Labs. *IEEE Robotics and Automatization Magazine* , 25-32.

Izak, P., & Hrianka, M. (kein Datum). Biomedical Image Analysis by Program "Vision Assistan" and "LabView". *Advances in Electrical and Electronic Engineering* , 233-236.

Papadopoulos, E., & Misailidis, M. (2008). Calibration and planning techniques for mobile robots in industrial environments. *Industrial Robot: An International Journal* , 564-572.

Reinders, M. (1997). Eye Tracking by Template Matching using an Automatic Codebook Generation Scheme. *Third Annual Conference of ASCI* .

Seong-Min, K., Young-Choon, L., & Lee, S.-C. (18. Octuber 2006). *SICE-ICASE* , 1508-1512.

Wyszecki, G., & Stiles, W. (1982). *Color Science: Concepts and Methods Quantitative Data and Formulae.* New York: John Wiley & Sons.

15

Remote SMS Instrumentation Supervision and Control Using LabVIEW

Rafael C. Figueiredo[1], Antonio M. O. Ribeiro[1],
Rangel Arthur[2] and Evandro Conforti[1]
[1]Department of Microwave and Optics - University of Campinas (FEEC/Unicamp),
[2]Division of Telecommunication Technology (FT/Unicamp),
Brazil

1. Introduction

The hot emergence of remote monitoring and control systems in recent years is closely related to the outstanding advance in electronics and instrumentation techniques. As one of the earliest examples, the telemetry experiments using satellite-relay systems for remote hydrologic data collection (Glasgow et al., 2004) in the 70's should be remembered. Since then, a fast and continual appearance of real time monitoring systems occurred, new devices and tools have kept coming up, and more and more powerful resources are available with decreasing prices. Hence, remote monitoring and control systems are gaining market-share in diversified areas such as industry, security, education and even in health-care applications.

In every distinct area it is possible to evince different advantages and applications when using remote systems. To exemplify the industrial field, a remote data acquisition may be used to monitor machine health and energy consumption in environments where it is difficult to access or to use wired data acquisition systems (Khan et al., 2004). As another example, a remote fault diagnostic system to check machines status including data, image, and video trough the Internet and mobile terminals by wireless application protocol (WAP) (Wang et al., 2007) was implemented. In the security area, a robot can inspect home environment giving general information and alarms about dangerous situations using wireless network (Zhang et al., 2007). In addition, real-time remote health monitoring systems can acquire and process data to evaluate long bridge structure reliability (Jianting et al., 2006). Regarding the educational field, there is a web-based remote control laboratory that employs a greenhouse scale model for teaching greenhouse climate control techniques using different hardware and software platforms (Guzmán et al., 2005), and also a virtual laboratory that permits remote access via Transmission Control Protocol/Internet Protocol (TCP/IP), enabling control and supervision through the Internet (Garbus et al., 2006). In addition, the results of an evaluation of remote monitoring in home health care show a reduction in nursing visit and hospitalization rates in the remote monitoring patient group (Rosati, 2009).

The example list can be much longer. The technological advances allow development of systems with more and better resources and higher transmission rates, consequently increasing its complexity and budget. However, in various applications we just need to control or monitor simple tasks, which can be performed by less complex and cheaper systems. In some cases there is a very small amount of data being collected and the necessary command to perform a specific action can be sent in a simple text message with a few characters. In this context, the short message service (SMS) used in cellular networks is being adapted to several remote applications. Despite some restrictions, such as the limit of 160 characters per message without a user-friendly graphical interface, the SMS is widely available throughout the digital cellular network. It can be used by any 2G cell phone, it is a low cost service, and it does not overload the network since this service does not consume much network resources. These and other advantages led to the development of diversified remote applications using SMS. Among many examples, the SMS can be used to monitor and/or control remotely the functions of an automotive alarm (Figueiredo et al., 2008), the ambient temperature in regions of difficult access (Zarka et al., 2006), a computer network (Sarram et al., 2008), an electronic switching system (Zahariah et al., 2009), as well as the status of power earth lines (Xiao et al., 2009).

Addressing now the main focus of this chapter, the Laboratory Virtual Instrumentation Engineering Workbench (LabVIEW) is a graphical programming environment from National Instruments that deserves attention not only on remote systems, but in a wide range of applications. Originally released in 1986, LabVIEW is commonly used to develop sophisticated measurement, test, and control systems; and its graphical language permits the development of programs even by inexpert programmers. The popularity of this platform has been increasing. Some years ago it was included in the curriculum of electrical engineering students by practical approaches involving experiments in electronics (Alsaialy et al., 2003; Higa et al., 2002). It is also possible to highlight a long list of applications using LabVIEW, among which we cite a system to analyze and monitor the mechanical vibration of industrial machines (Lita et al., 2005); a remote-accessed instrumentation laboratory for digital signal processors training on the Internet (Gallardo et al., 2006); a solution of data acquisition/distribution designated for remote process control and long distance learning (Sgârciu & Stamatescu, 2010); a tele-health system that detects changes in heart rate and blood pressure of the patient in advance and sends an alert SMS to the doctor (Sukanesh et al., 2010); and a low cost system to monitor and control laboratory instruments remotely by SMS (Figueiredo et al., 2009). This chapter will be developed based on this last application, focusing on the necessary steps for the LabVIEW-based software development and describing all the programming details for creating a remote monitoring and control system using LabVIEW and SMS. Additionally, at the end of the chapter, an example of system applicability is illustrated in a measurement procedure, validating the developed tool and demonstrating the implementation in a specific application.

In general terms, a computer running LabVIEW is connected to a Global System for Mobile Communication (GSM) modem via RS-232 serial communication. This GSM modem is controlled by AT commands, which is a standard-command set with instructions used for modem control, detailed in Section 2 of this Chapter. The GSM modem enables the user to monitor and control a specific instrument while away from it, using a cell phone that sends and receives text messages through SMS. As an example to be discussed here, the instrument can be connected to LabVIEW via IEEE-488 General Purpose Interface Bus (GPIB), but it can also be easily adapted for other communication forms.

The chapter is organized as follows:

- Section 2 aims to provide basic knowledge about issues that will be raised during the system development. The text brings basic information about LabVIEW, SMS and AT commands, always focusing on the resources that will be applied in this particular project;

- Section 3 describes the system architecture. Also, the program created in LabVIEW will be fully detailed;
- Section 4 presents a case study in which the designed tool is applied to an 1.8-GHz narrow band envelope measurement made in an urban area to characterize the coherence bandwidth between two frequency-spaced radio mobile signal (Ribeiro et al., 2007), demonstrating the remote SMS system operation and results.;
- Section 5 gives the concluding remarks followed by acknowledgments in Section 6;
- Section 7 comes with the references.

2. Background

As mentioned earlier, the purpose of this Section is to provide a basic understanding of the issues to be raised throughout the chapter. Initially, the SMS will be briefly addressed, followed by some explanation of AT commands, listing the main commands that will be used to control the GSM modem. Lastly, some basic LabVIEW concepts related to the development of our remote application will be quickly described.

2.1 Short Message Service (SMS)

The SMS technology evolved from the GSM standard in the early 90's. It is currently available in the entire GSM network and can be accessed by practically every cell phone. The service enables the user to send messages with the maximum length of 160 or 140 characters when using 7-bit or 8-bit encoding, respectively. The system can segment messages that exceed the maximum length into shorter messages. In this case, it must use part of the payload for a user-defined header that specifies the segment sequence information. When a text message is sent from a user to another, the phone actually sends it to a short message service center (SMSC), where the message is stored and delivered when the recipient is on the network. Namely, it is a store-and-forward operation. In this paradigm, the system keeps resending the message for some period of time until it is successfully received. The SMSC usually has a configurable time limit for how long it will store the message, and be able to resend it in case of failure in the previous attempts. Messages can be sent using text mode or protocol data unit (PDU). The text mode is a character-based protocol and it is the simplest mode to send messages, suitable for unintelligent terminals. The PDU may contain control information, address information, or data, i.e., this mode adds the convenience of binary data to be transmitted, not just characters (Peersman et al., 2000; Brown et al., 2007). In this project the exchanged messages will be composed only of ASCII characters. Therefore, the SMS text mode will be used, which, despite allowing only transmission of characters, it is simpler to work with.

In this project, the GSM modem is responsible for sending and receiving text messages. It can accesses the GSM network like a mobile phone, differing in the way it is controlled, which is accomplished through AT commands. The command set may vary according to the device manufacturers. Here, the GSM modem used was assembled with the Motorola G24 module, whose operation and main AT commands are described below.

2.2 AT commands

AT or Hayes commands are a set of data stream commands for communication between computers and modems. Originally developed by Hayes Microcomputer Products in the beginning of modem communications, the AT commands became a standard for modem control. AT is the prefix for almost every command-line set; it is derived from the word "attention" and tells the modem that a request is coming. Requests can be made to accomplish a particular action, to change or query a specific parameter and they are sent to the modem through strings (Figueiredo et al., 2008; Jawarkar et al., 2007; Zhicong et al., 2008).

An AT command line may be composed by one or more commands, but it must not exceed 140 characters. Extended commands are preceded by the "+" symbol and are separated on the same line by a semicolon, whereas basic commands can be separated by a single blank space. The syntax of an extended command enables to query or change more than one sub-parameter, but the sub-parameters that will not be modified can be omitted from the command line. In order to clarify the structure of an AT command line, an example is shown in Figure 1, where the suffix <CR> is the ASCII (American Standard Code for Information Interchange) character to "carriage return". After a query, the modem responds with a result code that can include the current values and the range of possible values of the consulted parameter. The result code is also emitted after a request, informing the success or failure of the execution through the strings OK or ERROR, respectively. An example of the result code is shown in Figure 2, where <LF> is the ASCII character to "line feed" (Figueiredo et al., 2008; Motorola, 2008).

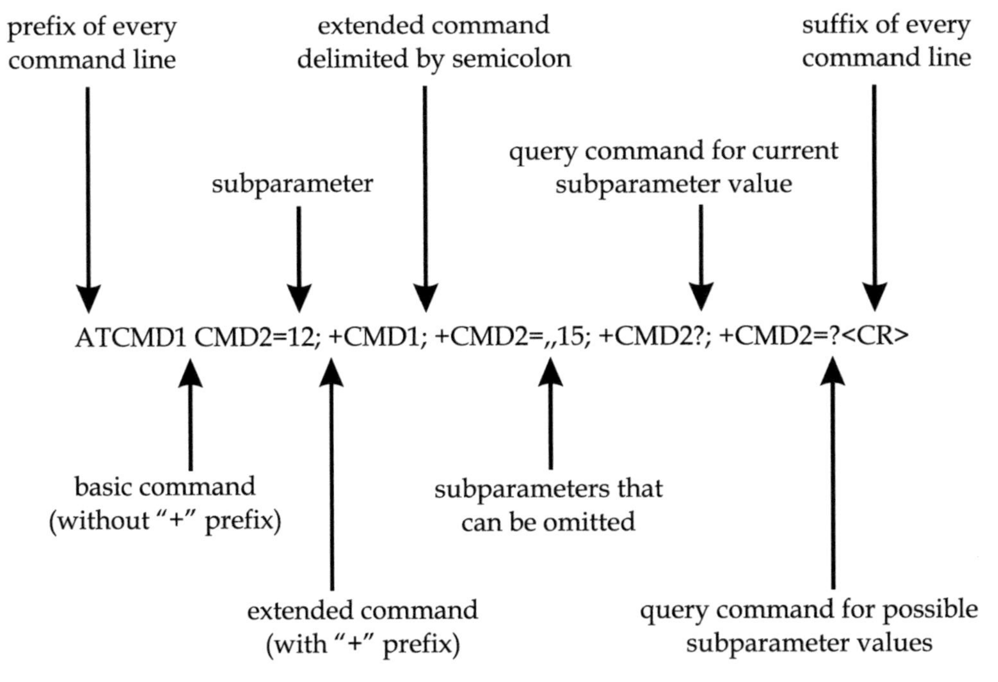

Fig. 1. Basic structure of an AT command line [adapted from (Motorola, 2008)].

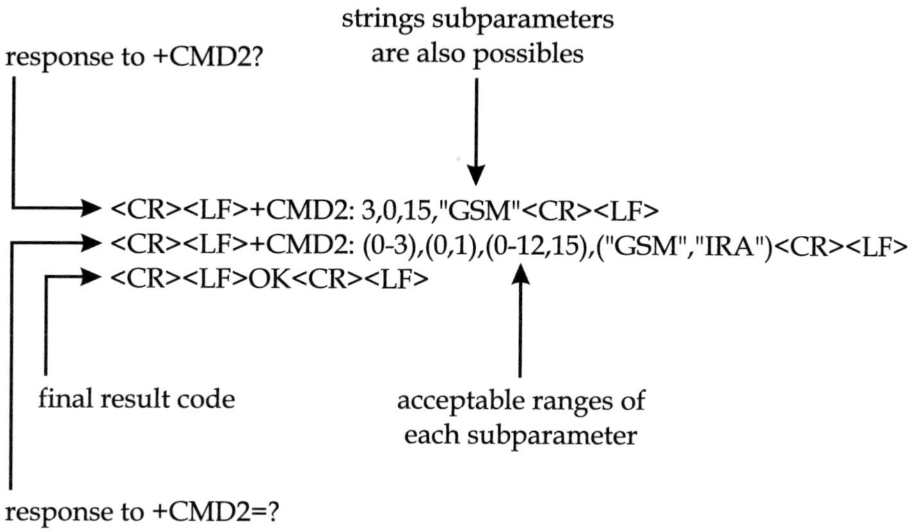

Fig. 2. Basic structure of result codes [adapted from (Motorola, 2008)].

2.2.1 Main AT commands

The list of all AT commands available for a particular device can be obtained from its manufacturer. Here we listed only the main commands that were used to develop this project and for the specific employed modem (Motorola, 2008).

- **AT&K0**: this command disables the flow control and must be the first command sent when the serial communication cable does not have the pins to transmit the RTS (request to send) and CTS (clear to send) signals;
- **ATE0**: disables the echo from the modem, i.e., the ASCII characters sent are not repeated back;
- **AT+CSQ?**: queries the modem signal intensity and ranges from 0 (no signal) to 31 (maximum signal);
- **AT+CMGF**: configures the message format; "AT+CMGF=1" sets to text mode, where the body of the message and its headers are given as separate parameters;
- **AT+CNMI**: configures how incoming messages will be handled by the modem; "AT+CNMI=,2" routes incoming messages directly to the terminal in a result code with the prefix "+CMT". Analogously in a cell phone configured with this mode, instead of an incoming message warning, the content of the message is immediately displayed on screen;
- **AT+CNMA**: acknowledges the receipt of a message and when the "CNMI =,2" mode is configured this acknowledgment must be sent whenever a new message is received;
- **AT+CMGS**: sends a short message from the modem to a given recipient and its syntax is "AT+CMGS=<"*recipient number*">,<*call type code*>" followed by the message content, the call type code for local calls is "129".

2.3 LabVIEW

LabVIEW is a powerful platform for algorithm development, design, prototyping, and interfacing of embedded system with real-world hardware. LabVIEW uses graphical language (G) that enables the creation of programs in block-diagram form, which are called virtual instruments (VI). The main executable program is called the top-level VI and the programs used as modular subroutines are called subVIs. Every VI consists of two main components, the graphical user interface that is named front panel; and the graphical code that implements the functionality of the VI, called block diagram. Once a VI is created and saved, it can be used as a subVI in the block diagram of another VI, acting as a subroutine (Gan & Kuo, 2007; Oussalah & Djezzar, 2010; Sumathi & Surekha, 2007).

The front panel contains objects known as controls and indicators. Controls are the inputs that provide data to the block diagram, and indicators shows output data from the block diagram. These objects, such as buttons, switches, LEDs and graphs are selected from the controls palette. In the Figure 3, the controls palette and the front panel with some examples of controls and indicators are shown.

Front panel controls and indicators have a corresponding terminal block on the block diagram, which holds the graphical source code that defines how the VI will operate. A block diagram is built with terminals and nodes available in the functions palette and that are connected by wires. An example using the same controls and indicators used in the front panel is illustrated in the Figure 4; the colors indicate the data type, e.g., numerical indicators are blue and floating-point ones are orange.

The block diagram code executes based on the principle of dataflow. The rule of dataflow states that functions execute only when all of their required inputs are populated with data. This programming architecture allows both sequential and parallel execution to be easily defined graphically. When a node completes execution, it supplies data to its output terminals on the right, and follows the dataflow imposed by the wires connecting the block diagram objects (Gan & Kuo, 2007; Sumathi & Surekha, 2007).

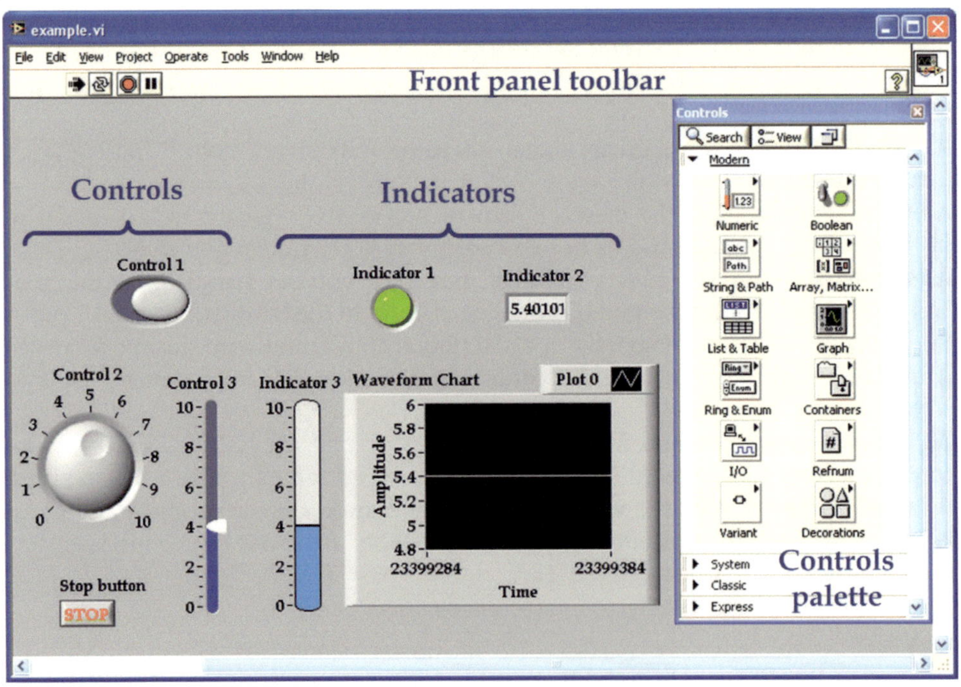

Fig. 3. LabVIEW front panel example and the controls palette.

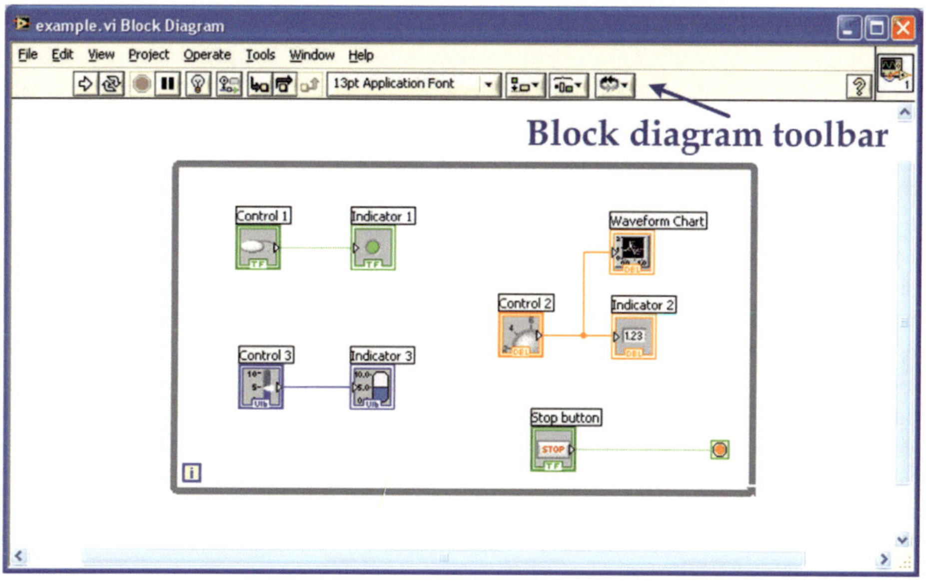

Fig. 4. LabVIEW block diagram example with the controls and indicator showed in the above front panel.

2.3.1 Some programming structures

The LabVIEW structures are graphical representations of the loops and case statements of text-based programming languages. Structures are found in the functions palette and used on the block diagram to repeat blocks of code and to execute code conditionally or in a specific order. Among various structures available in LabVIEW, the While loop will be briefly described in this subsection, including the case structure, and sequence structures. Illustrations of those graphical LabVIEW structures are shown in Figure 5.

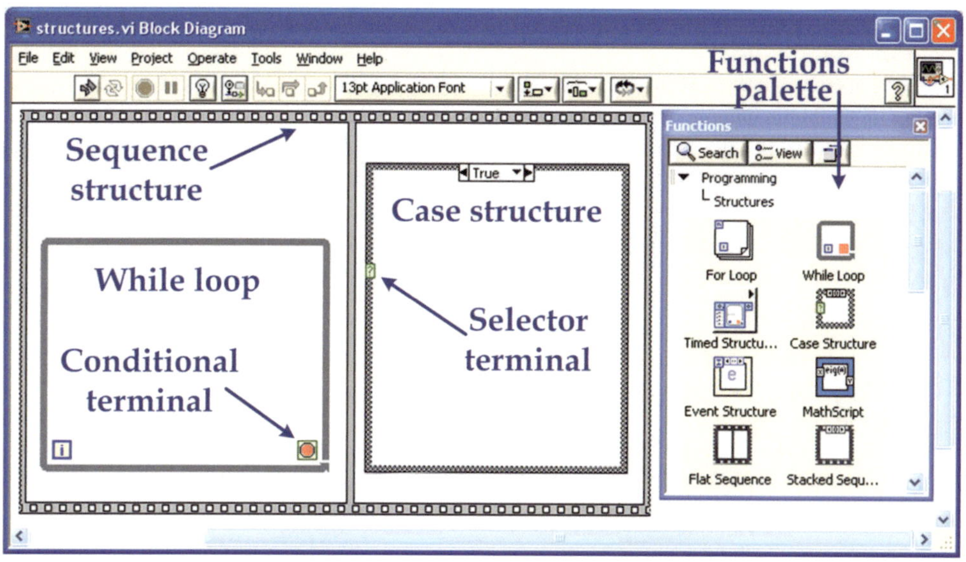

Fig. 5. Some LabVIEW programming structures and the functions palette.

- **While loop**: structure that executes the subdiagram inside its borders, until the Boolean value wired to its conditional terminal be "false". The conditional terminal value is checked at the end of iteration, and if the value is "true" the iteration repeats. Since the default value of the conditional terminal is "false", the loop iterates only once if left unwired, but it is possible to change this default status. Hence, the looping "while true" can be modified to loop unless it is true (Sumathi & Surekha, 2007).
- **Case structures**: they have two or more subdiagrams and only one of which will be executed, depending on the value of the Boolean, numeric, or string value wired to the selector terminal. If a Boolean value is wired to the selector terminal, the structure has two cases, "false" and "true". If a numeric or string data type is wired to the selector, the structure can have almost unlimited cases (Sumathi & Surekha, 2007).
- **State Machine**: programming concept to provide an intelligent control structure and that revolves around three concepts: the state, the event, and the action. In simple terms, a state machine in LabVIEW is a case structure inside a While loop. The While loop provides the ability to continuously execute until the conditional operator is set "false" and the case statement allows for variations in the code to be run (Bitter et al., 2006).
- **Sequence structures**: these types of structure are used to control the execution order of nodes that are not data dependent on each other by arranging its elements in a certain sequence that is called control flow. The sequence structure looks like a frame of film, and executes first the subdiagram inside the first frame, followed by the subdiagram in the second, until the last frame (Sumathi & Surekha, 2007).

3. System development

This Section presents the basic system architecture, an overview of the program, and all the necessary steps for the development of the main program and its subVIs, which constitute the programming framework for the SMS system.

3.1 System architecture

The system architecture is relatively simple, consisting of a GSM modem and a computer with LabVIEW. This main block is then connected to the instruments that will be monitored and/or be controlled. The interface between the user and the system can be accomplished by any 2G phone, which will be responsible for the communication with the modem, as illustrated in Figure 6. In this project, in particular, the Version 8 of the LabVIEW platform was used, and a GSM modem was assembled with the Motorola G24 module, as displayed in Figure 7.

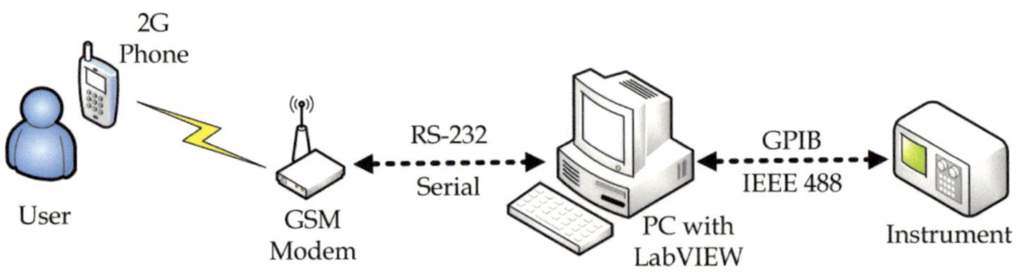

Fig. 6. SMS system architecture diagram.

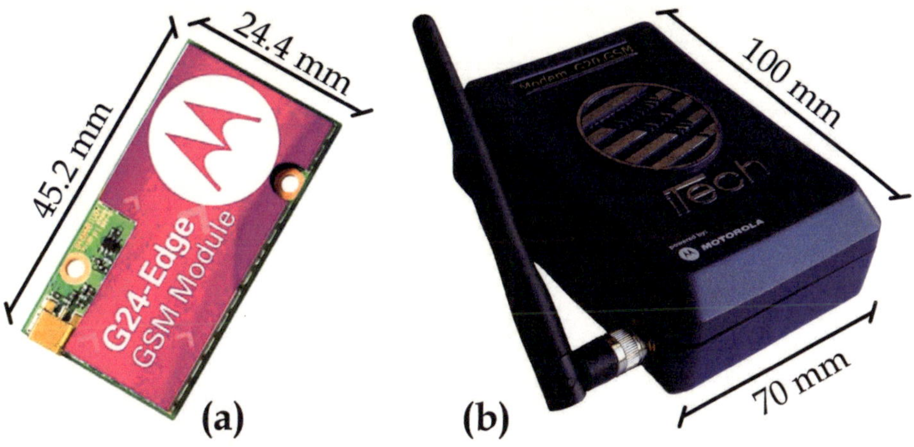

Fig. 7. (a) The G24 module [adapted from (Motorola, 2008)] and (b) the GSM modem used in the project, with their respective dimensions.

3.2 Program overview

In general terms, the program will perform the initial settings of the GSM modem; prepare it for sending/receiving messages; wait for commands sent via SMS; execute the requested action; and re-await a new text message with another command. The basic flowchart of these actions is illustrated in Figure 8. An overview of the block diagram program created in LabVIEW is shown in Figure 9.

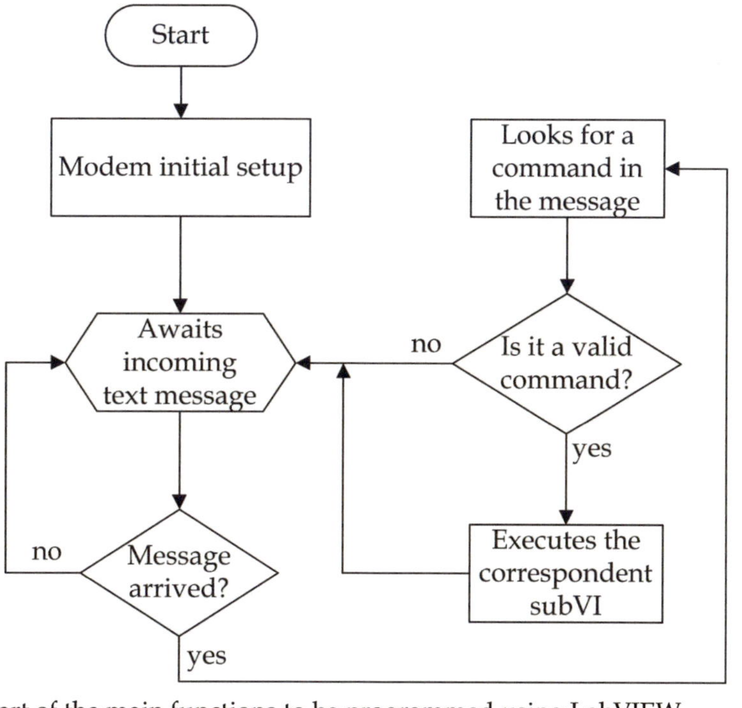

Fig. 8. Flowchart of the main functions to be programmed using LabVIEW.

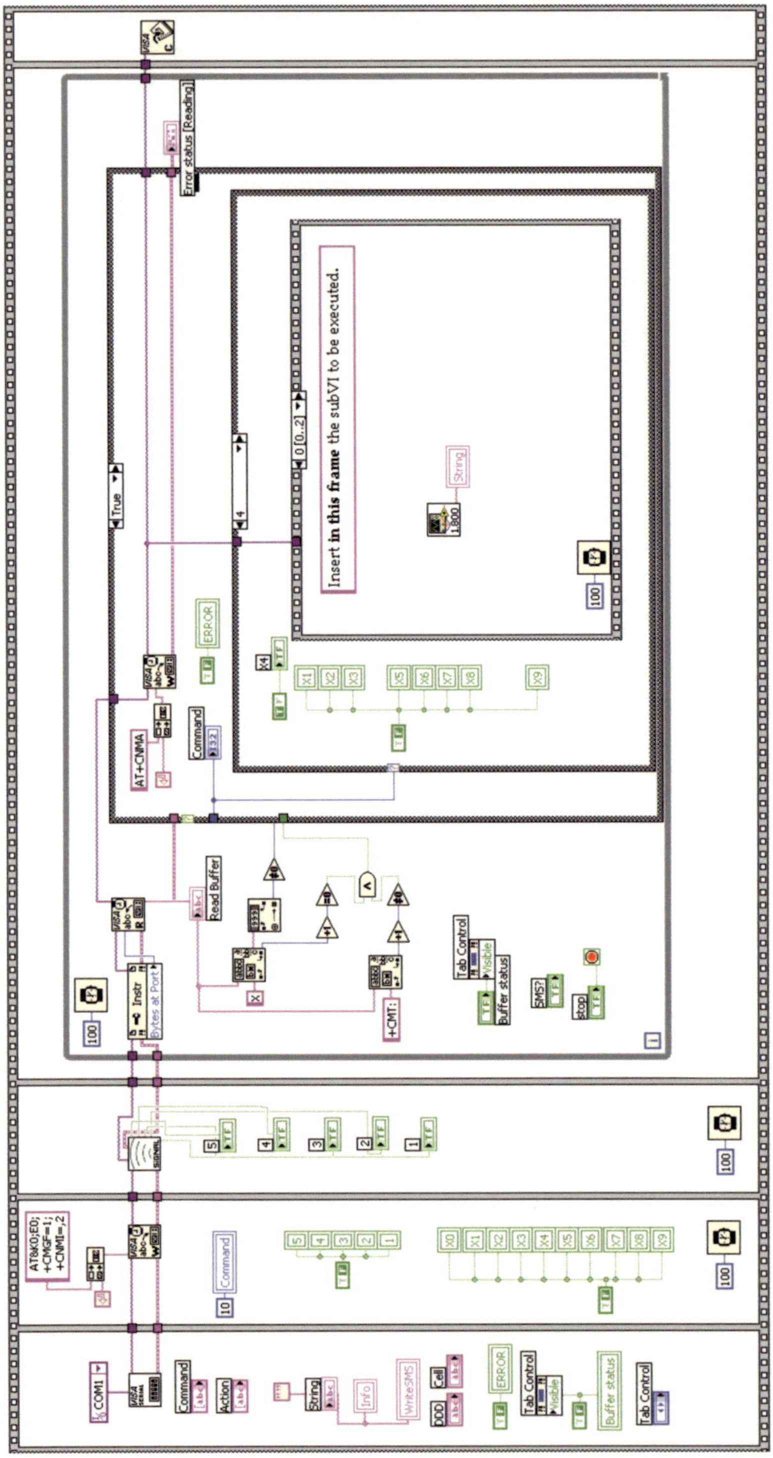

Fig. 9. Main program overview.

In addition to these actions, the user can choose to receive text messages confirming the execution of the requested actions. Also, there are some additional settings that need to be performed in a specific sequence, such as serial communication port settings and GSM modem signal intensity checking. Hence, the LabVIEW main program was implemented in a flat sequence structure, as shown in the above picture. In the figure it is not possible to identify clearly all the details, but for now the purpose is to provide only an overview of the programming framework, since each step of the program will be detailed in the following subsections.

3.3 Block diagram

The graphical source code will be explained following the sequence structure in which it is inserted, that is, from left to right. Likewise, the subVIs will be described at the moment they appear in the code sequence.

3.3.1 Program initialization

The code piece responsible for the program initialization is shown in Figure 10.

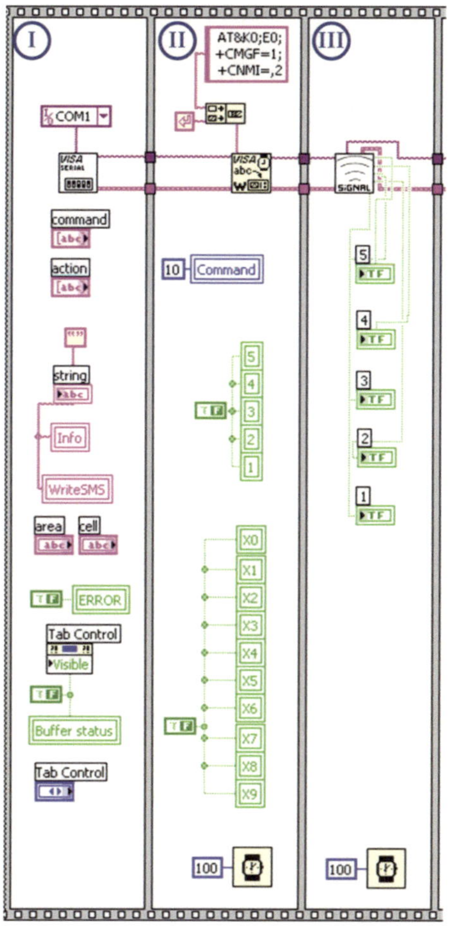

Fig. 10. Frames responsible for the communication port and modem initialization.

In frame I, explaining in a top-down approaching, there is a VISA block to configure the serial communication port. VISA is a standard application programming interface that can control GPIB, USB, serial or other communication protocols, making the appropriate driver calls. So the user does not have to learn the instrument communication protocol. In this block it is necessary to inform only the port used for communication, "COM1" in this case. For the other settings the block default options are used, which are 8 data bits, 1 stop bit, no flow control, no parity, and baud rate of 9600 bps. The arrays "command" and "action" are placed under the VISA block, forming a table in the front panel where the user is able to write the actions performed by each code. This is followed by the array "info", which is initially filled with an empty string. But later, it will be used to display an execution confirmation message, which is the text to be sent for the user, if this confirmation option (to be explained later) is activated. Continuing, there are the arrays "area" and "cell", through which the user should inform the area code and the phone number for which the confirmation messages aforementioned will be sent. At the bottom of the frame there is a tab control setting, which allows the visualization of what is being read and written in the serial buffer. It is useful to be used during the program development, although when the application is working correctly this tab is not very helpful. Therefore, a button was created that allows users to either view it or not.

The key function of Frame II is to configure the GSM modem by sending it the AT commands to disable the flow control and the echo; configure the SMS to text mode; and adjust the incoming messages settings, as described early in the subsection 2.2.1. The commands are sent by serial communication using the "VISA write" block in LabVIEW. This frame also adjusts the value of the global variable "command" to 10, but this functionality will be explained later, in subsection 3.3.3. In addition, the Boolean value "false" is attributed to the global variables representing the GSM modem signal intensity and the commands codes available in the program. These global variables correspond to LED indicators, which will be seen on the front panel.

The frame III checks the GSM modem signal intensity through a subVI, described below.

3.3.2 SubVI to check signal intensity

The routine to check the modem signal was bundled into a subVI, shown in Figure 11. In general terms, this subVI queries the signal intensity from the GSM modem via serial communication in the first frame and reads the answer in the second frame. Then, the Boolean value "true" is attributed to indicators 1 to 5, representing LEDs on the front panel in a manner analogous to the indicators of mobile phone screens.

To check the signal intensity, the corresponding AT command is sent through a "VISA write" block. Next, a property node is used to read the number of bytes of the modem response and use it as an input parameter of a "VISA read" block, and then the decimal number corresponding to the signal intensity is extracted from the string received by the modem. When this number is zero, there is no signal. If the number is between 1 and 9, there is a weak signal corresponding to one signal bar. A number greater than 9 indicates two signal bars, greater than 19 indicates three bars, greater than 29 indicates four bars, and a number greater than 30 indicates the maximum signal level, with five bars.

Next, the parameters obtained in this subVI are forwarded to the indicators of the main program.

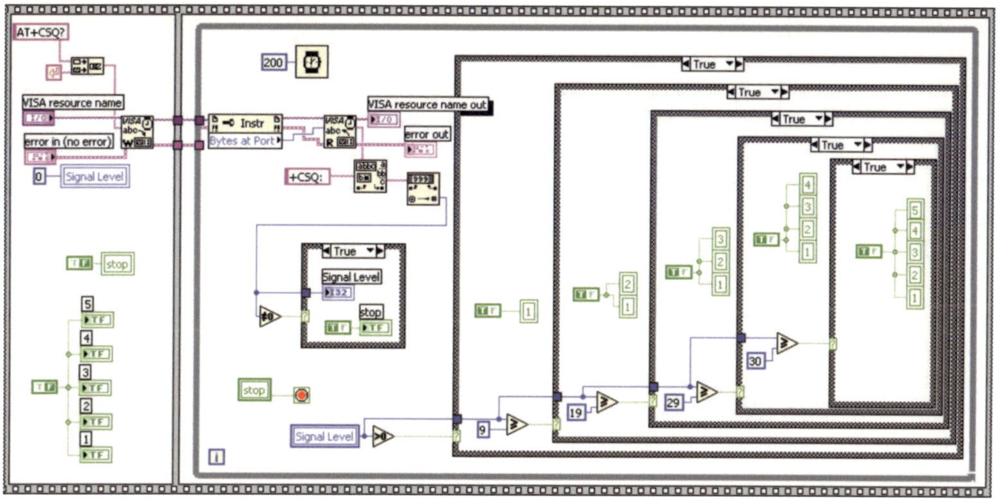

Fig. 11. Block diagram of the subVI to check the GSM modem signal intensity.

3.3.3 Recognizing and executing SMS commands

This part of the graphical source code was designed as a state machine. It can be considered the heart of the system and subdivided into two main stages. The first recognizes the code in a message received by the modem and the second selects the action to be performed, according to the command received.

In the first stage, shown in Figure 12, the program is within a While loop waiting for incoming text messages. When a message is received, the property node informs its number of bytes to the "VISA read" block, from where the message goes to the "read buffer" array, to be shown in the front panel tab. The message content also goes to "match pattern" blocks, where it is performed the search for a valid command code in the message text. At this point Boolean results are generated, which will be used in the second stage.

The message received by the modem is composed by several other characters besides the text informed by the user, such as date and number of the sender. Therefore, to recognize a command in the received message it is necessary to create a code table. In this project the codes are represented by the character X followed by a decimal digit from 0 to 9, and they were chosen to avoid confusion with the header message characters and to be easily typed on the keypad mobile phone (Figueiredo et al., 2009).

Furthermore, in this first stage a control variable is created that will be displayed on the front panel as a switch, allowing the user to choose whether it is desired or not to receive confirmation messages after the execution of a requested command. In the While loop, is also checked whether the user has enabled the view of the "tab control" mentioned earlier.

At the beginning of the second stage, shown in Figure 13, the acknowledgment AT command "+CNMA" (required after each received message) is sent to the modem. Next, the program enters into a case structure, according to the Boolean results obtained from the "match pattern" blocks of the first stage. If the block does not find a valid code, the program goes to a "false" case structure shown in Figure 14. This will return an invalid code message to the front panel, through the array "info". It will also send the user mobile phone a warning via SMS, if the confirmation option is active. When a valid command is received, the program enters into a second case structure, according to the decimal number after the X character. In this step, one of the X0 to X9 indicators will receive Boolean value "true", in accordance with the received code, turning on a LED indicator on the front panel, representing the code that is running. After that, still inside this case structure, the program runs a stacked sequence structure, where it must be placed the subVI to be executed for each code. Thus, in the case #0, it is placed the subVI to be executed when the X0 command is sent to the GSM modem via text message. In the case #1 the subVI is placed in such a way that will run for the received code X1 and so on, until the last code, which is X9 in this project. Besides the case structures being used, it is necessary to create an additional case, which is left blank and enabled as default. In this case, the empty structure is the eleventh one. For this reason the number 10 was assigned to the global variable "command" mentioned earlier in subsection 3.3.1.

Increasing the number of codes available for execution is not a difficult task. However, it is necessary to increase the number of cases in the structure and modify the Boolean routine that enters in the case structure, in order to make it able to interpret the new codes.

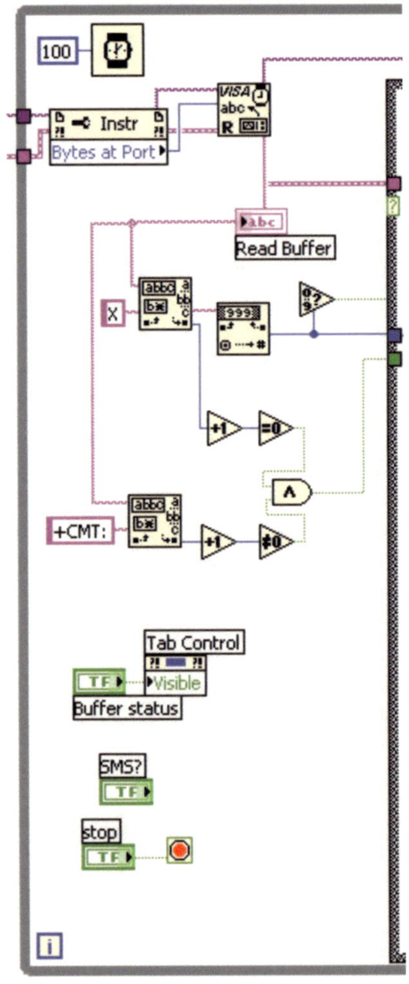

Fig. 12. Code that searches for a valid code in the message received by the modem.

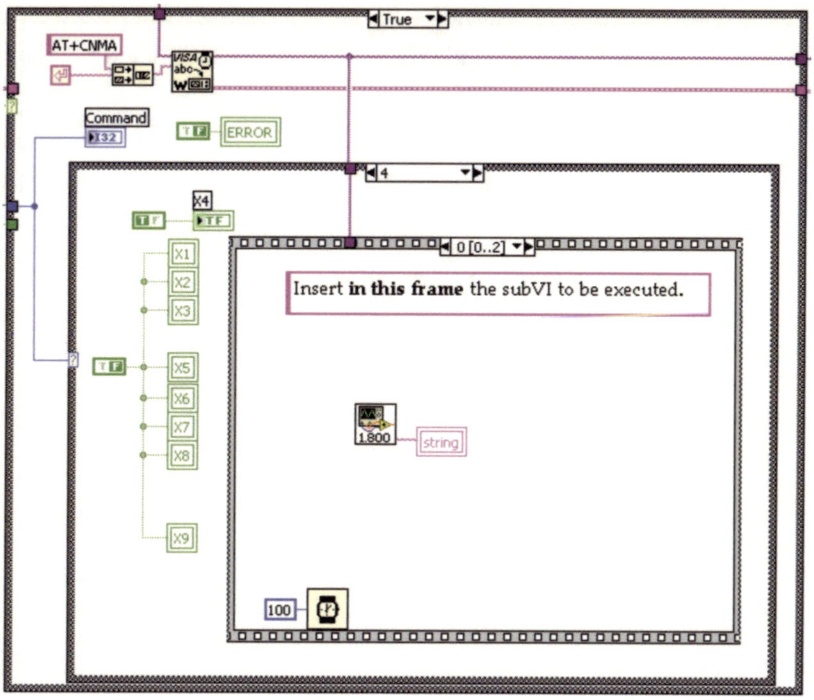

Fig. 13. Structure that executes the subVI corresponding to the received command.

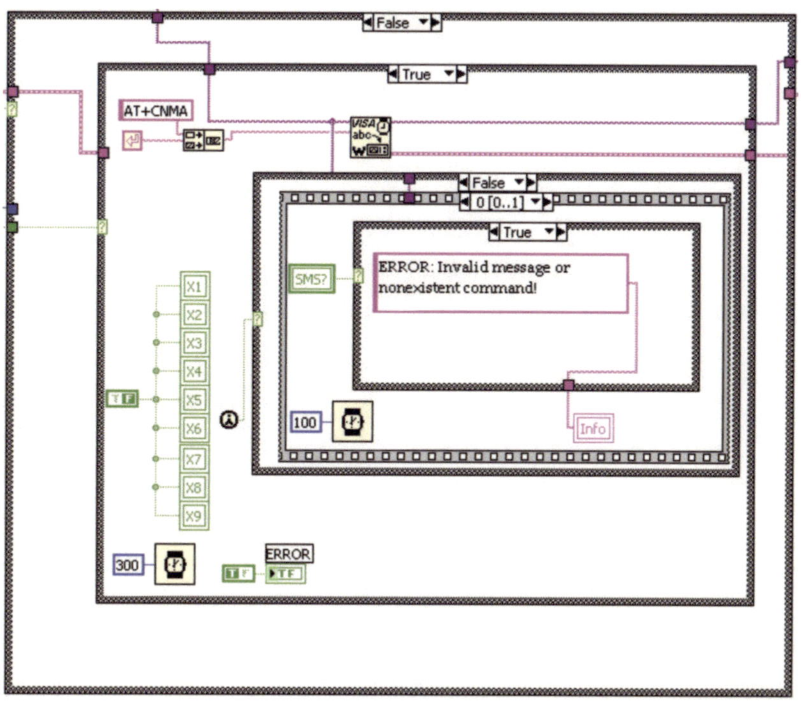

Fig. 14. Routine that deals with cases where an invalid command is received by the modem.

The subVIs to be executed for each command must be placed within the first frame (frame zero) in the sequence structure that is inside the case structure, as illustrated above in Figure 13. After running the subVI, the next frame assembles a text that confirms the execution of the requested action and sends it to the front panel, through the "info" indicator, as shown in Figure 15. This same text is used by the modem to send the user mobile phone a message via SMS. This text message is sent through a subVI that runs only if the confirmation option is active, and it is detailed in the next subsection.

3.3.4 SubVI to write message

This subVI is built in a sequence structure, numbered from I to VII, as shown in Figure 16. The frame I specifies the resource to be opened informing the VISA name to a "VISA Flush I/O Buffer" block, in this case the resource to be opened is the serial communication port COM1. The frame II gets the phone number informed by the user and passes it to the frame III, where it is assembled in the AT command to send a text message from the GSM modem. Frame IV only transmits the ASCII code for "carriage return", enabling the entry of the characters that form the message payload, which is transmitted in the frame V. In frame VI the "\1A" ASCII characters, which correspond to the "CTRL+Z" command, are sent to the modem, indicating that the message was written, and enabling the modem to send the SMS. In this frame is used a large time delay for allow the modem to send the text message.

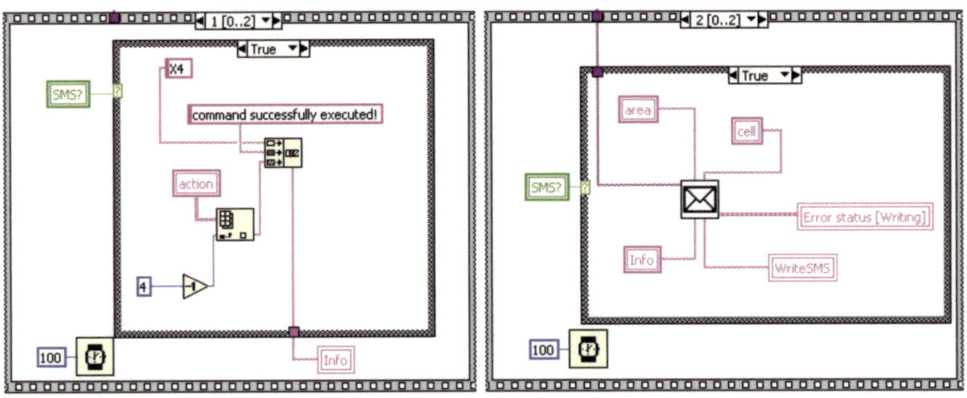

Fig. 15. Sequence structure that assembles and sends the text message.

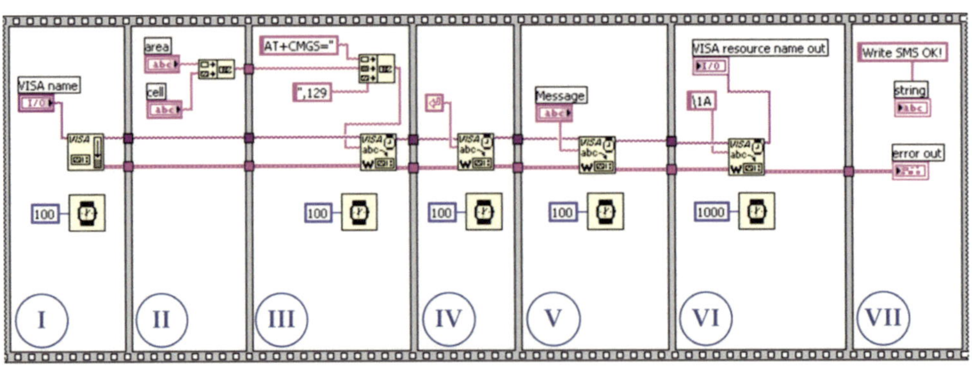

Fig. 16. SubVI to send messages from the GSM modem to the user mobile phone.

The frame VII just informs that the subVI for writing and sending the message was executed correctly, showing this information in the "tab control" placed on the front panel.
All procedures described as the heart of the system are inside a While loop. Hence, after performing all these actions described, the program returns to the point where it awaits for the arrival of new text messages by the modem. When a message arrives, this whole process is repeated until the user press the stop button located on the front panel.
When the stop button is pressed, before the program stops running completely, it goes to the last frame of the sequence structure, which can be seen in Figure 9 shown earlier. This last frame function is just to close the communication with the COM1 port through the "VISA close" block, leaving it available for other possible activities that need to use this communication port.
At this point it is possible to redesign the flowchart showed earlier in Figure 8, adding now all program features and also the routine hierarchy, including the subVIs, as shown in Figure 17. Thus, the block diagram explanation is closed with a summarized review of its overall operation.
As seen in Figure 17, the computer communication port and GSM modem settings are the first tasks accomplished. Then, the signal intensity of the modem is checked and the program enters in a routine waiting for incoming text messages. When a message arrives, the program searches for a valid command in the text, and once it has been found, the corresponding subVI is executed. Next, if the confirmation option is active, a text message is sent the user mobile phone by the modem, confirming the action execution. Lastly, when the program is stopped, the serial communication port is closed and liberated for other applications.

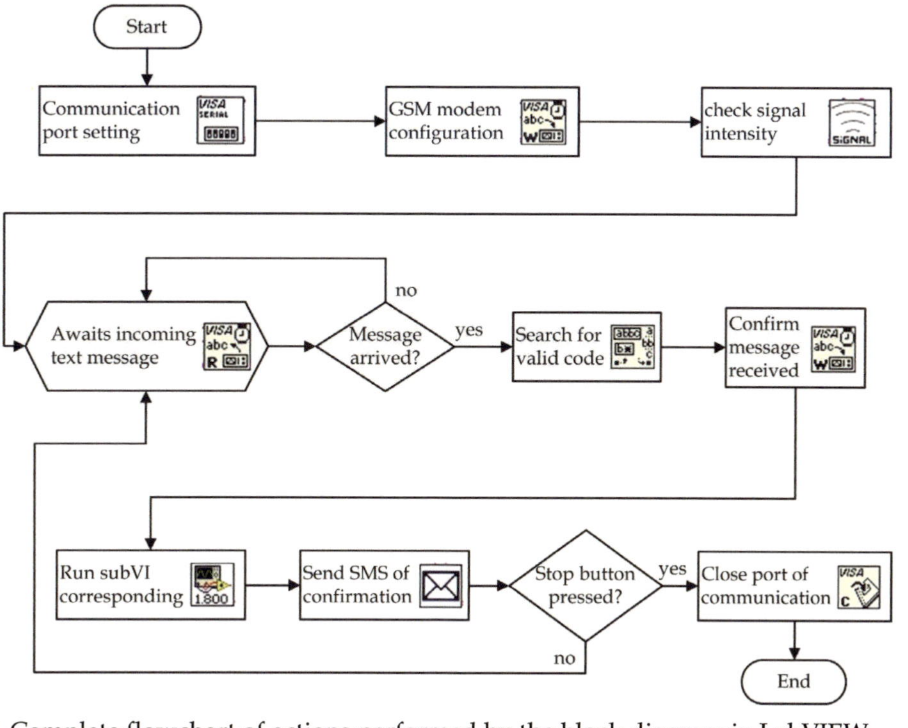

Fig. 17. Complete flowchart of actions performed by the block diagram in LabVIEW.

3.4 Front panel

The front panel of the program developed in LabVIEW is shown in Figure 18, and its resources are explained below.

The graphical programming allows the creation of detailed interfaces and with high iteration levels. However, in this application it is not necessary to provide many resources in the graphical user interface (GUI), because the user will use it only to start the program and after will work in the distance using SMS. The functions available on the front panel designed for this project will be explained according to the numbered blocks showed in Figure 18.

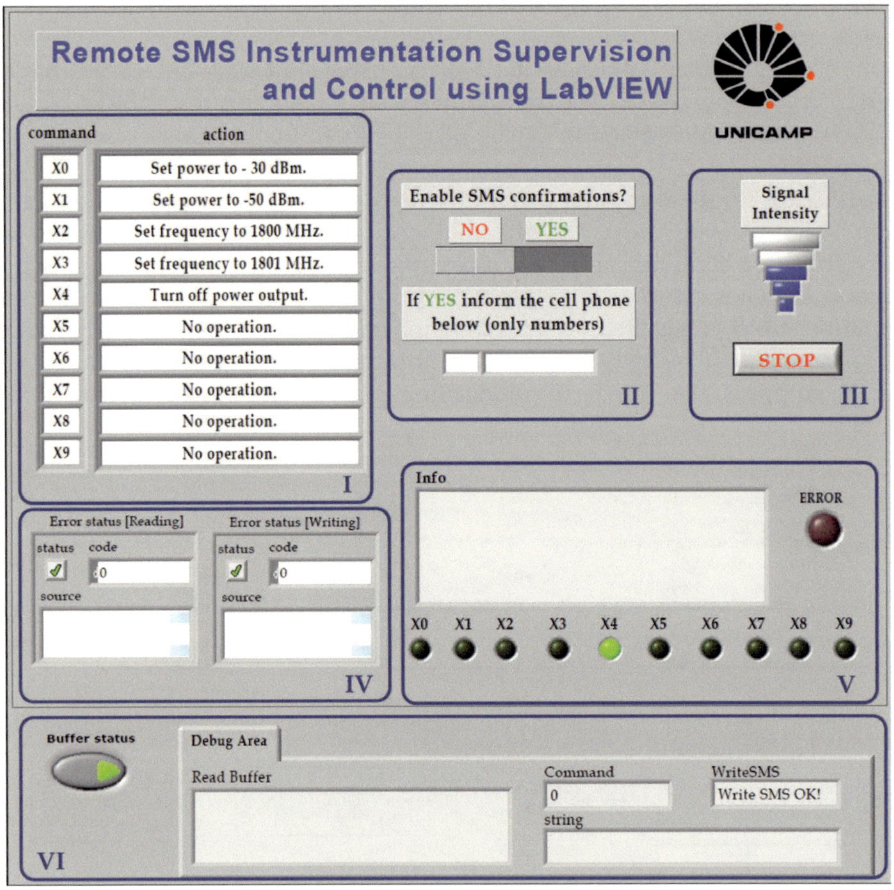

Fig. 18. The application GUI created in the LabVIEW front panel.

Block I is composed of a table created by the arrays "command" and "action". The user should fill the array "action" with a brief description about each code function. Subsequently, the text of these fields will be used to assemble the confirmations messages sent to the user.

In Block II there is the switch that lets the user choose whether to receive or not the confirmation messages after running a requested command. This feature will send the user mobile phone a text message reporting success or failure of the requested action. Therefore, it is necessary to inform the phone number to which the confirmations will be sent. Since the

sending of messages implies in additional charges, the switch was designed to enable or disable this feature.
In Block III there are the signal intensity indicator and a button that closes the program. As explained before, the indicator is processed through a subVI and its operation is similar to that seen in cell phones displays: the stronger the signal, the greater the number of bars. The inactive bars are gray and the active bars are represented in the blue color.
Block IV is formed by the errors indicators. Although there were no failures during the tests performed in this project, errors may occur during the program execution while reading or writing in the serial communication buffer, and the error description is displayed in the corresponding box. Besides, when an error occurs the red LED indicator located in block V is turned on.
Block V is also composed by information about the program execution. In the "info" box appears the text of the confirmation messages, which will be sent the user mobile phone by the GSM modem if the switch of this resource is activated. The indicators X0 to X9 indicate the last command executed, by turning the corresponding LED to green.
The Block VI is a tab with information about the serial communication channel. The buffer content is displayed in the "read buffer" box, and the remaining fields show if a valid code was found in a received message, besides the current string sent to the buffer, and if the subVI for writing and sending messages was performed correctly. This tab information is very useful to the programmer, because allows to analyze the status of the serial communication and locate possible errors with the modem communication. However, it has no great value to the user, so it is possible to hide the tab by using the button on the left.
Thus, the creation of a user-friendly panel with some basic features allows the user to put the program to run and accesses its key information without the need to access the block diagram. It permits to evaluate if everything is fully operational before start to operate the program remotely via SMS. Moreover, such panel can be useful if there is the need to publish a web page to monitor the program via Internet.
Once explained the whole operation and programming of the remote SMS system using LabVIEW, the application will be evaluated in a measurement process described in the next section.

4. Case study

The objective of this case study is to test and evaluate the proposed remote SMS control and monitoring. Hence, the developed system was applied to an 1.8-GHz radio mobile envelope measurement carried out in an urban area. This section will describe the measurement process and how the SMS tool was used in these measurements, followed by the achieved results.

4.1 System and measurement description

In the mobile radio channel, signal propagation frequently takes place in a typical urban environment. In such a situation, there is normally no line-of-sight condition between the transmitter and mobile receiver and multipath propagation is the predominant phenomenon. This fact leads to frequency selectivity, since the frequency response of the channel is no longer flat over all frequencies. One measure of the channel frequency selectivity is the coherence bandwidth. The coherence bandwidth refers to the frequency separation between two signals, which results in a given level of correlation between their envelope amplitudes. Here, the aim of the measurement process is to characterize the coherence bandwidth between two frequency-spaced radio mobile signals, based on narrow-band 1.8-GHz field trials carried out in an urban open area. The equipment list of the transmitter setup is composed by two signal generator, an amplifier, and a Yagi antenna. On the other side, the receiver setup is composed by a monopole antenna, a preamplifier, a splitter, two spectrum analyzers, a trigger signal, and a laptop with the LabVIEW software installed. The schematic diagram of the measurement systems is shown in Figure 19 (Ribeiro et al., 2007).

In the transmitter, two frequency-separated continuous wave signals (CW) around 1.8 GHz are combined and then amplified to about 30 dBm in power. This signal is transmitted from a 12-dBi vertically polarized Yagi antenna with 33° and 36° E- and H-plane 3-dB beam widths, respectively. The transmitting antenna is located 10 m above the street level on the rooftop of a laboratory building (Ribeiro et al., 2007).

The receiver setup is onboard in a vehicle driven along the local area streets. The signal is received with a 3-dBi monopole antenna, located on the vehicle roof, and then amplified before being split into two branches. Each signal branch is fed to a spectrum analyzer to separately detect and record the envelopes of each frequency. In order to simultaneously record the two frequency-spaced envelopes, the sweep of each analyzer is time-synchronized by the same external trigger signal (Ribeiro et al., 2007).

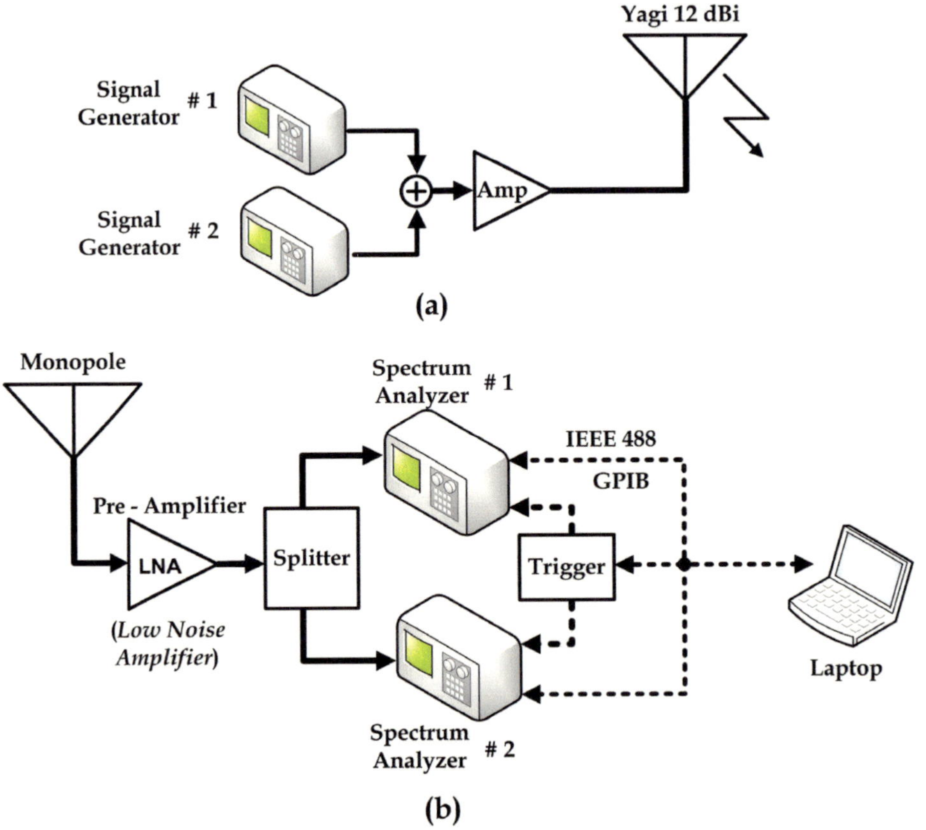

Fig. 19. Measurement system schematic of the (a) transmitter and (b) receiver setup.

The recorded envelopes are stored in a personal computer for latter analysis. In the vehicle, the configuration and control of the equipments, as well the data acquisitions are carried out using programs developed in LabVIEW. The communication between the instruments and the laptop is performed via GPIB using an USB/GPIB interface (Ribeiro et al., 2007).

4.2 Applying the SMS tool in the measurement process

The measurements are acquired with the vehicle in movement at a distance of about 1 km from the transmitter, and frequently it is necessary to change the parameters of one of the generators located at the laboratory. As a consequence, a person need to stay in the laboratory to perform this function or the one who is in the vehicle has to return to there whenever a parameter has to be changed. However, this role can be attributed to the remote SMS instrumentation supervision and control. Hence, the person who is performing the measurements in the vehicle can send a text message by a cellular phone to the GSM modem that transmits the message to the computer with LabVIEW by serial communication, where the message is interpreted and translated in a command, which is finally sent by GPIB to the signal generator. Thus this procedure saves time, since there is no need to return to the laboratory for changing parameters, and there is no need of an additional person in the laboratory (Ribeiro et al., 2007; Figueiredo et al., 2009).

For this purpose, the configuration shown previously in Figure 6 is added to that shown in Figure 19 (a). At this point it is necessary to create a subVI for each signal generator parameter that will be changed and insert it in the appropriate place within the SMS main program, indicated previously in Figure 13. One can argue about the need to make a program for each action, but, making the first one, the next subVIs can be made using this first as model, and no more than one GPIB command needs to be changed, which is a relatively simple task. In one measurement set it is necessary to vary the signal frequency in a specific range, in this case from 1800 MHz to 1801 MHz, in steps of 0.1 MHz. To do this, ten subVIs were designed and placed in the appropriate frame of the case structure, where each subVI sets the frequency in a determined value according to Table 1, which was also written in the program front panel.

The block diagram of a subVI that adjusts the frequency at 1801 MHz is shown as an example in Figure 20.

Code	Action
X0	Set frequency to 1800.1 MHz
X1	Set frequency to 1800.2 MHz
X2	Set frequency to 1800.3 MHz
X3	Set frequency to 1800.4 MHz
X4	Set frequency to 1800.5 MHz
X5	Set frequency to 1800.6 MHz
X6	Set frequency to 1800.7 MHz
X7	Set frequency to 1800.8 MHz
X8	Set frequency to 1800.9 MHz
X9	Set frequency to 1801 MHz

Table 1. Command list to be executed via SMS in the signal generator.

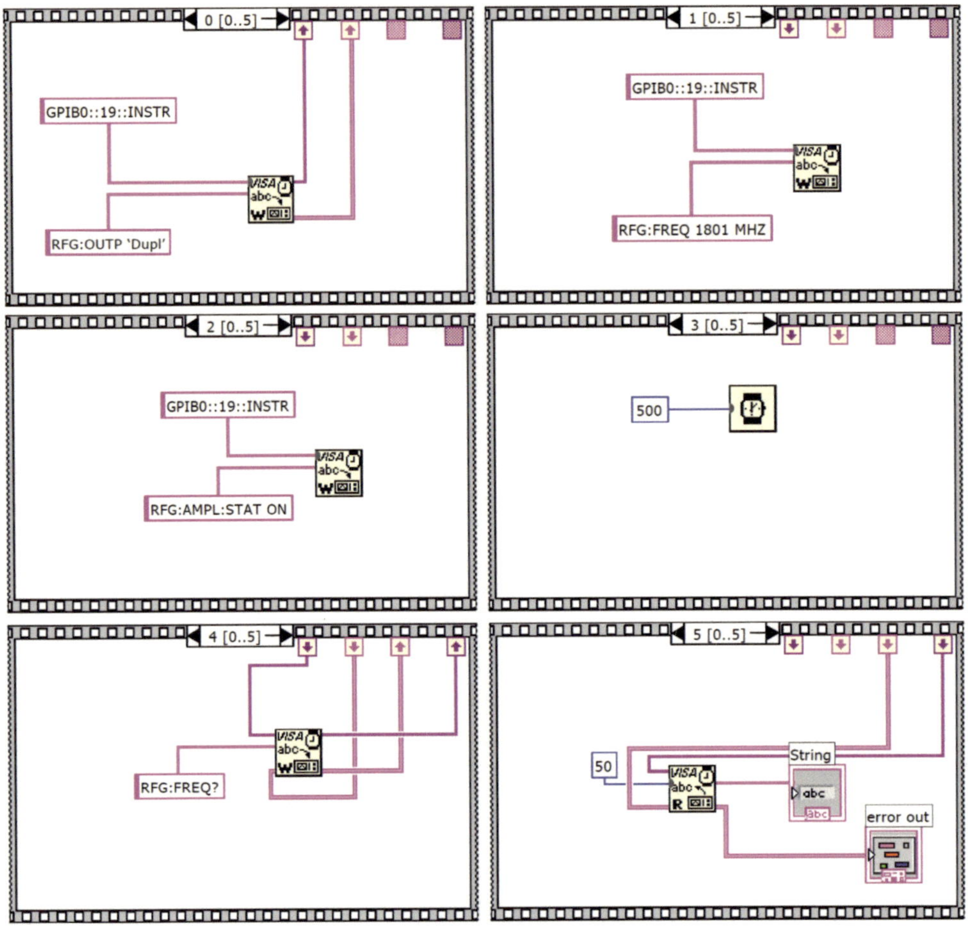

Fig. 20. All frames of the subVI that sets the signal generator frequency at 1801 MHz.

The program was developed in a sequence structure with six frames, saved as a subVI, and inserted in the main program. In the frame 0 the initial instrument configuration is done by setting its RF output port to duplex, the frame 1 sets the frequency; the frame 2 turns on the amplifier output; the frame 3 is just a time delay in the subVI running; the frame 4 queries the current signal generator frequency; and the last frame reads the answer from the instrument. After this first subVI, the other nine were obtained changing the frequency value in the frame 1. In this case, ten subVIs were used, but the number of available options can be increased, as explained previously.

4.3 Results

The first tests were conducted with a simplified setup, entirely mounted within the laboratory. The tests were basically done by sending the commands and examining whether the requests were properly executed by observing the parameter changes in the instruments. To measure the full response time of an execution, the confirmation messages were chosen to be received. Each command showed in Table 1 was sent several times throughout a week, and the execution time was measured from the moment the message with a command was sent until the moment when the confirmation returns. Thus it was possible to analyze how long the system took to receive, interpret and execute the command, and then assemble and send the confirmation message to the user. Accounting for the delays intentionally inserted into some LabVIEW routines, the execution times were around thirty seconds. Additional tests were performed during times of network congestion and the full response time of an execution did not show large variations (Figueiredo et al., 2009).

Further tests were performed in the vehicle, during the measurement process, in different days and times. In these tests the confirmation messages were disabled, because it is possible to note if the action was executed through the spectrum analyzer screen in the vehicle. As in the previous tests, all requests were correctly executed with times below thirty seconds, since in this case there are no times of confirmation messages included.

In addition to the tests conducted for this case study, preceding tests were executed for controlling and monitoring of car alarm functionalities via SMS, where the results were satisfactory, and with runtimes similar to those obtained here (Figueiredo et al., 2008). Furthermore, measurements conducted by other authors investigated the transmission time and message loss probability, in order to analyze the SMS reliability for emergency warning systems. The measurement results have shown that it is possible to use SMS in such systems, since there was no message loss and almost every message was received within a short time, increasing the trustworthiness of applications based on SMS (Pries et al., 2006).

5. Conclusion

Considering the growth of remote monitoring and control systems and knowing that a large number of such applications can be achieved using simple text messages, this Chapter has presented the feasibility of a flexible and low cost monitoring and control solution using SMS, which can be easily applied and adapted to various applications.

The system is LabVIEW-based and uses standard interfaces for communication. So, it does not require expert programmers to perform adjustments in the program. It requires basically a computer with LabVIEW, and a GSM modem, besides the instruments to be controlled and/or monitored. The access to the system can be carried out using any 2G cell phone without the need to use high cost devices.

This Chapter showed all the details of how to develop the programming framework with detailed instructions of each routine within the main program, which makes easier the task of adapting the system for applications different from that illustrated here.

The developed system was applied to a RF signal procedure measurement saving time and staff in this process. The tool development and its use in a specific application showed the LabVIEW versatility. Furthermore, the results showed that SMS is suitable and reliable for several kinds of applications.

At last, the remote SMS instrumentation supervision and control using LabVIEW allows a wide range of future work, because it is just needed to adapt the program in accordance with the requirements of any application where it is desirable to control or monitor instrumentation remotely, and this Chapter gives the necessary foundation for such work.

6. Acknowledgment

This work was supported in part by the Brazilian agencies FAPESP (*Fundação de Amparo a Pesquisa do Estado de São Paulo*), CAPES (*Coordenação de Aperfeiçoamento de Pessoal de Nível*

Superior), and CNPq (*Conselho Nacional de Desenvolvimento Científico e Tecnológico*), under CEPOF-FAPESP, FOTONICOM and TIDIA-Kyatera programs.

7. References

Alsaialy, S.D.; Tawy, D.M & Lord, S.M. (2003). Introduction to LabVIEW two-part exercise, *Proceedings of the 33rd Annual Frontiers in Education (FIE)*, Vol. 1, pp. T4E-1—6, ISBN 0-7803-7961-6, Nov. 5-8, 2003

Bitter, R.; Mohiuddin, T. & Nawrocki, M.R. (2006). *LabVIEW Advanced Programming Techniques* (2nd edition), CRC Press, ISBN 978-0-8493-3325-5, Boca Raton, FL, USA

Brown, J.; Shipman, B. & Vetter, R. (2007). SMS: The Short Message Service, *Computer*, Vol. 40, No. 12, pp. 106-110, Dec. 2007, ISSN 0018-9162

Figueiredo, R.C.; Arthur, R.; Bonani, L.H. & Arnold, F.J. (2008). Wireless Control System Based on SMS, *Proceedings of IEEE Andean Region IV International Conference (ANDESCON)*, Cusco, Peru, Oct. 15-17, 2008

Figueiredo, R.C.; Ribeiro, A.M.O.; Arthur, R. & Conforti, E. (2009). Remote instrumentation control and monitoring based on LabVIEW and SMS, *Proceedings of the 35th Annual Conference of the IEEE Industrial Electronics (IECON)*, pp. 2477-248, ISBN 978-1-4244-4648-3, Porto, Portugal, Nov. 3-5, 2009

Gallardo, S.; Barrero, F.; Toral, S.L. & Duran, M.J. (2006). eDSPlab: A remote-accessed instrumentation laboratory for digital signal processors training based on the Internet, *Proceedings of the 32nd Annual Conference of the IEEE Industrial Electronics (IECON)*, pp. 4656-4661, ISBN 1-4244-0390-1, Paris, Nov. 6-10, 2006

Gan, W.S. & Kuo, S.M. (2007). *Embedded Signal Processing with the Micro Signal Architecture* (1st edition), Wiley-IEEE Press, ISBN 978-0-471-73841-1, Hoboken, NJ, USA

Garbus, R.U.; Aguirre, I.J.O.; Sanchez, R.C. & Pureco, O.R. (2006). Virtual Remote Lab for Control Practices, *Proceedings of Electronics, Robotics and Automotive Mechanics Conference*, Vol. 2, pp. 361-366, Sept. 26-29, 2006

Glasgow, H.B.; Burkholder, J.M.; Reed, R.E.; Lewitus, A.J. & Kleinman, J.E. (2004). Real-time remote monitoring of water quality: a review of current applications, and advancements in sensor, telemetry, and computing technologies, *Journal of Experimental Marine Biology and Ecology*, Vol. 300, No. 1-2, March 2004, pp. 409-448, ISSN 0022-0981

Guzmán, J.L.; Berenguel, M.; Rodríguez, F. & Dormido, S. (2005). Web-Based Remote Control Laboratory Using a Greenhouse Scale Model, *Computer Applications in Engineering Education*, Vol. 13, No. 2, Jul. 2005, pp. 111-124, ISSN 1099-0542

Higa, M.L.; Tawy, D.M. & Lord, S.M. (2002). An introduction to LabVIEW exercise for an electronics class, *Proceedings of the 32nd Annual Frontiers in Education (FIE)*, Vol. 1, pp. T1D-13—T1D-16, ISBN 0-7803-7444-4, Nov. 6-9, 2002

Jawarkar, N.P.; Ahmed, V. & Thakare, R.D. (2007). Remote Control using Mobile through Spoken Commands, *Proceedings of International Conference on Signal Processing, Communications and Networking (ICSCN)*, pp. 622-625, Feb. 22-24, 2007

Jianting, Z.; Hanmin, H.; Shanglian, H.; Weiming, C.; Zhen, J.; Zhixiang, Z. & Simeng, L. (2006). Remote Real-time Health Monitoring and Evaluation System for Long Bridge Structure, *Proceedings of the Multiconference on Computational Engineering in Systems Applications (IMACS)*, pp. 1751-1755, Oct. 4-6, 2006

Khan, S.; Islam, M.R. & Khalifah, O.O. (2004). Wireless and wired remote measurement unit design and applications, *Proceedings of 39th International Universities Power Engineering Conference (UPEC)*, pp. 1282- 1285, Sept. 6-8, 2004

Lita, I.; Visan, D.A.; Mujea, G. & Ghita, D. (2005). LabVIEW Application for Analysis of Mechanical Vibrations from Industrial Environment, *Proceedings of the 28th International Spring Seminar on the Electronics Technology: Meeting the Challenges of Electronics Technology Progress*, pp. 463-467, ISBN 0-7803-9325-2, May 19-20, 2005

Motorola, Inc. (June 2008). Motorola G24 Developer's Guide - AT Commands Reference Manual, In: *M2M Wireless Modules*, 11.Mar.2011, Available from http://motorola.com/web/Business/Products/M2M%20Wireless%20Modules/G24%20Lite/_Documents/static%20files/AT_Commands_Reference_Manual2.pdf

Oussalah, S. & Djezzar B. (2010). Automated MOS Transistor gamma Degradation Measurements Based on LabVIEW Environment, In: *LabVIEW - Modeling Programming and Simulations*, Riccardo de Asmundis, pp. 163-176, InTech, ISBN 978-953-307-521-1, Rijeka, Croatia

Peersman, G.; Griffiths, P.; Spear, H.; Cvetkovic, S. & Smythe, C. (2000). A tutorial overview of the short message service within GSM, *Computing & Control Engineering Journal*, Vol. 11, No. 2, pp. 79-89, Apr. 2000, ISSN 0956-3385

Pries, R.; Hobfeld, T. & Tran-Gia, P. (2006). On the Suitability of the Short Message Service for Emergency Warning Systems, *Proceedings of the IEEE 63rd Vehicular Technology Conference (VTC)*, pp. 991-995, May 7-10, 2006

Ribeiro, A.M.O.; Castelli, C.S.; Barrientos, E.M.M. & Conforti, E. (2007). Coherence bandwidth in a 1.8-GHz urban mobile radio channel, *Proceedings of Microwave and Optoelectronics Conference (IMOC)*, pp. 599-602, ISBN 978-1-4244-0661-6, Oct. 29 - Nov. 1, 2007

Rosati, R.J. (2009). Evaluation of Remote Monitoring in Home Health Care, *Proceedings of the International Conference on eHealth, Telemedicine, and Social Medicine (eTELEMED)*, pp. 151-153, Feb. 1-7, 2009

Sarram, M.; Ghasemzadeh, M. & Aghaei, V. (2008). Remote Control and Overall Administration of Computer Networks, Using Short Message Service, *Proceedings of the International Conference on Information and Communication Technologies: From Theory to Applications (ICTTA)*, pp. 1-5, April 7-11, 2008

Sgârciu, V. & Stamatescu G. (2010). Distance Process Monitoring using LabVIEW Environment, In: *LabVIEW - Modeling Programming and Simulations*, Riccardo de Asmundis, pp. 67-88, InTech, ISBN 978-953-307-521-1, Rijeka, Croatia

Sukanesh, R.; Gautham, P.; Arunmozhivarman, P.T.; Rajan, S.P. & Vijayprasath, S. (2010). Cellular phone based biomedical system for health care, *Proceedings of the IEEE International Conference on Communication Control and Computing Technologies (ICCCCT)*, pp. 550-553, ISBN 978-1-4244-7769-2, Oct. 7-9, 2010

Sumathi, S. & Surekha, P. (2007). *LabVIEW based Advanced Instrumentation Systems* (1st edition), Springer, ISBN 978-3-540-48500-1, New York, NY, USA

Wang, W.; Tse, P.W. & Lee, J. (2007). Remote machine maintenance system through Internet and mobile communication, *The International Journal of Advanced Manufacturing Technology*, Vol. 31, No. 7, Jan. 2007, pp. 783-789, ISSN 0268-3768

Xiao, J.; Xu, S. & Wu, G. (2009). Monitor System of the Intelligent Power Earth Lines Based on GSM SMS Protocol, *Proceedings of the International Conference on Electronic Measurement & Instruments (ICEMI)*, pp. 3-178-3-181, Aug. 16-19, 2009

Zahariah, M.; Mardiana, B.; Hazura, H.; Fauziyah, S. & Hanim, A.R. (2009). Designing a Low Cost Electronic Devices Switching System Controlled by Short Message Service, *Proceedings of the International Conference on Computer Technology and Development (ICCTD)*, Vol. 2, pp. 292-295, Nov. 13-15, 2009

Zarka, N.; Al-Houshi, I. & Akhkobek, M. (2006). Temperature Control Via SMS, *Proceedings of the International Conference on Information and Communication Technologies: From Theory to Applications (ICTTA)*, Vol. 2, pp. 2678-2683, April 24-28, 2006

Zhang, R.; He, F.; Du, Z. & Sun, L. (2007). An Intelligent Home Environment Inspecting Robot, *Proceedings of the International Conference on Mechatronics and Automation (ICMA)*, pp. 1683-1688, Aug. 5-8, 2007

Zhicong, Q.; Delin, L. & Shunxiang, W. (2008). Analysis and Design of a Mobile Forensic Software System Based on AT Commands, *Proceedings of the IEEE International Symposium on Knowledge Acquisition and Modeling (KAM) Workshop*, pp. 597-600, Dec. 21-22, 2008

16

Lightning Location and Mapping System Using Time Difference of Arrival (TDoA) Technique

Zulkurnain Abdul-Malek[1], Aulia[1,2], Nouruddeen Bashir[1] and Novizon[1,2]
[1]Universiti Teknologi Malaysia,
[2]Universitas Andalas,
[1]Malaysia
[2]Indonesia

1. Introduction

Lightning strike is a dangerous natural phenomenon that can cause various problems. Telecommunication subscriber lines (TSLs) and electrical power lines are two systems that are almost always affected by nearby lightning strikes. Voltages in the telecommunication subscriber line (TSL) do get induced by nearby lightning strikes. The induced voltage can be carefully measured and lightning parameters such as the lightning current wave shape, lightning peak current and strike locations be reproduced. Better designs of lightning protection systems can be realised if data on lightning strike distribution in a given region is known. Commercial lightning mapping or locating systems are based on several technologies (Araujo, 2001; Kenneth, 2003). The two most popular methods are those based on the Time of Arrival (ToA) and the Directional Finder (DF) principles.

An example of the lightning locating system (LLS) based on the ToA method is the country-wide LLS owned by the Malaysian national power company (TNB). The system is capable of determining the coordinates of the cloud-to-ground lightning strikes within 500m accuracy. However, for a localised distribution of lightning, say within 1 square km area, this accuracy is too large for the data to be meaningful.

In this work, a new method to determine the coordinate of any cloud-to-ground lightning strike within a certain localised region is presented. The system is suitable for determining lightning strike distributions for a small area by measuring the induced voltages due to lightning strikes in the vicinity of an existing overhead telephone lines (Aulia, 2008a; Aulia, 2008b; Sorwar, 1997; Tominaga, 2003). LabVIEW was employed to measure and acquire lightning parameters such as peak current, wave shape; strike location as well as map the location of the strikes.

A mock telecommunication subscriber line system (MTSL) was designed in the field to capture the lightning induced voltages. The model for the MTSL was developed based on the concept shown in Figure 1. If a cloud to ground lightning strike occurs near an overhead telecommunication cable, and if the location of the strike is placed exactly in the middle of the telecommunication cable, then the induced voltage on the cable due to the strike will not only travel in opposite direction toward the cable ends, but also both waves will arrive at the cable's end at the same time. In other words, there is no difference in the time of arrival, or the time difference of arrival (TDoA) is equal to zero.

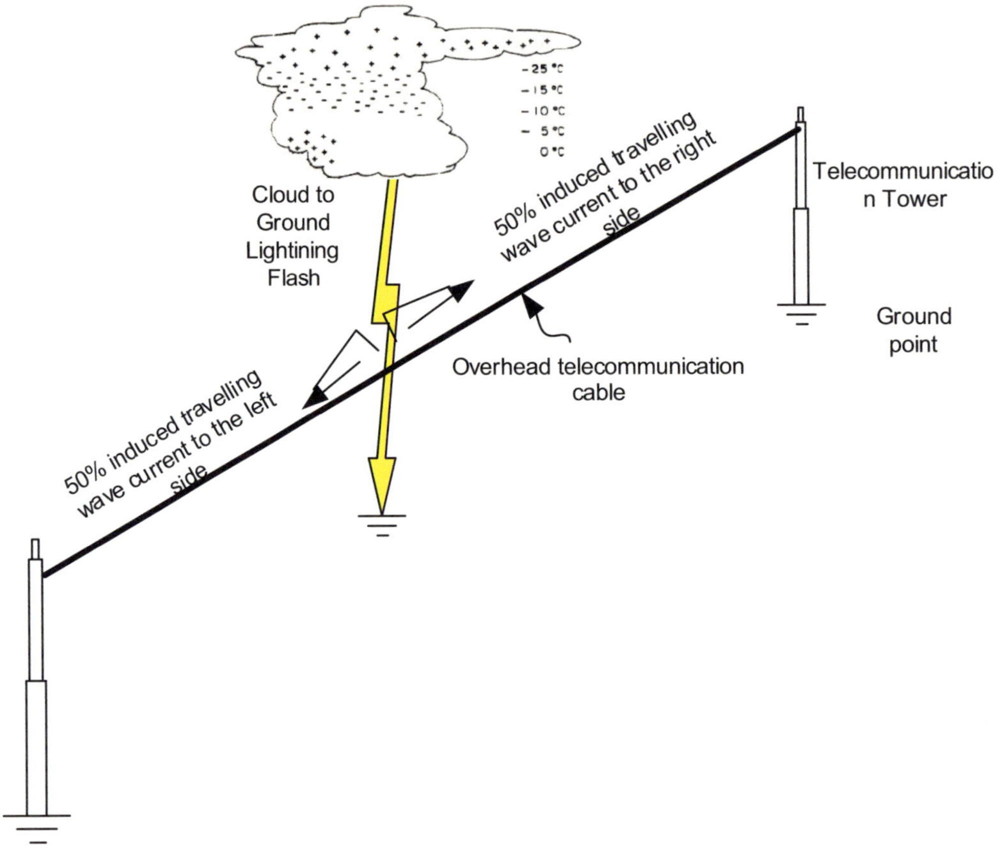

Fig. 1. Cloud to ground lightning strike model adopted for developing the localized lightning locating system (LLLS) using the existing overhead telecommunication cable

2. Lightning detection technique based on the time difference of arrival

In this work, the mapping of the lightning strike locations was done based on the time difference of arrival (TDoA) of the travelling waves. Lightning induced voltage causes a transient on a cable. The point of induction could be treated as a transient source or a fault source. Figure 2 show the Bewley Lattice diagram depicting what happens to the induced voltages based on travelling wave theory (Piantini, 2007). Points A and B are the points of induction caused by lightning strike near the cable.

For an induced voltage at point A, in the first half of the cable $X < L/2$ Figure 2a, the point of induction could be determined using the following formulas:

$$td_1 = 3T_1 - T_1 = 2T_1 = 2(X / V)$$

$$td_2 = T_2 - T_1 = (Y / V) - (X / V)$$

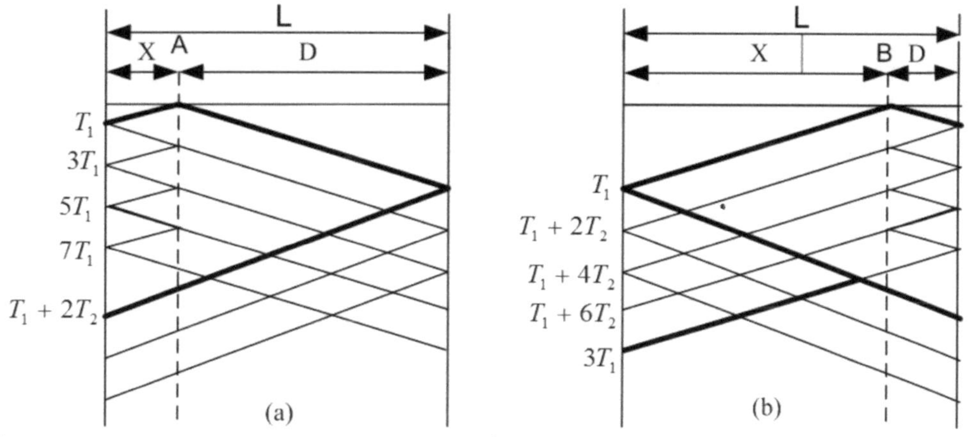

Fig. 2. (a) Bewley Lattice diagram for a fault at (a) first half section of the line at A (b) second half section of the line at B.

By eliminating V, results in

$$X = L * \frac{(1/2)}{(1 + (td_2 / td_1))} \text{ m} \tag{1}$$

where $L = X + D$

T_1 the time for the wave to travel distance X

T_2 the time for the wave to travel distance Y

(td_1) transient time between the first and the second spikes at the first side (sending end);

(td_2) transient time between the initial arrivals of the travelling wave at both sides of the cable (sending and receiving ends);

V travelling-wave velocity;

L total length cable line in meters.

For an induced at point B in the second half of the cable at ($X > L/2$), as shown in Figure 2b, the distance could be calculated using the following equation:

$$X = L * \left(1 - \frac{(1/2)}{(1 + (td_2 / td_1))}\right) \text{ m} \tag{2}$$

Both equations are independent of the velocity of propagation. This fact makes this technique very powerful compared with other traditional techniques.

3. Small scale model

A small scale model was set-up to test and verify the LLS concept. The cloud-to-ground lightning flash was simulated by a purposely-made surge current generator. The generator consists of a high voltage DC generator, and an impulse waveshaping circuit as shown in Figure 3. A series resistor (5-10 Ω) was added in series to limit or control the lightning current.

The height of the copper strip was 2 m. A pair of RG 59 coaxial cable was laid horizontally to mimic the TSL in a certain distance, d, and height, h. The impulse current was measured using a Rogowski coil that has a sensitivity of 0.01 V/A. The induced voltage on the cable was measured through a 50 Ω resistor at the cable's end. A Tektronix 3052 oscilloscope was with a 10m cable was used to measure the induced voltage, the time scale was set to nanosecond range. In this experiment, the end of the cables closer to the copper strip were left opened and the other end was terminated through resistor for measuring purpose.

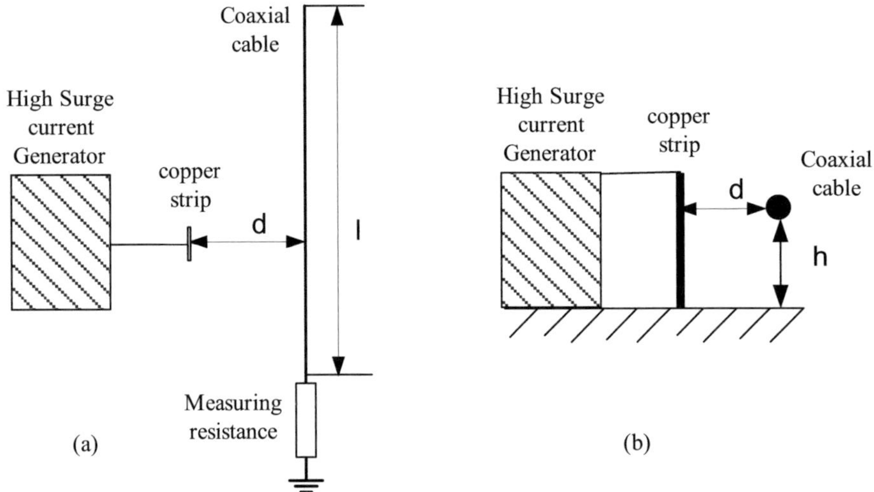

Fig. 3. The circuit connection to simulate the lightning induced voltage on a coaxial cable for reduced scale model (a) top view and (a) side view, where d is the distance between copper strip and the coaxial cable and h is the height of cable laid down above the ground or floor.

4. Travelling wave speed

The speed of the travelling wave in the cable was calculated based on the experimental result as follows:

$$v = l / t \tag{3}$$

where v = velocity,

l = distance travelled, and

t = time travelled

The velocity, v refers to the induced voltage signal speed in telecommunication cable. In this work, the speed was calculated based on the measurement results.

Figure 4 shows the set-up to determine the travelling wave velocity in the telecommunication and coaxial cables. The lengths of cable 1 and cable 2 were varied. Table 1 shows the tabulated results. Figure 5 shows the correlation between difference of distance (DoD) and time diference of arrival (TDoA) of twisted telephone line (in Figure 5a) and RG 59 coaxial cable (in Figure 5b). Based on the measurements, it can be concluded that an average TDoA of 4.6 ns and 5.1 ns represents 1 m propagation for the telecommunication cable and coaxial cables respectively.

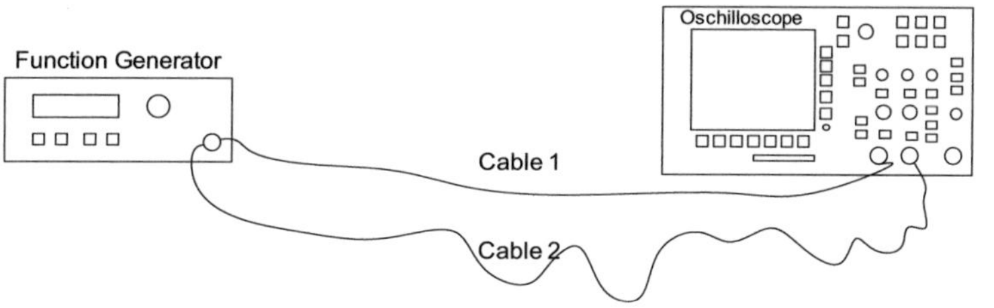

Fig. 4. The speed of travelling wave measurement in the cable to get the TDoA/m

Do D (m)	0	1	2	7	8	9	10	11	18	19	20
TDoA (ns)	0	4.64	9.28	33.5	37.12	41.53	46.4	51.04	84.6	88.2	92
DToA per meter (ns/m)	0	4.64	4.64	4.79	4.64	4.614	4.64	4.64	4.7	4.64	4.6
DToA in avarage (ns/m)	4.660										

(a)

DoD (m)	0	1	2	7	8	9	10	11	18	19	20
TDoA (ns)	0	5.2	9	35.6	41.6	45.8	52.4	57.6	91.8	96.6	101
TDoA per meter (ns/m)	0	5.2	4.5	5.09	5.2	5.089	5.24	5.236	5.1	5.084	5.1
TDoA in avarage (ns/m)	5.082										

(b)

Table 1. Time difference of arrival (TDoA) and the travelling wave speed in (a) Telecommunication Subscriber Line (b) RG 59 coaxial cable.

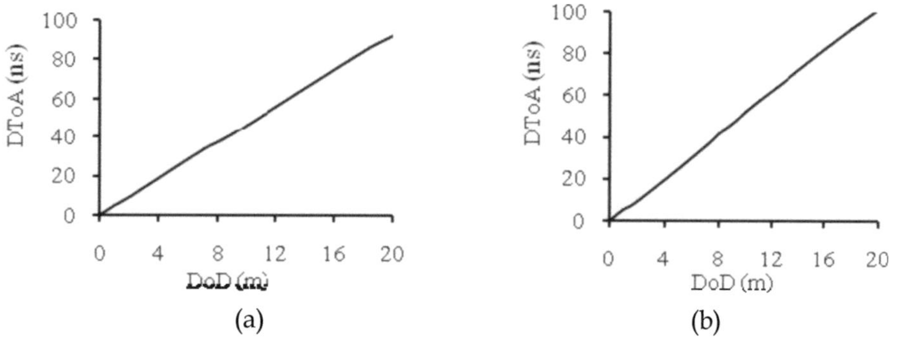

Fig. 5. The correlation between difference of distance (DoD) and time diference of arrival (TDoA) of (a) twisted telephone line and (b) RG 59 coaxial cable

5. Impulse current generator

Two types of impulse current generators were used in the research work. Firstly, a manually set up impulse generator described in (Aulia, 2008a and Aulia, 2008b) and secondly a commercial impulse generator manufactured by Haefely. The former was used during working with the small scale system while the latter was used during the calibration process of MTSL. Pictorial view of the impulse generators are shown in Figure 6.

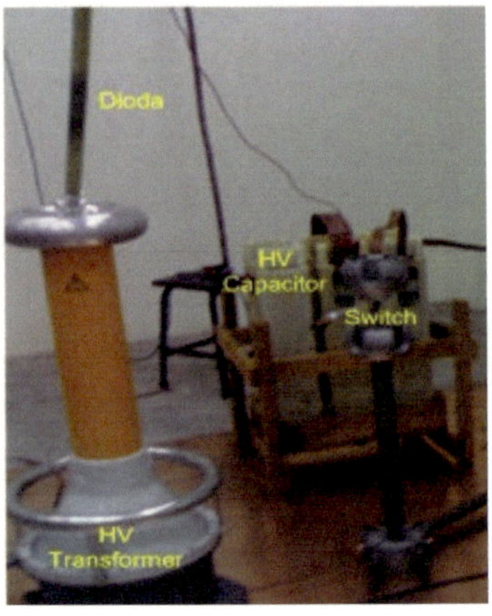

(a)

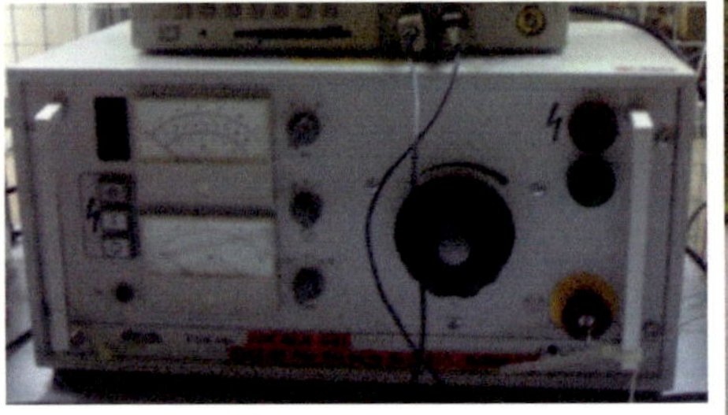

(b)

(c)

Fig. 6. (a) The manually set up impulse current generating unit, (b) the corresponding input voltage control unit, (c) Commercial impulse current generator

6. The measurement, transmission and central processing station

Several types of voltage transducers installed at the line ends can be used to measure the induced voltage due to lightning strikes (Altafim, 1992). In this work, specially modified voltage transducers were used. Since the lightning strike coordinate was calculated based on the arrival time delays of various induced voltage impulses, any delay or interference in the transmission of the induced impulses can influence the calculation. Therefore, the transmissions of data from the voltage transducers to the central processing station (within P06 building) were implemented using optical fibres. Optical transmitters and receivers (transceivers) similar to the ones described by (William, 2006; Kurata, 2007) were used. Apart from the optical receivers, the central processing station consisted of a LabVIEW-enabled four-channel high speed oscilloscope and a personal computer (PC).

The block diagram of the measurement and data acquisition system for this work is shown in Figure 7 and the typical flowchart for the data acquisition implementation is as shown in Figure 8. LabVIEW 8.5 software was used for the control of the data acquisition system.

All measuring equipment was physically checked to make sure they have been correctly connected and installed. Referring to Figure 8, when the system is switched on, it will initialize and be in standby mode waiting for a trigger. In the event of a trigger data will be acquired and then verified. If the correct signal has been captured, the system determines the lightning time of arrival, induced voltage, current and map the lightning location in the Cartesian. On the other hand if the signal captured was not correct the system will be in standby mode and waits for another event. The location will then be mapped in the Cartesian system. These parameters will then be stored and printed. If another lightning event is to be captured, the system returns back to standby mode else stops.

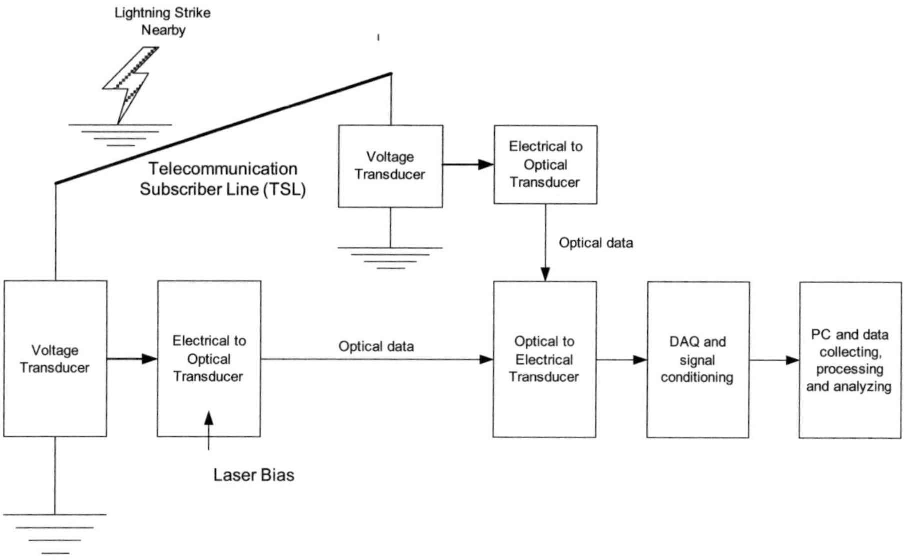

Fig. 7. The measurement and data acquisition system of the LLLS

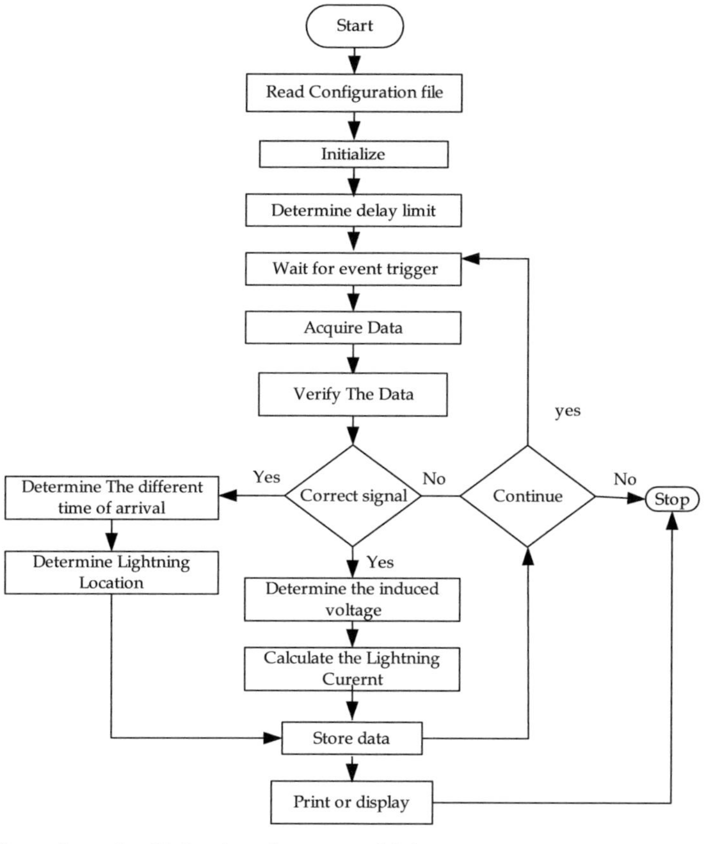

Fig. 8. Typical flow chart for lightning data acquisition system

6.1 Measuring equipments

In this work, the key measuring equipments used were digital storage oscilloscope, high current transducer and Picoscope.
The oscilloscopes were used for the purpose of measuring the induced voltage both in the laboratory and field tests. A high current transducer with a 0.01 V/A sensitivity was used to measure the current generated from the impulse generator.

6.2 Data acquisition system

All data was acquired, analysed and save in the data acquisition system which consisted of a Picoscope and LabVIEW program. Picoscope is a device that resembles the functions of an oscilloscope but runs on computer. Usually, Picoscope comes with software that turns it into a PC oscilloscope. In order to connect with LabVIEW, a virtual instrument (VI) interface was developed. LabVIEW Picoscope VI program links the Picoscope with LabVIEW software. To accommodate the need of very high speed data acquisition, the new version of Picoscope Technology, 5203 series having maximum data capturing speed of 200 MS/s was used. Data can be saved in temporary memory and erased each time capturing data restarted. Alternatively, the captureed data could be saved in the Excel readable files or using Picoscope accompanied software.

7. The mock telecommunication subscriber lines and cartesian model

Lightning induced voltages on overhead lines could be studied using models (Piantini, 2007). Piantini studied the lightning induced voltages on overhead lines of power distribution systems using a scaled down model. However, this is prohibitively complex to be treated theoretically. The scale model was successfully implemented at the University of São Paulo, São Paulo, Brazil. A similar approach was adopted and implemented in this work.

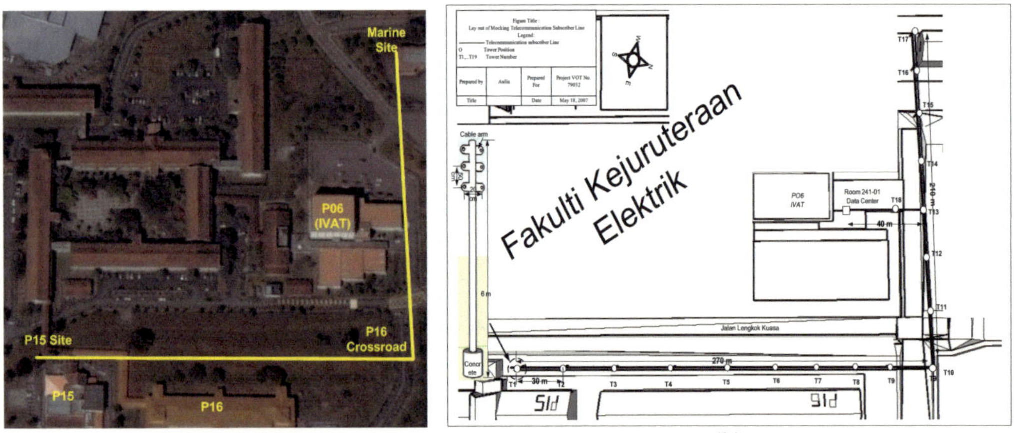

(a) (b)

Fig. 9. (a) Aerial view of the mock TSLs location (Google Earth June 4, 2008) (b) Diagrammatic layout of the mock TSLs

The MTSL was installed in a chosen area at the Institute of High Voltage and High Current (IVAT). Figure 9 a shows details of the site (Google Earth dated June 4, 2008) and Figure 9 b shows the schematic diagram of the mock TSLs. The coordinates of various spots are given as follows: P15: latitude 1°33'30.51"N and the longitude 103°38'36.31"E; P16 (crossroad):

latitude 1°33'37.72"N and longitude 103°38'38.90"E; and Marine Building: latitude 1°33'39.72"N and longitude 103°38'32.60"E. Two types of cables were laid down on the top of the seventeen installed telecommunication towers having heights of 6 m from the ground. Ten towers (T1-T10) with a total cable length of 270 m were installed alongside P15 to P16 buildings. This line route was designated as Line I. Perpendicular to this, the rest of the seven towers (T11-T17) with a total cable length of 210 m were laid alongside P06 to Marine buildings. This line route was designated as Line II.

The cable types were twisted telephone and coaxial cables. The two perpendicular lines form a Cartesian system. Line I represents the X-axis and Line II the Y-axis. Using this purposely made Cartesian system, any lightning strike occurring within the square region made up by the two perpendicular lines can therefore be determined.

The cables installed at the back of P15 to P16 crossroad and P16 crossroads to Marine site do not form the perfect Cartesian system and therefore needed to be corrected. The correction was done by adding an additional line perpendicular to P16 crossroad to Marine site as shown in Figure 10. The simplified diagram of the MTSL for lightning detection system mapping is shown in Figure 11.

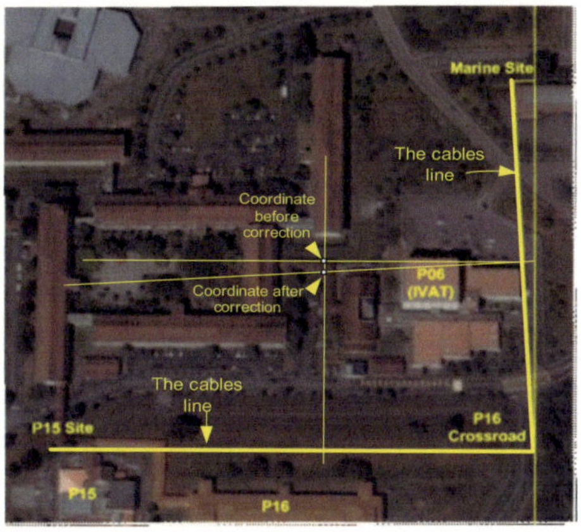

Fig. 10. Correction for the Y-axis of the 'imperfect' Cartesian system

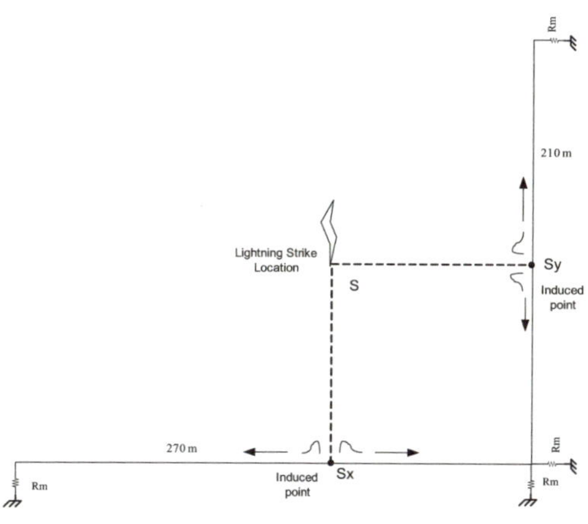

Fig. 11. The simplified diagram of mock telecommunication subscriber line (MTSL) for lightning detection system.

Referring to Figure 12, the lightning is assumed to strike a certain place S, nearby in the area. Consequently, electromagnetic field is generated as a result of the strike which then induces the cables. The closest point of induction is a point that is perpendicular with lightning strike location, S_x and S_y. At the point of induction, the induced current is separated into two signals that travel in opposite direction, 180° phase in difference, towards the ground. At the ends the cable, a measurement resistor, R_m, and voltage transducer is installed to measure the voltage across it.

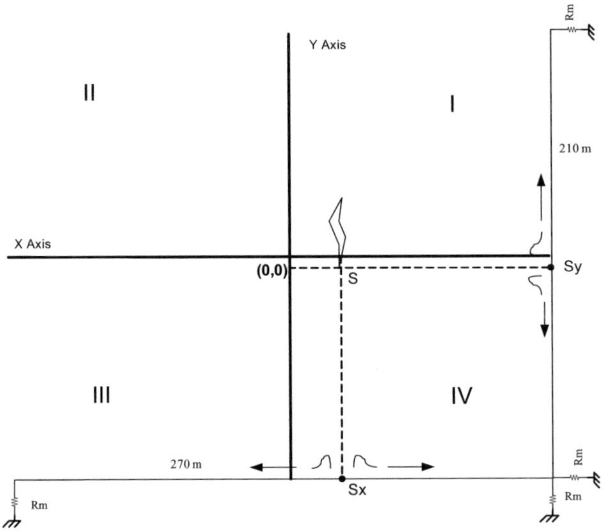

Fig. 12. Four quadrants of the Cartesian system covering the LLLS square area

The time difference of arrival (TDoA) method was used to determine the lightning strike coordinate. Clearly, the arrival time of the induced voltage or surge is dependent on the distance travelled. Hence, for the strike location (0,0), the distance travelled along the (x,y) coordinates is (270/2, 210/2) or (135,105). For this case, the TDoA shall be (0,0) since the induced voltages arrived at the same time on both cable ends and hence no net time difference of arrival. If the TDoA is positive in both cable X and Y, say (x,y), the strike location is in quadrant I, where x and y represent the Sx and Sy respectively. If for example, the TDoA is negative in cable X but positive in cable Y, that is (-x,y), the strike location is in quadrant II as illustrated in Figure 12.

8. The implementation of lightning locating and mapping system in LabVIEW

Several subVIs from LabVIEW library were used to implement the lightning mapping and locating system. Below are the SubVI that were used to locate and map the lightning strikes. The detail explanation could be found in help menu of the LabVIEW software.

a. Simulate Signal

Simulate Signal SubVI contains many options to simulate the signals. In this work, the Simulate Signal SubVI was used to generate signals representing the lightning strike signals. This subVI could generate different types of signal waveforms in different frequency and magnitudes. In Dialog Boxes, the sine wave, square wave, saw tooth wave, triangle wave, or noise (DC) with different frequencies and amplitudes could be simulated. The other options are timing, time stamp, reset signal, signals name and result preview. The icon on the Simulate Signal is shown in Figure 13.

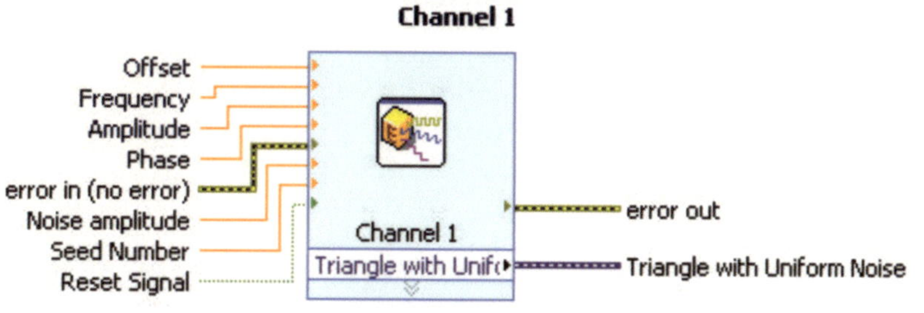

(a)

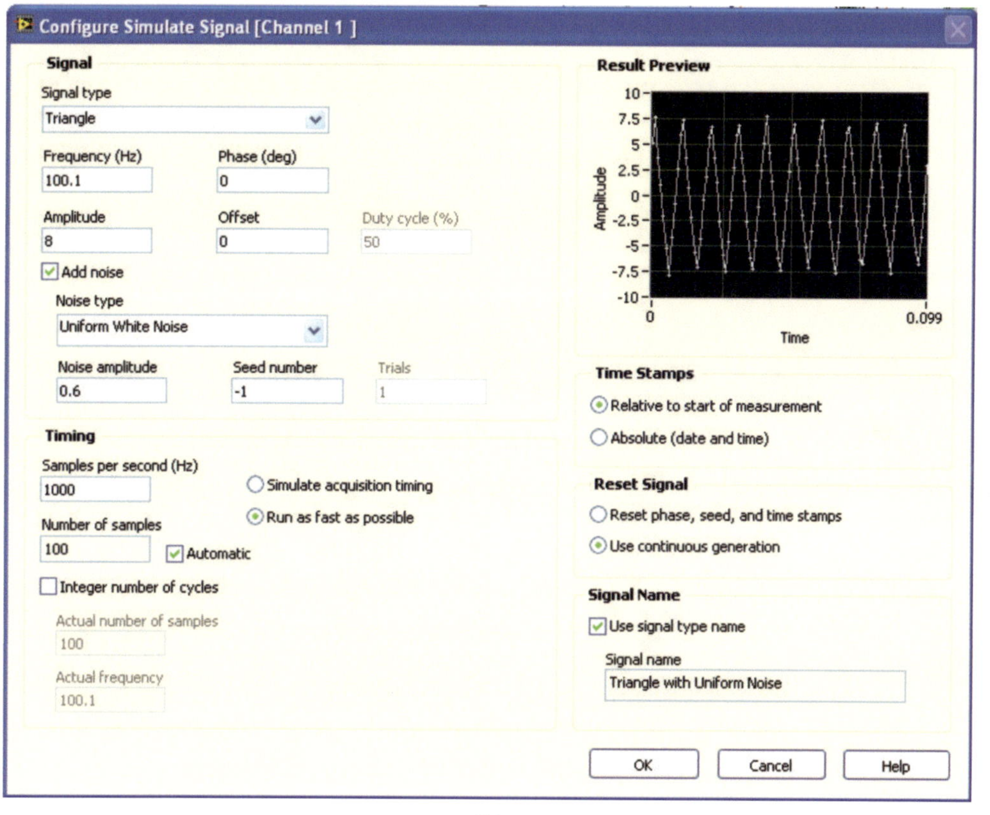

(b)

Fig. 13. Simulate signal generator SubVI (a) Icon (b) Dialog box

b. Amplitude and Level Measurement

Amplitude and level measurement (ALM) measures some wave features such as peak voltage, minimum peak voltage, peak to peak voltage, cycle average, cycle RMS, DC and RMS. The icon on the ALM is shown in Figure 14. This SubVI was used to measure the maximum voltage of generated signals as well as the maximum induced voltage of the real lightning strike.

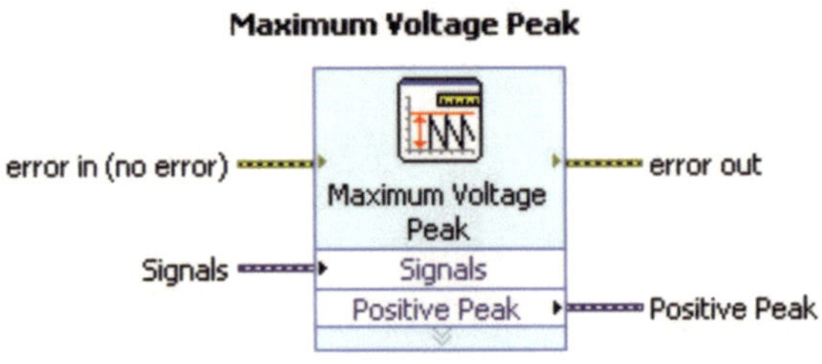

(a)

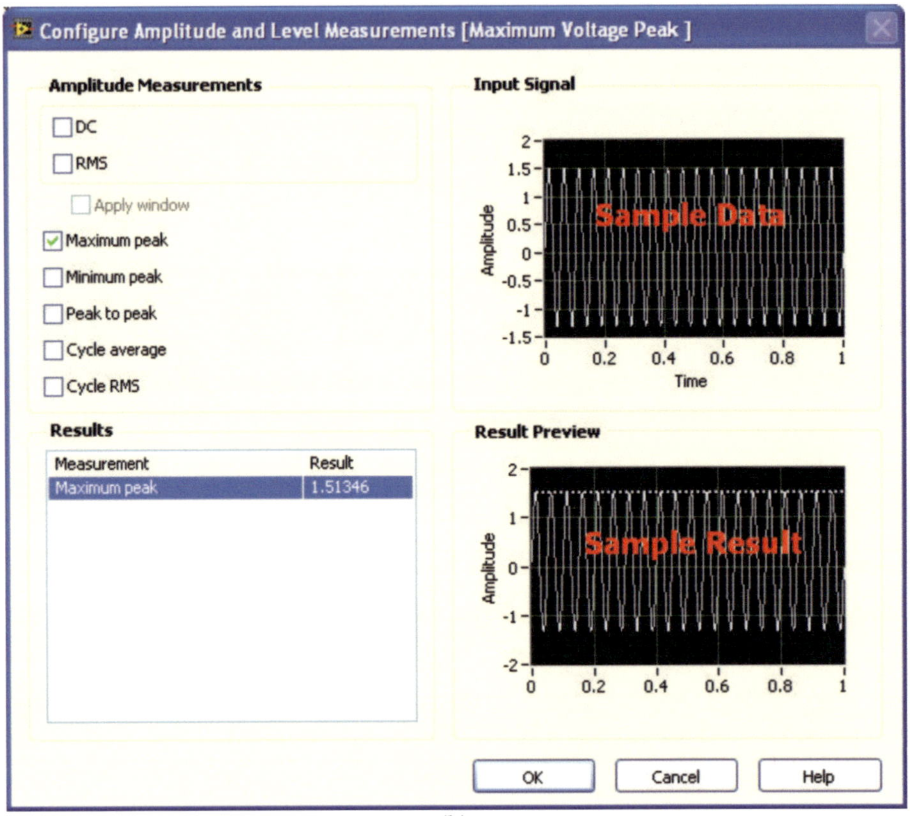

(b)

Fig. 14. Amplitude and level measurement SubVI (a) Icon (b) Dialog box

c. Subtract

Subtract SubVI subtracts numeric values such as the maximum voltage that was measured by ALM. Figure 15 shows the icon.

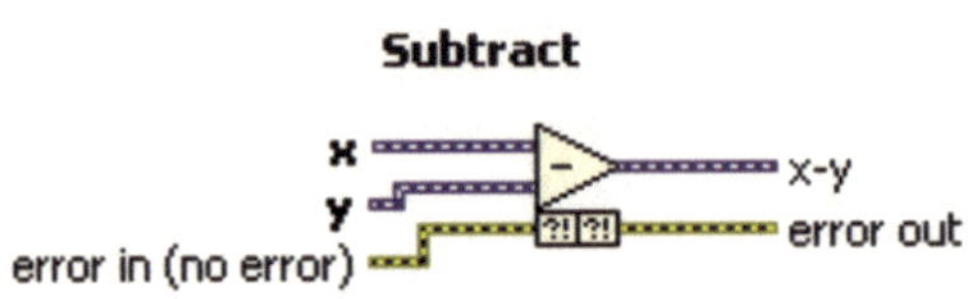

Fig. 15. Subtract SubVI icon

d. ConFig Comparison

The calculation result of lightning strike distance does not always suit with the actual distance of X axis or Y axis values of the Cartesian system. Only the values in acceptable range of data were treated as valid values and passed to next step of programming process. The ConFig. Comparison SubVI was used in this work for this purpose. ConFig. Comparison SubVI filters the values that are fed into it in different logical condition like equal, not equal, greater, greater or equal, less, less or equal, equal within tolerance, in range and out of range. The output will result in one result per data point, one result per channel and one result for all channels. This VI is shown in Figure 16.

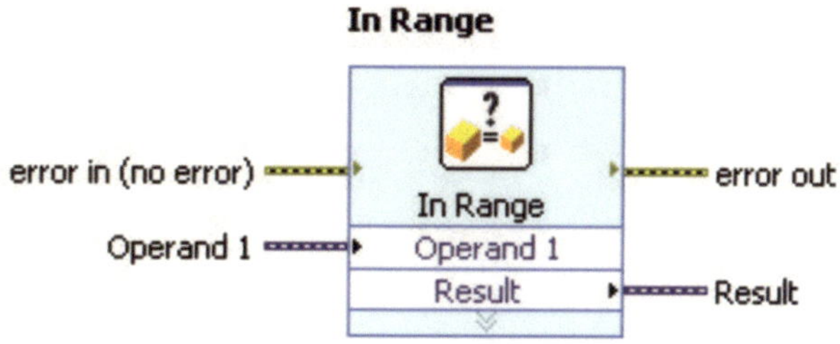

(a)

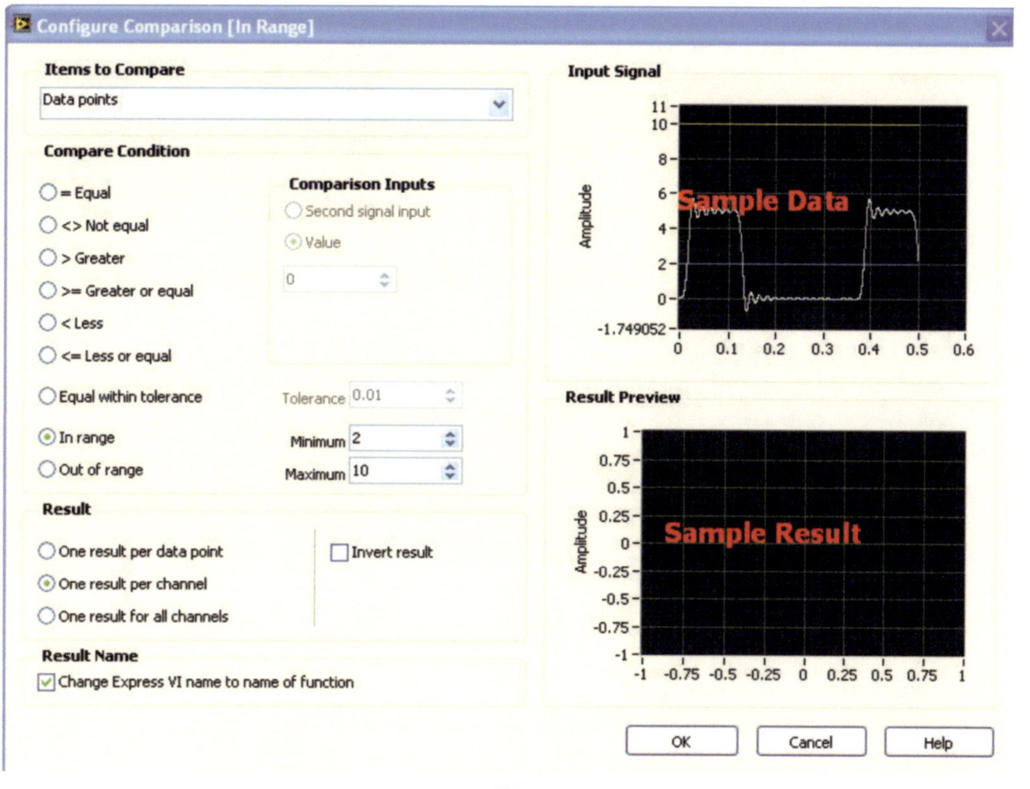

(b)

Fig. 16. ConFig. Comparison SubVI (a) Icon (b) Dialog box

e. ConFig. Statistic

Timing of the maximum voltage measured by ALM is very crucial in calculating the TDoA. Inaccurate timing will give the wrong information of the lightning strike location. To determine the TDoA, the ConFig. Statistic SubVI was used. The ConFig. statistic icon returns the selected parameter of the first signal in a waveform. The icon SubVIs ConFig. statistic is shown in Figure 17. The type of data that will be stored and processed further was managed in this block.

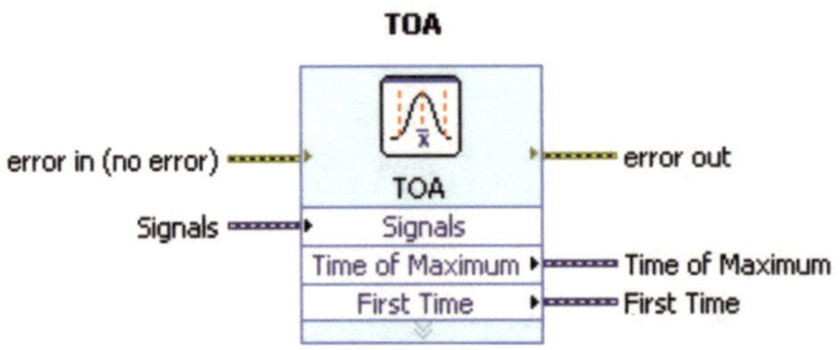

(a)

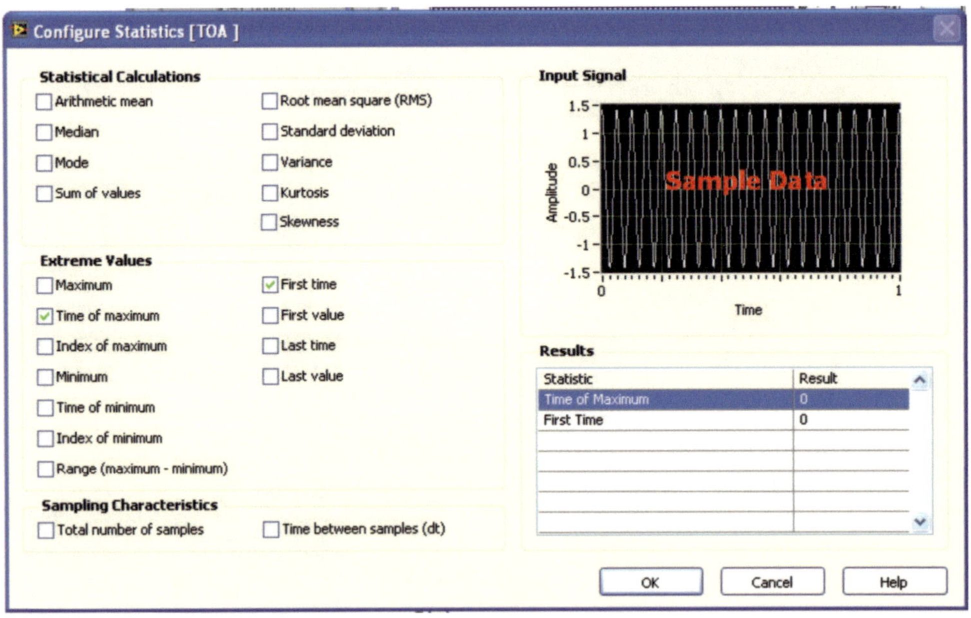

(b)

Fig. 17. SubVI ConFig. statistic (a) Icon (b) Dialog box

f. ConFig. Write to Measurement

This SubVI was used for data logging or saving the lightning data in a file for future analysis. The file type could be in text data or in a binary data. Both data could be exported to a compatible Excel file. To store the data, write to Measurement File SubVI in a CSV files was used. These files could be read out again using Read from Measurement File SubVI. The icon on the Write to Measurement File SubVI is shown in Figure 18.

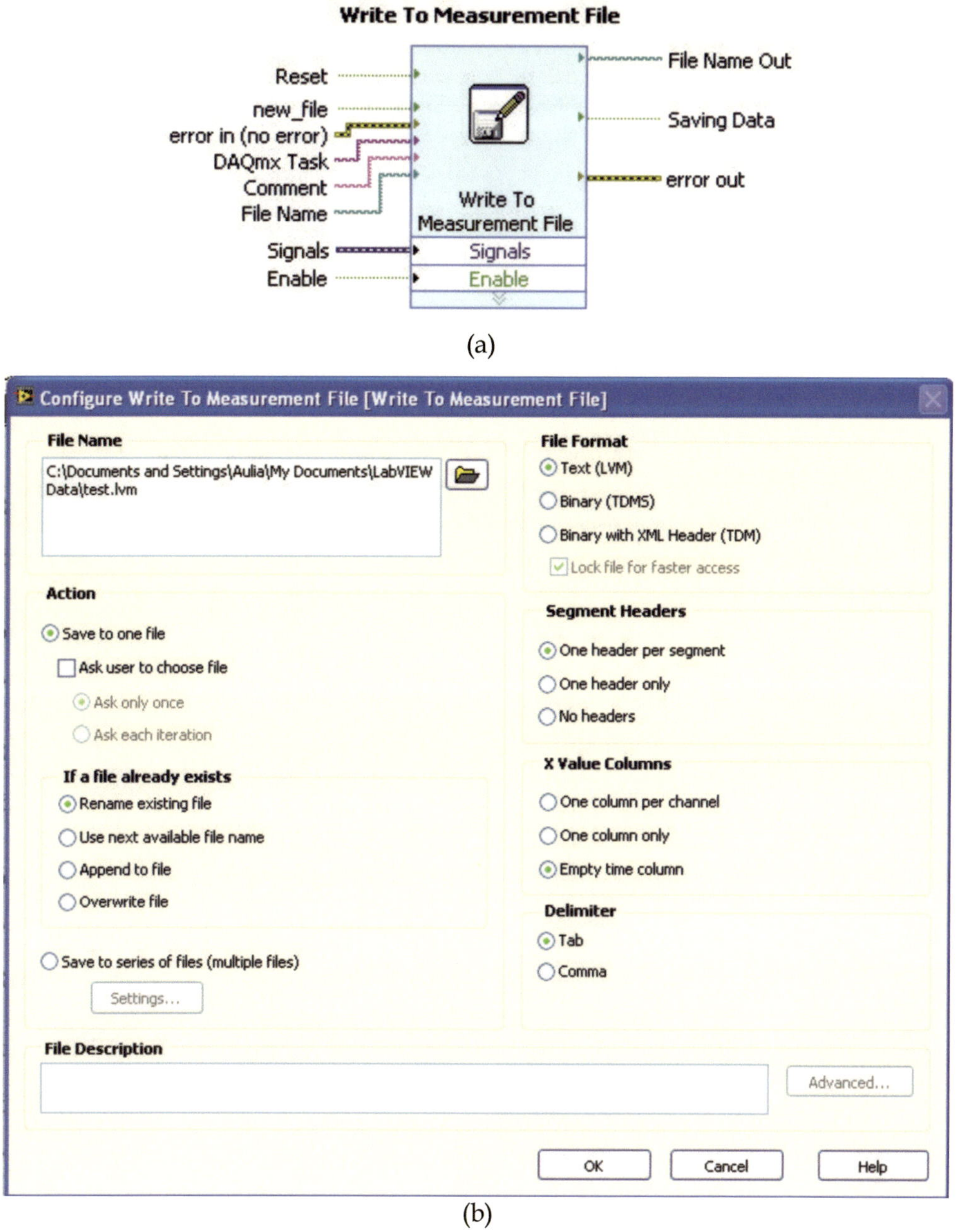

Fig. 18. Write to Measurement File SubVI (a) Icon (b) Dialog box

g. ConFig. Formula

The ConFig. Formula uses a calculator interface to create mathematical formulas to perform most math functions that a basic scientific calculator can compute. The input is represented by x1. x2,....x8 that could be labeled by any mathematical expression. The SubVI of ConFig. formula is shown in Figure 19. In this work the distance was calculated using this block. The distance in X axis was calculated based on TDoA from time of maximum voltage of Channel

1 minus time of maximum voltage of Channel 2 to get the x coordinate. The same process for Channel 3 and Channel 4 was done to get distance in Y axis to plot the y coordinate.

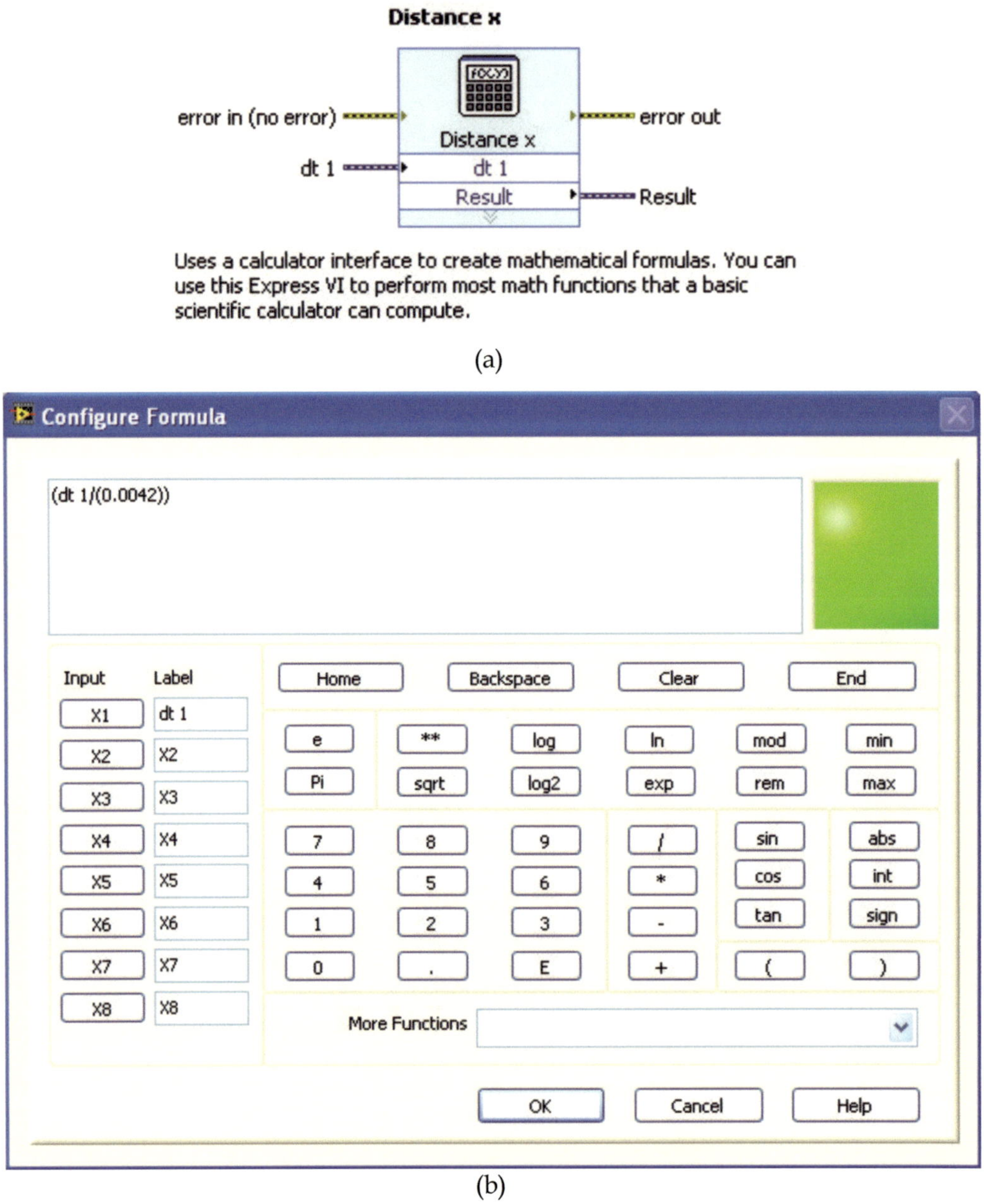

Fig. 19. Configuration formula SubVI (a) Icon (b) Dialog box

h. Display

Lastly the important thing is to display the lightning strike location. The appropriate type of graph in LabVIEW is the XY graph representing the Cartesian system and lightning strike location area. LabVIEW has 5 different types of graphs and charts. These include the

Waveform Graphs and Charts, XY Graphs, Intensity Graphs and Charts, Digital Waveform Graphs and Mixed Signal Graph to display the data. In this work, the first two types, Waveform Graphs Charts and XY Graphs were used. The waveform graph and chart was used to display the waveform of the lightning strike waveform or generated signals, while the XY graph was used to display the lightning strike location. These types of graphs are shown in Figure 20.

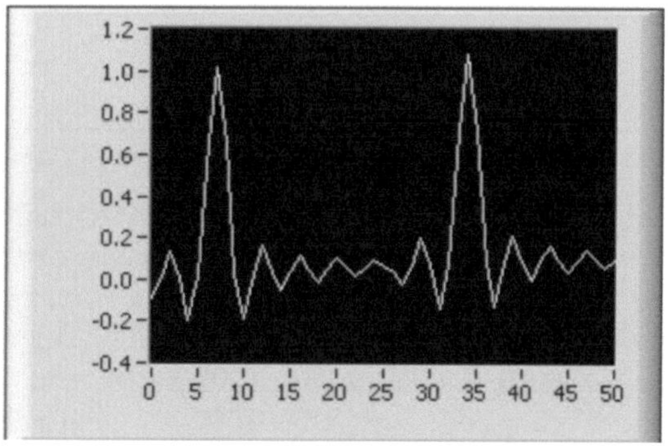

(a)

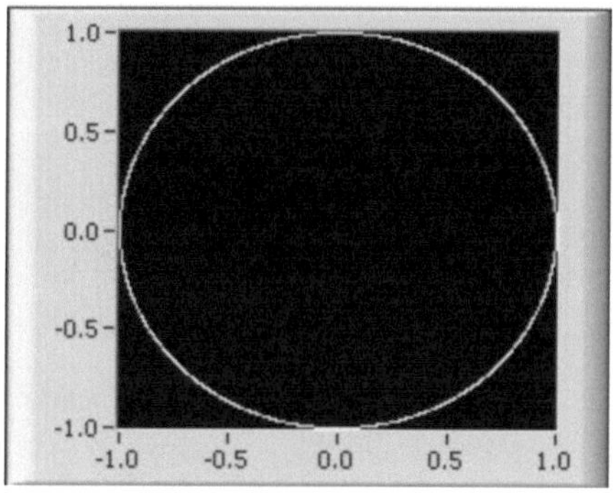

(b)

Fig. 20. LabVIEW Graph (a) waveform graph and (b) XY graph

The XY graph is a general-purpose, Cartesian graphing object that plots multivalued functions, such as circular shapes or waveforms with a varying time base. The XY graph displays any set of points that are either evenly sampled or not.

The XY graph accepts three data types for single-plot XY graphs. The XY graph accepts a cluster that contains an x array and a y array. Refer to the (X and Y arrays) Single Plot graph in the XY Graph VI in the labview\examples\general\graphs\gengraph.llb for an example of a graph that accepts this data type.

9. The lightning locating and mapping system

Figure 21 shows the general process of lightning locating and mapping system. The real lightning strike was detected using induced voltage lightning detector that consists of series of resistor that are installed at the ends of telecommunication lines. The induced voltage in this measurement resistor was measured remotely through a measurement cable and then captured by oscilloscope or Picoscope. However in this chapter, the lightning strike was simulated by signals generated from the Simulate Signal SubVI to demonstrate the workability of the LLLS system. The crucial data are the peak voltages and the related time stamp. These data were used to calculate the TDoA and DoD respectively to locate the lightning strike.

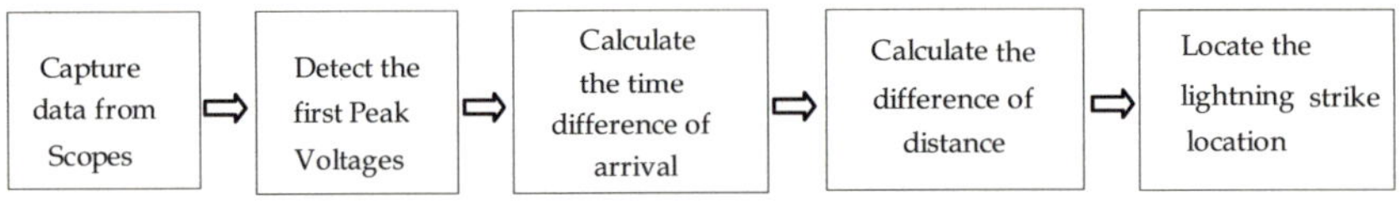

Fig. 21. The general process of lightning locating and mapping system

Figure 22 shows how the LabVIEW system work for two channels data acquiring to generate the X coordinate in the current work. From the figure, Channel 1 and Channel 2 in the section SubVI 1 are Simulate Signal SubVI that was used to generate signals with different shape, amplitude, frequency and noises added. For the acquisition of real data, these channels are replaced with the Picoscope 5203 series and high resolution storage oscilloscope TDS3052 (two channel) and TDS5104B (4 channel). The communication between the devices and computer was interfaced by a driver related to each device (not discussed in this chapter).

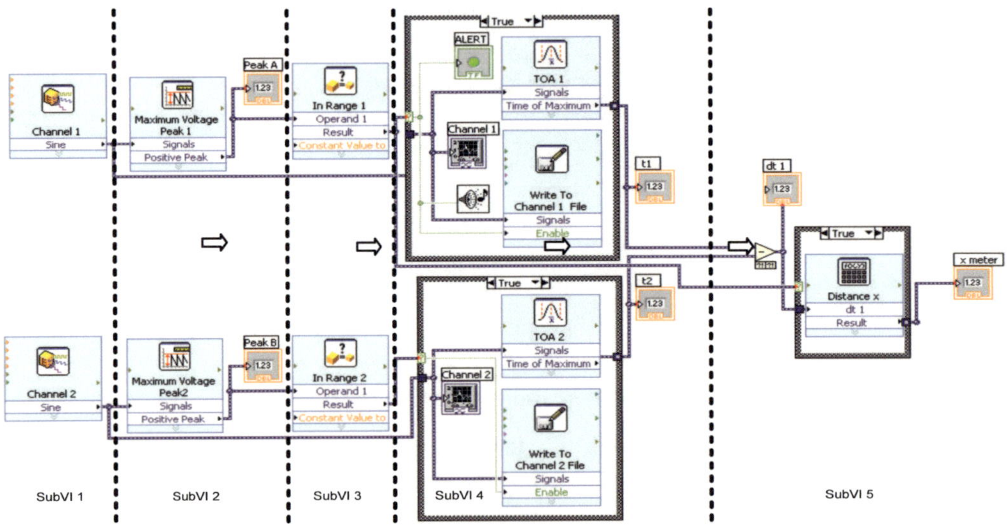

Fig. 22. SubVI block in the LabVIEW environment to generate the X coordinate

SubVI 2 is the measuring block that measures the maximum voltage of Channel 1 and Channel 2. SubVI 3 takes the value of the two signals and first of maximum time of maximum voltage occur. These times were recorded in SubVI 4 to get t_1 and t_2 and then t_1 was subtracted by t_2 to determine TDoA. The result is then passed to the mathematical block to calculate the distance in X axis to get X coordinate in SubVI 5. The same process was conducted to generate the Y coordinates. Lastly, the values of X and Y were plotted to get (x,y) coordinates in the Cartesian System. All of the data are then stored in MS Excel readable files.

Figure 23 shows a typical output screen showing lightning strike coordinates within the four quadrants using simulated data. The output panel also shows the corresponding captured induced voltage surges, in this case represented by the simulated sources.

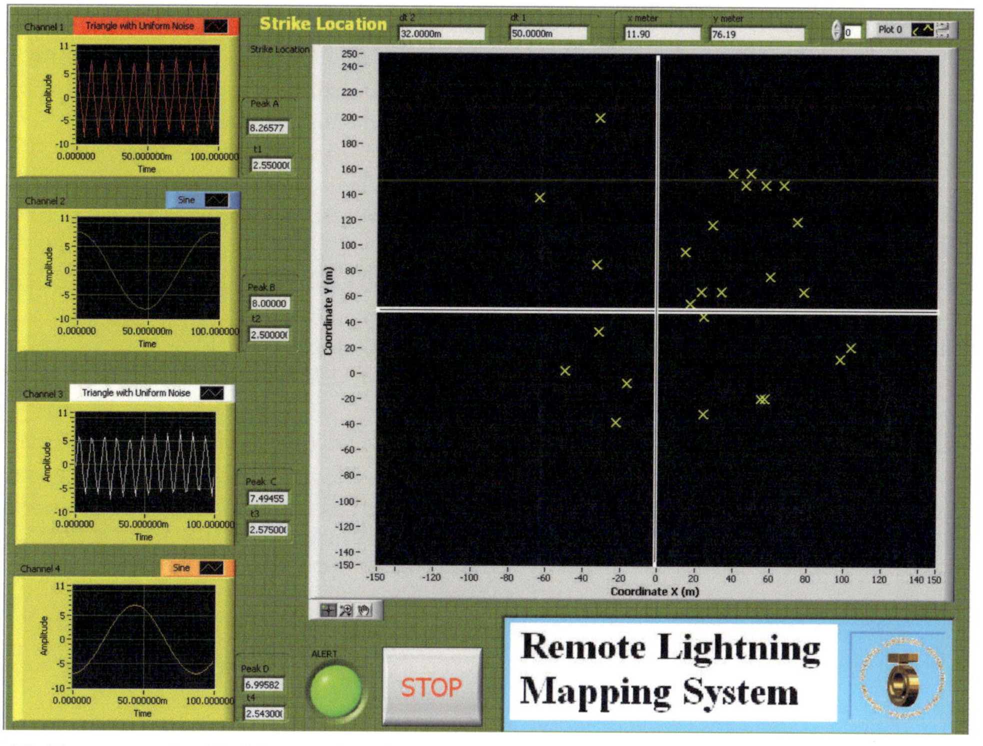

Fig. 23. Front panel of LabVIEW for the LLLS display

10. Conclusion

In this work, a new localized lightning location system (LLLS) has been developed. The LLLS detects, locates and maps cloud-to-ground lightning strikes due to the voltages induced on Telecommunication subscriber lines using the Time Difference of Arrival (TDoA) Technique. The software part of the LLLS was successfully implemented in LabVIEW for the location and mapping of lightning strike incidences.

11. Acknowledgment

The authors would like to thank Ministry of Science, Technology and Innovation (MOSTI) Malaysia and Research Management Centre (RMC), Universiti Teknologi Malaysia, for the financial and management support.

12. References

Altafim, R.A.C. et al. (1992). An Electret Transducer for Impulse Voltage Measurements, *IEEE Trans. Indus. App.* Vol. 28, No. 5, pp. 1217 - 1222, 0093-9994.

Araujo, A.E.A. et al. (2001). Calculation of lightning-induced voltages with RUSCK's method in EMTP: Part I: Comparison with measurements and Agrawal's coupling model. *Electric Power Systems Research*, Vol. 60, No. 1, pp. 49 - 54, 0378-7796.

Aulia et al. (2008). Lightning Induced Voltage as a Lighting Detection System, A New Approach, Proceedings of Commet, Johor Bahru, Johor, Malaysia, January 2008.

Aulia et al. (2008). The Surge Induced Voltage on a Small Scale Model of Telecommunication Subscriber Lines (TSL) in Different Height and Distance: Experimental Approach, Proceedings of Commet, Johor Bahru, Johor, Malaysia, January 2008.

Kenneth, L. et al. (2003). Overview of Lightning Detection in the VLF, LF, and VHF Frequency Ranges, In: *ILDC 2001*, June 19 2007, Available from :<https://www.thelightningpeople.com/htm/about/events/ildc/ildc 2000/docs/03_CUMMINS.pdf>

Kurata, K. and Kami, N. (2007). US, Pat No. US 7,165,653 B2. Washington DC: U.S. Patent and Trademark Office

Piantini, A. et al. (2007). A Scale Model for the Study of the LEMP Response of Complex Power Distribution Networks, *IEEE Trans. Power Delivery*, Vol. 22, NO. 1, pp. 710 - 720, 0885-8977

Sorwar, M.G. (1997). The Analysis of Induced Surge on Overhead Telecommunication Subscriber Line Due to Lightning Return Stroke, Master Thesis, UTM, Malaysia.

Tominaga, T. et al. (2003). Characteristics of Lightning Surges Induced in Telecommunication Center in Tropical Area, *IEEE Trans. Elect. Comp.*, Vol. 45, No.1, pp. 82 - 91, 0018-9375.

William et al. (2006), US Patent, Pat No. US 7,073,960 B2. Washington DC: U.S. Patent and Trademark Office

Computer-Based Control for Chemical Systems Using LabVIEW® in Conjunction with MATLAB®

Syamsul Rizal Abd Shukor, Reza Barzin and Abdul Latif Ahmad
University Sains Malaysia,
Malaysia

1. Introduction

Current trend and characteristics in chemical industries has become more complex, hybrid and intensified in nature thus requiring faster and more powerful control systems to perform adequate control action for optimal performances (Charpentier, 2005). The time would not be more suitable to accommodate this advancement in the chemical industries with the existence of more powerful computer technologies either hardware or software. This development of more advanced and powerful computer architecture provides a better alternative to address the problems of performing optimally for the state-of-the-art chemical industries. Thus, computer-based control systems become the inevitable platform for fast, precision and close control of chemical processes. The advanced, powerful and user-friendly programming environment enables the process control engineers to easily design appropriate controller with minimal time and at lower cost, eventually implementing the designed controller directly on the actual systems via these tools. MATLAB® and LabVIEW® are amongst the most powerful and useful software that can be extremely helpful in this regard. MATLAB® is a very powerful mathematical tool, which enables us to use its powerful controller design toolboxes and also perform simulation in SIMULINK® environment with ease. Nonetheless, interfacing the control equipments such as measurement devices and control valves via MATLAB® is not an easy task. In contrast, LabVIEW® is among the best available software for communicating with the hardware in PC based systems. Utilising LabVIEW® facilitates easy data acquisition from the hardware and sending the corresponding signal to the final control element.

The idea of incorporating the two software for the computer-based control system would enable us to have an easy data acquisition (getting signal from all measurement devices and processing the signal to the desirable form) using LabVIEW® and then the signal is transferred to MATLAB® which conventionally acts as the controller to perform control calculation. Finally, the output signal from the controller is transferred back to LabVIEW® software to be applied to the final control element to perform adequate corrective action. In order to connect these two software, there are number of toolboxes in LabVIEW® which can help the user to easily connect them based on the needed environments. For example, using SIMULINK Interface Toolkit (SIT), LabVIEW® can easily communicate with SIMULINK environment in a continuous mode.

The proposed combination of these two powerful software not only can help researchers to design and implement their designed controller in various forms in a very short time but also in some cases it facilitates operation under conditions that might not be possible using conventional systems. For example, controlling of miniaturized intensified systems is a very challenging issue (Abd Shukor and Tham, 2004, Etchells, 2005) where traditional control approaches were found to be very difficult in achieving sufficiently fast control (Luyben and Hendershot, 2004, Bleris et al., 2006) which is due to the sampling speed limitation of the industrial controllers and slowness of the mentioned systems. However, using the proposed combination software in tandem, we have the opportunity to choose a wider range measurement of the analytical devices and additionally the controller is not restricted to specific sampling range and even more important, the same controller can be used for both simulation studies and actual controller (because the developed controller in MATLAB® is used for both parts)(Barzin et al., 2010).

This chapter will provide some insights of the proposed utilization of the two software (MATLAB® and LabVIEW®) for proper control of a microreactor-based miniaturized intensified system. An overview of the designed miniaturized intensified systems will be described and followed by the description of traditional control method limitations on the control of the described system. Then, the structure of the proposed system is described in order to show the data flow on the system. This is followed by interfacing the control components with LabVIEW® and the required low level programming steps. Then, controller design in MATLAB® and SIMULINK as well as the data flow between LabVIEW® and SIMULINK® are discussed in detail and finally, the controller performance of the system using the proposed system is presented which shows the successful implementation of the proposed system.

2. Overview of the microreactor-based system

The designed system as presented in Fig. 1 consists of a single slit interdigital micro mixer (SSIMM) with volume of 0.23 ml as the reaction chamber (A) which is capable of performing very fast reactions. Having very small holdup, residence time can vary from fraction of a second to 3 seconds which can be extremely useful for fast reactions or reactions that need precise residence time in order to achieve high selectivity. In this study, a simple week acid (phosphoric acid, 0.1 Molar) and strong base (sodium hydroxide, 0.1 Molar) reaction will be taken as the case study.

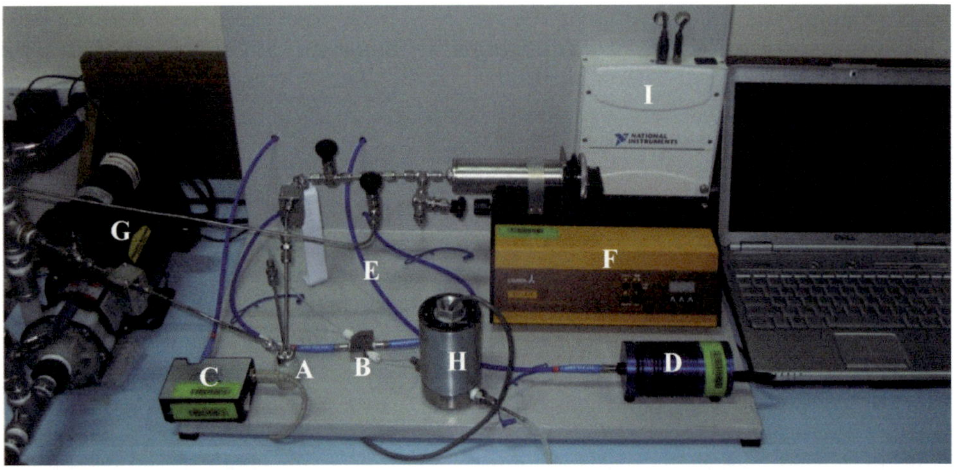

Fig. 1. Experimental rig and components

In order to perform measurement of the reactor outlet, the reaction part is connected to the Z-flow through cell (B) which is connected to a USB 2000+ (Ocean Optics, USA) spectrometer (C) and a HL-2000 (Ocean Optics, USA) tungsten halogen light source (D) via optical fibers (E). The spectrophotometric setup is used to perform online pH measurement from the reaction product every few milliseconds (Barzin et al., 2010). A 100 ml stainless steel LAMBDA VIT-FIT syringe pump (Lambda Laboratory instruments, Switzerland) (F) is used as the final control element in order to manipulate the flow rate of the injected strong base into the SSIMM microreactor. A centrifugal pump (G) is used to provide continuous and pulsation free flow of the weak acid into the micro reactor. In order to measure the total flow rate which passes through the micro reactor, a FMTD4 nutating micro flow meter (DEA Engineering Company, USA) (I) is used. A NI DAQ-Pad 6015 (J) is also used in order to carry out data acquisition from the micro flow meter and to send the controller output signal from the controller to the final control element (syringe pump).

3. Limitations of traditional control systems

Traditional chemical industries usually operate in a high residence time (in the range of few minutes to few hours), hence, conventional measurement system which having much lower residence time than the process able to provide adequate measurement for optimal control of the process. This is not the case for miniaturized intensified system as the conventional measurement system would definitely have higher residence time than the intensified process (Jones and Tham, 2006). This would then hamper the control system to work efficiently as the measurement is very slow in response to the fast reaction in the micro system. Thus, such system necessitates a much faster measurement systems and controllers to provide sufficiently fast measurement. Having a controller with a sampling time of 10 seconds for industrial systems would be considered fast enough whereas for miniaturized intensified systems,it is considered very slow and makes the system difficult to control.

This can be concluded that miniaturized intensified systems need some requirements in order to be able to be controlled properly. For instance, the controller should has a very high sampling rate, the measurement also should be capable of performing measurement every few milliseconds and eventually the obtained results from the measurement need to be transferred to the controller in a very high transfer rate. The proposed spectrophotometric measurement system can provide a very fast measurement. However, not having a suitable control system and also a mean to transfer the collected measurement data to the controller and back to the final control element would hamper a successful control performance to be achieved. To overcome this problem, LabVIEW® provides an excellent solution as it is amongst the powerful software for interfacing and communicating with instruments.

4. Software design

The feedback control loop was built in SIMULINK®, MATLAB® 2006a software. A number of simulations were carried out to study the performance of the designed controller at different controller setting. To better evaluate the controller performance on real system, it is essential to use exactly the same controller on the experimental setup. On the other word, it is preferable to use MATLAB as our controller. However, as mentioned earlier MATLAB has a very limited functionality for interfacing with the hardware. For instance, PC based data acquisition with MATLAB® is limited to the hardware supported by the MATLAB® DAQ toolbox. Moreover, a number of complicated steps have to be taken to communicate with the hardware.

Thus, in order to use MATLAB® as the controller and also easily communicate with the components of the rig, the current study uses MATLAB® software to build the feedback control loop and LabVIEW® software to communicate with the hardware. A low level programming using SIT were used to provide communication between MATLAB® and LabVIEW®. The following sections show the needed for both to interface the hardware and communicate with the designed controller in MATLAB® environment using LabVIEW® software.

5. Interfacing rig components with computer using LabVIEW®

In the case study, syringe pump, spectrophotometer, flow meter and NI-DAQ, are interfaced with the embedded controller in the computer. This can be clearly seen in Fig. 2 depicting the interfacing of the experimental rig with the supervisory control system.

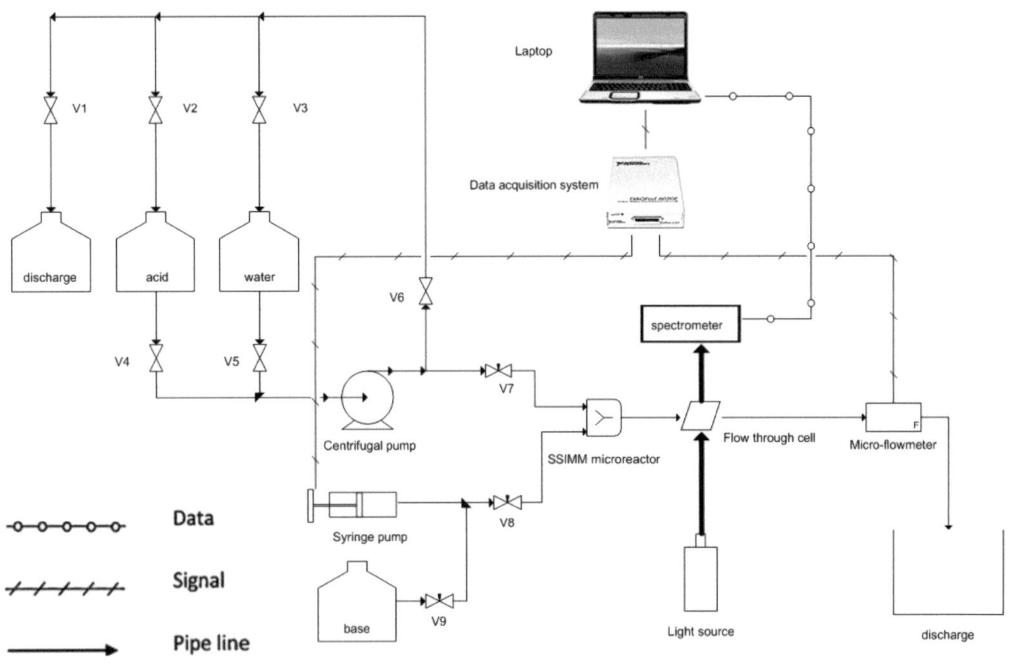

Fig. 2. Schematic diagram of the designed and developed rig

As can be observed from the figure, syringe pump and micro-flow meter are using analog signals to communicate whereas the spectrophotometer uses digital signals to send measurement results to the computer. NI USB-6009 (National Instruments, USA) data acquisition system has been chosen which is amongst the basic products of National Instrument. It can be seen from Fig.3, NI USB-6009 offers analog input with positive and negative polarity suitable for communicating with the flow meter and it also provides two analog out which can be used for the syringe pump.

Module	Terminal	Signal, Differential Mode
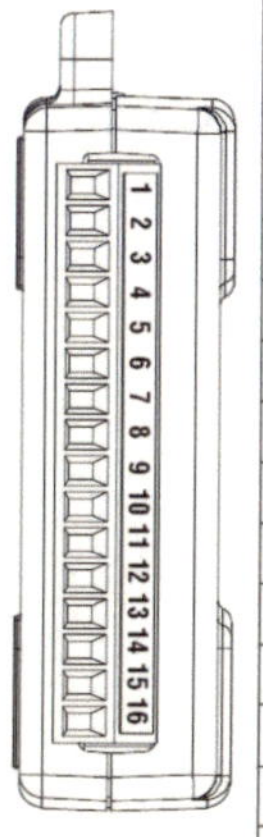	1	GND
	2	AI 0+
	3	AI 0–
	4	GND
	5	AI 1+
	6	AI 1–
	7	GND
	8	AI 2+
	9	AI 2–
	10	GND
	11	AI 3+
	12	AI 3–
	13	GND
	14	AO 0
	15	AO 1
	16	GND

Fig. 3. USB-6009 with corresponding terminals (NI, 2008)

The NI-DAQ can be connected easily to the computer using USB cable which is automatically detectable and do not require installing. In order to setup the connected NI-DAQ, *Measurement and Automation Explorer* (MAX) is required. Launching the MAX provides access to all National Instruments devices as shown below:

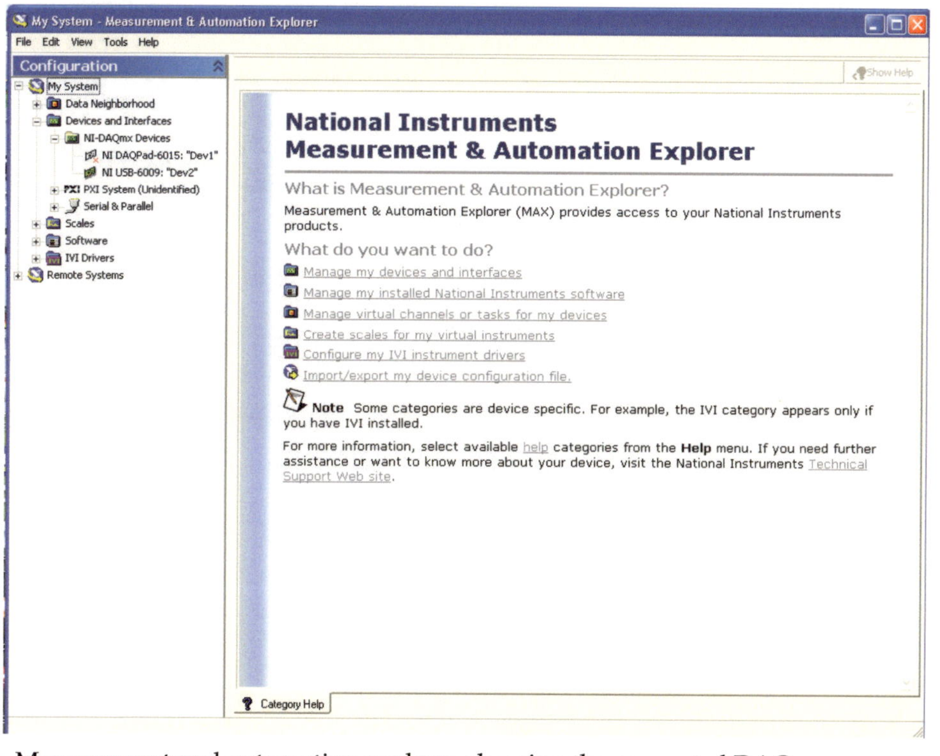

Fig. 4. Measurement and automation explorer showing the connected DAQ.

The connected NI device can be observed in MAX as NI-USB 6009 is shown in green color which means that it is connected properly. Further DAQ setting can be done later at the programming stage which will be discussed in the following.

5.1 Interfacing the syringe pump

The pump offers multiple control options such as RS232 and RS485 or through analog signals (0-10 V or as an option: 0-20 mA or 4-20 mA) which is one of its big advantages over similar products. Based on the available connectors on the DAQ system, voltage signals are selected to manipulate the flow rate of the syringe pump.

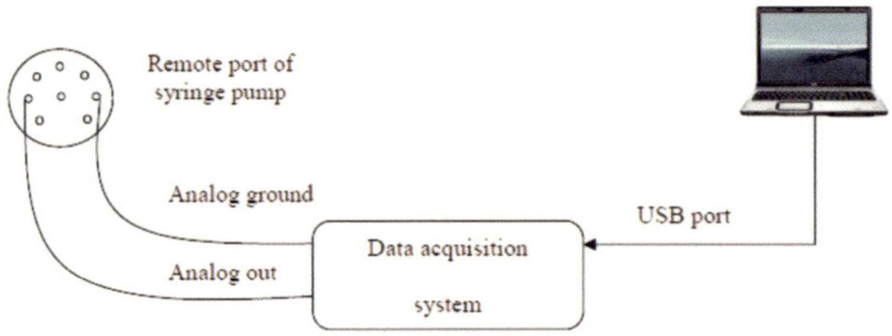

Fig. 5. Electrical connections from computer based controller to the data acquisition system and to the syringe pump

In order to connect the syringe pump to the DAQ, we need to identify the signal type and also the corresponding connector. This can be done easily using DAQ assistant and selecting the proper output type and also the range of applicable voltage for the pump as can be observed in Fig.6.

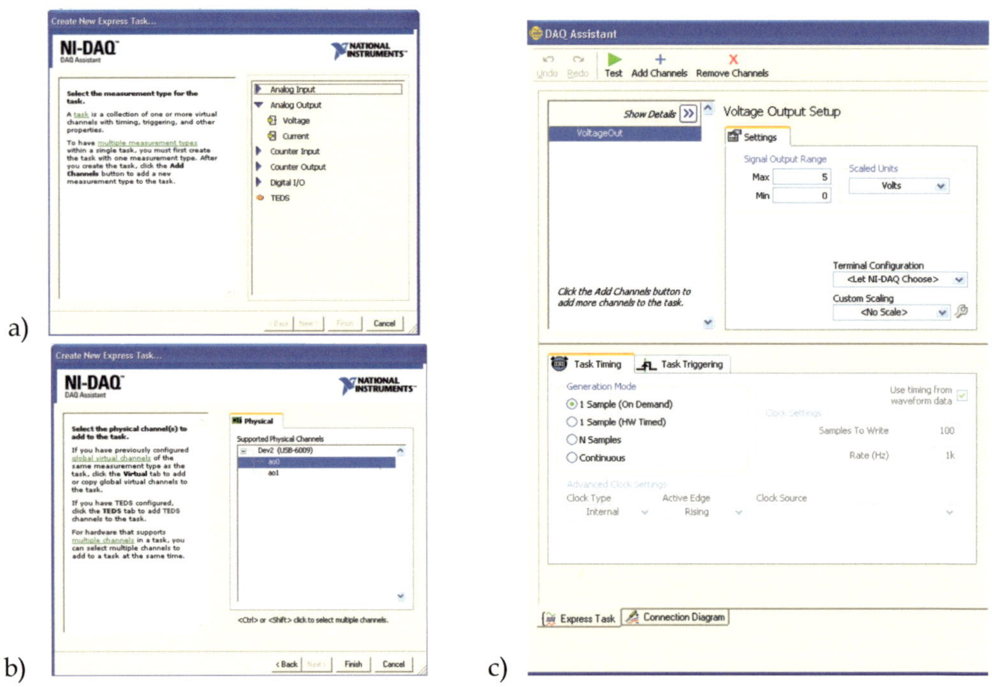

Fig. 6. Syringe pump interfacing steps, a) signal type b) connector selection c) signal settings

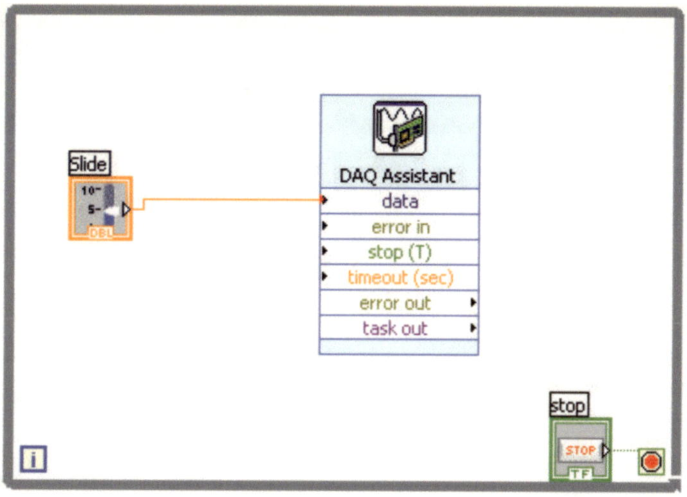

Fig. 7. DAQ connected to a slide bar to test the syringe pump.

Then, using a *while loop* and a slide bar we can actually check if the desired signal is being received by the syringe pump as shown above. This shows that LabVIEW®easily facilitates sending the desired signal to the final control element by just doing 4 simple steps.

5.2 Interfacing the micro-flow meter

In this study, FMTD4 nutating micro flow meter (DEA Engineering Company, USA) was used which has an operation range of 1-250 ml/min in order to measure the flow rate of the system. The flow measurement principle is shown in Fig. 8.

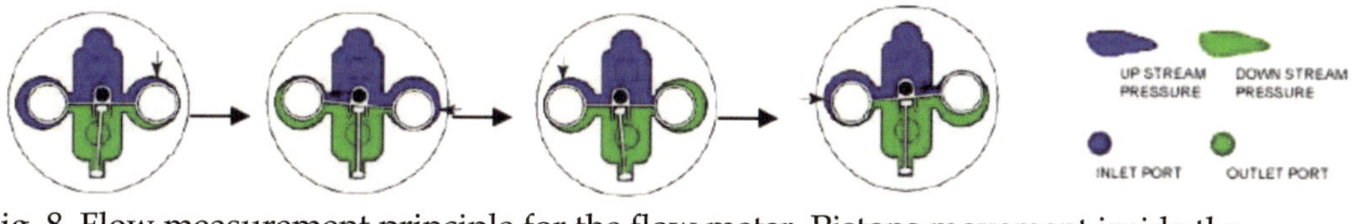

Fig. 8. Flow measurement principle for the flow meter. Pistons movement inside the chamber while the liquid passes through the flow meter (DEA, 2008)

The pistons inside the flow meter chamber rotate in a cycle motion while the flow passes through the flow meter. Each cycle displaces approximately 0.02 ml. Signal detection is accomplished by light interruptions of a photo emitter/detector device. A ferromagnetic wire tracks the magnet in the nutator (through a pressure tight barrier) causing these interruptions. The interruptions are electronically shown as sine waves. The obtained sine waves can be conditioned by conventional electronic means to provide a square wave output as shown in Figure 9. However, the flow meter is not designed to directly measure flow rate and it only gives raw data using 5 volt pulses for each cycle. Therefore, a code need to be developed in LabVIEW® environment to calculate the actual flow rate based on the obtained pulses from the flow meter.

In order to address the problem, NI-DAQ receives the analog voltage in pulse form as can be observed in figure 9 then, these number of pulses are calculated every seconds and consequently, the flow rate passing through the flow meter. The appropriate block diagram in LabVIEW® environment is presented in Fig. 10.

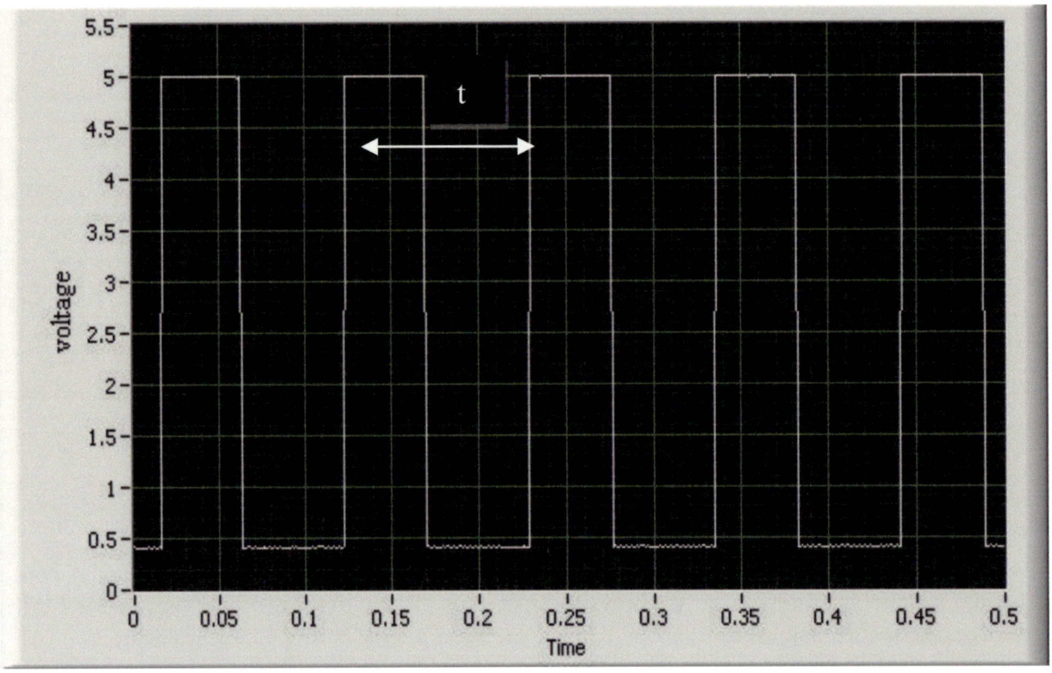

Fig. 9. Obtained pulses from the flow meter while the flow passing through the flow meter

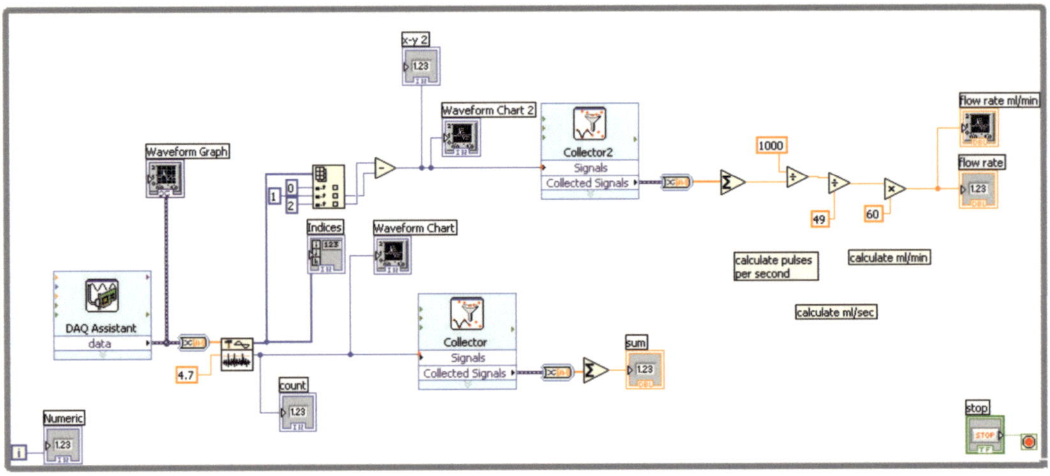

Fig. 10. Block diagram for micro-flow meter interfacing

5.3 Interfacing the spectrophotometer

The spectrophotometer is connected to the computer using USB connection to provide fast data transmission from the spectrophotometer. It uses 2 MHz A/D converter, and the absorbance of the liquid is captured and transferred to the computer at every millisecond via the USB port. In order to capture data from spectrophotometer, OmniDriverSPAM™ was used to acquire the data from spectrophotometer using the developed code in

LabVIEW® environment. However in order to suit the developed code into our application, some changes need to be made.

OmniDeriveSPAM™ provides the code in order to get the full spectrum data from the spectrophotometer and in order to get the value of the required wave length which is the corresponding value needed to found from the input data which has been done in the first step as can be presented in Fig. 11. Second step, calculates the intensity of light at each wavelength (based on the spectrophotometer's manual). Third step, calculates the mean value for specific number of irritation in order to have less noisy measurement and finally at the final step, the pH value can then be calculated via simple calculations (Liu et al., 2006, Martz et al., 2003). It can be observed that the transmission of the raw data in to the required data form was done in few simple steps.

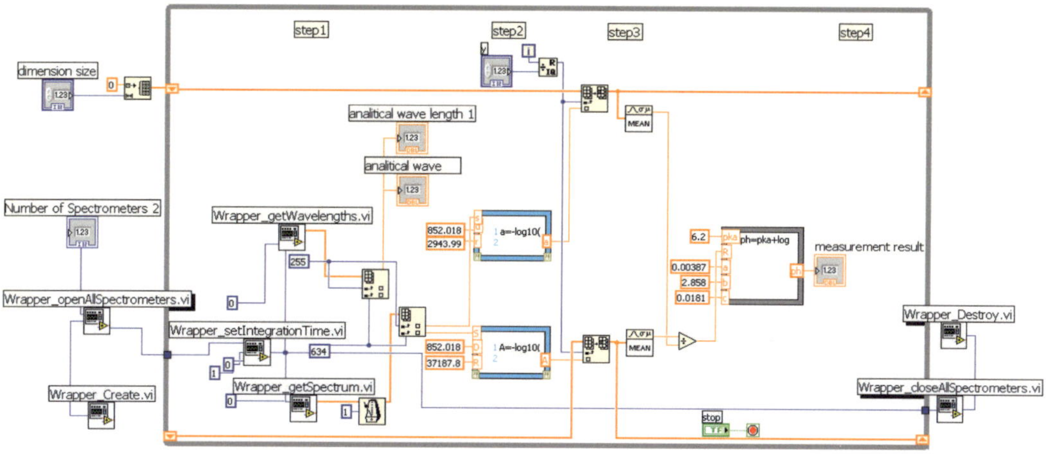

Fig. 11. Block diagram for spectrometer interfacing

6. Building a LabVIEW® user interface for a Simulink® model

As mentioned earlier, controller was developed in SIMULINK® environment and thus in order to be able to control the developed experimental setup, the connection between the designed controller in MATLAB® and LabVIEW® is essential. Thus, a low level programming using SIMULINK® interface toolkit (SIT) is applied in order to provide communication between MATLAB® and LabVIEW®.

The SIT, provides a platform not only to run any simulation in SIMULINK® environment via LabVIEW® but also to read and write data from SIMULINK® blocks as the simulation is running. Figure 12 shows that using SIT, we can locate and run any SIMULINK®'s `.mdl` file. In addition, any desired value can also be fed into any specific block in that `.mdl` file. For instant, Fig. 12 shows how any desired value can be written into "constant2" block in the `mdl` file. Then using `read.vi`, we can get output from any block in the mdl file.

Using this valuable tool, SIMULINK® can be used as the controller while the measurement data is feed into the measurement blocks in SIMULINK® using LabVIEW® and controller output signal also can be easily transferred to LabVIEW® and conditioned then sent to the final control element to do the corrective action.

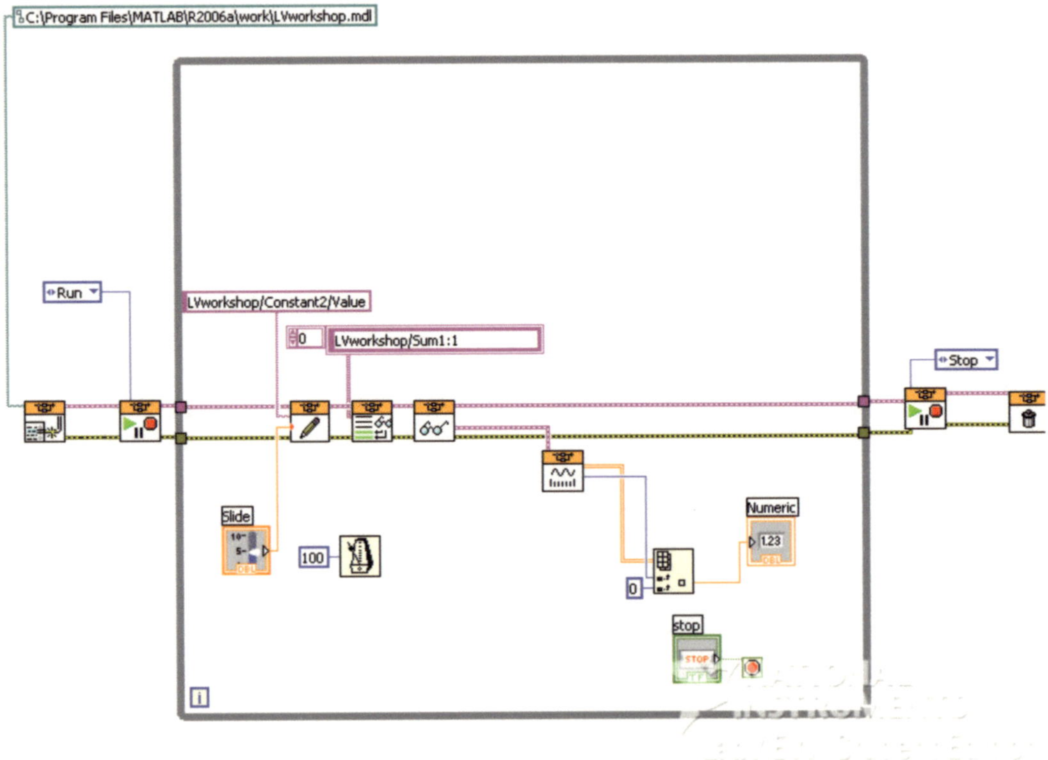

Fig. 12. Block diagram for linking SIMULINK using SIT

7. Control system

After interfacing all the control components using LabVIEW® and also linking LabVIEW® to SIMULINK environment, it is essential to include all the parts in a single VI and provide suitable connections for each part. Figure 13 shows the schematic diagram for data communication of the experimental rig. As can be observed from the diagram, SIMULINK® and LabVEIW® environment can communicate via the SIT toolkit. It is clear that LabVIEW® acts as interface between the experimental rig components and the embedded controller in SIMULINK.

A signal probe need to be placed in SIMULINK model in order to enables SIT to communicate with the file as can be observed from Fig. 14. A PID plus first order low pass filter design is used as the controller of the system (Barzin et al., 2010).Using the developed structure using SIT, the controller output can be taken from the `Sum` block in the SIMULINK® file and transferred to LabVIEW® to be sent to the final control element (syringe pump). In order to be able to apply the step change to the system, set-point value should be adjustable while the SIMULINK® model is running. To address this problem, set-point input block is also connected to LabVIEW® which enables the user to make any change in set-point value. Measurement input signal can also be transferred to the measurement block in the control loop via LabVIEW®. Thus, the controller easily can access to the updated measurement results every 50 milliseconds as the `.mdl` file is running.

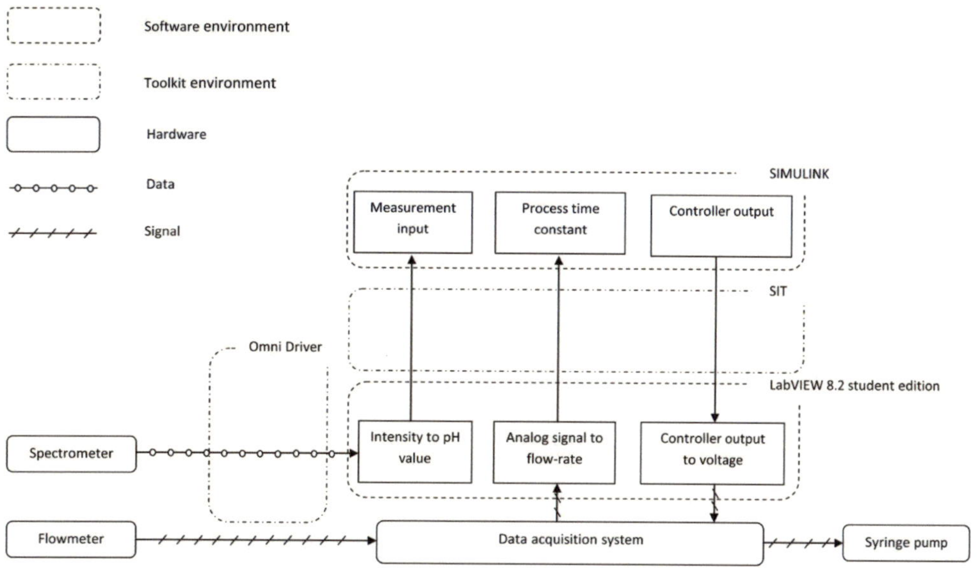

Fig. 13. Schematic diagram for data communication of the experimental rig.

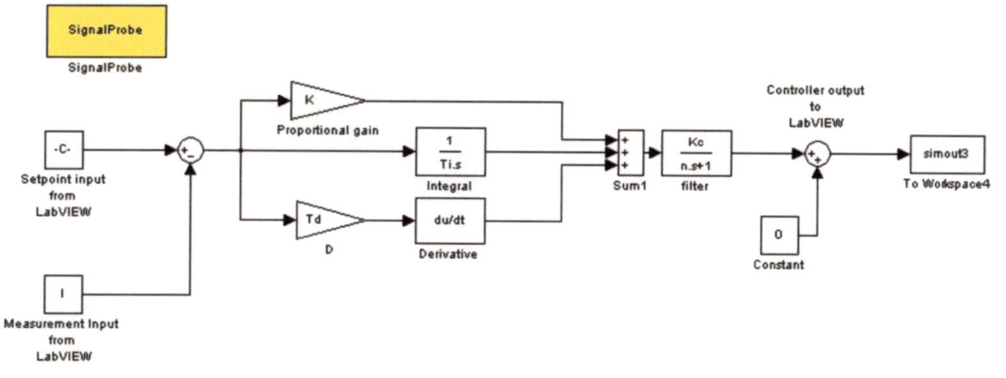

Fig. 14. Controller in SIMULINK environment showing the input and output block

Figure 15 shows the final code in LabVIEW® which is a combination of previously presented VIs. When the VI starts, simultaneously it initiates the `controller.mdl` file in SIMULINK®. Measurement results of the spectrophotometer are transferred from the "*Measurement Results*" block to the write block in SIT. Write block transfers the data from the spectrophotometer to the "*measurement input from LabVIEW*" block presented at Fig. 14. At the same time, selected set-point value (which can be set using the slide knob in LabVIEW®) is transferred to the "*set-point input from LabVIEW*" block which is the set-point value of the control system. This enables for performing any set-point change such as introducing step-change, ramp and impulse while the system is running. Then the controller performs the corrective calculation and the controller output signal is transferred back to the LabVIEW® using the read VI which needs to be transmitted and conditioned to the proper format that can be sent to DAQ system. Controller output signal then sent to the DAQ system using DAQ assistant block which transmits the received signal to its equivalent voltage as has been set up earlier in the syringe pump interfacing section.

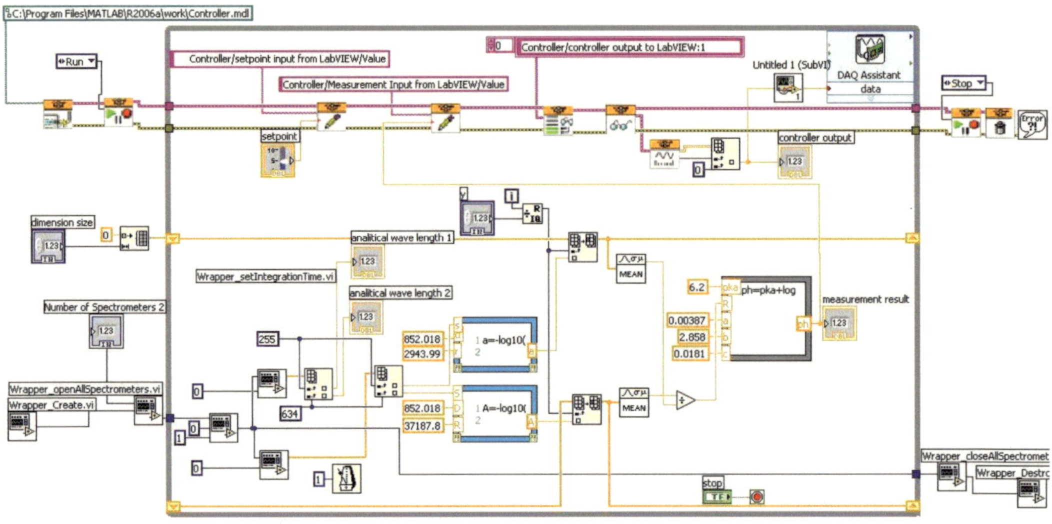

Fig. 15. Low Level LabVIEW® code including SIT and Measurement parts.

Figure 16(a) shows the pH changes of the designed PID controller using λ values equal to 4 and 1.5 which are presented in dotted line and solid line respectively. The step change was performed from pH equaled 5.85 to 6.85 at t=10 seconds as denoted by the dashed dotted line. Using λ value equals to 4 seconds (dotted line), the pH gradually increases from 5.85 to 6.85 with no overshoot or under shoot. However, decreasing the λ value to 1.5, faster controller response can be achieved which results in an impressive settling time of 4.2 seconds. Fig. 16(b) shows the controller output during the step change.

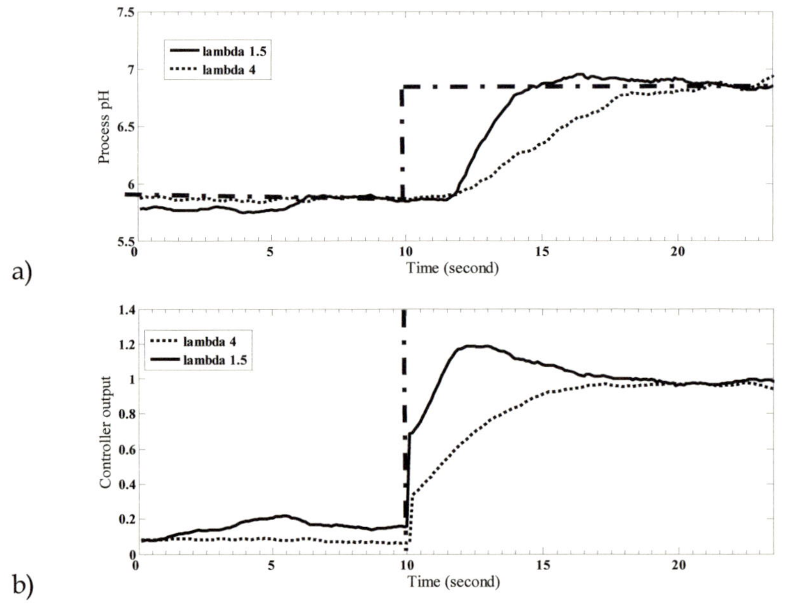

Fig. 16. Experimental results for step change in the set-point of the system at desired closed loop time constant equal to 4 and 1.5 seconds. a) process pH, b)controller output of the system.

Controller output transmitted to corresponding voltage in LabVIEW® and then applied to the final control element to increase or decrease the flow rate of the manipulated variable of the system (which is sodium hydroxide in this case study). From the figure it is clear that for λ equal to 4, the controller output increases gradually. As a result, input voltage to the final control element and consequently the flow rate of the strong base increases steadily, thus, the pH value of the system does not change too fast. Whereas for λ equal to 1.5 seconds, an abrupt change can be observed at the controller output which resulted in much faster change In pH value of the system.

Desired closed loop time constant λ	Controller gain (K_c)	Rise time	Settling time
4	0.27	11	8.3
1.5	0.52	4.7	4.2

Table 1. Effect of λ on the controller parameters

Table 1 shows that using λ equals to 4 results in a small controller gain (K_c=0.27). As a result of using a low value for K_c, a slow set-point tracking with a corresponding rise time and settling time equals to 11 seconds and 8.3 seconds is achieved respectively. Reducing the λ to 1.5 increases the controller gain to 0.52 and consequently a faster setpoint tracking with a corresponding settling time of 4.7 and rise time seconds of 4.2 seconds is obtained.

8. Conclusion

This study presented the difficulties of process control for miniaturized intensified systems and in order to address the problem, LabVIEW® and MATLAB® is proposed to be used tandem to provide suitable mean perform suitable control action on the system. It is presented that interfacing different measurement and final control elements can be speeded up using LabVIEW® software. Additionally, using SIT toolkit enables user to transfer measurement data from LabVIEW® to the embedded control in SIMULINK and also apply the controller output to the system via LabVIEW®. High performance of the proposed software structure (LabVIEW® as interface and MATLAB as controller) also demonstrated using the experimental results.

9. References

ABD Shukor, S. R. & Tham, M. T. (2004) Performance Envelopes of Process Intensified Systems. *Proceedings of International Symposium on Advanced Control of Chemical Processes.* Hong Kong.

Barzin, R., Shukor, S. R. A. & Ahmad, A. L. (2010) New spectrophotometric measurement method for process control of miniaturized intensified systems. *Sensors and Actuators, B: Chemical,* 146, 403-409.

Bleris, L. G., Garcia, J., Kothare, M. V. & Arnold, M. G. (2006) Towards embedded model predictive control for System-on-a-Chip applications. *Journal of Process Control,* 16, 255-264.

Charpentier, J. C. (2005) Four main objectives for the future of chemical and process engineering mainly concerned by the science and technologies of new materials production. *Chemical Engineering Journal,* 107, 3-17.

Etchells, J. C. (2005) Process intensification: Safety pros and cons. *Process Safety and Environmental Protection,* 83, 85-89.

Jones, R. W. & Tham, M. T. (2006) Control strategies for process intensified systems. *2006 SICE-ICASE International Joint Conference.* Busan.

Liu, X., Wang, Z. A., Byrne, R. H., Kaltenbacher, E. A. & Bernstein, R. E. (2006) Spectrophotometric measurements of pH in-situ: Laboratory and field evaluations of instrumental performance. *Environmental Science and Technology,* 40, 5036-5044.

Luyben, W. L. & Hendershot, D. C. (2004) Dynamic Disadvantages of Intensification in Inherently Safer Process Design. *Industrial and Engineering Chemistry Research,* 43, 384-396.

Martz, T. R., Carr, J. J., French, C. R. & Degrandpre, M. D. (2003) A submersible autonomous sensor for spectrophotometric pH measurements of natural waters. *Analytical Chemistry,* 75, 1844-1850.

National instuments (2008) [online].[Access 22thMay 2008] available on World Wide Web: http://zone.ni.com/reference/en-XX/help/371361B-01/lvanlsconcepts/aliasing/

DEA, (2008) [online]. [Access 9th Nov 2008] available on World Wide Web: http://www.deaengineering.com/Operation.html

18

Dynamic Wi-Fi Reconfigurable FPGA Based Platform for Intelligent Traffic Systems

Mihai Hulea, George Dan Moiş and Silviu Folea
Technical University of Cluj-Napoca, Romania

1. Introduction

This chapter proposes a software and hardware platform based on a FPGA board to which a Wi-Fi communication device has been added in order to make remote wireless reconfiguration possible. This feature introduces a high level of flexibility allowing the development of applications which can quickly adapt to changes in environmental conditions and which can react to unexpected events with high speed. The capabilities introduced by wireless technology and reconfigurable systems are important in road traffic control systems, which are characterized by continuous parameter variation and unexpected event and incident occurrence.

Intelligent Transportation System (ITS) is the term commonly used to describe the employment of electronic devices for the management of road traffic and other types of transportation networks for improving decision making by operators and users. There are many new available technologies which can be used for increasing the efficiency of road systems and many cities are introducing ITS models as pilot schemes to test their effectiveness.

Reconfigurable hardware offers many benefits and this led to its use in the ITS field also. Traffic light systems implemented on FPGAs were developed and examples can be found in the literature (El-Medany & Hussain, 2007; Zhenggang et al., 2009). This research led to the conclusion that FPGA based devices can be a good solution for this type of systems conferring them scalability, adaptability and stability, and increasing their efficiency (Zhenggang et al., 2009). FPGAs had also been used in vehicle-to-vehicle communication (V2V), the authors of (Sander et al., 2009) presenting a V2V communication system based on this technology and special mechanisms that exploit its benefits. The result consists of a modular and flexible framework for software routines which in the same time supports critical tasks with special hardware accelerators. The modularity achieved with the help of FPGA technology allows the system to react to changes in the environmental conditions or in the user demands.

2. Background

2.1 FPGA reconfigurable systems

FPGA is the acronym for Field Programmable Gate Array and it represents a silicon chip which has an internal scheme that can be "changed". Together with the class of programmable logic devices (PLDs), without a clearly defined distinction among them, they form the programmable Application-Specific Integrated Circuit (ASIC) group of devices (Smith, 1997).

A FPGA is a device that consists of an array of basic logic cells that can be configured after fabrication using a certain programming technology. The logic cells are interconnected by wires and switch boxes with each other and with special input/output blocks (Mitra et al. 1998). Other important components include, but are not limited to multipliers, embedded block RAM and digital clock managers. The configurable logic blocks, or logic cells, are made up of two basic components: flip-flops and look-up tables (LUTs). The LUT is a storage block having the capacity of one bit that acts as a programmable gate. The input represents the address lines of the storing element and the output represents the value contained at this address. The input and output data can be synchronized with the clock signals. When programming the FPGA, one actually specifies the logic function of each basic logic cell and configures the connections represented by the switch boxes within the device. FPGA devices can be divided in two main classes: one time programmable FPGAs which are based on an antifuse approach and reconfigurable FPGAs which usually employ SRAM cells (Lyke, 2002). The SRAM cells contained in the device will not keep the stored information when the supply power is turned off and this way the configuration will be lost. Depending on its generation, the FPGA allows static or dynamic reconfiguration. In the case of static reconfiguration, the FPGA is programmed in the compiling phase and it cannot be reconfigured during operation, while in the second case, the FPGA can be reconfigured at any point in the lifetime of the application. Furthermore, dynamic reconfiguration can be total, when the entire device is reconfigured, or partial, when only a part of an operating FPGA is reconfigured.

By using the hardware to its maximum capabilities and due to their truly parallel nature, FPGAs are able to assure better performance as compared to conventional processors (National Instruments[1], 2011). They can be used in digital signal processing (DSP) systems where they can provide more complete solutions than the ones represented by traditional DSP implementations (programmable digital signal processors or ASICs) (Tessier & Burleson, 2001). Despite being slower than ASICs, the hardwired circuits realized by FPGAs have a speed advantage of several orders of magnitude over the software solutions on general purpose processors (Reis & Jess, 2004). Other applications which employ FPGA devices include space and defence systems (Tessier & Burleson, 2001; Altera, 2011), prototyping systems (Banovic, 2005), medical systems (Altera, 2010) and many other relatively new developed markets such as language recognition, bioinformatics (HPCWire, 2009), cryptography (Prasanna & Dandalis, 2007) etc.

The capacity of reprogramming the hardware during operation allowed programmable logic to take over a central role in digital systems. The most important feature that results from the ability to reconfigure digital circuits is flexibility (Compton & Hauck, 2002). Among other things, it provides the possibility that a system might adapt to changing operating contexts or to unforeseen events (Lyke, 2002) in order to be able to fulfil its originally assigned tasks. Although this important feature, the flexibility of "on-field" re-programming without going through re-fabrication with a new design (Xilinx, 2010), along with the FPGA based systems' low-cost and short time-to-market come at a considerable price, namely significant area overhead, increased delay and power consumption (Kuon et al., 2007), this did not affect their development and large scale usage.

Systems that make use of user-reprogrammable logic elements such as FPGAs were studied (Patel & Moallem, 2010; Kalte, 2002) being well suited for applications with high dependability (Straka & Kotasek, 2008); Bolchini, et al., 2007). Reconfigurability allows the implementation of mechanisms that improve overall system performance and dependability: in the field hardware upgrades, runtime reconfiguration, adaptive hardware algorithms, continuous service applications and system adaptation to unexpected events and environmental conditions.

The utilization of FPGAs in applications where the reach to the target device is impractical and difficult through wires (e.g. the system is not stationary, a portable embedded system) (Andretzky, 2005) lead to the need for the wireless configuration of FPGAs. In the literature we can find several implementations for the configuration process (Maye, 2005; Adly et al. 2010). The work in (Maye, 2005) achieves the wireless configuration of FPGA based components of a Modular Robot through Bluetooth. This is possible because each one of the modules that make up the system contains a FPGA board and a Bluetooth board. The authors in (Adly et al. 2010) developed a flash memory configuration controller for configuring a FPGA wirelessly from a flash memory. The design of a programmable chip working as a configuration controller which receives configuration bits through a wireless link, stores them into a flash memory and afterwards recalls them to configure the FPGA was developed in this case.

2.2 LabVIEW development platform

LabVIEW, the short name for Laboratory Virtual Instrument Engineering Workbench, is a graphically based programming language developed by National Instruments (Bitter et al., 2006). An appropriate description is given by Simon Hogg: "LabVIEW is a highly productive development environment for creating custom applications that interact with real-world data or signals in fields such as science and engineering" (National Instruments[1], 2010). LabVIEW, as a programming language, is a powerful tool that is ideal for test and measurement (T&M), automation, instrument control, data acquisition, and data analysis applications (Bitter et al., 2006).

The LabVIEW software development environment consists of several valuable components such as G Programming, Hardware Support, Analysis and Technical Code Libraries, UI Components and Reporting Tools and Models of Computation, which reduce the amount of time and people needed for project completion (National Instruments[1], 2010). It provides a number of add-on modules for extending the graphical development platform to target a wide range of hardware devices. One of these add-ons is the NI LabVIEW FPGA Module which makes custom measurement and hardware control possible without prior knowledge of low-level hardware description languages or board-level design. It uses LabVIEW VIs for defining the FPGA logic instead of low-level languages such as very high speed integrated circuit hardware description language (VHDL) (National Instruments, 2007). By using this module, applications that employ field-programmable gate arrays on NI reconfigurable I/O (RIO) hardware can be developed (National Instruments[2], 2011). The parallelism and data flow in LabVIEW are very similar to the ones in a FPGA implementation, therefore running LabVIEW code on FPGAs leads to true, simultaneous, parallel processing (National Instruments, 2007; National Instruments[2], 2011).

The LabVIEW FPGA VIs are created on a computer and afterwards compiled and run on reconfigurable hardware. Because the compiling time can range from minutes to hours depending on design complexity, LabVIEW provides a FPGA Device Emulator for executing the VI on the Windows development computer for verification purposes. While the typical FPGA design flow includes program creation, translating design files (design entry), synthesizing and mapping design elements to device resources, placing and routing design resources, performing timing analysis and generating programming file (Altera, 2009), LabVIEW offers an intuitive and simplified solution for this action. The development process for creating FPGA applications in LabVIEW consists of: the creation of the FPGA VI, emulation on PC for testing if necessary, compilation to FPGA and the creation of host VIs for communicating with the reconfigurable hardware (National Instruments[2], 2010). Actually, the configuration of the FPGA device's operation is performed by programming in LabVIEW. Another useful characteristic is represented by the fact that when a specific FPGA device is targeted, LabVIEW displays only the functions available in the FPGA (National Instruments[2], 2010).

3. Wi-Fi FPGA based reconfigurable platform for ITS

3.1 General system overview

The general structure of the proposed platform is presented in the figure bellow. As it can be seen, the platform is composed of the two main components: the FPGA board at which level the application's logic algorithms are implemented and the Tag4M board which has Wi-Fi communication capabilities and which executes the reconfiguration and communication algorithms needed for making remote access possible. The presented platform can be installed on vehicles or on the road traffic infrastructure equipment (like traffic lights and dynamic signs). The presented platform can communicate with a Configuration Server which is responsible for performing the reconfiguration operations in order to set-up new applications at the FPGA platform level. It can also communicate with Traffic Servers in order to report traffic data or to receive commands.

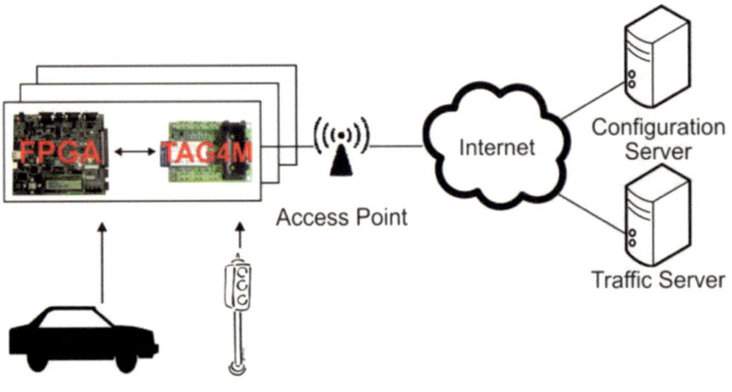

Fig. 1. General system structure

By attaching the Tag4M Wi-Fi extension to the FPGA board a versatile computing device with communication capabilities which has numerous applications in the ITS field is obtained. This provides the FPGA device not only with the capacity to communicate over the Internet with remote servers or other devices but also the possibility to dynamically change its functionality depending on the current application's requirements.

This flexibility is particularly important in dynamic environments represented by road traffic systems. A FPGA platform installed in a vehicle can play multiple roles and the same hardware can be used in multiple traffic scenarios without the need of having direct access to the device installed in the field or on the vehicle. The device can be easily accessed by using remote servers to which it communicates and which perform the configuration procedures. While the vehicle is entering the highway, a configuration server can load into the vehicle device an application for automatic toll collection eliminating the need for the vehicles to slow down while passing the checkpoints. When the vehicle exits the highway the previously loaded toll collection program can be replaced with a road traffic control module which makes the vehicle capable of communicating with other vehicles or with infrastructure equipments in order to provide peers information for achieving traffic fluidization. At a later time, when the vehicle is entering a parking zone the on-board FPGA platform can be loaded with a parking advisory system in order to guide the driver to the closest parking place and to keep track of the parking time.
The same FPGA equipment can be used as the infrastructure controller for managing the traffic lights and other dynamic traffic signs. By using its Wi-Fi communication capabilities it is easy to integrate these pieces of equipment into the distributed road traffic monitoring and control system.

3.2 Wi-Fi Tag4M device

The Tag4M device which is used for FPGA reconfiguration is presented in Figure 2 (scale 1:1). This is a Wi-Fi RFID (Radio-Frequency Identification) active device with measurement capabilities. By attaching sensors to its I/O terminal blocks in a similar manner as for a data acquisition device, the user can build wireless proof-of-concept sensor solutions for a wide range of applications. The system has the advantage of reduced dimensions (4.7 cm x 7.0 cm) and of a limited weight of 50 g and can run on battery power, making it a portable solution. It is a complete Wi-Fi and networking solution, incorporating a 32-bit CPU, a memory unit, an eCos real-time operating system and a UDP or TCP/IP stack. Other included components are the analogical sensor interface, the power management unit, the hardware cryptographic accelerator and the real time clock (G2 Microsystems[1], 2008).

Fig. 2. Tag4M Data Acquisition System

The hardware architecture of the device is presented in Figure 3. In this version, 8 analogical and 10 digital channels and 2 serial ports are available. A general interface was implemented to allow the acquisitions from different sources like: 3-axis accelerations, 3-axis gyroscopes, magnetic sensors and more other parameters, which can be combined for obtaining a wide range of configurations (G2 Microsystems[3], 2008).

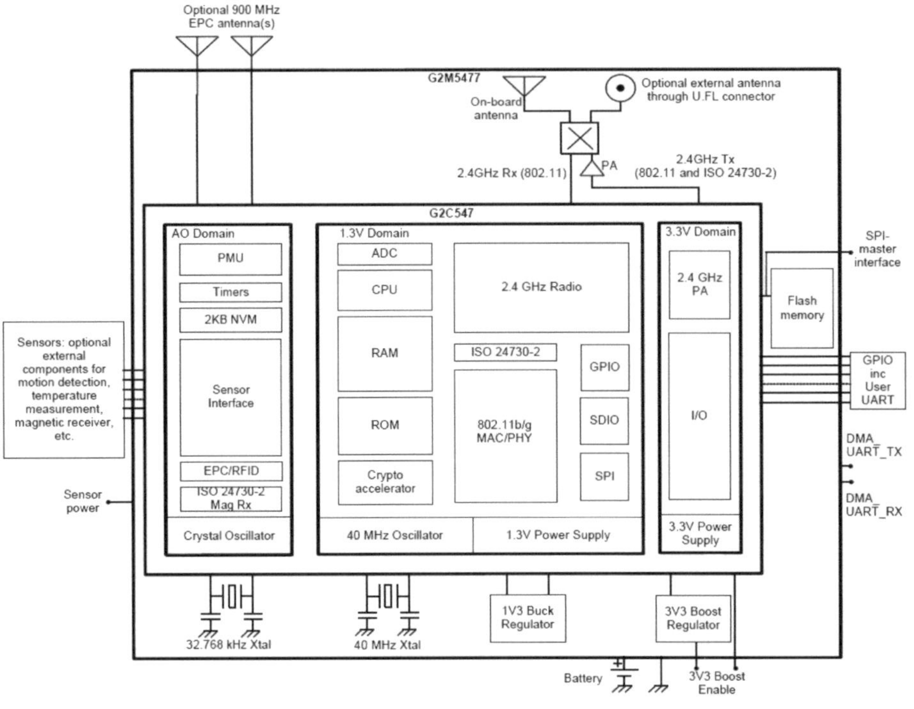

Fig. 3. The Hardware Architecture of the Tag4M Data Acquisition System

3.3 Wi-Fi Tag4M software stack

In this section, the software stack installed on the Wi-Fi Tag4M is described. The device is powered by a G2C547 module from G2 Microsystem (bought by Roving Networks). It has an eCos real-time operating system installed on ROM which boots up when the system is powered on (G2 Microsystems[2], 2008).

The eCos operating system runtime provides full preemptibility, low latency, synchronization primitives, scheduling policies and interrupt handling mechanisms which are useful in real-time applications. The embedded applications can also take advantage of other eCos functionalities such as device drivers, memory management mechanisms, exception handling, math libraries and many more others. The OS also includes all the necessary tools for developers, namely: build tools, compilers, assemblers, linkers, debugger and simulators.

Programming microcontroller devices raise a unique set of challenges in general and the Tag4M device is not an exception. First, there are several points of failure. The Wi-Fi Tag4M device itself may fail. There can be transient or permanent communication errors between connected devices and the microcontroller device like overlapping signals, accidental disconnection etc. The C Application on the Wi-Fi Tag4M device itself may fail, but this is unlikely to happen. A communication failure between the Wi-Fi Tag4M device and the application server could also occur. An application for the Tag4M device needs to handle these multiple points of failure and hide its complexity from the end user.

Secondly, device programming requires much more debugging and testing iterations than normal application development because of the direct low-level interaction with the underlying hardware.

The application needs to provide robust error handling capabilities. Automatic error correction codes must be incorporated for correcting several types of transient errors. This minimizes maintenance requirements and user intervention.

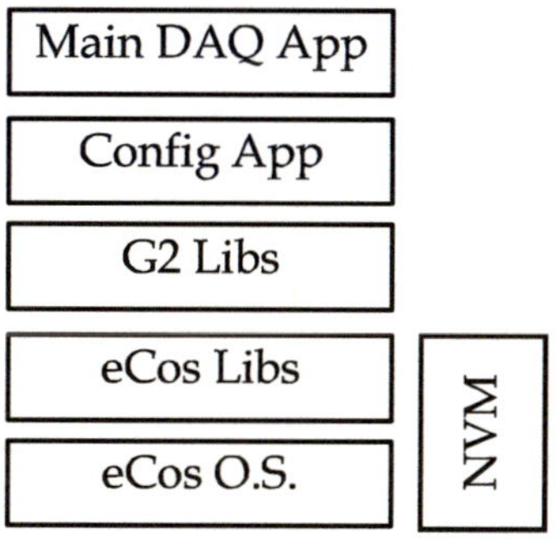

Fig. 4. Tag4M Device Software Stack

As it is shown in Figure 4, the Wi-Fi Tag4M device software stack is composed of the eCos operating system, eCos libraries for accessing low level services, the G2 library for accessing sensors and measurement services and two user applications (Main DAQ App and Config App) which are stored in the non-volatile memory (NVM).

3.4 FPGA configuration process

The prototype architecture represented by Figure 5 uses a Spartan-3E Starter Kit board which can be configured in serial mode (Xilinx, 1998). The upgrade of the design in the field over a wireless network is made possible by using the Tag4M as a microcontroller and as a Wi-Fi receiver. The signals used are the DIO lines 0 to 4 of the Tag4M and the FPGA IO lines (-PROGRAMM, CCLK, DIN, -INT and DONE).

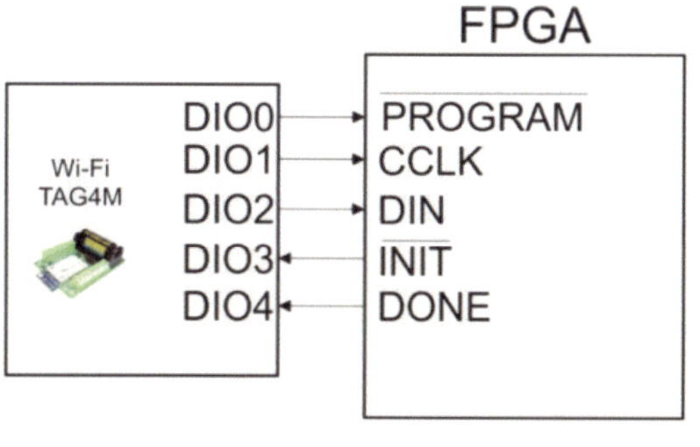

Fig. 5. The connection between the FPGA and the Tag4M device

Spartan-3E

The Spartan-3E Starter Kit Board we used provides a powerful development platform for designs targeting the Spartan 3E FPGA produced by Xilinx. It features the Xilinx XC3S500E FPGA having 500K gates. Some of the Spartan-3E FPGA family features include: parallel NOR Flash configuration, SPI Serial Flash Configuration, Master and Slave Serial configuration, etc. The FPGA chip on the board can provide up to 232 user-I/O pins and over 10000 logic cells in a 320-pin FBGA package (Xilinx, 2006).

Configuration Process

Serial mode was chosen for configuration because of the reduced number of interface signals needed (a minimum of four: DIN, CCLK, -PROGRAM and -INIT) and because of the relative ease of implementation. The microcontroller that initiates the configuration process and which sends configuration data, the Tag4M, acts as the "master" and the Spartan-3E board plays the role of the "slave" device, being the one receiving data.
A brief description of the configuration process is given in the following paragraphs. The four steps that make up the configuration flow are: the clearing of the configuration memory, initialization, configuration and start-up.

Clearing Configuration Memory

The first step is performed either automatically at system power-up or by applying a Low-level pulse to the -PROGRAM input. This is useful when the "master" initiates the configuration at any time during device operation. When -PROGRAM changes to High, the last clearing operation takes place. After this step, in the initialization phase, -INIT goes High to confirm that the memory is cleared. It is not recommended for -PROGRAM to be held low for more than 500μs and it should not be used for delaying the configuration process. The entrance in the configuration step can be delayed by holding the -INIT signal Low.

Initialization

At this point, the selected configuration mode is identified by sampling the mode pins which indicate the slave serial mode (M[g_SR_2:0]=<1:1:1>). Now, the device can pass to the configuration step. By holding -INIT low, the entry to the configuration step can be delayed.

Configuration

After -INIT goes High, the controller begins to send data on the DIN line from the memory block along with clock pulses, this action taking place in the configuration phase. A small pause having the duration between 55 and 275μs is needed before sending clock signals and data bits. After the last bits for configuration are sent, some additional clock cycles are needed, and then the Start-Up step takes place and the Spartan device starts normal functioning (Xilinx, 2009).

Start-Up

The events taking place during Start-Up are: the DONE pin goes High, the I/Os go active and the Global Set/Reset (GSR) Net is released. The DONE pin is optional because the "master" knows the number of configuration bits it has to send, but it can be used as an indicator for problems with configuration: its failure to go High means that an error had occurred (Xilinx, 1998). In this phase, several additional clock cycles must be provided, for synchronizing the events that take place at this time.
The following figure presents the general configuration process of the Spartan-3 devices (Xilinx, 2009).
When a FPGA board installed on a vehicle or on the road side needs to be configured, a *Start Programming* message is sent to the associated Tag4M device, which in turn initializes the configuration procedure for the FPGA device. As a result of this first set of messages exchanged, the Configuration Server receives an ACK message if the FPGA board is ready for receiving the new program or ERR in case an error occurred. In the case in which the ACK message was received, the Configuration Server will decompose the program in small packages and will send them sequentially over Wi-Fi to the Tag4M device, and from there to the FPGA board. In the case in which a package is lost (and an ERR message received), the

respective package will be resent. The programming procedure will end with a *Stop Programming* command.

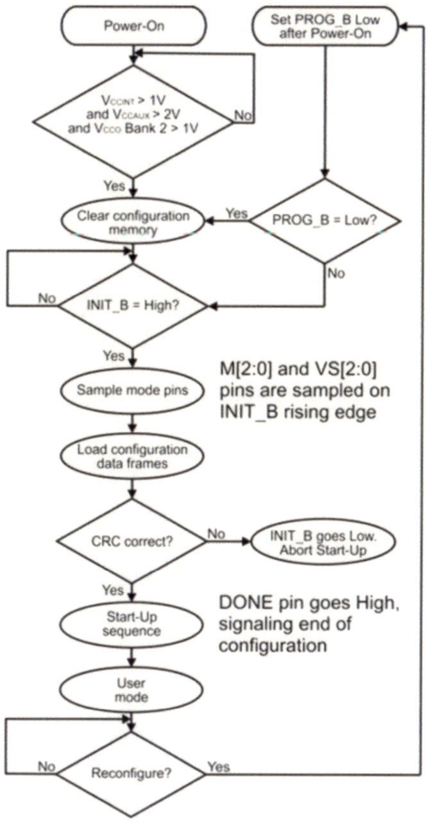

Fig. 6. General configuration process (Xilinx, 2009)

The messages exchanged between the entities involved in the FPGA configuration process is presented in the following figure.

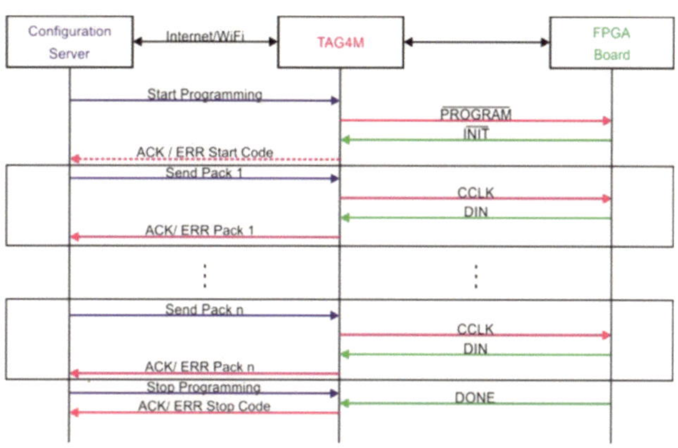

Fig. 7. Description of the communication protocol

The application installed on the Tag4M device is responsible for performing the FPGA programming procedure. The application has an event-driven architecture with a main loop (presented in Table 1) in which events are handled.

```
activateAnalogDigitalLines();
startDHCP();
whiel(1){
        evntID = getNextEvent();
        case START_PROGRAMMING:
                startFpgaProgramming();
                postEvent(REPORTING_EVENT);
                break;
        case PACKAGE_RECEIVED:
                fpgaPackageSend();
                postEvent(REPORTING_EVENT);
                break;
        case STOP_PROGRAMMING:
                fpgaStopProgramming();
                postEvent(REPORTING_EVENT);
                break;
        case REPORTING_EVENT:
                sendReport();
                break;
        case FIND_ACCESSPOINT_EVENT:
                associate();
                break;
        case DHCP_COMPLEAT:
                dhcpConfigure();
                initializeMeasureTimer(frequency);
        case DHCP_RENEW:
                dhcpConfigure();
                break;
        case WATCHDOG_RESET:
                restartApplication();
}
```

Table 1. Events executed in the main application thread

Without entering into implementation details, the basic activities implemented at Tag4M level are presented in this paragraph. When the application is started, the first action performed is the search for an available access point (AP). If one AP is found, the application will acquire a dynamic IP address and then will wait for messages from the Configuration Server. When a new message is received by the Tag4M device, it will be decoded, and depending of its content a new event will be fired. For example, when a *Start Programming* message is received this will result in firing a START_PROGRAMMING event which will be detected and handled by the event loop described in the table above. As described in the *Configuration* section, the FPGA configuration bits are sent on the rising edge of the CCLK signal (the clock is generated on the DIO1 line) using the FPGA DIN line (which is connected to the Tag4M DIO2 line). The bit sending process is implemented in the *fpgaPackageSend()* function.

4. Applications of the Wi-Fi FPGA platform for ITS

4.1 Detecting vehicle location using Wi-Fi RSSI

The simplicity and cost efficiency of the Received Signal Strength Indicator (RSSI) based localization makes it the best candidate for specific applications like tracking systems and dynamic networks where precision is not crucial.

In the following paragraphs an application implemented in LabVIEW for vehicle localisation using a FPGA and a Tag4M device is presented.

A "scan" operation which finds all access points and reads the corresponding RSSI values is implemented at Tag4M level. These values are packed and sent to the FPGA using a serial communication link where the localisation algorithm is implemented.

Table 2 presents a scan operation result. In this case four APs are detected. The corresponding RSSI values (in dBm) measured by the Tag4M are reported for every AP.

```
> scan
>
RSSI Scan Results: 4
 Time        SSID        Ch Ad-Hoc    Sec WPS   MAC Address     ERP WMM  R
SSI Supported Rates (Mbit/s, *Mandatory)        Crypto Suites      CW Max/Min

AP_SCAN,Hawk,-57 dBm,
AP_SCAN,Helicopter,-50 dBm,
AP_SCAN,tag4m,-68 dBm,
AP_SCAN,witagserver,-45 dBm,
```

Table 2. A sequence of results for the "scan" operation executed on the Tag4M device

The program for reading the RSSI values from the Tag4M device was implemented in LabVIEW2010. Three APs (which are placed on a crossroad) named witagserver, Hawk and Tag4M, are displayed by the application in this case.

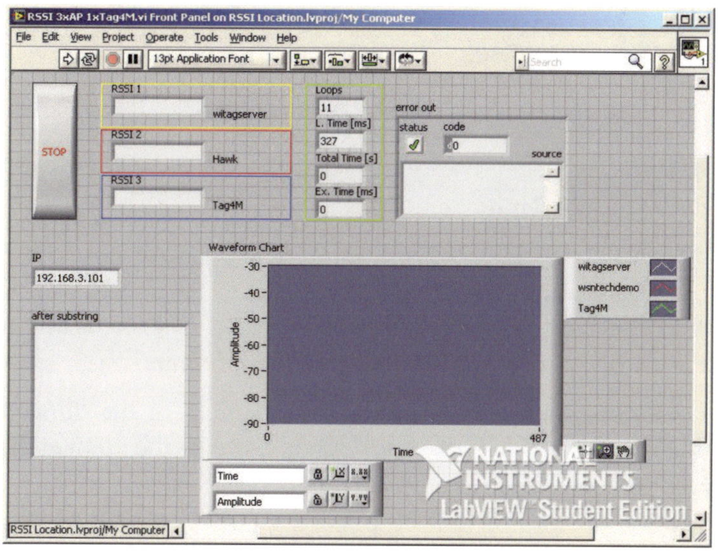

Fig. 8. Front Panel of the program for reading RSSI values

The data received by the program are parsed and only data from APs which we are interested in are processed. The RSSI values are converted to distance values using formula (1).
The value of the received signal strength is a function of the transmitted power and the distance between the sender and the receiver. The received signal strength will decrease when the distance increases as the following equation shows (Aamodt, 2006).

$$RSSI = -(10n \cdot \log_{10} d + A) \tag{1}$$

Where:

- n represents the signal propagation constant, also named propagation exponent,
- d represents the distance from the sender,
- A represents the received signal strength at a distance of one meter.

The distance values are grouped into an array which is sent to another application using a Shared Variable. This option offers the possibility for the user to read the location from his application which runs locally on a Touch Panel Computer (TPC) installed on the car or on a mobile phone.
The program for localization using the Wi-Fi FPGA platform was implemented in LabVIEW2010. The application displays the distances between the Wi-Fi FPGA placed in a car and the three APs placed on a crossroad. The number of APs can be increased for obtaining a more accurate position estimate. The distances between the Wi-Fi FPGA and each AP are represented as circles having the centre in the AP locations which have previously known coordinates.

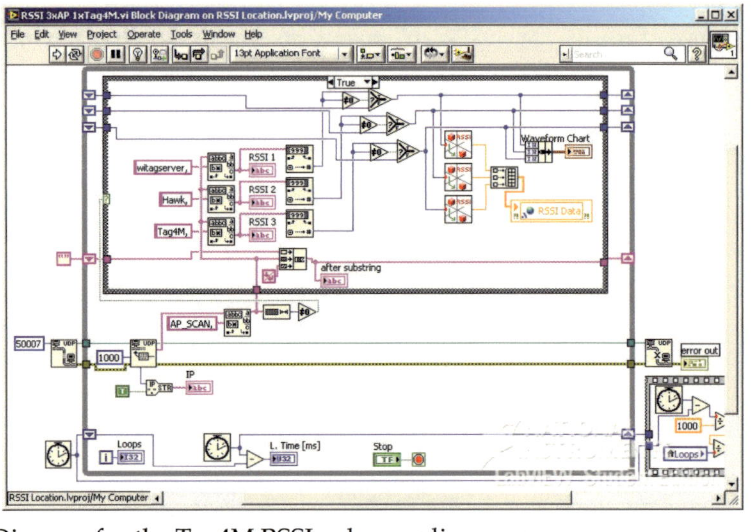

Fig. 9. Block Diagram for the Tag4M RSSI value reading program

The application was tested for only one crossroad because of the difficulty of placing a larger number of APs on a road. The car's position is given by the point at the intersection of the three circles.
The distance data are received from the program that reads the RSSI values using a Shared Variable. The local applications which run on a TPC or mobile phone convert the data to graphical representations which are afterwards displayed.

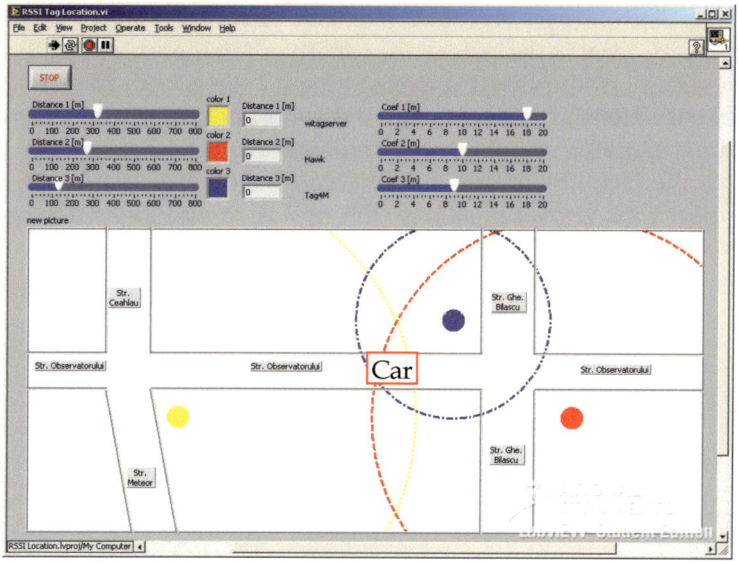

Fig. 10. Front Panel of the localisation program

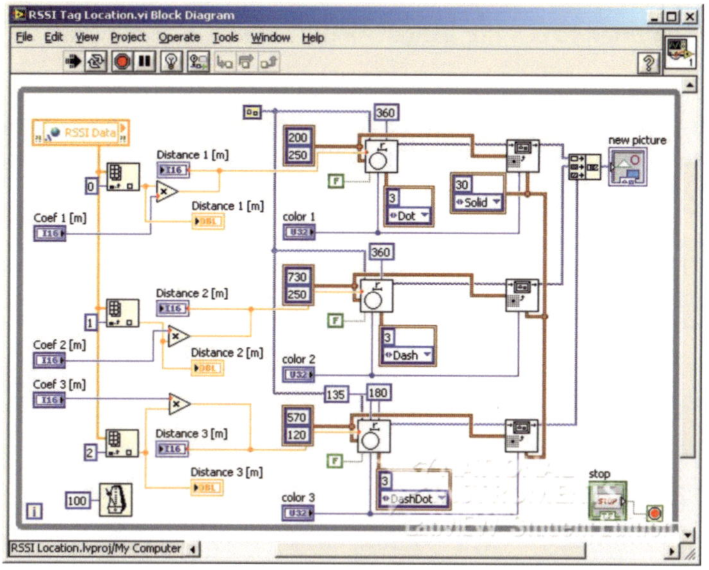

Fig. 11. Block Diagram of the localisation program

4.2 Detecting vehicle movement using accelerometer and the gyroscope sensors

Another application of the presented FPGA platform can be used for detecting the dynamic vehicle parameters. By attaching a gyroscope sensor and a 3-axis accelerometer to the FPGA board, the implementation of an application for determining the vehicle's state (moving or stopped, running on a straight road or making a turn) is possible. A LabVIEW application was implemented and installed on a FPGA in order to determine the vehicle's dynamic behaviour.

A correlation between the signals from a 3-axis accelerometer and a 2-axis gyroscope is realized in order to determine the state of the car. The signals acquired by the accelerometer and gyroscope sensors were filtered implementing a Butterworth filter (Figure 12) which has an essential characteristic: a smooth and monotonically decreasing frequency response (National Instruments, 2009). The Butterworth filter is available in LabVIEW FPGA, and the Express VI from the Help documentation and configure panel is presented in Figure 12 along with the settings. LabVIEW allows the operative and rapid change of the filter parameters and the usage of other types of filters.

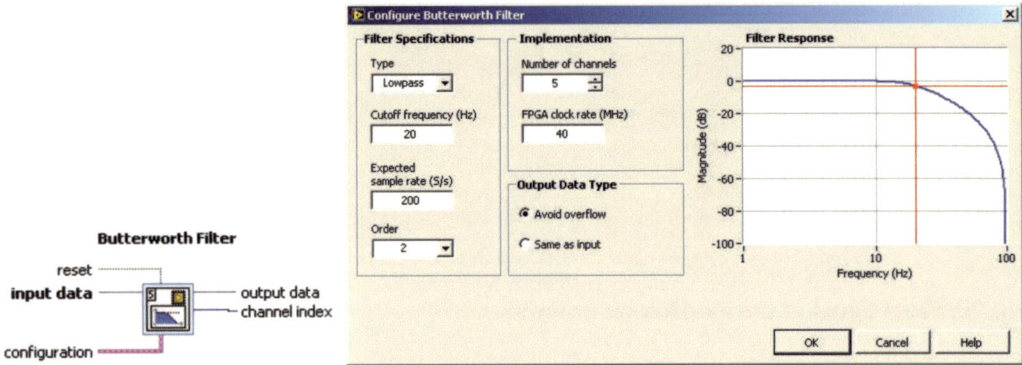

Fig. 12. Butterworth filter, FPGA implementation

3-Axis Acceleration Sensor

The acceleration sensor (Figure 13) allows the measurement of static or dynamic acceleration (in ±3g range) on three axes. The ADXL330, iMEMS type, from Analog Devices was chosen to be used for this purpose.

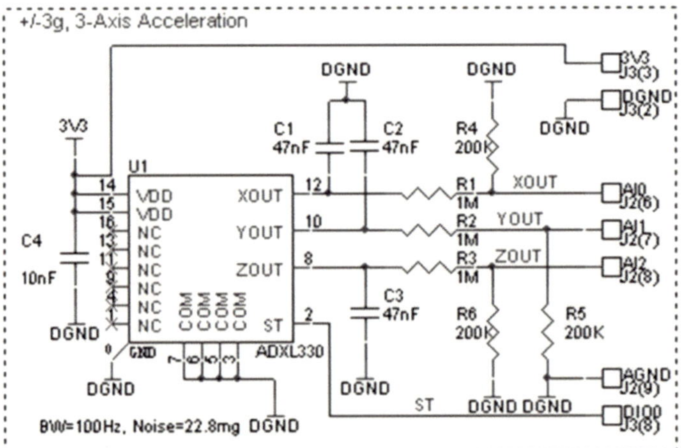

Fig. 13. Acceleration sensor scheme

External components are used for establishing the period of the output signal between 2 and 1000 ms, and the frequency band is limited to values between 0.5 and 1.6 kHz. The typical noise level is 280 μg/√Hz rms and allows the acquisition of signals under a 5 mg level (Analog Devices, 2006).

2-Axis Gyroscope Sensor

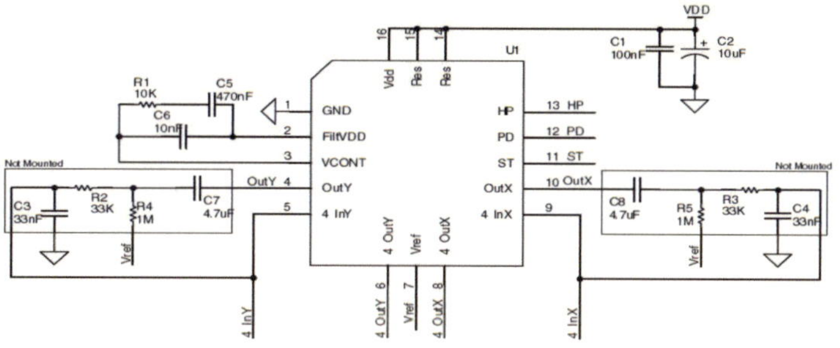

Fig. 14. Gyroscope sensor scheme

The gyroscope chosen to be used (LPR530AL) integrates one actuator and one accelerometer in a single micro machined structure. It is based on the Coriolis principle and it is able to react when an angular rate is applied to the sensing element which is kept in continuous oscillating movement (STMicroelectronics, 2009). The electric scheme is presented in Figure 14. It has a full scale of ±300 °/s and it is capable of detecting rates of up to 140 Hz with a -3 dB bandwidth.

A series of tests has been performed in order to determine a correlation between the vehicle's movement and the signal generated by the two sensors.

The program for displaying data acquired by the Wi-Fi FPGA platform from the 3-axis accelerometer and the 2-axis gyroscope was implemented in LabVIEW2010 and the application panel is presented in Figure 15. The application displays the signals received from the two sensors.

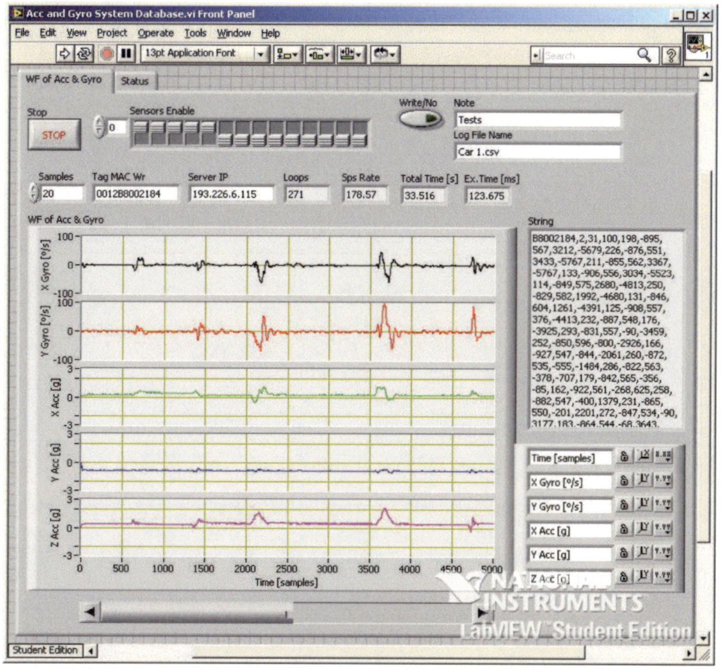

Fig. 15. Front Panel of the "Display Data" program

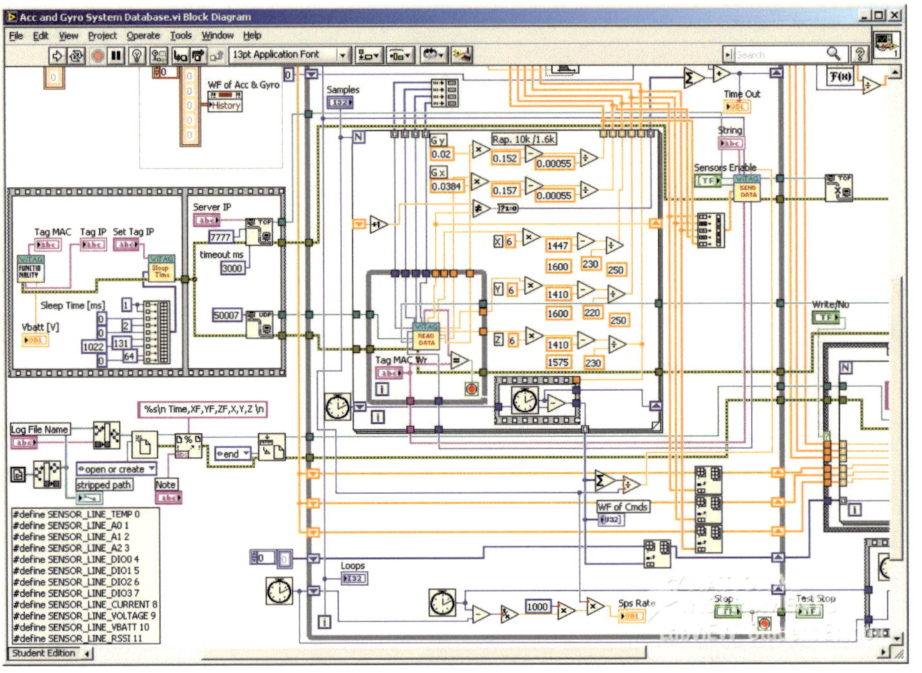

Fig. 16. Block Diagram of the "Display Data" program

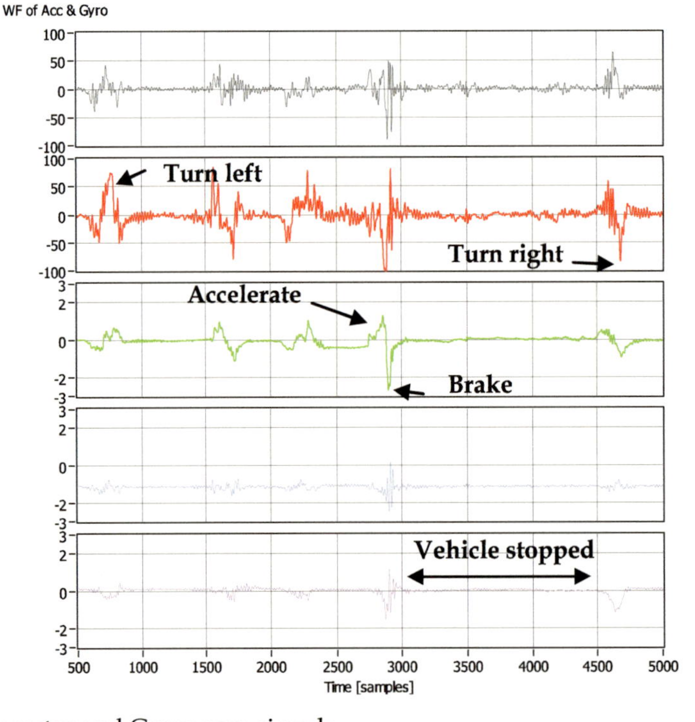

Fig. 17. Accelerometer and Gyroscope signals

In this case, the Tag4M device is used as a serial RS232 to Wi-Fi gate between the FPGA board (Spartan-3E Starter Kit) and the PC application that runs on the server. The block diagram of the PC application is presented in Figure 16.

One initialization step is necessary for reading the data from the Tag4M device. During this stage, the Tag4M sends a package containing the IP received through DHCP from the AP. This IP is used in the application for sending commands to the Tag4M device after the initialization step. The data are read in a loop and are validated if they are received from a previously known MAC address which is used as a validation mask. The latency determined after performing a number of experiments lies between the value of 5 and 20 milliseconds and it depends on the RSSI values. The values of the latency are greater in case of a poor signal.

Figure 17 presents the experimental results obtained from an IVU device installed on a vehicle performing a series of manoeuvres in a test field.

The length of the "Vehicle stopped" period is of 1500 samples which represent 7.5 seconds at a rate of acquisition of 200 Sps.

5. Conclusion

The first part of this paper presents a solution for remote Wi-Fi FPGA reconfiguration using Tag4M devices. The resulting system represents a versatile equipment with multiple applications in various fields, including ITS.

In the second part two applications developed for a FPGA platform that can be used in road traffic systems are presented. The first application exemplifies the way in which a vehicle can be tracked by using access points installed in the field and by using the Tag4M device which can read the RSSI values for each of them. The approximate of the vehicle's location is computed by applying a triangulation algorithm.

In the second application, the dynamic behaviour of a vehicle is determined by using a gyroscope and an accelerometer sensor attached to a FPGA board.

The work outlines the advantages provided to the developer and to the user by the employment of the FPGA technology and the features of the LabVIEW programming language in an Intelligent Transportation System. The reconfigurable systems' flexibility and the simplified way of creating programs for FPGAs by using the LabVIEW platform lead to a system that allows facile in the field hardware upgrades, runtime reconfiguration and adaptation to unexpected events or to changing environmental conditions.

6. References

Aamodt, K. (2006). CC2431 Location Engine, Application Note AN042, from http://focus.tij.co.jp/jp/lit/an/swra095/swra095.pdf

Adly, I.; Ragai, H. F.; Al-Henawy, A. & Shehata, K. A. (2010). Wireless Configuration Controller Design for FPGAs in Software Defined Radios, *The Online Journal on Electronics and Electrical Engineering (OJEEE)*, vol. 2, no. 3, pp. 293 - 297.

Altera (2009). AN 307: Altera Design Flow for Xilinx Users, from: http://www.altera.com/literature/an/an307.pdf.

Altera (2010). Medical Imaging Implementation Using FPGAs, *White Paper,* from http://www.altera.com/literature/wp/wp-medical.pdf

Altera (2011). Military End Market, from

http://www.altera.com/end-markets/military-aerospace/mil-index.html
Analog Devices (2006). Small, Low Power, 3-Axis 3g MEMS Accelerometer", Technical Report, from http://www.analog.com/en/mems-sensors/inertial-sensors/adxl330/-products/product.html
Andretzky, B. (2005). FPGAs Build Bridges To Wireless Connectivity, from http://electronicdesign.com/article/embedded/fpgas-build-bridges-to-wireless-connectivity9820.aspx
Banovic, K.; Khalid, M.A.S. & Abdel-Raheem, E. (2005). FPGA-Based Rapid Prototyping of DSP systems, *48th Midwest Symposium on Circuits and Systems*, pp. 647 - 650, Covington, KY.
Bitter, R.; Mohiuddin, T. & Nawrocki, M. (2006). *LabVIEW Advanced Programming Technique*, CRC Press, second edition.
Bolchini, C.; Miele, A. & Santambrogio, M. D. (2007). TMR and Partial Dynamic Reconfiguration to mitigate SEU faults in FPGAs, *Proceedings of the 22nd IEEE International Symposium on Defect and Fault-Tolerance in VLSI Systems*, pp.87 - 95, Rome, Italy.
Compton, K. & Hauck, S. (2002). Reconfigurable Computing: A Survey of Systems and Software, *ACM Computing Surveys*, vol. 34, no. 2, pp. 171 - 210.
El-Medany, W.M. & Hussain, M.R. (2007). FPGA-Based Advanced Real Traffic Light Controller System Design, *4th IEEE Workshop on Intelligent Data Acquisition and Advanced Computing Systems: Technology and Applications (IDAACS 2007)*, pp. 100 - 105, Dortmund, Germany.
G2 Microsystems[1] (2008). G2C547 SoC, Technical Report, from www.g2microsystems.com
G2 Microsystems[2] (2008). G2C547 Software, Example Application. Technical Report, from www.g2microsystems.com.
G2 Microsystems[3] (2008). G2M5477 Wi-Fi Module Data Sheet, Technical Report, from www.g2microsystems.com.
HPCWire (2009). FPGA cluster accelerates bioinformatics application by 5000×, from http://www.hpcwire.com/offthewire/FPGA-Cluster-Accelerates-Bioinformatics-Application-by-5000X- 69612762.html
Kalte, H.; Langen, D.; Vonnahme, E.; Brinkmann, A. & Rückert, U. (2002). Dynamically Reconfigurable System-on-Programmable-Chip, *Proceedings 10th Euromicro Workshop on Parallel, Distributed and Network-based Processing*, pp. 235 - 242, Canary Islands, Spain.
Kuon, I.; Tessier, R. & Rose, J. (2007). FPGA Architecture - Survey and Challenges, *Foundations and Trends® in Electronic Design Automation*, vol. 2, no.2, pp. 135 - 253.
Lyke, J. (2002). Reconfigurable Systems: A Generalization of Reconfigurable Computational Strategies for Space Systems, *2002 IEEE Aerospace Conference Proceedings*, vol. 4, pp. 4-1935 - 4-1950.
Maye, J.; Supervisors: Upegui, A. & Prof. Ijspeert, A. J. (2005). Bluetooth Configuration of an FPGA: An Application to Modular Robotics, *Semester Project*, from http://birg.epfl.ch/webdav/site/birg/users/147507/public/semester/report.pdf
Mitra S.; Shirvani, P. P. & McCluskey, E.J. (1998). Fault Location in FPGA-Based Reconfigurable Systems, *IEEE Intl. High Level Design Validation and Test Workshop.*

National Instruments (2007). *CompactRIO™ and LabVIEW™ Development Fundamentals Course Manual*, Course Software Version 8.2.

National Instruments (2009). Working with LabVIEW Filtering VIs and the LabVIEW Digital Filter Design Toolkit Vis, , from http://zone.ni.com/devzone/cda/tut/p/id/4851

National Instruments[1] (2010). *What is LabVIEW?*, from http://zone.ni.com/devzone/cda/pub/p/id/1141

National Instruments[1] (2011). FPGA Technology, from http://www.ni.com/fpga_technology/

National Instruments[2] (2010), *Building Programmable Automation Controllers with LabVIEW FPGA*, Tutorial, from: http://zone.ni.com/devzone/cda/tut/p/id/3068

National Instruments[2] (2011). NI LabVIEW FPGA, from http://www.ni.com/fpga/

Patel, P. & Moallem, M. (2010). Reconfigurable system for real-time embedded control applications, *IET Control Theory and Applications*, issue 11, pp. 2506 - 2515.

Prasanna, V. K. & Dandalis, A. (2007). FPGA-based Cryptography for Internet Security, *Online Symposium for Electronics Engineers (OSEE)*, pp. 1- 6.

Reis, R. & Jess, Jochen A. G. (2004). *Design Of System On A Chip: Devices & Components*, Kluwer Academic Publishers.

Sander, O.; Glas, B.; Roth, C.; Becker, J. & Muller-Glaser, K. D. (2009). Design of a Vehicle-to-Vehicle Communication System on Reconfigurable Hardware, *International Conference on Field-Programmable Technology (FPT 2009)*, pp. 14 - 21, Sydney, NSW, Australia.

Smith, M. J. S. (1997). *Application-Specific Integrated Circuits*", Addison-Wesley Pub Co.

STMicroelectronics (2009). LPR530AP MEMS motion sensor: dual axis pitch and roll 300/s analog gyroscope, Technical Report, from http://www.st.com/internet/com/-TECHNICAL_RESOURCES/TECHNICAL_LITERATURE/DATASHEET/CD00237209.pdf

Straka, M. & Kotasek, Z. (2008). Design of FPGA-Based Dependable Systems, *Proceedings of the 4th Doctoral Workshop on Mathematical and Engineering Methods in Computer Science*, pp. 240 - 247, Znojmo, Czech Republic.

Tessier, R. & Burleson, W. (2001). Reconfigurable Computing for Digital Signal Processing - A Survey, *Journal of VLSI Signal Processing*, vol. 28, issue 1/2, pp. 7 - 27.

Xilinx (1998). The Low-Cost, Efficient Serial Configuration of Spartan FPGAs, XAPP098, Application Note by Kim Goldblatt, November 13 (Version 1.0), from http://www.xilinx.com/support/documentation/application_notes/xapp098.pdf

Xilinx (2006). Spartan-3E Starter Kit User Guide, User Guide, (Version 1.0), from http://www.xilinx.com/support/documentation/boards_and_kits/ug230.pdf

Xilinx (2009). Spartan-3E FPGA Family: Data Sheet, Product Specification, August 26 (Version 3.8), from http://www.xilinx.com/support/documentation/data_sheets/ds312.pdf

Xilinx (2010). Partial Reconfiguration User Guide, from http://www.xilinx.com/-support/documentation/sw_manuals/xilinx12_1/ug702.pdf

Zhenggang, L.; Jialong, X.; Mingyun, Z.; Jun, Y. & Hongwei, D. (2009). FPGA-Based Dual-Mode Traffic Light System Design, *1st International Conference on Information Science and Engineering (ICISE)*, pp. 558 - 561, Nanjing, China.

Part 6

Programming Techniques

19

Extending LabVIEW Aptitude for Distributed Controls and Data Acquisition

Luciano Catani
Istituto Nazionale di Fisica Nucleare (INFN) - Sezione Roma Tor Vergata
Italy

1. Introduction

LabVIEW is probably the most comprehensive environment for setting up a control/data acquisition system (CS) for a scientific/laboratory experiment. It provides ready to use solutions for both control and data acquisition for a large number of equipments and for the analysis of various types of data.

In the scientific environment, especially, these features are particularly useful because CS are frequently developed and managed by scientists willing to spend more time in operating their experimental apparatuses than in maintaining software for controlling components and reading instruments outputs.

In a scientific laboratory, or a medium/small experimental apparatus, typical selection of equipments is unavoidably heterogeneous: scopes, digital I/Os, motors, digital cameras and, quite often, a mixture of new and relatively old technologies for connecting devices to the computer managing the system.

Moreover, CS for scientific experiments are quite often far from being developed once forever; instead they are continuously updated by replacing and/or introducing new components in order to follow the evolution of the apparatus.

LabVIEW easy to learn graphic programming and its large number of instrument drivers and libraries for data analysis and graphical display, successfully fulfill the above requirements.

When the scientific apparatus became larger and more complex a single computer may not be sufficient for the management of all the components. Additionally, in some environment the equipments need to be operated from remote or it might be preferable to separate data acquisition from on-line analysis in order to optimize the performances of both.

In other word the single computer CS needs to be upgraded to implement a distributed control system (DCS).

LabVIEW provides quite a number of solutions also for the development of DCS by offering tools for remote control of Virtual Instruments (VI) and sharing of data across the network by means of dedicated LabVIEW components that allow communicating with remote computers and devices.

Developers can easily find ready to use solutions for their needs among these resources although, in some cases, they might either lack in flexibility or cannot offer the required compatibility with all the software components of the DCS.

In these situations a communication solution for the DCS should be necessarily based on the widely accepted standard protocols ensuring highest compatibility.

There exist numerous possible alternatives. One such model is Microsoft's component object model COM(mscom, 2011) and its associated distributed component object model DCOM which allows COM objects to run and communicate in a distributed manner. Also from Microsoft is the .NET environment, supporting Internet-based connectivity between components.
Another option is offered by the CORBA(corba, 2008) proposed by the Object Management Group (OMG). CORBA is a software standard for component-based development that has been quite successful among developers of DCS.
Yet another model is the Java-based proposal by Sun Microsystems, which encompasses basic infrastructure such as Java Beans and Enterprise Java Beans and remote method invocation (RMI) but also more ambitious solutions for interoperation of distributed intelligent systems such as Jini(jini, 2006).
The aim of this paper is to present the development of a communication framework for distributed control and data acquisition systems, optimized for its application to LabVIEW distributed controls, but also open and compatible with other programming languages because it is based on standard communication protocols and standard data serialization methods. In the next Paragraph the LabVIEW tools for Distributed Systems and their field of application will be briefly presented. In Paragraph 3 the general purpose communication framework will be discussed, with particular attention to the problem of data serialization and the definition of the communication protocol. Paragraph 4 and subsequents will discuss in details the implementation of the communication framework in LabVIEW, focusing on the development strategies and the solutions for achieving the performances required for this field of application.

2. LabVIEW tools for distributed systems

LabVIEW offers a number of tools for transferring, via network, data between the components of a distributed control/data acquisition system.
The Table 1 shows some solutions provided built-in by LabVIEW, a subset of the networking features suggested by National Instruments for developing distributed control systems (Lima et al., 2004). Common to all these solutions is the ease of implementation because they have been designed to require very limited programming effort.
Shared Network Variable, DataSocket, VI Server, VI reference, TCP/IP and UDP communication libraries and also interfaces to .NET and ActiveX are the main communication tools offered by LabVIEW. They are powerful and well suited for many applications but, with the exception of TCP/IP and UDP, are not flexible enough to allow the implementation of a real communication protocol.
Shared Variable and Data Socket, for instance, basically provide data sharing across the network, others (VI Server, VI reference) allow access to remote VI, with some relevant restrictions in some cases, and their use is limited to LabVIEW environment.
In addition the LabVIEV Internet Toolkit includes a HTTP server and the possibility to operate the VIs (Virtual Instruments, i.e. the LabVIEW applications or subroutines) as CGIs that a client can invoke using the HTTP protocol to execute particular procedure on the server side. This is a relatively flexible solution but offers low performances and limited features.
In conclusion it's hard to find the best candidate for developing an open, general purpose communication framework because the before mentioned solutions are either offering limited features or performance, or they are proprietary so that, for instance, integration with the control system of a nearby experiment or with a bigger apparatus, that could have been

Networking Feature	Use Case	Programming Required	Multiple Writers/ Readers	Transmission Delay	Transfer Rate
Shared Network Variable	Share live data with other VIs on a remote computer, or deployed to a target.	No	Many-to-Many	Low	High
DataSocket	Share live data with other VIs on a remote computer, or deployed to a target.	Yes	Many-to-Many	Low	High
Application Control VIs and Functions	Programmatically control VIs and LabVIEW applications across a network by way of the TCP protocol and VI Server.	Yes	One-to-one	Medium	Medium
Remote Front Panels on the LabVIEW Web Server	View and control a VI front panel remotely using LabVIEW or a Web browser.	No	One-to-Many	Medium	Low
Web Services on the Application Web Server	Deploy LabVIEW applications as Web services.	No	Many-to-Many	Medium	Low
HTTP Client VIs	Build a Web client that interacts with servers, Web pages, and Web services.	Yes	One-to-Many	Medium	Low
TCP VIs and Functions	Communicate with an instrument that uses a protocol based on TCP.	Yes	One-to-One	Medium	High
UDP VIs and Functions	Communicate with a software package that uses a protocol based on UDP.	Yes	One-to-Many	Low	High

Table 1. LabVIEW most relevant communication features (excertp from Communication Features table from LabVIEW on-line manual).

developed with different software solutions, would be hard to manage or even impossible. On the other side, an example of requirements for the communication framework is given by the list of communication modes it should allow, like for instance the four cases shown in Fig.1.

The *case 1* is the typical client/server model: a client application asks for data to a remote controller and receives from it the required information that could be, for instance, the most recent value of an I/O channel, the history of that value, a bundle of data of different types. The *case 2* is similar to the remote procedure call (RPC) model: a client application needs to execute a subroutine or procedure on a device attached to another controller without the programmer explicitly coding the details for this remote interaction. It could be the change in the set point of a remote equipment, the execution of a measurement. etc.

For the above mentioned modes of communication a programmer can relay on the predictability of type of data handled and on the limited set of action to be taken on the server and client side. It that would have been the case, DataSocket or VI Server will probably solve

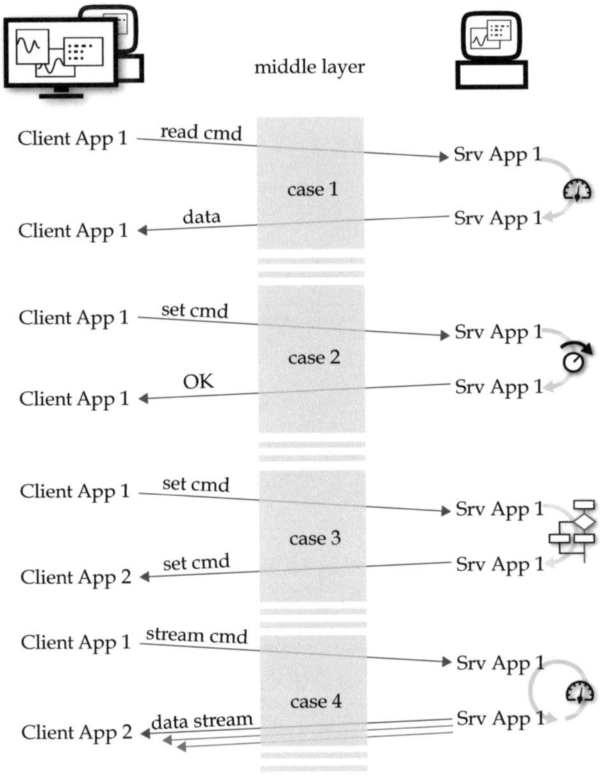

Fig. 1. Modalities of interaction between components of DCS to be supported by the communication framework.

the communication problem.
The *case 3* and the following *case 4* introduce a more elaborated way of interaction. In the first one a request originated from a client application in turn requires an execution of a command on the client side according to the response received by the remote unit. The *case 4* extends the example in *case 1* to another modality of communication that is a continuous stream of data from a server application upon request from the client.
These are just few examples but they are sufficient to confirm and strengthen the requirement for a communication framework that should be based on a versatile and well established communication solutions, to achieve high compatibility and, at the same time, it should allow information to be transferred as different format, i.e. requests or commands, responses and data of different type.

3. A general purpose communication framework

When compatibility and flexibility is an issue, TCP/IP and UDP socket communication might be the natural choice. Network socket communication libraries are available for all main programming languages and the simplicity of the protocol ensures a wide compatibility.
Indeed, LabVIEW provides tools for interfacing with other devices on a TCP and UDP network with standard socket communication protocol by means of TCP/IP and UDP VI and functions.

The set of functions LabVIEW provides for TCP/IP and UDP communications, similarly to other implementations of network socket libraries, supports few elementary operation: *open, close, listen, read* and *write*.

The first three are used to establish connections between client and server, the last two for transferring data in the form of buffers of given length (VI in the *Networking/TCP&UDP* section of LabVIEW examples show some possible implementations of network socket communication).

If data to be transferred is not as simple as either a string of characters or an array of bytes, the communication framework should be equipped with tools for packaging and parsing data, regardless their type, size and complexity.

This process, known as serialization, converts any complex data structure into series of bits that can be easily transmitted across a network connection link and later restored in the original or equivalent form. This result is achieved by adding some kind of descriptor (meta-data) to the payload. Hopefully, the impact of meta-data on the size of serialized data structure and the coding/parsing execution time on the overall data throughput should be limited.

Different types of serialization strategies can be used to flatten object(s) into a one-dimensional stream of bits suited for their transmission by means of socket communication functions.

XML (xml, 2000) (eXtensible Markup Language) is a popular way of coding data especially when interoperability and compatibility between platforms and programming languages is an issue. Client/server communication protocols based on this coding exist, among these the more interesting are SOAP(soap, 2007) and XML-RPC(xmlrpc, 1999). The latter it's basically a remote procedure call(rpc, 1988) that uses HTTP, or other TCP/IP and UDP protocols, as the transport and XML to serialize data allowing complex, and relatively large, data structures to be transmitted and then un-marshaled at destination.

Services provided by the server are called *methods* that a client can invoke by issuing `method Call` to the server. The latter, in turn, replies sending the result in the form of `method Response`. Fig.2 shows an example of messages passed between a client and a server in the XML-RPC protocol. They include header with declarations and `methodCall` or `method Response` fields.

The `methodCall` contains, enclosed with the correspondent tags, the name of the method to be executed on the server side (`methodName`) and optional parameters (`params`). The `methodResponse`, being the reply message from the server to the client contains, enclosed by the (`params`) tag, the data produce by the execution of the *methodName*.

XML-RPC can be easily implemented in LabVIEW by using the before mentioned socket communication libraries; it will be discussed in details in the following Paragraphs.

Socket communication sessions are defined upon the couple IP address and port number that are chosen, on the local and remote computer, for that particular session. That means in a distributed control system with several computers the local application willing to send a command or receive data to/from another application running on a remote computer should be informed on the IP address and the port number that is used by the remote application for listening incoming connections, or equipped with instruments permitting to obtain this information from some kind of repository.

Actually, from the client application point of view, i.e. display consoles, measurement application etc. the DCS should better be seen as a distributed set of components: actuators, diagnostic components, equipments etc. and client applications could be unaware of their physical location or the details of the communication protocol.

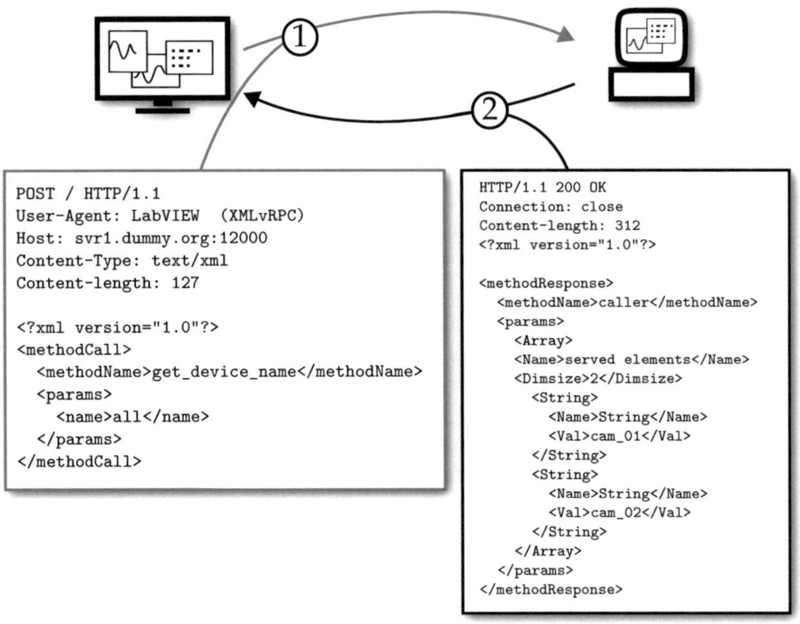

Fig. 2. `methodCall` (left) and `methodResponse` (right) in the XMLvRPC protocol.

In order to be addressed uniformly components need to be integrated in a standardized way such that the communication framework can be developed on top of a generic component model.
It means the network socket communication libraries should be the basis for a general purpose communication framework, a middle-layer between the top level with display or client programs and the front-end layer with device controllers, providing a simplified access to data and commands transfer across the network by hiding the transport layer implementation details.
In the next paragraphs definition of the middle layer and data serialization will be discussed in details.

4. Distributed controls with XMLvRPC

Although it has been basically developed for web services, XML-RPC provides a number of features that fit with the requirements of a simple and flexible communication framework for the distributed control system under development. In particular XML-RPC:

- uses a well established human readable data serialization
- can be easily implemented in LabVIEW by using the standard TCP/IP and UDP libraries
- allows a good flexibility in defining the communication between client and server
- offers high compatibility having a large number of implementations with different programming languages

A communication protocol named XMLvRPC, based on XML-RPC and optimized for LabVIEW distributed controls, was introduced by the author in a previous paper (Catani, 2008).

4.1 Client/server communications

The main components of the XMLvRPC protocol are the *XMLvRPC_Server.vi and XMLvRPC _Client.vi*. Fig.3 schematically shows an example of a data request from a client application to a XMLvRPC server running on a remote controller.
The client application calls the *XMLvRPC_Client.vi* providing the TCP socket information that identify the server side, the remote method to be invoked and optional parameters. The *XMLvRPC_Client.vi* encode the information as a standard XML-RPC call and send it to the server specified (1).
The *XMLvRPC_Server.vi* extract the `methodName` and call the correspondent VI providing "as it is" the information enclosed by the `params` tags in the `methodCall` (2). The VI that implements `methodName` is instructed to parse the data in `params`; it executes its task accordingly and replies to *XMLvRPC_Server.vi* that encode the information in a `methodResponse` that is finally returned to XMLvRPC_Client.vi (3).
As final step the *XMLvRPC_Client.vi* outputs to the calling application the content of `params` enclosed in the `methodResponse`.
At this point XMLvRPC shows a first difference respect to standard XML-RPC.
While the latter always assumes, at least so far, that `params` returned from the server will be directly used by the calling application, XMLvRPC allows the *XMLvRPC_Client.vi* to dynamically call another application, different from the one that issued the `methodCall`, for handling the data received from the remote server.
This is possible because, similarly to `methodCall`, also `methodResponse` includes a `methodName` field for specifying the application (a LabVIEW VI, in this case) that must be invoked to handle the enclosed data.
For this purpose, a number of different solutions can be implemented according to user's needs: all *method.vi* can be either pre-loaded at start-up to optimize execution time or loaded when called and released after execution or optionally cached in memory. Since *method.vi* are programmatically loaded and run, this also means that when a new method is added to a server (similarly on a client) the server source-code doesn't need to be modified to include the call to this new VI. It will be sufficient to copy the VI that serves this new method to the directory where the server *XMLvRPC_server.vi* searches for the *method.vi* implementing the particular `methodCall` requested from the client.
This feature simplifies implementation of new methods: once the client and the server side routines (i.e. LabVIEW VIs) of the method have been developed, they just need to be copied into the specified directories to be immediately available to the control system.
Fig.4 provides more information about the *XMLvRPC_Server.vi* by showing a portion of its block diagram where the main steps of execution are presented.
Let assume that during phase (0) the server has been listening for connection requests. When it finally established a connection after a client request, in (1) the *XMLvRPC_Read_request.vi*

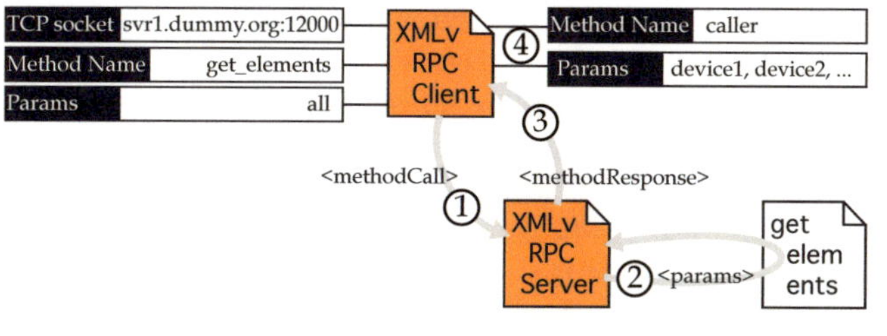

Fig. 3. Main components in a XMLvRPC client/server communication.

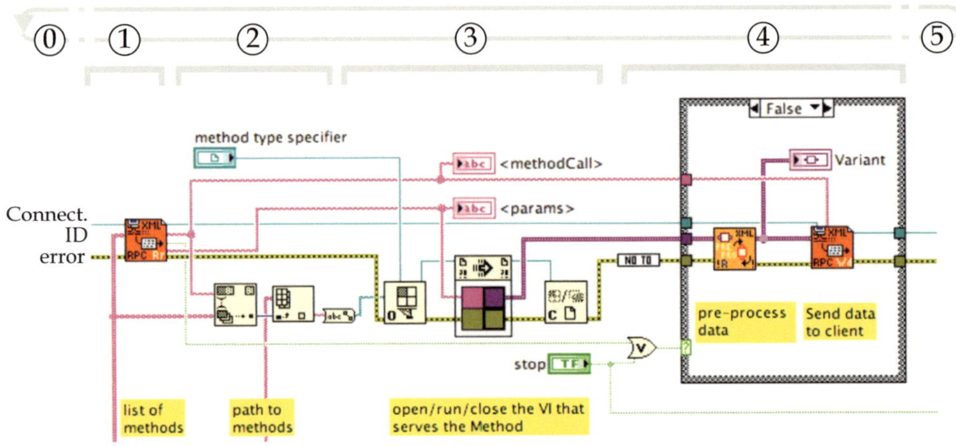

Fig. 4. Portion of block diagram of the the XMLvRPC_Server.vi showing the execution of the server loop.

receives the `methodCall` from the client and parses it, looking for `methodName` and `params`. The `methodName` is then used (2) to find out the full path of the VI that serves that particular method, that is expected to be stored in a dedicated directory with the other *methods* available for that particular server. The full path allows to dynamically load and run the target VI with `Call by Reference Node`.

This solution simplifies very much the server's structure. Methods don't need to be placed directly on the block diagram provided they all have the same connector pane because the `Call By Reference Node` requires a strictly typed VI refnum.

Fortunately this isn't a severe limitation. In fact, since data provided as input for the method execution are serialized onto the `params` string of the XML coding, for VI implementing any of XMLvRPC methods, basically, only one input connector (a String control) is sufficient. Similarly, data produced by the methods, either a single value or a complex data structure, are returned from a single output connector.

In the following paragraph it will be explained why a Variant indicator is used as output instead of a String data type. At this point it is sufficient to mention that Variant data do not conform to a specific data type allowing a program to pass it from one VI to another without specifying what kind of data type it is at compile time.

In LabVIEW, variant data type differs from other data types because it stores the control or indicator name, the information about the data type from which was converted, and the data itself, allowing to correctly convert the variant data type back to the original or to another one.

As for the input connector, the Variant allows methods VIs to output any type of data, or combination of thereof, after the `Call By Reference Node`.

For that reason the *XMLvRPC_Server.vi* is a generic server for requests issued by clients and it doesn't need to be specialized for a particular controller, i.e. for a particular set of tasks to be executed or components to be controlled, because the methods are not statically linked subVI calls. The VIs implementing the methods only need to be available at run time, ready to be loaded and executed upon request of the remote client.

Block diagram of *XMLvRPC_Client.vi* is even simpler, as shown in Fig.5 (next page).

In conclusion XMLvRPC client and server are based on four symmetric functions.

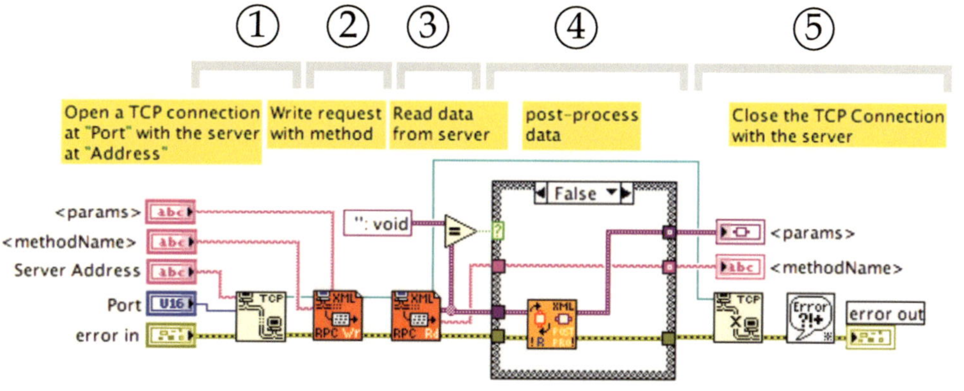

Fig. 5. Block diagram of the the XMLvRPC_Client.vi.

The VIs implementing these functions are, on the server side, *XMLvRPC_ReadRequest.vi* and *XMLvRPC_WriteResponse.vi*, on the client side, *XMLvRPC_WriteRequest.vi* and *XMLvRPC_ReadResponse.vi*.

These VIs, depending to their specific function, perform coding or parsing of XML request or response or network socket read or write operations. The block diagram of *XMLvRPC_WriteRequest.vi* is shown as example in (Fig.6 next page).

4.2 Data serialization

Before going into details of data serialization for XMLvRPC, it should be noted that XML is not the unique choice for providing a human-readable serialization of a given data structure. Another option for text-based serialization is, for instance, JSON(JSON, 2009) derived from Java Script syntax and, as well as XML, well supported from many programming languages. Compared to XML, JSON is more lightweight though, probably, a bit less readable.

Similarly to XML-RPC, a remote procedure call protocol based on JSON encoding has been proposed with the name of JSON-RPC(JSONRPC, 2009). The XML-RPC `methodCall` and `methodResponse` examples shown in Fig.2 would translate to JSON-RPC as the following:

Request from Client: `{"jsonrpc": "2.0", "method": "get_elements", "params":[all], "id": 1}`

Response from Server: `{"jsonrpc": "2.0", "result": ["cam_01", "cam_02"], "id": 1}`

Clearly JSON coding, being less verbose and more compact, provides a clear advantage with respect to XML when used for web services.

However, taking into account all the possible data structures that are routinely transferred across the network in the case of distributed controls for scientific applications, neither XML nor JSON can address the crucial problem for the final size of serialized data that is the coding of large binary arrays that client applications may receive from some particular devices.

Typical example could be the read out of the buffer of a digital scope, consisting of few hundreds of floating point values or, what's worse, raw images produced by a digital monochrome camera consisting of hundreds of thousand pixels, eight or more bits each.

In this case, the text-based serialization produced by either JSON or XML could be really unfavorable because of the large number of single values to code and, especially, because of the much larger size of the serialized data with respect to the original.

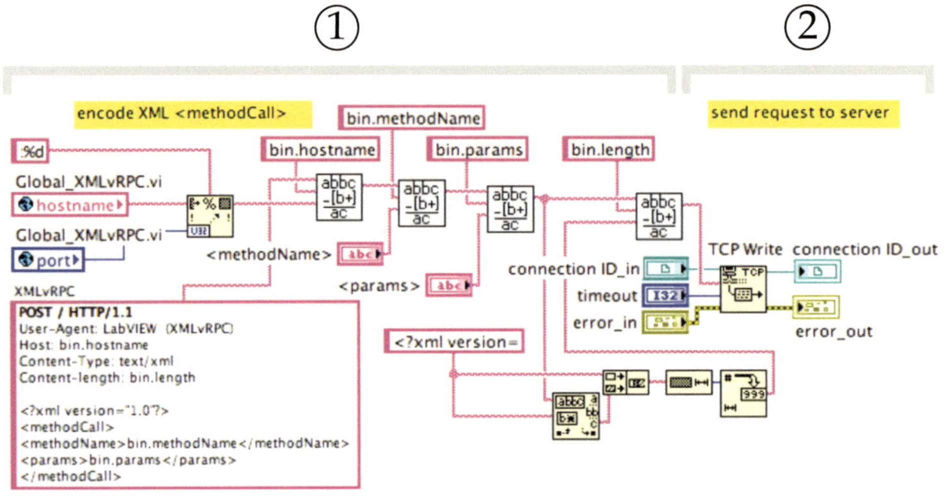

Fig. 6. Block diagram of the the XMLvRPC_WriteRequest.vi.

4.2.1 Binary arrays management

Embedding of binaries in XML format has different options. Binary data, for instance, can be enclosed with the XML `CDATA` tag, a special tag for processing data that isn't going to be parsed during XML processing.

Unfortunately, this method is not perfectly safe and might lead to messy results as, for instance, when binary data contains the `]]>` sequence, which would indicate to the XML parser the end of the non parsed data even though it's not the end of the binary data.

Another option is binary encoding, a process that changes the binary bytes into ASCII bytes using relatively simple algorithms. The two most popular binary encoding algorithms are *UUencode* and *base64*(base64, 2006) encoding. They are commonly used when binary data needs be stored and transferred over media that are designed to deal with textual data.

However, binary encoding introduces some processing overhead and, moreover, it expands 3 bytes into 4 characters, thus leading to an increase of data size by one third.

In other words, a well recognized and efficient standard for handling binary data in text-based serializations is not available, at least so far, and since this work is aimed to developing a communication framework for LabVIEW based distributed systems, it's worth trying to find a suitable solution among the LabVIEW features.

The natural approach to an efficient serialization of large binary arrays is to flatten the binary data into characters and then handle the result as any other string in XML.

In LabVIEW this data transformation is provided by one of the *flatten to string* functions that convert to string either variants or directly any kind of data type.

LabVIEW *flatten to string* transforms numeric arrays, as well as any other data type, to strings of binary digits in big-endian form. In the case of arrays, the binary sequence of the data is preceded by the record of the size, in elements, of each of the array dimensions.

Obviously, an arbitrary flattened data or data structure can be specified in an XML-RPC communication as the content of a `<String>` element, i.e. its associated `<Val>` container, as long as any special characters such as "<" are represented as entities ("<").

XML provides five pre-declared entities that can be used to escape special characters(xml, 2000) in an XML encoded document. This process is under the responsibility of the server

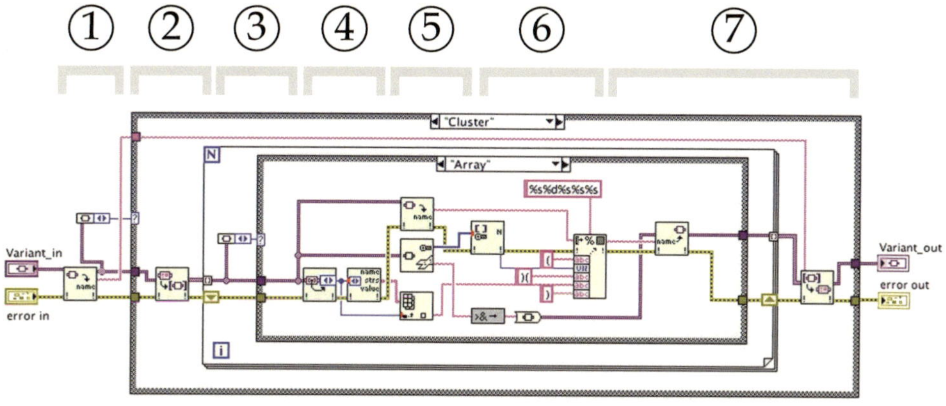

Fig. 7. Pre-processing of LabVIEW data converted to Variant to replace binary arrays with correspondent flattened strings.

side application after encoding the data it has to send, while the client receiving the flattened data will need to check the binary sequence to replace the escaped characters before it process the flattened string to recover the original binary stream.
To preserve compatibility with standard LabVIEW XML functions, instead of introducing modification in the XML coding to process binaries as previously mentioned, it is worth to pre-process the LabVIEW data before it's converted to XML by inserting a VI that inspects the input data structure and replace, when it finds it, any binary array with the equivalent as flattened to string.
Because the pre-processor, similarly to the XML coding tool, must be ready to accept any possible type of data structures as input, the latter is first converted to LabVIEW *Variants*, that sort of type-less container for any (simple or structured) data type that has been introduced in Par.4.1. The *Any-to-Variant* function converts any LabVIEW data to this particular format that can be passed between VIs and manipulated independently from the original data type.
A Variant can be unpacked, its content modified (adding, deleting or replacing data, for instance) and at the end converted back to a "standard" LabVIEW data (numeric, text, array, cluster, etc. or any combination thereof).
The pre-processor developed for XMLvRPC is a VI that recursively searches for nested binary arrays into a LabVIEW data structure, previously converted into a Variant, and replace them with the correspondent flattened strings.
Since the binary array(s) in the Variant structure is(are) flattened and coded into a XML string the reduction in size, with respect to the non pre-processed data, can be significant especially when size of the binary array is large.
In Fig.4 the *XML_preR-processor.vi* is executed just before the *XMLvRPC_WriteResponse.vi* that serialize the LabVIEW data into an XML format and then send the *MethodResponse* to the caller.
In Fig.7 a portion of the block diagram of *XML_preR-processor.vi* is shown. The VI inspects the input Variant (1) looking for either a *Cluster* or a *Array* data type. When a *Cluster* is found the VI recursively inspects its inner elements (2). If, at some point, an *Array* is found (3), it's flattened to string (5), checked to escape special characters, and finally replaced to the original *Array* (7) into the *Cluster*.
Later, the XML encoder will handle the string corresponding to the flattened binary array as well as any other string type data, i.e. by encoding the data into a <*String*> element and by

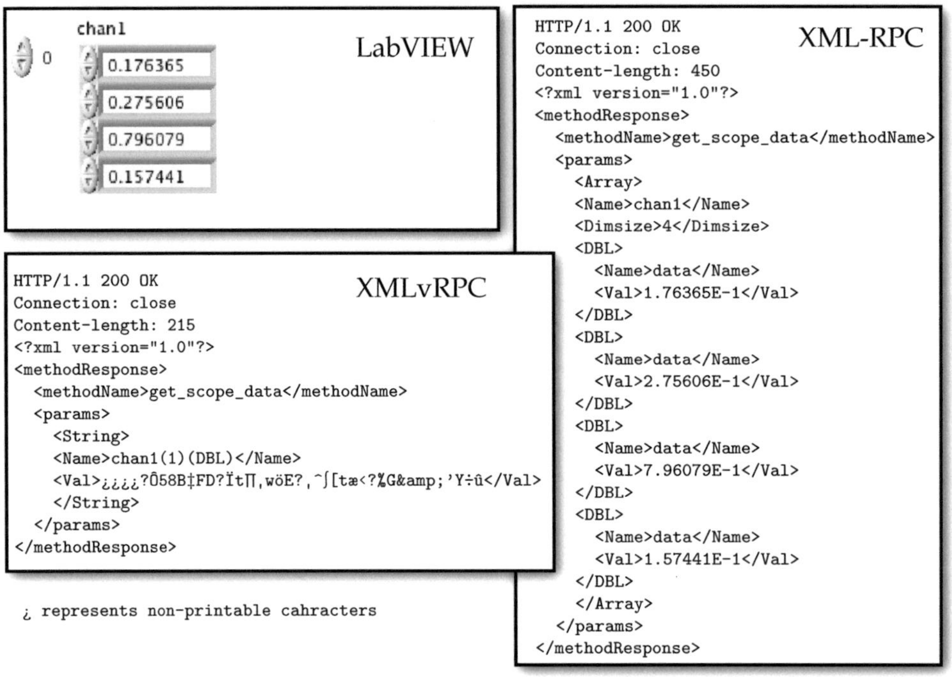

Fig. 8. Binary arrays coding in XML and XMLvRPC.

enclosing the string as it is in *Val* tags (Fig.8)

As consequence, compared to standard XML, the quantity of bytes to be transferred on the network is very much reduced, overhead is almost negligible and the throughput of the communication protocol become compatible with the requirements of a control system.

If considering, for instance, XML coding of a data structure (e.g. a LabVIEW cluster) that includes a 640x480 2D-array of unsigned-bytes, a typical pixels map of a raw image produced by a CCD camera, the reduction in size obtained by applying the pre-processing just described can be a factor 100 or more with respect to standard XML.

It should be mentioned that development of the XMLvRPC's pre and post-processor has been significantly simplified by complementing the LabVIEW functions with the OpenG(Jim Kring, 2003) LabVIEW Data Tools library providing a number of useful functions for manipulating Variants.

Fig.9 presents the execution time in ms for the pre-processing and post-processing VIs as function of the size of the input array. The latter is a 2D-array of unsigned-bytes with equal sizes in both dimensions. In Fig.9 values in abscissa are the (equal) dimensions of the 2D-array. Since pre and post processing are executed separately by the two partners in the communication process (data sender does pre-processing while receiver post-processes data received), their contribution (green and light blue areas) to the total time budget (blue) has been evidenced.

Total execution time, well below 10 ms even for large binary arrays, is comparable to the typical time needed to transfer the same amount of data through the network (from few to several tens of milliseconds).

It must be noted that when a LabVIEW binary array is flattened into a string, some relevant information about the original array is lost. As consequence reconstruction of a binary

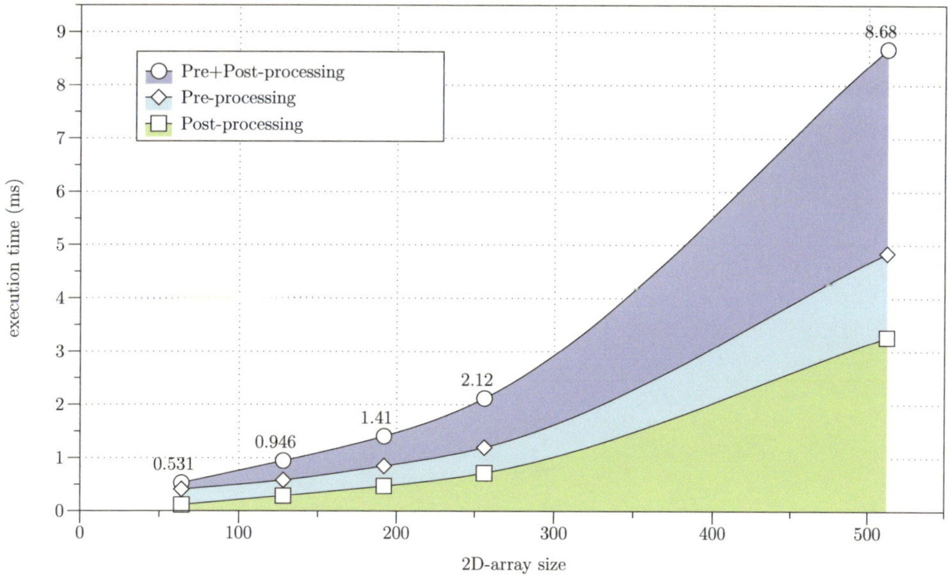

Fig. 9. Perfomances of pre-processing and post-processing routines for different sizes of 2D binary array. Values in abscissa (2D-array size) represent the two equal sizes of a 2D array, e.g. the value 128 corresponds to a 128x128 U8 binary array given as input to processing routines.

array on the receiver (client) side is not possible unless it is supplied, by other means, the dimension(s) of the array and its data type and size. It has been already mentioned that the number of elements for each dimension is included by LabVIEW in a header of the flattened string.

The solution that has been chosen for XMLvRPC serialization is straightforward: the missing information, i.e. the dimensions of the array and its data type (U8, U32, I32 etc.), properly coded and formatted is appended to the name of the variable. This part of the procedure corresponds to step (6) in the block diagram of Fig.7.

As an example, the variable `image`, being the 640x480 2D unsigned-bytes array previously mentioned, after the pre-processing procedure transforming it into a string will change its name into `image(2)(U8)`. On the receiver side a post-processor parses the LabVIEW Variant obtained converting the XML data. It selects the strings that it recognizes, by their particular names, as flattened binary array and un-flatten them into an array having the indicated dimensions (2) and data type (U8).

As alternative additional XML elements can be introduced into `<String>`, e.g. `<ArrayDim>` and `<ArrayDataType>` to specify the original array structure.

Results of some tests have been carried out to evaluate the performance of the communication protocol are shown in Fig.10.

To the overall command execution time shown in the graph contribute, beside the time needed to transfer data-in and data-out from/to client to/from server, the execution time of the *method.vi* on the server side and time needed to open/close communication sockets for the transmission of the `methodCall` and the `methodResponse` between client and server. Performance, especially when dealing with large data sets, can be improved by optimizing the network parameters (e.g. ethernet packet size) as evidenced by the two curves resulting

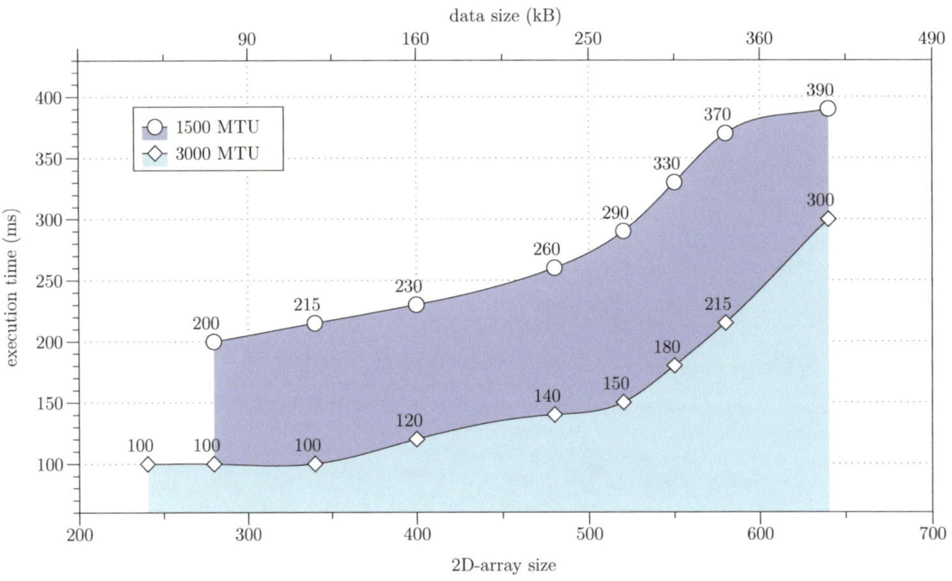

Fig. 10. Time needed to complete a client/server `methodCall` and `methodResponse` as function of different data size returned by the server. The two curves correspond to results obtained with different settings of Maximum Transmission Unit (MTU, i.e. Ethernet maximum packet size) on the network interface of the client computer in a 100 MBps switched network.

from different settings of MTU.

Moreover, when a continuous flow of large data buffers needs to be implemented as, again, in the case of streaming the output of a digital camera, one can consider to implement a dedicated streaming-like communication between server and client(s) that can be initiated/terminated on demand by XMLvRPC commands.

4.2.2 Enhancing the client/server communication

It was mentioned before that the XMLvRPC protocol supports asymmetric `methodCall`/ `methodResponse` communications. It means that on the client side the *method.vi* that is required to handle the data received from the server can be different from the one that originated the `methodCall`.

The `methodResponse` can indicate another method (i.e. another client application) to deal with the response on the client side, according to the data produced from the *method.vi* on the server.

The client's `methodRequest`, for instance, might ask for the newest data on the controller, i.e. the most recently updated value among the I/O channels read from equipment assigned to this particular controller. In this case the result will have a data format that cannot be defined a-priori and needs the appropriate client application to be displayed. Another example of asymmetric XMLvRPC communication will be given later in Par.5 when the services registration procedures will be discussed in details.

Interestingly, this feature of XMLvRPC can be employed for extending the client/server communication discussed so far by introducing another option for data transfer between a server and the client application.

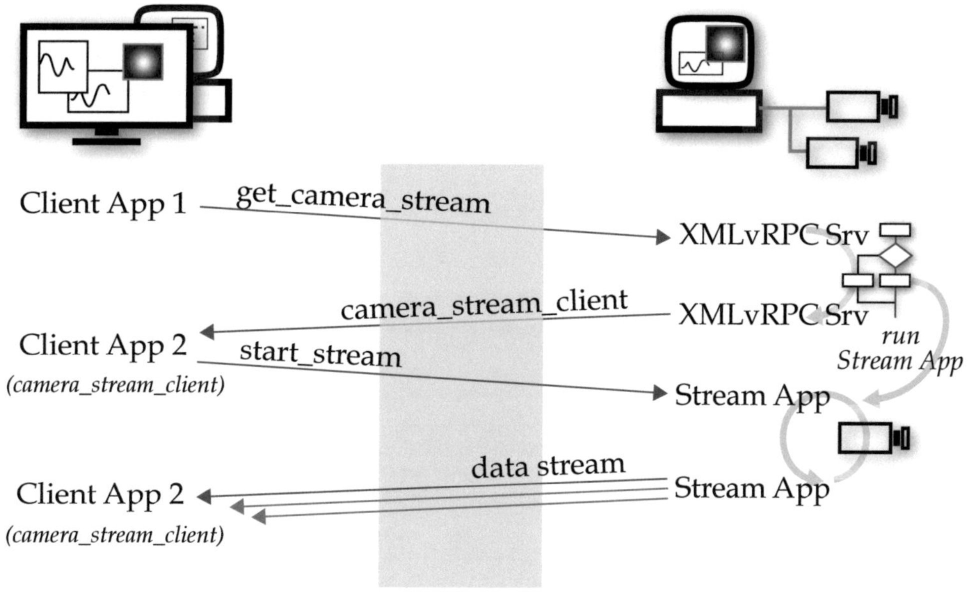

Fig. 11. An example of asymmetric communication in XMLvRPC establishing a streaming of image data from a controller of a digital camera to a client application.

When, for instance, a display or a measurement application is expecting to receive continuous updates of a value for a given time, it would be more efficient to open a socket connection between the two parts and keep it open, as long as needed, instead of forcing the client to continuously send identical *methodRequest*s to the server.

This is even more significant when the data to be transferred each iteration is large. In this case data serialization can be optimized in such a way to reduce the overhead by XML coding/parsing and, as consequence, avoiding the pre/post-processing.

Fig.11 shows an example of asymmetric communication in XMLvRPC aimed to establishing a streaming of image data from a controller of a digital camera to a client application.

As first step the client application sends a `methodCall` to the controller by issuing the method, e.g. `get_camera_stream`, that starts the image stream server. As soon as the stream server is running, the XMLvRPC server replies to the client with `camera_stream_client` as `methodName` providing, as parameters, its IP address and port number for the socket connection, and other optional information. The client, as consequence of the `methodResponse` dynamically opens and runs the display application, i.e. the client-side method, `camera_stream_client`.

Block diagrams of both the client and server side of the data stream connection are shown in Fig.12.

On the server the Stream Application starts listening for incoming requests. When connection is established the inner loop read data from the device controller and, in this particular case, push the 2D array with raw image data to the client.

Since server and client are specialized for handling a particular type of data, i.e. a 2D unsigned-bytes array, serialization and de-serialization are very much simplified compared to what has been previously shown for XML coding. The string sent to the client is obtained by simply appending the 2D array, previously flattened to a string, to the 4-bytes string being

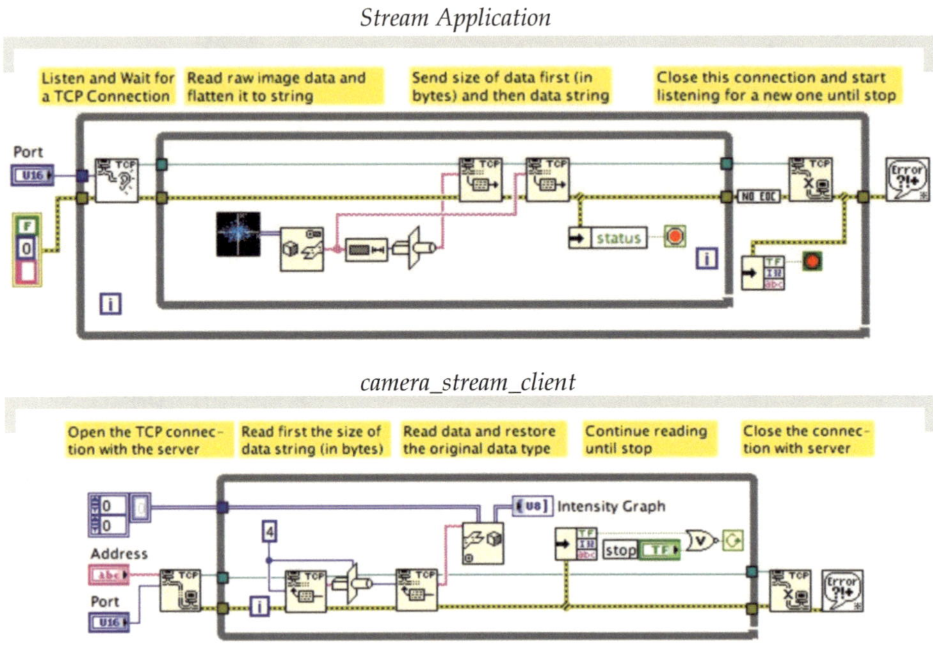

Fig. 12. LabVIEW diagrams of server (top) and client (bottom) applications in a data stream session.

the flattened U32 size of the 2D array.
This information is needed to the client application to inform the *TCP Read.vi* about the size of the buffer it's going to receive from the server.
Finally, a *Type cast* allows to restore the original 2D unsigned-bytes array.
As expected this approach allows better performances than XMLvRPC, around a factor 2 faster, and very simple programming.

5. Inizialization and registration of services

On Par.3 it was mentioned that the final goal of this development should be the realization of a *middle-layer* providing a set of functions allowing (top) client applications communicating with (bottom) hardware equipment via XMLvRPC.
Actually, what has been presented so far already provides a fairly complete solution for small or medium size CS where the number of components to be controlled, and that of controllers and client consoles, is limited. In this case it shouldn't be too difficult to organize a simple list, or a spreadsheet table, with a catalog of components managed by each controller, their I/O channels, IP addresses of network units etc. Then, each client application could relay in this catalog to search for information such as the controller in charge for a particular component and its IP address, the list of methods it provides and optional parameters for a correct formatting of a `methodCall`.
An improvement of the system configuration procedure can be achieved by implementing either a central configuration service or a sort of service location protocol allowing components of the CS to find services and components without prior configuration.

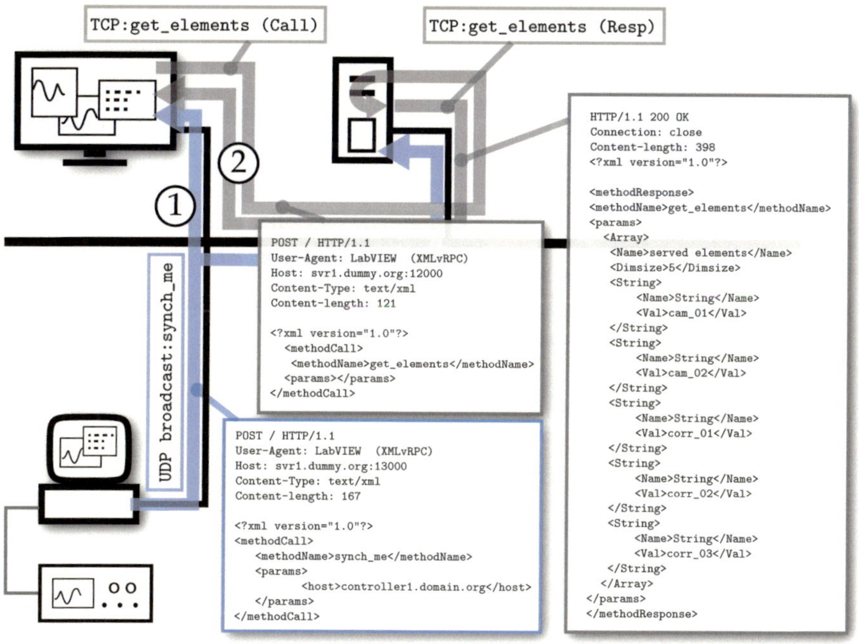

Fig. 13. Synchronization of a controller with the Configuration database either at startup by means of UDP-broadcast (1) or run time by using dedicated XMLvRPC `methodCall` (2).

Fig.13 introduces a new component, the Configuration DataBase, to the DCS depicted so far. Its role is the management of the configuration of components in the distributed control system.

At startup each controller sends a UDP-broadcast to register on the Configuration DataBase by issuing `synch_me` or `register_me` (Fig.13).

The method `register_me` is used if the controller has been configured with all its methods and elements. The method `synch_me` is used if some methods (and elements) are provided by the Configuration DataBase. If the system has more than one Configuration DataBase, for redundancy purposes, both will receive the request to register the controller in the system. The Configuration DataBase detects the UDP-broadcast and then sends to the controller a TCP/IP `get_elements` `methodCall` and then a `get_element_conf` for each element listed in the previous methodResponse received from the controller.

Practically, local services (i.e. those specific for a class of elements) are configured directly on each controller while global services (e.g. back-up, restore etc.) can be configured centrally in the Configuration Database.

Consoles and high level applications rely on the Configuration DataBase to locate the controller in charge for a particular element. They use an UDP broadcast to find the Configuration DataBase, i.e its IP address. At this point the client can either decide to receive the complete configuration of the system at once and refresh it periodically or inquire that service each time an application needs to identify the controller in charge of a particular I/O channel or service.

The Configuration DataBase can run either on a dedicated server (as shown in the picture) or any client, or controller, of the the DCS.

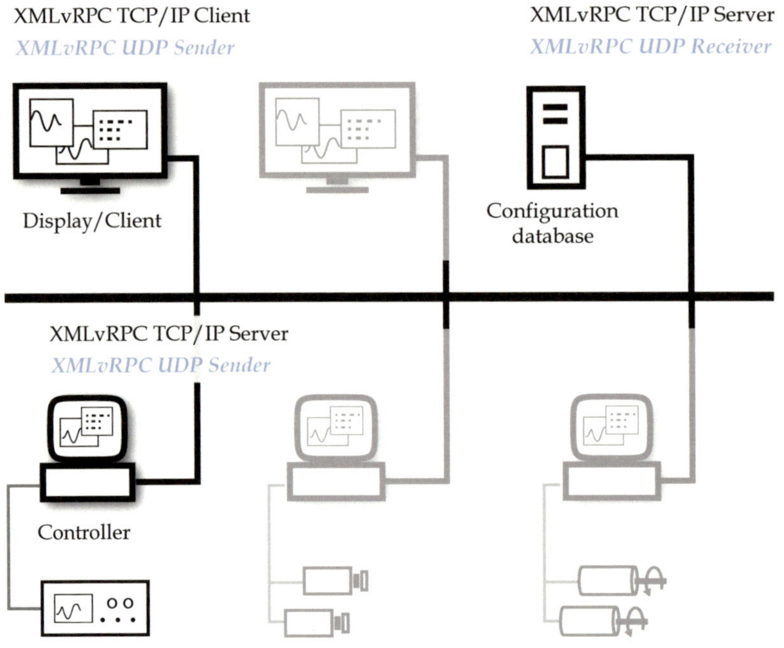

Fig. 14. Typical components in a XMLvRPC based distributed control system. Services running on each component are also shown.

6. Components in a XMLvRPC distributed control system

Fig.14 shows an example of components in a XMLvRPC distributed control system. Controllers run front-end applications: they are either the interface to equipment or provide general services.

Displays, or consoles, run user applications or analysis and measurement procedures. They directly connect to controllers to run remote procedure provided they know (the IP address of) the controller in charge for the particular I/O channel (or service) and the methods made available for it.

This information is provided by the Configuration Database on request from the Console (or any another client). The Configuration Database is thus the repository of the system configuration files collected from any controller at the time they start-up and register to the system.

To summarize, TCP/IP and UDP services in XMLvRPC are the following:

XMLvRPC TCP/IP Server: runs on each controller and on the Configuration DataBase serving XMLvRPC `methodCalls` issued by clients. For each controller, valid `method Names` correspond to VIs listed in the *XMLvRPC_ClientServer/methods_svr* directory. Elements under control are listed in *XMLvRPC_ClientServer/elements_svr* directory.

XMLvRPC TCP/IP Client: runs on each console (a client, in general); it sends XMLvRPC `methodCall` to XMLvRPC TCP/IP Server as consequence of some action on the console panels or from measurement application.

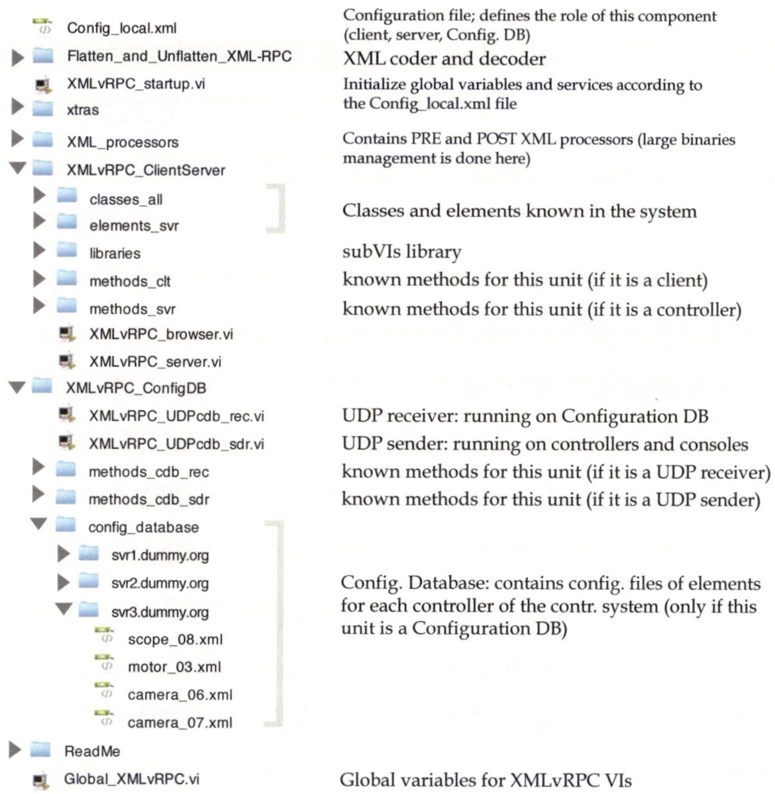

Fig. 15. Directories, VIs and configuration files in the XMLvRPC package

XMLvRPC UDP Receiver (Configuration DataBase): runs on the Configuration DataBase to serve `synch_me` or `register_me` `methodCalls` sent by controllers or `locate_cdb` sent by consoles at startup.

XMLvRPC UDP Sender: runs on controllers and consoles at startup. It sends `synch_me` or `register_me` `methodCalls` to Configuration DataBase for registering the new controller in the system. Consoles use it to locate the Configuration DataBase.

Configuration DataBase: is the repository of the configuration; it supplies clients (e.g. display/measurements applications) with information about the controller in charge for a given element.

6.1 The XMLvRPC suite of VIs

Fig.15 shows the structure (directories, VIs and configuration files) of the XMLvRPC software package.
The installation can be identical for any component of the XMLvRPC DCS because the role assigned to each component (i.e. server or client) and the services it will provide are configured by *XMLvRPC_startup.vi* according to the settings in the configuration file *Config_local.xml*.
If the local computer runs a Configuration Database the methods to be used for this service are

PHP script

```php
<?php
include("xml-rpc.class.php");
function get_tag($string, $tag){
    $tagstart = "<".$tag.">";
    $tagend = "</".$tag.">";
    $string = " ". $string;
    $ini = strpos($string,$tagstart);
    if ($ini == 0) return "";
    $ini += strlen($tagstart);
    $len = strpos($string, $tagend, $ini) - $ini;
    echo $tag.": ".substr($string, $ini, $len)."</br>";
    return substr($string, $ini + $len);
}
$thisHost = "client1.dummy.org";    //client hostname
$thisPort = 12000;                  //client port
$server = "svr1.dummy.org"          //remote server hostname
$serverPort = 12000;                //remote server port
$socket = Socket::singleton();      //create socket
$socket->connect($server, $serverPort); //connect to remote server
//template for methods without params, e.g. get_elements, get_methods, get_timestamp
$str1 = "POST / HTTP/1.1\nUser-Agent: LabVIEW  (XMLvRPC)\nHost: "      ;
$str2 = "\nContent-Type: text/xml\nContent-length: ";
$str3 = "<?xml version=\"1.0\"?>\n<methodCall>\n<methodName>";
$str4 = "</methodName>\n<params><name>none</name>\n</params>\n</methodCall>";
$methodName = "get_elements";                   //set method's name
$length = strlen($str3.$methodName.$str4);  //length of payload string
//format methodCall
$methodCall = $str1.$thisHost.":".$thisPort.$str2.$length."\n".$str3.$methodName.$str4;
//print methodCall
echo "<b>methodCall sent to server:</b></br>".
 str_replace("\n", "</br>", htmlspecialchars($methodCall)."</br>"."</br>");
//send method and get response
$socket->sendCmd($methodCall);
$response = $socket->getMultilinedResponse();
echo "<b>methodResponse from server:</b></br>";  //print methodResponse's name and Values
$resp = get_tag($response, "methodName");
while (strlen($resp)) $resp = get_tag($resp, "Val");
?>
```

HTML output

```
methodCall sent to server:
POST / HTTP/1.1
User-Agent: LabVIEW (XMLvRPC)
Host: client1.dummy.org:12000
Content-Type: text/xml
Content-length: 122
<?xml version="1.0"?>
<methodCall>
<methodName>get_elements</methodName>
<params><name>none</name>
</params>
</methodCall>

methodResponse from server:
methodName: get_elements
Val: scope_08
Val: motor_03
Val: camera_06
Val: camera_07
```

Fig. 16. PHP script (left) for issuing an XMLvRPC `methodCall` from a web browser and the HTML output of the values in the `methodResponse` (rigth).

in *methods_cdb_rec*. The *system_database* directory contains a directory with the configuration files of the controlled elements for each of the controllers (servers) which registered to the system.

Adding an element, for instance a new device or service, is as simple as creating, and properly editing, the corresponding configuration file in the controller directory of the *system_database* folder. Similarly, a method can be added to a server, or a client, by including the correspondent VI in the *methods_svr*, or *methods_clt*, directory respectively. In both cases there is no need to modify either source code or global configuration file since these directories are scanned at start-up to identify services and elements available to this component of the control system.

Development of a VI for a new method can start from a common template since they all present an identical interface (i.e. the connector pane) to the calling application.

7. Interoperability

The communication framework described so far, although it has been designed and optimized for a LabVIEW-based DCS, exhibits a clear attitude to interoperate with network applications developed by using different programming language and/or running on diverse hardware platforms or operating systems.

First of all it is, essentially, a fairly customized version of the XML-RPC protocol, yet compatible with all its implementations at least for what concerns the client/server communication and the basic structure of the body of the request.

That means any XML-RPC compatible client can issue a well-formed `methodCall` to an XMLvRPC server and receive a `methodResponse` that, afterwards, it will be able to parse to properly extract the XML elements.

Handling of binary arrays that have been serialized as described in Par. 4.2 will be under responsibility of the application that required the data. Even if the latter wouldn't be equipped with tools for restoring the original format of the serialized binary array, these data will be still

recognized as a valid string element, though meaningless.
A lower, hence more general, level of compatibility is the network socket communication that is at the basis of the XMLvRPC protocol.
Libraries for socket communication are available for, practically, any existing programming language and it very easy, as it was with LabVIEW, writing a piece of software for implementing a socket communication session.
An example is shown in Fig.16 allowing to request and display data received from an XMLvRPC server on a web browser.
The simple PHP script on the main frame is used for composing and issuing a `methodCall`, to read the reply of the XMLvRPC server and finally parse the `methodResponse` for printing the main information such as the value elements in the `<params>`.

8. Conclusion

The communication framework presented in this paper has been described in details to provide a ready to use solution for implementing a distributed control system with LabVIEW. Nevertheless, it could also be seen as a collection of strategies that instead of being adopted as a whole may be individually replaced by, or integrated with others if those are found to be best suited for some particular application or requirement.
It was mentioned, for instance, that XML could be exchanged with other rules for formatting data and also that binary array serialization can be based, as alternative, on the referred standard encoding algorithms.
All the development strategies that have been presented share in the intention to exploit and take advantage from the great features of LabVIEW for delivering an overall solution that still offers the expected compatibility with other programming languages and with other well-established communication solutions.

9. References

COM: Component Object Model Technologies *Microsoft Corporation*, http://www.microsoft.com/com/default.mspx

Catalog Of OMG CORBA/IIOP Specifications *Object Management Group, Inc.*, http://www.omg.org/spec/CORBAe/1.0/

Jini Architecture Specification *jini.org*, http://www.jini.org/wiki/Jini_Architecture_Specification

T.Bray, et.al. (2008). Extensible Markup Language (XML) 1.0 (Fifth Edition) *W3 Consortium*, http://www.w3.org/TR/REC-xml

SOAP Version 1.2, *World Wide Web Consortium (W3C)*, http://www.w3.org/ TR/soap12-part1/

XML-RPC Specification, *Scripting News, Inc.*, http://www.xmlrpc.com/spec

Remote Procedure Call Protocol Specification v.2, *Network Working Group, Sun Microsystems, Inc.*, http://tools.ietf.org/html/rfc1057

Catani, L. (2008). An XML-based communication protocol for accelerator distributed controls, *Nuclear Instruments and Methods in Physics Research Section A: Accelerators, Spectrometers, Detectors and Associated Equipment*, Volume 586, Issue 3, 1 March 2008, Pages 444-451.

Lima et al., (2004). Choosing among LabVIEW Communication Features. *LabVIEW 2010 Help Manual*, Part Number: 371361G-01, June 2010

Jim Kring, (2003). OpenG LabVIEW Data Tools. *OpenG.org website,* http://wiki.openg.org/Oglib_lvdata

Crockford, D. (2006). JSON format specifications. *Internet Engineering Task Force,* http://www.ietf.org/rfc/rfc4627.txt?number=4627

JSON-RPC Working Group, (2009). JSON-RPC 2.0 Specification proposal. *JSON-RPC Google Group,* http://groups.google.com/group/json-rpc/web/json-rpc-1-2-proposal

Josefsson, S. (2006). The Base16, Base32, and Base64 Data Encodings. *Network Working Group,* http://tools.ietf.org/html/rfc4648

20

Graphical Programming Techniques for Effective, Fast and Responsive Execution

Marko Jankovec
Faculty of Electrical Engineering,
University of Ljubljana,
Slovenija

1. Introduction

Graphical programming languages (G-language) in LabVIEW provide easy and intuitive coding, where even a beginner without any programming skills can build simple software and get results back quickly. The versatile collection of blocks providing most functions needed for a general user and simple graphical representation of dataflow that resembles flow charts are main advantages of G-language over text-based programming. However, when project grows and the complexity increases, the one dimensional programming space in text based languages starts to show advantages since it allows program flow in vertical direction only making it easier to follow and organize. The programming space in case of G-language is at least two dimensional with no data flow direction constraints. Furthermore, the use of structures for data flow manipulation (e.g. sequence, event structure etc.), at least one additional dimension is introduced.

Thus, a project that started as a simple and easy task that could be handled by a non-programmer quickly becomes vast and hard to understand. Usually the graphical code quickly grows over one computer screen making data flow very hard to follow and it becomes difficult to insert or change any functionality later on. Finally, it comes to a point, when one asks himself whether it would not be better to start all over again keeping in mind all the required software functionality. At that stage, the programmer already has much more clear ideas how his software should work and thus he can build the software from beginning in a better, much more organized way that it would be easy to modify and upgrade later on.

This happens quite often to beginners and for that reason it is good to know some common graphical programming rules. They are recommended to follow from the beginning of graphical code development in order to avoid such problems and save a lot of valuable time later on when the code grows.

When making software where very fast execution is required, (eq. handling fast data stream in real time) a detailed knowledge of memory and execution time requirements is essential. By knowing how LabVIEW handles data, one can build the program in a way that handles the data effectively without any unnecessary memory or execution overhead.

Software that interacts with the end user needs a kind of a user interface, which is one of the most important features of LabVIEW. The controls and indicators on front panel even substitute variables in text-based languages. User interface thus grows together with program code and cannot be apart from each other. The execution flow of a simple LabVIEW code is basically linear from data source over some processing nodes to the indicators with regard to data flow. Advanced software usually has to provide more functionality by executing various pieces of code when pressing buttons or performing other actions on front panel. This is well handled in LabVIEW by Event structure, which is constantly gaining more and more functionality since version 7.1. Nevertheless, there are several issues still present with regard to the responsiveness of the user interface when time consuming operations are performed in the background or in the case of slow or even none response of hardware, such as external instrument.

2. Graphical programming techniques for better VI performance

An efficient LabVIEW application is designed without unnecessary operations, with minimal memory occupation including code, data, block diagram and front panel, GUI updates and data manipulations. The VI profiling tools in LabVIEW offer a detailed overview of execution time and memory occupation of the main VI and its SubVIs and should be used to find and correct all execution issues of designed application. Even though graphical programming looks trivial and bullet proof many rules are good to follow in order to achieve memory efficient and fast code.

2.1 Execution order

The execution order is solely defined by dataflow and not by position of the nodes in the diagram as one would intuitively presume. If no data dependency exists to determine the dataflow, a sequence structure can be implemented for that purpose, as shown in Fig. 1.

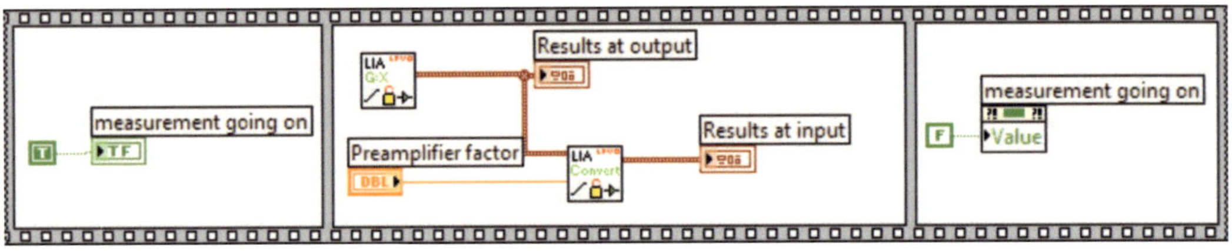

Fig. 1. Determining the execution order with flat sequence structure

In the presented case an indicator is lit before the measurement starts. The indicator goes off when data collection and calculation is finished. In such a case, the use of a sequence structure is appropriate.

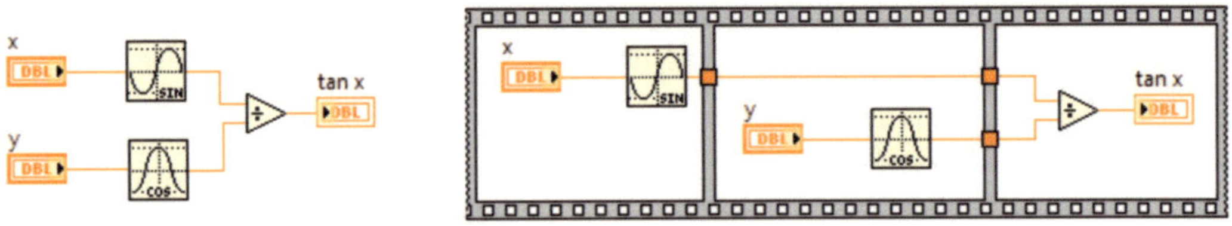

Fig. 2. By using sequence structure (right) the execution order is forced undermining possible data execution parallelism (left)

If the execution order is not important it is undesirable to use sequence structures just to save space in the diagram (e.g. stacked sequence - in Fig. 2 flat sequence is shown for better readability), since they undermine data flow principals and reduce the efficiency of code optimisation in the scope of LabVIEW's compiler. LabVIEW can distribute execution of parallel data paths applying them to more processor threads making code execution much

faster. Therefore it is advisory to use native dataflow principle to determine the execution order and leave parallel data paths if possible. Parallel data paths are desirable to use but one has to be careful if specific execution order is required.
Another chance of messing with dataflow is using local and global variables or property nodes. They can be used to write and read data of front panel controls and indicators at any desirable place and time in the block diagram. They make the code readability much harder and even cause some undesired dataflow issues leading to race conditions and software misbehaviour (Fig. 3).

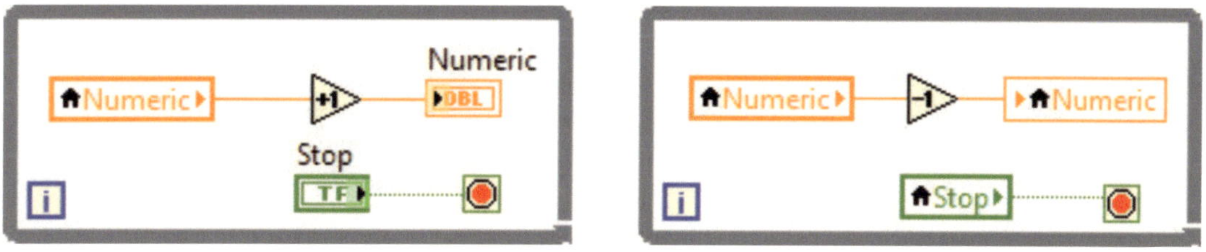

Fig. 3. A simple example of race condition using local variables that are changed in two independently running loops

If no particular data is passed to the nodes to be executed next one can use an error wire instead of sequence structure to define dataflow order. For that all used SubVIs should have error inputs and outputs at least. Besides defining dataflow direction, a consistent usage of error handling greatly improves reliability and responsiveness of software, especially when software execution depends on external hardware.

2.2 Execution speed

When working with LabVIEW it is quite easy to forget how data is handled and how they are stored in memory. This is often one of the reasons for slow execution speed that can be dependant of many factors such as time elapsed since last program launch, amount of data already processed and similar.
In order to explore the effectiveness of using different variables in LabVIEW a test was performed, where the simple algorithm was repeatedly executed in a loop and the total loop execution was measured using "Tick count" functions just before and after the loop by using sequence structure, as shown in Fig. 4. The number of loop iterations in our case was set to one million times so that the time difference in ms scale could be measured accurately enough and that execution time of "Tick count" function is negligible with respect to the total loop execution time.

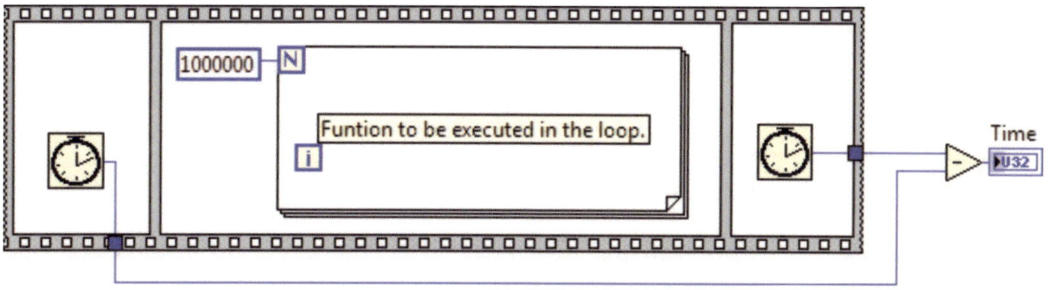

Fig. 4. Experiment of measuring execution time of one loop iteration

The execution priority of the VI was set to Highest (time critical priority) in order to eliminate the influence of operating system as much as possible. During the execution speed test no other programs were running and no disk or mouse activities were performed. The computer used for test has Intel Core i540 2.53 GHz processor, 4 GB RAM and Nvidia NVC 5100M graphic adaptor. The test was performed in 64-bit LabVIEW 2010 running on 64-bit Windows 7 Enterprise operating system. A test algorithm was the following: A random number between 0 and 1 is generated inside the loop and compared to a pre-set test value. In each loop iteration occurrences of test result are counted according to the outcome by two separate variables.

Beginners frequently use local and global variables in LabVIEW as they are used to text based programming languages. Besides already mentioned data flow undermining they are also slower to access and they increase memory occupation. Each local or global variable makes a copy of data of original control or indicator in memory, which becomes important when the data occupies large memory blocks.

Initially, front panel indicators named "less" and "more or equal" were used as counters (Fig. 5.). Local variables are used to read data from indicators. The VI was executed 100 times to get a good approximation of the average execution time. In this case the average time for 1 loop iteration was 680 ns.

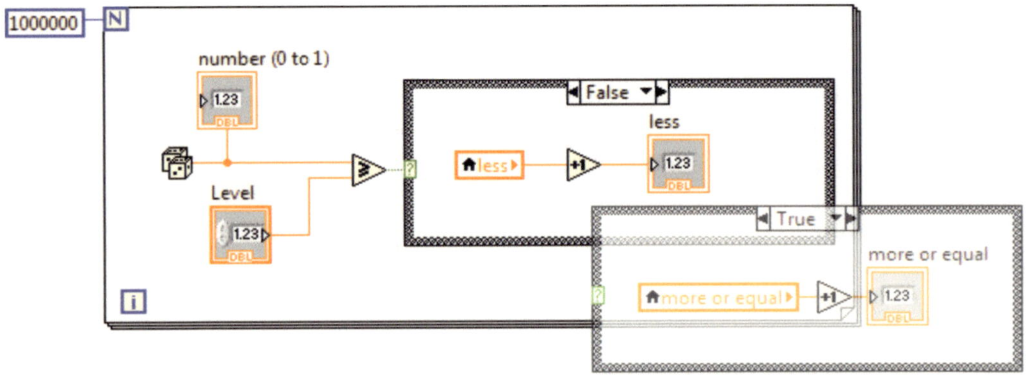

Fig. 5. An example of using local variables to read values of front panel indicators

Another possibility to read or write values of front panel controls and indicators is to use their "Value" property nodes. By that no additional memory allocation is needed to store variable data, since you write or read directly to variables' memory block. The downside of using property nodes is that they turn out to be extremely slow. By replacing local variable with "Value" property nodes in the presented case slowed down the execution to enormous 300 μs, which is much slower than using local variables. For that reason it is strongly advised not to use property nodes in places where fast execution is required.

Nevertheless, in many cases it is possible to avoid using local variables as well. A better solution of this simple problem is to use shift registers to store data instead, as shown in Fig. 6. They are inherent loop structures and thus perform much faster. Additionally, no front panel activities are necessary to update the counters' values. Measured time needed for one loop iteration was 83 ns on average. Further optimisation is possible by removing the indicator "number 0 to 1" out of the loop. Displaying this number inside the loop for each iteration is meaningless since no one can perceive updates at such rate. Execution time of one loop iteration thus drops significantly to only 41 ns. On the contrary, if we replace it with a more complex indicator e.g. Waveform Chart, the execution time would increase to 133 ns.

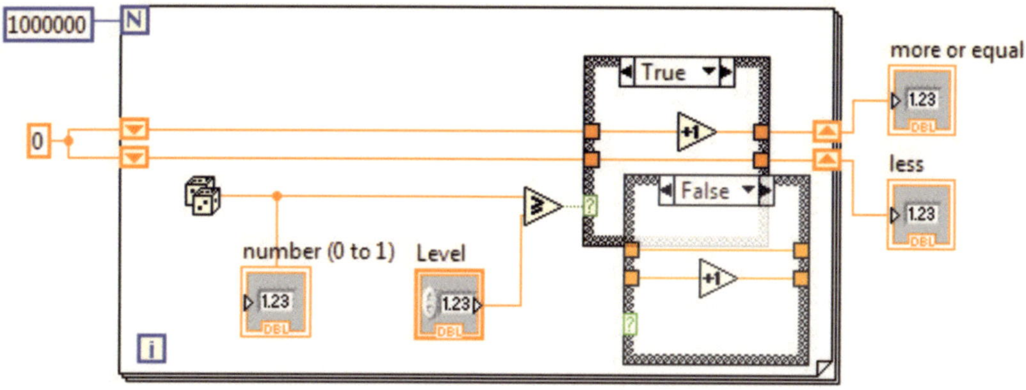

Fig. 6. An example of using shift registers to store values from previous loop iteration

When choosing data type the least time and memory consuming variable type that still complies with the algorithm should be used. If we replace the type of both counters from Double to 32-bit Integer, the execution time decreases from 41 ns to 35 ns. Finally, if "Level" control is not required to change during the loop iteration it is better to put it outside the loop so the control is read only once and after that its value is read from the input tunnel of the loop in each iteration. This further decreases the execution time to 33 ns.

It is important to avoid all unnecessary operations that are performed repeatedly within loops. All constants and calculations that are placed in a loop and result in constant values should be put outside. If possible also avoid data type coercions (marked by small red dots) since they insert additional operation and extra memory buffer that stores the new variables' data.

2.3 Memory management

Memory and disk operations are the main source of latencies in computes. If memory requirements are known in advance, memory can be allocated statically. When you launch the application, memory is allocated according to known global memory requirements of the application and it remains allocated while the application runs. Static memory allocation is simple to work with because the compiler handles all the details.

However, in most application it is impossible to determine what would be the memory requirement in advance. With dynamic memory allocation, memory is reserved when needed and freed afterwards when not used anymore. Dynamic allocation though requires more processor time than static, especially if memory consumption grows during the execution of an application, which results in slower execution speed and fragmented memory. LabVIEW utilises special Memory management module, which is a set special routines for allocating and deallocating memory. It can statically or dynamically allocate, manipulate and deallocate memory as needed and the developer doesn't have to concern about that as would be the case of using conventional C or C++ programming. However, although LabVIEW takes care of all memory management details, a serious developer should be aware of when the memory allocation is performed and how to tailor the code in the way that the particular data memory is reused instead of copied to a new allocated memory block.

Large amount of data is usually stored in a form of arrays or strings, where string is physically stored as an array of unsigned 8-bit integer. Both data types are stored in continuous memory blocks. Conversion of string to unsigned 8-bit array or back is performed by function "String to Byte Array" or "Byte Array to String" which does not actually change the data stored in memory but only changes its representation. This operation is similar to "Type Cast" function which changes the memory interpretation to or from any kind of variable type. In general type casting is very useful to interpret the data in a binary format that are usually read from external devices, e.g. instruments. Binary data transfer is often used since it greatly improves the utilisation of the communication bandwidth of the bus, such as RS-232 or GPIB. However, typecasting does the same operation as flatten to string and unflatten from string and the new temporary buffer is allocated if data have to be reinterpreted and this cannot be avoided even by "In Place Element" structure that is intended to prevent new buffer allocations in the data flow.

When manipulating with arrays LabVIEW can utilise the same memory block of the source array to store the result, if possible. This is very important if the size of array is large saving a lot of time and memory needed for memory allocation and data copying. However, this is not always possible and depends also on the developer's approach of problem solving.

LabVIEW 2010 offers a tool called Show Buffer Allocations, found under Tools->Profile menu. By this tool you can actually see at which points in the diagram new memory buffers are allocated and let the developer to tailor his software in a way that allocated memory is reused more efficiently.

LabVIEW inherently tries to minimize new buffer allocations by analysing the data flow. An example in Fig. 7 shows two almost identical cases. An 8-bit integer array is initialised and after that each element is multiplied with a "Numeric" control value. A case in the right hand side uses 32-bit integer type of "Numeric" control to multiply the array elements. This requires array type conversion to 32-bit integer data type followed by a new memory allocation to store it. If the left diagram requires 1 MB to process the array data and 1 MB to display it (2 MB all together), the right one requires 1 MB for initialised array, 4 times that much to convert it to 32-bit integer and the same amount to display it (9 MB all together).

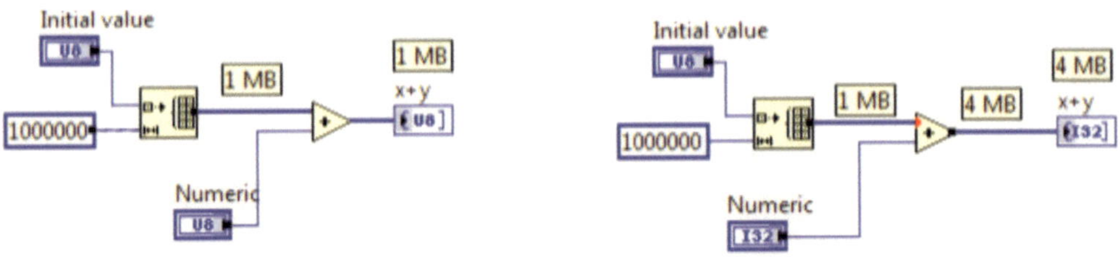

Fig. 7. An example of data type conversion (red dot at the upper input of addition function) requiring new buffer allocation (black square at the output of addition function)

It is clearly seen from results in Fig. 7 that one should avoid type conversion if large amount of data is processed. Developer should use consistent data types for arrays and watch for coercion dots when passing data to functions. Furthermore, displaying large arrays and strings on front panel also increases memory consumption since the array indicator uses its own memory buffer for data storage. In order to decrease memory consumption one should avoid using front panel indicators to store large amount of data. If the VI is used as a SubVI front panel should stay closed if not used thus the required memory block for front panel objects would not be allocated. However, if some property nodes connected to any front panel object are used in the diagram, the front panel memory allocates completely. Since

LabVIEW also uses front panel information to determine possible optimizations, wiring front panel controls holding large amount of data to the connector pane can reduce the number of buffer allocations.
LabVIEW tries to minimise the number of buffers according to the dataflow and functions used to process the data. If dataflow fans out to several branches the new buffer allocations are made according to the node functions that these branches are connected to. An example shown in Fig. 8 manipulates the same array data by functions in parallel.

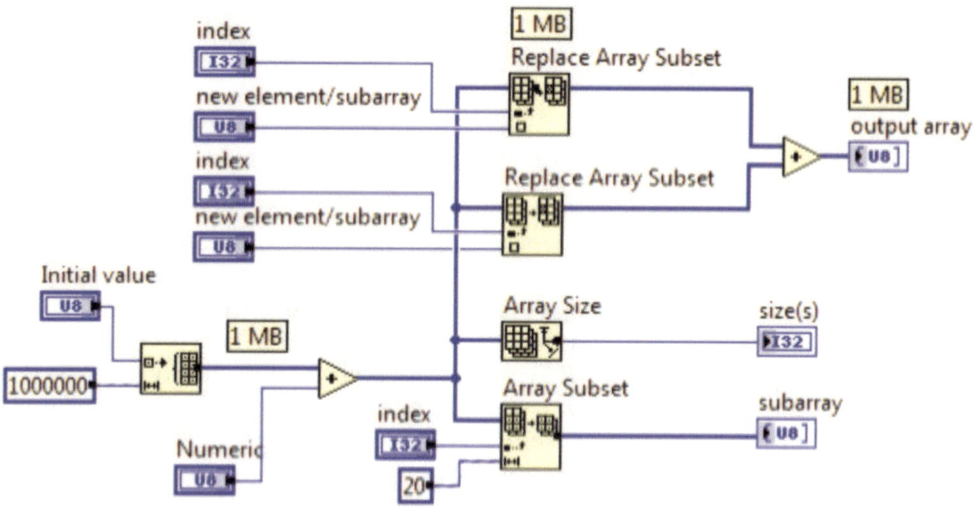

Fig. 8. An example of data path fan out and possible buffer allocations (denoted as small black squares in the block diagram)

Functions that do not alter content of the array can operate over the same buffer (Array Size, Array Subset, …) and allocate their own buffers to store their output data, which are usually smaller. The functions that alter the content of the array can also operate on the same buffer, if possible. Since array data at fan out flows in parallel, no execution order is forced in any way and LabVIEW can decide which function to execute first. In order to retain the required functionality without new buffer allocations LabVIEW chooses first to execute functions that don't alter the array data and afterwards all others. However, if two functions (e.g. Replace Array Subset) that alter the data are used in parallel an additional buffer copy has to be allocated since outputs of both functions must be consistent with the input data. Thus the example shown in Fig. 9 uses 3MB of memory to store the data. If only one "Replace array subset" was used for the same purpose, the additional 1MB buffer would not be allocated.
When designing the block diagram, a designer has to be aware of any areas where the size of data changes frequently in a flow, such us increasing of array or string size. Since strings and arrays are stored in a continuous memory blocks, at each node that increase the data size a new memory allocation occurs leading to fragmented memory which gives a lot of work to LabVIEW Memory Manager.
For array initialisation it is most convenient to use "Initialise Array" function if elements of constant value are permitted. If array values have to be dynamically generated the most efficient way is to use loops with output tunnels with enabled indexing. If loop count is known in advance the memory block of the requested size is allocated only once just before

entering the loop. If the array size is not known in advance (e.g. wiring the control to the count terminal), the memory is allocated dynamically during the loop iterations. However LabVIEW is smart enough not to allocate one array element at each loop iteration but rather allocates larger blocks of memory at each *n*-th run of the loop reducing the time overhead and memory fragmentation to minimum.

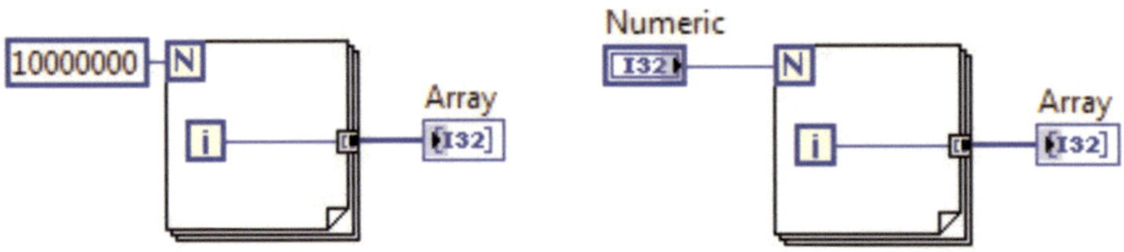

Fig. 9. Examples of the most efficient ways of creating arrays.

One of the problems that often occur is reading some data from external instrument in a continuous manner and storing it to an array. In such cases usually the amount of data is not known in advance and thus memory buffer cannot be preallocated. Fig. 10 shows a simple solution that is not recommended if large amount of data is expected to be read. The "Build array" function continuously increases the array size by allocating new and new chunks of memory as data are passed from the "485 read" SubVI. After a while the array that is passed by shift registers through loop iterations would be stored in a fragmented memory that would require more and more time for LabVIEW Memory Manager to allocate. This would finally start to slow down loop execution resulting in buffer overflows and possible data loss.

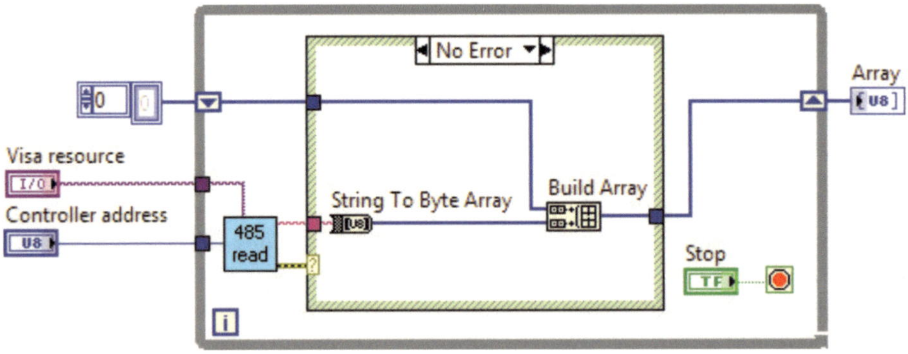

Fig. 10. The easiest but the least efficient solution to continuous data reading and storage in a dynamically allocated array.

In such cases it is advisory to avoid applying concatenate string and build array functions to large strings or arrays since every execution changes the size of data and requires new buffer allocation. A developer should use "replace string/array subset" functions instead and initialise data at the beginning if size is known in advance. If not, then increase the size of the array in large increments when necessary as the loop runs and use "replace array subset" otherwise. An example of improved algorithm for continuous data storage is shown in Fig. 11.

In this solution the current array write index has to be stored separately for "Replace Array Subset" function. Initially an empty array of certain size is allocated and passed to shift register. After each execution of "485 read" SubVI the size of the stored data in the array together with the size of the returned data is calculated and compared to the total array size. If the returned data do not fit in the array the "Build array" function is called to increase the array. Initial array size should be chosen according to the expected data size, returned by "485 read" function and total amount of data. Smaller value means more often buffer allocations while larger value can lead to unnecessarily oversized buffer for array data storage.

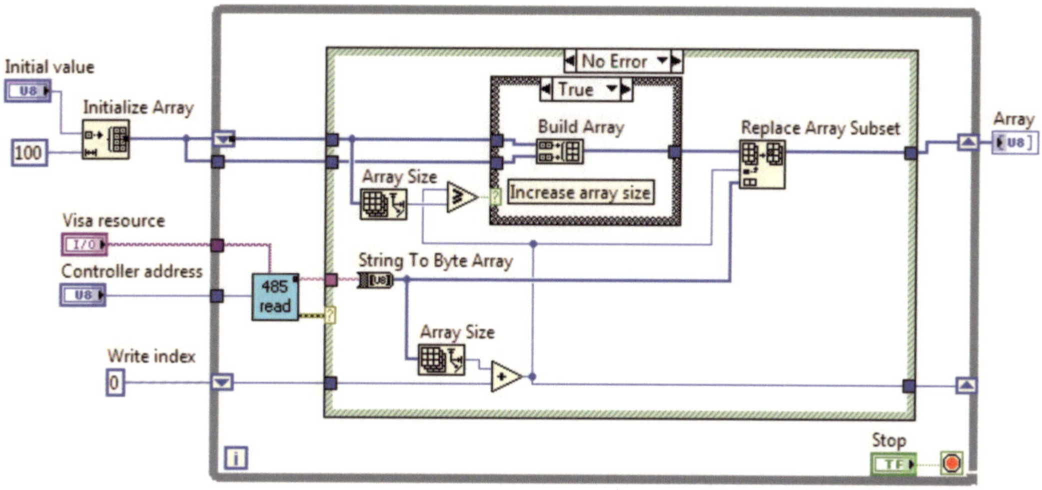

Fig. 11. An efficient way of dynamic memory allocation for data that are continuously read.

3. Organising the LabVIEW code

Dataflow concept of LabVIEW's code execution is very close to the engineering way of thinking and solving problems. Nevertheless, no one can expect a successful result without basic problem solving skills, regardless of how easy and user friendly the software environment is. LabVIEW offers many ways to solve the problem from beginning to an end and it is a developer's choice which way to follow. This is the first trap in which one can be caught. It is smart to ask yourself a question: Which way to take? And the answer would be: "It depends of the problem."

Let's presume that a problem is well defined. By knowing the problem one should have a clear idea of what are the required functionalities of the software. The requirements are usually formed together with an end user at the beginning but they can also evolve during the software development. A very common problem that people have is that they start to develop software by not knowing exactly what the requirements are. And the result is often a wasted effort when the software has to be partly or even completely rewritten when some new features need to be added that are slightly out of the chosen concept. Therefore, the first step in LabVIEW application development should be a clear definition of all requirements that are completely understood, agreed, approved by all partners and documented.

Starting from that point a developer can identify the inputs, outputs and finally design the algorithm. When the algorithm is well defined it is the right time to run the LabVIEW and start to translate the algorithm into code. The developer has to choose the most efficient way of applying it in to a graphical code, maximising readability and performance of the code.

LabVIEW provides several options to choose from; each optimal for a specific target application.

3.1 Linear data flow

If the problem is trivial and the software is intended for one's own use, linear data flow programming style can be used. This suits for cases, where you have some input data that have to be processed and results written out. The algorithm can have some loops or other structures implemented, but the solely task of the software is, that it executes once and then terminates, passing results to some outputs. From definition of dataflow execution concept it is obvious that every diagram node executes when all of its inputs are present and after the execution it passes data forward to other nodes. The dataflow is linear and defined by wire connections. In Fig. 12 an example of a linear dataflow code is shown that reads one single measurement from data acquisition (DAQ) interface.

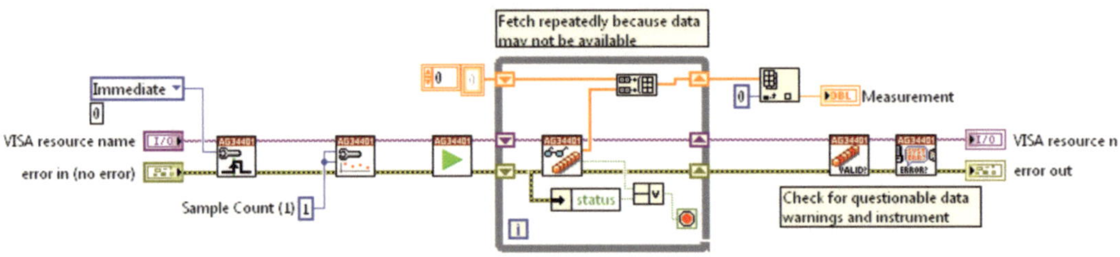

Fig. 12. Example of a linear dataflow programming style (taken from NI DAQ example)

Linear data flow style is usually the first approach that beginners start with regardless of the nature of the problem to be solved. In most cases this leads to several execution, memory and readability problems when the code evolves. In Fig. 13 an example is presented, showing such software, made in the linear data flow programming style. It evolved from simple task as shown in Fig. 12 and then expanded adding various features later on.

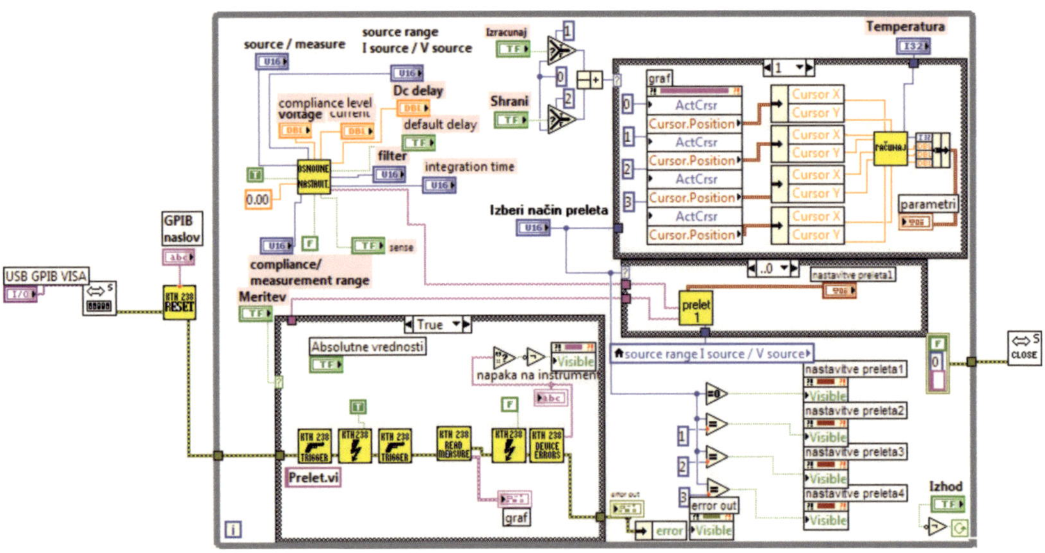

Fig. 13. External instrument driver via GPIB by using linear data flow programming style

This block diagram is well organised, all building blocks are aligned, dataflow direction goes from left to right as we are used to and errors are properly handled, but it is still pretty clumsy in the sense of its expandability. The software development started as a simple task to control an external instrument via GPIB and return measurement results. Although not intended at beginning it finally resulted in a top level application that interacts with end user via controls and indicators on front panel. Unsuitable design used at the very beginning resulted in a bad user experience:

- Initialisation of the GPIB interface is outside the main loop. The software has to be restarted in the case of GPIB connection error or just to update GPIB device changes.
- All user interfacing is done via buttons on front panel which is not common in modern computer application (e.g. File saving).
- The main loop is polling the values of front panel controls as fast as it can, thus taking much of the processor time that could be available to other applications. The same fact states for updating front panel indicators.

For that reason this software was completely overwritten making majority of the invested effort fruitless.

3.2 Handling events

Events represent the core functionality of any contemporary operating system. Introducing event handling in LabVIEW is almost inevitable when the target software has emphasis on user interface. Such an example is shown in Fig. 14. The event structure, which handles events that are generated from user activities on front panel, is placed in the main program loop. The software controls full colour LED reflector by sending appropriate string commands via USB interface.

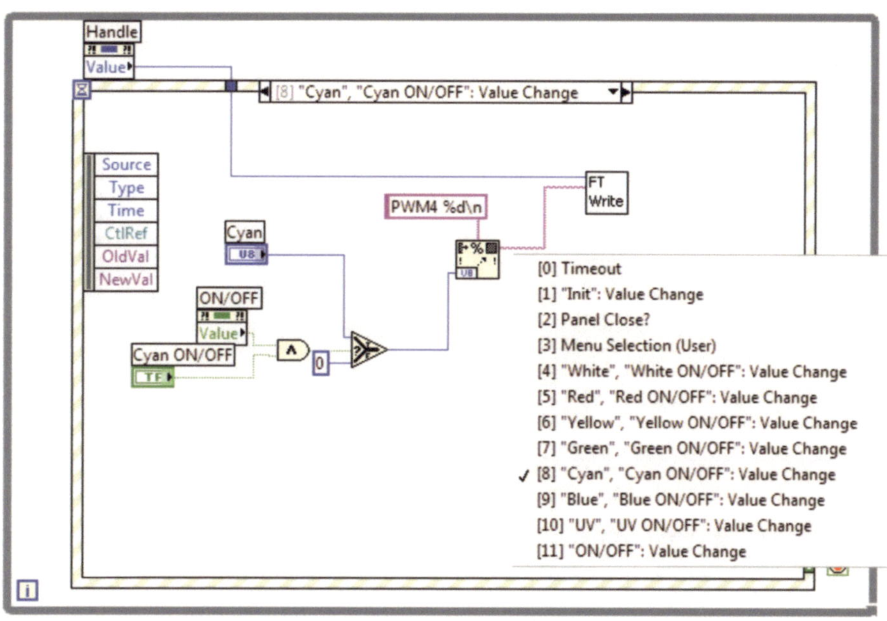

Fig. 14. Example of handling the user interface activities by event structure.

Each event case is assigned to one or more events that can be triggered by front panel object by user or code itself. In this particular case seven sliders control seven LEDs of different

colours together with ON/OFF knobs for each colour. USB write function (FT write) ends immediately if the write operation is not successful making this software responsive even if USB device is malfunctioning. USB interface is initialised in the "init:Value Change" case, which is assigned to a hidden "init" button. The dataflow is made in such a way that the "init:Value Change" event is triggered automatically when the software starts by "Value signaling" property node.
If the USB interface initialisation fails, it runs the same event again until initialisation completes or user closes the software as shown in Fig. 15. Making user defined events in such a way has lot of possibilities. Besides (hidden) front panel objects that can be used solely for software user event triggering LabVIEW offers special user event VIs that can generate software events. This makes event handling very versatile. The problem however occurs if a piece of code inside some event case gets stuck. This often happens trying to read data from external hardware that does not respond. The whole event structure waits till the individual event case completes and it cannot be interrupted with other events pending. Certainly, it is wise to implement a timeout in the functions that read data from external instruments. However, this only partly solves the problem since timeouts for some instruments are required to be in the range of 10 seconds or more.

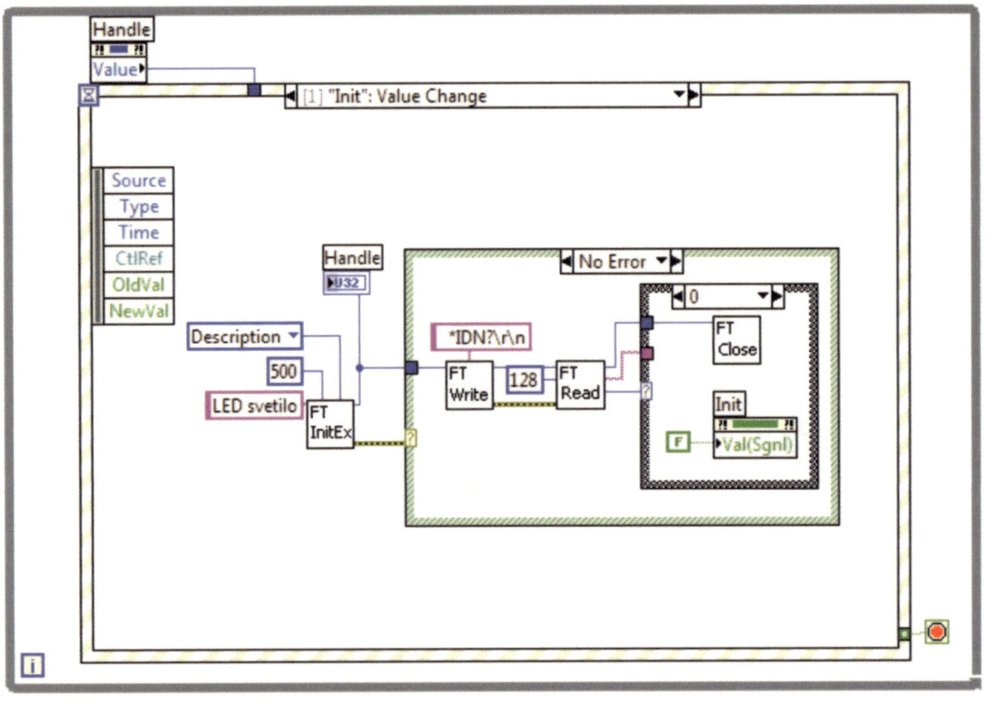

Fig. 15. "Init" case, where the USB interface is initialised and if it fails, the same event is called again by "Value signaling" property node of "Init" button

3.3 State machine

State machines in LabVIEW basically do not differ from other implementations. They represent the solution to a problem in a form of a state diagram, providing most clear and robust solution. In contrast to event handling, state machines are meant for fast execution and data content handling in cases, where user's interaction is small or even not present. The implementation of a state machine is shown in Fig 16. It consist of a while loop, where for each state a separate case is defined. The state is stored in a shift register, which can hold any type of data in general. Nevertheless, the most appropriate data type would be (enumerated) integer allowing fastest loop execution and lowest memory occupation. The inner while loop passes the state value from previous to next iteration together with other relevant data via shift registers. In each case a code is executed according to the state specifications and the next state number is chosen based on the results.

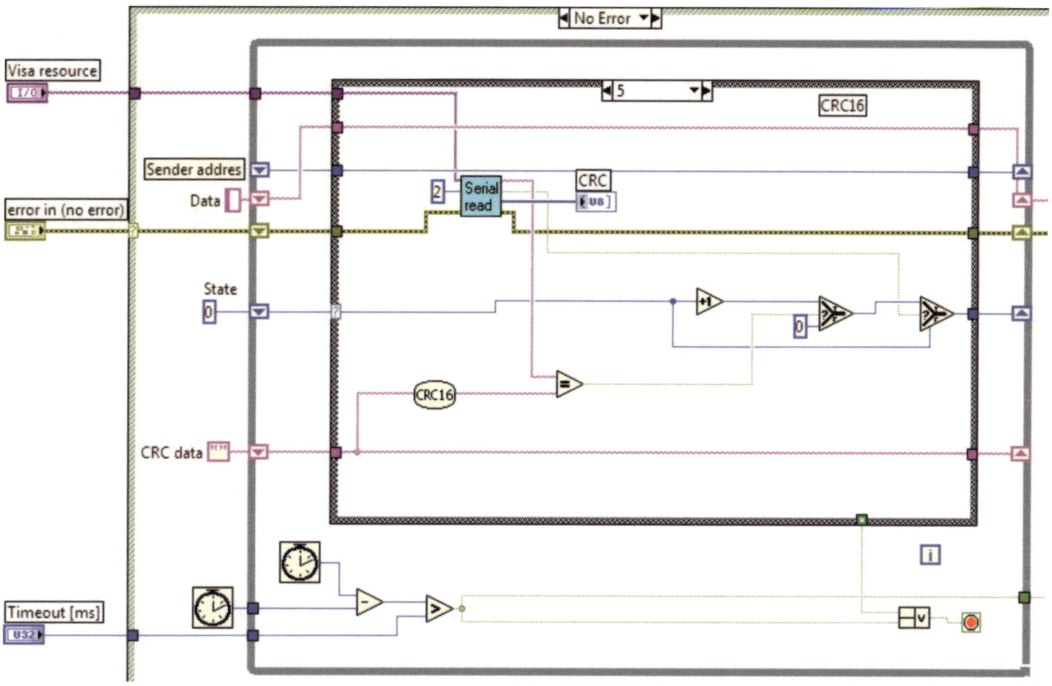

Fig. 16. Example of a state machine for handling RS-485 serial communication protocol

This particular state diagram handles data that are read from RS-485 port according to communication protocol requirements. The presented state reads 16-bit CRC value from input data stream and compares it to the calculated value. If the results match the next state is chosen, otherwise the state returns to 0, at which it waits for the first byte of the communication frame. If the "Serial read" function returns no data i.e. the data have not arrived yet, the same state repeats. Timeout is implemented by reading time in ms before entering the loop for a reference time and comparing it to a time inside loop iterations. Since the timer function returns ms timer value in 32-bit unsigned integer format it can overflow. For that a subtraction is performed of both timer values prior comparison thus eliminating the overflow problems.

By using state machine programming style it is very easy to change or add some new features, but it is not convenient for handling user interface actions. The main reason is that in every state all relevant buttons have to be handled resulting in unnecessary processor load. Furthermore, if several states are present it is a lot of work to add additional user interface features. For user interface event handling a separate default state can be defined in which all buttons and other front panel object states can be polled. In such a way the user interface actions are polled only when no other operation is going on. Such an approach is easier to implement but prone to become irresponsive if state machine doesn't enter the default state frequently enough or stays in some other state for a longer time.

3.4 Master-slave design style

Most of the main applications require user interface handling with fast response and also fast code execution in the background. For that at least two parallel dataflows are required. They are arranged in two main loops, where the first (master loop) handles front panel activities usually by event structure and second (slave loop) executes all other software activities. An example is shown in Fig. 17. To assure parallel executions of both loops they shouldn't be connected by wires in the way that dataflow would force sequential execution of loops. In order to pass data between both loops the queue functions are most appropriate to use. The only connection between both loops is the obtained queue reference wire, which is the input data of both queues and thus parallel execution is allowed. Although the queue data can be of any type, the easiest way would be a string type in which any text message can be passed or an enumerated integer.

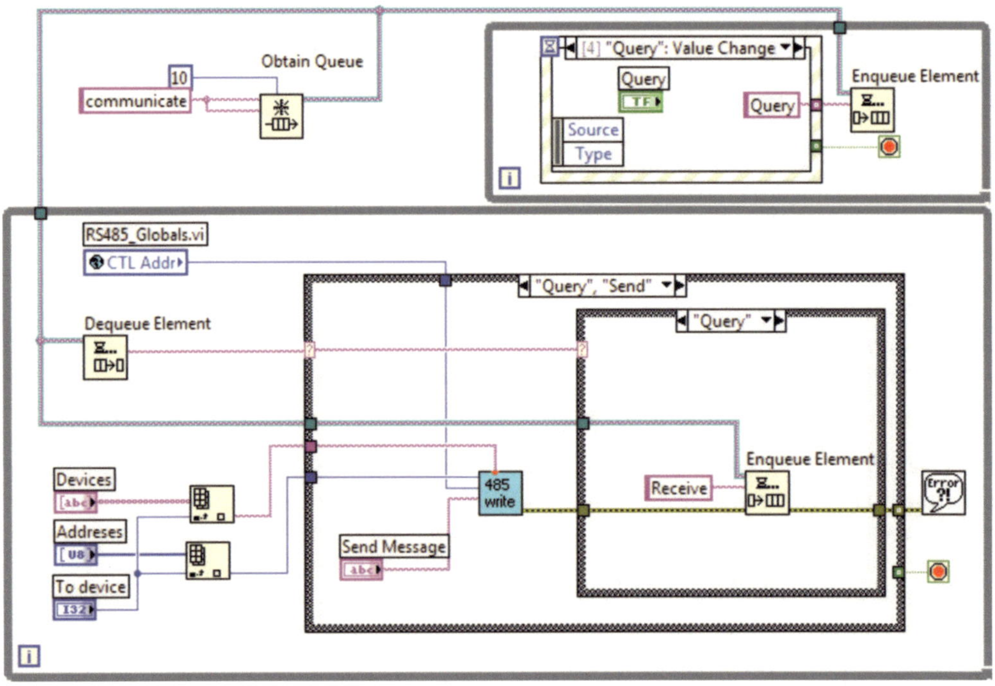

Fig. 17. Master-Slave design with two loops that run in parallel

In Fig. 17 a top level application is presented that acts as a communication terminal over RS-485 bus. Case structure in the slave loop executes different cases according to the de-queued string. Strings that are used as commands can be queued anywhere. In this particular case a value change event of query button (Button pressed) sends "Query" command to slave loop, where a "Query" case is executed. The same case executes also when "Send" command arrives, since both are required first to send message over RS-485 bus. But additionally in the case of "Query", the "Receive" command is additionally queued if no error occurs. In the next run of slave loop the "Receive" string is dequeued and a corresponding case is executed. The advantage of this approach is that the front panel event handling is disconnected from code execution, allowing that both run independently. The problem can be divided into simple actions that can be easily implemented in the slave loop and these actions are then executed according to the front panel events and results of previous executions (e.g. error outputs or other). This makes such an approach much more versatile since many combinations of different cases and events are possible. Furthermore, if execution of a certain case freezes for longer time (waiting for receive communication timeout), the master loop is still running and captures front panel events. The problem of software responsiveness however is only partially solved since the slave loop still doesn't respond until the function in the failed case is timed out.

Thus we need to implement a way of breaking the execution of a SubVI, which waits for timeout. One way to do that is to read the queue size, i.e. number of elements pending for de-queuing. If the queue size is a larger than zero it means that a front panel event is pending and the current execution in the slave loop should break and continue to service another string in a queue. But this approach allows only one queued message at a time which can be quite a limitation in some cases. A special break message can also be reserved for slave loop breaking at which any slave function would break the execution. It can be queued from master loop by a special cancel key or event on exiting the software or similar.

4. Conclusion

Programming in LabVIEW looks easy, since the dataflow, functionality of execution nodes and data types of wire connections are visually presented. Peoples' graphical perception is much more efficient and faster way of acquiring information comparing it to textual, which makes graphical programming so attractive. However, an experienced LabVIEW developer should be aware of all possible pitfalls that are hidden behind the neat wires and functions. This chapter provides beginners and advanced developers with some general rules illustrated by examples taken out from real life applications. A developer should check his software with LabVIEW Profile tools on regular basis, isolate and correct the issues. It is not good to waste time striving to perfect every detail but rather isolate main problems that slow down the software execution and increases memory usage. These problems lie in complex or large memory data structures that are improperly handled and in frequently executed parts of the software that perform unnecessary calculations.

5. References

Bishop, R. H. (2004). *Learning with Labview 7 Express*, Pearson Prentice-Hall Int., ISBN 0-13-117605-6

Gorup, Ž. (2006).*Uvod v Labview*, Fakultetazaelektrotehniko, ISBN 961-243-036-5, Ljubljana, Slovenija

Hogg, S. (November 2010). What is LabVIEW? In: NI developers zone, Available from http://zone.ni.com/devzone/cda/pub/p/id/1141

Kerrry, E. (April 2011) Memory management in LabVIEW 8.5, In: NI developers zone, Available from http://zone.ni.com/devzone/cda/pub/p/id/241

NI Tutorial. (October 2006). LabVIEW and Hyperthreading, In: NI developers zone, Available from http://zone.ni.com/devzone/cda/tut/p/id/3558

Travis, J.&Kring, J. (2006).*LabVIEW for Everyone: Graphical Programming Made Easy and Fun (3rd Edition)*, Prentice hall, ISBN 0-13-185672-3

The Importance of a Deep Knowledge of LabVIEW Environment and Techniques in Order to Develop Effective Applications

Riccardo de Asmundis
Istituto Nazionale di fisica nucleare, Section of Napoli,
Physics Departement University "Federico II",
Italy

1. Introduction

LabVIEW development system is spreading out in many applicative fields: industry, research fields, controls and monitoring designs; automatic measurement systems as well as machine controls or robotics; FPGA design associated with real time applications, artificial vision and enhanced controls in industrial processes. These circumstances create the need to prepare many people in the correct approach in the design, manipulation and management of both simple, complex and extensive LabVIEW Applications and Projects.

All these conditions imply the necessity of having good programmers involved in such a job: very often this statement is not at all reflected by the real working conditions with evident critical consequences on the resulting style and quality of the Applications delivered. You must be aware from the easy paradigm of the type "I understood, it's easy to do", without investing time and human resources to correctly study the development system before making Applications of a high level (Bishop 2009). Programming in LabVIEW must be considered as a serious job exactly like programming in any other language; expertise and professionalism play an essential role in the correct design in order to accomplish the final result of having a solution which is effective, robust, scalable in the future, reliable and pleasant to use or manage. If these conditions are unsatisfactory I would suggest either avoid programming in LabVIEW or delegating someone else with the correct expertise in making programming on it, or spend some time on your own in learning and becoming proficient in this knowledge process in order to obtain the best results for your Applications.

1.1 What the bad programmer loses?

A bad programmer is usually not conscious of being a bad programmer. Just like the mistakes made while learning a new human language, a bad programmer isn't aware of the mistakes he is making, either since he does not know about different solutions or he is not conscious of using a bad one, or he underestimates the consequences of an erroneous or poor design; these consequences are frequently "masked" by the exceptional quality of the G-Compiler, Memory Manager or other elements contained in the Run Time Engine, or the machine performance and whatever is done behind the scenes in helping arrive at a final successful execution and good apparent behaviour: in other words, LabVIEW is strongly "robust against stupidity" and the programmer often doesn't see it. Please, try to avoid the principle of "whatever works is ok for me".

The most evident damages of bad programming can be visible in both the short and long terms: in the short term the programmer can undergo a possible personal stress in manipulating the generally extended front panels, with poorly identifiable objects onto it; complex block diagrams are usually related to them and have typical drawbacks: for instance they do not fit into the PC window of the screen and oblige the programmer to move the window up-down and left-right continuously, creating incredible difficulties in following the wire routing. Under these conditions it becomes hard to include new parts of code to extend functionalities, for both loss in space into the diagram and loss in technicalities which help in this process. As a result the solution is unsatisfactory and the programmer will dislike the development system and probably the language itself, or, worse, he will continue to design Applications in this way without taking advantage of the advanced tools and clean designing which are all possible in LabVIEW (Essic 2008) (Johnson G. W. 1994).

On the other hand, the heritage of such a badly written code by a different programmer is usually a shocking event whose solution passes several times through a complete redesigning of the Project. In the long term, developers like these do not encourage the use of the system at all: they tend not to choose LabVIEW because they finally don't know how the system really works and how to use it in terms of programming. They think it is not sufficiently clear, that the desired results cannot be easily reached, and sometimes that "LabVIEW is slow". All these bad opinions come uniquely from their own responsibility: the one of not knowing the system correctly and, sometimes, of simply having to accept the fact that they will have to spend sufficient time in learning all its features.

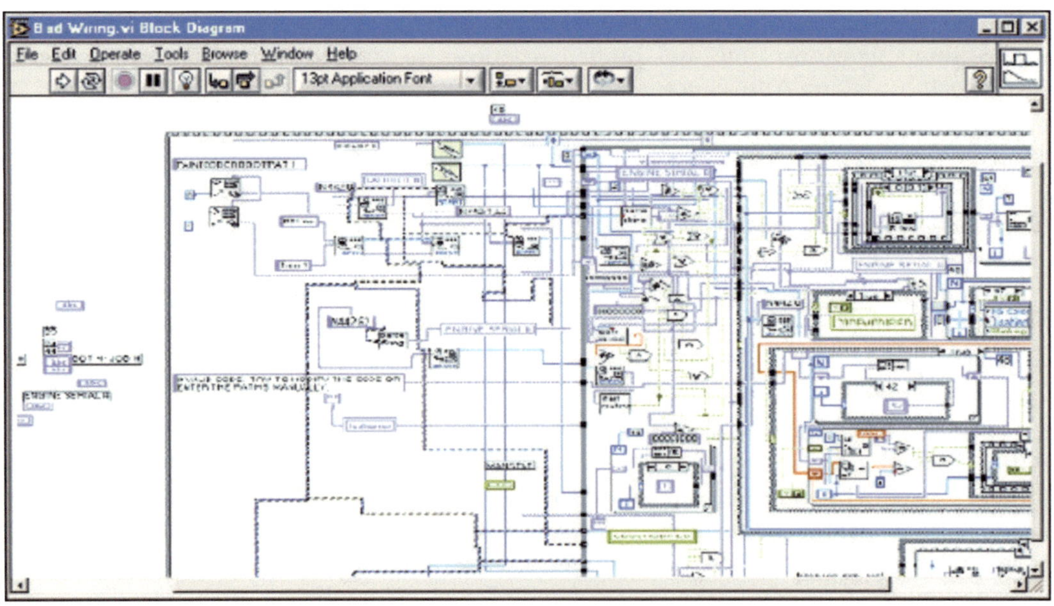

Fig. 1. Example of a typical result of a "badly designed" block diagram.

Lot of recommendations come even from official LabVIEW courses: if you look at the Figure 1 the example reported comes from one of the official LabVIEW Intermediate courses just as an example of what *should never happen* when programming in LabVIEW (National Instruments 2010).

From here I wish to start with my series of recommendations, which I will try to indicate in such a way in order to allow the reader to keep track of them and use them in the future as a reference.

Recommendation 1) Don't allow diagrams to go out of the development window sizes; if this cannot be avoided for grouping reasons ([1]) do it in a single direction, the best would be in the horizontal one.

Avoid diagrams whose development goes out of the screen. If your diagram is starting to have an aspect similar to the ones in Figure 1 (out of the screen, too many wires, too many superposition, confusion,...), stop your development and think about the right solutions: adopt the modularity model typical of LabVIEW by using SubVIs. Open a new VI and start to write your code into it. Then you will define the final character and finality of the SubVI you are developing in order to include it into the whole project (main VI) as a subpart. In other words *think modularly!*

1.2 The data dependency model

LabVIEW uses a "Data Dependency Model". This concept is strongly stressed into all main and basic courses like the LabVIEW Core 1 course. Self-teaching developers tends to underestimate this concept, even if they have seen it in the Core 1 self-course. If the developer does not adequately consider the data dependency he will experience several problems. One is to

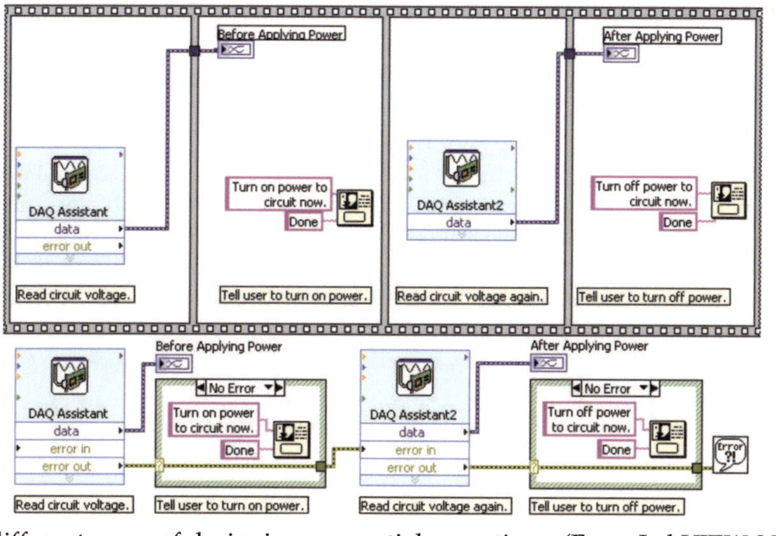

Fig. 2. Two different ways of designing sequential operations. (From LabVIEW 2009-Core 1 course manual, Lesson 8 "Using Sequential Programming").

[1] Like a SubVI which has to complete some operation in a whole (i.e. a complete communication with an instrument or a complete access to a file,...)

arrange the parts of his VI badly, which have to be executed in sequence: hyper-usage of Sequences Structures generally indicates a non-understanding of the data dependency issues, poor management of the available structures, a strong mental conditioning coming from classical text-based programming languages probably utilized in the past. And here we can introduce the next recommendation:

Recommendation 2) Avoid using the Sequence Structures. Sequences are not considered in the official courses unless for marginal purposes: they overcome the data dependency paradigm which is the main point of force in LabVIEW. Make the effort in using data dependency instead. Mainly **use the error cluster** to create data dependency which forces the sequence of execution and, at the same time, takes care of produced errors.

Error cluster is a main topic in the LabVIEW environment. Their use is not only recommended but is vital for good programming structures and final reliability of the application. Lots of aspects have to be analysed concerning the Error treatments and a specific paragraph will be dedicated to it. In the Figure 2, the contrast between the two indicated solutions to create a sequence is shown. The first is "forced" by the flat sequence structure; the second is naturally invited to be sequential thanks to the data dependency: the error cluster makes the operations naturally in sequence and its usage allows it to act with the right messages to the user in case of error/no-error. Try to comprehend this example to amplify the concept of data dependency model: *LabVIEW executes nodes as data are available at its entrance.*

Finally the Sequence Structures have another drawback: several developers tend to affectionate to them avoiding using of most of the existing alternatives: State Machines, for examples, can be used in the place of many Sequences Structures, with the big advantage of letting the program flow to "choice" the step to be performed, which is, on the contrary, fixed for the Sequences.

1.3 The development environment: project explorer and the organization of the proper job

In my daily experience I see many programmers who don't have good organization of their work in terms of the storing resources in the PC: precise rules should be used for the locations in which the VIs related to a project or VIs coming from third parts (like Instruments Drivers) must be stored (Sumathi, Surekha 2007). Very frequently people can be confused regarding this issue, and this causes problems: the most frequent problem is losing control of what version of certain SubVI the developer is using: this aspect can lead to very serious problems, like the non-functioning of a VI (even the "main one") that worked the day before! Such a situation can happen if a version conflict is engaged due to different and old versions of VIs on the machine.

Here are some suggestions to consider for good organization for a correct outcome:

Rule 1) Decide an "official" area on the machine in which a**ll LabVIEW Projects or Applications must be stored** and use that area at all times.

a. **Do not use the Windows "Desktop"** to store work, or folders located on the desktop.
b. Chose a **subfolder of the main "Document"** folder relative to the developer account, which must have Administrator's privileges.
c. As an alternative to point b., use the **"LabVIEW Data" folder,** automatically created by the LabVIEW installation.

Rule 2) **Create a subfolder for every project** you develop: all material developed uniquely for that project must be stored in that folder.
Rule 3) **Subdivide the folder of the project into several subfolder**, each of them containing VIs, Controls, Menu, etc. for specific tasks: see figure 3 for an example.
Rule 4) **Use the project explorer:** the project explorer must reproduce the organization you are keeping in the file system. See figure 4 for the aspect of the project explorer related to the Project.

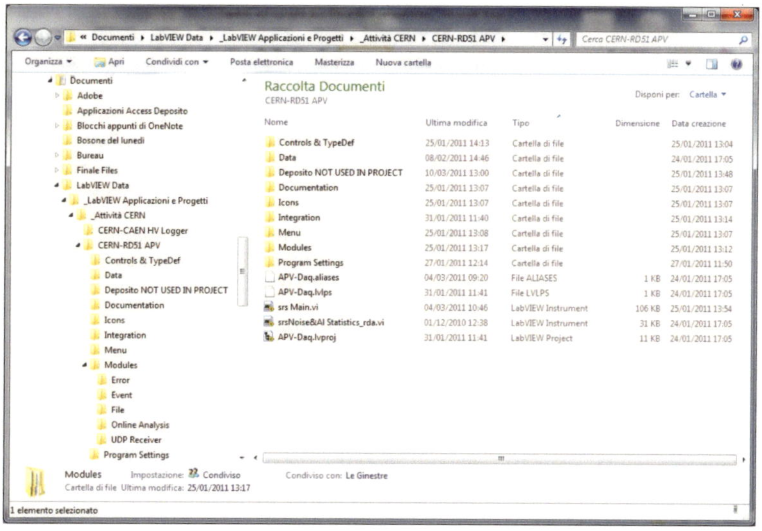

Fig. 3. An example of a folder containing a project. Remark the readability in such an organization created thanks to a subdivision in lower subfolder.

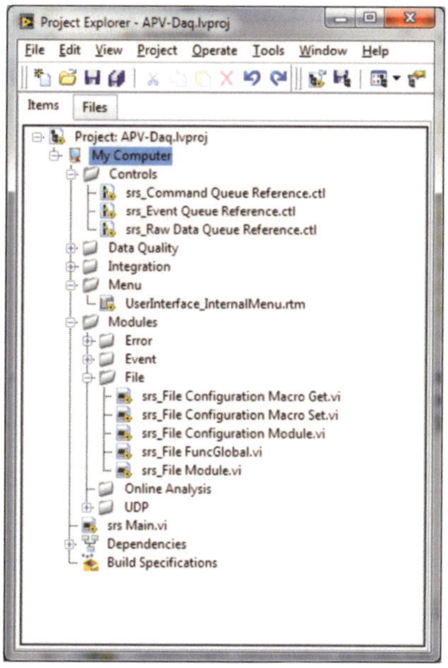

Fig. 4. Aspect of the Project Explorer window relative to the example above.

Project Explorer not only allows you to keep track of the organization of all files (VIs, data files, LabVIEW menus, other accompanying files for documentation too) but also gives several instruments not available in other ways: building a stand-alone Application is an example, as well as creating and managing Shared Variables.
Remember that you have at least two ways to create subfolders in the Project Explorer: the "Virtual Folder" and the "Auto populating Folder". The latter replicates what you do in the actual Windows directories, while with the former you need to explicitly manipulate them in the Project Explorer in order to organize the materials. The former is not always preferable: in my example I used Virtual Folders (i.e. "manual" organization) only.

Rule 5) Be careful if you save new versions of SubVIs with the same name but under different location. It's possible that, at a new reload of the Project, the system links an older version of these SubVI's, causing incomprehensive malfunctioning. If you need to change the location only of a sub-VI, **pay attention in removing the old version by deleting it** or, if useful for future references, move them to a storage area called "deposit" or similar, with a different name (i.e. "mySubVI_**OLD**.vi").

Rule 6) Last: if you need to use a third part software like Instruments Drivers, take care that the **whole driver folder is located in the official Instruments directory of LabVIEW,** like C:\Program Files\National Instruments\LabVIEW 2009\instr.lib, depending on the LabVIEW version you have. Official subdirectory must be "**instr**" folder. This allows LabVIEW to look at the existing drivers and to create the appropriate buttons in the Functions Palette window. Drivers stored there, are not erased when you uninstall the LabVIEW version in view of installing a new one: you just need to copy the whole driver folder to the new "instr" subfolder of the new installation (National Instruments 2010).

2. The correct design of front panels

Front Panels represent a critical job that is very often underestimated. It is true that, in case of a VI used as a quick, short and "fast" check, it is not worth spending a long time on the front panel: the problem is that from those poorly designed front panel, used in temporary VIs, we frequently evolve towards a large public utilization of the VI. The VI becomes from a short test, a "final user VI" and for this reason it must be correctly designed.
Poorly designed front panels usually suffer from the following drawbacks:

1. They are **larger than the screen size** and need to move window positioning bars, both horizontal and vertical.
2. They use lot of **"single" controls or indicators**, not separated among them well, creating confusion in the input and output objects.
3. They use **insupportable colours** on the objects or parts of the objects.
4. They use **inconsistent character sizes** and/or styles.
5. Controls and indicators **are labeled by their default names** (numeric 1, array 2,...).
6. They are not **user-friendly**.

In the Figure 5 you can see an example of a badly-designed front panel. Here a certain confusion exists in the destination of controls and indicators which are not organized well or logically and several character styles are used together (National Instruments 2010).

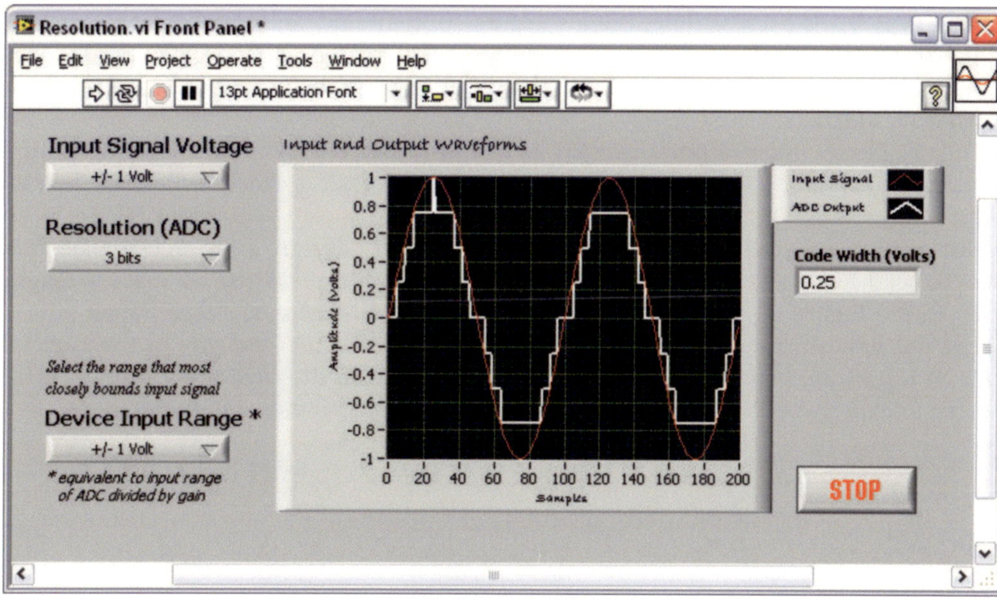

Fig. 5. A badly designed Front Panel. The use of different character styles, the non-clear assignment of controls and indicators cause confusion in the final user. (From National Instruments 2009-Core 1 Course presentation slides, Lesson 4 "implementing a VI").

Try to adopt certain rules in designing front panels. We can distinguish two categories of rules: the aesthetical ones and the functional ones. The problem is the two categories interfere each other. We try to resume in the following:

Aesthetical rules:

Rule 1) Avoid front panels that are bigger than the screen size. If more elements should be included use:

a. Tab Control to separate the elements in different logical context (i.e. all input/instrument settings, run control, output, error or alarm list, etc.).
b. Different windows as SubVIs which open for the running period only (i.e. small windows for setting, controlling etc.).

Rule 2) **Clearly organise controls and indicators for their correct purpose**: do not mix them in short space, but explicitly separate them for their functions. Regroup controls and indicators that are related to the same element (i.e. all controls of an instrument should be collected together in an unique portion of the screen or a specific tab of a Tab Control.

Rule 3) **Do not play with colours**: use default colours when possible. If an emphasis must be done use the light colours only and be uniform for entire parts (i.e. all controls of an instruments=light-blue).

Rule 4) Try to put yourself under the **final user point of view**; try to check the panel by thinking that the user has never seen it before. If necessary ask a colleague to check if the panel is easily understandable.

Functional rules:

Rule 5) Use specific labels for controls and indicators: **do not use default names** (numeric 1, 2, array 1, 2,…). Always give a representative name to the objects.

Rule 6) If labels became long, use a short one (mnemonic) and use **Caption instead on the front panel objects**. Establish your own rules for the name assignment for labels and/or captions and respect it. Example: Label CSM_BField; caption "Common Switch Magnet, Magnetic Field (Tesla)".

Rule 7) **Panels must respond quickly to any stimulus from the user** (coming from the mouse, TAB key,...) and must appear as animated (ex. a clock indicating day/time running).

The last point of the above list is strictly related to a correct design of the block diagram, but is very crucial for a good implementation. We will return on it when we discuss diagram issues. In the Figure 6 you can see an example of a well-designed Front Panel: note the absence not only of the displacement bars but also of all extra elements in the LabVIEW Menu on top of the window; such a solution contributes to the clearness of the VI and in avoiding unexpected behaviour at run time due to an improper use of the commands.

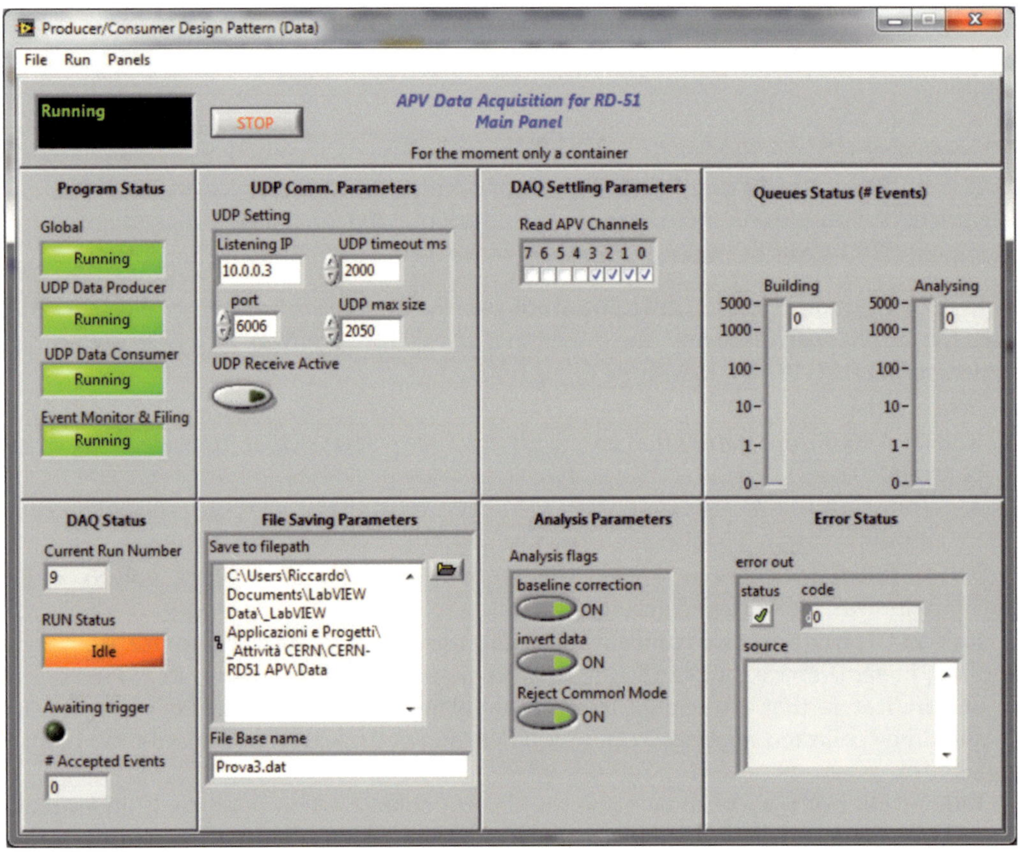

Fig. 6. An example of quite a good design for a Front Panel. Please note the subdivision of the panel into boxes clearly indicating the category or specificity of the elements included (from APV Data Acquisition System for CERN-Geneve, by R. de Asmundis).

In this case the VI presents only an overview of the execution status, indicating all the relevant elements involved: data are presented in separate panels. This solution has been adopted to further separate the logical aspect of the final Application.

In most cases, when a front panel must be revisited, **you may need a stop** to your development process, taking your time to decide how to reorganize it. Pressing in a fast design is the most dangerous aspect that can cause a bad design.

2.1 Custom menus

Usually all commands to be sent to a VI are implemented as graphical controls: buttons as Booleans, simple numeric controls or slides, dials etc. represent a natural "way of thinking" in LabVIEW. Nevertheless, if the number of implemented commands starts to be too high, basically on the main VI, different solutions are suggested. In this context **Custom Menus becomes a very useful alternative**. Custom Menus allow you to define your own menu items and organize them as you desire. Your custom menu is shown at run time on the VI window allowing the user to select from the menu voice the required function: the VI diagram has to handle the menu item voice by voice, by executing the related command, just as you would do by using Boolean buttons. Use event structure to handle, in an unique event case, all menu items. There are several useful examples concerning the menus which can be used as a starting point: this issue is quite a rich one and must be carefully studied. In the Figure 6 again, a custom menu is visible on top of the window, while in the figure 7, a possible programming solution for menu choice handling is shown.

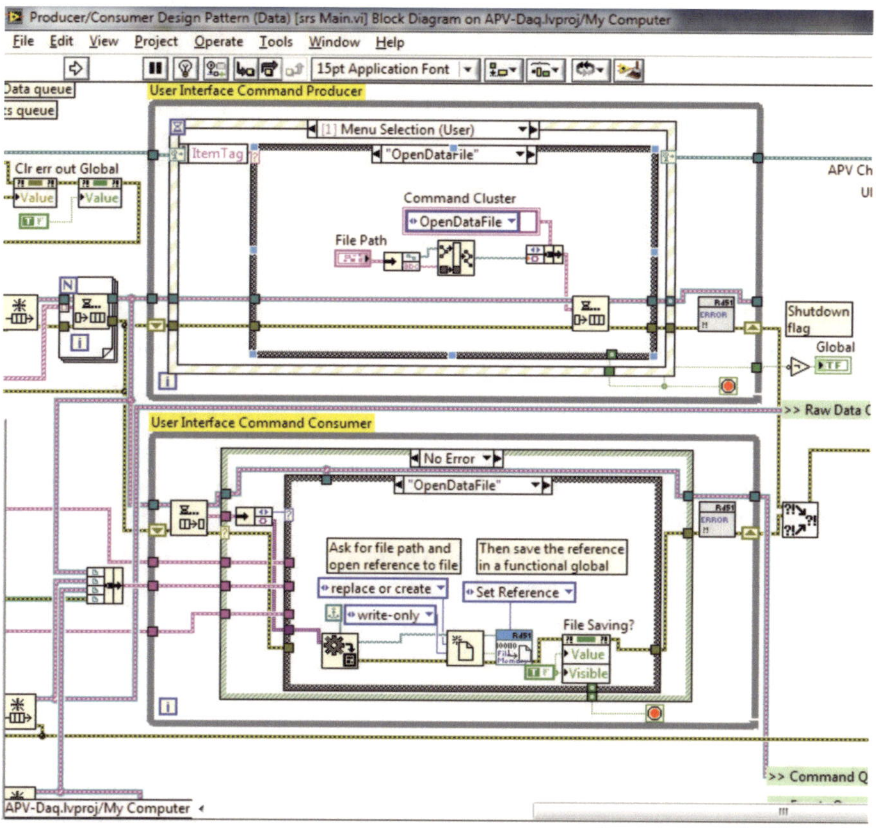

Fig. 7. Portion of the diagram which handles the Menu Item selection and acts in consequence. The bottom most loop handles the request coming from the top one (from APV Data Acquisition System for CERN-Geneve, by R. de Asmundis).

This handling is performed via a queue command exchange between the top and the bottom loop in Figure 7.

3. Elements of language: why to ignore them?

Several aspects related to the basic knowledge of LabVIEW language are, for some mysterious reason, often ignored by beginners. This is really a pity and demonstrates the weakness in which several people approach the language: they tend to underestimate the possibility offered and to overestimate their capability in developing with the few elements of language learned. We can individuate the following objects which are often misused, not well understood or completely ignored:

- **Relating data: Arrays and Clusters**. Correct use of them in several situations.
- **Shift register, a precious tool:** their "active" utilization instead of under staying to the needs of them.
- **Auto indexing of arrays into For** and (marginally) While Loops.
- Advanced data manipulation: Variant, bit manipulation, cast type, etc..
- The **References to objects** and their use in the Property Nodes setting actions.

A deep discussion on all of these topics would make this Chapter too long, so, for some of them, I can only make a citation.

3.1 Arrays

These elements are often misused. Cluster not used at all. Let me try to give some suggestions.
Arrays and Clusters are "musts" in LabVIEW environment: Arrays constitute a mandatory data structure for several situations, like data acquisition coming from samplings (at slow or high rates), oscilloscopes and data sampling equivalent acquisition cards, blocks of data to be processed and so on. Even weak programmers undergo the experience of using arrays because of their "natural" introduction by lots of drivers-VIs, subVIs or LabVIEW functions that only treat arrays. Nevertheless very often arrays are badly used since most of their mechanisms are not well understood. The most powerful of these mechanisms is the **auto indexing principle**: Arrays are, by default, **auto indexed when entering or leaving any** *For Loop* **structure,** while they are optionally auto indexed in *While Loops*. When using arrays, programmers must think from the "array point of view" and always considering auto indexing not only as an useful instrument, but also as the best way with which we treat arrays. Arrays tend naturally to be treated by auto indexing mechanisms (Travis 2004).
As an example consider the following problem: we want to generate a 10 by 10-elements matrix of random numbers where each row contains a random in the range 0-10^n, where "n" is the row index starting from 0. Then we want to extract the main diagonal of this matrix into a second output array. In other words, each row of the 2D-matrix, will contain random numbers in the range 0-1, 0-10, 0-100,…0-10^9. In the following figure the two different solutions are reported:

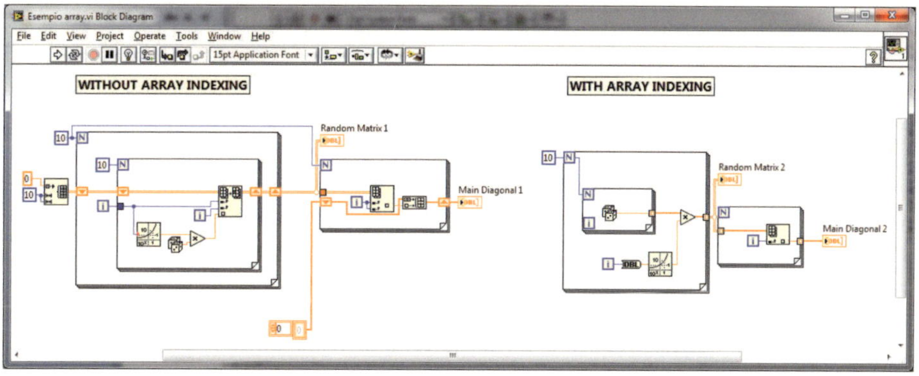

Fig. 8. Contrast between two different solutions in the use of indexing of arrays. Remark the elegance of the second (the right) solution.

In the leftmost solution auto-indexing of array is not used and more functions are involved, the structure is more complicated and the readability of the diagram lower. In particular, the second loop generates an array starting from an empty one by using a build array function in concatenate mode: this solution, although quite practical, is memory and time consuming for the machine and should be adopted only if strictly necessary.
The solution on the right uses auto-indexing **which is implicit in the For Loop structures**: the compactness and the elegance of the solution, in particular in the extraction of the main diagonal, is evident.
So, definitively:

- **Auto-indexing** should be used as frequently as possible when manipulating Arrays.
- Sometimes auto indexing **can be useful with While Loops** too (example to record the history of some parameters once the loop has terminated): be careful in this case, because While Loops can run for extremely extended time and accumulation of array on the border is greatly memory consuming in those conditions. For this reason auto indexing in While Loops is disabled by default.

We cannot spend very long on arrays since there are a lot of other issues to be considered in the Chapter. Anyway, make the effort to think and plan better and better when working with the arrays, even by investing some time in understanding related functionalities.

3.2 Clusters

Clusters are basically ignored by most beginning programmers. This is a paradox since the cluster is the **equivalent in LabVIEW to the "Structures" in C or C++ languages, or Records in Pascal**. Roughly speaking, ignoring clusters is exactly like ignoring one of the most important data structure of programming languages: it is like completely cutting out an entire vital existence of LabVIEW. People who do so often make incorrect sentences like "data structures in LabVIEW are complicated and too many wires and connections are necessary to move data". Reasons for this lack of knowledge always comes from the approximated way of learning the language, without spending any time in the pure study of it, but going directly to "try to develop" something: it becomes natural that in such cases, people use what they have learned until that time and tend not to go on in their acquisition of knowledge.
So, stop for a while and **study Clusters. Then use them as frequently as possible** to represent data which is **logically related one another**. Clusters are extremely useful, for

instance, for grouping setting parameters for an instrument, variables coming from the same source that must be displayed together, entire groups of data to be presented like atmospheric parameters in an environmental control, and so on. Moreover many internal structures in LabVIEW are clusters, like data handled by X-Y graphs, so you must know them. Clusters allow:

1. The **collection of several variables** (In or Out) in an unique container; by choosing to "clusterize" variables which are logically coherent, you have a natural way of logic separation of data into different categories.
2. **Wiring becomes simpler**: very complex data can be exchanged using a single wire.
3. Clusters can be **assembled or disassembled by name**: this introduces an intrinsic clearness into the diagram, by citing the name of the variable transported.
4. Uniform clusters (i.e. all numbers, all characters) can be **sent directly to mathematical (or character) operations** thanks to the polymorphic nature of the functions, so it is not necessary to unbundle and re-bundle them.
5. Clusters allow **improvement in clearness of front panels**. A Front Panel organized in clusters is clear, compact, logically subdivided in a natural way and simpler to maintain.

Consider, as an example, the front panel showed in Figure 9 it is quite well designed, but **it does not use Clusters**. Besides the hard work to obtain it (all boxes around Controls are put by hand), the real problem is into the diagram (Figure 10) where values coming from different controls are picked up in an apparently spread out way. Clusters would help a lot in grouping together the data and make the diagram more friendly, as you can see in the bottom part of Figure 10, where two Clusters have only been introduced. Notice the *Unbundle by Name* function which greatly increases visibility of the diagram. You can imagine the advantage in using Clusters for **all Controls and Indicators** in this diagram.

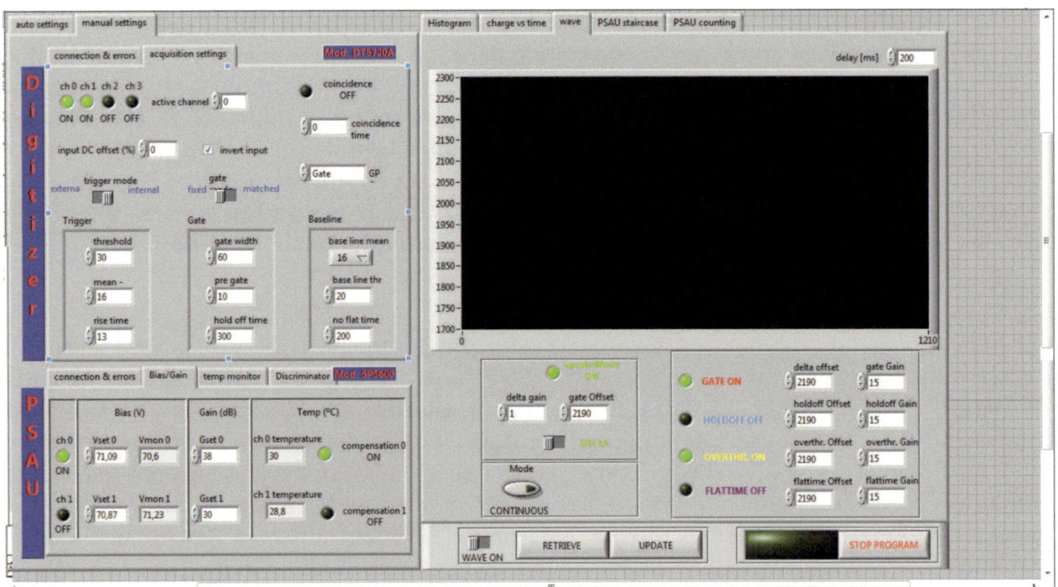

Fig. 9. Example of a front panel which do not use Clusters: even if it appears quite good, a lot of time has been spent to obtain this result. Boxes around groups of Controls or Indicators have been put in by hand: Clusters would provide a natural way of doing this.

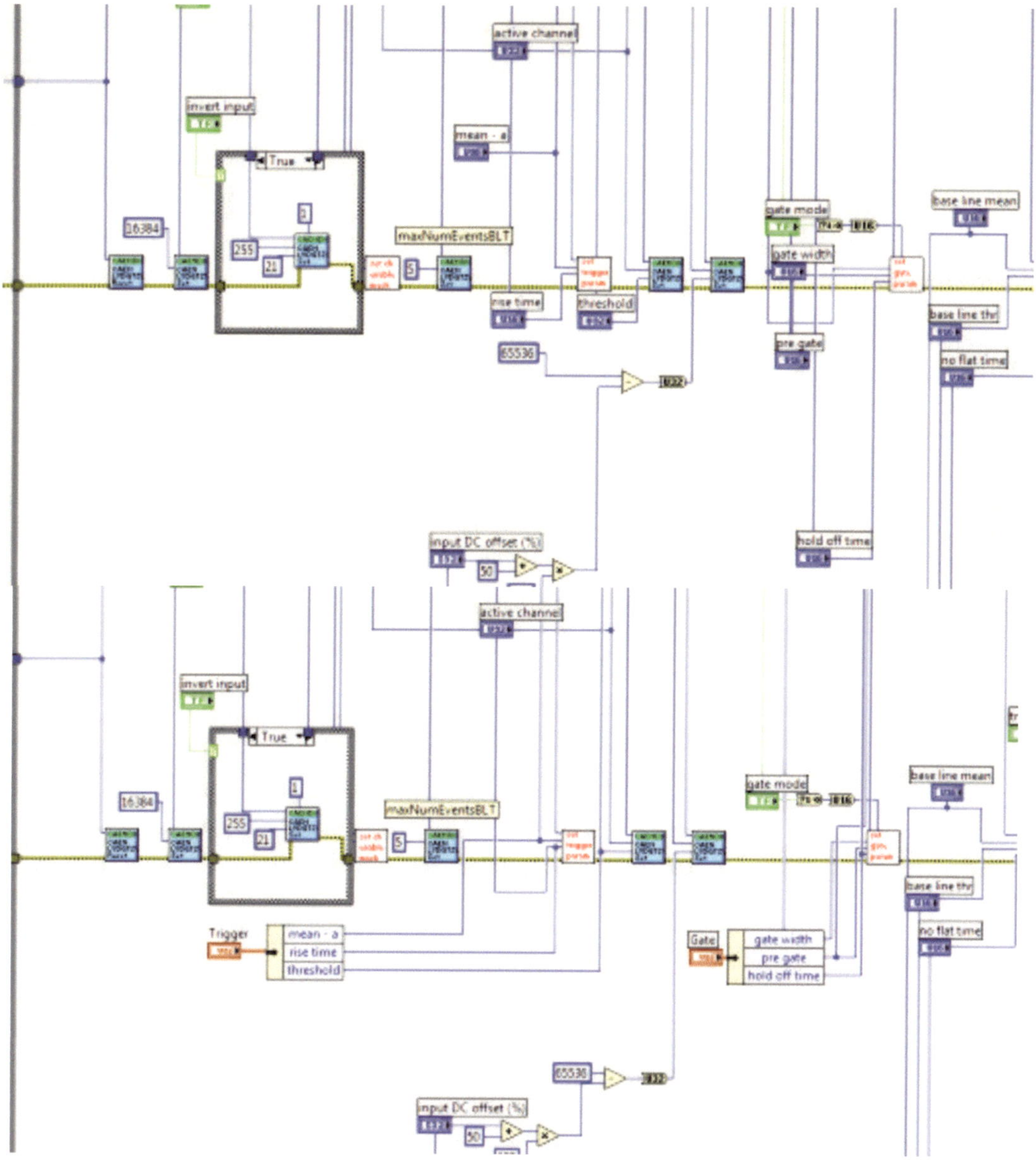

Fig. 10. On top a portion of the diagram relative to the Figure 9. In the bottom the same portion in which only two clusters, each containing three elements, have been introduced. You have to imagine the final result when the clusterization of data is completed.

3.3 Type definitions

Clusters, but not only them, are often involved in **Type Definitions**. If Clusters are "seen but ignored", type definition are often **not known at all**. Again this is a paradox, since they are the equivalent, in C/C++, of "Typedef" statement. In particular C-statement "typedef struct" **is translated in LabVIEW as** "Type definition made using Clusters". For this reasons, Clusters and Type Definitions are often used together.

Use type definition to **create your own data type for your Applications.** Include type definitions into your project using a specific folder. Once you create a Type Definition, you can use **instances** of it wherever you want in all VIs of your Project. Instances are **bound** to the original Type Definition, so that, if you modify it, all instances are automatically updated.

Type definitions are made **by using the Control Editor** and this may be the reason for which they are so ignored: editing of Controls are, in fact, considered as a "far" item, not useful in the daily practice and to be used rarely. Although it is true that we do not modify controls to create our own controls every day, Type Definitions can be manipulated in this environment only.

It can be convenient to try with the following suggestions:

Suggestion 1) If you think a control/indicator, even a simple one like a small cluster expressly prepared, is subject to be used several time, then **define it as a Type Definition.**

Suggestion 2) To do so, simply select your control, go to "Edit → Customize Control" menu item. The Control Editor window will open. Select "Type Definition" or "Strictly typed Type Definition" as the type of control you are editing. Customize it if necessary and save it as a new, separate type. When you close the Editing window, answer YES to the question asking if old control must be bound with Type Definition.

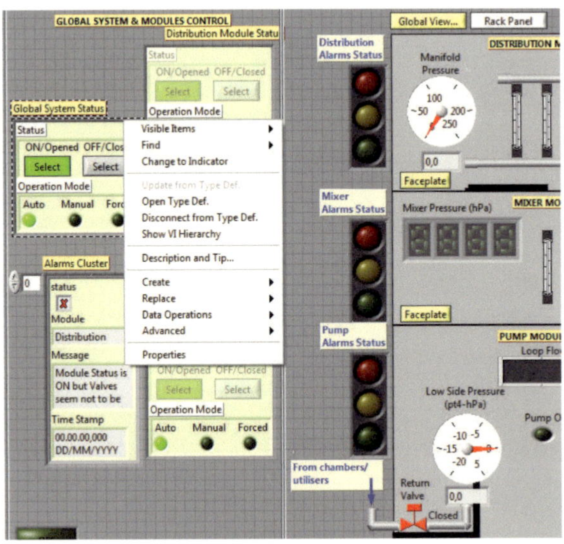

Fig. 11. Example of a Control Panel which uses several Type Definition. Remark the contextual menu with relative voices like "Open Type Def" or "Disconnect from Type Def". If the pointed Cluster is modified in the Control Editor as Type Def, all instances are automatically updated (from a Real Time Gas Control System implemented in the INFN Naples, R. de Asmundis)

In the example of Figure 11 several Type Definitions are present. On one of them the contextual menu is opened. All Type Definitions are Clusters, and this is not by chance: if a cluster must be repeated in several points of the VI because it has several utilization, it is convenient to define it as Type Definition.

- Remember that if you need to change anything in your Type Definition, **just open it and make your modifications**: all instances will be automatically updated.

One of the most useful aspects of adopting Type Definition is in the case of advanced Design Patterns into diagrams. We will return to this in the relative paragraph.
Remember: it is not convenient to ignore Type Definitions.

3.4 Local and global variables. Using shift registers as Global Variables

Shift Registers represent a very powerful tool generally used to report, in repetitive structures (For or While Loops) data coming from previous cycles. We do not enter in the details because shift registers are so useful that they are surely known even by beginners. Almost every repetitive structure uses shift registers because of the needs of the process itself.

Don't forget that Shift Register **are actually a memory storage** for any type of data. Consequently we can use Shift Register as a memory storage to pass data among VIs or part of a VI. This solution, strongly recommended by National Instruments knowledge base, is called "**Functional Global Variable**".

The reader surely knows Local and Global Variables: they are an useful way of accessing to Controls and Indicators in different parts of a diagram or among SubVIs. Excessive use of Variables is, indeed, to be strongly avoided. I have seen several beginners using local variables in the place of drawing wires to transmit data within the diagram. Well, this is **a very incorrect way of programming** for several reasons:

1. You lose the main principle of LabVIEW language, again the **Data Dependency** paradigm. LabVIEW performs operation once data is available at the input of functions. Variables alter this paradigm, by inducing an immediate **availability of data, but with no guaranteed it will be up to date.** This leads to 2.
2. **Race conditions** can be introduced: a function (far) uses data (picked up from a Variable) that has not been updated yet, because, in another point of the diagram, the Variable is still waiting to be updated., In this way we *planned* to send correct data to the target VIs or portion of diagram, but this is not the case.
3. Race condition **must be avoided** since they represent big "bugs" in your program. Diagrams can run correctly even thousands of times and fail at a thousand and one!

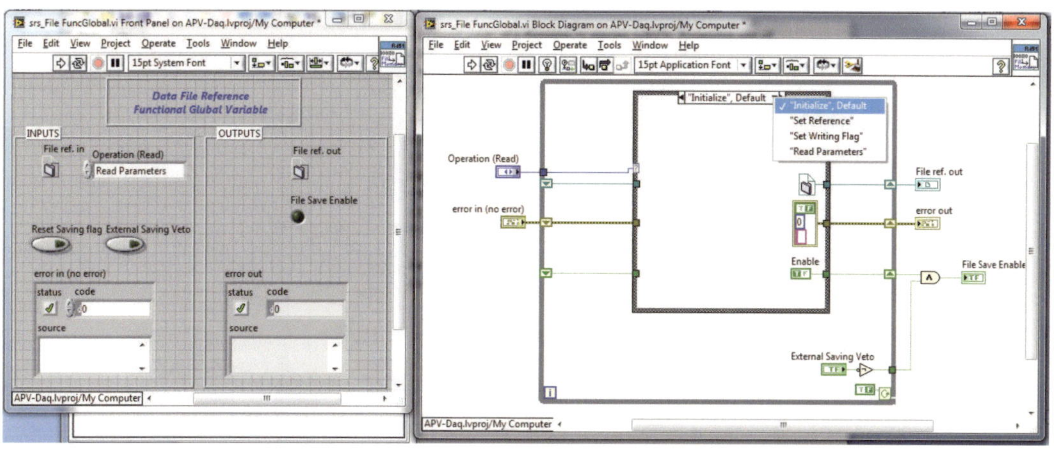

Fig. 12. Example of a Functional Global Variable (FGV). To be noted, the different choices with which the FGV can be called: "initialize" to clear the output, "Set Reference" to save values to be successively used, then "Read Parameters" to use them.

Please consider Figure 12. the front panel and diagram of a Functional Global variable which uses shift registers to store data is represented. The problem solved here is the following: in a professional application, the User can decide when saving *streams* of data onto a file and when not to. Where to open and handle the file in such a process? Usually data streaming consists in opening the file before a loop, writing continuously within the loop and closing it after (see paragraph on the "files" in this Chapter). If the diagram is quite complex and this sequence for file handling is not convenient to be designed in the standard way, the *opening and closing* of the file only can be done in the command section of the diagram: there a **Functional Global Variable is used** to store the **file reference** and, if needed, other information too. Then, in the part of the diagram which writes the file, the **same functional global** is used to read the file reference number and whatever is needed. You can, in this way, store and retrieve information at different locations in a diagram without using a variable. Since Functional Globals are SubVI the data dependency paradigm tend to be correctly applied, automatically avoiding race conditions.

4. References and variants

References and Variants represent two other data type which is often ignored in LabVIEW. We encountered **References** in the above paragraph, talking about files. References do not apply to files only: basically each object can be referenced, and actions can be taken on the objects by using references. References are *numbers* which we do not decide, create or define: just **use.** References are created by right click on terminals in the diagram and from there on, this number can be used for several purposes:

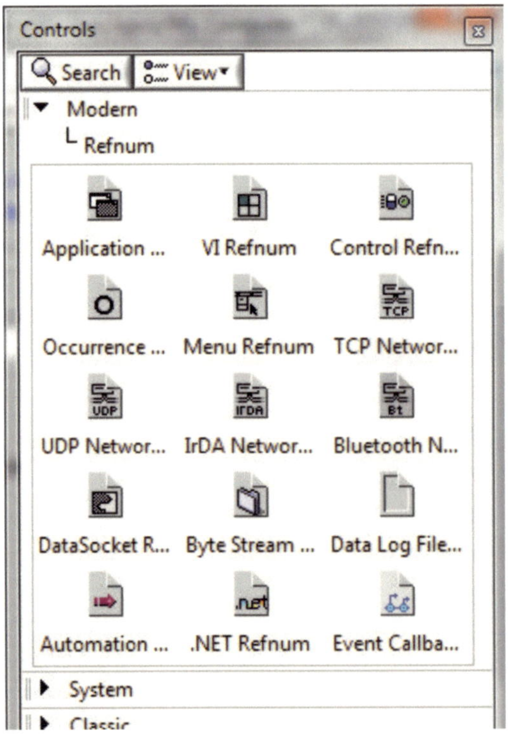

Fig. 13. The "Reference" palette menu.

Reference to a file, as above, to write, read and do any other special operation on file; reference to an object on the front panel can be used to access it and programmatically modify **any attribute it has**. It is difficult here to collect all situations where References can be used or are useful. Just as an example, consider using the **property nodes** to change property programmatically (i.e. changing the colour of an indicator depending on data, make a control active or inactive greyed-out and so on). Property Nodes need a considerable space in the diagram and it can be useful to move them in a SubVI. In that case **References** to the modifying objects must be sent to the SubVI: it will be received in the SubVI as a "Control Reference". Figure 14 shows a cluster of reference created to send compactly references to SubVIs.

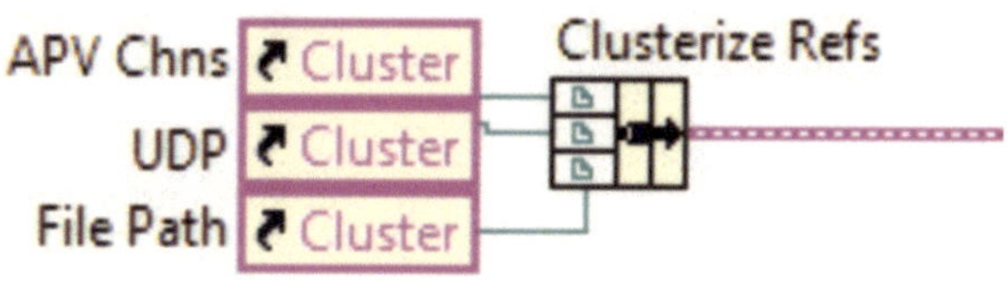

Fig. 14. A Cluster of Reference is created in order to transmit compactly References to specific SubVI.

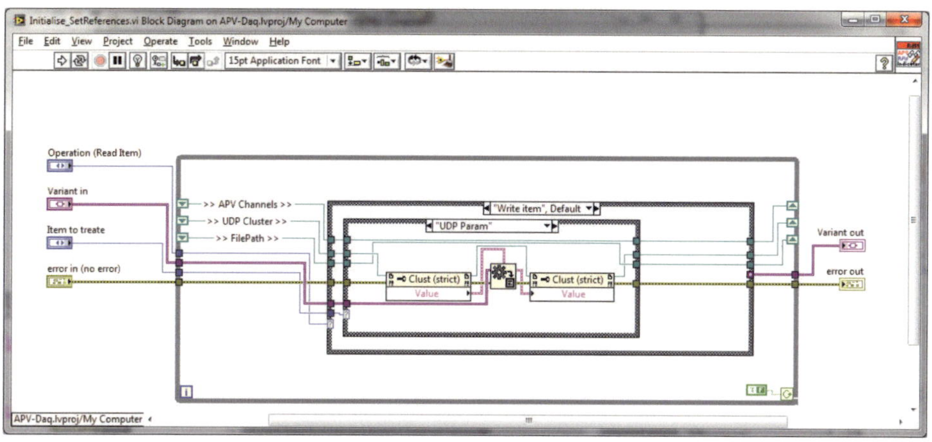

Fig. 15. The subVI in which these References are used.

Figure 15 shows the diagram of a SubVI which uses these References: note the Property Node which accesses to the object and read/write data on it, remotely (i.e. in a SubVI) and again without using Global Variables. Property nodes act in a better way on objects with respect to Variables, and allow Error treatment.

In the same figure also a **Variant** is used. Variant can be very practical, and it is another item defined in most programming languages. It simply contains "any" kind of data. You can use Variants when you need to send various-shaped data using a single "channel". An example is the handling of a user menu choice: depending on the selected menu item, you need to send different data types to a consumer into the diagram. You simply send a Variant at **every menu item,** so the structure to send data is always the same: the receiver must interpret the Variant by knowing what data type is associated with it in order to reconvert. Variants are a very flexible way of data exchange for several situations. It is useful to spend some time in testing and learning them in view of an advantageous utilization starting from available built-in examples on Variants.

5. The hierarchy

LabVIEW is conceived as a **hierarchical environment**: different tasks or jobs can be performed in different subprograms, namely different SubVIs. It often happens that programs are written without using SubVI, writing everything in an unique diagram, namely the main VI. This is not a good choice. In this way diagrams tend to quickly become too big, going over the screen size and incomprehensive; it becomes difficult to manage, to be updated and is not as scalable as it should be. In my opinion there are two main reasons for this tendency:

1. There is insufficient familiarity in creating SubVIs at the beginning, so their usage is not taken into account.
2. Developers do not "think hierarchically", meaning they have not figured it out, before writing the code, the best way of organizing the diagram and basically on how to **subdivide tasks.**

Regarding the first point, it is sufficient a simple tour in creating some SubVIs, be careful where to store them or giving the correct names to SubVIs, correctly choose the data in/out and the terminal connection and so on.

As for the second point, don't forget that SubVIs are the equivalent of Functions and Subroutines in text-based programming languages (C, C++, Pascal,...). When learning C, for instance, one of the first points stressed is the use of Functions: C and C++ that are **made by Functions**. Pascal pushed this concept to the extreme: Functions and Subroutines had to be declared in the main program. All these aspects force the developer to "think hierarchically": when a C developer has a specific task that the main program has to do, a specialized one or a task which has to be repeated several times, he/she immediately starts to define a new **C Function.** It must be the same in LabVIEW: **opening a new VI** and making it a SubVI should be a natural process.

In the Figure 16 we can have an idea of what a disastrous diagram can come out when not constructed with the principle of a good planned hierarchy.

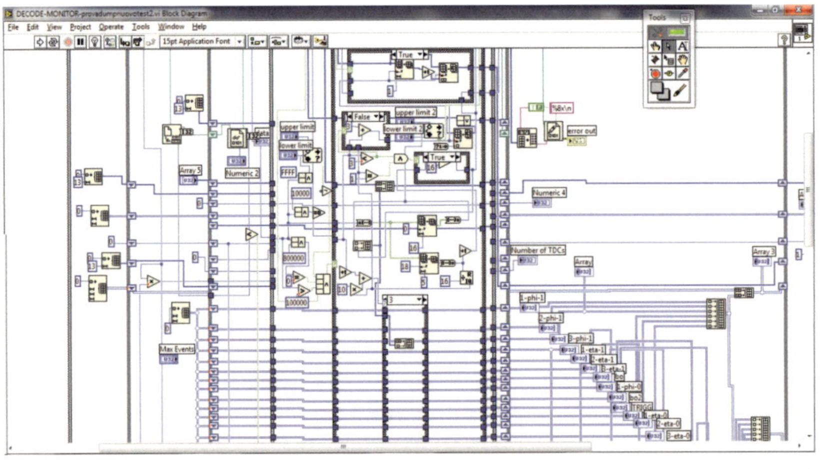

Fig. 16. An example of a very badly designed diagram in which no use of SubVIs has been adopted.

Situations like the diagram of Figure 16 lead to serious difficulties in understanding and possibly rescaling the program (i.e. the diagram) for future developments. It can be impossible to understand it even after reopening just two months later: the confusion can be total and the robustness is strongly compromised.

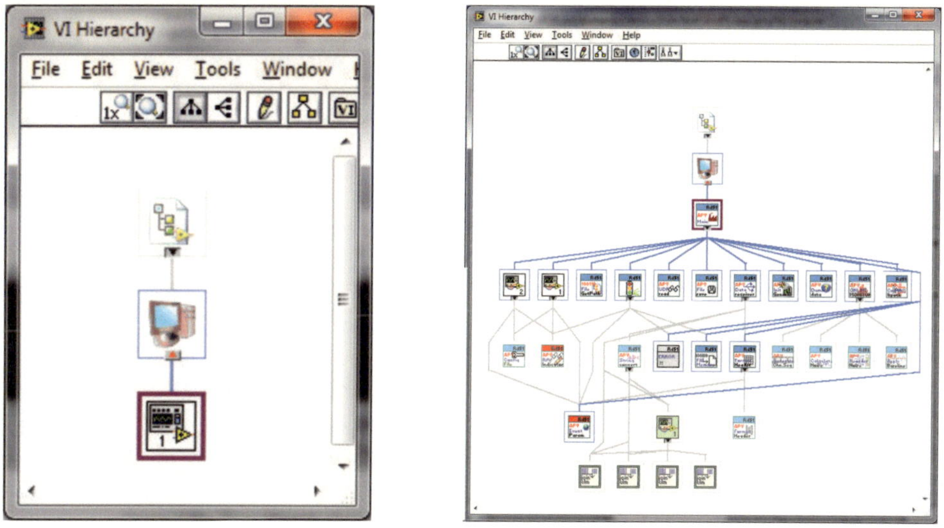

Fig. 17. Left: the "Hierarchy Window" of the above diagram has no meaning due to the poor hierarchical design. On the right a Hierarchy Window for a correct designed Application which adequately uses SubVIs.

The **Hierarchy Window** helps a lot in keeping the control of the development process. It would be useful to refer to it during hierarchy definition. Starting from the **first SubVI** you introduce into your application, open the Hierarchy Window to have a look at the modularity you are adopting in creating your Application. SubVIs can be easily accessed to open their front panel, to set VI properties, to edit their icons.
Here are some possible hints about Hierarchical developing and SubVIs in general:
Suggestion 1) Whenever you have a "sub-problem" in the sense that a certain task can be seen as independent, **open a new VI and use it as a SubVI.** You can develop robust, clear, independent VI that can be used as SubVI in several points of your Application.
Suggestion 2) SubVIs allow you also to create parts of your program that can be tested and debugged independently from the whole Application: once your SubVIs work fine you are saved from one of the most frequent source of bugs in your Application.
Suggestion 3) When your main diagram starts getting too big, individuate a part that can be performed by SubVs: then select that part and make **"edit→ create SubVI" command from menu.** Then re-organize your SubVI (terminals, Icon, etc.).
Suggestion 4) When you open a new VI to be used as a SubVI, **immediately drag the icon terminal** pane in the main VI: this immediately imposes the desired hierarchy, and the SubVI is visible in the Hierarchy Window. You organize your hierarchy even before finish developing of your SubVIs.
Suggestion 5) The last hint is somewhat more complicated: think **what you don't want to see** into the diagram of the Main VI of your Application and what you do see. For example **decide what not to have in the main VI** as, for instance, low level functions: file open, write/read, close; access to instruments drivers; TCP/UDP access; etc. Decide that **all low level functions** of any kind **must be written in SubVI.** This solution allows you to create a **"Layers" Hierarchy** in which you can have different visibility of your work: it is a great help for big Projects and Applications.
Obviously most of these hints must be checked and a lot of experience must be done to absorb them. But please, start to adopt these strategies immediately.

5.1 Documenting VIs

VI documentation is another missing point: basically all developers, also experienced ones, tend to skip this step completely. Diagrams are poor in explanations, notes or internal documentation. This is another mistake. VIs without any documentation are hard to understand and if you mix this with the general weakness in the diagrams clarity the result is hard to understand.

LabVIEW is a self-documenting environment and you do not need a lot of work to create a good documentation. It is sufficient to keep in mind some standard steps to adopt during the development processes to get an automatically documented code. Documentation issues include:

- A **correct name** given to the VIs.
- A **correct allocation** of VIs in your file system (as already described).
- A correct **naming of Controls and Indicators** on the Front Panels.
- Designing of **a good Front Panel**, in order to self-guide the user in understanding it. This should be a good practice for SubVIs too, even **if they are not normally open or visible to the final user**.
- Good aspect of **VIs Diagrams**.
- An adequate choice and design of the **VIs Icons**.
- A **correct positioning of input and output** terminals on the SubVIs Connection Panes.
- Some words in the "documentation" tab of the **VI Properties page for all VIs involved**.

Most of the above issues are clear to understand. For others, further clarification may be useful. As you can see, basically, all these rules do not imply extra-work to your job. They must become habitual. When you open a new VI, for instance, the first thing to be done **is saving it in the right folder and giving it a good name** which is indicative of its attitudes.

The same thing when you introduce any Control or Indicator: the name label is automatically selected to allow you to input the specific name: please, do it. Do not leave "numeric 1, numeric2, array1"… names.

For VI icons you can have suggestions by the same Figure 17 right side, in which two icons only must still be designed. There is a logic in the choice of the icons:

1. **An icon Template** has been adopted: it is a simple framework design (two rectangles in light blue in Figure 17) with a short explanation as a short name of the Project or the activity for which the Project has been made. Create it and save it as an Icon Template (from version 2009 on).
2. One specific **Template should be used for each Project**, giving a signature to the project.
3. The background colour is modified into **two-three options** (Red or Pink) to locate different purposes of SubVIs: normal VIs are in the original colour (blue); Functional Global variable are in Red and Type Definitions are in Pink.
4. At **every icon of the SubVI in the Application** three lines of text, one glyph and the cited framework identify the purpose of the SubVI itself.
5. Icons that are different in styles **come from the LabVIEW system** (as internal functions made by SubVIs) or from my personal "User Library": obviously they keep their old icon design.

In the two figures 18 and 19 you can see the front panel and diagram of a SubVI **that is normally closed**, but optionally opened and shown to the User.

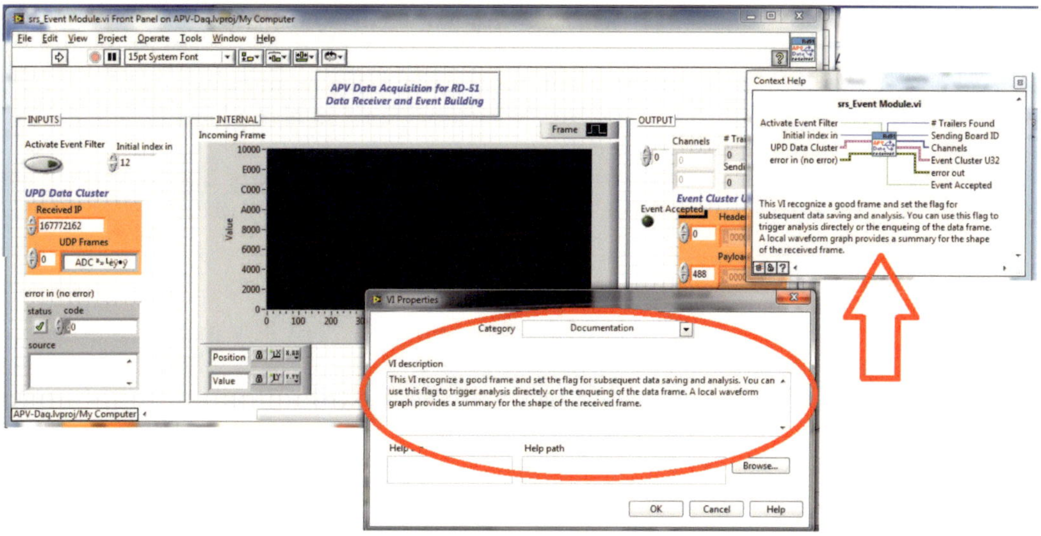

Fig. 18. Example of a documentation introduced in a SubVI.

Note the care taken in the arrangement of the objects on the front panel: Input, Internal and Output frames create a visual impact which immediately guides the user; the coloured object are Type Definitions and this strategy is useful to locate them in panels; the message written in the "Description" page (indicated by the oval (in figure 18)) of the VI-Property window is automatically shown in the LabVIEW Context Help.

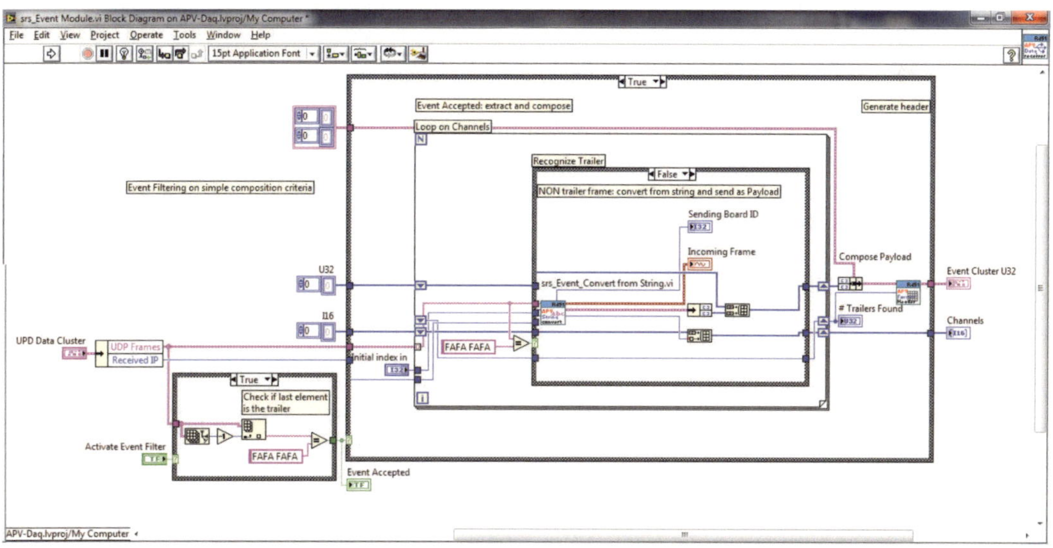

Fig. 19. The diagram of the SubVI of figure 18.

In the second figure the corresponding diagram is shown. Note the presence of several free labels used as internal documentation of the diagram itself. They help a lot in reminding the purpose of objects used, of SubVIs etc. Here are some hints concerning the diagram:

Suggestion 1) It is useful to document specific operations by choosing to **show the label on structures** (For and While Loops, Events structures), giving them a clear name which

indicates the function. You can do the same on some function (it is done on a Bundle Function in the Figure 19).
Suggestion 2) Using **free labels** to document the diagram is highly suggested.
Suggestion 3) From version 2010 on **use the "wire label tool"** to give a label to single wires, indicating the data transported.
With a well-organized and documented set of SubVIs you do not risk that even after two months, when you reopen your project, you will not remember what you did.

6. Data filing in LabVIEW

Data filing is not a trivial job in any programming language: LabVIEW makes no exception in this regard. There is, in fact, a very wide range of choices concerning how you can save your data on files, and the decision of using one format instead of another must be steered by the following two points:

- **What kind of data**, in a "logic sense" you are saving.
- What is the **future utilization** of this data?

These two points are not clear at all to the novel developer, and sometimes even to an experienced one.
Typically, once learned how to save data onto spread-sheet files, the tendency is to continue using spread-sheets even in cases that would require a more convenient solution: the Spread-sheet format is supported by the fact that it is Excel compatible, in the sense that files can be directly read by Excel and eventually transformed into Excel format. But we mustn't forget that there exist a lot of other possibilities whose utilizations can be strongly recommended.
First of all, let's try to give some explanations of the statements above.

- The "logic sense" of data to be saved means a sort of category to which data needed or produced by an Application belong. Here is a possible list reported as a series of examples:
  a. [configuration data] The physical channels to which the program must acquire data from the field via ADCs or other related hardware.
  b. [configuration data] On-Off status which decide if some Data Acquisition Channels must be taken or not (to temporary inhibit DAQ from certain channels).
  c. [Internal data] Information related to the user (ID, account, a possible password).
  d. [internal logging] Log information concerning the correct functioning of an Application for debugging purpose.
  e. [internal logging] Journal file of actions taken by the user / Journal file of actions taken by the Application for getting a strong redundancy on delicate processes.
  f. [log raw data] Real (physical) data acquired that must be saved on disc for future analysis.
  g. [log analysed data] Online analysis is performed and we want to save basics results of analysed data.

The list is far from being complete. Pay attention to the fact that we are not speaking about **the format**. The format, in fact, **is an independent choice:** all the logical categories of data indicated in the above list are subject to be saved into different formats, but there are no fixed rules for this. One must clarify, **before deciding the format**, what is the logical aspect of data to be saved. For each of them a different and more indicated solution is suggested.

- The second point is in some way related to the first and, from a certain point of view, the choice must be done by considering both aspects. Saved file can be:

a. Successively used as source of data **to be analysed**.
b. **Retrieved intact**, just as they have been written.
c. Subject to be **archived** in a long term historical archive and sometimes retrieved for future reference.
d. Hidden because it is used **by the program itself** for its internal setups (typical case of Configuration Files).
e. Subject to be used on the **same machine** which took it or moved to be opened/used on a **different machine**.
f. Their destination is on the same **Operating System** or on a different one.

And this list could also continue.

Another aspect is the format: **text file or binary file**? What exactly is the difference? What is more convenient and for what reasons? I found that sometimes even experienced people make some trivial mistakes by choosing a wrong solution on this point.

6.1 An overall analysis of the file functions

The File Functions are very well divided and organised in LabVIEW. After an overall analysis of them we will switch to a series of useful hints for deciding file saving in LabVIEW. The Figure 20 represents the main File Function palette at the centre with four sub-palettes opened. The first row of the main palette contains the "basic" File Functions, the ones you use when you don't want to worry about *how*, technically speaking, *you are saving* your files.

6.1.1 Basic file functions

This first line provides two different and pre-ordered ways of file saving: spread-sheet file (Write and Read respectively) and express VIs which use LabVIEW Measurement file format.

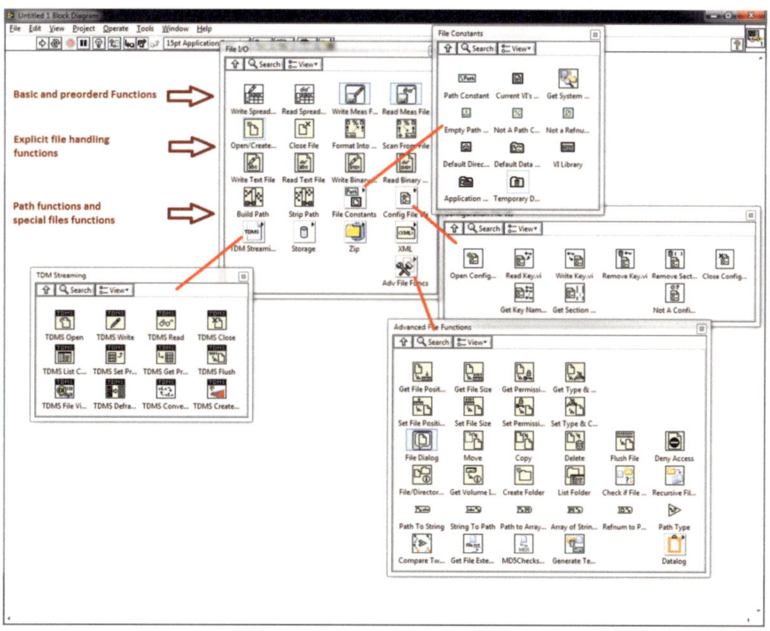

Fig. 20. The very extended and rich File Functions palette of LabVIEW.

Even if these two methods are useful in several situations, they suffer from some drawbacks:

- Spread-sheet file

a. Spread-sheet files **can only save numeric values** in double precision representation. Moreover some old LabVIEW versions saved these data as single precision representation. If your floating data are usually treated in double precision, **a loss of representation or loss of data** can be introduced if you saved them with the Write to Spread-sheet File Function.
b. You **cannot write on your file any other auxiliary information** like strings, Booleans, annotations etc.: you **cannot save date and time string** information; date and time can only be saved as floating point, i.e. using the absolute timestamp of LabVIEW, but that is to be decoded by another program and is not clearly understandable by human operators if written as a double number and not interpreted.
c. The machine format is a text file, whose fields are separated by tab character. This means that huge files can be created even for not such a large amount of data to be stored.
d. When you record spread-sheet files you must be careful in developing the file **towards bottom** direction instead of to the right one: in other words, spread-sheets must grow toward the bottom by appending **lines**, avoiding too many columns on the right. In this case, spread-sheet programs can fail in opening these files.
e. The numeric precision can be lost because **you chose the number of significant digits** at the moment of the file save, just as in a print-out sheet.

The last point is particularly significant when critical numerical data must be saved. It is an important issue concerning text file which will be considered later.

- LabVIEW Measurement files. They can be very useful, but I suggest to adopt this solution for a relatively small amount of data. They are driven by an Express VI, so a specific setup panel is opened when you introduce these functions into your diagram. The main advantage of using LabVIEW Measurement Files is the rapidity in defining the file and obtaining it. The read-back of the file is also easy.
  Here are some drawbacks:
  a. They are usually text file unless you select "binary (TDMS)" into the setup page, so they reflect the usual problems of text files.
  b. Their utilization is basically foreseen as a LabVIEW tool, being incompatible with any other analysis software or platform.
  c. Files can grow a lot if you try to save uncontrolled data banks, like big multi-dimensional arrays and so on.

The last point can be a very critical issue. Often the data size treated by an Application is hidden by the apparent ease in which the diagram handles it: a simple array, for instance, **can grow to hundreds of Megabytes** without any particular indication or problem. This aspect is so transparent that risks can be under evaluated by the developer: in the case of saving such an amount of data, very huge files can be abruptly created, causing slowness in the machine response.

In conclusion use the **first line of File Function** if you have little data, in small or moderate Applications, or to do initial tests of data saving of a new Application. Then consider using a **more sophisticated method** for **file saving** even for moderate Applications and whenever more control and care must be taken in saving data.

6.1.2 Owner's file functions

The second and third lines (on Figure 20) provide a complete control of file writing and reading which should be well understood. These functions are able to manipulate files as you want: you can open, write/read data repeatedly and finally close. You can use these function for every situations of data I/O to disc. You can decide:

- If the file is a text or a binary file;
- The data representation in the case of binary files;
- The number of characters/data elements to be read;
- The adoption of **data streaming** technique.

6.1.3 File Constants Palette

The upper right palette of figure 20 is the **File Constant Palette.** It is an important series of tools useful for path definition and handling. Consider using them to create the correct path to access the disc area in which files are stored (the whole path to the actual folder). In particular the "Current VIs Path" function is extremely useful for getting the current path in which the VI is acting: wherever you move the VI, on different machines also, the function shows you the current and complete path to locate the VI. From there, with the **strip and building path functions**, you can define your own path.

6.1.4 Advanced file functions

This is a very plenty toolkit with all sorts of functions: you can move within an (opened) file, by positioning the "pick up head" wherever you choose, calculate file sizes, list directories, create or destroy folders or files, and so on. These functions are not frequently used, but when needed they are really useful. A typical use is the positioning within a file with Get/Set File Position functions, which allows you to move in binary files like on a tape recorder. **Some experience is needed to use these functions; always start with little tests**: create new, small VIs to do the test and study the effects and the results. Then integrate the test VIs as SubVIs into your final application. This process is the only way to learn and clarify the utility of these functions kit. Since the functions are **low level Functions**, you can almost do anything on your File System, even delete important System Files! They must be used carefully.

6.1.5 Text files or binary files?

At this point in our discussion, some time must been spent on the format. Text files are usually preferred to binary ones, at least because when we open them with a text editor we can *see the contents*. The same thing does not happen for binary files which are somehow unreadable. A binary file can only be read by using the same procedure as when it was written: the same data type must be declared when we read and the number of bytes of *elements* must be input to the read function.

But what is the real difference between the two types ?

Consider that a file (binary or text) is composed of a sequence of bytes, groups of 8 bits on the disk (independently from how the File System of the machine has fragmented them on the disk). A single byte can have a value that, if translated into integer, goes from 0 to 255.

Well, a file which can potentially contain all combinations of the 8 bits within the bytes, i.e. bytes which contain all values from 0 to 255, is called a **binary file.** On the contrary, if the values are limited to a certain subset of the range 0..255, they are called **text files**. The subset is a precise one: "allowed codes" cover all ASCII printable characters (form 'space' to 'z', numerically 32..127 code range) and some other "control character" which indicates line or page feed, carriage return etc.. Under certain points of view there is not a big difference between the two categories, but practically the difference is enormous.

The following table reports some hints concerning the possible choices for file saving:

Table of suggestions for choosing format of files	
Use Text files when	**Use Binary files when**
You do not have big amount of data to be saved.	The amount of data starts to be significant.
You want to have the "feel" on the data just saved by watching them.	Your utilization of data in the future is for analysis or archiving purposes.
You are not concerned about space on the disc.	You are concerned about saving space on the disc: Binary files are extremely more compact than Text ones.
You don't have to worry about speed in data writing or reading, since text file operations are slow.	You are concerned about speed: if you need to get data quickly and save on disc "into the loop" Binary files is the only solution, often accompanied with the "data streaming technique" (see later).
You don't have to worry about machine overload: text files are somehow a heavy process for it.	You are concerned about machine overload: writing in binary is a light process and no data conversion is needed.
You do not care about precision for saving numerical data: suppose you have a 15 significant digits number to be saved. When saving it in a text file you de facto print it on the disc by using a character representation. If you, by mistake, ask for 5 significant digits to be saved, the remaining 10 digits are definitively lost.	You are interested in definitively storing data with the original precision or the original conditions (i.e. all data must be saved "as they are").
Your data must be read from other programs, different machines or different Operating Systems.	Your data must be read in the same environment (LabVIEW); some extra work is needed as a specifically-written program into a different Language (C, C++, …), even on a different Operating System, in order to read binary file on other platforms.

Table 1. A compendium of indications for steering the choice of a correct file format.

Binary files seem to be more complicated or difficult to manipulate. Well, it is not so: they are quite simple and easy to understand. Consider the following example. We have the following eight numbers (as signed integers) to be saved:
667283 -134452 235567 7894451 -5569852 7789663 -3363331 -445874
Each of them, to be stored in memory, needs a 32 bits Integer (I32) representation and takes 4 bytes in the computer memory.

- If we save them into a Text file, we need approximately 67 bytes: each digit is, in fact, transformed in an ASCII character (1 byte) and **we do not save numbers** but their representation in a character writing. It is like **printing a sheet of paper and saving it on the disc**. The text files need some control characters like 'tab' to move from one number to the next, 'EndOfLine' to end the rows and so on.
- If we save them into a Binary file, the effective file size containing data is 32 bytes: 8 numbers times 4 bytes each, simply the dump of the memory onto the disc. Negative numbers are already taken into account thanks to the two's complement representation.

Try to figure out how they work: take some time before deciding and do not make rapid decisions which usually end up in text files.

6.1.6 TDMS Files

In recent years, starting from version 7, National Instruments introduced the LabVIEW Measurement Files format (LVM files). We already cited this format while talking about the Basic Files Functions: it is a text file well organized to record on disc "sessions" of data taking under the form

[Date-Time] | [X] | Channel 1 | [Channel 2] | ...

Where '[]' means optional fields. The format and storing parameters (name, paths, automatic naming,...) can be set up by Express VIs. A prefix header can be optionally recorded to store further descriptions.

A few years later the TDMS format was introduced, together with the TDM Streaming palette (the bottom-left palette in figure 20). TDMS File format is an evolution of LVM, recorded in **binary mode** and optimized for search and access thanks to a specific indexing technique. The details of how the files are stored or indexed are transparent to the developer, who can take advantage from the intrinsic structures and handling related to this format. TDMS is a LabVIEW "internal" format, in the sense that it is conceived as an efficient method for **data storage and retrieving in LabVIEW environment**: you can save large amounts of data, perform data streaming and classify your data into different channels and categories. This choice can be particularly useful in several situations in which you have a consistent amount of data and/or numerous sources of it (i.e. several channels which produce data).

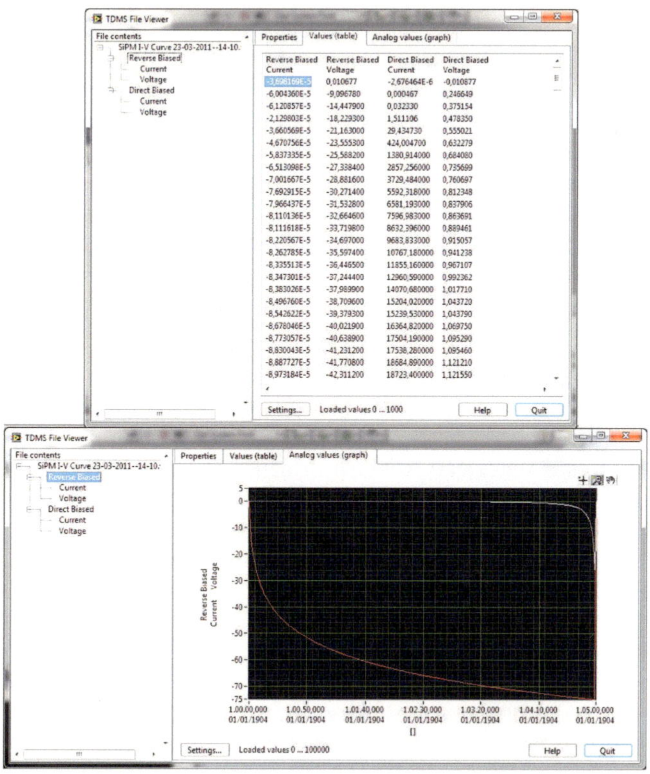

Fig. 21. An example of the TDMS file Viewer in which some data is shown.

In the Figure 21, two screenshots of the "TDMS File Viewer" (the bottom-left VI in the TDM palette of figure 20) are shown. I'm indicating here two possible presentations of data: table form and graph form. You can imagine that the number of channels visible as in the top table can increase, or the number of curves on the same graph could increase as well. It depends on how you organise the data saving operation in your writing VI and on how you access to their view by using the TDMS File viewer: this function works as an interactive browser that you can expressly open or programmatically open from a VIs.

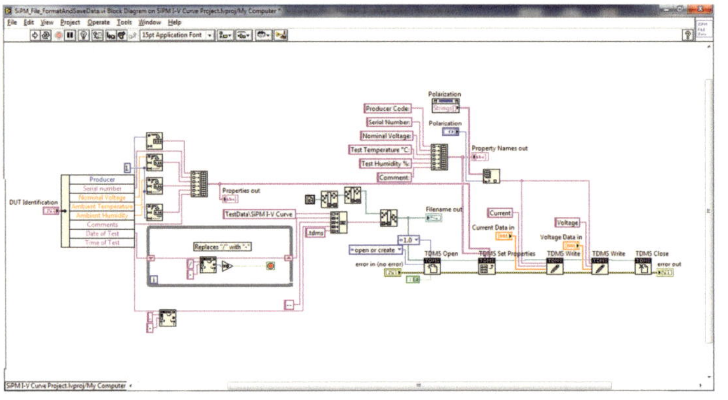

Fig. 22. Portion of file writing VI which saved data of figure 21.

In the Figure 22 you can see how the data are saved into a TDMS file: two writing operations are used ("TDMS Write" to create the two Channels "Voltage" and "Current"), while the same Group Name is used (coming from "Polarization" string set). Note that before writing the file, a series of auxiliary data is stored by using "TDMS Set Properties" function: it is a very useful feature that allows you to store a header on the file whose format is completely custom. The parameters, conditions and serial number of the device under test are written in the header in the test bench Application chosen for this example.
In conclusion: if you have a consistent amount of data that must be visible internally in LabVIEW, **without any doubt use TDMS Files**. In the case you need to extract data and use it in a different environment (i.e. convert to ordinary binary or to text file) it is easy to write a conversion program.

6.1.7 Configuration and Datalog Files

We have yet to speak about two special categories of files: Configuration files and Datalog Files.
Use **Configuration Files** if you need to store **internal characteristics or parameters of your VIs or Application**: examples are initial setup of a panel or of a bench instrument, different configurations for instruments or for any connected hardware; choices of taking or not data from certain channels of your field and so on. Configuration files resemble the old ".ini" files in Windows: they are text files in which a series of "Sections" are listed and, within any "Section", information is identified using "Keys". One advantage is that they can be opened in a text editor and, if needed, edited by hand (even if this is not a suggested action) and one can always keep track and "understand" what is written. One disadvantage is that, as the number of Keys and Sections grows, writing and reading the file can start to be tedious because you need to expressly call the "Read Key", "Write Key" or similar VIs for every Section and Key you have. It is convenient to organize the Configuration File reading and writing process well:

1. Perform Read and Write on Configuration files in **specifically written SubVIs**; it is not convenient to implement this aspect into the Main VI.
2. Carefully chose the **Sections** (how many and their names) to be used and **Keys** within sections.
3. If possible **use automatic naming in For Loops** for assigning names to Keys or Sections. Automatic naming can be formed by a base (i.e. "Voltage_") followed by the index of the loop iteration

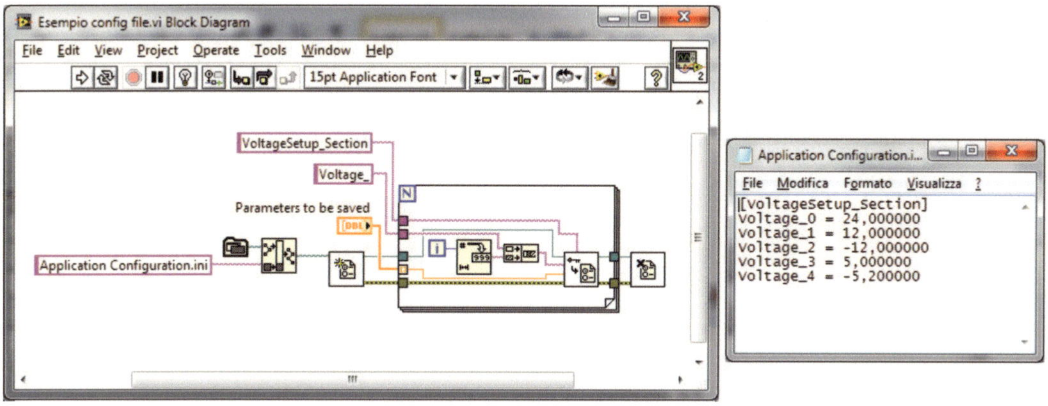

Fig. 23. Example of Configuration File write using an iterative technique and its result.

To have an idea, the Figure 23 reports the code to write a DBL floating point array to a Configuration File in iterative mode, together with the resulting file. All types of information needed by your application can be collected in configuration files: integers, doubles, Booleans, etc., even Variants data type. One should decide to use **Variants** when the amount of data to be stored and retrieved is quite consistent. Variants are stored as a series of codes and strings, where the former classify the type of data contained in the latter. Information can be reconstructed using the Variant as data type to be read from the file and finally by reconverting Variants to the original type using the "Variant to Data" function. Using Variants allow you to quickly write and read on configuration files, but the result is somewhat incomprehensible at a first glance.

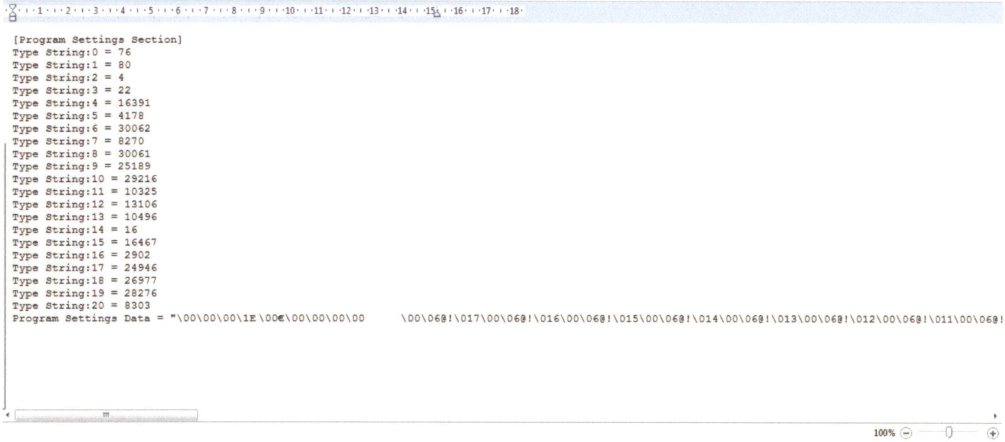

Fig. 24. Example of the aspect of a Configuration File using a Variant writing.

Use **Datalog Files** when a series of data organized as "Records" must be saved. Datalog files are a special kind of binary files basically conceived for storing Clusters contents: suppose you want to save a group of inhomogeneous data, like the content of a cluster composed by a timestamp, some Boolean, integers, strings, and so on, and several times during your execution. Datalog file makes a single Record at every saving action and stores it in this way. Single records can be accessed when reading back the Datalog file, by specifying its index: the first, second record etc.. Moreover the record position can be specified before reading, avoiding a sequential access which is usually slow.

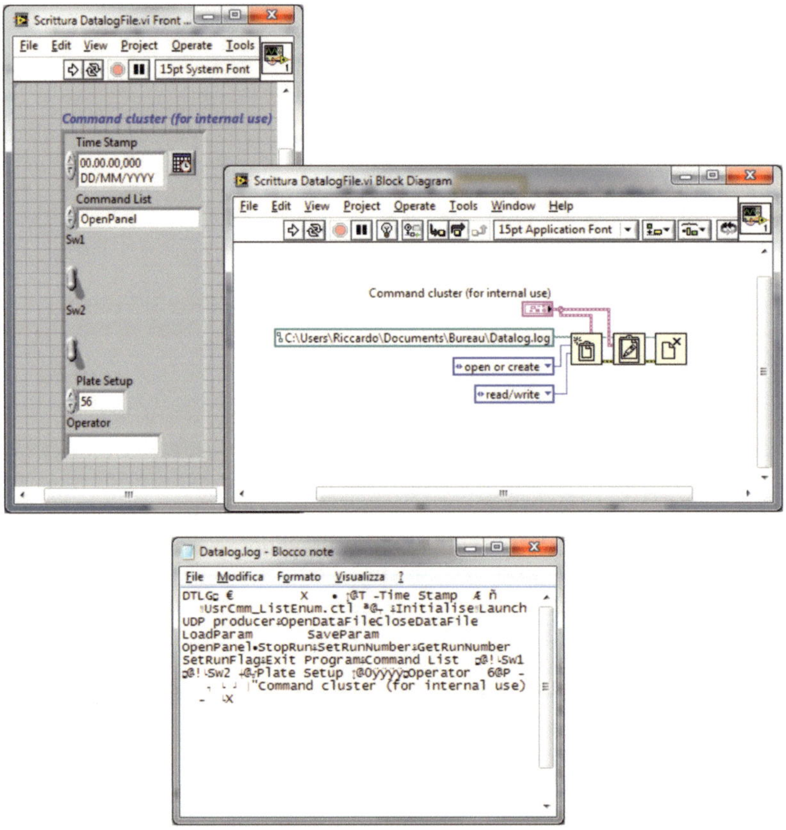

Fig. 25. Example of use of a Datalog File. The cluster is transcript as records in the file. The resulting file contents (which is binary) is also represented.

6.1.8 The concept of the "Data Streaming"

A very important concept which is typically ignored by new or inexperienced LabVIEW developers is the **Data Streaming.** If an Application produces a flux of data whose duration in time or size is long, the Data Streaming technique is almost a "must", to save data. New developers tend to accumulate data internally in the VIs, under the form of arrays of different sizes: then, at a certain moment in the program, they "save" these arrays into some files. This is not a good solution for several reasons:

- First, accumulation of large amounts of data in some structures of the VI is not convenient for the machine overload it can create, in particular regarding the LabVIEW Memory Manager.

- Second, if the program halts or is subject to an internal error which induces the VI to abort, all accumulated data can be corrupted or is lost.
- Third, since accumulation memory cannot be infinite, you need to stop some processes to dedicate machine time to write the data in a shot: the writing time can have, unfortunately, a duration of several seconds in the case of a large amounts of data to be saved. This situation can be attenuated with the correct handling of **parallel processes**, which constitute another important aspect of good programming in LabVIEW.

For all these reasons, in similar cases, use **Data Streaming**. The concept is simple and is based on the following processes:

1. open your data file
2. enter a loop which takes data and write immediately into the file, usually in binary format
3. stop the loop when finished and close the data file
4. check for errors.

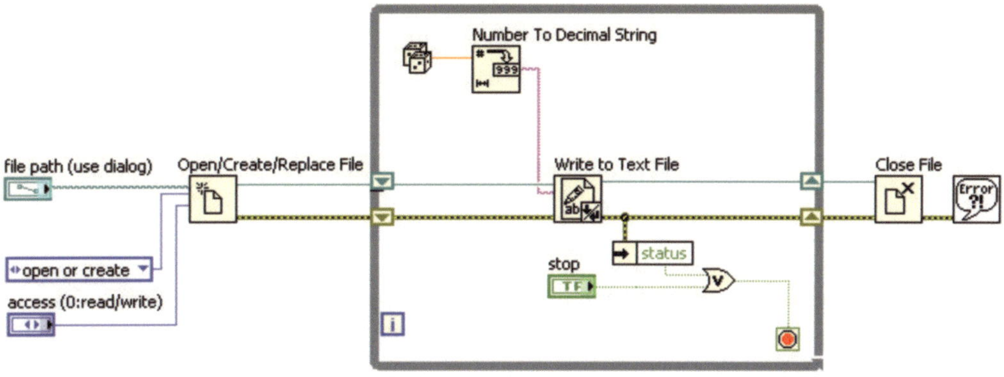

Fig. 26. Example of a simple Data Streaming implemented with a text file. (From National Instruments 2009-Core 1 Course presentation slides, Lesson 6 "Managing Resources").

In the Figure 26 the simplest data streaming technique is reported, in this case made by writing on a text file. Such a structure must be implemented as an independent one with respect to the rest of a VI, like parts which operate on the User Interface, for instance. The next paragraph will present some complex structures and Design Patterns which help for such a kind of design.

6.2 A conclusion concerning the files

Filing in LabVIEW (and in all programming languages) is a very extensive topic which has lots of implications. A mistaken choice in file format or recording technique can cause serious problems in using the data stored in your DAQ systems. It often happens that a series of conversion programs (under the form of several new VIs in the case of LabVIEW) must be written just to convert data files in order to make them compatible with some analysis system. A list of suggestions follows:

Suggestion 1) **Plan carefully** regarding your file format before starting to write code abruptly.

Suggestion 2) Decide, on the basis of the amount and type of data to be stored, **how many files you need to write** "in parallel": LVM files, Configuration, TDMS, Datalog, actual row Data Files, analysed results, etc..

Suggestion 3) **Choose carefully the files locations** (folders) related to your application, and use an automatic naming technique for data files which is based on a correct archiving logic:

for example a basic file name followed by date and time of your DAQ and a standard file extension.
Suggestion 4) **Decide about the format** for your data file: text file or binary ones. Both of them have advantages and disadvantages. A binary file is compact, rapid to write and read, and reports the actual values taken during DAQ; if correctly formatted, it can be read under different platforms too, even if this is an advanced task. Text files are nice because they are comprehensible, but take more time to be written and read, they need more space on the disc and limit the numerical precision because you cast your native precision by an "internal printing" operation.
Suggestion 5) **Save files in streaming mode** using an adequate structure if the DAQ or related processes are long term processes. Avoid accumulating large amounts of data and save them at the end of your process or from time to time by interrupting your DAQ.

7. Structures and parallel programming in LabVIEW

Structures in LabVIEW include For and While (Timed or not) loops, Case and Event structures and Sequences (flat or staked). Most beginners use structures in an incorrect way: they superimpose one structure over another by adding pieces which try to satisfy the increasing demands in the features of the application under development, again without any planning.
First of all **try to avoid using the Sequences Structures.** All LabVIEW programs can be done without them, and data dependency can fully substitute the sequencing of operations in most cases. Sequence Structures must be used in very restricted cases, when, for example, stringent timing issues are present during, suppose, a dialogue with an instrument. Sequences Structure is in contrast with the data dependency paradigm typical of LabVIEW, and must be used expressly to circumvent it **when necessary.** They tend to hide code in different frames, generating poor diagrams not clearly understandable.
Bad usage of structures implies several problems and under-utilization of LabVIEW system features. LabVIEW is an implicit **parallel environment** in the sense that it is designed to generate parallel and optimised code without particular intervention of the developer: but the latter **must know how to arrange structures** in order to induce LabVIEW to work parallel.
A last point is that Structures are related to the so-called **Design Patterns** techniques: this topic is a very important point which is expressly studied in several official LabVIEW courses (from Core 1 on).

7.1 Parallel processing issues

Putting more than one loop structure on the same diagram, automatically generates parallel code in LabVIEW, **if no data dependency exists among the loops.** Loops (While or For, but the usefulness is basically on While ones) cannot be interconnected to one another with wires, because this would create a data dependency, and the second loop should wait for the end of the previous to start its execution. Even transmitting a "STOP" flag needs a specific technique. LabVIEW compiler optimizes code in order to be executed in separate threads of the Operating System or, if it is the case, in separate sub-processor of a multi-core system.
Similar precautions must be taken to transmit **data** among parallel loops, and for this aspect several synchronization VIs are available (see the "Synchronization Function" palette). We cannot do a large *excursus* here, but I want to show you some general principles in order to encourage you to continue in carefully study and learn about these techniques.

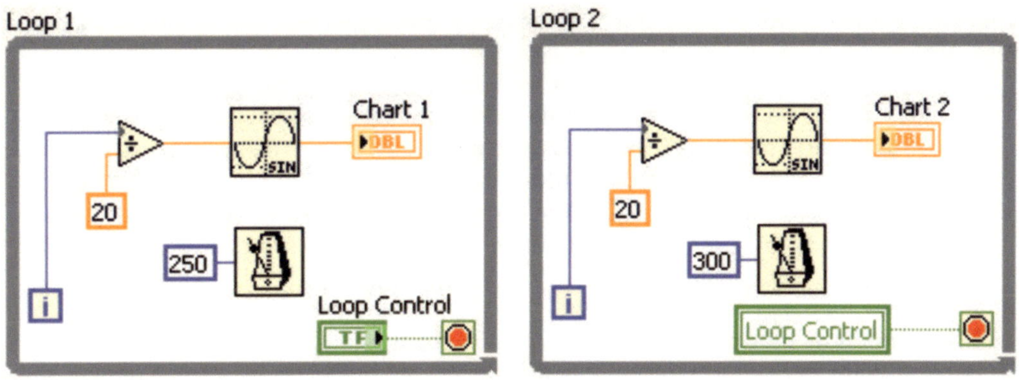

Fig. 27. Example of a very simple parallel structure. The Stop signaling must be passed via Local Variable (as in the case of figure), Global or Shared Variable or Propery node (on Value item). (From LabVIEW 2009-Core 1 course presentation slides, Lesson 9 "Using Variables").

Consider the example in Figure 27 the two loops are timed using the metronome function and the stop signal is sent via local variable. This is the simplest way for implementing parallel processing.
If you need to send data from one loop to another, which is the case for some particular **design patterns**, you must use Synchronization Functions.

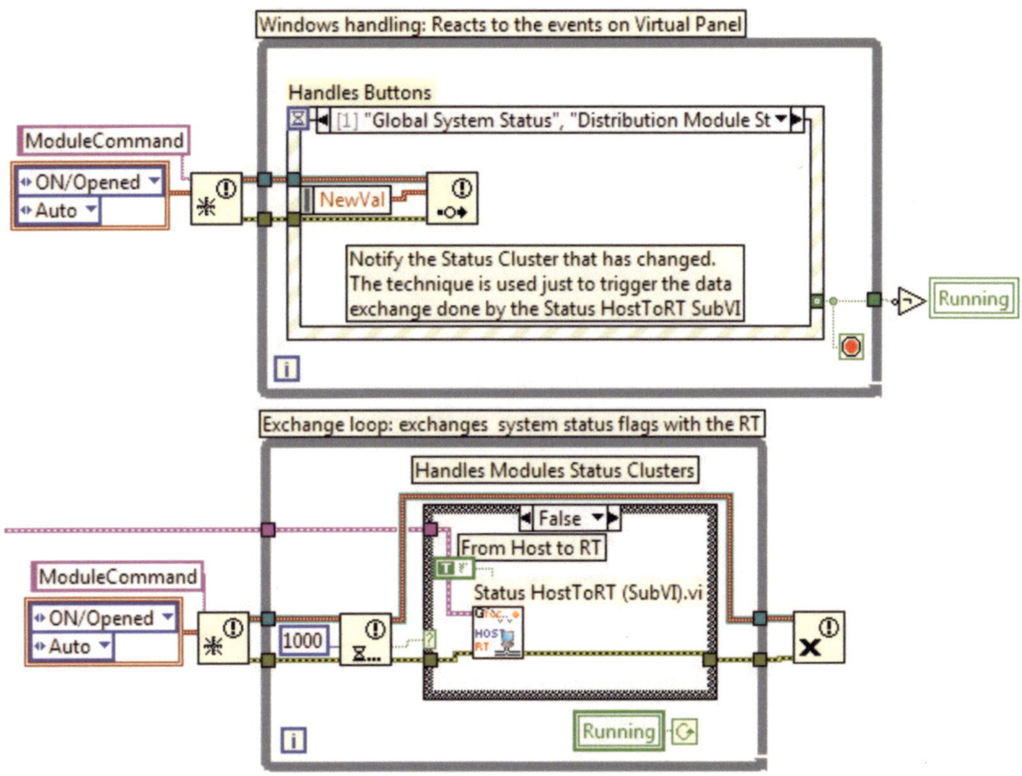

Fig. 28. Two parallel processes which exchange data via Notification Functions and control the end of process using the "Running" flag.

By looking at the Figure 28, several techniques for parallel processing and data exchange are presented:

1. The loops exchange information using **Notification VIs Functions.**
2. Notifiers allow you to pass a **single data** to the receiver.
3. The data can be of any type: here a cluster containing two enumerated types is passed.
4. You can ask to create "the same notifier" (whose name here is "ModuleCommand"): it will be created only once by the first Create Notification Function which is executed. Using multiple initializations with the same notifier name adds clarity to the diagram.
5. The upper loop signals the action of the user that has been taken into account by the Event Structure, by writing the "new value" of the notified variable (the cluster) into the notifier reference.
6. The lower loop receives the data and processes it. You have the possibility of tracing, in the lower loop, if any data has arrived, thanks to the "timeout" technique: the Boolean coming out from the notification receiver (lower loop) is the timeout flag.
7. Both loops need no timing: the upper one waits for an event from the users that is processed by the Events Structure (typical way of functioning for this structure); the lower loop uses the timeout of the notification function as internal timing, and performs different operations in the case the notifier has sent a data or not (timed out or not).

This technique is an application of the so called "**Master-Slave Design Pattern**", in which a short information, like a sort of flag, is sent from a "Producer" loop to alert a "Consumer" loop to do something.

An extension of this technique is the "real" **Producer-Consumer Design Pattern** in which **Queues Functions** are used instead of Notification Functions. Use Producer-Consumer design patterns, when more data must be sent from an acquisition loop to a data treatment loop, for example. Using notifier can cause data to be lost since it can treat one item at a time: queue functions, on the contrary, allow you to send streams of data from a producer loop to a consumer loop without losing any.

In the figure 29 **Data Consumer** is the bottommost loop. It is a state machine which "knows", from outside, if a Data Acquisition Process is in action or not.

- In the first case it provides to extract data packets from the queue, analyse and write them into an archiving data file **using data streaming on a binary file**; it finally sends formatted events (I mean *physical events*) data to a second queue for event monitoring purpose: a third loop (not represented in the figure) provides for this extraction and online presentation.
- In the second case it just does a monitoring of the incoming events.

This example is extracted from an actual Data Acquisition System for the "RD51" research activity at CERN (Geneva, Switzerland), on a Data Acquisition System for MicroMGas particle Detectors. This example carries several technicalities into it: two queues are used, one for UDP (raw) data and the second for pre-analysed data (built physical events). A Producer-Consumer design pattern is used where the consumer features a state machine which handles Run status on the experiment: state machine stays "idle" if no Run is active, and makes a series of operations (like initialization, file opening, flags settings,...) when a Run is started. Then it takes data, analyse it creating actual physical events and save it into formatted, binary streaming file; and eventually sends events to the online monitor via the second queue.

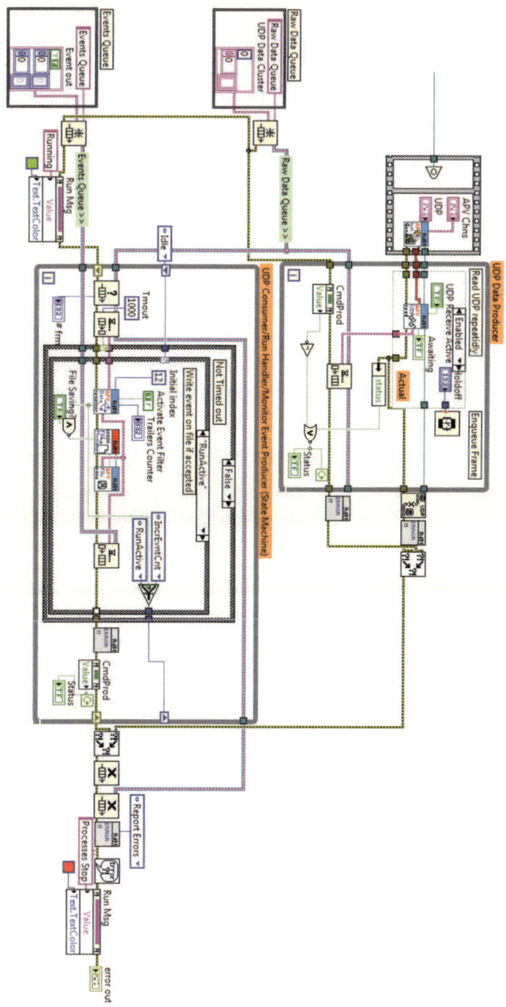

Fig. 29. A more complex example of parallel loops in a "Producer-Consumer" Design Pattern.

Using design pattern is extremely advantageous for a lot of reasons:

1. It is clear at the beginning of the development operation, how to implement things in the VIs.
2. Design patterns feature the logic and the "place" for implementing all that you need in an Application: from User Interface which gets commands from the User and formats information toward the "Command Consumer" which actually executes the command, to data getting and distributing onto secondary processes.
3. The design becomes clear and standard: a known framework helps to insert code. You already know where and how to process an User command, for instance, where to get data or write a file.

Definitively the **work can be well organised in a rational, standard way**. Future extensions of code can be added easily, but also reusing of code in new applications, since the framework is basically the same.

8. Conclusions

This Chapter does not want to substitute official LabVIEW courses, but, on the contrary, pushes in the direction of encouraging following some course, at least Core 1 and Core 2 if you are a beginning programmer. It is only a collection of considerations and suggestions in the direction of improving the knowledge in what a developer should know as a minimum to develop rational, well organized and effective Applications. Extending Applications in the future, which is a common job for programmers, can be done without altering the existant structure with the risk of obtaining a non effective solution. Remember that it is not convenient that diagrams go over the screen size, for clarity and readability: if that is not important make sure that the Diagram goes out of the screen in one direction only; horizontal direction is preferred. If you are starting to go over the screen, stop for a while and reorganize by creating more SubVIs, compacting structures and wiring and so on. Avoid excessive usage of local and global variables and sequence structures, since these features overcome the data dependency paradigm.

Many other suggestions can be made. A lot of other topics exist in LabVIEW programming, from Active-X usage to priority setting of SubVIs, from extensive use of Variants to complex data structures, from interaction of machine with the external field (via specific hardware) to Instrument Driver designing techniques. This list can be basically infinite.

I hope this work can stimulate new or inexperienced developers in adopting a well-planned strategy for development their job, in the direction of creating effective Applications which are finally understandable, reliable and scalable. This strategy starts from a good knowledge of the language features that can only be reached by a careful study before and during LabVIEW development process. In this way a complete experience can be accumulated which make, at the end, a very capable LabVIEW programmer.

In the end I would like to conclude with a final remark. The Figure 16 is an indication in understanding to which level of difficulty a diagram can arrive, when the developer *thinks to "know everything" concerning* LabVIEW. Several people, in particular if coming from the scientific environments, are convinced that just by giving few spots on the LabVIEW development system they are capable of doing everything: this is a big mistake, and anyone who wants to develop effective Applications in LabVIEW should have the ability to stop at a certain point and take the time to *study* LabVIEW.

9. References

Bishop R.H. (2009) *LabVIEW 2009 Student Edition*, National Instruments

Essic J. (2008) *Hands-On Introduction to LabVIEW for Scientists and Engineers*, Oxford Press

Johnson G. W. (1994) *LabVIEW® Graphical Programming*, Mc Graw Hill

National Instruments (2010) *LabVIEW Core 1 Course Manual and presentation slides*, ©National Instruments

National Instruments (2010) *LabVIEW Core 2 Course Manual and presentation slides*, ©National Instruments

National Instruments (2010) *LabVIEW Core 3 Course Manual and presentation slides*, ©National Instruments

Sumathi S., Surekha P. (2007) *LabVIEW based Advanced Instrumentation Systems*, Springer-Verlag

Travis J., Kring J. (2004) *LabVIEW for everyone*, Prentice Hall